McGRAW-HILL's

LSAT

McGRAW-HILL's

LSAT

Curvebreakers™

SECOND EDITION

McGraw-Hill

New York / Chicago / San Francisco / Lisbon / London / Madrid / Mexico City
Milan / New Delhi / San Juan / Seoul / Singapore / Sydney / Toronto

2 3 4 5 6 7 8 9 0   QPD/QPD   0 1 2 1 0 9 8 7

ISBN: P/N 978-0-07-149261-4 of set
        978-0-07-148571-5

MHID: P/N 0-07-149261-5 of set
        0-07-148571-6

Printed and bound by Quebecor/Dubuque.

McGraw-Hill books are available at special quantity discounts to use as premiums and sales promotions, or for use in corporate training programs. For
more information, please write to the Director of Special Sales, McGraw-Hill
Professional, Two Penn Plaza, New York, NY 10121-2298. Or contact your
local bookstore.

This publication is designed to provide accurate and authoritative information in regard to the subject matter covered. It is sold with the understanding that neither the author nor the publisher is engaged in rendering legal,
accounting, or other professional service. If legal advice or other expert assistance is required, the services of a competent professional person should be
sought.

*—From a Declaration of Principles jointly adopted
by a Committee of the American Bar
Association and a Committee of Publishers*

LSAT is a registered trademark of the Law School Admission Council, which
was not involved in the production of, and does not endorse, this product.

CONTENTS

Editor

Chris Keenum

Special Thanks

Nick Degani
Patrick Keenum
Evan Magers
Matt Ott
Josh Salzman
Aman Solomon

Additional Thanks

Dave Gaston
Nathan Kitchens
Ken Reinker
The Whigs

Get Extra Help Online at the Curvebreakers Web Site!

This book has been prepared by Curvebreakers, a group of current and former Harvard Law School students who aced the LSAT and who have pooled their test-taking expertise to help future LSAT takers. Your purchase of this book entitles you to a FREE three-month access to the Curvebreakers Web site, where you'll find additional LSAT help, special discounts, and late-breaking LSAT information. You'll also be able to purchase supplementary LSAT practice materials.

Visit the Curvebreakers Web site if you

- **Don't understand something about a particular kind of LSAT question.** If there is something about the test that you still do not understand, you can get answers to your questions at the Web site. Having someone explain LSAT problems to you may be more helpful than reading explanations in a book.

- **Keep making the same kind of mistake.** If you consistently have trouble with a particular kind of Logic Game or Logical Reasoning question, you can purchase supplementary practice materials for every question type at the Web site.

- **Need to improve your test-taking speed.** If you are having time troubles with a particular section or if you would just like to improve your speed so that you'll have extra time to spend on difficult questions, you'll find *speed workshops* at the Curvebreakers Web site. These workshops contain practice problems from all test sections that will help you step up your speed on each section.

- **Need to improve your test-taking stamina.** The LSAT is essentially a mental marathon. It requires you to pay attention to minute details and to apply logical reasoning to these details over a span of four hours. This process is incredibly exhausting, and untrained test takers may do progressively worse from one section to the next solely because of fatigue. You can gain an easy 5- to 15-point increase in your test score simply by building up your test-taking stamina. Curvebreakers recommends that its students take the equivalent of an LSAT on five out of seven days of the week for three weeks before the test. This mental training builds up your mental strength so that you will not grow weary and begin making careless errors during the later parts of the test. Supplementary materials for this training program are available on the Curvebreakers Web site.

www.curvebreakers.com

McGRAW-HILL's

LSAT

PART I

GETTING STARTED

CHAPTER 1

INTRODUCTION TO THE LSAT

In this chapter you will learn:

- When to take the LSAT and how to register for the test

- The format of a typical LSAT

- How the LSAT is scored

- The three main types of LSAT questions

- Why it makes sense to guess if you cannot answer a question

- How to use this book to make the most of your study program

LSAT Basics

The Law School Admission Test (LSAT) is required for admission by the more than 200 law schools in the United States and Canada that are members of the Law School Admission Council (LSAC). Many law schools that are not LSAC members also require applicants to take the LSAT.

According to the LSAC, the LSAT is designed to measure certain skills that are considered vital to success in law school. These include the ability to read and understand complicated text passages, to draw reasonable inferences and conclusions from them, to think critically, and to evaluate logical arguments.

When the LSAT Is Given. The LSAC administers the LSAT four times each year at designated test centers in the United States and Canada and throughout the world. The four test dates are typically on Saturdays in February, June, October, and December. Many law schools require that you take the LSAT by December if

you are applying for admission the following fall. However, applicants are often advised to take the test earlier than December, that is, in October or even June of the year before they expect to begin law school.

How to Register. You can register for the LSAT by mail, by telephone, or online. A registration fee is charged. Regular registration takes place until approximately 30 days before the test date. Late registration is allowed until about three weeks before the test date, but a higher fee is charged. You cannot register for the test on the day it is given.

To register, contact the Law School Admission Council at the following address:

Law School Admission Council
662 Penn Street
Box 2000
Newtown, PA 18940-0998
Tel. (215) 968-1001 (service representatives are available on weekdays only)
For online registration: www.LSAC.org

Registration forms are included in the *LSAT and LSDAS Registration/Information Book*, a booklet that is usually available in college and university guidance offices or by mail from the LSAC. If you are registering by mail, fill out the forms in the booklet and mail them in the enclosed, preaddressed return envelope. Faxed registration forms are not accepted.

When you register, you will have the opportunity to select a first-choice and second-choice test center located near you. If both centers you select are full or unavailable, the LSAC will assign you to another center located as near to you as possible.

Alternative Testing Arrangements. If you observe Saturday Sabbaths, you may take the LSAT on the Monday following the regular Saturday testing date. To do so, you must submit to the LSAC a letter from your rabbi or minister on official stationery confirming your religious affiliation.

Special testing accommodations are also available for test takers with documented disabilities. To request these arrangements, obtain an accommodations request packet by contacting the LSAC either by mail or online. The LSAC urges test takers who wish to request special testing accommodations to do so well in advance of the registration deadline.

Obtaining Your Score. If you have an online account with the LSAC, you will receive your LSAT score by email about three weeks after taking the test. There is no charge for doing so, and this is the fastest way to obtain your score. You can also obtain your score by telephoning TelScore at (215) 968-1200 approximately three weeks after taking the test. You will be asked to pay a $10 fee by credit card. Approximately four weeks after each test, the LSAC mails score reports to test takers. If you have an online LSAC account, you will be charged a $25 fee for hardcopy mailings of the score information available to you online.

Taking the Test More Than Once. You may take the LSAT up to three times within any two-year period. However, the LSAC advises test takers to take the test again only if they believe that their first test score was negatively affected by a circumstance such as anxiety or illness. For most test takers, taking the test again does not result in a substantially different score, and test takers should keep in mind that their second or third score might actually be lower than their first. If you do take the test more than once, your score report will show all your scores. In addition, an average score is calculated and reported.

Reporting Scores to Law Schools. Nearly all American Bar Association–approved law schools require test takers to make use of the Law School Data Assembly Service (LSDAS), a service provided by the LSAC. To take advantage of this service, you must provide the LSDAS with school transcripts and letters of recommendation. The LSDAS combines that information with LSAT scores and copies of your writing sample and creates a complete report that is provided to every law school to which you apply.

What's on the LSAT

The LSAT is one of the most demanding standardized tests in existence. It tests your ability to answer questions that involve difficult logical transitions, syllogisms, and inductive reasoning—and to answer them quickly. The funny thing is that if given enough time, most people would be able to work through the questions and get most of them right. However, the LSAT gives you nowhere near enough time to do this. Instead, you are forced to operate under severe time pressure. Most test sections have between 24 and 27 questions that you are required to answer in a 35-minute time span. This is an average of about 1 minute 25 seconds per question. This is not a lot of time, and it is not surprising that most people do not finish many sections of the test. One main purpose of this book is to teach you how to answer LSAT problems quickly and accurately despite their difficulty.

Format of the Test. The LSAT includes five sections of multiple-choice questions. Of these, only four are graded: two Logical Reasoning sections, one Logic Games section, and one Reading Comprehension section. Another section is what is called "an experimental section." You are not told which section this one will be, but it can be any of one of the three question types and it will not count toward your grade. The experimental section is used only to test questions for future versions of the test.

Another part of the test that is not graded is the writing sample. In this test section, you have 30 minutes in which to write a short essay based on a given scenario. The writing sample is given at the very end of the LSAT, after you have completed all the other sections. It does not contribute to your LSAT score, but it is sometimes read by the admissions committees at the schools to which you apply. The writing sample gives committee members an idea of how well you write and take sides in an argument.

The following chart summarizes the format of a typical LSAT.

Typical LSAT Format

Section*	Number of Questions	Time Allowed, minutes
1 Logic Games	24	35
2 Logical Reasoning	24–26	35
3 Reading Comprehension	27	35
4 Logical Reasoning	24–26	35
5 Writing Sample	—	30
Total	101	170

*Graded sections only.
Note: All sections except the Writing Sample may appear in any order. An ungraded experimental section is also included in each test form.

LSAT Scores

There are typically about 101 questions that are graded on the LSAT. There are usually about 50 in the two logical reasoning sections, 25 in the logic games section, and 27 in the reading comprehension section. If you add up the total number that you get correct on these sections, you will have your **raw score**. No points are deducted for wrong answers, and all questions count the same.

Some LSATs are easier than others, and some are more difficult. To account for this variation, a statistical procedure is used to convert your raw score to a **scaled score**. Scaled scores range from **120 to 180**.

LSAT scores also include a percentile rank. This rank indicates the percentage of test takers who scored below your reported test score.

LSAT Question Types

The three types of multiple-choice questions on the LSAT are logic games, logical reasoning, and reading comprehension.

Logic Games. The Logic Games section of the LSAT consists of a series of "games," each of which specifies certain relationships among a group of variables. The questions ask you to deduce additional relationships based on the given facts. Generally, math majors and others who are good at analytical reasoning do well on this section.

Here is a sample of a logic game:

> Anna, Bill, Claire, Dale, Emily, and Fanny are flying in an airplane. They sit in six seats that are aligned in two columns of three:
>
> 1   2
> 3   4
> 5   6
>
> Their seating order is determined by the following constraints:
> Anna sits in a lower-numbered seat than Bill.
> Claire sits immediately behind Fanny.
> Dale does not sit in the same row as Fanny or Emily.
> Bill sits in the same column as Emily.

Following this setup there will be five to eight questions, each of which will ask you to make a logical deduction based on the information and the rules ("constraints") of the game. Here is a typical question:

> 1. If Dale sits in seat 2, then which of the following must not be true?
>
> (A) Fanny sits in seat 1.
> (B) Anna does not sit in seat 3.
> (C) Claire sits in seat 5.
> (D) Bill sits in seat 4.
> (E) Emily sits in seat 6.
>
> Correct answer: A

Test takers who prepare carefully for the logic games section can significantly improve their scores. Certain diagramming techniques and ways of setting up the games can greatly increase both speed and accuracy in this test section. Chapter 3 of this book will provide examples and solution techniques for the following eight types of LSAT logic games:

1. Formal Logic
2. Sequencing
3. Linear
4. Complex linear
5. Grouping
6. Mapping
7. Minimized variables
8. Maximized variables

Logical Reasoning. In the Logical Reasoning sections of the LSAT, each question starts with a short passage (the "squib") that discusses a given issue or presents a particular argument. The question then asks you something about the reasoning behind the

issue or the argument. Here is a sample logical reasoning question:

> Forest Ranger: Bigfoot is an abominable creature that is larger than any bear and certainly larger than any human being. We are pleased to announce that Bigfoot was spotted yesterday in the park's canyon near the waterfall. Several campers were out eating their lunch on a picnic table near the top of the waterfall when they heard growling and strange noises coming from the base of the waterfall. They looked over the edge to the base of the waterfall and saw a big hairy mammal jump into the pool of water about 200 yards away. The campers screamed in surprise and the creature looked up, shook itself dry, and then ran off into the wilderness.
>
> Which of the following, if true, would undermine the Forest Ranger's contention that the creature spotted was Bigfoot?
>
> (A) Bigfoot likes bathing in waterfall pools.
> (B) A camper did not have her glasses with her when looking down to the bottom of the falls.
> (C) Bigfoot roams through northern parklands only during the winter months.
> (D) No hairy mammals were present in the park yesterday besides bears and humans.
> (E) Bigfoot is scared of people, especially when he is spotted and they scream at him.
>
> Correct answer: D

To answer logical reasoning questions correctly, you need to have good critical reading skills and you must be attentive to details. Sometimes small issues present in a long squib can be pivotally important when test takers are deciding between answer choices. Remembering and being able to understand such details is the key to successfully answering logical reasoning questions. Chapter 4 of this book will provide examples and solutions for the following seven types of LSAT logical reasoning questions:

1. Conclusion
2. "Resolve"
3. "Strengthen"
4. "Weaken"
5. Reasoning strategy
6. Analogous reasoning
7. Controversy

For each of these seven question types, there are different things to watch for in the squib and different solution strategies. That is why you need to study each type carefully and to practice with sample questions. All that study takes time, but the payoff is higher scores on two of the four graded LSAT sections—fully half of your total LSAT score!

Reading Comprehension. The Reading Comprehension section contains questions of a type that you have most likely seen before on other standardized tests. The SAT has reading comprehension questions, and those on the LSAT are similar in form. A 400- to 500-word passage is presented and followed by six to eight questions that ask about the passage.

Here is an example of part of a reading comprehension passage and a question based on its content:

> As a personification of England, John Bull became a popular caricature during the nineteenth century. John Bull originated as a character in John Arbuthnot's *The History of John Bull* (1712). He became widely known from cartoons by Sir John Tenniel published in the British humor magazine *Punch* during the middle and late nineteenth century. In those cartoons, he was portrayed as an honest, solid, farmer figure, often in a Union Jack waistcoat, and accompanied by a bulldog. He became so familiar that his name frequently appeared in books, plays, periodical titles, and as a brand name or trademark. Although frequently used through World War II, since the 1950s John Bull has been seen less often.
>
> 1. Which of the following best expresses the main idea of the first paragraph?
>
> (A) Uncle Sam, the personification of America, is used in the same way that John Bull is used in England.
> (B) John Bull is a figure that emerged as a character in a cartoon in a British humor magazine called *Punch*.
> (C) John Bull, a personification of England, was popular during the nineteenth century but has appeared less often since the 1950s.
> (D) John Bull was a farmer figure who wore a Union Jack waistcoat and was commonly accompanied by a bull dog.
> (E) The English people were big fans of John Bull and strongly identified with him as a national figure.
>
> Correct answer: C

To answer reading comprehension questions correctly, you must pay careful attention to details when you read the passages. Chapter 5 of this book will provide examples and solutions for the following six types of LSAT reading comprehension questions:

1. Main point
2. Author's/character's opinion
3. Claims
4. Syntax
5. Inference
6. Support/undermine

You'll learn all about each question type and what to look for when answering questions of each type. You'll also learn techniques to help you retain more information when you read the lengthy reading passages. These techniques can give you the edge you need to succeed on the Reading Comprehension section.

Should You Guess?

On the LSAT, no points are deducted for wrong answers. Therefore, if you really do not know the answer to a question, there is no reason not to guess. In fact, if you are running out of time at the end of a section and there are questions you have not been able to answer, guess an answer for each one and mark your answer sheet accordingly before time is called. You have nothing to lose!

Keep in mind too that you can use the process of elimination to your advantage. Because the LSAT is a multiple-choice test, the correct answer to each question is right in front of you. If you can identify one or more answer choices as obviously wrong and then make your guess, your chances of being correct will be greatly increased.

How to Use This Book

The LSAT is a very difficult test, and your preparation time may be limited. That is why it is important to use your study time wisely. This book provides a comprehensive review of everything you need to know for the test, and it has been organized to make your study program practical and efficient. It will help you

- familiarize yourself with the test format and test question types
- learn the logic tools and diagramming tools you'll need to score high
- develop solution strategies by reviewing samples of every question type with step-by-step solutions
- practice your test-taking skills using sample LSATs

The following four-step study program has been designed to help you make the best use of this book.

STEP 1: TAKE THE DIAGNOSTIC TEST

Once you have read through this chapter, start your preparation program by taking the Diagnostic Test. This test is carefully modeled on the real LSAT in terms of format, types of questions, and topics tested. Take the Diagnostic Test under test conditions and pay careful attention to the time limits for each section. When you complete the test, score yourself using the scoring information at the end of the test. Then read through the explanations to see which question types gave you the most trouble. Look for patterns. Did you miss particular types of questions? Did specific question formats give you trouble? When did you need to guess at the answer? Use your results to identify the question types that were most difficult for you. Once you know your strengths and weaknesses, you'll know which question types you need to focus on as you review for the test.

STEP 2: STUDY THE LSAT QUESTION TYPES

Chapters 3, 4, and 5 of this book provide an in-depth look at each of the multiple-choice question types on the LSAT. Within each type, the questions can be divided into specific categories. You'll learn the characteristics of each category, how to recognize each one, and how to use this knowledge to your advantage. Each category is illustrated by numerous examples, and detailed, step-by-step solutions are provided. For each category, you'll see typical question setups, typical questioning words and phrases, and the kinds of correct answer choices, incorrect-but-plausible "second-best" choices, and obviously wrong answers that you'll encounter on the actual LSAT. The more you know about each question category and the more examples you study, the more confidant you'll feel and the better you're likely to do on test day.

Chapter 6 of this book focuses on the Writing Sample, an essay-writing exercise that is part of the LSAT but which is not scored. In this section of the book you'll find out what the test writers are looking for, you'll learn valuable essay-writing tips, and you'll see a sample of a typical high-scoring writing sample.

You do not need to work through these chapters in the order in which they appear. Skip around if you like, but remember to focus on the question types that gave you the most trouble on the Diagnostic Test.

Make a study schedule. Take the time to work through Chapters 2 through 5 at your own pace, studying all the

examples and explanations to make sure that you understand them thoroughly. If you have the time, after you have finished reading each chapter, go back and rework a selection of sample questions to make sure that you mastered each solution strategy. Be sure to set aside enough time at the end of your schedule to take the practice tests at the end of the book. However, if you do not have much time before the test, you may want to shorten your review time and focus instead entirely on the practice tests.

STEP 3: LEARN STRATEGIES FOR ANSWERING EACH QUESTION TYPE

As you work through Chapters 3, 4, and 5, you'll learn proven strategies for answering each LSAT question type. The examples will show you exactly how to use each strategy to reason your way to the correct answer. You'll learn how to use:

- simple diagramming techniques that make it easy to solve the LSAT's complex logic games
- time-tested logic tools that will give you the ability to answer the toughest logical reasoning questions
- scholarly reading techniques that will help you organize and remember the information you need to answer LSAT reading comprehension questions

STEP 4: TAKE THE PRACTICE TESTS

Once you have worked through Chapters 3 through 6, get ready for the real exam by taking the six practice tests at the back of this book. When you take each test, try to simulate actual test conditions. Sit in a quiet room, time yourself, and try to work your way through the entire test without interruption. The tests are ideal for practice because they have been constructed to be as much like the real test as possible. The directions and practice questions are very much like those on the real test. You'll gain experience with the LSAT format, and you'll learn to pace yourself so that you can earn the maximum number of points in the time allowed.

Explanations for all questions can be found at the end of each test. If you get a question wrong, you'll want to review the explanation carefully. You may also want to go back to the section in the earlier chapters that covers that particular question category.

At the end of each test you'll also find scoring information. Calculate your raw score, then use the table provided to find your approximate scaled score. The scaling on the real test may be slightly different, but you'll get a good idea of how you might score on the actual test.

The Curvebreakers Method

This LSAT guide is based on the test-preparation techniques developed by Curvebreakers, a group of current and former students at Harvard Law School, each of whom scored in the 99th percentile or better on the LSAT. By using this guide, you will benefit from the numerous advantages that the Curvebreakers techniques have over those used in other test-preparation courses.

Most other LSAT guides and courses offer mainly generic test-taking advice applicable to broad categories of LSAT questions. In truth, however, each of these broad categories actually includes a variety of different question types, each with its own individual characteristics and pitfalls. The Curvebreakers techniques focus on each of these specific types in turn, analyzing each one in depth and giving you targeted problem-solving strategies and/or diagramming tools for that specific question type. You also get intensive practice with each question type, so you can familiarize yourself with the kinds of tricks specific to that type. By working your way through the following pages, you'll master each and every LSAT question type, you'll quickly improve your test-taking skills, and you'll raise your LSAT score on test day.

Get Extra Help Online. If you need additional practice beyond what is available in this book, you can find it on the Curvebreakers Web site, www.Curvebreakers.com, where you can access entire "books" dedicated to each question type. This kind of extra practice is a good idea if you find yourself having trouble with a particular question type.

Curvebreakers Recommendations

I. WORK HARD

The LSAT is a test that can be mastered if you are dedicated to improving yourself and getting a good score. Passively reading through lessons is not going to do much good. Instead, be sure to work through the problems in this book when you are wide awake and can give them full attention. If you do this consistently, your score will progressively improve. It is that simple.

2. Make a Study Plan

You should make an LSAT study plan that you can stick to. For example, it is a good idea to take a practice test each weekend on Saturday morning in order to simulate actual LSAT testing conditions. You should also map out consistent times each week when you will be able to work through at least part of each lesson.

3. Read Critically

On the LSAT, the test writers often bury important points beneath piles of meaningless words and irrelevant sentences. Almost every question contains a pitfall that is intentionally designed to trap unwary test takers. To prevent those pitfalls from trapping you, train yourself to read critically. Practice this kind of reading every time you sit down to study for the LSAT.

4. Identify Your Weaknesses

After you take each of the sample tests in this book, make sure to go back and study the questions that you got wrong. If you have the version of this guide that includes sample tests on CD, use the CD to analyze the question types that you commonly miss. These simple steps can make all the difference in your LSAT preparation program. They will enable you to identify your weaknesses and focus your study so that you will not make the same mistakes in the future.

5. Do Not Worry about Time!

Take your time as you work through the lessons in this book. Focus on learning the characteristics of the different question types instead of worrying about how quickly or how slowly you are answering the questions. You can work on improving your test-taking speed when you take the practice tests at the back of this book. If you need further practice, use the materials on the Curvebreakers Web site for speed drills.

CHAPTER 2

DIAGNOSTIC TEST

In this chapter you will:

- Take a full-length sample LSAT under actual test conditions

- Practice with every type of LSAT question

- Read explanations for every question

- Review your results to identify your strengths and weaknesses

- Develop a personal study plan

The following test has been carefully modeled on the actual LSAT in terms of number of questions, types of questions, and degree of difficulty. You can use it to identify your strengths and weaknesses as you begin your LSAT preparation program.

The chart shown below summarizes the organization of this Diagnostic Test.

When you take this Diagnostic Test, try to simulate actual test conditions. Find a quiet place where you will not be disturbed. Set aside enough time so that you can complete the entire test without being interrupted.

Follow the time limits for each test section. Use the Answer Sheet to record your answers.

When you are finished, check your answers against the Answer Key located at the end of the test. Then follow the instructions to calculate your score. Review the answers and explanations that follow, especially for those questions you missed. Use your results to plan your LSAT preparation program. A suggested study plan is provided to help you make the best use of the materials in this book.

Diagnostic Test

Section Number	Question Type	Number of Questions	Time Allowed, minutes
1	Logical Reasoning	25	35
2	Logic Games	24	35
3	Logical Reasoning	25	35
4	Reading Comprehension	27	35
	Total	101	2 hrs, 20 min

ANSWER SHEET

SECTION 1	SECTION 2	SECTION 3	SECTION 4
1. Ⓐ Ⓑ Ⓒ Ⓓ Ⓔ	1. Ⓐ Ⓑ Ⓒ Ⓓ Ⓔ	1. Ⓐ Ⓑ Ⓒ Ⓓ Ⓔ	1. Ⓐ Ⓑ Ⓒ Ⓓ Ⓔ
2. Ⓐ Ⓑ Ⓒ Ⓓ Ⓔ	2. Ⓐ Ⓑ Ⓒ Ⓓ Ⓔ	2. Ⓐ Ⓑ Ⓒ Ⓓ Ⓔ	2. Ⓐ Ⓑ Ⓒ Ⓓ Ⓔ
3. Ⓐ Ⓑ Ⓒ Ⓓ Ⓔ	3. Ⓐ Ⓑ Ⓒ Ⓓ Ⓔ	3. Ⓐ Ⓑ Ⓒ Ⓓ Ⓔ	3. Ⓐ Ⓑ Ⓒ Ⓓ Ⓔ
4. Ⓐ Ⓑ Ⓒ Ⓓ Ⓔ	4. Ⓐ Ⓑ Ⓒ Ⓓ Ⓔ	4. Ⓐ Ⓑ Ⓒ Ⓓ Ⓔ	4. Ⓐ Ⓑ Ⓒ Ⓓ Ⓔ
5. Ⓐ Ⓑ Ⓒ Ⓓ Ⓔ	5. Ⓐ Ⓑ Ⓒ Ⓓ Ⓔ	5. Ⓐ Ⓑ Ⓒ Ⓓ Ⓔ	5. Ⓐ Ⓑ Ⓒ Ⓓ Ⓔ
6. Ⓐ Ⓑ Ⓒ Ⓓ Ⓔ	6. Ⓐ Ⓑ Ⓒ Ⓓ Ⓔ	6. Ⓐ Ⓑ Ⓒ Ⓓ Ⓔ	6. Ⓐ Ⓑ Ⓒ Ⓓ Ⓔ
7. Ⓐ Ⓑ Ⓒ Ⓓ Ⓔ	7. Ⓐ Ⓑ Ⓒ Ⓓ Ⓔ	7. Ⓐ Ⓑ Ⓒ Ⓓ Ⓔ	7. Ⓐ Ⓑ Ⓒ Ⓓ Ⓔ
8. Ⓐ Ⓑ Ⓒ Ⓓ Ⓔ	8. Ⓐ Ⓑ Ⓒ Ⓓ Ⓔ	8. Ⓐ Ⓑ Ⓒ Ⓓ Ⓔ	8. Ⓐ Ⓑ Ⓒ Ⓓ Ⓔ
9. Ⓐ Ⓑ Ⓒ Ⓓ Ⓔ	9. Ⓐ Ⓑ Ⓒ Ⓓ Ⓔ	9. Ⓐ Ⓑ Ⓒ Ⓓ Ⓔ	9. Ⓐ Ⓑ Ⓒ Ⓓ Ⓔ
10. Ⓐ Ⓑ Ⓒ Ⓓ Ⓔ	10. Ⓐ Ⓑ Ⓒ Ⓓ Ⓔ	10. Ⓐ Ⓑ Ⓒ Ⓓ Ⓔ	10. Ⓐ Ⓑ Ⓒ Ⓓ Ⓔ
11. Ⓐ Ⓑ Ⓒ Ⓓ Ⓔ	11. Ⓐ Ⓑ Ⓒ Ⓓ Ⓔ	11. Ⓐ Ⓑ Ⓒ Ⓓ Ⓔ	11. Ⓐ Ⓑ Ⓒ Ⓓ Ⓔ
12. Ⓐ Ⓑ Ⓒ Ⓓ Ⓔ	12. Ⓐ Ⓑ Ⓒ Ⓓ Ⓔ	12. Ⓐ Ⓑ Ⓒ Ⓓ Ⓔ	12. Ⓐ Ⓑ Ⓒ Ⓓ Ⓔ
13. Ⓐ Ⓑ Ⓒ Ⓓ Ⓔ	13. Ⓐ Ⓑ Ⓒ Ⓓ Ⓔ	13. Ⓐ Ⓑ Ⓒ Ⓓ Ⓔ	13. Ⓐ Ⓑ Ⓒ Ⓓ Ⓔ
14. Ⓐ Ⓑ Ⓒ Ⓓ Ⓔ	14. Ⓐ Ⓑ Ⓒ Ⓓ Ⓔ	14. Ⓐ Ⓑ Ⓒ Ⓓ Ⓔ	14. Ⓐ Ⓑ Ⓒ Ⓓ Ⓔ
15. Ⓐ Ⓑ Ⓒ Ⓓ Ⓔ	15. Ⓐ Ⓑ Ⓒ Ⓓ Ⓔ	15. Ⓐ Ⓑ Ⓒ Ⓓ Ⓔ	15. Ⓐ Ⓑ Ⓒ Ⓓ Ⓔ
16. Ⓐ Ⓑ Ⓒ Ⓓ Ⓔ	16. Ⓐ Ⓑ Ⓒ Ⓓ Ⓔ	16. Ⓐ Ⓑ Ⓒ Ⓓ Ⓔ	16. Ⓐ Ⓑ Ⓒ Ⓓ Ⓔ
17. Ⓐ Ⓑ Ⓒ Ⓓ Ⓔ	17. Ⓐ Ⓑ Ⓒ Ⓓ Ⓔ	17. Ⓐ Ⓑ Ⓒ Ⓓ Ⓔ	17. Ⓐ Ⓑ Ⓒ Ⓓ Ⓔ
18. Ⓐ Ⓑ Ⓒ Ⓓ Ⓔ	18. Ⓐ Ⓑ Ⓒ Ⓓ Ⓔ	18. Ⓐ Ⓑ Ⓒ Ⓓ Ⓔ	18. Ⓐ Ⓑ Ⓒ Ⓓ Ⓔ
19. Ⓐ Ⓑ Ⓒ Ⓓ Ⓔ	19. Ⓐ Ⓑ Ⓒ Ⓓ Ⓔ	19. Ⓐ Ⓑ Ⓒ Ⓓ Ⓔ	19. Ⓐ Ⓑ Ⓒ Ⓓ Ⓔ
20. Ⓐ Ⓑ Ⓒ Ⓓ Ⓔ	20. Ⓐ Ⓑ Ⓒ Ⓓ Ⓔ	20. Ⓐ Ⓑ Ⓒ Ⓓ Ⓔ	20. Ⓐ Ⓑ Ⓒ Ⓓ Ⓔ
21. Ⓐ Ⓑ Ⓒ Ⓓ Ⓔ	21. Ⓐ Ⓑ Ⓒ Ⓓ Ⓔ	21. Ⓐ Ⓑ Ⓒ Ⓓ Ⓔ	21. Ⓐ Ⓑ Ⓒ Ⓓ Ⓔ
22. Ⓐ Ⓑ Ⓒ Ⓓ Ⓔ	22. Ⓐ Ⓑ Ⓒ Ⓓ Ⓔ	22. Ⓐ Ⓑ Ⓒ Ⓓ Ⓔ	22. Ⓐ Ⓑ Ⓒ Ⓓ Ⓔ
23. Ⓐ Ⓑ Ⓒ Ⓓ Ⓔ	23. Ⓐ Ⓑ Ⓒ Ⓓ Ⓔ	23. Ⓐ Ⓑ Ⓒ Ⓓ Ⓔ	23. Ⓐ Ⓑ Ⓒ Ⓓ Ⓔ
24. Ⓐ Ⓑ Ⓒ Ⓓ Ⓔ	24. Ⓐ Ⓑ Ⓒ Ⓓ Ⓔ	24. Ⓐ Ⓑ Ⓒ Ⓓ Ⓔ	24. Ⓐ Ⓑ Ⓒ Ⓓ Ⓔ
25. Ⓐ Ⓑ Ⓒ Ⓓ Ⓔ	25. Ⓐ Ⓑ Ⓒ Ⓓ Ⓔ	25. Ⓐ Ⓑ Ⓒ Ⓓ Ⓔ	25. Ⓐ Ⓑ Ⓒ Ⓓ Ⓔ
26. Ⓐ Ⓑ Ⓒ Ⓓ Ⓔ	26. Ⓐ Ⓑ Ⓒ Ⓓ Ⓔ	26. Ⓐ Ⓑ Ⓒ Ⓓ Ⓔ	26. Ⓐ Ⓑ Ⓒ Ⓓ Ⓔ
27. Ⓐ Ⓑ Ⓒ Ⓓ Ⓔ	27. Ⓐ Ⓑ Ⓒ Ⓓ Ⓔ	27. Ⓐ Ⓑ Ⓒ Ⓓ Ⓔ	27. Ⓐ Ⓑ Ⓒ Ⓓ Ⓔ
28. Ⓐ Ⓑ Ⓒ Ⓓ Ⓔ	28. Ⓐ Ⓑ Ⓒ Ⓓ Ⓔ	28. Ⓐ Ⓑ Ⓒ Ⓓ Ⓔ	28. Ⓐ Ⓑ Ⓒ Ⓓ Ⓔ
29. Ⓐ Ⓑ Ⓒ Ⓓ Ⓔ	29. Ⓐ Ⓑ Ⓒ Ⓓ Ⓔ	29. Ⓐ Ⓑ Ⓒ Ⓓ Ⓔ	29. Ⓐ Ⓑ Ⓒ Ⓓ Ⓔ
30. Ⓐ Ⓑ Ⓒ Ⓓ Ⓔ	30. Ⓐ Ⓑ Ⓒ Ⓓ Ⓔ	30. Ⓐ Ⓑ Ⓒ Ⓓ Ⓔ	30. Ⓐ Ⓑ Ⓒ Ⓓ Ⓔ

SECTION 1
Time—35 minutes
25 questions

<u>Directions:</u> The questions in this section are based on brief statements or passages. Choose your answers based on the reasoning in each passage. Do not make assumptions that are not supported by the passage or by common sense. For some questions, more than one answer choice may be possible, so choose the *best* answer to each question—that is, the one that is most accurate and complete. After you have chosen your answer, mark the corresponding space on the Answer Sheet.

1. Julian must have his mother's consent in order to go to the movies. His mother will not agree to let Julian go unless he has already done all his homework. Julian has finished his homework but has left it at Elizabeth's house and has no way to retrieve it. Julian's mother says that she must check his homework in order to consider it complete. Sometimes, however, she lets Julian go to the movies on the basis of his promise that he has done his homework, but only if he agrees to wash the dishes for her.

Which of the following scenarios would enable Julian to go to the movies?

(A) Julian tells his mother that he has done his homework.
(B) Elizabeth calls and tells Julian's mother that Julian has done his homework.
(C) Julian washes the dishes for his mother.
(D) Elizabeth promises to bring the homework to Julian's house.
(E) Julian washes the dishes and promises his mother that his homework is complete.

2. Advertising executive: One in every six Americans chews gum on a daily basis. Out of this number, seven out of ten choose chewing gum, two out of ten choose bubble gum, and one out of ten states no preference. Our client's share of the market will be most increased, therefore, if we focus our television advertising campaign on our client's chewing gum product rather than its bubble gum.

Which of the following, if true, most seriously weakens the executive's argument?

(A) Nine out of ten chewing gum chewers claim not to be affected by the advertising of brand rivals.
(B) Bubble gum chewers do not watch television.
(C) Fewer Americans chew gum now than 20 years ago.
(D) Chewing gum chewers do not watch television.
(E) Most people already prefer his client's chewing gum to its bubble gum.

GO ON TO THE NEXT PAGE

3. Beleaguered author: The future of publishing is cloudy at best, as it seems that no one cares to read books these days. Instead, everyone has turned to digital media and schlock entertainment for the instant gratification they are no longer taught to find in a book. There is even talk of the book industry itself becoming digital, with people turning to their computers and the Internet when they choose to read, instead of picking up a real, printed volume. How much of the aesthetic of the experience, indeed, the journey we know as a book, will be lost when this change is fully complete?

Which of the following can be inferred from the beleaguered author's statements?

(A) Online books will soon be the only kind people read.
(B) People are less intelligent than they used to be, since they seek instant gratification instead of deeper satisfaction.
(C) People were once taught to find instant gratification in reading a book, but this is no longer the case.
(D) People no longer care about aesthetics.
(E) The publishing industry prefers digital books to printed ones.

4. Politician: It is wrong for a government to infringe upon the liberty of an individual, except in those cases when to fail to restrict a person's liberty would directly result in another person being harmed. However, no ethical or legal statement may well be made regarding the responsibility of a government to protect a person from harming him- or herself; such a responsibility falls to that person alone.

Which one of the following can be properly inferred from the politician's statements?

(A) It is wrong for an individual to harm him- or herself.
(B) It is not morally wrong for a government to make suicide illegal.
(C) A government should interfere with a person's liberties only when that person's actions will lead to harm of any sort.
(D) A person may legally harm him- or herself as long as no one else is harmed.
(E) It is always wrong for a government to restrict an individual's liberties.

5. A happy household is one in which all members of the family dine together at least four nights out of the week. In order for a family to dine together on such a regular basis, one of two conditions must exist: the family members must not have busy schedules, or they must each be willing to make an effort to sacrifice time for one another. No one without a busy schedule is truly happy, since human beings must work in order to be happy. And a household may not be happy if its members are not happy.

If the information above is accepted as true, which of the following must be true of a household in order for it to be happy?

(A) The family members must not be happy individually.
(B) The family members must not be busy.
(C) The family members must take pride in their work.
(D) The family members must sacrifice time for one another.
(E) The family members must communicate regularly.

GO ON TO THE NEXT PAGE

6. Painters who create works of great artistic merit are often more highly valued by other artists than by the rest of the population. This is because members of the population who are not artists are often unable to appreciate the artistic merits of great paintings when compared to other paintings. For this reason, artistically great paintings often sell for less money than paintings with larger mass appeal. Therefore, if I wanted to collect a room full of paintings of great artistic merit, it would probably be less expensive than if I wanted to collect works with higher mass appeal.

Which of the following, if true, would resolve the discrepancy between cost and artistic merit noted above?

(A) Works of great artistic merit are often not works with great mass appeal.
(B) Artists are inclined to spend large amounts of money on works that they like.
(C) People who appreciate works of mass appeal tend to also appreciate works of great artistic merit.
(D) Paintings done by great artists are often not offered up for sale to members of the general public.
(E) Paintings that sell for very little money often do not have mass appeal or artistic merit.

7. Governments that subsist by fostering cultures of fear in the population have a tighter control over their citizens. These governments' laws are more strictly adhered to, governmental officers are given more deference by the people, and the president is viewed more as a monarch than a person of the people. Elections are not held in these tightly controlled societies, and presidents perpetually stay in office. But the average number of years that presidents are in office is less than the average number of years that monarchs rule in monarchical societies.

Which of the following resolves the discrepancy noted above?

(A) Presidents of tightly controlled societies are sometimes overthrown.
(B) Monarchical societies do not give monarchs the same type of deference that other societies give to their presidents.
(C) Presidents of tightly controlled societies tend to be less popular than monarchs, and they are often voted out of office.
(D) Monarchs come to power at a much younger age than presidents.
(E) Elections are held in monarchical societies.

GO ON TO THE NEXT PAGE

8. People who walk along downtown streets late at night run the risk of being robbed. Several factors are at play here. First, people who walk along streets at night are more likely to be walking alone. And people who are walking alone are more likely to be robbed. Second, given the opportunity, robbers are more likely to rob someone at night. Third, downtown streets are higher-crime areas than other streets in the city. Based on these factors, it is apparent that someone who is walking along downtown streets at night is more likely to be robbed than someone concurrently walking anywhere else in the city.

Which of the following, if true, would most support the conclusion?

(A) In all areas of cities except downtown, people are robbed only during daylight hours.
(B) Robbers are more likely to rob people in downtown areas than they are in suburban areas.
(C) People walking along a downtown street at night tend to have more money than people walking elsewhere.
(D) There are more burglars downtown than there are in most other parts of the cities.
(E) Buses at night carry burglars from outer regions of the city into the downtown area.

9. Presidential addresses are often pivotal moments in a nation's history. These are the points when the country's chief executive elucidates his or her plans to help the nation progress, heal its problems, and become more unified. Strangely, the same is not true of the addresses of important senators. Even though the addresses of these senators illuminate their plans to help the nation, these addresses are almost never pivotal moments in the nation's history because the plans of the senators are much less likely to come to fruition than are the plans of the president.

Which of the following, if true, would tend to strengthen the argument?

(A) Presidents are often more eloquent than senators and evoke a more emotional response from their audience than senators.
(B) Presidents' plans are ratified 95% of the time, whereas important senators' propositions are ratified only 4% of the time.
(C) It is counterintuitive to believe that plans of some people are not actualized but plans of other people are.
(D) Presidential addresses are not always pivotal moments but they are always historically noteworthy, whereas senators' addresses are sometimes ignored by the public.
(E) Competition between presidents and senators often causes presidential proposals to be rejected.

GO ON TO THE NEXT PAGE

10. I. Houses that have dogs get fleas.

II. People who live in houses with fleas get fleas themselves.

III. If a person does not live with fleas, then he or she does not have a cat.

Which of the following makes it logical to claim that Bill has fleas?

(A) Bill has a cat.
(B) Bill has a dog.
(C) Bill lives in an apartment with fleas.
(D) Bill does not have fleas himself.
(E) Bill's brother, who lives in a house, has fleas.

11. Mount Kilaboo will more than likely erupt this year. The fact is that it has erupted every year of the past three and every decade of the past eight. This increase in volcanic activity means that the pressure within the mountain is growing and will soon result in a monumental eruption the likes of which Mount Kilaboo has never produced before. If this occurs, then the villages that are located within 100 feet of where the lava flow reached last year will have to be evacuated before the lava pours over the village.

Which of the following is assumed by the argument?

(A) Mount Kilaboo will cause a village evacuation this year.
(B) If a monumental eruption occurs, lava will extend at least 100 feet farther than it did last year.
(C) Mount Kilaboo's imminent monumental eruption will be larger than any previously recorded in the world.
(D) Pressure within a volcanic mountain will increase until the entire mountain explodes.
(E) Increased volcanic activity increases the chance that lava flow will not occur.

12. Realtor: A great place to invest is not in the stock market; it is in Marlagos beachfront property! Past history has shown that in 10 years the beachfront properties here on Marlagos Island have quadrupled in value. What a great investment it would have been to buy these properties 10 years ago. I certainly wish I had! There is nothing to suggest that this trend of price increase will not continue for long into the future, so all people with the funds should buy, buy, buy!

Which of the following, if true, would tend to support the argument of the realtor?

(A) The amount of tourism on the island will increase by 30 times in the next 10 years.
(B) The stock market has been very flimsy lately when compared to the bond market.
(C) People who buy beachfront property on the island will never lose all their money.
(D) Property investments in general yield lower returns than stock market investments.
(E) Buying land is a good way to diversify a person's financial portfolio.

GO ON TO THE NEXT PAGE

13. Aliens have visited this world. They invaded Area 51, and they have picked up many people from farms and homes throughout the region and taken them onto their ships in order to study them. Of course the aliens have not officially announced their presence. What good would this do them? If they are going to invade, they would not want to alert us to this fact so that we could prepare. And if they just wanted to study humans, then they would not want to announce their presence because then we would change our behavior and ruin their observations.

Which of the following is assumed by the passage?

(A) Aliens have not been technologically able to visit all regions of the Earth.
(B) Aliens have invaded worlds before ours and might invade ours.
(C) Humans would benefit if the aliens announced their presence to us.
(D) It is possible for aliens to get important information about humans through their study of us.
(E) Aliens would be interested only in invading the world or studying humans.

14. Grass has to be mowed every week during the summer but only about once every month during the winter. This is because during the summer the days are longer and the light from the sun is more intense. Both these factors combine to allow grass to glean more energy from the summer sunlight that reaches its leaves. Plants in general react the same way as grass does during the summer—they grow longer faster for the same reasons that grass does. People just do not realize this because, unlike growing grass that needs to be mowed, the growth spurts of other plants do not require reciprocal actions.

Which of the following is assumed by the argument?

(A) Juniper bushes do not need extra pruning during the summer months.
(B) Grass grows faster in the spring than in the winter.
(C) Increases in light always lead to increases in plant growth.
(D) Mowing is a task that is not completely necessary during the winter when grass does not grow.
(E) If there were no extra hours of sunlight during the summer, plants would still grow faster because of the sun's extra intensity.

GO ON TO THE NEXT PAGE

15. Exceptional football stars exit college and then enter the professional leagues with the desire to make money and also to bring about some good in the world through their stardom. If Kevin Kennedy played football, he would be this "exceptional" type of player because he entered college with the desire to bring about good.

Which of the following, if true, would undermine the conclusion of the passage?

(A) It has been well documented that Kevin Kennedy plays the European version of football, known as soccer.

(B) Football stars who truly realize their potential never have the goal of making money through their fame.

(C) People who enter college with the desire to bring about good in the world leave without that desire.

(D) People who play professional football are almost never able to bring about any real good in the world.

(E) Football stars become exceptional only after they have played football for a minimum of five years.

16. Photographers are condemned to living life vicariously through black and white, color-coded, and panoramic still frames. Instead of enjoying special moments while and when they occur, photographers try to capture these moments. But by the effort of concentrating their sight through a small circular peephole, photographers irrevocably lose sight of the captured moment and leave themselves with no redress but the infinite opportunity to bask in a small photographic eclipse of the full moment that once occurred in a brilliant and broad range of living motion. Is an infinite ability to regard the zenith of a special moment worth more than a transitory opportunity to regard the whole timeframe in its vast living glory?

Which of the following, if true, would undermine the argument's contention that photographers lose moments when they capture them?

(A) Photographers do not decide whether they will capture or observe a moment until right before it occurs.

(B) Photographers gain greatly from captured moments, because not only do they record those moments but they are also paid for capturing them.

(C) People often do not take the opportunity to observe the full beauty of an instantaneous moment in the way that photographers do.

(D) Photographers are able to enjoy the full benefits and character of an occurring moment through the lens of their camera.

(E) When viewed through photographs, certain types of moments appear to be better than they actually were.

GO ON TO THE NEXT PAGE

17. Anthropologist: It is inevitable that a species of ant will take over the world if we let ant colonies subsist into the next evolutionary era. The facts that imply this turn of events are clear and corroborated. First, the total ant population is hundreds of times greater than the human population. Second, ants are smaller and need less food per individual and therefore will be less susceptible to overpopulation. Third, the ant's exoskeleton will allow it to adapt to any environment. Fourth, the ant's shorter life span causes it to evolve faster than the human population. In conclusion, there is simply no way for humans to halt a future ant takeover if we do not stop them now.

Which of the following, if true, would be the best evidence to counter the anthropologist's final conclusion?

(A) Ants do not possess the rational capacity to form sentient thoughts and therefore will never be able to exert the kind of global domination that humans do.
(B) Most arthropod species could not be eradicated right now even if humans were to decide to try to do so.
(C) In the future, human nations will be able to stop any ant takeover by setting off a series of atom bombs that will create a nuclear winter.
(D) Ants are not the most highly sophisticated arthropod that humans should be worried about—grasshoppers and crickets are much more dangerous.
(E) Aliens could arrive on Earth during the next evolutionary era, and they will probably subdue all species of ants.

18. Populist: Modern art resembles the drawings that my child brings back from preschool every afternoon. These scribbles are not fascinating! They are not genius! It is amazing that so-called artists have brainwashed an entire culture into believing that they are creators, when it's clear that their children's work is worth no more than a chocolate chip cookie, a pat on the back, and a glass of milk after coming home from school each day.

Which of the following, if true, would counter the Populist's fundamental proposition?

(A) Children are unable to reproduce "modern art" pictures.
(B) The elitist's child would make a fortune if his art were sold at modern art auctions.
(C) Even the most unaccomplished of modern artists never have children.
(D) Unless harassed, a modern artist will never admit that she has sold one of her children's drawings.
(E) Many adults cannot draw as well as the children of prominent artists.

GO ON TO THE NEXT PAGE

19. Guitars are musical instruments of diminished importance in the pop music era. Synthesizers and drumbeats have been brought to the forefront of music compilations and consequently have edged out classic rock's staple electric guitar. Recordings now focus mainly on background noise and reverb, rather than on the eloquent sounds of the master guitarist. If classic rock is to survive, then its fans will need to find a way to bring its flagship instrument back to center stage in this decade's new musical genres.

Which of the following, if true, would undermine the conclusion of the passage?

(A) The popularity of classic rock is not dependant upon any trait or aspect of any new musical genre.

(B) Classic rock will survive only if electric pianos are given greater significance and placed stage front.

(C) Classic rock will never be extremely popular again, even if the guitar is brought to the forefront in tomorrow's music genres.

(D) Blues music is not superior to classic rock, but it will survive longer than other jazz and some other genres.

(E) An unusual number of pop musicians play classical guitar and would enjoy exploiting its versatility in their music.

20. Historian: In order to build the pyramids, the Egyptians had to move large blocks of rock that weighed hundreds of tons over large distances. The question of how this feat was achieved puzzles the modern-day historian. Some people claim that the Egyptians built the pyramids using wind power; they attached a type of kite to the block, and the force of the wind allowed a small group of people to push the block along toward its destination. However, this is impossible, because, as anyone who has visited the country today knows, Egypt is entirely devoid of wind.

Which of the following identifies a flaw in the argument?

(A) It ignores the fact that Egyptians could have used kites for things other than capturing the wind.

(B) It assumes the continuation of a condition that might have changed from several thousand years ago.

(C) It neglects to mention that millions of people would have been working on the project regardless of the wind.

(D) It claims that using wind would be a necessary condition for moving the blocks.

(E) It fails to account for the long amount of time that Egyptians took to build each pyramid.

GO ON TO THE NEXT PAGE

21. My science book says that when liquid A and liquid B are mixed, liquid C is formed. When more liquid A than B is mixed, liquid C will have yellow color. When more liquid B than A is mixed, liquid C will have green color. Tomorrow, our teacher will mix liquid A and B to form a liquid that is either green or yellow in color.

    Which of the following identifies an error of reasoning in the passage?

    (A) It assumes that liquid C is formed by the mixture of liquids A and B.
    (B) It assumes that a chemical reaction will occur in a similar way to the way it did in the past.
    (C) It assumes that the teacher will add some other liquid to the mix in addition to A and B.
    (D) It assumes that the teacher will not mix equal parts of liquid A and B.
    (E) It assumes that the liquid will not be hidden by the teacher before the class sees what color it has become.

22. It has been demonstrated that people who heavily consume alcohol are more stressed than people who are less intensive drinkers. Studies show the same for cigarette smokers. People who smoke tend to have a higher incidence of stress than the population of nonsmokers. Studies show a huge overlap between groups who drink heavily and smoke. Studies also demonstrate a relationship between strained interpersonal familial relationships and drinking. Therefore, in order to curb familial problems, people should find ways to cut down on their stress levels.

    A flaw of the reasoning in this passage is that it:

    (A) neglects to mention that use of illegal drugs is tied to interpersonal problems
    (B) assumes that stress levels create interpersonal problems and not the other way around
    (C) identifies the implications of drinking and smoking in the argument's conclusions
    (D) omits revealing the causal relationship between stress and cigarette smoking
    (E) infers that stress leads to interpersonal problems, which lead to alcohol consumption and smoking

GO ON TO THE NEXT PAGE

23. Self-deprecating humor is the funniest kind as long as a listener is able to get the jokes. It is a type of humor that allows a comic to make commentary based on an introspective view of the wheels and cogs that turn his or her own psyche. Comedians who are unable to view their inner workings effectively are incapable of using this sort of humor, but those who have the inner awareness to be self-deprecating gain access to stockpiles of jewels that can be brought out for a crowd at any moment. It would make sense, therefore, that audience members who are not self-knowledgeable enough to understand their own psyches are not capable of enjoying humor that is self-deprecating.

Which of the following techniques is used by the author in drawing the argument's conclusion?

(A) comparing comedians to stockpiles of jewels that can be brought out for the crowd at any moment

(B) implying that comedians who are able to think introspectively are able to make funnier jokes than comedians who do not think introspectively

(C) questioning the validity of a certain assumption by professing the merits of a competing assumption

(D) making assumptions about the capabilities of audience members based on the capabilities of comedians

(E) humorously misapplying the key term "funniest" in determining the quality of a comedian's jokes

24. The judgment that a person is a "good" person always rests on an appraisal of the quality of a number of acts that he or she has previously engaged in. A series of virtuous acts is the only test for a person's "goodness." Therefore, saying that a person is "good" is only to summarize a series of his or her acts, and labeling a person as "good" provides no basis for predicting the quality of that person's future or unknown acts.

Which of the following is logically flawed in the way most similar to the argument above?

(A) A manager is known to be a manager only because he or she has engaged previously in managerial acts. Therefore, nothing can be determined about a person known as a manager solely based on his or her having the title of manager.

(B) A sports psychologist talks to sports players and would not be employed if he or she did not talk with sports players. Therefore, nothing can be determined about a sports psychologist who does not talk to sports players.

(C) A baseball player's being called a successful hitter is determined only by the number of balls that he has hit well in his games to date. Therefore, no judgment can be made about the future quality of the hitting of someone who has become known as a successful hitter.

(D) Politicians are judged to be politicians only on the basis of their being elected by the people. Without being elected, a person would not be a politician. Therefore, predictions can be made about a person's future as a politician by knowing the future opinions of the populace.

(E) Swiss trains have earned the reputation of being "punctual." Without constantly being on time, they would have never gained this reputation. Therefore, you can predict the nature of the trains based on their reputation.

GO ON TO THE NEXT PAGE

25. Robert: People who invest in the stock
        market should be surprised when their
        investments suddenly diminish. After all,
        companies portray themselves to be safe
        and good investments. When it turns out
        that they are not, people have every
        reason to be astonished.

    Amanda: People should be surprised only
        when companies make bad decisions
        that would have negative implications on
        their stock prices. It is the job of
        executives to prevent companies from
        doing this, and yet sometimes the
        companies still do so.

Which of the following, if true, would tend to
support Robert's argument?

(A) Surprise is a reaction that should be
     reserved for the most extraordinary
     circumstances, such as earning money.
(B) It should be unsurprising when good
     investments mature to produce really
     good returns.
(C) Immature stock funds should never be
     divested until they have an opportunity
     to mature.
(D) People should not expect companies to
     have qualities that are different from the
     ones those companies portray to
     investors.
(E) CEOs are always surprised when
     stockholders' portfolios decline.

S T O P

IF YOU FINISH BEFORE TIME RUNS OUT, CHECK YOUR WORK ON THIS SECTION ONLY.
DO NOT GO ON TO ANY OTHER TEST SECTION.

SECTION 2
Time—35 minutes
24 questions

<u>Directions:</u> The questions in this section are divided into groups. Each group is based on a set of conditions. For each question, choose the answer that is most accurate and complete. For some questions, you may wish to draw a rough diagram to help you select your response. Mark the corresponding space on your Answer Sheet.

Questions 1–6

At a local boat race, six boaters, Anna, Ben, Chris, Dan, Emily, and Fanny, are competing for the watercourse title. Each boater has his or her boat in one of six starting slots.

Every boat starts in a slot, and no boat shares a slot with any other boat.
The starting slots are numbered from 1 to 6.
Chris is in a slot three numbers below Dan's.
Ben is in a slot three numbers below Anna's.
Fanny is in a slot with a lower number than Emily's.

1. Which of the following is a possible order for the boaters to start in?

    (A) Fanny, Ben, Chris, Emily, Dan, Anna
    (B) Chris, Fanny, Ben, Dan, Emily, Anna
    (C) Ben, Anna, Emily, Dan, Fanny, Chris
    (D) Chris, Ben, Fanny, Anna, Dan, Emily
    (E) Ben, Chris, Emily, Anna, Dan, Fanny

2. If Fanny is in slot 3, then who could start in slot 2?

    (A) Anna or Dan
    (B) Ben or Chris
    (C) Chris or Anna
    (D) Dan or Emily
    (E) Emily or Ben

3. If Chris is in a lower-numbered slot than Ben, then which of the following could be true?

    (A) Dan is in a higher-numbered slot than Anna.
    (B) Fanny is in a higher-numbered slot than both Dan and Anna.
    (C) Neither Fanny nor Chris is in slot 1.
    (D) Chris and Ben are not in consecutive slots.
    (E) Neither Emily nor Dan starts in slot 4.

4. If Anna starts in a slot numbered one lower than Dan's slot, then which of the following must be true?

    (A) Ben starts in the slot numbered one lower than Chris's slot.
    (B) Emily starts in slot 4.
    (C) Dan starts in a lower-numbered slot than Emily.
    (D) Either Anna or Chris starts in slot 3.
    (E) Chris and Fanny start in consecutive slots.

5. If Chris, Emily, Anna, and Dan start in consecutive slots in that order from least to greatest, then which of the following CANNOT be true?

    (A) Fanny starts in slot 1.
    (B) Two boaters start in higher-numbered slots than Emily's slot.
    (C) Ben and Chris do not start in consecutive slots.
    (D) Anna starts in slot 5.
    (E) Ben does not start in slot 3.

6. If Ben starts in slot 1 and Chris starts in a higher-numbered slot than Fanny, then which of the following could be true?

    (A) Nobody starts in slot 5.
    (B) Fanny starts in a slot three numbers below Emily's.
    (C) Emily starts in a higher-numbered slot than Dan.
    (D) More than one slot separates Chris and Emily.
    (E) A person whose name begins with a vowel starts in slot 3.

GO ON TO THE NEXT PAGE

Questions 7–11

In an ancient Greek town, there are eight huts that exist in two perfectly parallel rows. The arrangement of the huts resembles the following diagram:

```
        A      B      C      D
Row 1:  ■      ■      ■      ■

Row 2:  ■      ■      ■      ■
        R      S      T      V
```

Animals tread between these huts wearing out the grass, so the chief of the town has decided to pave paths between the huts with a primitive form of concrete. He keeps in mind several rules when planning these roads:

> Each hut in row 1 is connected to one and only one hut in row 2.
> Each hut in row 2 is connected to one and only one hut in row 1.
> Roads can connect huts in one row to other huts in the same row.
> All roads are perfectly straight lines, and none extends beyond the town.

7. What must be true if there are zero intersections of roads?

  (A) There are four roads total.
  (B) A connects with C.
  (C) T connects with V.
  (D) B connects with S.
  (E) C connects with D.

8. What must NOT be true if there is only one intersection?

  (A) A connects with S.
  (B) D connects with T.
  (C) R connects with C
  (D) V connects with T.
  (E) V connects with D.

9. What must be true if there are only two intersections and B is connected to T and A is connected to R?

  (A) S is connected to D.
  (B) C is connected to S.
  (C) V is connected to T.
  (D) T is connected to C.
  (E) B is connected to A.

10. What must NOT be true if R connects to D and there are only three points of intersection?

  (A) S connects to A.
  (B) D does not connect to V.
  (C) B connects to T.
  (D) C does not connect to V.
  (E) T does not connect to A.

11. If B connects with T and D connects with R, then which of the following could be true?

  (A) S connects with B.
  (B) T connects with D.
  (C) V connects with T.
  (D) R connects with B.
  (E) D connects with V.

GO ON TO THE NEXT PAGE

Questions 12–17

A group of aliens walks across the Texas plains until it come upon an oil well. Thinking that it is a sentient being, each alien decides to try and shake its hand. Some aliens are bolder than other aliens, but all of them eventually touch the oil well. No alien touches the oil well at the same time as any other alien. The order in which aliens A, B, C, D, E, F, G, and H touch the oil well is governed by the following constraints:

D touches the well before B and C.
G touches the well after A and H.
C touches the well before E and F.
A touches the well after F and E.

12. Which of the following could be the order in which the aliens touch the well, from first to last?

(A) H, D, C, B, F, E, A, G
(B) D, B, E, F, C, A, H, G
(C) D, C, B, F, H, E, G, A
(D) D, C, B, A, E, F, H, G
(E) H, D, B, E, C, F, A, G

13. Which pair contains two aliens either of whom could touch the oil well seventh?

(A) G, F
(B) B, H
(C) E, A
(D) B, C
(E) A, F

14. How many different aliens could touch the well third?

(A) 1
(B) 2
(C) 3
(D) 4
(E) 5

15. Which pair could never touch the oil well consecutively in any order?

(A) H, E
(B) B, A
(C) E, C
(D) D, C
(E) E, G

16. Which of the following must be true if B touches the oil well third and H touches the oil well fourth?

(A) F touches sixth.
(B) A touches seventh.
(C) E touches sixth.
(D) C touches first.
(E) G touches sixth.

17. If F and E do not touch the oil well consecutively, then which of the following must NOT be true?

(A) H touches seventh, and B touches second.
(B) F touches third, and E touches fifth.
(C) A touches seventh, and H touches fifth.
(D) B touches fourth, and E touches third.
(E) D touches first, and G touches eighth.

GO ON TO THE NEXT PAGE

Questions 18–24

A Girl Scout troop of seven girls, A, B, C, D, E, F, and G, is broken up into three groups to distribute cookies. Group 1 has two scouts, group 2 has three, and group 3 has two. Due to interpersonal difficulties, the scout master arranges the groups according to the following constraints:

> A is in a group with G.
> B is not in a group with C or D.
> E is not with C or D.

18. If A is in group 2, then which of the following could be true?

   (A) C is in group 1, and D is in group 3.
   (B) B is in group 1, and E is in group 3.
   (C) F is in group 2 with A and G.
   (D) G is in group 3 with B.
   (E) C is in group 1, and E is in group 1.

19. If G is in group 1 or in group 3, then which of the following must be true?

   (A) F is in group 2.
   (B) B is in group 3.
   (C) E is in group 2.
   (D) B and E share a group with F.
   (E) C is in group 1 or 2.

20. If A and E are in group 2, then which of the following must be true?

   (A) G shares a group with D.
   (B) F shares a group with B.
   (C) D shares a group with F.
   (D) C and D are in group 3.
   (E) E does not share a group with G.

21. If F is in group 3, then which of the following is impossible?

   (A) A is in group 2.
   (B) E is in group 3.
   (C) D is in group 2.
   (D) B is in group 2.
   (E) G is in group 1.

22. If F and E are in group 1, then which of the following must be true?

   (A) B is in group 2.
   (B) G is in group 3.
   (C) D and A share a group.
   (D) A is in a higher-numbered group than C.
   (E) C and D do not share a group.

23. If A is in group 2 and F is in group 1, then how many possible arrangements are there for the variables?

   (A) two
   (B) four
   (C) six
   (D) eight
   (E) ten

24. If F is not in a group with A, B, or E, then which of the following must be true?

   (A) F is in group 2.
   (B) F is in a group with C or D.
   (C) F is in a group with G.
   (D) B is in group 3.
   (E) C and D are in group 3.

STOP

IF YOU FINISH BEFORE TIME RUNS OUT, CHECK YOUR WORK ON THIS SECTION ONLY.
DO NOT GO ON TO ANY OTHER TEST SECTION.

SECTION 3
Time—35 minutes
25 questions

<u>Directions:</u> The questions in this section are based on brief statements or passages. Choose your answers based on the reasoning in each passage. Do not make assumptions that are not supported by the passage or by common sense. For some questions, more than one answer choice may be possible, so choose the *best* answer to each question, that is, the one that is most accurate and complete. After you have chosen your answer, mark the corresponding space on the Answer Sheet.

1. People who are concerned citizens know and abide by the rule that if their pets want to go into the park during the daytime, the animals should be kept on a leash so that their excitement does not become a problem and disturb people who are in the park to enjoy the quiet nature of the outdoors. Alex is a concerned citizen, but he never leashes his dog when they go into the park together during the daytime.

Which of the following can be inferred from the passage?

(A) No one else is in the park when Alex enters the park.
(B) Alex's dog gets excited, but not very excited when he is in the park.
(C) People who are in the park are concerned citizens.
(D) All cats should be leashed before they are allowed to enter the park.
(E) Alex's dog never wants to go into the park.

2. Computers have always been modeled to perform in the same ways as the mind of a human. Addition, calculation, syllogism, and all other computational mental activities were carefully deciphered in the human brain before any engineer ever tried to transcribe these processes to the hard-wiring of circuitry boards. This trend will continue: As we learn more about the human brain, we will transfer more of our mental capacities to our electronic counterparts—the computers. Eventually, the central processing unit (CPU) of a computer will perfectly mirror the mentality of a human brain. Surely, this perfect computer will attain self-knowledge.

Which of the following, if true, would invalidate the argument's conclusion?

(A) Even if a computer did attain self-knowledge, there would be no way for a human being to ever realize it.
(B) Compositions of electronic circuits will never be able to gain a rational capacity that would amount to the possession of self-knowledge.
(C) We do not currently have the capability of producing a CPU that mirrors even 1/100 of the processes in the human brain.
(D) Some human beings do not possess what one could call self-knowledge, so it is not likely that a computer will ever possess it.
(E) Self-knowledge is a mental gift that is only enjoyed by holy people and therefore can be transferred only to excessively spiritual computers.

GO ON TO THE NEXT PAGE

3. In 2004, 60 million Americans worked for more than 40 hours a week on average, and approximately 55 million Americans found their jobs to be unreasonably demanding. These figures demonstrate that a relatively small portion of those who worked for more than 40 hours per week on average did not find their jobs to be "unreasonably demanding."

Which of the following is a logical flaw of the argument?

(A) It draws a conclusion based on evidence that could support several conclusions.
(B) It overlooks the possibility that there is little or no overlap between groups.
(C) It provides no information regarding groups of workers who worked over 50 hours per week.
(D) It juxtaposes two pieces of concluding text regarding groups with bivariate tendencies.
(E) It makes a conclusion based on premises that contradict each other.

4. Somnambulist: A person should invest a serious amount of time in choosing a bed. Instead of ordering a bed from a catalog or just going to the store to look at one, a person should bring a new mattress home for a couple of days and sleep on it before buying it. This will give the person a good idea about whether he or she will be comfortable sleeping on the purchase from then on. Many people do not realize that they can become unconsciously disgruntled with their bedroom selection, and that it will cause incessant troubles for them in their subconscious life. People should realize that humans spend half their lives asleep.

Which of the following functions does the last sentence play when the entire passage is considered?

(A) It is the main point toward which the argument as a whole is directed.
(B) It is an irrelevant piece of evidence included merely to summarize the passage.
(C) It is a premise on which the argument as a whole is based.
(D) It is an assertion that supports the conclusion.
(E) It clarifies the meaning of an ambiguous sentence in the passage.

5. Professor: A healthy prenatal environment is the most vital factor in producing an intelligent offspring. The steroids, minerals, and vitamins that are transferred into prenatal brains jump-start cranial enlargement and neurodevelopment. There is simply no way for infants who experience malnourishment in their prenatal environments to catch up with other children who were not malnourished.

Doctor: Practically speaking, very few children experience malnourishment in their prenatal environment. A much larger portion of the population experiences malnourishment in their neonatal environment. On average, this neonatal inadequacy of diet holds larger implications for the intelligence of offspring than the specifics of the prenatal environment.

Which of the following is the point at issue between the professor and the doctor?

(A) the negative implications that malnourishment holds for a child's intelligence
(B) the importance of a child being adequately nourished within its prenatal environment
(C) the relative importance of neonatal nourishment in producing intelligent offspring
(D) the need for doctors and professors to monitor the nourishment of a child through both prenatal and neonatal stages
(E) the inability of children to overcome the inadequacies of their environments

GO ON TO THE NEXT PAGE

6. Many critics believe that music causes emotions. The lyrics, chords, and melodies of songs inspire our souls and pluck at our heartstrings, making listeners respond with a passion and zeal for life that cannot be similarly produced by any other human endeavor. It has not been until recently, however, that we as a culture have been able to realize this quality of music, because only since the 1920s has music been commercially available. Hundreds of millions of sales of CDs, tapes, and phonographs make it apparent that music is incredibly evocative and can be factored into people's lives, wherever and whenever they want it, by the simple pressing of a "play" button. Before music's commercialization, a person could not have had such easy access to music, and therefore, it was not possible for music to have such a huge impact on anyone's life.

Which of the following, if true, would most support the conclusion that society has only recently realized the evocative quality of music?

(A) More CDs have been sold than tapes, 8-tracks, and phonograph records combined.
(B) The commercialization of music was necessary for society to realize music's emotional effects.
(C) Music inspires emotion only if it is not played at CD-level digital quality.
(D) People long ago could go to their local pub or dance hall to feel the emotional effects of good music.
(E) People who played instruments in ancient Greece could not appreciate the emotions that music inspires.

7. Lobbyist: The airborne pollution made by automobiles has little to no effect on people's everyday lives. After all, increases of the CO_2 concentration in breathable air affect only those living in big cities, because by the time the city air has diffused to the countryside, trees have been given the time to filter out excess CO_2 and replace it with pure oxygen. Therefore, there is no reason to strengthen the regulations on vehicular exhaust fumes.

Which of the following would most weaken the lobbyist's argument?

(A) People living outside of the city have less tolerance for high CO_2 concentrations than people in the city.
(B) It would be very costly to force the auto industry to make more environmentally friendly automobiles.
(C) Exhaust fumes from factories have been proven to have detrimental effects on the everyday lives of city inhabitants.
(D) An environmental group runs a study that details the negative effects of CO_2 pollution.
(E) There are other pollutants that are created by car exhaust fumes besides CO_2 that negatively affect people's lives.

8. All basketball players hate the rain. All people who hate the rain do not like cats. Many tall people are basketball players.

Which of the following would need to be assumed in order to reach the conclusion that everyone who owns a cat is not a basketball player?

(A) All tall people do not own a cat.
(B) If you own a cat, then you dislike cats.
(C) Everyone who dislikes cats does not own a cat.
(D) Some people who hate the rain do not own a cat.
(E) No one who likes the rain owns a cat.

GO ON TO THE NEXT PAGE

9. The great Roman Julius Caesar was hated by all Roman citizens. This animosity is shown by historians through multiple documents describing the circumstances surrounding Caesar's death. These documents reveal that in the end even his best friend, Brutus, wanted to kill him. Roman politicians and senators also conspired to bring about his death.

A flaw in the argument is that the author

(A) assumes that whatever is true of a group is true of a sample of that group
(B) argues for a course of action that is counterproductive
(C) makes a conclusion based on a small and unrepresentative sample of a group
(D) makes an appeal to the opinion of an implausible authority
(E) treats a failure to prove a claim as proof of a denial of the claim

10. It has been claimed that many people who own video game systems do not use them. This is preposterous because it is impossible for someone to own something that would bring so much happiness and not use it constantly.

The flawed reasoning above is analogous to the reasoning in which of the following?

(A) A statement has been issued that the country of Minishu has nuclear weapons. Minishuan officials claim that they will never use the weapons, but this is unlikely since the only reason to have weapons is to use them.
(B) Bernie claims that he never listens to his Jeff Buckley CD. However, he is lying because the CD brings too much aural satisfaction not to be listened to repeatedly.
(C) Absalom claims that he loves his father dearly. However, based on the actions of the biblical figure of Absalom, his claim is not likely to be true.
(D) It has been claimed that tigers will eventually become extinct. However, this is unlikely because they have sharp claws and teeth that will always aid them in catching prey.
(E) It has been argued that many people who own cars do not use them enough. This claim is inarguable because it is impossible to determine how much a car should be used.

11. Captain: The Bermuda Triangle is a place of great danger, where the seaweed has eyes, where there are ghost ships in the fog, where grisly squid will envelop a boat and pull it and its crew into the depths. My crew will never return to this dreadful place, no matter how thirsty they may be for adventure and riches.

First Mate: Captain, I respect your wishes and utterly agree with you about the dangers of the Triangle, but as soon as we return home, you are scheduled to sail through the Bermuda Triangle to Africa. Am I to cancel this voyage for you?

Which of the following is the point at issue between the captain and the first mate?

(A) whether the captain will return to the Bermuda Triangle
(B) whether the first mate will return to the Bermuda Triangle
(C) whether the crew will return to the Bermuda Triangle
(D) whether the Bermuda Triangle holds no danger for sailors
(E) whether the members of the crew will cancel their future voyages through the Triangle

GO ON TO THE NEXT PAGE

12. Musician: People enjoy music because it stirs the native passions latent in everyone's soul. Even the most uptight and rigid person relaxes when hearing a good jazz tune. The most depressed human being lightens at the sound of Bach's "Air in G." Music fills a person with any emotion he or she would like to feel. All someone has to do is pick a song and play it to suddenly be filled with the emotion that the song was designed to evoke in its listeners. In the next voting term, people should vote to raise school spending on music programs.

Which of the following roles does the assertion that people should vote for increasing school spending on music programs play in the argument?

(A) It is the main point toward which the argument as a whole is directed.
(B) It is a claim that is largely unsupported by evidence.
(C) It is a premise that will be validated if listeners agree with the main point of the argument.
(D) It reformulates a previously stated argument in the passage.
(E) It juxtaposes expenditure and particular ways of enjoying music.

13. The American Revolution was at first greeted with widespread cynicism. Almost no one truly believed that a bunch of disheveled American soldiers could defeat the English army, an army that was more than likely the world's most powerful one since the early Renaissance. Eventually as the war wore on, Americans realized that they would not really have to defeat the English army; they would just have to force them into a stalemate through the use of guerrilla warfare. After realizing this, Americans began to feel very positive about the revolution. They foresaw that America could cause England to lose its resolve and that eventually the king would relinquish his efforts to dominate American soil.

Which of the following is the main point of the passage?

(A) The leaders of the American Revolution were initially met with a large amount of skepticism.
(B) The American army was doomed if it tried to battle the English army in a head-on attack.
(C) Guerrilla warfare was the only way to successfully fight the English army.
(D) The English king would eventually tire of his efforts to dominate America if the Americans used guerrilla warfare.
(E) American sentiment toward the Revolution changed for the better as the war wore on.

GO ON TO THE NEXT PAGE

14. Sports gambling is a dangerous hobby because you have no real control over the outcome of a particular game. Sure, you can study statistics and injury reports, but when it all comes down to it, the majority of outcomes are determined solely by chance. Bookies employ groups of people who, for a living, study the odds of every betted game in order to make sure that the bookie will make money. Some people assume that they can guess at the odds better than these hired statisticians, but, in general, it is impossible to improve a bettor's chances. This is why gambling on sports is almost always a waste of time and money.

Which of the following can be concluded from the paragraph?

(A) Sports gamblers would be better served by playing poker for a living.
(B) Investing in the outcomes of sports games is like investing in the stock market.
(C) Bookies are able to determine the odds on games better than any other group of people.
(D) Dangerous hobbies can be physically dangerous in addition to being monetarily risky.
(E) Most sports gamblers could do something more constructive with their money than bet on sports.

15. Journalist: Choosing a new pope is a difficult decision because the church desires a person who is very experienced in the faith and also someone who can lead the faith well in modern times by being in touch with modern times. The problem is that people who are very experienced in the faith are often very old, and people who are very old tend to be out of touch with modern times, so it appears that there is almost never a pope chosen that fits both criteria. The best decision would be for the church to choose a pope who is young enough to be in touch with modern times and who will likely become a person very experienced in the faith.

Which of the following can be concluded about the journalist's opinion from the passage?

(A) Having a pope who is in touch with modern times is more important than having a pope who is very experienced in the faith.
(B) The pope should never be a person who is inexperienced in the faith, even if he is in touch with modern times.
(C) Popes who are both in touch with modern times and very experienced in their faith are best able to serve as ambassadors.
(D) People who are very experienced in the faith and who are in touch with modern times should always become the pope.
(E) Priests who dislike the pope would be best served by voicing their opinions before he is elected rather than after.

GO ON TO THE NEXT PAGE

16. A park officer reports that in the previous year, 30% of the bear population in the park was determined to be excessively aggressive toward humans. This year, a full 60% of the bear population has been found to be excessively aggressive. However, bear attack statistics show that in the past 12 months there have been only 3 bear attacks on humans, whereas last year there were 12 such bear attacks over the same time period.

Which of the following would help to resolve the apparent discrepancy present in the passage?

(A) Throughout the nation, there have been fewer bear attacks this year than in previous years.

(B) More people have been bringing knives to parks in order to protect themselves during attacks.

(C) Fifteen people have decided not to visit the park this year because of the risk of bear attacks.

(D) At the end of last year, three-quarters of the park's bear population was permanently deported to a far-off park.

(E) A local news anchorman has decided to make peace with the bears by feeding them honey on the day of the summer solstice.

17. Financial support for the chamber music hall in every city in America rests largely on the shoulders of a few wealthy individuals. If these individuals did not offer their support to the music halls, then the halls would be forced to close and the musicians would be out of work. Based on this general review, it appears that music halls would not be able to maintain operations in communist societies where there are no individually wealthy people.

Which of the following, if true, most calls the argument's conclusion into question?

(A) People in communist societies love music and would be strongly in favor of attending music halls.

(B) In communist societies, there are other groups besides the wealthy who might find it beneficial to bear the financial burden of supporting music halls.

(C) Wealthy individuals from noncommunist countries might desire to fund the operations of music halls in communist nations.

(D) Music halls are not needed in communist nations since musicians find work by playing in people's homes.

(E) Music halls are very expensive to maintain and often considered excessive, so a communist nation would view them as an unnecessary financial burden.

GO ON TO THE NEXT PAGE

18. Political races should be completely subsidized by the government. This would allow for candidates to spend less time fundraising and more time differentiating themselves from their opponents based on substantive issues. It would also free candidates from owing any favors to big corporations once they get into office. When elected under this subsidized system, officeholders would be able to make impartial decisions about corporate acts without feeling as if they had a vested interest in the success of a particular company that had donated large sums of money to their campaign. Fully subsidizing races would equalize the playing field, since every candidate would have an equal amount of money with which to campaign. All these results would greatly improve the political environment of our nation, and in order to enjoy each of these advantages, we only need to lobby the government to completely subsidize political races.

Which of the following principles, if established, provides a basis for supporting the argument above?

(A) Political races should be based on the candidates' views, not the ideas of other people.
(B) It is more important for the populace to hear substantive issues than propaganda if the people are to successfully choose a candidate.
(C) Politicians should not owe any favors to corporations.
(D) Large sums of money should not determine who wins a political race.
(E) Governments should not get involved with candidates at election time.

19. Singer: People who listen to music consistently become able to emphatically feel the beat of the world moving around them. They begin to take pleasure in the cosmic pendulum that swings them back and forth through the progression of their days. They learn to appreciate the beginnings and the endings of their spirituality and see where it interfaces with their existence in mortal life. By interpreting and enjoying the movement of songs, a whole new mode of existence is opened up to them.

Pragmatist: The people of whom you speak do tend to be more emphatic and emotional than other people, but the abstract and diverse nature of the effects that you claim are simply impossible to tie to any one cause.

Which of the following is the point at issue between the singer and the pragmatist?

(A) the breadth of the effects that listening to music holds for its listeners
(B) the specific musical genre responsible for the effects that the singer claims
(C) whether listening to music creates numerous positive effects
(D) whether anything that is abstract can be tied to a cause that is wholly concrete
(E) the merits of advising people who are not music listeners to listen to music

GO ON TO THE NEXT PAGE

20. Entomologist: The purple dung beetle has gained its remarkable color through several generations of evolution. Originally, this dung beetle had small, dull, purplish streaks that ran down the length of its dorsal exoskeleton, but some members of the population had more prominent coloring than other beetles. This coloring pattern allowed them to be more noticeable to female beetles roaming through the dung looking for mates. It was so much easier for females to spot vividly striped beetles than beetles of more traditional coloring patterns that the latter were bred out of the gene pool.

Which one of the following, if true, would most support the argument?

(A) Prominently colored dung beetles are more evident to predators and have a much lower life expectancy than traditionally colored dung beetles.

(B) Female dung beetles are very attracted to, and will mate with, dung beetles that are painted bright yellow.

(C) Purple dung beetles have larger mandibles and are stronger than traditional dung beetles.

(D) The colors of dung beetles' exoskeletons have no implications for anything other than their attractiveness to the females of their population.

(E) Purple dung beetles tend to eat more, reproduce more, live longer, and grow larger than traditionally colored dung beetles.

21. Street luge is an extreme sport that combines the basic idea of the Olympic ice luge with wheels and an asphalt hill to roll down. People who engage in luging on ice are subject to very dangerous conditions due to the high speed of their bodies next to areas that are very hard and abrasive. If lugers fall on ice, they get hurt badly, but if street lugers fall, then they get hurt even worse. This is because people are able to slide on ice.

Which of the following can be concluded from the passage?

(A) There are more injuries from street luge than ice luge.

(B) Bobsled racers are hurt more often than lugers.

(C) Street luging is more dangerous than ice luging.

(D) Asphalt is a harder and more abrasive surface than ice.

(E) The hills that ice lugers travel down are of a grade similar to those traveled by street lugers.

22. Movie stars fraternize with other movie stars for several reasons. First of all, they meet each other at work on the movie sets. Secondly, they lead similar lives and have similar job paths, so they feel as if they can understand each other. Finally, they associate with each other in hopes of picking up another movie deal through their networking. In conclusion, the social habits of a movie star are complex, but they can be boiled down to the fact that there are numerous positive reasons for a movie star to associate with another movie star.

Which of the following is the main point of the passage?

(A) There are no negative aspects to movie stars associating with other movie stars.

(B) There are at least several reasons why movie stars associate with each other.

(C) Movie stars fraternize together because they work in the same industry.

(D) Movie stars are likely to get new movie parts by socializing with other movie stars.

(E) Some movie stars do not socialize with other movie stars.

GO ON TO THE NEXT PAGE

23. Protester: Children are taught from birth that fighting and violence toward others is immoral, but even so, it is no small wonder that this peaceful moral imperative is not assimilated by the majority in our nation. As adolescents, children are allowed to watch violent TV shows that feature characters who are idolized solely because of their violent tendencies. As adults, our people are governed by leaders who impose their wholly unprovoked imperialistic tendencies on seemingly peaceful nations. Even though the moral backdrop of our childhoods should bolster a predilection toward peace, the righteous moral framework of our culture is constantly subverted by important role models within our society. Until our role models reform their behavior, our society can never really claim that it promotes peace.

Which one of the following, if true, would most undermine the protester's argument?

(A) All role models believe that by engaging in a small amount of violence, they will promote a substantial amount of peace.
(B) The penchant to engage in violence to achieve peace is not morally sustainable for any society.
(C) Children should not be taught that peace is achievable because personal convictions are unsustainable when confronted with opposing mindsets.
(D) TV characters and the leaders of society have little to no effect on prenatal children.
(E) Harmonious discourse between societies will not be achieved until there is a multinational movement categorically to promote the value of peace in place of violence.

24. Salespeople are a special breed. They live off their skill at convincing people to part with one of their most prized possessions: money. To do this, salespeople have to be fairly slick, well put together, eloquent, and mentally quick. Otherwise, many buyers would become disinterested in the salespersons' products and the salespeople would lose business. Some salespeople work on an hourly rate in addition to a commission, but most earn nothing more than a percentage of the price of the products that they sell. Sam the salesman has not sold a product in years, but he still is getting paid. He sells figurines of rabbits for a major pottery maker in West Virginia. The figurines are designed to sit on the desks of salespeople in order to function as good luck charms.

Which of the following is the best inference that you can make from this argument?

(A) Sam is not paid by commission.
(B) Sam is a good salesman with a bad product.
(C) Sam should quit his job to find one with a better product.
(D) Sam is paid an hourly rate.
(E) Sam understands that it's difficult selling products to other salespeople.

GO ON TO THE NEXT PAGE

25. In China, side-by-side comparisons between the staple crops of rice and corn reveal that rice always produces more food per cultivated acre than corn can produce. This fact demonstrates that the United States would be best served by switching its agricultural focus from corn to a completely rice-based production scheme that would be sure to provide enough food for our growing population.

    Which of the following, if true, would cast doubt on the recommendation in the argument?

    (A) The United States has a variety of different climates and soil types that are able to support corn.
    (B) Corn crops are able to subsist in more diverse geographic locales than rice.
    (C) Corn crops are demanding on the soil and therefore can only be successfully cultivated every three years on a particular plot.
    (D) Most regions in the United States do not have climates that would be able to support rice crops.
    (E) Corn is more susceptible to disease and crop blights than rice.

S T O P

IF YOU FINISH BEFORE TIME RUNS OUT, CHECK YOUR WORK ON THIS SECTION ONLY.
DO NOT GO ON TO ANY OTHER TEST SECTION.

SECTION 4
Time—35 minutes
27 questions

Directions: Each passage in this section is followed by a group of questions. Answer each question based on what is stated or implied in the passage. For some questions, more than one answer choice may be possible, so choose the *best* answer to each question. After you have chosen your answer, mark the corresponding space on the Answer Sheet.

For a long time, Americans tended to think that knowing English was sufficient for all their needs. As a result, Americans developed an image as the people who cannot say even the most rudimentary
(5) phrase in any other language. Fortunately, however, many business, political, and educational leaders are belatedly realizing that the whole world does not speak English, and that even many of those who have learned English as a second language prefer to
(10) converse, to do business, and to negotiate in their native tongue.

Not long ago learning a foreign language was considered to be merely a part of a liberal education or an intellectual exercise through the study of
(15) grammar and literature. It was automatically assumed that anyone studying a foreign language as a major field was going to be a teacher, an interpreter, or a translator and had no other career options. There is still a need for people in those
(20) professions. There is also a growing need for individuals who possess advanced skills in foreign languages and are trained in various technical areas. This is a result of increased activity in international business, the influx of large amounts of foreign
(25) capital to the United States, increased internationalization, and an expanded awareness of the need to conduct not only business but also diplomatic relations in the language of the host country.
(30) A second language is now becoming a vital part of the basic preparation for an increasing number of careers. Even in those cases where the knowledge of a second language does not help graduates obtain a first job, many report that their foreign language
(35) skills often enhance their mobility and improve their chances for promotion. In addition to any technical skills that foreign language students choose to develop, they also have further tangible advantages in the job market. In a recent study that

(40) sought to ascertain which college courses had been most valuable for people who were employed in the business world, graduates pointed not only to career-oriented courses such as business management but also to people-oriented subjects
(45) like psychology and to classes that had helped them to develop communication skills. Foreign language students, whose courses focus heavily on this aspect of learning, often possess outstanding communication skills, both written and oral.
(50) Furthermore, recent trends in the job marketplace indicate a revived recognition of the value of general liberal arts training in an employee's career preparation.

1. Which one of the following best states the main idea of the passage?

   (A) In recent years, fluency in a foreign language has become an important educational asset and a distinct advantage in the job market.
   (B) People who study foreign languages are probably going to be teachers, interpreters, or translators.
   (C) Foreign language skills are likely to improve an employee's chances for promotion.
   (D) Increased internationalization in the American business world has necessitated the hiring of more foreign language speakers.
   (E) Greater knowledge of a foreign language means a greater paycheck.

GO ON TO THE NEXT PAGE

PART I / GETTING STARTED

2. The author argues that studying foreign languages is

    (A) necessary for world travel
    (B) an internationalizing experience
    (C) the way into business school
    (D) merely one part of a liberal education
    (E) becoming crucial to career preparation

3. The second paragraph primarily serves to

    (A) explain how the United States can obtain more foreign capital
    (B) tell the reader about the public view of foreign language study
    (C) explain how and why old, widely held misconceptions should change
    (D) argue that many Americans have overlooked the power of a strong foreign language background
    (E) propose that foreign language studies help us learn more about our own language

4. Which of the following statements would the author of this passage be LEAST likely to agree with?

    (A) The rise in demand for foreign language speakers in the job market is paralleled by the rise of international business.
    (B) Knowledge of a second language does not always help students obtain a first job.
    (C) Foreign language students still have many job options even without possessing another technical skill.
    (D) Studying a foreign language also builds a student's communications skills in his or her first language.
    (E) The recent increase in demand for foreign language speakers in the job market is only temporary.

5. The passage suggests which of the following about foreign language study in the past?

    (A) The lack of it held back American business.
    (B) It seemed a frivolous part of a general liberal arts education.
    (C) It was limited to European universities.
    (D) It was as pertinent to any student as it is now.
    (E) It was seen as a valuable experience in improving one's communication skills.

6. Of the following, the author's primary purpose in writing the passage most likely is to

    (A) call attention to the increasing importance of foreign language studies in the job market
    (B) argue that foreign language studies are not the superficial exercise they once were thought to be
    (C) enlist students to study to become translators and foreign language teachers
    (D) debate the effects of internationalizing business
    (E) search for modern reasons to study foreign language

GO ON TO THE NEXT PAGE

The Search for Extraterrestrial Intelligence ("SETI") is still no trivial task. Our galaxy is 100,000 light-years across, and contains a hundred thousand million stars. Searching the entire sky for

(5) some faraway and faint signal is an exhausting exercise.

Some simplifying assumptions are useful to reduce the size of the task. One is to assume that the vast majority of life-forms in our galaxy are

(10) based on carbon chemistries, as are all life-forms on Earth. While it is possible that life could be based around atoms other than carbon, carbon is well known for the unusually wide variety of molecules that can be formed around it. The presence of

(15) liquid water is also a useful assumption, as water is a common molecule and provides an excellent environment for the formation of complicated carbon-based molecules that could eventually lead to the emergence of life. A third assumption is to

(20) focus on Sun-like stars. Very big stars have relatively short lifetimes, meaning that intelligent life would not likely have time to evolve on planets orbiting them. Very small stars provide so little heat and warmth that only planets in very close orbits

(25) around them would not be frozen solid, and in such close orbits these planets would be tidally "locked" to the star, with one side of the planet perpetually baked and the other perpetually frozen.

About 10% of the stars in our galaxy are Sun-

(30) like, and there are about a thousand such stars within 100 light-years of our Sun. These stars would be useful primary targets for interstellar listening. However, we know of only one planet where life exists, our own. There is no way to know

(35) if any of the simplifying assumptions are correct, and so as a second priority the entire sky must be searched. Searching the entire sky is difficult. To find a radio transmission from an alien civilization, we also have to search through most of the useful

(40) radio spectrum, as there is no way to know what frequencies aliens might be using. Trying to transmit a powerful signal over a wide range of wavelengths is impractical, and so it is likely that such a signal would be transmitted on a relatively

(45) narrow band. This means that a wide range of frequencies must be searched at every spatial coordinate of the sky.

There is also the problem of knowing what kind of signal to listen for, as we have no idea how a

(50) signal sent by aliens might be modulated, and how the data transmitted by it would be encoded. Narrow-bandwidth signals that are stronger than background noise and constant in intensity are obviously interesting, and if they have a regular and

(55) complex pulse pattern, they are likely to be artificial. However, while studies have been performed on how to send a signal that could be easily decoded, there is no way to know if the assumptions of those studies are valid, and

(60) deciphering the information from an alien signal will be very difficult.

7. Which one of the following best expresses the main idea of the passage?

(A) We have not yet found sentient life on any other planet.

(B) The search for extraterrestrial life is difficult and requires scientists to create simplifying assumptions in order to attempt the task.

(C) Radio waves are an excellent means of finding life on other planets where the life-forms use radio waves to communicate.

(D) Our galaxy is too large to find intelligent life.

(E) By employing a large number of techniques, we will expand our potential for finding intelligent life in the future.

8. According to the passage, the author asserts which one of the following about the roles of stars in SETI?

(A) Stars like our Sun usually are orbited by planets rich in carbon-based molecules.

(B) Midsized stars like our Sun are most conducive to supporting life in their solar systems.

(C) It would be impossible for any life to exist on a planet orbiting a very big star.

(D) As long as planets in a small-star solar system aren't tidally "locked" to the star, they are favorable for the production of life.

(E) Intelligent life probably exists in 10% of the solar systems in our galaxy.

GO ON TO THE NEXT PAGE

9. The author of the passage would be LEAST likely to agree with which one of the following statements about SETI?

(A) Intelligent life does exist on some other planets.
(B) It is remotely possible that other life-forms would be based on chemistries other than carbon.
(C) The possibility for the existence of life on Earth is a result of the convergence of several relatively unique conditions on one planet.
(D) Assumptions that simplify the complexity of SETI are not always realistic enough to be helpful.
(E) Alien radio signals would probably be transmitted over a range of different wavelengths.

10. The passage suggests which one of the following about the "interstellar listening" (lines 32–33) cited in the third paragraph?

(A) It is a much more complicated task than one would initially expect.
(B) Aliens probably code a radio signal in much the same way we do.
(C) The most difficult task would be initially deducing whether a signal was natural or artificial.
(D) If done thoroughly, it is a sure way to discover if life exists elsewhere in the universe.
(E) Complicated radio signals can be produced by any number of natural events in the galaxy.

11. The author of the passage suggests which one of the following about the concerns of SETI?

(A) If Earth is the only place in the universe where life exists, the search will be both endless and fruitless.
(B) The universe may be too large to ever find another set of conditions as conducive to life as those on Earth.
(C) The creation of fallible assumptions in order to simplify the search may be a necessary risk.
(D) If extraterrestrials were based on an element other than carbon, our simplifying assumptions might discount them as real life.
(E) Because of the inductive basis of our assumptions, it is unlikely that any of them are actually correct.

12. The author mentions that the only planet we currently know that has life is our own (lines 33–34) in order to

(A) demonstrate that if we know of one place where life exists in the universe, it must exist elsewhere as well
(B) point out the appropriate size of our Sun as a star supporting a planet with life-forms
(C) argue that if our assumptions are true for us, they must be true for any life in the universe
(D) explain the uncertainty in our assumptions because of their limited base
(E) dissuade readers from thinking that the search for intelligent life in the universe should end with Earth

13. The passage is primarily concerned with

(A) drawing attention to the uniqueness of the coexistence of all the conditions necessary for life to exist on our planet
(B) suggesting that some simplifying assumptions made in SETI are necessary, even though possibly misleading
(C) explaining how SETI is important to the survival of the human race
(D) arguing that SETI is a valuable motivational tool for advancement in several different scientific fields
(E) proposing that, to make the search easier for ourselves, we have underestimated the helpfulness of simplifying assumptions in SETI

GO ON TO THE NEXT PAGE

Since 1993, the Department of Justice ("the Department") has made fighting fraud and abuse in the health care industry one of its top priorities. Health care fraud and abuse drains billions of
(5) dollars from Medicare and Medicaid, which provide essential health care services to millions of elderly, low-income, and disabled Americans. The impact of health care fraud and abuse cannot be measured in terms of dollars alone. While health
(10) care fraud burdens our nation with enormous financial costs, it also threatens the quality of health care. The Department has developed a balanced and responsible program to fight health care fraud and abuse. The first component of the Department's
(15) program focuses on enforcement efforts, including the use of criminal and civil tools. The second component emphasizes prevention and deterrence, through compliance initiatives for the health care industry and through public education to empower
(20) individual patients to be vigilant in identifying and reporting potential health care fraud schemes.

The Department's enforcement actions have proven results. In 1998, $480 million was awarded or negotiated as a result of criminal fines, civil
(25) settlements, and judgments in health care fraud matters. Under the requirements of the Health Insurance Portability and Accountability Act of 1996 (HIPAA), $243 million was returned to the Medicare Trust Fund to support future beneficiary
(30) payments. Additionally, the Department reported that there were 326 defendants in 219 criminal cases who were convicted of health care fraud and abuse. At the same time the U.S. Department of Health and Human Services excluded more than
(35) 3000 individuals and businesses from participating in federal health programs, many due to criminal convictions.

The Department continues to prevent fraud and abuse in a number of ways: by encouraging
(40) providers to police their own activities through compliance programs; and by sponsoring consumer outreach initiatives, such as the consumer fraud hotlines, to involve patients with first-hand knowledge in the detection of fraudulent practices.
(45) Settlement agreements with providers also emphasize future prevention efforts. Settlements in 1998 included 231 corporate integrity agreements, where providers agreed to change their operations so as to prevent fraud from recurring in the future.
(50) The pace of legislative and industry change is altering the landscape of health care delivery and payment, presenting new challenges that must be planned for, both in prevention and enforcement efforts. The Department's continuing challenge in

(55) the future is to change the behavior of health care businesses so that they will take effective measures to prevent health care fraud schemes, while keeping enforcement efforts cognizant of the adverse impact of provider's conduct on the welfare of their
(60) patients

14. Which one of the following best describes the overall organization of the passage?

(A) A generalization is made, it is argued against with counterexamples, and it is rejected.
(B) A problem is described, solutions are introduced, and the effectiveness of these solutions is explained.
(C) An assumption is made, the validity of the assumption is tested by comparing it to what is known to be true, and the assumption is then verified.
(D) A challenge is presented, plans of action are recommended, and the potential effectiveness of each plan is debated.
(E) A particular government department is introduced, its shortcomings are discussed, and its reconstruction efforts are acclaimed.

15. Which one of the following statements regarding health care fraud is best supported by information presented in the passage?

(A) It is an unsolvable problem.
(B) It has no effect on those who do not pay Medicare taxes.
(C) It has been decreasing in occurrence every year since 1998.
(D) It has both economic and social consequences.
(E) Since the 1980s, the Department of Justice has made the fight against health care fraud a top priority.

GO ON TO THE NEXT PAGE

16. The author mentions each of the following as possible preventive efforts against health care fraud EXCEPT

(A) denial of incidental Medicare claims
(B) public education
(C) the use of civil tools to aid in enforcement
(D) exclusion of some former convicts from health program work
(E) compliance initiatives for the health care industry

17. Which one of the following is a claim that the passage makes about deterrence efforts?

(A) For the Department of Justice, these efforts have been successful, though there is still much to be done.
(B) As the landscape of health care payment evolves, the Department's current efforts will weed out more and more fraud.
(C) The Health Insurance Portability and Accountability Act of 1996 has had the greatest effect on reducing health care fraud in America.
(D) So far, these efforts have been too ineffectual to make much of a difference.
(E) While they have caused a decreased number of fraud incidents, the amount of money lost to health care fraud continues to increase.

18. By using the terms "compliance initiatives" (line 18) and "compliance programs" (line 41), the author shows that the Department is trying to

(A) teach health care patients to pay more attention to details in their dealings with insurance companies
(B) make health care providers become more structurally alike so that prevention efforts will not have to be so diverse
(C) settle many health care fraud criminal cases out of court so as not to damage the reputation of any companies involved
(D) present continuing challenges to be dealt with in the future
(E) convince health care providers to abide by certain government suggestions to curtail the possibility for fraud

19. Which one of the following generalizations about fraud is most analogous to the author's points in the first paragraph about health care fraud?

(A) Fraud is a social vice without equal.
(B) Fraud is a drain on the economy as well as society.
(C) Fraud hurts both the victim and the perpetrator of the crime.
(D) Fraud can only be fought directly by its victims, so public education should be our primary goal.
(E) Vigilance alone is the most powerful weapon against fraud.

20. This passage was written primarily to

(A) explain how health care fraud affects people on every level of society, from individuals in hospital beds to multibillion-dollar insurance companies
(B) offer ways to deal with health care fraud as a victim
(C) prescribe changes in the health care system that could effectively end health care fraud in America
(D) call to attention the climbing rates of health care fraud in America and debate some proposed ways to curb this climb
(E) describe the Department's successful fight against health care fraud in the past several years and its plans for continued success in the future

GO ON TO THE NEXT PAGE

A healthy man in his early 60s begins to notice that his memory isn't as good as it used to be. More and more often, a word will be on the tip of his tongue but he just can't remember it. He forgets
(5) appointments, makes mistakes when paying his bills, and finds that he's often confused or anxious about the normal hustle and bustle of life around him. One evening, he suddenly finds himself walking in a neighborhood a couple of miles from
(10) his house. He has no idea how he got there.

Not so long ago, this man's condition would have been swept into a broad catchall category called "senile dementia" or "senility." Today, the picture is very different. We now know that
(15) Alzheimer's disease (AD) and other illnesses with dementia are distinct diseases. Armed with this knowledge, we have rapidly improved our ability to accurately diagnose AD. We are still some distance from the ultimate goal—a reliable, valid,
(20) inexpensive, and early diagnostic marker, but experienced physicians now can diagnose AD with up to 90 percent accuracy.

Early diagnosis has several advantages. For example, many conditions cause symptoms that
(25) mimic those of Alzheimer's disease. Finding out early that the problem isn't AD but is something else can spur people into getting treatment for the real condition. For the small percentage of dementias that are treatable or even reversible, early
(30) diagnosis increases the chances of successful treatment. Even when the cause of the dementia turns out to be Alzheimer's disease, it's good to find out sooner rather than later. One benefit is medicinal. The drugs now available to treat AD can
(35) help some people maintain their mental abilities for months to years, even though they do not change the underlying course of the disease. Other benefits are practical. The sooner the person with AD and family know about the disease, the more time they
(40) have to make future living arrangements, handle financial matters, establish a durable power of attorney, deal with other legal issues, create a support network, or even make plans to join a research study. Being able to participate for as long
(45) as possible in making decisions about the present and future is important to many people with AD.

Finally, scientists also see advantages to early diagnosis. Developing tests that can reveal what is happening in the brain in the early stages of
(50) Alzheimer's disease will help them understand more about the cause and development of the disease. It will also help scientists learn when and how to start drugs and other treatments so that they can be most effective.

21. Which one of the following best states the main idea of the passage?

(A) There are drugs on the market that help people maintain their mental faculties into their late 80s.
(B) Early diagnosis is currently the most important goal in the treatment of Alzheimer's disease.
(C) Older people often have trouble remembering things.
(D) It is easier to diagnose Alzheimer's disease today than it used to be.
(E) Current research is still a long way off from the ultimate goals of AD diagnosis.

22. In line 16, the author of the passage uses the word *dementia* in order to

(A) give an example
(B) dismiss an objection
(C) undermine an argument
(D) codify a system
(E) acknowledge a trait

23. Which one of the following best describes the author's attitude toward catch-all categorizations like *senility*?

(A) indifference
(B) disapproval
(C) commendation
(D) apathy
(E) befuddlement

24. Which one of the following is suggested as a medical benefit of early diagnosis of Alzheimer's disease?

(A) It is helpful in dealing with precautionary legal issues.
(B) It serves to make the disease less expensive to treat.
(C) It can help doctors prevent the disease from running its full course.
(D) It may help in slowing the progression of the disease.
(E) It aids in shortening the duration of the disease.

GO ON TO THE NEXT PAGE

25. The primary purpose of the first paragraph is to

(A) scare the reader into reading the rest of the passage
(B) establish the author's argument for early diagnosis
(C) explain that good general health will not prevent Alzheimer's disease
(D) introduce the topic in a personalized manner
(E) propose an action plan for the treatment of Alzheimer's disease

26. The passage provides inferential support for all the following generalizations about Alzheimer's disease EXCEPT:

(A) Early diagnosis can make Alzheimer's disease an easier condition to live with.
(B) Treatment for Alzheimer's disease can be a financial burden.
(C) Scientists have recently reached an impasse in Alzheimer's research.
(D) Alzheimer's disease is currently treatable, though a cure is not yet in sight.
(E) One of the symptoms of Alzheimer's disease is dementia.

27. The passage contains specific information that provides a definitive answer to which one of the following questions?

(A) What research has done the most to develop new treatments for Alzheimer's disease?
(B) What is the importance of early diagnosis for Alzheimer's disease?
(C) What is the greatest threat to an aging man who is still considered healthy?
(D) In what ways can Alzheimer's disease be successfully treated?
(E) What is the best thing a family can do for one of its members diagnosed with Alzheimer's disease?

S T O P

IF YOU FINISH BEFORE TIME RUNS OUT, CHECK YOUR WORK ON THIS SECTION ONLY.
DO NOT GO ON TO ANY OTHER TEST SECTION.

ANSWER KEY

Section 1	Section 2	Section 3	Section 4
1. E	1. B	1. E	1. A
2. D	2. B	2. B	2. E
3. C	3. D	3. B	3. C
4. D	4. A	4. D	4. E
5. D	5. C	5. C	5. B
6. A	6. B	6. B	6. A
7. D	7. D	7. E	7. B
8. A	8. C	8. C	8. B
9. B	9. A	9. C	9. E
10. A	10. D	10. B	10. A
11. B	11. C	11. A	11. C
12. A	12. A	12. B	12. D
13. E	13. B	13. E	13. B
14. A	14. E	14. E	14. B
15. C	15. E	15. A	15. D
16. D	16. B	16. D	16. A
17. C	17. A	17. B	17. A
18. C	18. C	18. C	18. E
19. A	19. A	19. A	19. B
20. B	20. B	20. D	20. E
21. D	21. E	21. C	21. B
22. B	22. A	22. B	22. E
23. D	23. B	23. A	23. B
24. C	24. B	24. D	24. D
25. D		25. D	25. D
			26. C
			27. B

Scoring Instructions: To calculate your score on this Diagnostic Test, follow the instructions on the next page.

CALCULATING YOUR SCORE

Now that you have completed the Diagnostic Test, use the instructions on this page to calculate your score. Start by checking the Answer Key to count the number of questions you answered correctly. Then fill in the table below.

Raw Score Calculator

Section Number	Question Type	Number of Questions	Number Correct
1	Logical Reasoning	25	_____
2	Logic Games	24	_____
3	Logical Reasoning	25	_____
4	Reading Comprehension	27	_____
		(Raw Score) Total:	_____

On the real LSAT, a statistical process will be used to convert your raw score to a scaled score ranging from 120 to 180. The table below will give you an approximate idea of the scaled score that matches your raw score. For statistical reasons, on real forms of the LSAT the scaled score that matches a given raw score can vary by several points above or below the scaled score shown in the table.

Write your scaled score on this test here:

Diagnostic Test scaled score: _____

Raw Score	Scaled Score	Raw Score	Scaled Score	Raw Score	Scaled Score
0	120	23	126	46	145
1	120	24	127	47	145
2	120	25	128	48	146
3	120	26	128	49	147
4	120	27	129	50	147
5	120	28	130	51	148
6	120	29	131	52	148
7	120	30	132	53	149
8	120	31	133	54	150
9	120	32	133	55	151
10	120	33	134	56	151
11	120	34	135	57	152
12	120	35	136	58	153
13	120	36	137	59	153
14	120	37	137	60	154
15	120	38	138	61	154
16	120	39	139	62	155
17	120	40	140	63	155
18	121	41	140	64	156
19	122	42	141	65	157
20	123	43	142	66	158
21	124	44	143	67	158
22	125	45	144	68	159

Raw Score	Scaled Score	Raw Score	Scaled Score	Raw Score	Scaled Score
69	159	80	166	91	174
70	160	81	166	92	175
71	160	82	167	93	175
72	161	83	167	94	176
73	161	84	168	95	177
74	162	85	169	96	178
75	162	86	170	97	179
76	163	87	170	98	180
77	163	88	171	99	180
78	164	89	172	100	180
79	165	90	173	101	180

ANSWERS AND EXPLANATIONS

SECTION I—LOGICAL REASONING

1. This squib is a sufficient-necessary question:

   1. Julian at Movies→Mother's Consent

   2. Mother's Consent→Mother Considers Homework Complete

   3. Mother Considers Homework Complete→ (Checks It Over) or (Julian Washes Dishes and Promises Homework Is Finished)

   This can be put into the following long chain:

   Julian at Movies→Mother's Consent→Mother Considers Homework Complete→(Checks It Over) or (Julian Washes Dishes and Promises Homework Is Finished)

   We know that Julian's mother cannot check over the homework since it is at Elizabeth's house.

   Question Type: Conclusion

   Correct answer: **E.** If Julian washes the dishes and promises that his homework is done, then sometimes his Mother will allow him to go to the movies.

   (A) Julian would also have to promise the homework was done and wash dishes.

   (B) Nothing in the squib supports the idea that Elizabeth's call has an effect.

   (C) Julian would also have to promise that the homework was done.

   (D) Julian's mother would still need to check the homework, or Julian would have to promise that it was done and wash dishes.

2. The advertising executive claims that most people who chew gum prefer chewing gum to bubble gum (or are undecided). Therefore, the executive says, *television* advertising efforts would have maximum effectiveness if advertisements focused on chewing gum instead of bubble gum.

   Question Type: "Weaken"

   Correct answer: **D.** If chewing gum chewers do not watch television, they will not see the advertisements for the client's chewing gum.

   (A) The chewing gum chewers may not be telling the truth, or they might be affected by this particular ad.

   (B–C, E) These statements are irrelevant.

3. The author claims that people no longer are taught to find instant gratification in books and that they therefore turn to other media for instant gratification.

   Question Type: Conclusion

   Correct answer: **C.** This statement is the crux of the argument.

   (A) The author says that this is possible, but not that it will surely happen.

   (B) In the squib, instant gratification is not compared to deeper satisfaction.

   (D) The author does not make this claim.

   (E) The author does not address the preferences of the publishing industry.

4. The politician claims that the purpose of law is to maximize a person's liberty so long as that liberty is not allowed to constrain the liberty of others. For this reason, there are no laws barring a person from harming himself or herself.

Question Type: Conclusion

Correct answer: **D.** The politician says that the government may restrict a person's liberty only when that liberty results in harm to another person. It is the individual's, not the government's, responsibility when he or she inflicts self-harm.

(A) The politician does not make this judgment.

(B) The politician implies the opposite.

(C) The politician specifies only harm to another person.

(E) The politician begins with an instance (harming another person) that contradicts this statement.

5. This is a sufficient-necessary question:

1. Happy Household→Members Dine Together

2. Members Dine Together→(~~Busy Schedules~~) or (Sacrifice Time)

3. ~~Busy Schedules~~ → ~~Individual Happiness~~; Individual Happiness→Busy Schedule

4. Household Happiness→Individual Happiness

Combine 3 and 4 to say: Household Happiness→ Individual Happiness→Busy Schedules.

This means that the family members in a happy household must have busy schedules. Therefore, in order to dine together and be happy, they must sacrifice time for one another.

Question Type: Conclusion

Correct answer: **D.** This statement is the correct answer, as demonstrated above.

(A and B) The opposite is true.

(C) The speaker does not refer to the family members' pride in their work.

(E) The speaker says nothing about communication.

6. The squib states that the average nonartist in our population is unable to differentiate between great paintings and other art. The squib then states that a person wanting to buy works with large mass appeal would have to spend more money than a person wanting to collect great art.

Question Type: "Resolve"

Correct answer: **A.** If paintings of great artistic merit do not have mass appeal, they would attract fewer members of the public, most of whom are nonartists, as purchasers. This would allow buyers to spend less on high-quality art when compared to art that is widely valued by the general public.

(B) This statement would not resolve the discrepancy.

(C) This statement would not explain why there are different price levels for high-quality art and mass-appeal art.

(D) Whether or not a painting is offered to the general public does not resolve the discrepancy between cost and artistic merit.

(E) The speaker says nothing about paintings that have neither artistic merit nor mass appeal.

7. According to the squib, governments that subsist by fostering fear in their citizens often are able to maintain a tighter control over their citizens than other types of governments, and the president is viewed as the equivalent of a monarch. However, presidents of these governments are likely to be in office for shorter periods than real monarchs.

Question Type: "Resolve"

Correct answer: **D.** The difference in average length of rule between presidents and real monarchs can be explained if monarchs come to power at a younger age than presidents.

(A) Monarchs are also sometimes overthrown.

(B) This statement is irrelevant.

(C) The squib says that elections are not held in tightly controlled societies.

(E) Although this statement may be true, it does not mean that the elections are for the position of monarch, which is not an elective office.

8. This squib states that for a number of reasons, people walking along downtown streets late at night have a high potential for being robbed. Based on these risks, the squib makes an unfounded assumption that people walking along downtown streets at night are more likely to be robbed than people walking anywhere else in the city at night.

Question Type: "Strengthen"

Correct answer: **A.** This statement validates the conclusion. The only robberies at night would occur downtown.

(B) But robbers may be equally, or even more, likely to rob people in uptown or midtown parts of the city.

(C) This statement is irrelevant.

(D) This statement does not support the conclusion. There may be other parts of the city that have as many burglars as downtown does.

(E) The burglars are not necessarily riding the buses to a robbery.

9. The squib claims that presidential addresses are often pivotal moments in history, but the same is not true of senatorial addresses because the plans espoused by the senators are not followed as often as the plans of the president are.

Question Type: "Strengthen"

Correct answer: **B.** The statement quantifies the fact that presidential plans are far more likely to be ratified than the plans of important senators. This would explain why a president's address is much more apt to take on historical meaning.

(A) A person's eloquence is not necessarily related to whether or not his or her plans get ratified.

(C) Actually, it is not counterintuitive to believe this. Some plans get actualized; others don't.

(D) This statement has nothing to do with whether the speaker's plans are ratified or not.

(E) This statement does not refer to the relative levels of ratification between senators' plans and presidents' plans.

10. This squib is a diagrammed sufficient-necessary problem:

    1. Dog in House→Fleas in House
    2. People Live in Houses with Fleas→People Get Fleas
    3. ~~People live with Fleas →Cat~~ ; Cat→People Live with Fleas

We want to conclude that Bill has fleas.

Question Type: Conclusion

Correct answer: **A.** If it is assumed that Bill has a cat, then number 3 makes us conclude that Bill has fleas.

(B) We are unsure if the dog lives in Bill's house or in his yard.

(C) Apartments with fleas have different properties than houses with fleas.

(D) We are trying to conclude that Bill *does* have fleas.

(E) It is immaterial that Bill's brother has fleas. Bill may not live in the same place.

11. The squib claims that Mount Kilaboo will soon produce a monumental eruption. Based on this idea, the squib claims that the villages located 100 feet beyond last year's lava flow will have to be evacuated.

Question Type: Conclusion

Correct answer: **B.** This statement explains why the evacuations will extend an extra 100 feet from last year's lava flow. It is assumed that the flows of the monumental eruption will extend 100 feet farther than the flows from last year's eruption.

(A) It is not stated that the monumental eruption will definitely occur this year.

(C) We do not know the comparison between the size of Mount Kilaboo's eruption and the eruptions of other volcanoes.

(D) The squib does not imply that the entire mountain will explode, nor does it state that such an explosion would make the lava flow extend 100 extra feet.

(E) The opposite is true.

12. The realtor claims that we should all invest in Marlagos beachfront property instead of the stock market. He or she claims that the prices of this real estate have been escalating at a huge rate and there is no reason to expect this trend to stop.

Question Type: "Strengthen"

Correct answer: **A.** If this statement were true, then properties would probably escalate in value again in the next 10 years.

(B) The bond market is unrelated to claims about real estate.

(C) This statement is irrelevant. It does not say that the price trend will necessarily continue.

(D) If true, this statement would tend to convince you to invest in the stock market, not Marlagos property.

(E) Such a diversification is not necessarily better than diversifying through the stock market.

13. This squib claims that the aliens would not benefit by announcing their presence here. The news would alert us to a possible invasion or hinder the aliens' studies of humans.

Question Type: Conclusion

Correct answer: **E.** Although it is possible that the aliens might want to befriend us or trade with us, the squib does not mention any other reasons why they have chosen to visit except to plan for an invasion or to study us.

(A and B) These two statements are not assumed. The squib says nothing about the aliens' technological ability, nor does it include their history of other invasions.

(C) If the aliens were here to study us, it might not be to our benefit to hinder their study. It would depend on what they were going to do with the information they acquired.

(D) Although it is implied that the aliens might want to study us, the squib does not mention that the aliens would actually succeed in getting important information.

14. According to the squib, people do not realize that, like grass, plants in general grow more quickly during the summer. People do not notice this because they do not have to take any actions to deal with the growth of plants other than grass.

Question Type: Conclusion

Correct answer: **A.** Since a juniper bush is a plant other than grass, its summer growth spurts do not require any reciprocal human actions.

(B) The squib says nothing about spring.

(C) Sometimes an increase in light levels can kill plants.

(D) The first sentence says that grass must be mowed about once a month in winter.

(E) The squib says that the factors combine to make plants grow faster. It is not stated what the result would be if only one factor were present.

15. Exceptional football players exit college with the desire to make money and bring about societal good. The squib claims that Kevin Kennedy would be an exceptional football player if he played football because he entered college with the desire to bring about societal good.

Question Type: "Weaken"

Correct answer: **C.** If this statement were true, it would mean that, when Kevin left college, he would have lost the desire to bring about societal good. According to the squib, then, he could not be an "exceptional" football player.

(A) The kind of football that Kevin plays is irrelevant.

(B) To "realize their potential" is a different variable than being "exceptional."

(D) This statement says nothing about their emotions and desire to bring about good.

(E) The information in the squib does not specify when a football player becomes "exceptional." This statement does not weaken the conclusion.

16. The squib states that photographers sacrifice the broad spectrum of the moments they live in order to capture part of that spectrum infinitely.

Question Type: "Weaken"

Correct answer: **D.** If photographers can fully enjoy the moment as it occurs, they do not lose any part of the broad spectrum of life just by looking through the camera's peephole. This statement weakens the squib's argument.

(A) This statement is irrelevant.

(B) Although they may earn income from their photos, photographers are not necessarily able fully to appreciate the spectrum of life in the moments they photograph.

(C) This does not mean that photographers are able to capture the full spectrum of living motion in moments they photograph.

(E) This statement is irrelevant.

17. The anthropologist cites a number of advantages that ants have over humans. Based on these advantages, she or he claims that there will be no way for humans to prevent a species of ant from taking over the world in the future.

Question Type: "Weaken"

Correct answer: **C.** According to this statement, the ant takeover can be stopped.

(A) Ants still may be able to exert a different kind of global domination from humans'.

(B) This statement supports, rather than weakens, the argument.

(D) The dangers of grasshoppers and crickets are immaterial. Ants might still be able to take over the world.

(E) The probability of aliens arriving on Earth seems to be remote, so this statement would not really weaken the passage.

18. This squib implies that the children of modern artists are the ones producing the work that is called modern art.

Question Type: "Weaken"

Correct answer: **C.** This answer would counter the speaker's proposition that modern artists are selling their children's artwork.

(A) This statement does not mean that children are unable to produce modern art initially.

(B) Rather than weakening the conclusion, this statement supports it.

(D and E) Both these statements are irrelevant.

19. The squib claims that the electric guitar is being edged out by other instruments. The conclusion of the squib is that for classic rock to survive, the electric guitar must gain prominence in today's new music genres.

Question Type: "Weaken"

Correct answer: **A.** If this statement were true, then even if the electric guitar were never used again in modern music, the popularity of classic rock would not be diminished.

(B) This is irrelevant to what will occur with the electric guitar.

(C) The squib refers to classic rock's survival, not its extreme popularity.

(D) This statement is irrelevant.

(E) The classical guitar is not the same as the electric guitar, so this statement is irrelevant.

20. The squib cites one explanation of how the ancient Egyptians built their pyramids, but then goes on to examine why that explanation is incorrect. The kites supposedly placed on the rocks would not perform because there is no wind in Egypt.

Question Type: Reasoning strategy

Correct answer: **B.** The flaw in the reasoning is that it does not consider the possibility that weather conditions might have changed over several thousand years.

(A) This statement does not explain why the squib's argument is flawed.

(C) However, the people might still have been helped by the wind, even though the squib argues that the kite explanation is impossible. You are looking for the flaw in the squib's argument.

(D) The opposite claim is implied; according to the squib, the Egyptians could not have used wind to move blocks, so wind was not a necessary condition.

(E) This statement is irrelevant.

21. This squib notes that there are two possible color outcomes when mixing liquid A and liquid B. Each outcome results when there is more of one liquid than the other. The squib "forgets" that it would be possible to mix equivalent amounts of the liquids.

Question Type: Reasoning strategy

Correct answer: **D.** We do not know what color will result if equal amounts of A and B are mixed.

(A and B) These are both reasonable assumptions.

(C) The squib does not mention any other liquid added to the mix, so this assumption is not made.

(E) This may or may not be a good assumption, but it is irrelevant. Hiding or not hiding the mixture would not affect the resulting color.

22. First, the squib relates information about smoking and drinking levels and stress levels. Second, the squib introduces information correlating strained interpersonal relationships and drinking. The squib recommends that people lower their stress levels in order to curb familial problems.

Question Type: Reasoning strategy

Correct answer: **B.** We are not sure whether stress leads to drinking, whether drinking leads to stress, whether strained interpersonal relationships lead to stress, or whether stress leads to strained interpersonal relationships. Causality is completely unaddressed in this squib.

(A) This choice is not a flaw of the squib.

(C) The identification of these implications is a well-fashioned part of the argument, not a flaw.

(D) This is true, but it would not be applicable to the conclusion of the argument. The argument is flawed for not revealing the causal relationship between alcohol, strained familial relationships, and stress.

(E) No causality was inferred about smoking. Also, the sequence of causality is not inferred.

23. This squib states that comedians who use self-deprecating humor have insights into their psyches. However, comedians who do not understand their "inner workings" are unable to use this sort of humor. The speaker assumes that audience members' ability to enjoy self-deprecating humor is similarly predicated on their insights into their psyches.

Question Type: Reasoning strategy

Correct answer: **D.** The author assumes that a person needs to understand his or her own psyche both to create and to enjoy self-deprecating humor.

(A) The jokes, not the comedians, are compared to stockpiles of jewels.

(B) The squib implies just the opposite.

(C and E) Neither of these techniques is used.

24. According to the squib, the judgment that someone is a "good" person is based only on that person's past acts. Since this is the case, the author claims that these past acts bear no implications for how the person will act in the future. This reasoning, of course, is not realistic.

Question Type: Analogous reasoning

Correct answer: **C.** In this statement, being called a good hitter is analogous to being called a good person in the squib. Like the squib, this statement claims that no predictions can be made about a person's future performance from his or her previous deeds.

(A) The squib refers to a person's acts, not his or her position. This statement does not speak about the manager's acts, but only his or her title.

(B) This statement refers to employment, not a person's acts.

(D and E) These statements claim that predictions can be made, but the squib states that predictions cannot be made.

25. Robert claims that people have grounds for being surprised when companies turn out to be different from the way they have portrayed themselves.

Question Type: "Strengthen"

Correct answer: **D.** If the opposite were true, then people would have no reason to be surprised if companies did not perform according to their expectations.

(A) This statement would support Robert's argument if it replaced "earning" with "losing."

(B) The squib relates only to the idea that people who lose money have grounds for being surprised.

(C) This statement is unrelated.

(E) CEOs' feelings are irrelevant to Robert's argument.

SECTION 2—LOGIC GAMES

Game 1: Linear

Initial Setup:

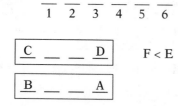

From this setup, we can infer that B and A can go in only three positions on the board. After drawing out these three scenarios, we can see that the C and D box can go only in two positions for each position that B and A are in. In all scenarios, the remaining two slots belong to F and E, with F in the lower one. This creates six possible scenarios for the game that we can draw as follow:

1. C B F D A E
2. F B C E A D
3. B F C A E D
4. B C F A D E
5. F C B E D A
6. C F B D E A

Now that you have completely tied down the variables in the game, you can turn to the questions.

1. Correct answer: **B**. This is the correct answer, as you can see from scenario 6.

2. Correct answer: **B**. If Fanny starts third, then it places us in either scenario 1 or 4. Looking in these scenarios to see who starts second, we see that either Ben or Chris starts second.

3. Correct answer: **D**. This is possible in scenarios 1, 5, and 6.

4. Correct answer: **A**. This is possible in scenarios 2 and 4. Ben's boat immediately precedes Chris's in both these scenarios.

5. Correct answer: **C**. This occurs only in scenario 2. Ben's boat must immediately precede Chris's boat.

6. Correct answer: **B**. This occurs only in scenario 3. But, in fact, Fanny starts three slots before Emily in all scenarios.

Game 2: Mapping

This game shows you the initial setup so you can go right to the questions.

7. Correct answer: **D**. There is only one way to follow rules 1 and 2:

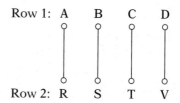

Huts in the same row may be connected to one another, so there may be more than just these four roads.

8. Correct answer: **C**. This sample diagram shows two possibilities in which a line from row to row would cause only one intersection. (The diagrams could also be flipped to apply to towns on the other side of the grid.)

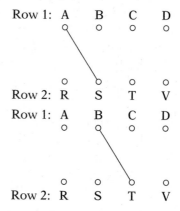

Two roads must connect to the towns directly across from them. R cannot connect with C because it would cause more than one intersection.

9. Correct answer: **A**. The following is the diagram that results from this situation:

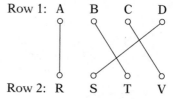

S must be connected to D.

10. Correct answer: **D**. Here is a picture of the scenario. If C did not connect to V, then the game would not be possible.

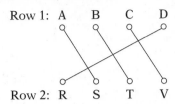

Row 1: A   B   C   D

Row 2: R   S   T   V

11. Correct answer: **C**. The only possibility is that V connects along the same row to T. The other choices all violate either rule 1 or 2. Here is a picture of the scenario:

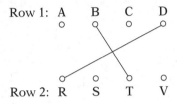

Row 1: A   B   C   D

Row 2: R   S   T   V

Game 3: Sequential

Initial Setup:

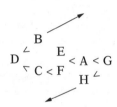

$$D \nearrow^{B} \searrow_{C < F} {}^{E}_{H} \nwarrow < A < G$$

12. Correct answer: **A**. Looking at our diagram, it is clear that H, D, C, B, F, E, A, and G could be an order.

13. Correct answer: **B**. Seventh is the second-to-last position, and G or B must always occupy the last position. The aliens that could go seventh are only A, B, G, or H.

14. Correct answer: **E**. There are five aliens who could touch the well third: B, C, E, F, or H.

15. Correct answer: **E**. H and B could touch the well consecutively with anyone, so we can eliminate answer choices (A) and (B). E and C or D and C could go consecutively. E and G, however, could never be consecutive because A must always be between them.

16. Correct answer: **B**. Here is the complete order for this scenario:

D	C	B	H	F/E	E/F	A	G
1	2	3	4	5	6	7	8

17. Correct answer: **A**. In this scenario, either H or B would have to fall between E and F. The following shows one possibility:

D	C	B	F/E	H	E/F	A	G

Game 4: Grouping

Initial Setup:

A = G   ☐1   ☐2   ☐3

B ≠ C, D   —   —   —

E ≠ C, D   —   —   —

Excess
—————   —
F

18. Correct answer: **C**. F could be in group 2 with A and G.

—   A   —

—   G   —

—

(A and B) These could not be true because then B or E would have to share a group with C or D.

(D) G must be in group 2 with A.

19. Correct answer: **A**. Here is an example of this scenario. (A and G could also be in group 3).

☐1   ☐2   ☐3

A   —   —

G

     F

F would have to be in group 2 to allow for B and E to avoid C and D.

20. Correct answer: **B**. B must be in a group with F, to avoid C and D. Notice that BF and CD could go in either group 1 or group 3, as long as the groupings are not changed.

☐ B   —   A   —   ☐ C
  F   G   D
       —   E   —

21. Correct answer: **E**. G could not be in group 1, because that would force B or group E to share a group with C or D.

—   A   F

—   G   —

—

22. Correct answer: **A.** In order to avoid being placed in a group with C or D, B must share group 2 with A and G.

5. $\underline{\text{F}}\quad\underline{\text{A}}\quad\underline{\text{C}}$
   $\underline{\text{E}}\quad\underline{\text{G}}\quad\underline{\text{D}}$
   $\qquad\underline{\text{B}}$

23. Correct answer: **B.** There are four different possible scenarios, which can be represented by the following two diagrams:

6. $\underline{\text{F}}\quad\underline{\text{A}}\quad\underline{\text{B}}$
   $\underline{\text{C/V}}\quad\underline{\text{G}}\quad\underline{\text{E}}$
   $\qquad\underline{\text{D/C}}$

   $\underline{\text{F}}\quad\underline{\text{A}}\quad\underline{\text{C}}$
   $\underline{\text{E/B}}\quad\underline{\text{G}}\quad\underline{\text{D}}$
   $\qquad\underline{\text{B/E}}$

24. Correct answer: **B.** If F cannot go with A, then F cannot go with G either. Since F cannot go with B or E, then F must share a group with either C or D. This forces B and E to go in a group together. F could share group 2 with both C and D or F could share group 1 or 3 with only one of them.

Section 3—Logical Reasoning

1. All animals that want to go into the park should be leashed. People like Alex who are concerned citizens know and abide by this maxim. Yet, Alex does not leash his dog when they go into the park together.

   Question Type: Conclusion

   Correct answer: **E.** We can infer that Alex's dog dislikes going to the park.

   (A) Even if this statement were true, the squib states that animals wanting to go into the park must always be leashed, regardless of who else is there.

   (B) This statement does not pertain to the logic of the squib.

   (C) Even so, this means that they keep their animals that want to go into the park on a leash.

   (D) According to the squib, only those cats that want to go into the park should be leashed.

2. This squib assumes that because we continue to progress in our understanding of the human mind, we will eventually be able to endow a computer with a sense of self-knowledge analogous to that held by humans.

   Question Type: "Weaken"

   Correct answer: **B.** If nothing electronic could gain self-knowledge, then the proposition of the squib would be invalidated.

   (A) This statement does not make the author's proposition untrue.

   (C) This statement does not mean that eventually we would not be able to do this in the "perfect computer."

   (D) As long as some humans *do* have self-knowledge, the computer could be mapped to emulate their brains.

   (E) This answer choice states that some computers will attain self-knowledge, thereby supporting the contentions of the passage.

3. This squib claims:
   1. 60 million Americans worked an average of more than 40 hours a week.
   2. 55 million Americans found their jobs to be too demanding.

   From these facts, the squib draws the conclusion that a small portion of the 60 million people working an average of more than 40 hours a week were satisfied with the demands of their job. This is an invalid conclusion because the groups of the study do not necessarily overlap. The people working more than an average of 40 hours a week could be completely different from those who find their jobs unreasonably demanding.

   Question Type: Reasoning strategy

   Correct answer: **B.** An overlap is not specified anywhere in the squib.

   (A) Although the squib may do this, it is not really the logical flaw in the specific conclusion drawn.

   (C) Such information would be irrelevant.

   (D) This answer is not applicable.

   (E) Although the premises may not be related to the same groups of Americans, they do not contradict each other.

4. The last sentence seeks to strengthen the conclusion that people should be very selective when choosing their beds. The fact that humans spend half their lives asleep (presumably in bed) would tend to support the idea that people should make a high-quality "bedroom selection."

Question Type: Reasoning strategy

Correct answer: **D.** The last sentence is a fact/claim that supports the squib's conclusion.

(A) The last sentence is definitely not the main point of the passage, which is that people should be selective about their beds.

(B) The last sentence is relevant, but it does not summarize.

(C) The whole argument is not based on this premise.

(E) The last sentence does not clarify the meaning of any other sentence.

5. The professor argues that the prenatal environment is the most important factor in a child's intelligence. The doctor argues that the neonatal environment is more important than the prenatal environment.

Question Type: Controversy

Correct answer: **C.** The professor and the doctor are arguing about the relative importance of the neonatal versus the prenatal environment.

(A) Both argue that malnourishment holds negative implications for a child's intelligence.

(B) Both agree that it is important for children to be adequately nourished in their prenatal environment.

(D) Nothing is mentioned about monitoring these different environments.

(E) The doctor does not contradict the professor's claim that children will not be able to recover from environmental inadequacies.

6. To put it briefly, this passage makes the claim that music was not very influential in human society before it came to be marketed as a commercial product.

Question Type: "Strengthen"

Correct answer: **B.** This answer choice essentially restates the conclusion: society did not fully realize music's effect before music became a commercial product.

(A) CDs, tapes, 8-track tapes, and phonograph recordings are all commercial products, so this statement is not relevant.

(C and D) Both these statements tend to undermine the conclusion of the squib.

(E) People in other parts of the world might have had such an appreciation.

7. The lobbyist claims that automobile pollution affects only those living in cities, since the CO_2 is filtered out of the air before it reaches the countryside. Based on this contention, the lobbyist claims that nothing should be done to curb the bad effects of pollution in the city.

Question Type: "Weaken"

Correct answer: **E.** The lobbyist's argument applies only to CO_2, not to other pollutants, which might not be absorbed by trees.

(A) According to the lobbyist, the CO_2 is filtered out of the air by the time it reaches people living outside the city. So the statement is irrelevant.

(B) The lobbyist's argument is about polluted air, not environmentally friendly automobiles.

(C) Exhaust fumes from factories, rather than cars, are not an issue here.

(D) Since this statement does not say what the study's conclusion is, the lobbyist may still be offering a valid argument.

8. This is a sufficient-necessary problem.

   1. Basketball Player→Hate Rain

   2. Hate Rain→Dislike Cats

   You can conclude: Basketball Player→Dislike Cats

   You are asked to find the assumption that justifies the conclusion that if you own a cat, you are not a basketball player. This conclusion is diagrammed as follows:

   Own Cat→~~Basketball Player~~

   Question Type: Conclusion

   Correct answer: **C.** Dislike Cats→~~Own Cat~~

This could be connected with the former conclusion to state:

Basketball Player→Dislike Cats→~~Own Cat~~

(A) We are not assured that all basketball players are tall.

(B) This assumption is nonsensical and does not connect with the given logic chains.

(D) The phrase "some people" does not lead to a conclusion about all basketball players.

(E) We know only that basketball players dislike the rain.

9. The squib claims that Julius Caesar was killed because all Roman citizens hated him. However, the only evidence given to support this idea is the historical documents referring to his death, in which only his friend Brutus and other politicians are mentioned. This is a very limited sample of the population.

Question Type: Reasoning strategy

Correct answer: **C.** The group that killed Caesar does not represent all Roman citizens.

(A) The killers are samples of the Roman population and not the other way around.

(B) The squib makes no argument for any course of action.

(D) Historical documents are likely to be highly authoritative.

(E) This strategy does not occur in the squib.

10. This squib claims that it is impossible for someone to own something pleasure-inducing and not use it.

Question Type: Analogous reasoning

Correct answer: **B.** The author of this answer choice makes the same mistake: assuming that Bernie must listen to the CD because if he did, then it would give him great pleasure.

(A and C) Neither of these statements makes mistakes analogous to the squib's.

(C) This answer choice does not make an analogous mistake.

(D) The mistake here is that tigers' claws and teeth may not aid them if their habitat changes. Although this statement uses logic similar to the claim in the squib, it is not as good a choice as B because it does not relate to pleasure.

(E) This answer choice is nonsensical in a way that does not mirror the squib.

11. The captain claims that his crew will never return to the Bermuda Triangle. The first mate reminds the captain that they are scheduled to return.

Question Type: Controversy

Correct answer: **A.** Since the captain is not a member of the crew who will "never return," the first mate is unsure whether the captain wants to return or not. This is the point at issue.

(B) The first mate is a member of the crew and if he returns to the Triangle, then that would clearly contradict the words of the captain. However, the first mate does not state that he will return.

(C) Both agree that the crew will not return.

(D) They agree that the Triangle holds many dangers.

(E) Only the captain, or first mate speaking for him, can cancel a voyage.

12. This squib talks largely about how music is emotionally evocative and able to produce any emotion in its listeners. Then, tacked on to the end of the squib, is an unsupported sentence claiming that music programs should be given more funding.

Question Type: Reasoning strategy

Correct answer: **B.** The claim is not supported by the rest of the squib.

(A) Although the final sentence is often a squib's main point, it is not so here.

(C) This is not true. Even if people agree that music is emotionally evocative, it does not mean they will agree that schools should spend more money on music education.

(D) It is completely unrelated to the argument that precedes it in the squib.

(E) The sentence does not juxtapose anything.

13. This squib claims that, initially, American popular sentiment toward the Revolution was cynical. As the war progressed, however, Americans began to see that an all-out victory would not be necessary. After this epiphany, American sentiment toward the Revolution improved dramatically.

Question Type: Conclusion

Correct answer: **E.** This is the thrust of the squib.

(A) This is a subsidiary claim but not the main point.

(B) This detail is not stated in the squib.

(C) Although this statement may be true, it was not stated in the squib, nor is it the main point.

(D) Americans hoped that this was true, but the statement is not the main point of the squib.

14. This squib refers to sports gambling. It claims that the common person can never consistently outpredict the statisticians that are hired by bookies. Since this is the case, most people will eventually lose the money that they devote to gambling.

Question Type: Conclusion

Correct answer: **E.** This conclusion can be drawn because, according to the squib, sports gamblers will inevitably lose their money.

(A) This statement might be true, but we cannot be sure that people would be better served by betting on a card game instead of a sport.

(B) Although the analogy may be tenable, it is not a conclusion that can be made on the basis of the squib.

(C) The statisticians that work for the bookies, not the bookies themselves, are the ones that determine the odds successfully.

(D) The squib does not refer to physical danger.

15. The squib states that popes are chosen based on two criteria:

1. Experience in the faith

2. Being in touch with modern times

The squib goes on to state that these criteria are often mutually exclusive, so the passage recommends satisfying the second and hoping that eventually the pope will also fit the former.

Question Type: Conclusion

Correct answer: **A.** This conclusion is true because otherwise the journalist would not recommend sacrificing experience in the faith for being in touch with modern times.

(B) This conclusion states the opposite of the conclusion in the squib.

(C) Ambassadors are not mentioned in the squib.

(D) This conclusion is not necessarily the case. There is no more than one pope, but it is likely that multiple people would fit both criteria.

(E) This statement is probably true, but it cannot be concluded from the information in the squib.

16. This squib tells us:

1. Last year, 30 percent of the bear population was aggressive, but this year 60 percent is aggressive.

2. Last year there were 12 bear attacks, but this year there have been only 3.

The discrepancy is that bears are more aggressive this year, but there have been fewer attacks.

Question Type: "Resolve"

Correct answer: **D.** If the bear population in general were lower, then that would explain why there are fewer attacks even though there is more aggression.

(A) This statement is irrelevant to what is going on specifically in the park.

(B) Having the ability to protect oneself during an attack will not prevent an attack.

(C) Fifteen is a number that will probably not be statistically significant.

(E) Even so, bears have been determined to be more aggressive this year than last year.

17. The argument makes several very tenuous claims. The first is that music halls would not be able to operate if there were no wealthy individuals in a society. The second is that there are no individuals or entities in communist societies that would have the same role as wealthy individuals in our country.

Question Type: "Weaken"

Correct answer: **B.** This statement points out the tenuousness of the claim that only the wealthy can support music halls.

(A) This statement does not refute the claim that it would not be financially viable to operate music halls.

(C) Although this statement might be true, it is not as compelling as answer choice B.

(D) This statement is irrelevant as to whether music halls would find financial support or not.

(E) The contentions of the squib are supported, not called into question, by this statement.

18. This argument claims that political races should be subsidized so that candidates would not owe favors to large companies, would be able to spend more time informing the public of their views, and would compete for office on an equal playing field.

Question Type: "Strengthen"

Correct answer: **C.** The squib cites this example as one reason that subsidized political races are desirable.

(A) This answer choice is nonsensical.

(B) Propaganda is not contrasted with substantive views in the squib.

(D) Even if this squib's recommendations were enacted, large sums of money would still determine who wins political races.

(E) The contention of the squib would be undermined if this principle were true.

19. The singer claims that numerous effects are derived from listening to music. The pragmatist claims that not all the effects can be tied to one cause.

Question Type: Controversy

Correct answer: **A.** The pragmatist does not agree that the entire breadth of effects is caused solely by listening to music.

(B) The singer and pragmatist disagree about music's responsibility in general, not the responsibility of a particular musical genre.

(C) They do not disagree about this point.

(D) Neither the singer nor the pragmatist argue that music is concrete.

(E) Both speakers might advise people that listening to music has some merit.

20. This squib claims that dung beetles with vivid coloring are more likely to be selected by females for breeding, because the females could see them better than they could see more traditionally colored beetles.

Question Type: "Strengthen"

Correct answer: **D.** The reason for coloring is pinpointed, and the implication is the one noted in the squib.

(A) If true, this fact would tend to argue against the selection of such dung beetles.

(B) This statement might support the argument, but it would not be as decisive as answer choice D. It says nothing about the color purple, which is the one at issue in the squib.

(C and E) These two statements would point to other explanations besides color for the prevalence of purple dung beetles.

21. This squib claims that all types of luging are very dangerous, but that people have the potential to be hurt more severely during street luging than ice luging because people do not slide as well on asphalt.

Question Type: Conclusion

Correct answer: **C.** Since there is more potential for injury in street luging than in ice luging, you can conclude that street luging is more dangerous.

(A) Although street luging is more dangerous, there are probably more injuries from ice luging because there are probably far more ice lugers than street lugers.

(B) You cannot conclude anything about bobsledders based on the squib.

(D) Asphalt may not be harder and more abrasive than ice, but it is harder to slide on.

(E) This statement is not supported by the squib.

22. This squib outlines three reasons why movie stars associate with each other.

Question Type: Conclusion

Correct answer: **B.** This answer is precisely what the squib states.

(A) The squib does not mention any negatives, but there may be some.

(C) This is a detail, not the main point.

(D) This is a detail, not the main point.

(E) Some stars may, indeed, avoid socializing with other stars, but the squib does not state this.

23. The protester argues that our society claims to teach peace, but in reality it is suffused with role models that emphasize aggression.

Question Type: "Weaken"

Correct answer: **A.** According to this statement, the situation is more complicated than the protester claims. Role models actually are aiming for peace by engaging in a small amount of violence. (So children should not interpret the violent actions they see solely as aggression.)

(B) The protester's argument is supported, not undermined, by this statement.

(C) This statement does not undermine the argument.

(D) However, these entities probably do have an effect on children who have been born.

(E) This statement does not relate logically to the protester's argument.

24. This squib mentions two ways that salespeople are paid: by commission or by an hourly rate (or by both). Sam has not sold anything for years, so if he is still getting paid, then he must be getting an hourly salary.

Question Type: Conclusion

Correct answer: **D.** If Sam were paid commissions, he would not be making any money, since he has made no sales in years. If he is being paid, it must be by an hourly rate.

(A) Sam could be paid by commission as well as by an hourly rate (although he would not have received any commissions recently).

(B) It's also possible that Sam is a poor salesman, or that the product is good but just not popular right now. You cannot be sure from the information in the squib.

(C) Based on information in the squib, you can't make any judgments about what Sam should do. Maybe he gets a great hourly rate and does not really have to do any work for it.

(E) This statement is not supported by the information in the squib.

25. This squib claims that because rice outproduces corn in China that corn should be replaced with rice in the United States, despite the fact that the United States has a climate that is different from China's.

Question Type: "Weaken"

Correct answer: **D.** Not having climates that can support a rice crop definitely argues against trying to switch an agricultural focus from corn to rice.

(A) This statement might also be true for rice, so it doesn't weaken the argument.

(B) However, the squib tells us nothing about whether the United States has many diverse geographic locales or whether some of those locales would be bad for rice.

(C) This statement would tend to support the claims of the squib.

(E) This statement would tend to support the claims of the squib.

SECTION 4—READING COMPREHENSION

1. Correct answer: **A.** The author uses every paragraph to back up the claim that education in a foreign language is becoming more useful than it used to be. Specifically, the author explains how knowledge of a foreign language is becoming a powerful tool in the workplace.

(B) The reference to the professions in lines 15–20 was made to describe a misconception people had of foreign language study. In addition, this reference is only a minor point made in the passage.

(C) The author makes this point, but it is not the main point of the entire passage.

(D) The author makes this point, but it is not the main point of the entire passage.

(E) Although this statement might be inferred, the author makes no direct claims about wages in the passage.

2. Correct answer: **E.** This answer paraphrases what is stated in lines 30–32.

(A) The author makes no mention of world travel in the passage. Be careful not to use inferences to answer a question that does not call for them.

(B) While the author states that the growing internationalization of American business is a good reason to study foreign languages, the author does not say that studying languages is the cause of this internationalization.

(C) The author makes no mention of business schools in the passage. Be careful not to use inferences to answer a question that does not call for them.

(D) The author is actually arguing nearly the opposite of this. In lines 12–15, the author is describing an old misconception that should be disregarded in America today.

3. Correct answer: **C.** The second paragraph starts by describing Americans' old view of foreign language study as almost a frivolity. The author then goes on to explain that today's reality is different from these old misconceptions because of changes in the relationship between America and the rest of the world. The paragraph therefore explains *how* the views should be modernized and *why* they are no longer true.

(A) There is mention of an influx of foreign capital into the United States in lines 24–25, but the paragraph includes no "how to" about it.

(B) This answer is essentially a summary of the first half of the paragraph.

(D) This answer is essentially a summary of the first half of the paragraph. Notice that this choice does not address the second half of the paragraph, which the author devotes to explaining *why*.

(E) This statement is an inference from a minor point made in the paragraph; however, it is not the primary purpose of the paragraph.

4. Correct answer: **E.** The author makes no mention of the time period of this increase. From the essay, though, it seems as if the changes causing this increase (lines 23–29) are long-term changes. So the resulting increase in demand is also likely to be long term. Therefore, the author would disagree with this statement.

(A) This is a relationship drawn in the second paragraph. See lines 23–24.

(B) This statement can be found almost verbatim in lines 32–34, in which the author seems to agree that foreign language study is not a foolproof way to get a first job.

(C) In lines 19–20, the author states that some foreign language students will still need to fill their traditional jobs. These jobs are those that generally require no other technical skills. Therefore, the author would agree with this statement.

(D) This statement is a paraphrase of author's ideas in lines 46–49.

5. Correct answer: **B.** The place to look for the answer to this question can clearly be narrowed down to the first part of the second paragraph, in which the author is discussing the old views of foreign language study. Of the choices, this statement best summarizes that section.

(A) This is an inference without any direct support from the passage. There is no claim that lack of foreign language studies held back American business.

(C) This is an inference without any direct support from the passage. There is no mention of European universities in the passage.

(D) This answer, if anything, runs contrary to the suggestions in the passage. The second paragraph is about changes from old times to new, and this statement says exactly the opposite of what is said in the passage.

(E) According to the author, foreign language study was not seen in the past as particularly valuable for improving everyday skills (such as communication).

6. Correct answer: **A.** Every part of the passage serves to build up the claim that "the whole world does not speak English," which is why foreign language skills are playing an increasingly important role in the job market. The author's primary purpose, therefore, must be to call this fact to the readers' attention.

(B) This is an argument the author does make, but it leaves out a major focus of the passage: business. The author continually connects foreign language study to its growing importance in the job market.

(C) The author is writing about how the job market is growing for foreign language students beyond the bounds of traditional careers for those students (such as translating and teaching). While the author does comment that there is still a need for people to fill jobs in those fields, the passage focuses mostly on using foreign language skills in the business world.

(D) The author writes about one effect of the increasing internationalization of business: a rising number of foreign language students in the business world. However, the author does not even bring up a second topic or opinion. Therefore, this passage was written to argue one specific point, not to debate several points.

(E) This answer can be immediately eliminated because it is not consistent with the tone of the passage, which is clearly not a reflective search for answers. Instead, it is an empirical argument that there is a growing need for foreign language skills in the American job market.

7. Correct answer: **B.** The first paragraph introduces SETI as a very difficult task. The following paragraphs explain some assumptions scientists make to try to simplify the task, and the author debates their worth. Nonetheless, the main idea of the passage is expressed well in choice B.

(A) While this statement is true and is a point made by the author, it by no means encompasses the main idea of the whole passage.

(C) Radio waves are mentioned only in the second half of the passage. In addition, this statement is argued against by the author, who describes how difficult interstellar listening is as a means of finding intelligent life.

(D) The author states that the size of our galaxy complicates the search, but does not say that the size of our galaxy bars us from success in SETI. Again, however, this is a relatively small point made by the author in relation to the main idea of the whole passage.

(E) This may be true, but it is not what the passage is truly written to discuss: the creation of debatably helpful assumptions in order to tackle the huge task of SETI.

8. Correct answer: **B.** In lines 19–28, the author explains why stars much bigger or much smaller than our own Sun tend to create conditions that are not supportive of life as we know it. In contrast, stars that are similar in size to our Sun are much more likely to support life in their solar systems.

(A) While the author writes about carbon-based life-forms and star sizes in the same paragraph, they are not interrelated other than by the fact that we base simplifying assumptions on both of them. Choice A is not supported in this passage.

(C) This answer is tempting, but the statement the author makes in lines 20–23 does not argue against any life, but only "intelligent life." Be sure to pay attention to details in tricky options.

(D) In lines 23–29, the author states clearly that planets not close enough to a small star to be tidally locked into orbits with that star are "frozen solid"—and, therefore, not favorable for the presence of life.

(E) About 10 percent of the stars in our galaxy are Sun-like, a condition that the author assumes is necessary for life. However, the passage does not say that a star probably sustains life just because it could possibly do so. This statement is a false inference from the passage.

9. Correct answer: **E.** The statement made in lines 41–45 directly contradicts choice E, so the author would be most likely to disagree with this statement.

(A) If the author considers SETI an important enough topic to write about (and is not clearly against it), then the author must consider it a worthwhile cause. Judging from the tone and argument, it is a fair inference to make that the author probably thinks intelligent life does exist elsewhere in the universe. The passage certainly does not contradict this inference.

(B) In lines 11–12, the author specifically states that choice B is plausible, albeit unlikely.

(C) This statement certainly seems to be a theme of the essay: that life, at least as we know it on Earth, is the result of several life-conducive conditions (such as the existence of water and survivable temperatures) shared in one place. In any case, the author would not disagree with this statement.

(D) The third paragraph debates the efficacy of the simplifying assumptions made in SETI. The author suggests that these assumptions may actually be leading the search astray, or at least blinding it to other possibilities. The author would agree with this statement.

10. Correct answer: **A.** In lines 34–37, the author makes a point that while our assumptions may seem to simplify the task, their lack of certainty means that the task may not be simple in the least. In other words, interstellar listening is definitely a more complex task than one might think.

(B) Repeatedly in the final paragraph, the author admits to uncertainty about how aliens might use radio waves and how inconsistent this may be with our own methods.

(C) In lines 52–56, the author explains a likely distinction between natural and artificial signals.

(D) Interstellar listening seems like the surest bet in SETI, despite its clear complexities. However, the author never ventures to make a statement as definite as choice D. It is too extreme an inference.

(E) Whether or not this statement is true, it is not mentioned in the passage. The only reference the author makes to natural radio signals in the universe is to refer to them as "background noise" (line 53).

11. Correct answer: **C.** The author describes the complexity and boundlessness of SETI and the assumptions we make to simplify the search. Although the author argues that some of these assumptions may be inaccurate, he or she suggests that, despite their imperfections, these assumptions may be necessary to designate "primary targets" (lines 31–33) for SETI.

(A) The author neither makes, nor hints at, this statement. See the explanation for question 9, choice A.

(B) While the vastness of the universe is an obstacle to tackle, this statement is contradictory to the tone of the passage. Again, see the explanation for question 9, choice A.

(D) Our simplifying assumptions might cause us to overlook a life-form that is not carbon-based, but not to *discount* it. As explained in the passage, our assumptions are used to narrow the areas in which we search for life, but not necessarily to determine what constitutes life.

(E) While the author does assert doubt about some of the assumptions scientists have made, he or she does not completely dismiss them. This statement is too strong an inference to be accurate.

12. Correct answer: **D.** In lines 33–34, the author is trying to show that our simplifying assumptions are inductive—the result of theories based on one set of circumstances that are inferred to be correct for other sets of circumstances. In other words, we know of only one way in which life exists and one set of life-forms existing that way. Therefore, to make assumptions that all life in the universe must exist in the same manner as this one set would be dangerously uncertain (because of the limited base of analysis).

(A) Though choice A is attractive, given the context of lines 33–34, it is not a good explanation of the author's reasoning.

(B) Choice B does not correctly reflect the context.

(C) The author is questioning the validity of choice C, not arguing for it.

(E) Choice E does not correctly reflect the context.

13. Correct answer: **B.** In the first paragraph, the passage introduces SETI as a very difficult task. The following paragraphs explain some assumptions scientists make to try to simplify the task, and the author debates their worth—are they more misleading or helpful, given the vastness of the universe? Choice B is the best answer.

(A) While the author does draw attention to the uniqueness of our planet, this is definitely not the primary focus of the passage.

(C) This statement is not made in the passage, nor is it logically inferable from it.

(D) This statement is not made or referred to in the passage, so it is certainly not the main focus of it.

(E) The author is more likely to say that we are overestimating, rather than underestimating, the helpfulness of the simplifying assumptions.

14. Correct answer: **B.** In the first paragraph, the author introduces the problem of health care fraud by describing its effects on society and two general approaches to dealing with it. In the following two paragraphs, the author offers more specific solutions to the problem and discusses their historical effectiveness.

(A) This explanation is very inconsistent with the tone and content of the passage. The focus of the first paragraph is not a generalization, and the rest of the passage does not offer counterexamples.

(C) This explanation is very inconsistent with the tone and content of the passage. The focus of the first paragraph is not an assumption, and the rest of the passage does not test the validity of an assumption.

(D) Choice D is not consistent with the verbal tense used in the passage, which primarily focuses on things that have been done or are being done, not on what is to be, or potentially could be, done.

(E) There is no talk of shortcomings in the Department of Justice or of any "reconstruction efforts." This is simply not a reasonable choice.

15. Correct answer: **D.** The author clearly states in the first paragraph: "The impact of health care fraud and abuse cannot be measured in terms of dollars alone. While health care fraud burdens our nation with enormous financial costs, it also threatens the quality of health care" (lines 7–12). The impact is therefore both on the economy and on society.

(A) The author certainly shows that health care fraud is a difficult problem to address but does not imply that it is an unsolvable problem.

(B) Choice B is simply not logically inferable from any details in the passage.

(C) The author references 1998 twice as a good year in the fight against health care fraud. However, nothing is said of the crime rate's increase or decrease, so although this may be a reasonable assumption given the tone of passage, it is an uncertain assumption. Therefore, this is not the best answer.

(E) The passage starts with "Since 1993, the Department of Justice ('the Department') has made fighting fraud and abuse in the health care industry one of the Department's top priorities." Therefore, the mention of "the 1980s" makes this statement incorrect.

16. Correct answer: **A.** There is no mention of denial of incidental claims anywhere in the passage.

(B) This point is mentioned in line 19.

(C) This point is mentioned in lines 15–16.

(D) This point is mentioned in lines 33–37.

(E) This point is mentioned in line 18.

17. Correct answer: **A.** The second and third paragraphs are both used to relate the success of current preventive efforts in the fight against health care fraud. The final paragraph is used to suggest that much is left to be done.

(B) The final paragraph suggests that as health care payment evolves, the Department will face continued challenges and must plan to change accordingly. Therefore, the current efforts of the Department may not be sufficient to halt all health fraud in the future.

(C) The passage only briefly references HIPAA, and while one can infer that it had a great effect on attacking American health fraud, it would be too strong an inference to say that HIPAA has had the greatest effect.

(D) This choice is counterintuitive to the tone and content of the passage. The focus of the second and third paragraphs is on how the efforts have made a difference.

(E) This is not stated anywhere in the passage, nor is it hinted at.

18. Correct answer: **E.** Especially in the context of line 41, the author is talking about the government's attempt to get providers to police their own activities against fraud. "Compliance programs" like this are ways for providers to avoid fraud without excessive government intervention.

(A) Given the phrasing in line 18, compliance initiatives are linked with the companies in the health care industry, not patients. This is reaffirmed by the phrasing in line 41.

(B, C, and D) These choices are not supported by the contexts in which the two terms are given. Be sure to pay careful attention to details. Some choices may sound familiar because they use words that were repeated throughout the passage, but be careful to examine each choice critically.

19. Correct answer: **B.** This point is discussed in the first paragraph. See the explanation for question 15, choice D.

(A) Although the author makes it clear in the first paragraph that health care fraud is a social vice, it would be too extreme an inference to say that it is "without equal."

(C) Again, the author makes it clear in the first paragraph that health care fraud hurts its victim financially and sometimes physically. However, the author says nothing about the perpetrator being hurt, except when caught.

(D) The word *only* eliminates this choice. Even in the first paragraph, the author makes the point that there is a plethora of ways to fight health care fraud.

(E) The first paragraph tells us that vigilance is an important weapon for patients who wish to protect themselves. However, it would be too strong an inference to say that vigilance is the most powerful weapon.

20. Correct answer: **E.** Given the organization of the passage, this is the best answer. There is a presentation of a problem in the introductory paragraph, and the following paragraph starts with the line: "The Department's enforcement actions have proven results." Finally, the passage closes with a paragraph about how the Department will continue to deal with fraud in the future.

(A) This point is made in the first paragraph; however, it would be an exaggeration to call it the reason the passage was written.

(B) This is touched on only briefly, and so it does not describe the author's purpose.

(C) The verbal tense used in this option implies that the passage was written to offer prevention plans for the future. However, much of the passage describes things that have already happened and are happening today.

(D) The passage gives the reader a sense that the incidence of health care fraud in America is actually declining. In addition, there is not any internal debate in this passage.

21. Correct answer: **B.** This passage begins with two introductory paragraphs that give some background about AD. The introductory material leads to an argument for the importance of early diagnosis in order to combat the disease. This argument is the main focus of the passage.

(A) This is a point made in the third paragraph, but it is clearly not the main point of the passage.

(C) This is a subsidiary point of the first paragraph.

(D) This point is made in the second paragraph, but the passage focuses on early, not just any, diagnosis.

(E) This answer is second best. However, scientific research is mentioned only as an afterthought in the final paragraph. Because of its brevity, it is not the main point of the entire passage.

22. Correct answer: **E.** Dementia is a trait of certain diseases that plague the elderly.

(A) *Dementia* is not an example; it is a generalization.

(B) There are no objections raised in the paragraph.

(C) *Dementia* is not used in this context to undermine an argument. Instead, it is a redefinition of an old scientific theory that lumped all diseases characterized by this trait into one general category.

(D) There is no system mentioned in the passage. Although the categorization of diseases could broadly be considered a system, the passage does not discuss the *dementia* as a way to codify these diseases.

23. Correct answer: **B.** A major part of the second paragraph strives to elucidate the fact that not all dementia diseases are the same. This paragraph seems to disapprove of the catchall categorization.

(A, C, and D) The author explains that the catch-all category is a misconception. Therefore, the author could not be characterized as indifferent, apathetic, or commending.

(E) The author is not befuddled about the catchall category, but rather explains how it was erroneous.

24. Correct answer: **D.** Of the choices, slowing the progression of the disease is the only medical benefit of early diagnosis mentioned by the author.

(A) Being able to deal with precautionary legal issues is a benefit of early diagnosis, but it is *not* a medical benefit.

(B) The passage does not mention the expense of treating the disease.

(C) The passage states explicitly that current treatments are unable to prevent the full course of the disease.

(E) The opposite is true: While doctors cannot stop the disease's progression, they can lengthen it through medicine and give the afflicted more years of cognizant living.

25. Correct answer: **D.** By starting the passage with this human story, the author introduces the topic in a manner that many readers can identify with.

(A) It would be a gross exaggeration to characterize the first paragraph as a scare tactic.

(B) Although the first paragraph precedes the author's argument for early diagnosis, it does not do anything to establish that argument. It merely sets the stage for a brief discussion of Alzheimer's disease.

(C) Neither the first paragraph nor the rest of the passage discusses the effects of good general health (or lack of it) on Alzheimer's disease.

(E) The passage does not propose any plan for treating Alzheimer's disease.

26. Correct answer: **C.** The opposite of this claim can be inferred.

(A) This inference is based on the medical, practical, and scientific benefits of early diagnosis.

(B) You can make this inference based on details in lines 38–42.

(D) This fact is stated explicitly by the passage (lines 34–37).

(E) Since AD was traditionally placed in the catchall category of "senile dementia," this inference is obvious.

27. Correct answer: **B.** The entire passage has been constructed to stress the importance of early diagnosis of AD.

(A) This question is not answered by the passage. Research is talked about only in a limited way.

(C) This question is unrelated to the passage.

(D) Even though the passage states that there are treatments for Alzheimer's disease, it does not discuss any specifics.

(E) Although answers to this question are hinted at in the passage, there is no information regarding the best course of action.

Your LSAT Study Plan

Now that you have taken the Diagnostic Test, you should have a good idea of what lies in store for you on the LSAT. It's time now to think about how to use *McGraw-Hill's LSAT* to make your preparation program the most effective it can be. You may also wish to consider supplementing the materials in this book with additional LSAT preparation materials from Curvebreakers.

The LSAT is above all else a test of your mental stamina. You need to train your mind to be able to work through the test in the time allowed without tiring and making errors, especially when you reach the final sections. That's why we recommend that you create and follow an intensive, week-by-week training course. Several days each week, you should make sure that you study at least one full LSAT's worth of material. Only by keeping up this pace will you be able to build the mental stamina you need to get a top LSAT score. That being said, the Curvebreakers LSAT course is more demanding and detailed than other LSAT courses, and you as a student will benefit dramatically from this intensity.

If you have purchased the book-only version of *McGraw-Hill's LSAT*, you have enough materials and sample tests for an intensive, five-week preparation program. If you have purchased the book-CD version, you have even more materials to get you ready for the exam. Here is a sample study plan that you can follow or adapt to meet your specific needs. This plan includes four days of intensive study every week. Try to have rest days in between the study days.

Week 1: Logic Games

Day 1: Go back and look carefully at the **Diagnostic Test** that you just completed. **Review the questions** that you missed and **identify** the sections that gave you the most trouble.

Day 2: Turn to Chapter 3 "Logic Games," and work through the logic games in the *Formal Logic, Sequencing,* and *Linear* sections. Answer the questions slowly and make sure that you understand the processes required for each diagramming technique.

Day 3: Work through the logic games in the *Complex Linear, Grouping,* and *Mapping* sections of Chapter 3, "Logic Games."

Day 4: Work through the logic games in the *Minimized Variables* and *Maximized Variables* sections of Chapter 3. **Review each section**. Rework a game of each type in order to ensure that you have learned the appropriate diagramming techniques for each type of game.

Week 2: Logical Reasoning

Day 1: Do the introductory exercises in Chapter 4, "**Logical Reasoning**." Work through the *Conclusion* logical reasoning question type.

Day 2: Work through the questions in the *Resolve* and *Strengthen* sections.

Day 3: Work through the questions in the *Weaken* and *Reasoning Strategy* sections.

Day 4: Work through the questions in the *Analogous Reasoning* and *Controversy* sections. **Review the material in the section** to make sure that you can accurately identify the question types and the correct way to solve them.

Week 3: Reading Comprehension

Day 1: Do the introductory exercises in Chapter 5, "**Reading Comprehension**." Work through the *Main Point* section, which deals with main point type questions. Be sure to read through the explanations of the answers that you miss and be sure to review your work.

Day 2: Work through the questions in the *Author's/Character's Opinion* and *Claims* sections.

Day 3: Work through the questions in the *Syntax* and *Inference* sections.

Day 4: Work through the questions in the *Support/Undermine* sections. **Review the material in this section** to make sure that you can accurately identify the question type and the correct way to solve it.

Week 4: Practice Tests

Day 1: Review the **Writing Sample** section.

Day 2: Take **Practice Test 1**.

Day 3: Review **Practice Test 1**. Look at your results, review your mistakes, and *identify the particular question types* for each section that you consistently miss.

Day 4: Take **Practice Test 2**.

Week 5: Practice Tests

Day 1: Review **Practice Test 2**. Look at your results, review your mistakes, and *identify the particular question types* for each section that you consistently miss.

Day 2: Take **Practice Test 3**. Look at your results, review your mistakes, and *identify the particular question types* for each section that you consistently miss.

Day 3: Take **Practice Test 4**. Look at your results, review your mistakes, and *identify the particular question types* for each section that you consistently miss.

Day 4: Take **Practice Test 5**. Look at your results, review your mistakes, and *identify the particular question types* for each section that you consistently miss.

IF YOU HAVE PURCHASED THE BOOK-CD VERSION OF *McGraw-Hill's LSAT*:

If you have purchased the book-CD version, you can take any or all of the practice tests listed above on your computer, where you will have the advantage of automatic timing, scoring, and score analysis. You will also have the following additional study materials:
- **Practice Test 6**
- **Practice Test 7**

SUPPLEMENTARY CURVEBREAKERS MATERIALS AVAILABLE

Because we believe so strongly in the importance of building stamina for the LSAT, we ardently recommend that you consider extending your training program by several additional weeks by ordering supplementary materials available from Curvebreakers at www.Curvebreakers.com. If you are fortunate enough to have **two months** before the test and are ready to start preparing right away, we recommend the following:
- During **Week 4** of the Study Plan outlined above, identify the **three** types of **logic games** and the **three** types of **logical reasoning** questions that you answer *incorrectly* the most often. Visit the Curvebreakers Web site and order the Supplementary Materials books relating to these question types, along with additional practice LSATs. If you order the books during week 4, you should have them when you are ready to start week 6.
- During **Week 6** of your study plan work through two supplementary logic games books and two supplementary logical reasoning books.
- During **Week 7** of your study plan work through a third supplementary logic games book and a third supplementary logical reasoning book. Then take two practice LSATs.
- During **Week 8** of your study plan take four additional practice LSATs.

THE WEEK OF THE TEST

Arrange your study program so that you take the LSAT **three days** after you take your final practice LSAT. You should do nothing related to studying in between the final practice LSAT and the actual LSAT since this will allow your mind to recover from the exertion of your study program. On the two days before the LSAT, go out and have fun with your friends in order to relieve stress, but be sure not to stay up past midnight and do not do anything that is physically or mentally exhausting.

PART II

SOLUTION STRATEGIES FOR EVERY LSAT QUESTION TYPE

CHAPTER 3

LOGIC GAMES

In this chapter you will learn:

- The eight major types of LSAT logic games

- How to use logic tools to understand each game

- How to create diagrams to clarify logic relationships

- Easy-to-follow solution steps for every game type

Logic games are often the hardest questions for LSAT takers, but the logic games section is also the section where people have the most potential for improvement if they consistently practice. Each game starts with a set of information called the *fact pattern*. This is followed by a set of rules called *constraints* that govern the fact pattern. Five to seven questions are based on the fact pattern and constraints. Achievement in logic games turns on the test taker's ability to remember and apply numerous rules and sets of facts. Few people have the innate ability to do this adeptly in the 8 minutes on average that you must spend per game in order to answer all questions in the 35-minute time limit. However, through systematic practice, anyone can learn the skills necessary to excel in logic games.

The following chart shows the eight major types of logic games on the LSAT. The types vary in difficulty and test different logical skills.

THE EIGHT TYPES OF LSAT LOGIC GAMES

1. Formal Logic
2. Sequencing
3. Linear
4. Complex Linear
5. Grouping
6. Mapping
7. Minimized Variables
8. Maximized Variables

This chapter will teach you how to master each type of logic game by applying logic tools and using accurate diagramming techniques.

You will be most likely to improve your score if you take the time to understand the tricks and idiosyncrasies of each question type.

Logic Games: Four General Strategies

The following four general strategies will help you to gain the maximum benefit from your logic game practice.

1. Use Logic Tools. The fact pattern and constraints of every game type can be broken down and modeled through the use of logic tools. These tools help you to remember the rules, to apply them in the correct way, and to choose the correct answer in the shortest amount of time. Here is a short list of the logic tools that this chapter will teach you:

- **Sufficient-Necessary:** Used for all types of logic games and some types of logical reasoning.
- **Logic Chains:** Used for formal logic, sequencing, linear, and grouping logic games. Also used on some types of logical reasoning questions.

- **Sequencing Chains:** Used for sequencing and linear logic games.
- **Box Rules:** Used for complex linear, linear, minimized variables, and grouping logic games.
- **Vacancy-Occupancy Rules:** Used for linear, advanced linear, minimized variables, and grouping logic games.

These tools apply to specific types of games, and they can also be used to map and solve difficult logical reasoning problems. A test taker who learns these tools will be able to discern the rules of a game more easily, understand hypothetical scenarios faster, and select responses more accurately than a test taker who does not take the time to learn them.

2. Diagram Every Logic Game. In order to use logic tools effectively, you must learn to use effective diagramming techniques. You should diagram before you even look at the questions, because many games can be so fully diagrammed that the correct answer choices for all the questions will be evident from your initial diagram. This is especially true of minimized variables logic games.

Get into the habit of diagramming the entire problem before you embark on answering the questions. Diagramming will enable you to process the rules of the game on a deeper level and increase the likelihood that you remember the rules or are reminded of them by your diagram. Some people hesitate to diagram because they feel that they do not have enough time, but the fact is that a little extra time up front will save you an abundance of time on each question. This fact plays into the third recommendation:

3. Work Through Examples Slowly. Time spent learning is not the same as time spent taking the test. In fact, learning time is and should be completely different. Even if you know that you will have only eight minutes to answer each logic game on the actual LSAT, you need to ignore this fact completely while practicing and initially learning logic tools. The reason is that you will need to spend a significant amount of time learning how to invoke the logic tools, to diagram them, and to apply them, at least at the beginning of your study program. Do not get frustrated if you need

to take 20 or 30 minutes per game when you first learn how to use each logic tool. You will be rewarded for you patience! Your speed will pick up naturally once you have slowly and diligently learned the logic tools required for each game.

Once you become skilled at using and applying logic tools, you can use the excellent resources available on the Curvebreakers Web site to increase your problem-solving speed.

4. Review Past Mistakes. Reviewing past mistakes is the best method for improving your understanding. This fact seems obvious, but still, many people do not go back and review the questions they missed on diagnostics and lessons. Without review of past mistakes, it is impossible to identify areas on which you should spend more time studying.

Going back to retake a logic game after several weeks is often worthwhile because much of the benefit from logic game practice centers on learning to set up the problem, and most people forget in a few weeks' time the preliminary setups for a specific logic game.

Studying This Chapter

Follow the recommendations in this section to gain an edge on your competition. The following sections cover each specific type of logic game, moving from the least complicated types to the most complex ones. Pay attention to which logic tools and diagramming techniques correspond to which types of games. As you learn to identify logic game types, you will eventually be able to guess the tricks that the test makers are likely to have written into the game. Go through these lessons slowly. Over time, you will increase your speed and eventually achieve a skill level that will allow you to dramatically increase your score.

---

1 Formal Logic Games

A formal logic game consists of a series of if-then statements. Based on the configuration of the statements, you will be required to deduce a series of consequences or possibilities. The following is an example of a formal logic game.

> Five children named Rufus, Samantha, Tyler, Uma, and Vern are scheduled to play together on Sunday morning. However, some of the children will not come if other children come, and some children will definitely come if other children come. The presence or absence of specific children is governed by the following constraints:
>
> Rufus will not come if Tyler comes.
> Tyler will come if Uma comes.
> Vern will come if Samantha does not come.

Logic Tools

Sufficient-Necessary. Various deductions and inductions can be made based on constraints such as the ones given in the sample game. In order to remember and build a framework of knowledge based on these constraints, you can use a logic tool called a *sufficient-necessary* condition. Here is an example:

> Traditionally, trade routes developed only through cities with castles. Through 200 A.D., French cities did not have castles. By that period, the Spanish cities all had castles. Spanish cities' castles were located within the center of the city and the roads of the trade routes spun through the castles' courtyards.
>
> If all of the statements in the passage are true, then which one of the following must also be true?
>
> (A) In 200 A.D., Spanish cities were the only cities with trade routes.
> (B) The development of trade routes caused the development of castles.
> (C) In 200 A.D., the French and the Spanish traded with each other.
> (D) After 200 A.D., French cities had castles and trade routes.
> (E) The French cities of the year 200 A.D. did not have trade routes.

By diagramming the conditions in the fact pattern, you will be able to make a series of deductions. The first sentence of the fact pattern states the following condition:

> *Trade routes ("TR") developed only through cities with castles ("C").*

To form a logical flowchart of this sentence, you need to understand which condition (*sufficient*) requires the presence of the other condition (*necessary*). These conditions are displayed in the form of:

Sufficient condition → Necessary condition

In this example, castles ("C") were necessary for the existence of trade routes ("TR"). This condition can be diagrammed in the form of a flowchart:

TR → C

This flowchart lets you state in an organized fashion that for a *trade route* to have *existed*, then it *required* the presence of a *castle*. Every time you start tackling a logic game, try making flowcharts like this one to map out all sufficient-necessary conditions that you are given.

Contrapositive. It is critical to note that this is not the only fact that the sentence reveals. It also tells you that:

> *Without a castle ("C"), there could have been no trade route ("TR").*

$\cancel{C} \to \cancel{TR}$

The fact above is not explicitly stated in the fact pattern, but it is true and it is called the statement's *contrapositive*. A statement's contrapositive is found through a logical reversal that you will learn momentarily, but for now it is enough to know that the contrapositive of any and every *true* statement is also a *true* statement. Every time you map out a sufficient-necessary condition, map out its contrapositive as well.

For the current question, the logical map that we are building looks like this:

TR → C $\cancel{C} \to \cancel{TR}$

Now let's look at the second statement in the fact pattern:

French cities ("FC") did not have castles ("C").

The sufficient-necessary condition in the statement is:

$$FC \rightarrow \cancel{C}$$

Its contrapositive is:

If there was a castle ("C"), then it was not a French city ("FC").

This can be written in the form:

$$C \rightarrow \cancel{FC}$$

So after you initially read the statement, you should write this logic chain down on your paper:

$$FC \rightarrow \cancel{C} \qquad C \rightarrow \cancel{FC}$$

Now let's look at the third statement:

Spanish cities ("SC") all had castles ("C").

The logical map of this statement looks like:

$$SC \rightarrow C \qquad \cancel{C} \rightarrow \cancel{SC}$$

This problem could be mapped out further, but in this case we have enough information to solve it already, so let's take a look at our complete logical map of the three sentences:

$$TR \rightarrow C \qquad \cancel{C} \rightarrow \cancel{TR}$$
$$FC \rightarrow \cancel{C} \qquad C \rightarrow \cancel{FC}$$
$$SC \rightarrow C \qquad \cancel{C} \rightarrow \cancel{SC}$$

Adding Logic Chains. Notice how some of these chains have the same ends and beginnings as other chains. These common variables can be connected to make longer sufficient-necessary chains, and one of these connections/deductions will be necessary to solve this problem:

$$TR \rightarrow C + C \rightarrow \cancel{FC} = TR \rightarrow C \rightarrow \cancel{FC} \quad or \quad TR \rightarrow \cancel{FC}$$

This can be read as:

"If there was a trade route, then there was no French city."

$$FC \rightarrow \cancel{C} + \cancel{C} \rightarrow \cancel{TR} = FC \rightarrow \cancel{C} \rightarrow \cancel{TR} \quad or \quad FC \rightarrow \cancel{TR}$$

This can be read literally as:

"If it was a French city, then there was no trade route."

This deduction will answer the question.

Now let's look at the answer choices to identify the correct answer based on our logic tools:

If all of the statements in the passage are true, then which one of the following must also be true?

    (A) In 200 A.D., Spanish cities were the only cities with trade routes.

You don't have enough information to support this answer choice.

    (B) The development of trade routes caused the development of castles.

This might seem correct until you map it out—the answer choice statement is equivalent to $C \rightarrow TR$. According to our facts, a castle was necessary to trade routes ($TR \rightarrow C$), not the other way around.

    (C) In 200 A.D., the French and the Spanish traded with each other.

You do not have enough information to support this answer.

    (D) After 200 A.D., French cities had castles and trade routes.

You are not told what happened to the French cities after 200 A.D., so you can't choose this answer.

    (E) The French cities of the year 200 A.D. did not have trade routes.

This is the correct answer as shown by our last deduction ($FC \rightarrow \cancel{TR}$).

You have now learned how to diagram a sufficient-necessary statement in order to map a constraint. You also learned how to deduce another piece of information called the contrapositive from the sufficient-necessary condition. Finally, you added two sufficient-necessary chains in order to form a larger chain that would allow you to answer the question correctly. This is a lot to learn in the span of a few pages, but don't worry; we will go through each of these logic tools many times in this chapter.

Incorrect Sufficient-Necessary Conditions and Contrapositives. Numerous mistakes can be made by anyone trying to identify sufficient-necessary conditions and their contrapositives. Test makers commonly include answers that fit these mistakes in the answer choices, so learning to avoid these pitfalls is very important.

Here are some examples of common mistakes made in forming sufficient-necessary conditions and contrapositives.

Statement:

All dogs ("D") are mammals ("M").

Correct sufficient-necessary condition:

$$D \rightarrow M$$

Incorrect sufficient-necessary condition:

M → D   (literally reads: If you are a mammal, then you are a dog.)

Always form the contrapositive by:

1. Switching the letters in the sufficient-necessary logic chain (M → D)
2. Reversing their positive or negative values ($\not{M} \rightarrow \not{D}$).

Correct contrapositive:

$\not{M} \rightarrow \not{D}$ (literally reads: If you are not a mammal, then you are not a dog.)

Incorrect contrapositives:

If you stop at step 1, then you will get an incorrect contrapositive:

M → D   (literally reads: If you are a mammal, then you are a dog.)

If you skip step 1 and move immediately to step 2, you will also get an incorrect contrapositive:

$\not{D} \rightarrow \not{M}$ (literally reads: If you are not a dog, then you are not a mammal.)

Sufficient-necessary conditions can be used to map out all if-then statements presented in LSAT Logic Games and Logical Reasoning Questions.

Here is a more difficult example:

Statement:

If the animal is in the pool (AP), then it is not a cat (C).

Correct sufficient-necessary condition:

$$AP \rightarrow \not{C}$$

Incorrect sufficient-necessary condition:

$\not{C} \rightarrow AP$ (literally reads: If it is not a cat, then the animal is in the pool.)

Correct contrapositive:

C → ~~AP~~   (literally reads: If it is a cat, then the animal is not in the pool.)

Incorrect contrapositives:

$\not{C} \rightarrow AP$ (literally reads: If it is not a cat, then the animal is in the pool.)

~~AP~~ → C   (literally reads: If the animal is not in the pool, then it is a cat.)

Neither of these statements is a conclusion that you can correctly draw.

Mastering sufficient-necessary conditions and contrapositives will allow you to solve LSAT problems more quickly and more accurately. You will also be able to avoid the incorrect answer choices based on incorrect sufficient-necessary conditions and incorrect contrapositives.

You have now learned:

- how to draw a sufficient-necessary logic chain
- how to form a contrapositive
- how to add logic chains together to make inductions

The following is a complete formal logic game. Solving it will require you to use each of the three skills that you have just learned. It is only practice, so take plenty of time to draw all of the conditions correctly and do all the possible logic chain additions before looking at the answer choices.

FORMAL LOGIC GAME I

Bulbs flicker on and off on a billboard equipped with exactly six light sockets, which are labeled lights 1, 2, 3, 4, 5, and 6. The billboard's circuitry causes the bulbs to light up according to the following conditions:

Whenever light 1 is on, light 4 is off.
Whenever light 2 is off, light 1 is on.
Whenever light 2 is on, light 5 is on.
Whenever light 4 is off, light 3 is on.
Whenever light 5 is on, light 6 is on.

1. If light 4 is on, which of the following is a complete list of the other lights that must be on?

    (A) light 3
    (B) light 5
    (C) lights 1, 2, and 4
    (D) lights 2, 3, and 5
    (E) lights 2, 5, and 6

2. If light 5 is off, which of the following lights could be on?

    (A) light 2
    (B) light 4
    (C) light 5
    (D) light 6
    (E) lights 2 and 3

3. If light 2 is on, which of the following is a complete list of other lights that must be on?

    (A) lights 5 and 6
    (B) lights 4 and 5
    (C) lights 4 and 6
    (D) lights 3 and 4
    (E) lights 1 and 6

4. If light 3 is off, then which light must also be off?

    (A) light 1
    (B) light 2
    (C) light 3
    (D) light 4
    (E) light 5

5. If light 5 is off, which light must be on?

    (A) light 2
    (B) light 3
    (C) light 4
    (D) light 5
    (E) light 6

6. If light 3 is off, which of the following is a complete list of the lights that must be on?

    (A) lights 2, 4, 5, and 6
    (B) lights 2, 4, and 5
    (C) lights 1, 5, and 6
    (D) light 1
    (E) light 4

USING THE LOGIC TOOLS

The questions in the formal logic game shown may seem difficult at first, but if you break the problem down slowly statement by statement through sufficient-necessary logic chains, you will be able to find the correct answers. In the following diagrams, the sufficient-necessary conditions are labeled 1a, 2a, and so on. The corresponding contrapositives are labeled 1b, 2b, and so on.

Statement 1:

> Whenever light 1 is on, light 4 is off.

Logic Chain:

1a. One → ~~Four~~   1b. Four → ~~One~~

Statement 2:

> Whenever light 2 is off, light 1 is on.

Logic Chain:

2a. ~~Two~~ → One   2b. ~~One~~ → Two

Statement 3:

> Whenever light 2 is on, light 5 is on.

Logic Chain:

3a. Two → Five   3b. ~~Five~~ → ~~Two~~

Statement 4:

> Whenever light 4 is off, light 3 is on.

Logic Chain:

4a. ~~Four~~ →Three   4b. ~~Three~~ → Four

Statement 5:

> Whenever light 5 is on, light 6 is on.

Logic Chain:

5a. Five → Six   5b. ~~Six~~ → ~~Five~~

Now that all the chains have been developed, it is time to link them together through logic chain addition:

I. (1a + 4a)

One → ~~Four~~ + ~~Four~~ → Three
= One → ~~Four~~ → Three

II. (2b + 3a + 5a)

~~One~~ → Two + Two → Five + Five → Six
= ~~One~~ → Two → Five → Six

III. (5b + 3b + 2a)

~~Six~~ → ~~Five~~ + ~~Five~~ → ~~Two~~ + ~~Two~~ → One
= ~~Six~~ → ~~Five~~ → ~~Two~~ → One

IV. (4b + 1b)

~~Three~~ → Four + Four → ~~One~~
= ~~Three~~ → Four → ~~One~~

Notice that several of these combined chains can be added even further to make longer chains that capture the entire problem and allow you to solve it with ease.

III + I

~~Six~~ → ~~Five~~ → ~~Two~~ → One + One → ~~Four~~ → Three
= ~~Six~~ → ~~Five~~ → ~~Two~~ → One → ~~Four~~ → Three

IV + II

~~Three~~ → Four → ~~One~~ + ~~One~~ → Two → Five → Six
= ~~Three~~ → Four → ~~One~~ → Two → Five → Six

Remember that you can move only to the right on logic chains. For instance, if light 6 is on, this does not tell you anything about the rest of the game. However, if light 3 is off, then we know the configuration of each lightbulb in the entire game.

The final two logic chains shown above denote two major possible configurations for the lights in the game, and solving the questions is easy by looking solely at these chains:

1. ~~Six~~ → ~~Five~~ → ~~Two~~ → One → ~~Four~~ → Three
2. ~~Three~~ → Four → ~~One~~ → Two → Five → Six

ANSWERING THE QUESTIONS

Question 1: If light 4 is on, which of the following is a complete list of the other lights that must be on?

(E) In the second logic chain, light 4 is on, so we look further down on the chain and see that lights 2, 5, and 6 must also be on. Therefore, the correct answer is E. Note that if light 4 is on, it does not mean that light 3 is necessarily off, because you can make deductions only by moving to the right on these logic chains, never to the left.

Question 2: If light 5 is off, which of the following lights could be on?

(D) In the first logic chain, light 5 is off. It follows that lights 1, 3, and also 6 could be on since light 6 precedes light 5 in the chain. The correct answer is D.

Question 3: If light 2 is on, which of the following is a complete list of lights that must be on?

(A) Light 2 is on in the second logic chain. We know for sure that lights 5 and 6 will be on. It is possible that lights 3, 4, and 1 might be on. The correct answer is A.

Question 4: If light 3 is off, then which light must also be off?

(A) Light 3 is off in the second logic chain. It follows that light 1 must be off. The correct answer is A.

Question 5: If light 5 is off, which light must be on?

(B) Light 5 is off in the first logic chain. Lights 1 and 3 must be on. Light 6 might be on. The correct answer is B.

Question 6: If light 3 is off, which of the following is a complete list of the lights that must be on?

(A) Light 3 is off in the second logic chain. Lights 4, 2, 5, and 6 must be on. The correct answer is A.

If this game seemed exceptionally hard, don't worry. If you are patient and take it slowly, you will be able to use these logic tools to answer questions in a game like this in five minutes or less when the actual LSAT comes around.

FORMAL LOGIC GAME 2

At the Ames town hall, a total of seven workers are employed. These workers follow a daily schedule that is constrained by the following conditions:

If Anna is working, then Bill is also working.
If Bill is working, then Claire is not working.
If Claire is working, then Dan and Emily are working.
If Fanny is working, then Dan is working.
If Gina is working, then Dan is working and Anna is working.

1. Which of the following is a complete list of people who could be working together?

    (A) Anna, Bill, and Claire
    (B) Gina, Dan, Anna, and Bill
    (C) Emily, Anna, Claire, and Bill
    (D) Gina, Dan, Anna, and Claire
    (E) Fanny, Dan, Gina, and Emily

2. If Gina is working, then who must NOT be working?

    (A) Anna
    (B) Bill
    (C) Claire
    (D) Dan
    (E) Emily

3. If Dan is not working, then which is a complete list of people who CAN NOT be working?

    (A) Claire and Emily
    (B) Bill, Anna, and Gina
    (C) Gina, Anna, and Bill
    (D) Gina, Emily, and Claire
    (E) Fanny, Claire, and Gina

4. If Emily is not working, then who of the following must not be working?

    (A) Claire
    (B) Dan
    (C) Bill
    (D) Gina
    (E) Anna

5. If Anna is working and Dan is not working, then which of the following people must be working?

    (A) Claire
    (B) Bill
    (C) Emily
    (D) Fanny
    (E) Gina

6. If Dan is working and Bill is working, then which of the following is a complete list of the other people who may be working?

    (A) Fanny and Gina
    (B) Anna, Gina, Claire, and Emily
    (C) Emily, Fanny, Gina, and Anna
    (D) Claire, Dan, and Bill
    (E) Emily, Gina, Anna, Claire, and Fanny

7. If the constraints were changed so that if Gina works, then Anna does not work, then which of the following is a complete list of people who could be working together?

    (A) Anna, Bill, Fanny, and Gina
    (B) Bill, Dan, Emily, Fanny and Gina
    (C) Anna, Bill, Claire, Dan, and Fanny
    (D) Fanny, Claire, Dan, and Bill
    (E) Bill, Fanny, Gina, and Emily

This second formal logic game will require you to utilize the same techniques that you just learned—the sufficient-necessary, the contrapositive, and logic chain addition. However, the game is more of an open game than the previous one, meaning that fewer constraints are imposed on the game up front in the fact pattern and more will be imposed by the answer choices. This means that your diagram should include a list of rules to which you should refer while answering each question.

SOLUTION STEPS

1. Transcribe the Constraints. Start by transcribing the separate sufficient-necessary conditions for the game into symbols. There are seven conditions:

1. $A \rightarrow B$		5. $F \rightarrow D$
2. $B \rightarrow \cancel{C}$		6. $G \rightarrow D$
3. $C \rightarrow D$		7. $G \rightarrow A$
4. $C \rightarrow E$		

Some people choose to diagram a constraint that says "If Claire is working, then Dan and Emily are working" like this: $C \rightarrow D, E$, but this is not a good idea for starters because this kind of formulation makes it harder to form contrapositives and to add the logic chains.

2. Add Logic Chains. You should add logic chains together wherever it is possible. If it is not possible to add chains, then now is the time to consolidate constraints. In the following diagrams, the combined

sufficient-necessary conditions are once again labeled 1a, 2a, and so on:

1a. $G \to A \to B \to \cancel{C}$ 2a. $F \to D$ with $C \searrow$ and $G \nearrow$ pointing to D

This means that the presence of any of the variables C, F, or G would lead to the presence of D.

3a. $C \to E$

3. Form Contrapositives.
Now form the contrapositives of the logic chains. These contrapositives are once again labeled 1b, 2b, and so on.

1b. $C \to \cancel{B} \to \cancel{A} \to \cancel{G}$ 2b. $\cancel{D} \to \cancel{F}$ / $\cancel{C}$ / $\cancel{G}$ 3b. $\cancel{E} \to \cancel{C}$

4. Finalize Chains and Make Inferences.
Finally, add together all chains that make inferences possible. You could combine all the variables into two long chains, but this is not as effective as connecting only those variables that will lead to and show future causal links. Here is an example of how this can be done:

$1b + 3a + 2a = C \to \cancel{B} \to \cancel{A} \to \cancel{G} + C \to E + C \to D$

$= C \to \cancel{B} \to \cancel{A} \to \cancel{G}$ with $\nearrow E$ and $\searrow D$

$1a + 2a = G \to A \to B \to \cancel{C} + G \to D$

$= G \to A \to B \to \cancel{C}$ with $\nearrow D$

Note that logical pieces of the problem could be combined still further, but the current level of combination is superior because if you see a variable on the left of the chain, then you know that all variables on the right will be caused by it. This is not true in the following diagram, which contains all the variables in two large and confusing mixed causality chains. For most test takers, it is best to avoid such overly complex chains.

1. $G \to A \to B \to \cancel{C}$ with $F \to D$, $\cancel{D} \to \cancel{G}$, $\nearrow \cancel{F}$, $\cancel{E} \nearrow$ 2. $C \to \cancel{B} \to \cancel{A} \to \cancel{G}$ with $\nearrow E$ and $\searrow F \to D$

Knowing when to combine variable chains is an important skill to learn. A good general guideline is that you should always combine variables into a larger chain as long as the variables were caused by something previous to them in the chain. If they

weren't, then leave them in their own chain. The five-factor diagram shown below is the most effective diagram for this game.

5. Create a Hierarchy of Chains.
The last step before moving to the answer choices is to organize the logic chains into a hierarchy that holds all pertinent information. It is a good idea to rank the smaller chains first in this hierarchy, because you are more likely to forget about them if they are included last.

1. $F \to D$ 3. $\cancel{D} \to \cancel{F}$ / $\cancel{C}$ / $\cancel{G}$ 4. $C \to \cancel{B} \to \cancel{A} \to \cancel{G}$ with $\nearrow E$ and $\searrow D$

2. $\cancel{E} \to \cancel{C}$

5. $G \to A \to B \to \cancel{C}$ with $\nearrow D$

Now that you have adequately diagrammed the game's constraints, you can move on to answering the questions.

ANSWERING THE QUESTIONS

Question 1: Which of the following is a complete list of people who could be working together?

(B) Diagram 5 shows that this is a possible group.

Question 2: If Gina is working, then who must NOT be working?

(C) Diagram 5 demonstrates that Claire does not work when Gina works.

Question 3: If Dan is not working, then which is a complete list of people who must NOT be working?

(E) Diagram 3 shows that if Dan is not at work then Claire, Fanny, and Gina must not be working.

Question 4: If Emily is not working, then who of the following must not be working?

(A) If Emily doesn't work, then Claire must not be working.

Question 5: If Anna is working and Dan is not working, then which of the following people must be working?

(B) Anna working means that Bill must be working and Claire must not be working. Dan's not working means that Claire, Fanny, and Gina must not be working. Emily's working is not connected to either of these variables, so she is able to work but only Anna and Bill must work.

Question 6: If Dan is working and Bill is working, then which of the following is a complete list of the other people who may be working?

(C) Bill's working requires Claire not to work. Dan's working does not affect any other variable. Therefore, everyone besides Claire is able to work.

Question 7: If the constraints were changed so that if Anna did not work, then Gina did work, then which of the following is a list of people who could be working together?

(B) This type of question is very unnerving since it changes the constraints just as you are about to finish the game. A good method for solving questions like these quickly is to use another constraint that remains in the game that was very determinative on the game in order to eliminate answer choices. A good one would be that Claire cannot work with Bill or Anna. This eliminates choices C and D. Another good constraint would be the one that was just imposed—Gina and Anna cannot work together. This eliminates

answer choice A. Answer choice E is not correct because it is incomplete—Dana could also work with this group. Therefore, answer choice B is the only complete answer choice.

Recap: Formal Logic Games

In this section you learned how to use

- the sufficient-necessary logical tool
- the contrapositive induction
- logical chain addition

---

2 Sequencing Games

Logic games that require sequencing can be fully diagrammed before you start to answer any question. A typical fact pattern and list of constraints for a sequencing game follows.

SEQUENCING GAME 1

Anna, Bill, Claire, Dave, Emily, Frank, and Gina are all working on their mathematics final. Each student hands his or her test to the professor at different times. The order in which their tests are submitted is governed by the following constraints:

> Anna turns in her test before Bill.
> Claire turns in her test after Bill
> Claire turns in her test before Dave.
> Emily turns in her test after Dave.
> Gina turns in her test before Emily and after Frank.
> Frank turns in his test after Bill.

The technique that you should use to map out sequencing problems is very similar to the five-step technique that you used to solve formal logic problems.

SOLUTION STEPS

1. Transcribe the Constraints. In a sequencing problem, the constraints can be arranged sequentially. For instance, "Anna turns in her test before Bill" can be transcribed as: A < B. Once you have read through all seven constraints, transcribe them into symbols as follow:

1. A < B	4. D < E	6. F < G
2. B < C	5. G < E	7. B < F
3. C < D		

When first transcribing the constraints, be careful to do two things. First, make sure that your "greater-than" signs consistently denote the same direction. Many test takers make careless errors by using a greater-than sign to represent "after" at the beginning of the problem and then switching to a "less-than" sign to represent "after" later in the problem. This is a serious mistake, so be sure to use a consistent ordering method in which you know the direction that each sign represents. Second, pay attention to "before" versus "after" and to use of the words *not* and *sometimes*. Test makers will throw in a "not after" or a "not before" just to try to confuse you. Also, they will

mix up saying "before" and "after" when referring to the same variables, hoping that you will confuse the two words. Finally, if the word *sometimes* is used, then the constraint really means nothing, because just as a variable could sometimes come before another, it could also sometimes come afterward. To sum up, figuring out the correct order of the variables before you begin transcribing is the most difficult step in solving sequence problems, If you take the time to determine the correct order, the rest of the problem will be easy.

2. Add Logic Chains. Consolidate the seven constraints through logic chain addition. Constraints 1 through 4 can be added together to make a linear chain:

$$A < B < C < D < E$$

Constraints 5 through 7 can be added to the linear chain to form a connecting chain that looks like this:

$$A < B < C < D < E$$
$$\llcorner F < G \lrcorner$$

This all-encompassing chain represents all the variables in the problem.

3. Figure Out What You Can Deduce Correctly. Before moving on to the questions, you should ask yourself what the chain and its variables mean. That is, what can you deduce from the chain? Several deductions are clear: A is less than E, F and G are less than E, B is less than G. However, there are several fallacious deductions that people often make when confronted with a chain like this. Here are a couple of *incorrect* deductions: F is less than D, G is greater than C, D is equal to G. When a chain branches like this, it is of the utmost importance to realize that you can deduce nothing about the order of a variable that is not connected in a direct chain. Watch out for branched chains and beware of making these false deductions.

Here is another chain. For practice, ask yourself the following question. What are some *false* deductions that a *test maker* would like to trick a *test taker* into making based on this diagram of the variables?

$$N < P < L$$
$$\llcorner \qquad \lor$$
$$M < K < O < J$$

Here are some examples of *false* deductions:

1. N < K
2. N < O
3. N < J
4. J < N

The principle is that there has to be a direct sequential link between the variables. If you are ever unsure of the sequential relationship, then start at one variable and try to make it to the next variable without either jumping the chain or having the sign change from "greater than" to "less than." For example, take N < O. Starting at N and trying to connect to O, you would move *greater* to P, but then you would have to go *less* to O. By trying to go the other direction, you would go *less* to M, then you would have to move *greater* to K and then to O. Making an assumption by switching from *less* to *greater* is impossible. Try to follow the order of logic of the correct deductions below.

Here are some examples of *correct* deductions:

1. M < L
2. K < P
3. M < J

See how you could start at M and consistently use the same chain to move *greater* to L. The following logic game will help you practice these techniques. Remember the order of operations. First, be careful while transcribing the constraints. Second, use logic chain addition. Finally, ask yourself what you can correctly deduce from your chain.

SEQUENCING GAME 2

Eight Olympic sprinters ran a 100-meter dash and finished in the following order:

Adam finished before Bill.
Frank finished before Evan.
Bill finished before Charles.
Dave finished after Charles and Bill.
Ham finished after George.
Evan finished before Charles and Dave.
George finished after Bill.

1. Which of the following is a possible order for the finishers to finish in from first to last?

    (A) Frank, Evan, Adam, Bill, George, Ham, Charles, Dave.
    (B) Dave, Charles, Evan, Frank, Ham, George, Bill, Adam.
    (C) Adam, Evan, Frank, Bill, George, Ham, Charles, Dave.
    (D) George, Frank, Adam, Evan, Bill, Ham, Charles, Dave.
    (E) Adam, Bill, Frank, Evan, Charles, Dave, Ham, George.

2. If Ham finishes after Charles, then how many runners must finish before Charles?

    (A) two
    (B) three
    (C) four
    (D) five
    (E) six

3. Which one of the following statements must be true?

    (A) George finishes after Charles.
    (B) Ham finishes before Dave.
    (C) Frank finishes after Adam.
    (D) Charles finishes after Dave.
    (E) Ham finishes after Bill.

4. If George finishes after Dave and Frank finishes after Bill, how many different orders could the racers finish in?

    (A) none
    (B) one
    (C) two
    (D) three
    (E) four

5. If Evan finished before George, then which of the following must be true?

    (A) George must finish after Charles.
    (B) Frank must finish after Bill.
    (C) Ham must finish after Frank.
    (D) Dave must finish after Ham.
    (E) Adam must finish first.

6. What is the total number of sprinters who could possibly finish first added to the number of sprinters who could possibly finish last?

    (A) none
    (B) one
    (C) two
    (D) three
    (E) four

7. If Frank finished after Bill and Ham finished before Charles, then how many possibilities are there for the race rankings?

    (A) four
    (B) five
    (C) six
    (D) seven
    (E) eight

SOLUTION STEPS

1. Transcribe the Constraints. The nine constraints should be transcribed as follows:

1. $A < B$	4. $C < D$	7. $E < C$
2. $F < E$	5. $B < D$	8. $E < D$
3. $B < C$	6. $G < H$	9. $B < G$

2. Add Logic Chains. Go through and see which pairs of variables share variables with other pairs. Make chains by adding a pair that ends with a given variable to a pair that starts with the same variable. Add chains together, making sure to cross off chains from your list as you combine them in order to keep track of which chains still need to be added.

Beware of misinformation, that is, information that tells you something twice so that you add the variable twice into your diagram, thereby convoluting it. An example is "Dave finished after Bill." You already knew this because Dave finished after Charles and Bill finished before Charles. Another example of misinformation is the statement that says "Evan finished before Charles and Dave." You know that Evan finished before Dave because it was specified that Evan finished before Charles, and you already know that Charles finished before Dave. Therefore, do not add a variable about

Evan twice in your chain, once before D and once before C, because the one before C is all that is needed.

Here is the complete and simplified diagram:

$$F < E$$
$$A < B < C < D$$
$$G < H$$

3. Figure Out What You Can Deduce Correctly.

You *can* assume that A is less than D or H. You *cannot* assume that A is less than F or E. You *cannot* assume that H is greater or less than C. You *cannot* infer any relationships between G and H or between F and E. You *cannot* assume that D is greater than G or H. Go through the diagram and ask yourself why you can assume certain things and why you cannot assume others. The following questions will expose errors and gaps in your knowledge if you do not correct them now. It is much safer to get a good grip on the diagram before giving questions the opportunity to trip you up.

ANSWERING THE QUESTIONS

Question 1: Which of the following is a possible order for the finishers to finish in from first to last?

(A) Looking at your diagram, it is clear that Frank, Evan, Adam, Bill, George, Ham, Charles, and Dave is a possible order. It is possible that Evan finishes before Adam, and it is possible that George and Ham finish before Charles. The rest of the ordering is mandated by the constraints.

Question 2: If Ham finishes after Charles, then how many runners must finish before Charles?

(C) If Ham finishes after Charles, then two runners must finish after him—Ham and Dave. It is possible that George finishes either before or after Charles. However, four people are required to finish before Charles—Adam, Bill, Evan, and Frank.

Question 3: Which one of the following statements must be true?

(E) Ham must finish after Bill. The other choices are only possibilities, except for D, which is impossible.

Question 4: If George finishes after Dave and Frank finishes after Bill, how many different orders could the racers finish in?

(B) There would only be one possible order—Adam, Bill, Frank, Evan, Charles, Dave, George, and finally Ham.

Question 5: If Evan finished before George, then which of the following must be true?

(C) This constraint would set up a chain that would look like this: F < E < G < H. Based on this chain, it is clear that Frank must finish before Ham.

Question 6: How many racers could have finished either first or last?

(E) Dave or Ham could finish last. Frank or Adam could finish first. Add them together and you get four people that could finish *either* first or last.

Question 7: If Frank finished after Bill and Ham finished before Charles, then how many possibilities are there for the race rankings?

(C) If this were true, then you know for sure that the order goes A, B, X, X, X, X, C, D. The Xs correspond to the places in the order in which F, E, G, and H can arrange themselves. You know that F must always precede E and G must always precede H. Keeping this in mind, write out the possibilities:

1. FEGH	3. FGHE	5. GFHE
2. FGEH	4. GHFE	6. GFEH

There are a total of six possible arrangements.

The next sequencing game will give you some more practice with sequencing logic tools. Try to set up the initial logic chain yourself before you look at the answer.

SEQUENCING GAME 3

A number of species faced extinction during the Mesozoic era. Species R, S, T, U, V, W, and X were species that all became extinct during this era, and scientists have determined that their extinctions occurred based on the following constraints:

W became extinct before X.
U became extinct after T.
S became extinct before T.
X became extinct before U.
V became extinct after U.
S became extinct before W.
R became extinct before S.

1. Which were the last two species to go extinct?

   (A) X, V
   (B) T, U
   (C) X, U
   (D) U, V
   (E) R, S

2. Which species could have been the fourth one to go extinct?

   (A) S
   (B) V
   (C) U
   (D) W
   (E) R

3. Which is the smallest number of species that could have gone extinct before T?

   (A) two
   (B) three
   (C) four
   (D) five
   (E) six

4. Which of the following must be true if X went extinct after T?

   (A) Two species went extinct before T.
   (B) Three species went extinct before T.
   (C) Three species went extinct after T.
   (D) Four species went extinct before T.
   (E) At least three species went extinct after T.

5. How many possible orders are there for the species' extinction pattern?

   (A) one
   (B) two
   (C) three
   (D) four
   (E) five

6. If the constraints were changed and X were not required to become extinct before U, then which of the following is a possible order for the species' extinction?

   (A) W, R, S, T, U, X, V
   (B) R, S, X, W, T, U, V
   (C) R, X, S W, T, U, V
   (D) R, S, T, U, V, W, X
   (E) R, S, T, X, U, W, V

SOLUTION STEPS

1. Transcribe the Constraints. There are seven total constraints:

1. $W < X$
2. $T < U$
3. $S < T$
4. $X < U$
5. $U < V$
6. $S < W$
7. $R < S$

2. Add Logic Chains. This problem illustrates that a vital part of logic chain addition is the elimination of repetitive variables. Depending on the order in which you add the chains, you will come up with different formations for two subchains. A common formation is the following:

1. $S < W < X < U$
2. $R < S < T < U < V$

S and U are variables common to both chains. These common variables signal that these are linkage points for the metachain. Here is what the metachain should look like:

$$R < S \overset{T}{\underset{W < X}{\diagup \diagdown}} U < V$$

3. Figure Out What You Can Deduce Correctly. The only pitfalls that you should watch out for are questions that try to get you to assume any sort of relationship between the variables X or W and the variable T. Other than that, the deductions you can make from this diagram are fairly straightforward.

ANSWERING THE QUESTIONS

Question 1: Which were the last two species to go extinct?

(D) The diagram shows that this had to have been U and V.

Question 2: Which species could have been the fourth one to go extinct?

(D) R must have been first. S must have been second. Either W or T could have been third. W, T, or X could have been fourth. Therefore, the answer is W.

Question 3: Which is the smallest number of species that could have gone extinct before T?

(A) R and S must go extinct before T. It is possible for W and X to go extinct before T also, but this does not matter since the question asks for the smallest number. Therefore, 2 is the answer.

Question 4: Which of the following must be true if X became extinct after T?

(E) Based on this fact, the order of extinction must be R, S, *, *, X, U, V. W and T correspond to *, because we do not know the relative order between them. It is possible for 2 or 3 groups to go extinct before T. It is possible for 3 or 4 groups to go extinct after T. Based on this limited information, the best answer choice is E, at least three species went extinct after T.

Question 5: How many possible orders are there for the species' extinction pattern?

(C) Based on our diagram, the possible orders for extinction are shown by R, S, *, *, *, U, V. * corresponds to the variables T, W, and X, and the only

constraint between these variables is that W must go extinct before X. From here you can write the possible orders:

1. WXT
2. WTX
3. TWX

There are three possible orders.

Question 6: If the constraints were changed and X were not required to go extinct before U, then which of the following is a possible order for the species' extinction?

(D) This would change your diagram to look like this:

$$R < S < T < U < V$$
$$W < X$$

The order R, S, T, U, V, W, X would be possible, since W and X could follow V.

Recap: Sequencing Games

In this section you learned:

- how to transcribe the constraints of the fact pattern carefully
- how to consolidate constraints while eliminating repetitive variables during logic chain addition
- how to take note of and avoid several false deductions that test makers use as tricks for the unwary

---

3 Linear Games

Linear logic games give you a number of constraints that determine places where variables can go along a linear continuum. To solve these games, start by drawing a linear continuum that represents all available spaces for the variables. A basic linear continuum diagram looks like this:

——— ——— ——— ——— ——— ———

Underneath your linear continuum, you can map out constraints in the fact pattern using box rules and vacancy-occupancy rules. These two new logic tools help simplify and keep track of constraints in linear and complex linear logic games.

Box Rules

There are many different varieties of box rules. Some are used much more often than others. Review the following list and commit all the different types to memory. That way, if you run into a difficult constraint, you will know how to model it.

Box Rule

Typical constraint:

J is next to and immediately after K: | K J |

This diagram lets you recognize that this box has to fit along the linear continuum with K immediately before J and nothing in between.

Switching Box Rule

Typical constraint:

J is next to K: | K J |⌐

The handle on top of the box denotes that K and J can be in any relative order, so long as they are situated right next to each other.

No-Box Rule

Typical constraint:

J is not immediately after K: | K/J |

The slash through the box tells you that these variables cannot be consecutive along the linear continuum.

Switching No-Box Rule

Typical constraint:

J is not next to K: | K/J |⌐

Expanded Box Rule

Typical constraint:

There are two spaces between K and J. J is after K: | K __ __ J |

This box greatly narrows the possibilities of where these letters can be used in the game. For instance, if this expanded box were in a game that had a six-space-long linear continuum, then K would have to go in the first, second, or third space, and J would have to go in the fourth, fifth, or sixth.

Switching Expanded Box Rule

Typical constraint:

There are two spaces between K and J:

This diagram keeps track of the fact that J and K are two spaces away from each other while also denoting that we do not know the spatial order of K relative to J.

Switching Expanded No-Box Rule

Typical constraint:

There are *not* two spaces between K and J:

The box rule diagramming techniques can be a little intimidating at first, but after you have worked through a couple of games, writing out the diagrams will become second nature and will improve your test-taking speed immensely. In fact, it would be wise to return to this section to review all the different varieties of rules. Now let's look at the next logic tool that will help you solve linear games.

Vacancy-Occupancy Rules

Once you have diagrammed a game's constraints, you can begin to make deductions about the possible placement of the letters along the continuum. To take

account of these possible occupancies versus vacancies, make notes beneath the continuum regarding each variable's ability to be present in particular spaces. Observe the notes in this example.

At a spelling bee, children sit down in four chairs that are numbered 1 through 4.

Two people sit between Anna and Bill. Chris sits in a lower-numbered chair that is next to Dave.

First, draw the continuum:

$$\overline{1} \quad \overline{2} \quad \overline{3} \quad \overline{4}$$

Next, diagram the first constraint: Two people sit between Anna and Bill.

$$\boxed{A \quad \underline{\quad} \quad \underline{\quad} \quad B}$$

Next, deduce vacancy-occupancy rules about where Anna and Bill can and cannot go.

With these deductions noted, your continuum should look like this:

$$\underline{A|B} \quad \underline{\quad} \quad \underline{\quad} \quad \underline{B|A}$$
$$\quad \quad \cancel{A} \quad \cancel{A}$$
$$\quad \quad \cancel{B} \quad \cancel{B}$$

Neither Anna nor Bill could go in either of the middle two chairs, because if they did then the box that we diagrammed could not fit into the continuum. Therefore, Anna and Bill must be in chair 1 and chair 4. This deduction should be noted by what is called a *dual option*. You know that either Anna or Bill must go in chair 1, but you don't know which, so mark it as in the diagram above. If further along in the problem you figure out that Anna is in chair 1, then the dual option that you diagrammed will remind you that you also know where Bill must go—chair 4.

Now diagram the second constraint: Chris sits in a lower-numbered chair that is next to Dave.

Now look at your diagram with this box in mind. It is clear that the CD box fits right inside your other box, making your continuum look like this:

$$\underline{A|B} \quad \underline{C} \quad \underline{D} \quad \underline{B|A}$$
$$\quad \quad \cancel{A} \quad \cancel{A}$$
$$\quad \quad \cancel{B} \quad \cancel{B}$$

There is only one unknown left in the problem—the order of Bill and Anna.

But what if the C and D constraint in this problem said only that "Chris sits in a lower-numbered chair than Dave, but not necessarily next to Dave"? And what if you diagrammed this constraint first?

The following would be your sequential logic chain (sequential chains along with sufficient-necessary conditions and contrapositives will all be used in future game types): C < D

Map out on the continuum where the letters cannot go:

$$\overline{\cancel{D}} \quad \overline{\quad} \quad \overline{\quad} \quad \overline{\cancel{C}}$$

These cross-outs are accurate because if Chris sits in a lower-numbered chair than Dave, Dave could not sit in chair 1. The same is true for Chris sitting in chair 4. Any time you have a sequential constraint, you can make inferences about the first and last couple of slots along the linear continuum in a linear game.

After mapping the sequential constraint, move on to mapping and diagramming the next constraint, which would demonstrate that C and D must sit in chairs 2 and 3.

In the following two linear logic games, use the diagramming techniques and logic tools that you learned for formal logic games, sequencing games, and the rest of this section thus far to simplify the fact pattern before moving on to answering the questions.

LINEAR GAME I

A film producer is arranging for a series of actors to appear during an awards show. The actors, Frank, George, Hillary, Iris, John, and Kelly, will fill six time slots during the show, and their appearances are subject to the following constraints:

Frank will go in a time slot before Iris.
Iris will not be scheduled for time slot 2.
Hillary will be in a time slot that is immediately after George.
Kelly will appear in a time slot that is two slots after Hillary.

1. In how many different time slots is it possible for John to appear?

   (A) two
   (B) three
   (C) four
   (D) five
   (E) six

2. If George is scheduled in time slot 3, then who of the following must be scheduled in time slot 5?

   (A) Frank
   (B) Hillary
   (C) Iris
   (D) John
   (E) Kelly

3. Which actors CANNOT be scheduled in time slot 3?

   (A) Iris and Kelly
   (B) Frank and John
   (C) John and Hillary
   (D) Frank and George
   (E) Kelly and Frank

4. If Frank and Iris were to be scheduled as far away from each other as possible, who would be scheduled in time slot 4?

   (A) Iris
   (B) George
   (C) John
   (D) Hillary
   (E) Kelly

5. If Frank is scheduled for time slot 3, then who must be scheduled in time slot 4?

   (A) George
   (B) Frank
   (C) Iris
   (D) John
   (E) Kelly

6. Which is the latest time slot that Frank can be scheduled for?

   (A) Time slot 2
   (B) Time slot 3
   (C) Time slot 4
   (D) Time slot 5
   (E) Time slot 6

SOLUTION STEPS

1. Transcribe the Constraints. There are four constraints:

1. F < I
2. I cannot go in 2. (Map this on the linear continuum.)
3. [G H]
4. [H __ K]

You can consolidate constraints 3 and 4 in the following diagram:

[G H __ K]

2. Draw Scenarios of a Cumbersome Constraint. Looking at the linear continuum, it is clear that the GH_K box is very cumbersome and can go in only a couple of places on the diagram. In situations where there is a constraint or box that is this cumbersome, it helps to go ahead and draw out the possible scenarios where the box could go:

__ __ G H __ K

__ G H __ K __

G H __ K __ __

3. Write Out the Vacancy-Occupancy Rules. Now that you have modeled the basic framework for the game, you should write out all vacancy-occupancy rules:

4. Make Deductions and Map Out Dual Options.
Based on the vacancy-occupancy rules, you can make deductions about the locations of certain variables. Also, there are dual options and triple options that can be mapped out to remind you of where specific variables may be present:

1. $\underline{\text{F/J}}$ $\underline{\text{J/F}}$ $\underline{\text{G}}$ $\underline{\text{H}}$ $\underline{\text{I}}$ $\underline{\text{K}}$
      J̸   J̸   F̸

2. $\underline{\text{F/J}}$ $\underline{\text{G}}$ $\underline{\text{H}}$ $\underline{\text{I/F/J}}$ $\underline{\text{K}}$ $\underline{\text{I/J}}$
      J̸   F̸

3. $\underline{\text{G}}$ $\underline{\text{H}}$ $\underline{\text{F/J}}$ $\underline{\text{K}}$ $\underline{\text{I/F/J}}$ $\underline{\text{I/J}}$
                     J̸   F̸

This diagram shows all possible configurations of the variables in the game. You can use it to quickly answer all the questions.

ANSWERING THE QUESTIONS

Question 1: In how many different time slots is it possible for John to appear?

(E) Looking at your diagram, it is apparent that he can appear in all six time slots.

Question 2: If George is scheduled in time slot 3, then who of the following must be scheduled in time slot 5?

(C) This question refers you to line 1 of your diagram where you made the deduction that Iris must appear in time slot 5 when George is in time slot 3.

Question 3: Which actors CANNOT be scheduled in time slot 3?

(A) Looking down column 3 in your diagram, it seems that G, H, F, and J can all appear in this slot. However, I and K cannot.

Question 4: If Frank and Iris were to be scheduled as far away from each other as possible, who would be scheduled in time slot 4?

(C) Line 2 of your diagram shows the situation in which Frank and Iris are scheduled as far away from each other as possible: Frank is in time slot 1 and Iris is in time slot 6. Time slot 4 might hold Frank, Iris, or John, but you know that in this scenario Iris and Frank are scheduled as far away from each other as possible, so John must be in time slot 4.

Question 5: If Frank is scheduled for time slot 3, then who must be scheduled in time slot 4?

(E) Look at line 3 of the diagram. When Frank is in time slot 3, Kelly must be in time slot 4.

Question 6: Which is the latest time slot that Frank can be scheduled for?

(D) In line 3 of the diagram, Frank is scheduled in time slot 5.

Now try the next linear logic game. This game is more open, meaning that less can be deduced from the constraints, but the same diagramming techniques will still help you to solve the questions.

LINEAR GAME 2

A camp counselor is holding tetherball practice for seven campers named Frank, George, Hillary, Iris, John, Kelly, and Lori throughout this week starting on Monday. Each camper will practice only once, and only one camper will practice per day.

Frank and John practice on either Tuesday or Saturday.
Hillary will practice on a day after Frank.
Lori will not practice either the day before or the day after Frank or John practice.
Kelly will not practice on the day immediately following the day that John practices.

1. If John practices before Lori, then who will practice on Sunday?

   (A) Lori
   (B) George
   (C) Hillary
   (D) Iris
   (E) Kelly

2. If Kelly practices on Friday, then who will practice on Thursday?

   (A) Kelly
   (B) George
   (C) Iris
   (D) Lori
   (E) Hillary

3. Who of the following CANNOT practice on Monday or Tuesday?

   (A) Iris
   (B) Hillary
   (C) Frank
   (D) Kelly
   (E) George

4. If George and Hillary practice before John, then who will practice on Sunday?

   (A) Iris
   (B) Lori
   (C) Kelly
   (D) Frank
   (E) George

5. If Kelly practices third, then we know which days that how many people practice, including Kelly?

   (A) Two
   (B) Three
   (C) Four
   (D) Five
   (E) Six

6. If George practices before John and John practices before Lori, then who will practice on Friday?

   (A) John
   (B) George
   (C) Kelly
   (D) Iris
   (E) Frank

SOLUTION STEPS

1. Transcribe the Constraints. Often when you transcribe the constraints, it is helpful to note what type of constraint each one is. This will allow you easily to determine at what step and where each constraint should be added to your diagram.

1. **Dual Option**—F practices on Saturday or Tuesday, and J practices on Saturday or Tuesday.
2. **Sequential Chain**—F < H
3. **Box Rule**— F/L   J/L
4. **Box Rule**— J/K

2. Draw Scenarios of a Cumbersome Constraint. A dual option is generally not considered to be a cumbersome constraint. However, in this problem, several different variables are changed by the different placements of F and J, so it would be a good idea to draw out these scenarios:

Mon	Tues	Wed	Thu	Fri	Sat	Sun
	F				J	
	J				F	

3. Write Out the Vacancy-Occupancy Rules:

Mon	Tues	Wed	Thu	Fri	Sat	Sun
	F				J	
H̶ L̶		L̶		L̶		L̶ K̶
	J				F	
H̶ L̶		K̶ L̶ H̶	H̶	H̶ L̶		L̶

4. Make Deductions and Map Out Dual Options.

Several deductions can be made. First, L must always practice on Thursday. Second, in line 2 of your diagram, H must practice on Sunday. After you have written in these two variables, you should remove the superfluous vacancy rules. That is, remove all vacancy rules referencing L in line 1 of the diagram and all vacancy rules referencing L or H in line 2 of the diagram because you know the definite location of both variables. Removing superfluous information helps you to keep in mind the information that is still important:

Mon	Tues	Wed	Thu	Fri	Sat	Sun
1. H̶	F	—	L	—	J	K̶
2. —	J	K̶	L	—	F	H

ANSWERING THE QUESTIONS

Question 1: If John practices before Lori, then who will practice on Sunday?

(C) This would put you in line 2 territory. Your diagram shows that H would practice on Sunday.

Question 2: If Kelly practices on Friday, then who will practice on Thursday?

(D) No matter when Kelly practices, Lori will always practice on Thursday.

Question 3: Who of the following CANNOT practice on Monday or Tuesday?

(B) You know for sure that the answer is not F or J. One of them is always practicing on Tuesday, so the question is really asking who out of the rest of the variables cannot practice on Monday. In line 1, Hillary cannot practice on Monday because she must practice after Frank. In line 2, you know that Hillary has to practice on Sunday to practice after Frank. Therefore, the answer is Hillary.

Question 4: If George and Hillary practice before John, then who will practice on Sunday?

(A) You know that Hillary practicing before John is impossible in line 2 of the diagram, so this must be a line 1 scenario. You know where the variables F, L, and J go, and none of them practices on Sunday. You know that G and H practice before Sunday, since they practice before J. You also know that K cannot practice on Sunday, since she cannot go immediately after J. I is the only variable left that could possibly practice on Sunday.

Question 5: If Kelly practices third, then we know which days that how many people practice, including Kelly?

(C) Kelly cannot practice third in line 2, so this is a line 1 scenario. Since you cannot make any more inferences based on Kelly's placement, the answer is 4.

Question 6: If George practices before John and John practices before Lori, then who will practice on Friday?

(C) J practices before L in line 2. We can infer that G practices on Monday in order to practice before J. There are two variables left—K and I. We know that K cannot practice on Wednesday in line 2, so she must practice on Friday.

Recap: Linear Games

In this section you learned:

- how to diagram box rules
- how to diagram vacancy-occupancy rules
- how to make deductions based on these rules

4 Complex Linear Games

Complex linear games are basically the regular linear games that you learned in the last lesson taken to two dimensions. All logic tools that you have learned thus far will be useful for these games, but in complex linear games, the techniques are all a little more complicated. Here is the fact pattern of a typical complex linear logic game:

COMPLEX LINEAR GAME I

Four subway lines will be inspected this Sunday—line 1, line 2, line 3, and line 4. One person from each of two groups of inspectors, the afternoon group and the morning group, will each inspect a subway line during the day. The morning group consists of Anna, Billy, Chris, and Dale. The afternoon group consists of Emily, Fanny, Greg, and Ham. No inspector will inspect more than one subway line, and every line will be inspected by one person in each group, according to the following constraints:

Anna inspects the same number line as Emily.
Billy inspects the line that is one number greater than the line inspected by Anna.
Chris inspects a higher-numbered line than Dale.
Fanny inspects a higher-numbered line than Emily.
If Chris inspects line 4, then Dale must inspect line 2.

SOLUTION STEPS

To solve this game, follow the same general steps that you did in regular linear games:

1. Transcribe the constraints.
2. Draw scenarios of cumbersome constraints.
3. Write out the vacancy-occupancy rules.
4. Make deductions and map out dual options.

Here is the general setup diagram for games like this:

	1	2	3	4
Group A A, B, C, D				
Group B E, F, G, H				

This diagram is a grid instead of the linear continuum that is used for linear logic games. The variables A through H will go inside the grid, and you can use the same vacancy-occupancy and dual option rules that you used for regular linear games. The diagramming tools are generally combinations of any number of the diagramming tools that you used in the last lesson.

1. **Transcribe the Constraints.** There are five basic constraints:

   1. **Sequential**—Chris inspects a higher-numbered line than Dale:
      $$D < C$$

   2. **Sequential**—Fanny inspects a higher-numbered line than Emily:
      $$E < F$$

   3. **Sufficient-Necessary**—if Chris inspects line 4, then Dale must inspect line 2:
      $$C_4 \rightarrow D_2 \quad ; \quad \cancel{D_2} \rightarrow \cancel{C_4}$$

It is a good idea to write the contrapositive automatically somewhere near the actual sufficient-necessary statement.

   4. **Box Rule**—Anna inspects the same number line as Emily:

      $$\boxed{\begin{matrix} A \\ E \end{matrix}}$$

   5. **Box Rule**—Billy inspects the line that is one number greater than the line inspected by Anna:

      $$\boxed{A \; B}$$

It is a good idea to go ahead and combine any constraints or logical chains immediately for these types of games. The box rules of constraints 3 and 4 can be combined to form a two-dimensional box that looks like this:

$$\begin{matrix} A & B \\ E & \end{matrix}$$

2. Draw Scenarios of a Cumbersome Constraint.

The A, B, E box can go in only three places in the diagram, so go ahead and draw out these scenarios:

1

	1	2	3	4
Morning	A	B		
Afternoon	E			

2

	1	2	3	4
Morning			A	B
			E	

3

	1	2	3	4
			A	B
			E	

3. Write Out the Vacancy-Occupancy Rules.

In this specific setup, writing out vacancy rules is not as important as it normally is because the placement of most of the variables is intuitive after you draw out the three possible hypotheticals. However, it is still good practice to write out the rules. Your diagrams would look like this:

1

	1	2	3	4
Morning	A	B	¢	Ø
Afternoon	E			

2

	1	2	3	4
	¢	A	B	Ø
		F	E	

3

	1	2	3	4
	¢	Ø	A	B
		F	F	E

4. Make Deductions and Map Out Dual Options.

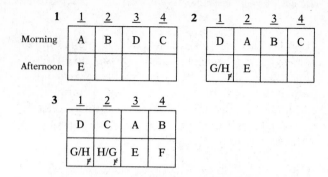

1

	1	2	3	4
Morning	A	B	D	C
Afternoon	E			

2

	1	2	3	4
	D	A	B	C
	G/H	E		

3

	1	2	3	4
	D	C	A	B
	G/H	H/G	E	F

According to the last constraint, however, when Chris inspects line 4, then Dale must inspect line 2. This is impossible in scenario 1 and scenario 2. So you can deduce that scenario 3 the only workable scenario in the game.

Many times in complex linear games you will be able to eliminate scenarios in this fashion. So make sure to ask yourself about the implications of all the game's sufficient-necessary conditions while you are making deductions. Here is the final diagram for this game:

	1	2	3	4
Morning (A, B, C, D)	D	C	A	B
Afternoon (E, F, G, H)	G/H	H/G	E	F

Try the following complex linear games using the diagramming techniques and logic tools that have been outlined. Do not forget to consider sufficient-necessary conditions when making your deductions.

COMPLEX LINEAR GAME 2

At a dance demonstration, women and men who are professional dancers pair off in couples. Each couple is placed in one of four consecutively numbered rooms in order to entertain the audience in each room. The men, Frank, Ham, Joel, and Lee, each pair with one of the women, Gina, Irene, Kelly, and Melissa. The formation of the pairs is governed by the following constraints:

The rooms are spatially arranged in the order of their numbers.
Each person dances only with his or her partner.
Each couple is the only couple in a room, and all four rooms have a couple.
Kelly does not dance in room 1.
Ham and Joel dance in consecutively numbered rooms.
Frank dances in the room numbered one lower than Gina's.
Gina dances in the room numbered one lower than Ham's.

1. If Kelly is paired with Frank, then who must be paired with Gina?

   (A) Frank
   (B) Ham
   (C) Joel
   (D) Lee
   (E) Irene

2. If Lee dances in room 4, then who must dance in room 2?

   (A) Gina
   (B) Kelly
   (C) Irene
   (D) Melissa
   (E) Ham

3. If Melissa dances in a lower-numbered room than Kelly, then with whom is Kelly unable to dance?

   (A) Frank
   (B) Ham
   (C) Joel
   (D) Lee
   (E) Irene

4. Who must always dance in a higher-numbered room than Frank?

   (A) Kelly
   (B) Joel
   (C) Lee
   (D) Melissa
   (E) Irene

5. If Melissa and Frank are the couple in room 1, then which of the following could be true?

   (A) Kelly dances in a room that is next to Frank.
   (B) Gina does not dance in a room next to Melissa or Kelly.
   (C) Ham dances in a room with Melissa.
   (D) Gina dances with Joel in room 3.
   (E) Lee does not dance in a room that is next to Frank

6. If Kelly does not dance in room 4, then which of the following is possible?

   (A) Gina dances in a room next to Lee.
   (B) Melissa's couple dances in room 3.
   (C) Either Lee or Joel is paired with Kelly.
   (D) Melissa dances in a higher-numbered room than Irene.
   (E) Frank's couple dances in room 3.

SOLUTION STEPS

1. Transcribe the Constraints. There are four constraints:

1. **Vacancy Rule**—Kelly cannot dance in room 1.

Keep this rule in mind so that you can immediately draw it into the grid in the next step.

2. **Box Rule**—Ham and Joel must dance in consecutive rooms:

3. **Box Rule**—Frank dances in the room numbered one lower than Gina's:

4. **Box Rule**—Gina dances in the room numbered one lower than Ham's:

Two of the box rules can be added together to form one box:

Some people choose to remember only that H and J go next to each other, as opposed to adding a third, *switching* box to these *static* boxes. If you choose to add all three boxes together, then make sure to remember that H is always in the same place, while J can move into either box next to H's static position.

2. Draw Scenarios of a Cumbersome Constraint.
If you draw all three box rules together, including the switching box rule, three scenarios are possible:

1

M / F, H, J, L	1	2	3	4
		F	J	H
F / G, I, K, M			G	

2

1	2	3	4
F		H	J
	G		

3

1	2	3	4
F	J	H	
	G		

3. Write Out the Vacancy-Occupancy Rules.
There is really only one in this fact pattern:

1

M / F, H, J, L	1	2	3	4
		F	J	H
F / G, I, K, M	I/M (K)		G	

2

1	2	3	4
F		H	J
I/M (K)	G		

3

1	2	3	4
F	J	H	
I/M (K)	G		

4. Make all Possible Deductions.
The only possible deduction is that L must go in the open square in the male group:

1

M / F, H, J, L	1	2	3	4
	L	F	J	H
F / G, I, K, M	I/M (K)		G	

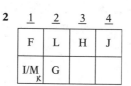

2

1	2	3	4
F	L	H	J
I/M (K)	G		

3

1	2	3	4
F	J	H	L
I/M (K)	G		

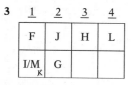

ANSWERING THE QUESTIONS

Question 1: If Kelly is paired with Frank, then who must be paired with Gina?

(C) This is possible only in scenario 1. In that scenario, J is paired with G.

Question 2: If Lee dances in room 4, then who must dance in room 2?

(A) This is possible only in scenario 3. In that scenario J dances in room 2.

Question 3: If Melissa dances in a lower-numbered room than Kelly, then with whom is Kelly unable to dance?

(E) In scenario 1, Kelly would be able to dance with F or H. In scenario 2, Kelly would be able to dance with J. In scenario 3, Kelly would be able to dance with L. Therefore, Kelly would be able to dance with all the male dancers but would still be unable to dance with a female dancer.

Question 4: Who must always dance in a higher-numbered room than Frank?

(B) The people who must dance in higher-numbered rooms than F are G, H, and J. So the answer is J.

Question 5: If Melissa and Frank are the couple in room 1, then which of the following could be true?

(E) This is possible in scenario 2 or 3. Option E refers to a possibility in scenario 3 and therefore is correct.

Question 6: If Kelly does not dance in room 4, then which of the following is possible?

(D) This means that Kelly must dance in either room 2 with F or room 3 with H. If this is true, then it would be possible for M to dance in a higher-numbered room than I in any scenario.

COMPLEX LINEAR GAME 3

In an auto shop that is open Monday through Friday, mechanics work on a series of cars. The mechanics are Frank, Gina, Hillary, Iris, and John, and they service one car from each of the following types: a Lamborghini, a Mercedes, a Neon, an omnibus, and a Porsche. Each mechanic works only one day of the week and none works on the same day. Each mechanic services only one car, and no car is serviced twice.

Hillary services the Neon.
Frank does not service the omnibus.
Gina works on a day earlier than the day John works.
One day and only one day is between the days that the Lamborghini and the Porsche are serviced.
If the Neon gets serviced on Tuesday, then Iris works on Thursday.

1. If Hillary works on Tuesday, then which of the following cars could NOT get serviced on Friday?

   (A) Omnibus
   (B) Lamborghini
   (C) Porsche
   (D) Neon
   (E) Mercedes

2. If the Neon gets serviced on the day after the Mercedes gets serviced, then which of the following could be true?

   (A) The Mercedes gets serviced on Wednesday.
   (B) Iris works on Thursday.
   (C) Gina works on Friday.
   (D) Hillary works on Thursday.
   (E) The Porsche gets serviced on Thursday.

3. If Hillary works on Tuesday, then which of the following would be impossible?

   (A) Neither John nor Gina works on Wednesday.
   (B) The Lamborghini gets serviced on Monday.
   (C) The Neon gets serviced before the Mercedes.
   (D) Iris services the Porsche.
   (E) John works after Hillary.

4. If the Porsche gets serviced on Friday and Iris works on Monday, then which of the following could be true?

   (A) The Neon gets serviced on Tuesday.
   (B) Frank services the omnibus on Thursday.
   (C) The Lamborghini gets serviced on Tuesday.
   (D) Gina services the Porsche.
   (E) Frank does not work on Wednesday or Friday.

5. If Gina and John work on consecutive days and neither services the Lamborghini or the Porsche, then which of the following must be true?

   (A) The Lamborghini gets serviced on Friday.
   (B) The Mercedes gets serviced by John.
   (C) Hillary works on Thursday.
   (D) Frank services the omnibus.
   (E) Neither the Lamborghini nor the Porsche gets serviced on Wednesday.

6. If the cars get serviced in the following order—Lamborghini, Neon, Porsche, Mercedes, and omnibus—for how many people do we know exactly which day they work?

   (A) none
   (B) one
   (C) two
   (D) three
   (E) four

SOLUTION STEPS

For this open game, you will follow a set of steps that are slightly different from the ones you have followed up to now.

1. Transcribe the Constraints. There are five constraints:

1. **Sequential**—Gina works on a day earlier than John:

$$G < J$$

2. **Sufficient-Necessary**—If the Neon gets serviced on Tuesday, then Iris works on Thursday:

$$N_{Tues} \rightarrow I_{Thurs} \qquad \cancel{I}_{Thurs} \rightarrow \cancel{N}_{Tues}$$

3. **Box Rule**—Hillary services the Neon:

$$\boxed{\begin{array}{c} H \\ N \end{array}}$$

4. **Box Rule**—Frank does not service the omnibus:

5. **Box Rule**—One day is between the days that the Lamborghini and Porsche are serviced:

There is no way to consolidate these rules further, which means that this is a very open game. In open games, you should make a list of the rules and be sure to keep them in mind for each question.

2. Draw a Diagram. There will not be much that you can put into your diagram initially, because the constraints are so unrelated. However, it will be useful to fill in what you do know before starting to answer the questions. Write out the vacancy-occupancy rules and place an asterisk on Tuesday to denote that a sufficient-necessary condition acts upon a variable that could possibly be present in this box.

	Mon	Tues	Wed	Thurs	Fri
Mech F, G, H, I, J	ȷ̸	*			ɢ̸
Car L, M, N, O, P					

3. Make a Hierarchy of Constraints. For open games like this one, organize the constraints into a hierarchy to which you can refer along with your diagram to solve the questions in the problem. List the lesser constraints first so that you do not forget them:

1. G < J
2. N$_{Tues}$→I$_{Thurs}$ I̶$_{Thurs}$→N̶$_{Tues}$

3. | H |
   |---|
   | N |

4. | F |
   |---|
   | O |

5. | L __ P |
   |---|

ANSWERING THE QUESTIONS

For open logic games, it is a good idea to write your general diagram in pen but use a pencil to sketch the possible scenarios described in the questions. That way you do not have to redraw the diagram every time a question asks about a different scenario; you just have to erase your pencil marks.

Question 1: If Hillary works on Tuesday, then which of the following cars could NOT get serviced on Friday?

(D) We know that the Neon does not get serviced on Friday because, according to constraint 3, Hillary services it on Tuesday.

Question 2: If the Neon gets serviced on the day after the Mercedes gets serviced, then which of the following could be true?

(B) There are two scenarios for placing MN because of the L __ P box in constraint 5:

	Mon	Tues	Wed	Thurs	Fri
Mech F, G, H, I, J	ȷ̸	H *		I ꜰ̸	ɢ̸
Car L, M, N, O, P	M	N	L/P	O	P/L

	Mon	Tues	Wed	Thurs	Fri
		ꜰ̸			H
	L/P	O	P/L	M	N

In scenario 1, Iris must work on Thursday due to the sufficient-necessary statement for which the asterisk serves as a reminder. So B is the correct answer.

Question 3: If Hillary works on Tuesday, then which of the following would be impossible?

(A) There are two places where the L___P box could go—Wednesday and Friday or Wednesday and Monday. Therefore, neither the Porsche nor the Lamborghini could be serviced on Thursday by Iris:

	Mon	Tues	Wed	Thurs	Fri
Mech F, G, H, I, J	ȷ̸	H		I	ɢ̸
Car L, M, N, O, P		N			

Question 4: If the Porsche gets serviced on Friday and Iris works on Monday, then which of the following could be true?

(E) This question is simple since it really asks only about constraints. To answer this type of question correctly, make sure to draw in each constraint on the diagram:

	Mon	Tues	Wed	Thurs	Fri
Mech	I	ȷ̸	*		ɢ̸
Car			L		P

Question 5: If Gina and John work on consecutive days and neither services the Lamborghini or the Porsche, then which of the following must be true?

(C) Scenario 2 is impossible since there is no place for H to go. Therefore we must look at scenario 1 to determine the answer:

1

G	J		H	
		L/P	N	P/L

2

	H̶		G	J
P/L	X̶	L/P		

It is clear that Hillary will have to work on Thursday.

Question 6: If the cars get serviced in the following order—Lamborghini, Neon, Porsche, Mercedes, and omnibus—for how many people do we know exactly which day they work?

(D) Drawing this scenario into the diagram, we see that we know exactly on what days H, I, and J must work:

G/F	H	F/G	I	J
L	N	P	M	O

Recap: Complex Linear Games

In this section you learned:

- how to apply box rules to a two-dimensional diagram
- how to apply sufficient-necessary and sequential logic tools to a two-dimensional diagram
- how to apply vacancy-occupancy rules to a two-dimensional diagram
- how to use your diagrams to map an open versus a closed game

5 Grouping Games

Grouping games are some of the most difficult games on the LSAT, and they are also some of the most prevalent. In general, they are more open than other types of games, leaving many deductions to be made while you answer questions. To succeed with these games, you need to organize and diagram the constraints in such a way that you will be able to remember them when you move from question to question.

Diagrams of grouping games are unique to each game and generally contain groups of a certain number. You should make slots under each group to map out the positions where the variables could go. Here is an example fact pattern for a grouping game.

GROUPING GAME I

In a casino there are three rooms and eight gamblers, Rufus, Sam, Thomas, Unger, Victoria, Wanda, Xavier, and Yolanda. The group of gamblers populating each room is determined by the following constraints:

> No more than three people can be in a room at one time.
> The blackjack room always has two people.
> Rufus is always in the poker room.
> If Sam is in the slots room, then Thomas is in the poker room.
> Rufus and Xavier cannot be in the same room.
> Yolanda and Unger must be in the same room.

SOLUTION STEPS

1. Transcribe the Constraints. As always, the first thing you should do to diagram the game is transcribe the six constraints. Some people might use box rules to map the final two constraints, but box rules are usually not a good idea for grouping games. It is better to use equals signs instead. Additionally, here for the first time you see what is called a numerical constraint. This type of constraint tells you how many people can be in each group.

  1. **Numerical**—No more than three people can be in a room at one time.

There is no logic tool available to represent this statement. It is best to remember numerical constraints and place them in your diagram at the next step.

  2. **Numerical**—The blackjack room always has two people.

  3. **Direct Placement**—Rufus is always in the poker room.

$$R = \text{Poker room}$$

  4. **Sufficient-Necessary**—If Sam is in the slots room, then Thomas is in the poker room:

$$S_{slots} \rightarrow T_{poker} \qquad \cancel{T}_{poker} \rightarrow \cancel{S}_{slots}$$

  5. **Grouping**—Rufus and Xavier cannot be in the same room:

$$R \neq X$$

  6. **Grouping**—Yolanda and Unger must be in the same room:

$$Y = U$$

2. Diagram What You Can. Make sure to put slots under each category so that you will know how many people could possibly go in each room according to the numerical constraints. Your initial diagram should look like this:

P	S	B
R	—	—
—	—	—
—	—	
X	—	

This diagram looks pretty empty, which is why it is so important to have your constraints handy in a list while answering questions. As you answer each question, you will have to go down your list in order to make sure that no answer choice violates any of the constraints. It is often a good idea to draw the above diagram in pen, and then write any hypothetical arrangement that is given in questions in pencil, so that you can easily erase the variables from one question's arrangement before moving on to the next question.

3. Order Constraints in a List. The numerical constraints and direct placement constraint have already been incorporated into the diagram, so you do not need to worry about them. The rest should be ordered into a list with the seemingly least important constraints going first so that you do not forget about them:

  1. $R \neq X$
  2. $Y = U$
  3. $S_{slots} \rightarrow T_{poker} \qquad \cancel{T}_{poker} \rightarrow \cancel{S}_{slots}$

Now let's solve some grouping games using this technique.

GROUPING GAME 2

A soft drink manufacturer conducts a taste test. Four people drink the diet cola, and three people drink the regular cola. Seven people participate in the taste test: Ryan, Sam, Tom, Uma, Vicki, Wanda, and Xavier.

If Sam drinks the diet cola, then Tom drinks the regular cola.

Uma does not drink the same type of cola that Vicki does.

Wanda does not drink the same type of cola that Xavier does.

1. Which of the following is a possible makeup for the diet cola group?

    (A) Ryan, Sam, Tom, Xavier
    (B) Wanda, Xavier, Tom, Sam
    (C) Xavier, Uma, Vicki, Tom
    (D) Wanda, Uma, Ryan, Tom
    (E) Ryan, Tom, Wanda, Xavier

2. If Uma is in the diet cola group, then which of the following is NOT possible?

    (A) Sam is in the same group as Tom.
    (B) Wanda drinks diet cola.
    (C) Xavier drinks diet cola, while Vicki drinks regular.
    (D) Wanda or Xavier drinks regular cola.
    (E) Sam drinks regular cola.

3. If Wanda and Vicki drink regular cola, then we know the identity of how many people who drink diet cola?

    (A) None
    (B) One
    (C) Two
    (D) Three
    (E) Four

4. If Tom is in a different group from Vicki and Vicki is in a different group from Xavier, then which of the following is possible?

    (A) Sam drinks regular cola, and Wanda drinks diet cola.
    (B) Vicki and Xavier drink regular cola.
    (C) Ryan and Sam drink diet cola.
    (D) Ryan and Vicki drink regular cola.
    (E) Xavier drinks a different drink from Tom.

5. If Ryan is assigned to a different group from Tom and Vicki, then which of the following is a group of people who could be assigned to the same group?

    (A) Ryan, Tom
    (B) Vicki, Sam
    (C) Xavier, Wanda
    (D) Uma, Tom
    (E) Wanda, Vicki

6. If Sam drinks diet cola, which of the following groups contains all the people who could drink regular cola?

    (A) Uma, Ryan, Wanda
    (B) Xavier, Uma, Vicki, Wanda
    (C) Uma, Wanda, Tom, Xavier, Vicki
    (D) Vicki, Tom, Wanda, Xavier, Uma, Ryan
    (E) Wanda, Vicki, Uma, Sam, Xavier

Solution Steps

1. Transcribe the Constraints. There are five constraints:

1. **Numerical**—Four people drink the diet cola.
2. **Numerical**—Three people drink the regular cola.
3. **Sufficient-Necessary**—If Sam drinks the diet cola, then Tom drinks the regular cola:

$$S_{diet} \rightarrow T_{reg}; \qquad \cancel{T}_{reg} \rightarrow \cancel{S}_{diet}$$

4. **Grouping**—Uma does not drink the same type of cola that Vicki does:

$$U \neq V$$

In a grouping game with only two groups, this type of constraint will become a dual option.

5. **Grouping**—Wanda does not drink the same type of cola that Xavier does:

$$W \neq X$$

2. Diagram What You Can. This problem seems to have very little to diagram. The following variables appear to be all that you can diagram:

Diet	Reg
U/V	V/U
W/X	X/W
____	____
____	

However, by writing out the dual options between U,V and W,X, you will be able to deduce that S and T cannot be in the same group either. There would not be enough spaces for them to be together in the Regular group, and because of the sufficient-necessary constraint, they would not be able to be in the Diet group together either. They have a dual option between the groups, and therefore Ryan will always have to drink Diet. None of these facts would be apparent without an attempt at diagramming the variables, which is why it is so important to draw out the groups based on the numerical constraints and dual option rules at the beginning of the game. After looking at this diagram's numerical configuration and the sufficient-necessary constraint, you will be able to make a diagram incorporating the following deductions:

Diet	Reg
U/V	V/U
X/W	W/X
S/T	T/S
R	

3. Order Constraints in a List.

Here is the constraint list that will come in handy in conjunction with the diagram while answering the questions. The sufficient-necessary condition is the only real condition that is not diagrammed already:

1. $S_{diet} \rightarrow T_{reg}$ $\cancel{T}_{reg} \rightarrow \cancel{S}_{diet}$
2. $U \neq V$
3. $W \neq X$

ANSWERING THE QUESTIONS

Question 1: Which of the following is a possible makeup for the diet cola group?

(D) The process of elimination is often the best way to answer these questions. Take the first constraint and see which choices violate it. Then take the second and do the same. Repeat this process until there is only one choice left. A and B violate constraint 1. C and E violate constraint 2. It is not immediately clear that E violates this constraint, but you must think about which variables are left to occupy the regular group. U and V would have to go together in this group if one of them is not present in the Diet group. D is the only choice left.

Question 2: If Uma is in the diet cola group, then which of the following is NOT possible?

(A) Due to constraint 1, it would be impossible for S and T to be in the same group. If S and T were both in the Regular group, there would not be enough spaces available in that group to ensure that U,V and W,X

were not in the same group. If S is in the Diet group, then T must be in the Regular group according to constraint 1. Therefore, having S and T in the same group is impossible.

Question 3: If Wanda and Vicki drink regular cola, then we know the identity of how many people who drink diet cola?

(D) Here is the diagram for that scenario:

Diet	Reg
U	V
X	W
S/T	T/S
R	

Based on the diagram, it is clear that we know the identity of three people drinking diet cola.

Question 4: If Tom is in a different group from Vicki and Vicki is in a different group from Xavier, then which of the following is possible?

(C) If this is true, then V must be in the same group as W and S. Also, T, U, and X must be in the same group. Ryan and Sam could drink diet cola together.

Question 5: If Ryan is assigned to a different group from Tom and Vicki, then which of the following is a group of people who could be assigned to the same group?

(E) The following diagram accounts for this scenario:

Diet	Reg
U	V
X/W	W/X
S	T
R	

Wanda and Vicki are the only two people out of the answer choices who could be assigned to the same group.

Question 6: If Sam drinks diet cola, which of the following groups contains all the people who could possibly drink regular cola?

(C) All variables present in the dual options could go in the Regular group. So it is basically everybody except Ryan and Sam:

Diet	Reg
U/V	V/U
X/W	W/X
S	T
R	

A look at your diagram clearly shows that the answer is T, V, U, W, and X.

GROUPING GAME 3

An ice cream company has three refrigerators holding different flavors of ice cream. The first two refrigerators have enough room for three flavors, but the third has only enough room for two. Each refrigerator is filled to its capacity with the flavors R, S, T, U, V, W, X, and Y.

If R is in refrigerator 1, then S is in refrigerator 3.
If X is in refrigerator 2, then Y is in refrigerator 3.
T is not in the same refrigerator as U.
V is in a different refrigerator from W.
Y and R are in the same refrigerator.

1. Which of the following is a group of flavors that could be in refrigerator 1 together?

   (A) R, Y, X
   (B) T, W, X
   (C) Y, R, T
   (D) V, W, S
   (E) T, U, X

2. If Y is in refrigerator 2 and S is in refrigerator 2, then which of the following flavors must be in refrigerator 1?

   (A) T
   (B) U
   (C) V
   (D) W
   (E) X

3. If neither W nor V is in refrigerator 2, then which of the following is a complete list of the flavors that could be in refrigerator 2?

   (A) Y, R, T, U, S, X
   (B) Y, R, U, S, T
   (C) Y, R, T, U
   (D) Y, R, U, S
   (E) Y, R, S

4. Which of the following is a pair of flavors that could NOT be in refrigerator 1 together?

   (A) T, V
   (B) W, U
   (C) X, T
   (D) R, V
   (E) S, V

5. If T and X are in refrigerator 2 together, then how many different configurations of the flavors are possible?

   (A) two
   (B) three
   (C) four
   (D) five
   (E) six

6. If neither V nor W is in refrigerator 3, then which of the following could be true?

   (A) Neither V nor W shares a refrigerator with U or T.
   (B) Y and X are in refrigerator 3.
   (C) T and U are in the same refrigerator.
   (D) S and T are in the same refrigerator.
   (E) R and X are in the same refrigerator.

7. If the constraint requiring Y to be in refrigerator 3 when X is in refrigerator 2 were removed, then which of the following flavors must be in refrigerator 3 when Y is in refrigerator 1?

   (A) T
   (B) U
   (C) S
   (D) V
   (E) W

SOLUTION STEPS

1. Transcribe the Constraints. There are seven constraints.

1. **Numerical**—Refrigerators 1 and 2 have enough room for three flavors.
2. **Numerical**—Refrigerator 3 has enough room for only two.
3. **Sufficient-Necessary**— If R is in refrigerator 1, then S is in refrigerator 3:

$$R_1 \rightarrow S_3 \qquad \cancel{S_3} \rightarrow \cancel{R_1}$$

4. **Sufficient-Necessary**—If X is in refrigerator 2, then Y is in refrigerator 3:

$$X_2 \rightarrow Y_3 \qquad \cancel{Y_3} \rightarrow \cancel{X_2}$$

5. **Grouping**—T is not in the same refrigerator as U:

$$T \neq U$$

6. **Grouping**—V is in a different refrigerator from W:

$$V \neq W$$

7. **Grouping**—Y and R are in the same refrigerator:

$$Y = R$$

2. Diagram What You Can. This game is extremely open, and very little is available to diagram. You should diagram the numerical constraints and then wait for questions to give further hypotheticals:

$$\begin{array}{ccc} 1 & 2 & 3 \\ \underline{} & \underline{} & \underline{} \\ \underline{} & \underline{} & \underline{} \\ & \underline{} & \underline{} \end{array}$$

3. Order Constraints in a List:

1. $Y = R$
2. $V \neq W$
3. $T \neq U$
4. $X_2 \rightarrow Y_3$ $\cancel{Y_3} \rightarrow \cancel{X_2}$
5. $R_1 \rightarrow S_3$ $\cancel{S_3} \rightarrow \cancel{R_1}$

Now you are ready for the questions.

ANSWERING THE QUESTIONS

Question 1: Which of the following is a group of flavors that could be in refrigerator 1 together?

(B) When a game is this open and it asks you a question that is also very open, it is best to use the process of elimination by going through your list of constraints. Constraint 1 eliminates none of the choices. Constraint 2 eliminates D. Constraint 3 eliminates E. Constraints 4 and 5 do not apparently eliminate any choices, so you must map out each possibility to find the correct answer.

Choice A:

$$\begin{array}{ccc} 1 & 2 & 3 \\ \hline R & \left(\begin{array}{c}T \neq U \\ T \neq U\end{array}\right) & S \\ Y & & V/W \\ X & W/V & \end{array}$$

This is incorrect, since T and U would be forced to be in the same refrigerator, which would violate constraint 3.

Choice B:

$$\begin{array}{ccc} 1 & 2 & 3 \\ \hline T & Y & S \\ W & R & U \\ X & V & \end{array}$$

Because this diagram is only for this specific question and the question asks only for a possibility, any configuration of variables that works would validate the answer choice. Thus, you can pretty much indiscriminately place variables so long as they do not violate any of the constraints. This specific placement is valid and therefore makes B the correct answer.

Choice C:

$$\begin{array}{ccc} 1 & 2 & 3 \\ \hline Y & X_* & S \\ R & V/W & W/V \\ T & U & \end{array}$$

This choice is incorrect, since in order for V and W to be in different refrigerators, then X would have to be in refrigerator 2. This would invoke the sufficient-necessary condition between X and Y and require Y to go in refrigerator 3. This diagram is impossible because of constraint 4, so this answer choice is not a workable scenario.

Question 2: If Y is in refrigerator 2 and S is in refrigerator 2, then which of the following flavors must be in refrigerator 1?

(E) Diagram this scenario, keeping your constraint list in mind:

$$\begin{array}{ccc} 1 & 2 & 3 \\ \hline V/W & Y & W/V \\ T/U & S & U/T \\ X & R & \end{array}$$

Based on the diagram, it is clear that V,W and U,T cannot be in the same refrigerators, thereby creating dual options. Therefore, X would have to go in refrigerator 1.

Question 3: If neither W nor V is in refrigerator 2, then which of the following is a complete list of the flavors that could be in refrigerator 2?

(B) After seeing that W and V cannot be in refrigerator 2, it becomes clear that there are only two places where the cumbersome YR box could go. You should draw out these scenarios:

$$1 \quad \begin{array}{ccc} 1 & 2 & 3 \\ \hline W/V & S & V/W \\ \boxed{Y} & T/U & U/T \\ \boxed{R^*} & X_* & \end{array}$$

The second scenario is not possible, because T and U must be in different refrigerators, so S could not go in refrigerator 3. This violates constraint 5. Also, X could not go in refrigerator 3, so Y would have to go in refrigerator 3 because of constraint 4. The diagram shows that this is impossible:

$$2 \quad \begin{array}{ccc} 1 & 2 & 3 \\ \hline W/V & \boxed{\begin{array}{c}Y\\R\end{array}} & V/W \\ \underline{} & S/T/U & \underline{} \\ & * & \end{array}$$

In this diagram, the only variable that could not accompany the YR box in refrigerator 2 would be X, since this variable would require Y to go in refrigerator 3 under constraint 4. Therefore, the variables that could go in refrigerator 2 are Y, R, U, S, and T.

Question 4: Which of the following is a pair of flavors that could NOT be in refrigerator 1 together?

(D) You need to use diagrams to answer this question. In diagrams for questions that ask which scenario is not possible, always place variables where you feel that they would be least likely to make a conflict. This is because some scenarios will not work in certain configurations but will work in others. You want to see what works as quickly as possible, so, for example, it is best to put the YR box in refrigerator 2 because some scenarios that work in general will not work when YR is in refrigerator 3:

A	T	Y	U
	V	R	X
	S	W	

For answer choice B, the variables W,U are functionally the same as T,V, which is the scenario that you just diagrammed. You know that this scenario works, so you really don't need to diagram it, but here it is just to demonstrate the fungibility of dual options:

B	W	Y	T		C	X	Y	S
	U	R	X			T	R	U
	S	V				V	W	

D	R	W	S
	V	T/U	U/T
	Y ←→ X*		

Diagram D does not work because putting R in refrigerator 1 will force S to go in refrigerator 3. In order for U,T to be in different refrigerators, X will have to go in refrigerator 2. This would require Y to go in refrigerator 3, which is impossible under the constraints of this answer choice. You do not need to diagram the final choice, and would not do so in order to save time on the test, but it is good to diagram it now while you practice.

E	S	Y	U
	V	R	W
	X	T	

Question 5: If T and X are in refrigerator 2 together, then how many different configurations of the flavors are possible?

(A) After diagramming this, you find that only two configurations are possible:

1	2	3
U	T	Y
S	X	R
V/W	W/V	

Question 6: If neither V nor W is in refrigerator 3, then which of the following could be true?

(D) Here is the diagram for D:

1	2	3
V/W	W/V	X
S	Y	U
T	R	

(A) This is impossible because W and V cannot share a refrigerator, and neither can T and U. For none of these variables to share refrigerators, there would have to be four refrigerators.

(B) This would be impossible since there are only two spaces available in every refrigerator and Y would have to be in the same as R. Therefore R could not be paired with any other variable.

(C) This is never possible because of the fundamental constraints of the problem.

(E) This would be impossible since there are only two spaces available in every refrigerator and Y would have to be in the same as R. Therefore R could not be paired with any other variable.

Question 7: If the constraint that requires Y to be in refrigerator 3 when X is in refrigerator 2 were removed, then which of the following flavors must be in refrigerator 3 when Y is in refrigerator 1?

(C) This constraint seems to change things, but as you diagram it, it becomes clear that S must be in refrigerator 3.

Recap: Grouping Games

In this section you learned:

- how to use grouping rules
- how to apply sufficient-necessary logic tools to grouping games
- how to diagram grouping games
- why you should wait until you tackle individual questions before diagramming open grouping games

---

Mapping games require you to draw diagrams that correspond to a real-world situation. Sufficient-necessary, direct placement constraints, and other logic tools that you learned in the earlier sections apply in certain places, but fitting them to each new diagram takes a certain amount of creativity. Mapping games introduce "mapping constraints" which are like grouping rules in that they determine which items can go near each other in the map. The following are some examples of mapping game fact patterns and constraints. You will examine and diagram several games without trying to answer any questions just because mapping games are all so different from each other.

MAPPING GAME 1

A square park in the middle of the city has trashcans situated along its perimeter according to the following diagram:

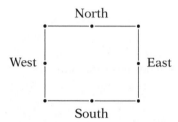

The trashcans are numbered clockwise from 1 to 8, beginning with trashcan 1 at the northwest corner, trashcan 2 at the middle of the north side, and so on until trashcan 8 at the middle of the west side of the park. The trashcans are either completely full or empty, depending on whether the sanitation worker has visited yet to empty the trashcans. The contents of the trashcans are determined by the following constraints:

> Trashcan 8 is full.
> If trashcans 4 and 7 are full, then so is trashcan 6.
> If trashcan 3 is full, then both trashcans adjacent to it are empty. If trashcan 3 is empty, then both trashcans adjacent to it are full.

SOLUTION STEPS

1. Transcribe the Constraints. The first thing that you should do, as in all games, is transcribe the constraints of the game. This mapping game makes use of sufficient-necessary statements and has three constraints:

1. **Direct Placement**—Trashcan 8 is full:

$$8 = \text{full}$$

2. **Sufficient-Necessary**—If trashcans 4 and 7 are full, then so is trashcan 6:

$$(4_{\text{full}} + 7_{\text{full}}) \rightarrow 6_{\text{full}} \qquad \cancel{6}_{\cancel{\text{full}}} \rightarrow (\cancel{4}_{\cancel{\text{full}}} + \cancel{7}_{\cancel{\text{full}}})$$

3. **Mapping Rule**—If trashcan 3 is full, then both trashcans adjacent to it are empty. If trashcan 3 is empty, then both trashcans adjacent to it are full.

The sufficient-necessary statements can be simplified into the following mapping rules:

$$3 \neq 4 \qquad 3 \neq 2$$

Since there are two potential configurations of the variables, empty or full and 2 and 4 vary solely according to 3's character, then 2 and 4 must have the same configuration:

$$2 = 4$$

2. Diagram What You Can. You should use the given diagram as a model in drawing your own diagram. At this stage, you should add all vacancy-occupancy rules, direct placement facts, and any deductions that you can make based on the facts. A good diagram for the problem would be the following:

$$
\begin{array}{ccccc}
 & & \mathbf{N} & & \\
 & 1 & 2 \neq & 3 & \\
 & & & \cancel{4} & \\
\mathbf{W} & 8=F & & 4 & \mathbf{E} \\
 & 7 & 6 & 5 & \\
 & & \mathbf{S} & &
\end{array}
$$

Mapping rules can generally be added creatively to diagrams as for 2, 3, and 4 above. Also, the dots are replaced with numbers so that you will immediately know to which number the questions refer.

3. Order Constraints in a List. As in most games, the final thing that you should do before moving on to the questions is order the constraints that were not put into the diagram in a list. This list will be very short:

$$(4_{\text{full}} + 7_{\text{full}}) \rightarrow 6_{\text{full}} \qquad \cancel{6}_{\cancel{\text{full}}} \rightarrow (\cancel{4}_{\cancel{\text{full}}} + \cancel{7}_{\cancel{\text{full}}})$$

MAPPING GAME 2

Six cars are parked facing each other in three rows of parking spots. The arrangement is shown by the following diagram:

Car 1	Car 2
Car 3	Car 4
Car 5	Car 6

The cars are either jeeps or sedans. They are either green or red. Lastly, they have either four-wheel drive or two-wheel drive. The cars' characteristics are governed by the following constraints:

All cars with four-wheel drive are jeeps.
All cars adjacent to three cars have four-wheel drive.
Car 6 is a sedan and is green.
All jeeps are adjacent to two and only two cars with four-wheel drive.
No car is the same color as any car directly adjacent to it.

Solution Steps

1. Transcribe the Constraints. There are five constraints.

1. **Direct Placement**—Car 6 is a sedan and is green.

$$6 = S,G$$

2. **Mapping**—All cars adjacent to three cars have four-wheel drive.

Understanding this constraint requires the understanding of what it means to be adjacent to something. Cars 2 and 3 are adjacent to car 1. Cars 2, 3, and 6 are adjacent to car 4. Car 4 and car 3 are the only cars that are adjacent to three cars, so these cars must have four-wheel drive.

$$4 = 4W \qquad 3 = 4W$$

3. **Mapping**—All cars with four-wheel drive are jeeps:

$$4W = J \qquad \cancel{J} = \cancel{4W}$$

Note that this does not mean that all jeeps have four-wheel drive.

4. **Mapping**—All jeeps are adjacent to two and only two cars with four-wheel drive.

This rule should be mapped out while keeping in mind that you know that cars 3 and 4 have four-wheel drive.

5. **Mapping**—No car is the same color as any car directly adjacent to it.

This rule should be mapped out, keeping in mind that you know what color car 6 is.

2. Diagram What You Can. You know many things about this diagram already, and drawing it will reveal more. What you should do first is draw on what you know by going down the list of transcribed constraints.

Initial Diagram:

1 _ _ _	2 _ _ _
3 _ _ _	4 _ _ _
5 _ _ _	6 _ _ _

There are three characteristics that you could know about each car—green or red, jeep or sedan, and four-wheel drive or two-wheel drive. Therefore, each box has three slots where it will be easy to fill in those variables. When filling out the variables, you should always keep them in the same order just to stay organized.

Constraint 1:   6 = S,G

1 _ _ _	2 _ _ _
3 _ _ _	4 _ _ _
5 _ _ _	6 <u>S</u> <u>G</u> _

Constraint 2:   4 = 4W
                3 = 4W

1 _ _ _	2 _ _ _
3 _ <u>4</u>	4 _ _ <u>4</u>
5 _ _ _	6 <u>S</u> <u>G</u> _

Constraint 3:   4W = J $\cancel{J}$ = $\cancel{4W}$

1 _ _ _	2 _ _ _
3 <u>J</u> _ <u>4</u>	4 <u>J</u> _ <u>4</u>
5 _ _ _	6 <u>S</u> <u>G</u> <u>2</u>

Constraint 4: All jeeps are adjacent to two and only two cars with four-wheel drive:

1 J _ 4	2 J _ 4
3 J _ 4	4 J _ 4
5 S _ 2	6 S G 2

Car 5 could not have four-wheel drive because it would then be a jeep that would only have the possibility of being adjacent to one car with four-wheel drive.

Constraint 5: No car is the same color as any car directly adjacent to it:

1 J R 4	2 J G 4
3 J G 4	4 J R 4
5 S R 2	6 S G 2

So it turns out that there are no unknowns in the game. Therefore, there is no reason to proceed to the third step of listing the constraints that you are unable to diagram. Note that the constraints will not always be arranged in an order that lets you make consistent and complete deductions by going down the list once. This was possible in this game, but it will not be in most future games. Instead, the constraints will be out of order, jumbled, and confusing. To eliminate this problem, keep in mind that each time you go down the list, you will be able to a make a new deduction until there are no more deductions left to be made. In order to be sure that you spot all inferences available, make sure that after each time you make a new deduction, you review the list one more time to see if there are any subsequent deductions you can make based on that deduction.

The last sample fact pattern is a so-called *circular game*.

MAPPING GAME 3

Six people are sitting around a conference table at a business meeting: Randy, Sue, Tom, Uma, Vern, and Yolanda. The table is completely circular and the seating arrangements are governed by the following conditions:

Randy sits across from Tom.
Sue sits immediately next to Uma.
Uma sits across from Yolanda.

SOLUTION STEPS

1. Transcribe the Constraints. Circular mapping games are simple as long as they are diagrammed properly. The constraints are composed of circular constraints and box rules:

1. **Mapping**—Randy sits across from Tom:

$$R\text{——}T$$

2. **Mapping**—Uma sits across from Yolanda:

$$U\text{——}Y$$

3. **Box Rule**—Sue sits immediately next to Uma:

2. Diagram What You Can. When diagramming these games, do not simply draw a circle. This is because, with a circle, it is hard to see who is sitting across from whom. Instead, you should diagram a wheel with spokes. Here is what it should look like:

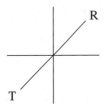

3. Order Constraints in a List. You know whom four people sit across from—R, T, U, and Y. So, you know that S and V sit across from each other:

1. R——T
2. U——Y
3. S——V
4.

Now try some logic games with questions using the mapping logic tools that you have just learned.

MAPPING GAME 4

R, S, T, U, V, and W are settlements in the wilderness. They are positioned in two straight rows.

	R	S	T
Row 1:	■	■	■
Row 2:	■	■	■
	U	V	W

R is across from U. S is across from V. T is across from W. People living in the settlements decide to clear the forest to make a continuous series of roads that connect all the settlements, according to the following constraints:

> One settlement cannot be connected to the same settlement twice.
> The roads consist of exactly five line segments.
> No roads cross each other, all of them are straight-line segments, and no settlement is connected to more than two roads.
> One road segment connects R and S, and another road segment connects U and T.

1. Which of the following settlements CANNOT be connected to each other?

   (A) V and W
   (B) U and S
   (C) T and W
   (D) S and V
   (E) R and U

2. If S connects directly to T, then which is a pair of settlements that do NOT have to be directly connected?

   (A) U and V
   (B) U and T
   (C) V and W
   (D) T and W
   (E) S and T

3. If S connects directly to U, then which is a pair of settlements that do NOT have to be directly connected?

   (A) W and V
   (B) R and S
   (C) T and U
   (D) V and T
   (E) S and U

4. If no settlement in row 1 is connected to the settlement in row 2 that is directly opposite it and S is connected to U, then which of the following segments must be connected?

   (A) T and V
   (B) R and U
   (C) U and V
   (D) V and U
   (E) S and T

5. If R connects to two roads and W connects to two roads, then which of the following could be true?

   (A) S connects to T.
   (B) V connects to U.
   (C) Only three settlements connect to two roads.
   (D) R does not connect to U.
   (E) T does not connect to V.

6. If only one road connects the settlements in row 1 to row 2, then which of the following is a settlement that can be connected to only one road?

   (A) R
   (B) S
   (C) T
   (D) U
   (E) V

7. How many different configurations of roads are possible?

   (A) two
   (B) three
   (C) four
   (D) five
   (E) six

SOLUTION STEPS

1. Transcribe the Constraints. There are six constraints.

1. **Numerical**—The roads consist of exactly five line segments.
2. **Mapping**—No roads cross.
3. **Mapping**—All roads are straight-line segments.
4. **Mapping**—No settlement is connected to more than two roads.
5. **Direct Placement**—One segment connects R and S.
6. **Direct Placement**—One segment connects U and T.

You can best view all these constraints by mapping them onto a diagram.

2. Diagram What You Can.
All that you can diagram based solely on the constraints is this diagram:

However, since we know that all settlements must be connected, that no roads can cross, and that no settlement can be connected to more than two roads, it appears that there are a limited number of configurations of roads that are possible, since there is one large road from U to T that splits the entire game. In games where there is a cumbersome constraint like this UT constraint, it is a good idea to go ahead and write out all possible configurations for the game.

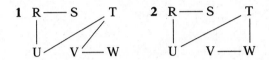

In the two above, R—U is connected while the line between T—W or T—V is changed.

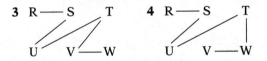

In the two above, S—U is connected while the line between T—W or T—V is changed.

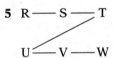

This final diagram is possible because if S connects to T, then U is free to connect to V.

3. Order Constraints in a List.
There are no constraints that we have not mapped in one of these five diagrams, so this step is not necessary.

ANSWERING THE QUESTIONS

Question 1: Which of the following settlements CANNOT be connected to each other?

(D) Based on your initial diagram, it is clear that S and V cannot connect because that would make a road that would cross U—T.

Question 2: If S connects directly to T, then which is a pair of settlements that do NOT have to be directly connected?

(D) This would mean that diagram 5 would be the correct map for the roads. T and W is the answer.

Question 3: If S connects directly to U, then which is a pair of settlements that do NOT have to be directly connected?

(D) This means that either diagram 3 or 4 accurately maps the roads. In diagram 4, V and T are not connected.

Question 4: If no settlement in row 1 is connected to the settlement in row 2 that is directly opposite it and S is connected to U, then which of the following segments must be connected?

(A) This would mean that diagram 3 would be the map of the roads. The answer is T and V.

Question 5: If R connects to two roads and W connects to two roads, then which of the following could be true?

(E) This means that diagram 2 is the map. The answer is that T does not connect to V.

Question 6: If only one road connects the settlements in row 1 to row 2, then which of the following is a settlement that can be connected to only one road?

(A) Diagram 5 is the map for the roads. The settlements that can be connected to only one road are R and W.

Question 7: How many different configurations of roads are possible?

(D) This question just asks you to add up all of your configurations. There are five total possibilities.

MAPPING GAME 5

In a zoo there are eight animal exhibits arranged in two rows as shown by the following figure:

1st: 1   2   3   4
_____

_____

2d: 5   6   7   8

Each exhibit faces the exhibit across from it in the opposing row. Each exhibit contains one of three types of animals—mammal, reptile, or bird.

Exhibits in the same row that are next to each other contain different animal types.

No mammal exhibit can be across from a mammal exhibit.

Every mammal exhibit has to have at least one bird exhibit next to it in its row.

Exhibit 2 has a mammal.

Exhibit 7 has a reptile.

1. Which exhibit of the following must have birds?

   (A) 3
   (B) 4
   (C) 5
   (D) 6
   (E) 7

2. If no reptiles are adjacent to mammals, then what is the maximum number of mammal exhibits that is possible?

   (A) two
   (B) three
   (C) four
   (D) five
   (E) six

3. If reptiles are in exhibit 3, then which of the following is a complete list of the exhibits that must NOT hold reptiles?

   (A) 2, 4, 5, 6
   (B) 4, 6, 7, 8
   (C) 1, 2, 4, 6, 8
   (D) 3, 5, 7
   (E) 1, 2, 3, 5

4. If there are only three bird exhibits, then which exhibit must have a bird?

   (A) 1
   (B) 3
   (C) 4
   (D) 5
   (E) 7

5. If there are three mammal exhibits, then which of the following could be true?

   (A) Every mammal exhibit is adjacent to or faces a reptile exhibit.
   (B) There are three reptile exhibits.
   (C) The 2d row contains only reptiles and birds.
   (D) The 1st row contains an animal facing an animal of the same type in the 2d row.
   (E) Every mammal exhibit faces a bird exhibit.

6. If no animal of the same type faces an animal of the same type, then we know the type of animal for how many exhibits?

   (A) three
   (B) four
   (C) five
   (D) six
   (E) seven

SOLUTION STEPS

1. Transcribe the Constraints. There are five constraints.

1. **Direct Placement**—Exhibit 2 has a mammal:

   2 = Mammal

2. **Direct Placement**—Exhibit 7 has a reptile:

   7 = Reptile

3. **Box Rule**—No mammal exhibit can be across from a mammal exhibit:

4. **Mapping**—Exhibits in the same row that are next to each other contain different animal types.

5. **Mapping**—Every mammal exhibit has to have at least one bird exhibit next to it.

This could be considered to be a box rule, but since there could be a number of exhibits that could house mammals, a switching box rule would not be as powerful as just listing this variable and trying to map its implications as well as you can in the next step.

2. Diagram What You Can.

Constraints 1 and 2:

1	2 M	3	4
5	6	7 R	8

Constraints 3 and 4:

1	2 M	3	4
5 ⋈	6 B ⋈	7 R ⋈	8 B ⋈

3. Order Constraints in a List.
The three constraints that will have further implications in the game and that cannot be completely captured by our current diagram are:

1.
M⁄
M̸

2. Exhibits in the same row that are next to each other contain different animal types.
3. Every mammal exhibit has to have at least one bird exhibit next to it.

ANSWERING THE QUESTIONS

Question 1: Which exhibit of the following must have birds?

(D) Exhibits 6 and 8 must have birds.

Question 2: If no reptiles are adjacent to mammals, then what is the maximum number of mammal exhibits that is possible?

(C) This is a good question to diagram:

1 B ⋈	2 M	3 B ⋈	4 M/R ⋈
5 R/M ⋈	6 B ⋈	7 R	8 B ⋈

The answer is four.

Question 3: If reptiles are in exhibit 3, then which of the following is a complete list of the exhibits that must NOT hold reptiles?

(C) Here is the diagram for this scenario:

B ⋈	M	R	B ⋈
M/R ⋈	B	R	B ⋈

Exhibits 3, 5, and 7 can hold reptiles, so the exhibits that cannot hold reptiles are 1, 2, 4, 6, and 8.

Question 4: If there are only three bird exhibits, then which exhibit must have a bird?

(B) Here is the diagram where there are three bird exhibits:

R ⋈	M	B ⋈	M/R
R/M ⋈	B	R	B ⋈

It would be impossible to have only three bird exhibits while having a bird in exhibit 1, so exhibits 3, 6, and 8 must have birds.

Question 5: If there are three mammal exhibits, then which of the following could be true?

(E) Here is the diagram showing three mammal exhibits:

R/B ⋈	M	B	M
M	B	R	B

The only choice possible is that every mammal exhibit faces a bird exhibit.

Question 6: If no animal of the same type faces an animal of the same type, then we know the type of animal for how many exhibits?

(C) Here is a diagram for this question:

R/B ⋈	M	B ⋈	R/M
R/M ⋈	B	R	B ⋈

You know the animal type for five exhibits.

Recap: Mapping Games

In this section you learned:

- how to diagram the different types of mapping games
- the best way to organize and understand mapping rules
- how to apply previously learned logic tools to mapping games

7 Minimized Variables Games

The term *minimized variable* describes more of a characteristic of a game than an actual game type. These games present huge difficulties for test takers who neglect to fully diagram games before tackling the questions because the positions of almost all the variables in a minimized variables game can be figured out from the fact pattern. Minimized variables games can also be linear, complex linear, grouping, or mapping games.

You can identify a minimized variables game by identifying a particularly cumbersome constraint. This is a constraint that can be configured in only one or two ways, and these different configurations each hold wide-ranging implications for the rest of the variables in the game. You have already worked through several minimized variables games, but so far they have been referred to as "closed games." The following fact patterns are examples of linear, grouping, and mapping games that are minimized variables games. Practice using the steps that you learned previously in this chapter to work through each type of game.

LINEAR MINIMIZED VARIABLES GAME

R, S, T, U, V, W, and X are all finalists on a popular game show. In order to win, each must sing in front of a live TV audience. Each person will sing on live TV on one day of this week, Monday through Sunday. Only one person will sing per day. The order in which people will sing is determined by the following:

   S sings later in the week than R, and there are three days between their performances.
   U sings the day after R.
   S sings the day after T.
   W and X sing before V.
   X cannot sing on Monday or Wednesday.

SOLUTION STEPS

1. Transcribe the Constraints. There are five constraints:

1. **Box Rule**—S sings later in the week than R, and there are three days between their performances:

$$\boxed{R \ \_ \ \_ \ \_ \ S}$$

2. **Box Rule**—U sings the day after R:

$$\boxed{R \ U}$$

3. **Box Rule**—S sings the day after T:

$$\boxed{T \ S}$$

4. **Sequential**—W and X sing before V:

$$W < V$$
$$X < V$$

5. **Vacancy-Occupancy**—X cannot sing on Monday or Wednesday:

$$X \neq Mon$$
$$X \neq Wed$$

Combination:

The box rules can be combined to form the following all-encompassing box rule:

$$\boxed{R \ \underline{U} \ \_ \ \underline{T} \ S}$$

2. Draw Scenarios of a Cumbersome Constraint.
The cumbersome constraint that makes this game a minimized variables game is the combined box rule:

$$\boxed{R \ \underline{U} \ \_ \ \underline{T} \ S}$$

Clearly, in a game in which there are only seven slots, this box rule can go in only three places, so you should draw it in those places and try to deduce whatever you can for each different scenario:

M	T	W	Th	F	S	Su
—	—	R	U	—	T	S
—	R	U	—	T	S	—
R	U	—	T	S	—	—

3. Write Out the Vacancy-Occupancy Rules.

M	T	W	Th	F	S	Su
		R	U		T	S
X̶X̶	X̶					
		R	U		T	S
X̶X̶		X̶				
R	U		T	S		
	X̶X̶				X̶	

4. Make Deductions. In this game, you can deduce the exact position of all of the variables in the entire game:

Mon	Tues	Weds	Thur	Fri	Sat	Sun
W	X	R	U	V	T	S
X̶ ✓	X̶					
W	R	U	X	T	S	V
X̶ X̶			X̶			
R	U	W	T	S	X	V
		X̶ ✓			X̶	

Any question asked about the game will refer to one of these three scenarios, so you will be able to answer any question very quickly with this diagram.

GROUPING MINIMIZED VARIABLES GAME 1

A troop of eight scouts is split up to go on different weekend activities. A group of three will go to the aquarium, and a group of four will go to the park. No scout can do more than one activity. The composition of the groups in determined by the following:

R cannot be in the same group as S.
T cannot be in the same group as U.
V cannot be in the same group as W.
Everyone but X or Y has to participate in one of the activities.
If S goes to the aquarium, then T and V go to the park.
If S goes to the park, then U goes to the aquarium and W goes to the park.

SOLUTION STEPS

1. Transcribe the Constraints. In this game there seems to be an overabundance of constraints. This fact will confound new test takers who have not learned proper diagramming tools, but it will allow you to order all the variables efficiently so that answering the questions will be quick and easy.

1. **Numerical**—Three will go to the aquarium.
2. **Numerical**—Four will go to the park.
3. **Grouping**—R cannot be in the same group as S:

$$R \neq S$$

4. **Grouping**—T cannot be in the same group as U:

$$T \neq U$$

5. **Grouping**—V cannot be in the same group as W:

$$W \neq V$$

6. **Direct Placement**—Everyone but X or Y has to participate in one of the activities.

You should wait and diagram this fact first. It essentially means that there is a dual option between X and Y in the "out" group.

7. **Sufficient-Necessary**—If S goes to the aquarium, then T and V go to the park:

$$S_{aqua} \to T_{park} \quad ; \quad \cancel{T}_{park} \to \cancel{S}_{aqua}$$
$$S_{aqua} \to V_{park} \quad ; \quad \cancel{T}_{park} \to \cancel{V}_{aqua}$$

8. **Sufficient-Necessary**—If S goes to the park, then U goes to the aquarium and W goes to the park:

$$S_{park} \to U_{aqua} \quad ; \quad \cancel{U}_{aqua} \to \cancel{S}_{park}$$
$$S_{park} \to W_{park} \quad ; \quad \cancel{W}_{park} \to \cancel{S}_{park}$$

2. Diagram What You Can. Diagram the direct placement constraint and the general group structure first:

A	P	Out
___	___	X/Y
___	___	
___	___	
	___	

Next, diagram the three grouping rules:

A	P	Out
R/S	S/R	X/Y
T/U	U/T	
V/W	W/V	
	Y/X	

Finally, diagram the only two possibilities for arrangements of the game, which are dictated by the two sufficient-necessary constraints:

A	P	Out		A	P	Out
S	R	X/Y		R	S	Y/X
U	T			U	T	
W	V			V	W	
	Y/X				X/Y	

3. Order Constraints in a List. There are no constraints that have not been fully input into the diagram, so there is no need to make this list. The above two scenarios completely represent the four possibilities for variable arrangements within the game.

An artist will paint 10 tiles on the floor in the colors green, red, and/or purple. The tiles are arranged in two symmetrical columns as in the following diagram:

1	2
3	4
5	6
7	8
9	10

The artist tells you that she will paint each tile a certain color according to the following conditions:

The corner tiles are painted red.
Tile 5 is painted red.
Every tile that borders two red tiles must be a green tile.
Every green tile must border a purple tile.

SOLUTION STEPS

1. Transcribe the Constraints. There are four constraints.

1. **Direct Placement**—The corner tiles are painted red:

   1, 2, 9, 10 = Red

2. **Direct Placement**—Tile 5 is painted red:

   5 = Red

3. **Mapping**—Every tile that borders two red tiles must be a green tile.

4. **Mapping**—Every green tile must border a purple tile.

2. Diagram What You Can. First, diagram the direct placement constraints:

R	R
R	
R	R

Next, diagram the first mapping constraint:

R	R
G	
R	
G	
R	R

Finally, diagram the last mapping constraint:

R	R
G	P
R	G/P
G	P
R	R

3. Order Constraints in a List. As you can see, this final step is not necessary because all the variables have been incorporated into your diagram that represents the game's two possibilities.

Now that you have seen how to diagram linear, grouping, and mapping minimized variables games, try the games with questions that follow. Notice how easy the questions are to solve once you have completely diagrammed the game.

MAPPING MINIMIZED VARIABLES GAME 2

In an executive box in a ballpark, there are nine seats. These seats are arranged in three equal rows that have three seats per row. The row with the lower number is closer to the field. Each seat in a row is on the right, in the center, or on the left.

	Left	Center	Right
1	___	___	___
2	___	___	___
3	___	___	___

Nine people sit in these seats based on the following constraints:

U and R sit on different sides.
T sits directly in front of S and in the same row as U.
R sits on the left side, immediately next to S.
V sits in the same column that S does and shares the row with W and X.
Z sits in a higher-numbered row than Y.

1. If Z sits in row 2, then who must sit in the center of row 3?

    (A) W
    (B) S
    (C) T
    (D) V
    (E) Y

2. If W sits in row 1, then which of the following could be true?

    (A) W, Y, and R sit on the left.
    (B) R, S, and Z sit in row 2.
    (C) V sits on the left side of a row.
    (D) Z shares a row with T and U.
    (E) W and X sit on the same side.

3. If Y sits closer to the field than W, then how many people could sit in row 3 on the right side?

    (A) zero
    (B) one
    (C) two
    (D) three
    (E) four

4. Which of the following is a complete list of the people who could share a row with either Y or Z?

    (A) T, U
    (B) T, U, R
    (C) T, U, R, S
    (D) T, U, R, S, V
    (E) T, U, R, S, V, W, X

5. If U sits on the right and R sits on the left immediately behind Y, then who could sit in front of Y?

    (A) V
    (B) T
    (C) W
    (D) U
    (E) R

6. How many different possible seating arrangements are there?

    (A) two
    (B) four
    (C) six
    (D) eight
    (E) ten

SOLUTION STEPS

This is a mapping game, so you will use the mapping techniques to solve it.

1. Transcribe the Constraints. There are six constraints.

1. **Box Rule**—T sits directly in front of S:

T
S

2. **Box Rule**—R sits on the left side, immediately next to S:

R	S

3. **Mapping**—T sits in the same row as U.
4. **Mapping**—U and R sit on different sides.
5. **Box Rule**—V sits in the same column that S does and shares a row with W and X.
6. **Sequential**—Z sits in a higher-numbered row than Y.

The first and second box rules can be added together to make this:

When you add constraints 3 and 4, you get this large box:

2. Diagram What You Can. There are two positions where the large box could go in the game. Based on this information, you can figure out the position of the rest of the variables by applying constraint 5 and then constraint 6:

1	Y	T	U		2	X/W	V	W/X
	R	S	Z̶			Y	T	U
	W/X	V	X/W			R	S	Z̶

3. Order Constraints in a List. This is not necessary since the constraints are evident in the scenarios of the diagrams.

ANSWERING THE QUESTIONS

Question 1: If Z sits in row 2, then who must sit in the center of row 3?

(D) This refers to scenario 1, and the answer is V.

Question 2: If W sits in row 1, then which of the following could be true?

(A) This refers to scenario 2. W, Y, and R sitting on the left is the only option that is possible.

Question 3: If Y sits closer to the field than W, then how many people could sit in row 3 on the right side?

(C) This questions refers to scenario 1. Two people, W and X, could sit in row 3 on the right side.

Question 4: Which of the following is a complete list of the people who could share a row with either Y or Z?

(C) Looking at both diagrams, you see the R, S, T, and U are the only people who can share rows with Y and Z.

Question 5: If U sits on the right and R sits on the left immediately behind Y, then who could sit in front of Y?

(C) This refers to either scenario. In the second scenario, X or W could sit in front of Y.

Question 6: How many different possible seating arrangements are there?

(B) Looking at your diagram, you see that there are two possibilities for each. Therefore, there are four total possibilities.

GROUPING MINIMIZED VARIABLES GAME 2

On a children's basketball team, the coach arranges six children into three groups. There will be three forwards, two defenders, and one child will sit out.

If W is a forward, then V is also a forward.
U is not in the same group as T.
R is not in the same group as S but is in the same group as U.
S is not in the same group as T.

1. Which of the following is a possible group of forwards?

   (A) R,U,W
   (B) W,V,R
   (C) R,U,S
   (D) S,W,V
   (E) T,S,V

2. Which of the following is a complete group of the children who could play defense?

   (A) R, U
   (B) R, U, W
   (C) R, U, T, W
   (D) R, U, T, S, W
   (E) R, U, T, W, V

3. Which of the following pairs could include a child who sits out?

   (A) R,W
   (B) S,W
   (C) V,U
   (D) R,V
   (E) R,U

4. Who may potentially be in only one group?

   (A) T
   (B) V
   (C) S
   (D) R
   (E) W

5. Which of the following pieces of information would allow you to deduce the entire configuration of the groups?

   (A) S sits out.
   (B) W plays forward.

   (C) R plays forward.
   (D) W is in the same group as V.
   (E) T plays defense.

6. Who is always in the same group as either S or T?

   (A) R
   (B) V
   (C) W
   (D) U
   (E) R and V

7. If S sits out, then which one of the following would NOT be possible?

   (A) T plays forward.
   (B) W and U play in the same group.
   (C) W plays defense.
   (D) R plays defense.
   (E) V and U play in the same group.

Solution Steps

This is a grouping game, so you will use the grouping logic games technique.

1. Transcribe the Constraints. There are five constraints.

1. **Sufficient-Necessary**—If W is a forward, then V is also a forward:

   $$W_{forward} \rightarrow V_{forward} \qquad \cancel{V}_{\cancel{forward}} \rightarrow \cancel{W}_{\cancel{forward}}$$

2. **Grouping**—U is not in the same group as T:

   $$U \neq T$$

3. **Grouping**—R is not in the same group as S:

   $$R \neq S$$

4. **Grouping**—R is in the same group as U:

   $$R = U$$

5. **Grouping**—S is not in the same group as T:

   $$S \neq T$$

2. Diagram What You Can. R and U have to be together. Since R and U could be together only as forwards or defenders, you should put them together in

each group to test what kind of deductions you can make based on each case:

1

Forward	Defender	Out
R	S/T	T/S
U	W	
V		
~~S~~ ~~W~~ ~~T~~		

2

Forward	Defender	Out
S/T	R	T/S
W	U	
V		

Since there are no constraints that have not been mapped, you can move on to answering the questions.

ANSWERING THE QUESTIONS

Question 1: Which of the following is a possible group of forwards?

(D) There are three possible groups of forwards: R, U, V or S, W, V or T, W, V.

Question 2: Which of the following is a complete group of the children who could play defense?

(D) Looking at your diagrams, it is apparent that R, U, S, T, and W could all play defense.

Question 3: Which of the following pairs could include a child who sits out?

(B) T and S are the only two children who can sit out in the game.

Question 4: Who may potentially be in only one group?

(B) V always has to be a forward.

Question 5: Which of the following pieces of information would allow you to deduce the entire configuration of the groups?

(E) The only unknowns in the game are the positions of T and S. If you found out either of their positions, then the rest of the variables in the game would be figured out. However, the correct answer is E and not A, because E specifies that you are in scenario 1, while the information in A could not tell you whether you are dealing with scenario 1 or scenario 2.

Question 6: Who is always in the same group as either S or T?

(C) The only people to share groups with S or T are W and V. W is always in a group with one of them.

Question 7: If S sits out, then which one of the following would NOT be possible?

(B) Regardless of what S does, it is impossible for W and U to play in the same group.

COMPLEX LINEAR MINIMIZED VARIABLES GAME

Four artists will use four colors of paint to paint on four canvases. The canvases will be ordered 1 through 4, and only one artist paints on each canvas. Each artist will use only one color of paint. The paint colors orange, red, purple, and green will all be used. The artists' names are Rufus, Sam, Tom, and Uma. Who paints on which canvas with which color is governed by the following constraints:

Canvases 1, 2, 3, and 4 are arranged next to each other consecutively.
Rufus paints on canvas 2.
The canvas that Rufus paints on is not next to a canvas that receives green paint.
If green is used on canvas 4, then Tom paints on that canvas.
Sam paints with purple.
The canvas that receives red paint is one before the canvas that receives purple paint.

1. Which artist could paint a higher-numbered canvas than the one Sam paints?

   (A) Tom
   (B) Uma
   (C) Rufus
   (D) Uma and Rufus
   (E) Uma and Tom

2. Who CANNOT use red paint?

   (A) Rufus
   (B) Sam
   (C) Tom
   (D) Uma
   (E) Tom and Rufus

3. Which of the following could be a list of the painters starting from canvas 1 and moving to canvas 4?

   (A) Sam, Rufus, Uma, Tom
   (B) Uma, Rufus, Tom, Sam
   (C) Tom, Rufus, Sam, Uma
   (D) Tom, Sam, Rufus, Uma
   (E) Uma, Tom, Rufus, Sam

4. Which is a full list of the paints that could be used for canvas 2?

   (A) orange
   (B) red
   (C) purple, orange
   (D) red, green
   (E) green, orange

5. Which of the following could be true if Rufus paints with red?

   (A) Tom paints with orange.
   (B) Uma paints a canvas with a higher number than the one Sam paints.
   (C) Sam and Tom do not paint consecutively numbered paintings.
   (D) The purple-painted canvas is not consecutive with the red-painted canvas.
   (E) The purple-painted canvas is one lower than the green-painted canvas.

6. Which canvas has the most possible painters?

   (A) 1
   (B) 2
   (C) 3
   (D) 4
   (E) 5

7. How many different total configurations are possible of painters, canvases, and paints?

   (A) one
   (B) two
   (C) three
   (D) four
   (E) five

SOLUTION STEPS

1. Transcribe the Constraints. There are five constraints.

1. **Direct Placement**—Rufus paints on canvas 2:

   $$Rufus = 2$$

2. **Sufficient-Necessary**—If green is used on canvas 4, then Tom paints on that canvas:

   $$G_4 \rightarrow T_4 \qquad \cancel{T}_4 \rightarrow \cancel{G}_4$$

3. **Box Rule**—Sam paints with purple.

S
P

4. **Box Rule**—The canvas that receives red paint is one before the canvas that receives purple paint:

R P

5. **Vacancy-Occupancy**—The canvas that Rufus paints on is not next to a canvas that receives green paint.

The box rules can be consolidated into the following box:

2. Draw Scenarios of a Cumbersome Constraint.

Because of the direct placement of Rufus, you know that there are only two places where the consolidated box can go:

1	2	3	4
	R	S	
	R	P	

1	2	3	4
		R		S
			R	P

3. Write Out the Vacancy-Occupancy Rules.

You know that Rufus cannot go next to green. You also know that there could be an invocation of the sufficient-necessary rule for painting 4:

1	2	3	4
	R	S	
ø	R	P	*

1	2	3	4
	R		S
	ø	R	P

4. Make Deductions and Map Out Dual Options.

Remember that when you have three boxes filled in for variables and there are four variables total, then you also know where the fourth variable goes. This seems like common sense, but it is a fairly common mistake.

From both scenarios, you can infer where green goes, and therefore you also know where orange will go. In the first scenario, you also know where Tom goes because of the sufficient-necessary rule that comes into play when green goes on canvas 4:

1	2	3	4
U	R	S	T
O ø	R	P ø	G *

1	2	3	4
T/U	R	U/T	S
O	G	R	P

ANSWERING THE QUESTIONS

Question 1: Which artist could paint a higher-numbered canvas than the one Sam paints?

(A) The only artist who could do this is Tom.

Question 2: Who CANNOT use red paint?

(B) Sam is the only person who cannot use red paint.

Question 3: Which of the following could be a list of the painters starting from canvas 1 and moving to canvas 4?

(B) The only list that is possible from the answer choices is Uma, Rufus, Tom, and Sam.

Question 4: Which is a full list of the paints that could be used for canvas 2?

(D) Either red or green could be used for canvas 2.

Question 5: Which of the following could be true if Rufus paints with red?

(E) This puts you in scenario 1 of our diagram. The only possible answer choice is that the purple-painted canvas is one lower than the green-painted canvas.

Question 6: Which canvas has the most possible painters?

(C) T,U could paint canvas 1. R paints canvas 2. S,U,T could paint canvas 3. T,S could paint canvas 4. Since three people could paint canvas 3, it has the most possible painters.

Question 7: How many different total configurations are possible of painters, canvases, and paints?

(C) There are three possibilities resulting from the dual option in scenario 2.

Recap: Minimized Variables Games

In this section you learned:

- How to solve open games in which there are numerous and very constrictive constraints
- how to do this with linear, complex linear, grouping, and mapping logic games

8 Maximized Variables Games

Games of this type are very open games—the variables can take on many different arrangements and configurations. Questions often ask you to place a variable in a certain place and then determine what *must*, *could*, or *cannot* go somewhere. To someone who is experienced in solving logic games, this is the hardest type because these games require a new diagram for every question, and sometimes for every answer choice within that question. Here is the best way to solve these games: (1) Transcribe the constraints. (2) Make a base diagram in pen. (3) Make a list of constraints that you could not put into the diagram. You must have the constraint list and the diagram handy for every question or you are very likely to forget one or more rules. When answering these questions on the LSAT, be sure to conserve space, since you know that you will have to make a lot diagrams. To give you a better understanding of these games, let's examine linear, grouping, and mapping/formal logic maximized variables games.

LINEAR MAXIMIZED VARIABLES GAME

There are eight cars scheduled to be washed by a carwash. The car in spot number 1 will be washed first, and the car in spot number 8 will be washed last. The cars are all of different types—S, T, U, V, W, X, Y, and Z. The order in which they get washed is determined by the following:

U will be washed before T.
Y will be washed immediately before Z.
If U gets washed fourth, then W will be washed second.
If V does not get washed fifth, then X will be washed third.
S gets washed last.

1. If X gets washed fourth, then which of the following must be true?

   (A) Z gets washed after S.
   (B) U gets washed fourth.
   (C) V must be washed fifth.
   (D) W gets washed second, and U gets washed third.
   (E) Y gets washed first, and Z gets washed second.

2. What CANNOT be true?

   (A) Either T or X gets washed before Y.
   (B) Both X and T get washed after U.
   (C) No car is washed before U.
   (D) U, T, Y, and Z get washed in consecutive order.
   (E) Y gets washed immediately before S.

3. If U gets washed fourth, then what must be true?

   (A) S gets washed before W.
   (B) Y gets washed before T.
   (C) U gets washed after Z.
   (D) X gets washed third.
   (E) U gets washed before X.

4. If Y gets washed fifth, then what CANNOT be true?

   (A) X gets washed second.
   (B) U gets washed before V.
   (C) Y and Z get washed after T.
   (D) W gets washed second.
   (E) Y and T get washed consecutively.

5. What is the latest that U could be washed?

   (A) fourth
   (B) fifth
   (C) sixth
   (D) seventh
   (E) eighth

6. If U gets washed fourth and Z gets washed sixth, then you know the exact position of how many cars?

   (A) four
   (B) five
   (C) six
   (D) seven
   (E) eight

SOLUTION STEPS

Normally, linear games are relatively closed, and you diagram their possibilities by (1) transcribing the constraints, (2) drawing the scenarios of a cumbersome constraint, (3) writing out the vacancy-occupancy rules, and (4) making deductions. In this case, however, there

are clearly no cumbersome constraints, so you will (1) transcribe the constraints, (2) diagram what you can, and (3) make a list of constraints.

1. Transcribe the Constraints. There are five constraints.

1. **Sequential**—U will be washed before T:

$$U < T$$

2. **Box Rule**—Y will be washed immediately before Z:

$$\boxed{Y\ Z}$$

3. **Sufficient-Necessary**—If U gets washed fourth, then W will be washed second:

$$U_4 \to W_2 \qquad \cancel{W}_2 \to \cancel{U}_4$$

4. **Sufficient-Necessary**—If V does not get washed fifth, then X will be washed third:

$$\cancel{V}_5 \to X_3 \qquad \cancel{X}_3 \to V_5$$

5. **Direct Placement**—S gets washed last:

$$S = 8$$

2. Diagram What You Can. The following diagram is the most that you can get from the constraints:

1	2	3	4	5	6	7	8
—	—	*X	*U	*V	—	—	S
$\cancel{Y}\cancel{Z}$							

3. List the Constraints. You should now list all the constraints that are not completely evident and incorporated into the diagram. These are:

1. U < T
2. $\boxed{Y\ Z}$
3. $U_4 \to W_2$ $\qquad \cancel{W}_2 \to \cancel{U}_4$
4. $\cancel{V}_5 \to X_3$ $\qquad \cancel{X}_3 \to V_5$

Now you can move on to the questions.

ANSWERING THE QUESTIONS

Question 1: If X gets washed fourth, then which of the following must be true?

(C) You know that, because of constraint 4, if X is anywhere besides 3, then V must be in 5. Here is a diagram for this situation:

$$\underline{\ \ }\ \underline{\ \ }\ \underline{\ \ }\ \underline{X}\ \underline{V}\ \underline{\ \ }\ \underline{\ \ }\ \underline{S}$$

Question 2: What CANNOT be true?

(E) Y can never be washed immediately before S because Y must go immediately before T.

Question 3: If U gets washed fourth, then what must be true?

(D) X must be washed third. This is because if V were to go fifth, then there would not be enough room for the YZ box and T which must precede U. This is the diagram for the workable situation:

$$\underline{V}\ \underline{W}\ \underline{X}\ \underline{U}\ \underline{T/Y}\ \underline{T/Y/Z}\ \underline{Z/T}\ \underline{S}$$

Question 4: If Y gets washed fifth, then what CANNOT be true?

(A) Here is a diagram of this scenario:

$$\underline{\ \ }\ \underline{\ \ }\ \underline{X}\ \underline{\ \ }\ \underline{Y}\ \underline{Z}\ \underline{\ \ }\ \underline{S}$$

X cannot be washed anywhere but third because then V would have to go fifth, and this would be impossible.

Question 5: What is the latest that U could be washed?

(C) T has to be washed later than U, and S is washed last, so the latest that U can be washed is sixth.

Question 6: If U gets washed fourth and Z gets washed sixth, then you know the exact position of how many cars?

(E) Your diagram from question 3 works here too:

$$\underline{V}\ \underline{W}\ \underline{X}\ \underline{U}\ \underline{T/Y}\ \underline{T/Y/Z}\ \underline{Z/T}\ \underline{S}$$

If you know that Z is washed sixth, then you also would know that Y is fifth and T is seventh. Based on this knowledge, you know the positions of all the cars.

GROUPING MAXIMIZED VARIABLES GAME

Students in a high school gymnastics class are practicing their skills at forming a human pyramid. R, S, T, U, V, W, X, and Y are in the class, and they each are in one part of the pyramid: the bottom, middle, or the top. One student can go on top, three can go in the middle, and four can go on the bottom. The placement of the students is governed by the following:

T is in the same layer as U.
R is not in the same layer as S.
If V is in the bottom layer, then W and Y are also in the bottom layer.
If X is in the middle layer, then T is also in the middle layer.

1. If both T and R are in the bottom layer, then which of the following must NOT be true?

   (A) U shares a layer with S.
   (B) V can go in the top or bottom layer.
   (C) W is higher in the pyramid than X.
   (D) S goes in the middle layer.
   (E) X and U go in different layers.

2. If X goes in the middle layer, then which of the following must be true?

   (A) X shares a layer with V.
   (B) W is in a higher layer than T.
   (C) V and U are in the same layer.
   (D) Either R or S is at the top.
   (E) Y goes in the middle layer.

3. If V does not go in the top or middle layer, then how many people could be the one at the top of the pyramid?

   (A) one
   (B) two
   (C) three
   (D) four
   (E) five

4. If T is in the bottom layer, then which of the following is a pair that could NOT share the middle layer?

   (A) R and V
   (B) Y and S
   (C) W and X
   (D) V and R
   (E) Y and W

5. If U is in a layer lower than R and S, then which of the following could be possible?

   (A) W and Y share a layer.
   (B) X is in a higher layer than V.
   (C) Neither R nor S is at the top of the pyramid..
   (D) T shares a layer with only two people.
   (E) Y shares a layer with V.

6. If W and Y do not share a layer, then which of the following must be true?

   (A) V is not in the bottom layer.
   (B) R and V are in the bottom layer.
   (C) T does not share a layer with U.
   (D) W is not at the top of the pyramid.
   (E) Y is in a higher layer than W.

SOLUTION STEPS

1. Transcribe the Constraints. There are five constraints.

   1. **Numerical**—One person can go on top, three can go in the middle, and four can go on the bottom.
   2. **Grouping**—T is in the same layer as U:

      $$T = U$$

   3. **Grouping**—R is not in the same layer as S:

      $$R \neq S$$

   4. **Sufficient-Necessary**—If V is in the bottom layer, then W and Y are also in the bottom layer:

      $V_{bottom} \rightarrow W_{bottom}$ $\cancel{W_{bottom}} \rightarrow \cancel{Y_{bottom}}$

      $V_{bottom} \rightarrow Y_{bottom}$ $\cancel{X_{bottom}} \rightarrow \cancel{V_{bottom}}$

   5. **Sufficient-Necessary**—If X is in the middle layer, then T is also in the middle layer:

      $X_{middle} \rightarrow T_{middle}$ $\cancel{T_{middle}} \rightarrow \cancel{X_{middle}}$

2. Diagram What You Can. There is not much that can be diagrammed in this game initially, but you should still get a main diagram ready to use as a reference for when you reach the questions:

Bottom	Middle	Top
___	___	$\cancel{T}\ \cancel{U}$
___	*X	
*V		

3. List the Constraints:

1. $T = U$
2. $R \neq S$
3. $X_{middle} \rightarrow T_{middle}$ $\cancel{T}_{middle} \rightarrow \cancel{X}_{middle}$
4. $V_{bottom} \rightarrow W_{bottom}$ $\cancel{W}_{bottom} \rightarrow \cancel{Y}_{bottom}$

     $V_{bottom} \rightarrow Y_{bottom}$ $\cancel{X}_{bottom} \rightarrow \cancel{Y}_{bottom}$

ANSWERING THE QUESTIONS

Question 1: If both T and R are in the bottom layer, then which of the following must NOT be true?

(A)

Bottom	Middle	Top
T	—	—
R	—	
U	—	
$\cancel{S}$		

This diagram shows that U would have to be on the bottom also and S could not be there since it cannot share a layer with R. Therefore, U cannot share a layer with S.

Question 2: If X goes in the middle layer, then which of the following must be true?

(D)

Bottom	Middle	Top
R/S	X	S/R
V	T	
W	U	
Y		

If X goes in the middle, then constraint 3 makes T go in the middle, which also makes U go in the middle. Since R and S cannot share a layer, one must be in the bottom layer and the other must be in the top layer.

Question 3: If V does not go in the top or middle layer, then how many people could be the one at the top of the pyramid?

(C)

R/S/X	T	R/S/X
V	U	
W	R/S/X	
Y		

This makes V go on the bottom, which would make W and Y also go on the bottom. T and U have to share a layer, and the only layer that would allow them to do this would be the middle. Therefore, R, S, and X could be in the top, middle, or bottom layers.

Question 4: If T is in the bottom layer, then which of the following is a pair that could NOT share the middle layer?

(C)

Bottom	Middle	Top
T	—	—
U	—	
—	$\cancel{X}$	
$\cancel{Y}$		

According to constraint 3, if X is in the middle, then T must also be in the middle. Therefore, X cannot share the middle with anyone in this scenario.

Question 5: If U is situated in a layer lower than R and S, then which of the following could be possible?

(E)

Bottom	Middle	Top
T	R/S	S/R
U	V	
X	Y/W	
W/Y	X	
$\cancel{Y}$		

R and S cannot share a layer, so U would have to be in the bottom layer. This would also require T to go in the bottom layer. X could not go in the middle because of constraint 3, and V could not go in the bottom because of constraint 1. This creates a dual option between W and Y. It is clear from there that Y could share a layer with V.

Question 6: If W and Y do not share a layer, then which of the following must be true?

(A) You could look to the previous diagram to help out with this question, but when looking at the answer choices, you immediately see that V cannot be in the bottom layer. This has to be true, because otherwise W and Y would be forced to share the bottom layer with V.

MAPPING MAXIMIZED VARIABLES GAME

Six lightbulbs are on a sign in the following arrangement:

| 1 | 2 | 3 |
| 4 | 5 | 6 |

Each bulb is either lit or not lit. Each bulb is either blue or green. The characteristics of each specific bulb are governed by the following constraints:

If bulb 3 is lit, then bulb 4 is not lit.
If bulb 6 is green, then bulb 2 is not blue.
If bulb 5 is not green, then bulb 1 is blue.
The characteristics of bulb 2 are the same as those of bulb 4.

1. If bulb 2 is lit, then which of the following must be true?

   (A) Bulb 4 is blue.
   (B) Bulb 6 is lit.
   (C) Bulb 3 is not lit.
   (D) Bulb 6 is blue.
   (E) Bulb 1 is lit.

2. If bulb 3 is lit, then which of the following must NOT be true?

   (A) Bulb 2 is lit.
   (B) Bulb 3 is blue.
   (C) Bulb 4 is not lit.
   (D) Bulb 5 is green.
   (E) Bulb 4 is green.

3. If bulb 5 is blue, then which of the following must be true?

   (A) Bulb 4 is green.
   (B) Bulb 1 is lit.
   (C) Bulb 2 and bulb 3 are different colors.
   (D) Bulbs 4 and 6 are blue.
   (E) Bulb 1 is not green.

4. If bulb 6 is not green, then what is the maximum number of bulbs that could be green?

   (A) one
   (B) two
   (C) three
   (D) four
   (E) five

5. If bulb 6 has at least one characteristic that is different from bulb 5, which is blue, then which of the following must NOT be true?

   (A) There are more green bulbs than blue bulbs.
   (B) There are three green bulbs.
   (C) There are more blue bulbs than green bulbs.
   (D) There are three blue bulbs.
   (E) Bulb 5 is on and bulb 6 is off.

6. Which of the following could be true?

   (A) Bulb 5 is the only blue bulb.
   (B) Bulb 2 is the only blue bulb.
   (C) Bulb 4 is the only lit bulb.
   (D) Bulb 3 is the only not lit bulb.
   (E) Bulb 1 is the only green bulb.

SOLUTION STEPS

1. Transcribe Constraints. There are four constraints.

1. **Sufficient-Necessary**—If bulb 3 is lit, then bulb 4 is not lit:

$$3_L \rightarrow 4_{NL} \qquad 4_{\cancel{NL}} \rightarrow \cancel{3}_{\cancel{L}}$$

Since you know that something that is "$\cancel{NL}$" is lit and that something that is "$\cancel{L}$" is not lit, the contrapositive of this statement is equivalent to:

$$4_L \rightarrow 3_{NL}$$

2. **Sufficient-Necessary**—If bulb 6 is green, then bulb 2 is not blue:

$$6g \rightarrow \cancel{2}_{\cancel{B}} \qquad 2_B \rightarrow \cancel{6}_{\cancel{G}}$$

It is now apparent that this logic game is asking you to recognize that there are only two options for each variable—lit or not lit and green or blue. Therefore, you can simplify the previous sufficient-necessary statement to say:

$$6_G \rightarrow 2_G \qquad 2_B \rightarrow 6_B$$

3. **Sufficient-Necessary**—If bulb 5 is not green, then bulb 1 is blue.

You should go ahead and simplify this sufficient-necessary statement immediately:

$$5_B \rightarrow 1_B \qquad 1_G \rightarrow 5_G$$

4. **Sufficient-Necessary**—The characteristics of bulb 2 are the same as those of bulb 4.

This requires you to rewrite your sufficient-necessary statements to include 2 wherever 4 is and 4 wherever 2 is:

$$3_L \rightarrow 4_{NL} \qquad 4_L \rightarrow 3_{NL}$$
$$3_L \rightarrow 2_{NL} \qquad 2_L \rightarrow 3_{NL}$$
$$6_G \rightarrow 2_G \qquad 2_B \rightarrow 6_B$$
$$6_G \rightarrow 4_G \qquad 4_B \rightarrow 6_B$$

You could consolidate this information into the following two statements:

$$3_L \rightarrow (4_{NL} + 2_{NL}) \qquad 4_L \rightarrow (3_{NL} + 2_L)$$
$$6_G \rightarrow (2_G + 4_G) \qquad 2_B \rightarrow (6_B + 4_B)$$

Remember that it is still important to transcribe the rest of the constraint:

$$2 = 4$$

There are contingencies that the previous two sufficient-necessary statements won't entirely cover that the equals sign will.

2. **Diagram What You Can.** There is not much that you can diagram except for the general setup:

$$\begin{array}{ccc} 1 & 2 & 3 \\ 4 & 5 & 6 \end{array}$$

There is no real need to include asterisks where the sufficient-necessary statements are, because every single number has a statement that pertains to it.

3. **List the Constraints.** As in all maximized variables problems, making a constraints list is what will carry you through the problem.

1. $3_L \rightarrow (4_{NL} + 2_{NL})$ $\qquad 4_L \rightarrow (3_{NL} + 2_L)$
2. $6_G \rightarrow (2_G + 4_G)$ $\qquad 2_B \rightarrow (6_B + 4_B)$
3. $5_B \rightarrow 1_B$ $\qquad\qquad 1_G \rightarrow 5_G$
4. $2 = 4$

ANSWERING THE QUESTIONS

Question 1: If bulb 2 is lit, then which of the following must be true?

(C) If bulb 2 is lit, then you know that bulb 4 is lit. If bulb 4 is lit, then 3 is not lit.

Question 2: If bulb 3 is lit, then which of the following must NOT be true?

(A) If 3 is lit, then both 4 and 2 are not lit.

Question 3: If bulb 5 is blue, then which of the following must be true?

(E) If 5 is blue, then 1 is blue. You know absolutely nothing about the rest of the game.

Question 4: If bulb 6 is not green, then what is the maximum number of bulbs that could be green?

(E) This means that 6 is blue. A look at the constraints clearly shows that there is nothing wrong with the rest of the bulbs being simultaneously green.

Question 5: If bulb 6 has at least one characteristic that is different from bulb 5, which is blue, then which of the following must NOT be true?

(C) Bulb 5 is blue, and because of the constraints of the question, bulb 6 must be green. If 6 is green, then because of constraint 2, bulbs 2 and 4 must be green. If 5 is blue, then 1 must be blue. We have three bulbs that must be green and two that must be blue. Bulb 3 is the only X factor, and it can go either way—making four greens and two blues or making three greens and three blues. There could not be more blue bulbs than green ones.

Question 6: Which of the following could be true?

(D) The only possibly true statement is that bulb 3 is the only bulb that is not lit. Note that it would not be possible for 3 to be the only lit bulb.

Recap: Maximized Variables Games

In this section, you learned:

- how to solve logic games that have fact patterns with very few constraints
- why you should wait to do certain parts of the diagramming until you tackle individual questions
- why you should always draw a base diagram and make a constraints list

---

LOGIC GAMES: TIPS FOR FURTHER STUDY

1. Be sure to use diagramming tools to set up the constraints of each game before answering the questions.
2. Identify the types of logic games that give you trouble. Repeat and rework practice logic games that were difficult for you the first time through.
3. Focus on improving your handling of grouping and advanced linear games since these are the ones most prevalent on the test.

CHAPTER 4

LOGICAL REASONING

In this chapter you will learn:

- The format of an LSAT logical reasoning question

- The seven major types of LSAT logical reasoning questions

- Easy-to-follow solution steps for every question type

Logical reasoning is the most demanding question type on the LSAT. There are two logical reasoning sections on the test, each with from 24 to 27 questions. That means that you have an average of only 1 minute and 20 seconds to answer each question. Most of the questions are relatively easy to solve if you read through them slowly and think through the answer choices carefully. However, many people are very stressed out on test day and have a hard time concentrating as fully as they should on each question. The only way to combat this stress is by practicing and making sure you are prepared.

Logical reasoning will determine half your total grade on the LSAT. Since there are two full sections of logical reasoning and just one section each of reading comprehension and logic games, you would be well advised to spend any extra time you have studying logical reasoning.

Logical reasoning questions have three parts: the *squib* (or *fact pattern*), the *question stem*, and five answer choices lettered A through E. The squib always precedes the question stem and the question stem always precedes the answer choices. Here is an example of a typical logical reasoning question:

Squib (fact pattern)

Politician: For a society to come into existence and perpetuate itself, a group of people must have first formed a government. If there is no society, then there is no way for people to interact together while feeling safe. Feeling safe is necessary for humans to live happily.

Question Stem

Which of the following is an inference that can be made from the passage?

Answer Choices

(A) The United States would be best served by ensuring its people's safety.
(B) If a government is created, then a society will be formed.
(C) If a society is happy, then it will not be safe.
(D) If people are living happily, then they have a government.
(E) Governments are only created by happy and safe societies.

The good news is that the sufficient-necessary tools that you just learned in the logic games chapter can be used to solve logical reasoning questions too. For example, you could use those tools to transcribe the facts from the squib into the following chains:

Society → Government ~~Government → Society~~
Feel Safe → Society ~~Society → Feel Safe~~
Live Happily → Feel Safe ~~Feel Safe → Live Happily~~

You could then add these chains to make one long deduction:

Live Happily → Feel Safe → Society → Government

This deduction allows you to choose answer choice D, since "Live Happily" requires the existence of "Government."

In this chapter you will learn about the seven types of logical reasoning questions. Do not speed through the sample questions or worry about how much time it takes you to answer them. Instead, work through each example slowly in order to understand how the questions work and what pitfalls they entail.

It helps to recognize the different question types because each one has its own variety of the following elements:

- **Reasoning Pattern.** Each question type follows a particular kind of reasoning pattern that you can understand and transcribe using the logic tools you learned in Chapter 3, "Logic Games." Once again, you'll be using sufficient-necessary constraints, the contrapositive, and so on.
- **Correct Answers.** Each question type also has a particular kind of correct answer. You'll start seeing the pattern once you begin working through the examples in this chapter. After a while, you'll start to get a "feel" for the right kind of answer to each question type. This is why it pays to be able to recognize each of the different question types the minute you see it.
- **Second-Best Choices.** Each question type also has its own kind of "second-best choices"— answer choices that are incorrect but that are nevertheless tempting to test takers. These choices are traps for test takers who do not read carefully or grasp what is going on in the squib or the answer choices. Each question usually has one second-best choice placed there purposely to sow confusion and delay. The idea is to cause test takers to narrow down their options to the correct choice and the second-best choice—and then choose the second-best choice if they are not careful. Once you practice with the questions in this book, you should begin to recognize the kinds of

second-best choices that appear in each logical reasoning question type. That's why once again it pays to recognize the different question types.
- **Clearly Wrong Answers.** Each question type also has its own kind of clearly wrong answers. These are choices that some test takers find compelling because they pick up key words from the squib or because they make a political statement that the test taker would support. The LSAT is a politically neutral test, so when you see a choice that makes a political or ethical statement (particularly an extreme one), you should be aware that that choice is probably not correct.

The more you practice answering logical reasoning questions, the better you will be at recognizing the different question types and knowing what kinds of reasoning patterns, correct answers, second-best choices, and clearly wrong answers to look for. One good way to practice is to visit the Curvebreakers Web site, which offers many sample logical reasoning questions categorized by question type. We recommend that you practice with one type at a time rather than tackling a mix of different types. You'll make faster progress and learn more efficiently by mastering the different question types one by one.

Below is a list of the seven logical reasoning question types. *Hint*: You'll always be able to recognize each different type by looking *solely at the question stem*.

Logical Reasoning Question Types

1. Conclusion Questions. These questions ask you to determine the conclusion, or main point, of an argument.

Common keywords in question stem:
- conclusion
- deduction
- main point
- inference
- must be true

Typical question stems:
- If the statements above are true, it can be *concluded* on the basis of them that . . .
- Which one of the following is most *strongly supported* by the information above?
- Which one of the following most accurately expresses the *main point* of the argument?
- If the scientist's claims are true, which one of the following *must also be true*?
- Which one of the following statements can be *inferred* from the passage?

2. "Resolve" Questions. These questions present a discrepancy between two opinions or a strange fact and require you to choose the best explanation for it.

Common keywords in question stem:
- resolve
- explain
- reconcile

Typical question stems:
- Which one of the following, if true, most helps to *resolve* the apparent discrepancy described above?
- Which one of the following, if true, most helps to *explain* the apparent inconsistency in consumer behavior described above?
- Which one of the following, if true, most helps to *reconcile* the restorers' decision with the goal stated in the passage?

3. "Strengthen" Questions. These questions ask you to identify different parts of an argument and choose the answer choice that would most *strengthen* a particular side of the argument.

Common keywords in question stem:
- support
- presupposes
- assumption
- strengthen
- premise
- principle

Typical question stems:
- Which one of the following, if true, *supports* the conclusion in the passage?
- In taking the position outlined, the author *presupposes* which one of the following?
- For the argument to be logically correct, it must make which of the following *assumptions*?
- Which one of the following, if it were determined to be true, would provide the best evidence that the journalist's decision will have the desired effect?
- Which one of the following *principles*, if accepted, would contribute most to Shanna's defense of her position against that of Jorge?
- The argument *assumes* which one of the following?

4. "Weaken" Questions. These questions ask you to identify different parts of an argument and choose the answer choice that would most *weaken* a particular side of the argument.

Common keywords in question stem:
- weakens
- conflicts
- casts doubt
- challenges
- undermines

Typical question stems:
- Which one of the following, if true, would most *weaken* the argument?
- Which one of the following, if true, would tend to *invalidate* use of the ratings for the agency's purpose?
- Which one of the following, if true, would *cast doubt* on the experimenter's conclusion?
- Which one of the following, if true, most seriously calls the conclusion above into question?
- Which one of the following, if true, most seriously *undermines* the scientists' contention?

5. Reasoning Strategy Questions. These questions ask you to identify the logical or illogical way that the author of the squib arrived at a particular conclusion.

Common keywords in question stem
- flaw
- error
- reasoning
- argument

Typical question stems:
- Which one of the following is a *flaw* in the argument?
- Which one of the following most clearly identifies an *error* in the author's *reasoning*?
- A *flaw in the reasoning* in the argument above is that this argument . . .
- Which one of the following most accurately expresses the *method used* to counter the automaker's current position?
- The passage employs which one of the following *argumentative strategies*?
- In the passage, the author does which one of the following?
- That homelessness is a serious social problem figures in the *argument* in which one of the following ways?

6. Analogous Reasoning Questions. This question type builds on the reasoning strategy question type. You must choose the answer choice that uses the same type of reasoning as the squib.

Common keywords in question stem:
- parallel
- similar flaw, argument, or logical structure

Typical question stems:
- Which one of the following most closely *parallels* the reasoning in the argument presented in the passage?
- Which one of the following, in its logical features, most closely *parallels* the reasoning used in the passage?
- Which one of the following arguments contains a *flaw* that is most *similar* to one in the argument above?
- Which one of the following has a *logical structure* most like that of the argument above?

7. Controversy Questions. The squibs are made up of opposing arguments from each of two people and the question stem asks you to point out what they are arguing about, what they would agree about, or the way one person has interpreted the other person's argument.

Common keywords in question stem:
- disagree about
- response
- point at issue

Typical question stems:
- Goswami and Nordecki *disagree* over the truth of which one of the following statements?
- Tina's and Sergio's statements lend the most support to the claim that they *disagree* about which one of the following statements?
- Which one of the following most accurately *characterizes* David's *response* to Alice's statement?
- Jean does which one of the following in her *response* to Anita?
- Which one of the following is a *point at issue* between Muriel and John?

QUESTION TYPE QUIZ

<u>Directions:</u> Based on the following question stems, determine which of the seven question types each item belongs to. Write a number from 1 to 7 in the space provided to indicate the question type.

_____ 1. Which one of the following, if true, would cast doubt on the scientist's conclusion?

_____ 2. Which one of the following most accurately expresses the main point of the argument?

_____ 3. Which one of the following, if true, most helps to explain the apparent inconsistency in the consumer behavior described above?

_____ 4. In the passage, the author does which one of the following?

_____ 5. Which one of the following, if true, most helps to resolve the apparent discrepancy described above?

_____ 6. The argument assumes which one of the following?

_____ 7. John's and Paula's statements lend the most support to the claim that they disagree about which one of the following statements?

_____ 8. Which one of the following, if true, most helps to reconcile the author's decision with the goal stated in the passage?

_____ 9. Which one of the following arguments contains a flaw that is most similar to one in the argument above?

_____ 10. For the argument to be logically correct, it must make which of the following assumptions?

_____ 11. If the statements above are true, it can be concluded on the basis of them that . . .

_____ 12. Which one of the following principles, if accepted, would contribute most to John's defense of his position against that of Paula?

_____ 13. Which one of the following, if true, would tend to invalidate use of the ratings for the agency's purpose?

_____ 14. If the scientist's claims are true, which one of the following must also be true?

_____ 15. Which one of the following, if true, would most weaken the argument?

_____ 16. Which one of the following most accurately characterizes John's response to Paula's statement?

_____ 17. A flaw in the reasoning in the argument above is that this argument . . .

_____ 18. Which one of the following, if true, most seriously calls the conclusion above into question?

_____ 19. Which one of the following, in its logical features, most closely parallels the reasoning used in the passage?

_____ 20. Which one of the following most clearly identifies an error in the author's reasoning?

_____ 21. Which one of the following, if true, supports the conclusion in the passage?

_____ 22. Which one of the following is most strongly supported by the information above?

_____ 23. Which one of the following, if true, most seriously undermines the scientists' contention?

_____ 24. Which one of the following is a flaw in the argument?

_____ 25. In taking the position outlined, the author presupposes which one of the following?

_____ 26. Which one of the following most accurately expresses the method used to counter the scientists' current position?

_____ 27. Which one of the following, if it were determined to be true, would provide the best evidence that the scientists' decision will have the desired effect?

_____ 28. Jean does which one of the following in her response to Anita?

_____ 29. That homelessness is a serious social problem figures in the argument in which one of the following ways?

_____ 30. Which one of the following most closely parallels the reasoning in the argument presented in the passage?

_____ 31. John and Paula disagree over the truth of which one of the following statements?

_____ 32. The passage employs which one of the following argumentative strategies?

_____ 33. Which one of the following statements can be inferred from the passage?

_____ 34. Which one of the following is a point at issue between Paula and John?

Quiz Answers

1. 4 ("Weaken")
2. 1 (Conclusion)
3. 2 ("Resolve")
4. 5 (Reasoning strategy)
5. 2 ("Resolve")
6. 3 ("Strengthen")
7. 7 (Controversy)
8. 2 ("Resolve")
9. 6 (Analogous reasoning)
10. 3 ("Strengthen")
11. 1 (Conclusion)
12. 3 ("Strengthen")

13. 4 ("Weaken")
14. 1 (Conclusion)
15. 4 ("Weaken")
16. 7 (Controversy)
17. 5 (Reasoning strategy)
18. 4 ("Weaken")
19. 6 (Analogous reasoning)
20. 5 (Reasoning strategy)
21. 3 ("Strengthen")
22. 1 (Conclusion)
23. 4 ("Weaken")
24. 5 (Reasoning strategy)

25. 3 ("Strengthen")
26. 5 (Reasoning strategy)
27. 3 ("Strengthen")
28. 5 (Reasoning strategy)
29. 5 (Reasoning strategy)
30. 6 (Analogous reasoning)
31. 7 (Controversy)
32. 5 (Reasoning strategy)
33. 1 (Conclusion)
34. 7 (Controversy)

1 Conclusion Questions

Conclusion questions all revolve around knowing and being able to identify the functional parts of an argument. In order to understand what the main conclusion is, it is necessary to understand the premises, supporting claims, facts/evidence, and subsidiary conclusions.

Identify the different parts of the argument for the following squib:

> The yellow Peruvian ant was an exceptional member of the arthropod phylum. It could lift many times its own weight. It was yellow. It was also the largest type of ant known in the 1890s. Unfortunately, its bright yellow exoskeleton made it an easy target for predators. Scientists think that it became extinct around 1956. Its extinction will forever be a loss to the genetic biodiversity of our planet.

The *main conclusion* is the last sentence:

> Its extinction will forever be a loss to the genetic biodiversity of our planet.

Everything else in the fact pattern supports this statement in some way. Let's look at the first sentence:

> The yellow Peruvian ant was an exceptional member of the arthropod phylum.

This sentence is known as a *subsidiary conclusion*. The following three sentences all support the truth of this statement. They can be termed *supporting claims* or *evidence*:

> It could lift many times its own weight. It was yellow. It was also the largest type of ant known in the 1890s.

These pieces of evidence support the subsidiary conclusion about how special the Peruvian ant was, which is used to justify the final conclusion that its extinction was a great loss to the genetic diversity of the planet.

The next sentence is merely a *claim* that provides evidence that tenuously supports the next subsidiary conclusion:

> Unfortunately, its bright yellow exoskeleton made it an easy target for predators.

Then comes the second subsidiary conclusion:

> Scientists think that it became extinct around 1956.

Finally, we come to the *main conclusion*. The first claims in the paragraph support the subsidiary conclusion about how special the ant was. The later claims support the conclusion that the ant has become extinct. Combine these two conclusions and you get the main conclusion: the ant's extinction is a great loss. To answer conclusion questions properly, you will need to be able to identify which conclusions are subsidiary conclusions and which conclusions are main ones. Also, you must be able to differentiate supporting statements (evidence) from conclusions. These skills will enable you to identify which statement the whole squib supports.

There are three versions of conclusion questions, as follow:
- *"Main point" version:* These questions ask you to identify the main point of the squib.
- *"Conclusion" version:* These questions ask you to draw a new conclusion based on the main point of the squib.
- *"Inference" version:* These questions ask you to make an inference based on some subsidiary conclusion within the squib.

The following sample questions will help you understand more about the three versions of conclusion questions.

Sample Conclusion Questions

1. Herman Hesse was one of the most renowned 20th century authors. He is remembered as the father of German modernist literature by virtue of his astounding literary achievements in the novels *Siddhartha* and *Steppenwolf*. However, some literary critics claim that Goethe was the greatest writer of the modern era from Germany due to his penchant for romanticism and lucid descriptive technique. These divergent opinions about great writers show how taste-specific the study of literature really is.

   What is the main point of the passage?

   (A) Herman Hesse is thought by many to be the greatest modern German writer.
   (B) German authors were the preeminent writers of the 20th century.
   (C) Some claim that Hesse was the most distinguished German writer while others claim that Goethe was the greatest.
   (D) Differences in opinion about the merits of literature demonstrate the fact that much of its worth is assessed subjectively.
   (E) One must study German literature in order to understand great writing.

Squib: The squib presents two alternate views regarding great authors, so clearly neither opposing view could function as a main conclusion. The conclusion must be an idea based on both opposing points. The only sentence that does not talk about only one of the authors is the final sentence, which discusses the taste-specific nature of literature.

Question stem: It asks for the main point inherent in the passage.

Correct answer: D. The whole squib leads up to the fact that literary criticism is largely subjective, as demonstrated by the fact that different literary critics have different opinions about two great writers.

(A) This was a subsidiary conclusion regarding the merits of Herman Hesse. Hesse is mentioned only in the first couple of lines, and, after that, the squib moves on to discuss other claims that are unrelated to this statement.

(B) This is a "clearly wrong answer." This information is not explicitly stated in the squib. Therefore it can never be the main point of a passage.

(C) This statement is a "second-best choice" because it is completely true based on the passage. However, it is merely a subsidiary point that is used to bolster the main point of the passage: These two different opinions demonstrate the subjective nature of literary criticism.

(E) This choice is a clearly wrong answer. While this information is possibly true, is not explicitly stated in the squib.

2. Sociologist: Theories of gender roles based on biological predisposition undervalue the influence of socialization on human psycho-social development. Such theories, which contend that males may be expected to seek throughout their lives more procreative partners than females, make such assertions wholly on the basis of biological assumptions, which in reality, are not only counterfactual but also indicative of the masculine hegemony and antifeminine bias inherent in the intellectual precedent established by the antiquated doctrine of Freud and Jung.

   Which of the following is the main point of the sociologist's argument?

   (A) Socialization rather than biological influences should be the prevailing model in gender studies.
   (B) Modern psychologists, drawing upon the Freudian and Jungian precedent, dominate the gender dialogue with their masculine bias.
   (C) Gender role explanations predicated entirely upon biology are not only erroneous but also inherently misogynistic.
   (D) Future psycho-sociology will prove that gender roles are indeed socialized.
   (E) It is a myth that females will seek fewer sexual partners in their lifetimes than will males.

Squib: The squib talks about theories of gender roles based on biological predisposition. It claims that gender roles and biology are not enough to make an accurate claim about the habits of a particular person. In fact, it goes on to state that theories seeking to do so demonstrate an antifeminine bias.

Question stem: This question asks for the main point of the squib.

Correct answer: C. The claim in choice C is the main point of the squib. It is supported by two supporting claims: (1) using biology to entirely explain gender roles is erroneous, and (2) psychologists' predilection to do so is based on misogynistic notions developed by Freud and Jung.

(A) The claim that socialization theory should be the main way to analyze gender roles is not made at all in the squib. Even though the squib berates models that are exclusively biological, it does not rule out a mixed biological and social model. Nor does it support a social model just because it condemns the biological model.

(B) This is the second-best choice. It restates a fact that is present in the squib. However, the squib does not talk about modern psychologists. Instead, it talks about the effects of Freud's and Jung's antiquated ideas on current gender theories. Furthermore, the point about those theories is a subsidiary conclusion, not the main idea of the squib.

(D) The choice is clearly wrong since the passage makes no predictions about the future. It merely states that some current ideas are counterfactual.

(E) This may be true based on the claims of the squib, but it is clearly not the main point of the squib. It is supporting evidence used to bolster the main point of the antifeminine bias present in the biological interpretation of gender roles.

3. The phenomenon of American artists of all races drawing on African-American musical influences is remarkable and far-reaching. Simply take a look at practically every major popular musical movement in the second half of the 20th century, and this becomes strikingly obvious. Had there been no Little Richard or Chuck Berry, there would never have been such luminaries as Elvis Presley, the Beatles, the Rolling Stones, or any other artists we herald as rock and roll masters or legends. Rock and roll can, in fact, be traced all the way back through early Roots Music, which never would have arisen if not for the nascent forms of rhythm and blues, which itself sprang from the Call-and-Response Songs popular among American slaves in the mid-19th century.

It can be concluded on the basis of the statements above that:

(A) Even early 20th-century popular forms of music, such as Big Band and Swing, owe a great deal to their black predecessors.

(B) No veritably original form of modern music does not have roots in early African-American music.

(C) Buddy Holly, a rock and roll legend, would not have been so had it not been for the influence from songs sung by slaves.

(D) Elvis Presley and the Beatles should not be considered as artistically great as Little Richard and Chuck Berry, since Richard and Berry preceded and influenced them.

(E) Caucasian artists will eventually dominate modern urban musical movements such as hip-hop and rap.

Squib: The main point of the squib is to make a claim that all forms of rock and roll have been strongly influenced by African-American music. In the middle of the squib, the claim is made that literally no great rock icon would be an icon had there not been the influence of African-American music to draw upon.

Question stem: This question asks for a conclusion that can be made based on the statements in the squib.

Correct answer: C. Buddy Holly is identified as a rock and roll legend in the answer choice. Based on this identification, you may conclude that he would not have been a rock and roll legend had he not had African-American musical influences to draw upon. This idea is stated explicitly with regard to Elvis Presley and the Beatles in the squib.

(A) While this might be true, it is certainly not the best inference that can be made from the statements in the squib. The squib solely concerns rock and roll music, not earlier 20th-century popular forms like Big Band or Swing.

(B) The squib makes claims only about rock and roll, not about all forms of modern music.

(D) The squib makes no judgments about the merits of Elvis Presley and the Beatles versus the merits of Chuck Berry or Little Richard.

(E) This mildly entertaining fantasy and improbable idea is not supported anywhere in the squib.

Conclusion Questions: Common Traits

Now that you have reviewed some sample conclusion questions, you should be able to recognize their common traits. These traits are listed in the following outline.

I. General Format

1. Squib is three to five sentences.
2. Word count: 56–121.
3. Each sentence in the squib states a proposition or presents a piece of information that is used to make further conclusions in the squib.
4. Questions constantly invoke sufficient-necessary problems.
5. Questions try to mislead test takers using
   a. incorrect statements of the contrapositive
   b. missing contrapositives
   c. false links in the logical chains
6. A sentence that is only distantly related to the topic as a whole may be included in the squib in order to throw test takers off.
7. *Unless, except*, and *not* are rife throughout the answer choices (one-fifth use one of these words) in order to trip up careless test takers.

II. "Main Point" Version

A. Sample Question Stem
1. Which one of the following most accurately expresses the **main point** of the argument?

B. Correct Answer
1. is the sentence or point to which every other sentence in the squib leads or contributes.

C. Second-Best Choice
1. is often a subsidiary point, that is, one required to reach the actual main point
2. may state an idea that is only generally related to the main idea of the squib
   a. *Example*: For a squib that talks about how great candy canes are, a second-best choice might say, "Candy in general is great."
3. offers a conclusion that tries to make a stronger claim than the squib actually does

D. Clearly Wrong Answers
1. make an invalid assumption based on the squib
2. conclude something that is related to but clearly not specified in the squib
3. conclude something that is not explicitly supported in the squib

III. "Conclusion" Version

A. Sample Question Stem
1. If the statements above are true, it can be **concluded** on the basis of them that . . .

B. Correct Answer
1. adequately uses the facts of the squib to formulate a tenable conclusion based on these facts

C. Second-Best Choice
1. makes a conclusion that is only possibly supportable or sometimes supportable based on the facts of the squib
2. functions like second-best choices of main point questions (see above)

D. Clearly Wrong Answers
1. may be based on a feeling or a moral imperative that lacks any real support in the squib
2. may state a conclusion that is directly opposed to the conclusion of the squib
   a. These are often present as a trap for careless readers who missed a *not, won't, unless*, or *except*.
3. may state a conclusion about a topic unrelated to the squib
4. function like clearly wrong answers of main point questions (see above)

IV. "Inference" Version

A. Sample Question Stems
1. Which one of the following is most **strongly supported** by the information above?
2. If the scientist's claims are true, which one of the following **must also be true**?
3. Which one of the following statements can be **inferred** from the passage?

B. Correct Answer
1. is a piece of information, however small, that can be gleaned from the squib
   a. The answer need not be the main point of the squib, but if there are two competing answer choices, one of which is closer to the main point, then that is the correct answer.

C. Second-Best Choice
1. incorrectly draws the contrapositive of a statement in the squib
2. makes an error of reasoning (Errors of reasoning are covered in depth in Section 5 of this chapter.)

D. Clearly Wrong Answers
1. state that something will definitely happen when it will only possibly happen
2. make an unsupported conclusion
3. incorrectly assume that the squib states something it does not

Now that you have seen some of the test makers' tricks, answer the following seven conclusion questions. Every correct answer and incorrect answer choice will match a particular point in the outline you just read.

DRILL: CONCLUSION QUESTIONS

1. According to many critics, Shakespeare's greatest gift to English literature was the introduction of the evolving character, that is, one who changes throughout the course of the work by virtue of his or her own words and thoughts. King Lear and Hamlet are two fine examples. Often, this achievement is what critics cite as justification for dubbing Shakespeare the greatest writer in the English language. However, it is a little-known fact that Chaucer achieved this very effect some 200 years before, with his masterfully penned pilgrims Alisoun of Bath and the Pardoner.

   Which of the following statements can best be inferred from the passage?

   (A) Chaucer was the greatest English writer.
   (B) Chaucer's Alisoun and the Pardoner resemble Shakespeare's Lear and Hamlet in more ways than one.
   (C) If whoever introduced the evolving character deserves the title of "the greatest writer in English," then Chaucer should hold that distinction.
   (D) The only reason Chaucer is not considered the greatest writer in the English language is because he wrote in Middle, and not modern, English.
   (E) "Greatest" is a term that cannot be applied to writers.

2. Politician: For a society to come into existence and perpetuate itself, a group of people must have first formed a government. If there is no society, then there is no way for people to be safe. Safety is necessary for humans to live happily.

   Which of the following is an inference that can be made from the passage?

   (A) The United States would be best served by ensuring its people's safety.
   (B) If a government is created, then a society will be formed.
   (C) If a society is happy, then it will not be safe.
   (D) If there is no government, then the society cannot be happy.
   (E) Governments are created only by happy and safe societies.

3. Not unlike their counterparts in Europe and parts of Asia, many American students are required to study a foreign language for two years, or often more, at the high school level. Quite frequently, these students continue their language study in college; the culmination of this study, the predicating assumption holds, is communicative competency formed through a method of tutelage in the areas of grammar, vocabulary, conjugation, and sentence structure. However, research shows that once students have been away from the classroom for over a year, the vast majority of them have failed to retain almost all of their foreign language skills.

   The argument above supports which of the following claims?

   (A) The American system of foreign language study pales in comparison to the competing systems of Europe and Asia.
   (B) The majority of language-learning programs in America need to strengthen their tutelage of grammar, vocabulary, conjugation, and sentence structure.
   (C) The methods of foreign language study in the American curriculum are in and of themselves insufficient to achieve retention.
   (D) American students should be immersed in a country that speaks the language they are studying in order to truly pick up the language.
   (E) American students feel less inclination to learn a second language, since English is currently the dominant imperial language.

4. The Russian Revolution could easily have been prevented had the czarist government been more cognizant of and attentive to the needs of its populace. A sentiment of unrest pervaded the Russian commoners for a long period of time preceding the revolution, which they expressed nonviolently for some years to no apparent avail. This was especially true in the potato fields, where thousands slaved away so that a few could gorge themselves on the fat of the land. Of course, the people eventually revolted. This model holds true for all governments; any leader would be wise to heed the example.

If the statements above are held to be true, it can be concluded that:

(A) If a government does not provide for its populace, the populace will revolt.
(B) The Russian commoners revolted because they were starving.
(C) Nonviolent expression of discontent is usually less effective than real action.
(D) A government must either meet the needs of the people or possess the military capacity to quell a potential revolt.
(E) If people choose to revolt against their government, the government will be forced to meet their needs.

5. In the 1920s, doctors advised that everyone over the age of eighteen should consume at least a third of a cup of pure butter each day, the theory being that doing so would help lubricate the arteries and therefore provide better circulation. As recently as the 1950s, physicians recommended that a person smoke a cigarette following each meal in order to facilitate better digestion. Modern physicians would balk at such suggestions, while wholeheartedly recommending dietary habits such as two glasses of wine per day, a low carbohydrate, high-fat and protein diet, and the substitution of artificially sweetened sodas and teas over more natural alternatives.

Which of the following is the main point of the passage?

(A) The claims and suggestions of modern medicine may one day seem as faulty as those of the past seem to us today.
(B) Medicine today puts many more restrictions on an enjoyable lifestyle than it used to.
(C) Fewer people die from preventable disease now than in the past because of the many advancements of medical study.
(D) Cigarettes and high-fat foods such as butter may not be as unhealthy as doctors tell us they are.
(E) Modern physicians contradict themselves quite often.

6. It is an irrefutable fact that no great pianists were not trained classically. Many jazz and rock pianists were not trained classically. Many great pianists are also jazz pianists. Only some rock pianists are great pianists. All great pianists, no matter what style they practice, are also great lovers of classical music.

If the information above is accepted as true, which of the following can be concluded?

(A) No rock pianists were trained classically.
(B) Great pianists are classically trained and love classical music.
(C) Jazz and rock pianists are inferior to classical pianists.
(D) All classical pianists learned their craft methodically.
(E) All great pianists eventually choose classical music over jazz or rock.

7. On a remote island in the South Pacific live a people known as the Yami. The Yami, to the average Western observer, would appear to epitomize the term "uncivilized"—clad in loincloths, living in dung hovels, and subsisting from day to day on the fresh dolphin they manage to spear in the mornings. And yet, an exhaustive cultural anthropological study of the tribe has revealed extensive and intricate mythological and religious beliefs and practices, a thoroughly functional and seemingly fair judicial system, and a language that technically rivals modern English in linguistic complexity and variance of structure.

Which of the following is the main point of the passage?

(A) We should be ashamed of the way we think of and judge cultures that differ from our own.

(B) When the Yami are more closely and intimately observed, it is clear that they are no less cultured than we are.

(C) We could learn much from studying cultures such as the Yami that we tend to think of as savage or uncivilized.

(D) The Yami, a people many would dismiss as savages, have societal elements rivaling some of those in Western civilization.

(E) Not enough people have studied the Yami to fully understand the intricacies of their culture.

ANSWERS AND EXPLANATIONS

Question 1

Squib: Note that Shakespeare has been called the greatest writer in the English language solely because he purportedly introduced the technique of the evolving character. The final sentence contradicts this widely held idea by introducing the little-known fact that Shakespeare did not introduce this technique. Instead Chaucer, another English writer, introduced the technique centuries before Shakespeare.

Question stem: This squib is an inference question that requires you to use some of the facts of the squib to make the following inference:

Chaucer, because he really first introduced the technique, would deserve any accolades that Shakespeare received for the introduction of the technique.

Correct answer: C. Chaucer was the first to introduce the technique. If the sole basis for bestowing the title of greatest writer in English is the introduction of this technique, then clearly Chaucer would deserve this distinction because he introduced it before Shakespeare.

(A) This claim cannot be made based on the information in the squib. Shakespeare contributed to the English language in many ways, so he may deserve the title of greatest writer even though it was Chaucer who introduced the evolving character technique.

(B) From the squib, we can infer that Chaucer's Alisoun and the Pardoner resemble each other in only one way: They were evolving characters.

(D) This answer is clearly wrong because there is nothing in the squib about Middle versus modern English.

(E) This answer is clearly wrong because it contradicts the facts of the squib, in which the term "greatest" is applied to Shakespeare.

Question 2

Squib: This question is very rigid and narrow. It starts off with several statements that you should recognize are sufficient-necessary statements. The squib should be diagrammed in the following fashion:

Happiness → Safety → Society → Government
~~Government~~ → ~~Society~~ → ~~Safety~~ → ~~Happiness~~

Question stem: It asks what can be inferred from this sufficient-necessary statement.

Correct answer: D. The sufficient-necessary technique reveals that a government is required for a happy society. Looking to the contrapositive, no government would mean that a society could not be happy: ~~Government~~ → ~~Happiness~~.

(A) This remark makes an assumption about information not present in the squib.

(B) This answer choice mistakes a sufficient condition for a necessary condition.

(C) The answer choice contradicts the statements in the squib. A happy society must also be safe.

(E) It is possible for an unsafe and unhappy society to create a government. A government is just necessary for the existence of happiness, safety, and a society.

Question 3

Squib: This squib starts off by saying that American students learn foreign languages in a classroom setting just like their European and Asian counterparts. It holds that the purpose of this teaching is "communicative competency." However, research has shown that this method of classroom teaching is incapable of ensuring that students will retain any skills in the language that they studied.

Question stem: It asks what can be concluded on the basis of this knowledge.

Correct answer: C. Since the main point of the paragraph is that the academic setting that American students now utilize to learn foreign languages is ineffective for retention, we can conclude exactly this in answer choice C.

(A) This is not stated in the squib. The converse was presented: American students are "not unlike their counterparts in Europe and parts of Asia."

(B) The strength of the academic technique is not addressed. The question is not whether American students can solve grammar questions during their school years, but rather why they do not retain this knowledge in later years.

(D) The squib does not propose that American students should do anything different to improve their retention. It merely states that current methods are ineffective. Always be aware of combining a factual squib with a normative statement such as "should," "would best be served by," or the like.

(E) This statement is completely unrelated to the squib.

Question 4

Squib: This squib discusses a period of time predating the Russian Revolution, when the czarist government refused to attend to the needs of the people. The people protested peacefully for a while in order to try and get the government to recognize their needs, but the government refused to respond, so eventually the people were forced to revolt violently. The final sentence states that this model will hold true for all governments: If they ignore the needs of their people, they will be overthrown.

Question stem: It asks what can be concluded on the basis of the above statements.

Correct answer: A. This choice states the conclusion exactly: The populace will revolt if the government does not adequately provide for them.

(B) This is not explicitly stated in the squib. The squib states that thousands slaved away, but not that they were not provided with some food for doing so.

(C) This answer choice is extremely ambiguous. It would require you to make an inference about not only nonviolent expression as applied to governments but also nonviolent means of expression in general. An inference this abstract and far-reaching will never be the correct answer to a question.

(D) The squib does state that a government must meet the needs of its people or they will revolt, but it says nothing about the need to have the military capacity to quell a revolt.

(E) This is not necessarily true because it is entirely possible for a government to quell a revolt before the revolt is effective.

Question 5

Squib: The squib introduces several pieces of information regarding the kooky habits and advice of doctors of old. It goes on to say that modern doctors would balk at these suggestions, but that they still recommend such questionable practices as drinking wine daily, following strange dietary requirements, and using artificial sweeteners.

Question stem: It asks for the main point of this information.

It is important to note that none of the answer choices really provides what could be considered the main point of the squib. In situations such as this, it is best to choose the answer choice that if added onto the squib as a final statement would be most fitting.

Correct answer: A. The squib suggests that modern medicine at times provides the same sort of kooky recommendations that were popular among doctors long ago but that have since been discredited. Based on this information, it would make sense to infer that in the future, some of the claims of modern medicine will seem just as kooky.

(B) This idea is not supported by the squib. The squib makes no normative judgment about the value of cigarettes or butter, and you as a test taker should never insert your own value judgments into the test.

(C) This idea may or may not be true; in any case, the squib has nothing on the subject to say one way or the other.

(D) This is not an inference that can be made on the basis of the statements in the squib.

(E) Modern physicians may or may not often contradict themselves, but the squib offers nothing to support either inference.

Question 6

Squib: This squib provides you with numerous true statements that you should recognize as sufficient-necessary statements. The only meaningful statements that you can glean from the passage look like this:

Great Pianist → Trained Classically
Great Pianist → Lover of Classical Music

Question stem: The stem asks for an inference that can be made based on the preceding true statements.

Correct answer: B. Based on the sufficient-necessary statement, if one is a great pianist, then one was classically trained and loves classical music.

(A) This is not an inference that the squib supports.

(C) These categories are not mutually exclusive. Nor was the category "classical pianist" ever mentioned. All that is mentioned is "classically trained" pianists.

(D) The category "classical pianist" is never mentioned, nor can you assume that classical pianists who were classically trained learned their craft methodically. They could have just as well learned it haphazardly.

(E) There is no statement regarding time in the squib.

Question 7

Squib: The point of this squib is that the Yami people appear to be very uncivilized when viewed solely on the basis of externals—the loincloths, the dung hovels, and the dolphin flesh. However, when viewed up close, they have extremely advanced philosophical ideas and language structure.

Question stem: The stem asks for the main point of the squib.

Correct answer: D. This choice presents the main point of the squib. It says that many would dismiss the Yami as savages, yet their society has some features that are as complex as certain ones in Western civilization.

(A) This is the type of normative judgment that can almost never be made for any LSAT question.

(B) This is not true because, according to the squib, the Yami rival Western culture in only two respects: religion and language structure. The West far surpasses them in many other ways.

(C) There is nothing in the squib about the need for Westerners to learn from the Yami.

(E) Nowhere does the squib suggest that the Yami have not yet been studied enough. In fact, it says that an "exhaustive anthropological study" was recently done on the tribe.

2 "Resolve" Questions

"Resolve" questions present you with a strange set of events, two opposing opinions, or sets of unusual facts and ask you to select the answer choice that would most explain the odd facts or the discrepancy between the opinions.

Here is an example squib for a "resolve" question:

> The Patriot Act, introduced in the year 2001, was designed to give police the authority to perform more types of searches with less evidence and lower levels of suspicion toward the person being searched. The idea was that giving police greater search powers would allow them to ferret out and prevent acts of terrorism. But despite this Act—an Act that liberals decry for its abrogation of individual freedom—the incidence of terrorism has increased fourfold on American soil.
>
> Which of the following, if true, would explain why the Act has not effectively decreased the overall incidence of terrorism in the United States?

The possible correct answers to this question are virtually limitless. Here are some possibilities:

> - The number of people trying to commit acts of terrorism on U.S. soil has increased tenfold since 2001.
> - The Act does not authorize police to search in enough new ways to effectively prevent terrorist acts.
> - The Act, while passed in 2001, will not take effect until 2008.
> - The Patriot Act was entirely repealed two months after its introduction.
> - The Search Subject's Rights Act, an act that increased peoples' ability to avoid being searched, was passed in conjunction with the Patriot Act.
> - Police have chosen not to utilize the powers granted to them under the Act.
> - People who could potentially be searched under the Act have found ways to elude the authorities.

Any of these answer choices could be a reason why the Patriot Act might have failed to decrease the overall incidence of terrorist acts. Incorrect answer choices would be ones that do not directly relate to terrorism or the Patriot Act and hold no real repercussions for either. Another kind of incorrect answer choice picks up ideas from the squib but posits an effect directly opposite to the one stated. Here is an example:

> - Working under the revised search laws, police captured 3,000 more terrorist suspects in 2001–2002 than they had in any previous year.

This answer choice implies that the Patriot Act was very effective—just the opposite of what is stated in the squib. Yet some test takers who did not read the question carefully might pick this choice just because it relates to both the Patriot Act and terrorism. Keep in mind that this kind of answer choice will never be correct.

Study the following sample "resolve" questions to learn more about this question type.

Sample "Resolve" Questions

1. Most broken limbs need to be treated and set by a doctor in order to heal properly. Otherwise, broken bones can ossify in the wrong places, and injured people will have limited functionality in the once-broken limbs for the rest of their lives. However, some doctors recommend against any treatment for broken bones in certain appendages.

   Which of the following, if true, explains this paradox?

   (A) Some doctors believe that bones in certain appendages heal better when left untreated.
   (B) At times, getting medical treatment for a broken bone disturbs the healing process.
   (C) Sometimes surgery can cause bones to heal less well than they would have without the surgery.
   (D) Many people would rather not have surgery if at all possible.
   (E) Few people cannot afford to pay for an operation to fix a broken bone.

Squib: This squib explains that it is usually to a patient's benefit to have broken bones treated professionally by a medical doctor. However, it contends that there are a number of doctors who consistently recommend that their patients get no treatment at all for broken bones in certain appendages. Why would this be? One of the answer choices will provide you with a good reason.

Question stem: It asks you to explain the paradox inherent in the squib.

Correct answer: A. This choice would definitely explain why some doctors would never advise their patients to receive treatment for certain kinds of broken bones. For example, many bones in the foot generally heal better without surgery or any type of treatment, so it would make sense that podiatrists often recommend that their patients leave broken foot bones untreated.

(B) This is a true statement and could explain some hesitancy on the patient's part in getting treatment. However, doctors realize that the majority of broken bones are greatly improved through medical treatment, so this would not adequately explain the paradox in the squib.

(C) This answer choice makes essentially the same argument as answer choice B. Therefore, it is incorrect for the same reason as B.

(D) This is true, and it would make sense that doctors would try to cater to the desires of their patients—but not to the extent that would be harmful to them. Therefore it seems that this fact would be negligible in determining whether or not to recommend surgery to a patient.

(E) If this statement were worded in the opposite way ("*Most* people cannot afford to pay for an operation to fix a broken bone"), then it could possibly be an explanation. However, it says that few people cannot afford surgery, so this fact would really have no affect on the decision to recommend surgery.

2. Scientists estimate that the Colombian rainforest holds about 100 million hectares of forestland. According to a survey based solely on models of the current rate of rainforest depletion, in 25 years' time all of this forestland will be gone. However, despite these models, Colombian scientists claim that there will be no more rainforests left in Colombia in as few as 15 years.

   Which of the following, if true, helps to best reconcile the scientists' conclusion with the survey's projection?

(A) Colombian scientists have a vested interest in increasing global awareness of the deforestation occurring in the Colombian rainforest.

(B) Colombian scientists take into account the fact that future technologies will probably speed up the rate of depletion.

(C) Farmers and loggers contribute to the current rate of deforestation, but farmers will not contribute to future rates.

(D) Rainforest regrowth will reduce the overall depletion rate if conservation groups actively plant new seedlings.

(E) The current depletion rates do not reflect data received from the boating industry, which uses Colombian wood for boating.

Squib: This squib presents a conflict between the claims of Colombian scientists and a survey based on the current rate of rainforest depletion. Colombian scientists claim that the rainforest will be destroyed in a much shorter time period than the survey suggests. You must choose the answer choice that explains this discrepancy.

Question stem: It asks you to reconcile the Colombian scientists' conclusion with the survey's projection.

Correct answer: B. A survey that merely extrapolated linearly using the current rate of depletion would not reflect new logging technologies that will likely speed up the deforestation process. Because the scientists' analysis takes these new technologies into account, its projected date for total deforestation is much sooner.

(A) This is a true statement since the scientists live in Colombia and will personally be disadvantaged by the destruction of their rainforest. However, this is not a reason for them to sacrifice their professional credibility by making claims unsupported by facts.

(C) If farmers actually stopped contributing to deforestation, then the rate of deforestation would slow and scientists would likely project a later date for complete deforestation than the date in the survey.

(D) Before even analyzing this statement, we must note that it is a hypothetical. Hypothetical statements are *almost never* correct answers to these questions because the question stem asks for an explanation, not a *possible* explanation. That aside, if the rate of deforestation were reduced, it would take more than 25 years for the forests to be fully depleted.

(E) This is the second-best choice to explain this scenario. However, it is probable that these data were not included because their effect was negligible. There is no reason to assume that the activities of a single Colombian industry would markedly affect rainforest depletion rates.

3. Most oil is transported around the world by sea in large oil barges. Along with this travel comes the small risk of a shipwreck that would spill the oil into the ocean, destroying the habitat of many sea creatures. The waters near Spain have had two major oil spills in the last year and a half. This summer, a third oil barge called to Spanish harbors requesting port since it was badly spilling oil. The captain wanted to stop this spill immediately, but even though the Spanish government highly values preventing oil spills, it did not allow the barge to dock and forced the captain to turn further out to sea.

Which of the following, if true, most explains the actions of the Spanish government?

(A) It costs more to clean up a spill that is far from the coast than a spill that is nearer to the coast.
(B) Most staunch environmentalists would have immediately given the barge permission to dock in a Spanish port.
(C) A leaking barge journeying to a Spanish port would destroy more sea life near Spain than one turning away to deeper waters.
(D) The barge was not spilling badly when it made the call, but the spill would eventually worsen if left untreated.
(E) The oil in the ship could not be salvaged and sold for a profit by the Spanish government.

Squib: Oil spills have been occurring near Spain, and it appears that the Spanish are tired of them. Therefore, when this particular captain asked for harbor in order to fix his spill, his request was rejected. The question asks us to choose a likely reason for the rejection.

Question stem: Explain the actions of the Spanish government.

Correct answer: C. The Spanish government most likely preferred that the damage from the leaky oil barge occur anywhere but in Spanish waters.

(A) This fact would actually have the opposite effect: It would incentivize people to bring the barge closer to shore.

(B) The preferences of a particular group of people who are not actually in charge of the situation have no bearing.

(D) This fact is not a reason why Spain would refuse to receive the ship. Most bad things eventually get worse if left untreated, but we do not know enough of the facts to say when the "eventually" in this situation would occur.

(E) This fact has no bearing on Spain's desires to help a ship in need and preserve the purity of its coastal waters.

"Resolve" Questions: Common Traits

Now that you have reviewed some sample "resolve" questions, you should be able to recognize their common traits. These traits are listed in the following outline.

I. **General Format**
1. Squib is three to five sentences.
2. Word count: 70–127.
3. May present two opposing opinions.
4. May present a paradox or strange set of facts.

II. **Standard Elements**
A. **Sample Question Stems**
1. Which one of the following, if true, best reconciles the apparently **discrepant facts** described above?
2. Which one of the following, if true, most helps to explain the **apparent inconsistency** described above?
3. Which one of the following, if true, most helps to resolve the **apparent paradox** in the passage?
B. **Correct Answer**
1. is the answer that explains the paradox or reconciles two groups' opinions
2. always explains the whole paradox or discrepancy and not just part of it
C. **Second-Best Choice**
1. is a possible explanation, that is, an explanation that under certain scenarios could explain the event. However, there is generally a better choice that explains the event more often than "sometimes."

2. may explain one speaker's opinion but not the discrepancy between speakers' opinions
3. may explain the existence of divergent facts but not offer a way to reconcile them

D. Clearly Wrong Answers
1. present facts that would not affect the given events or opinions
2. are intentionally slanted to elicit some moral reaction from the test taker but are not really logically related to the problem

Now that you have seen some of the test makers' tricks, answer the following seven "resolve" questions. Every correct answer and incorrect answer choice will match a particular point on the outline you just read. The same will be true for questions on the actual LSAT, so knowing the points on the outline will help you to identify correct answers quickly and consistently.

DRILL: "RESOLVE" QUESTIONS

1. A recent national ice cream survey shows that Marble Ice is the brand most strongly preferred by people throughout the United States. However, global sales figures for Marble Ice are lower than those of 23 of its top competitors.

   Which of the following, if true, best explains the discrepancy between brand preference and worldwide brand sales?

   (A) Sales for Marble Ice's top 10 competitors account for 99% of the global market.
   (B) Marble Ice is marketed mostly outside of the United States and its territories.
   (C) Glacier Ice, a competing brand, is the top ice cream seller in the United States.
   (D) Marble Ice is more expensive per gallon than 10 of its overseas competitors.
   (E) U.S. preferences for ice cream are markedly different from global preferences.

2. Early genetic research demonstrated that when beans with different traits are cross-bred, they produce offspring that possess the traits of the parents according to a specific pattern: The dominant trait will be displayed in all the offspring. There are two varieties of height in green beans, long and short. The short gene is recessive (not dominant), but when Sam breeds his green beans, the next season's offspring are always of the short variety.

   Which of the following, if true, would best explain why the offspring of Sam's beans are always short?

   (A) Sometimes mixes of beans produce beans that are of the short variety.
   (B) Sam would rather have short green beans than long green beans in his garden.
   (C) The dominant allele in black beans is the gene for short height.
   (D) Sam cross-breeds beans that only have the recessive trait for height.
   (E) Ten years ago, only short green beans grew in Sam's garden.

3. If two parents have type O blood, then all of their children will have type O blood. A happily married couple has had three children with type O blood and assumes that the fourth, due next May, will also have type O blood. However, after a blood test, the doctor informs them that their fourth child will have type A blood.

   Which of the following, if true, would best account for this turn of events?

   (A) The father of the family next door has type O blood.
   (B) People who do not have type O blood can have children with type O blood.
   (C) The three older children were born during the winter, while this child will be born during the summer.
   (D) Due to a genetic mutation, 2% of the children of type O parents will have type B blood.
   (E) Scientific documents regarding certain particularities of blood have been found to be untrue.

4. Many crops are grown in the same place and on the same soil for many years, so they naturally deplete the minerals in the soil. These minerals include nutrients that the crops need to survive. By using organic fertilizers, farmers can restore these vital nutrients. Some overeager farmers take fresh organic fertilizers and put them immediately on their crops. This often causes the crops to die within a week.

   Which of the following, if true, would help to resolve the unexpected finding reported in the passage?

   (A) Organic fertilizers must be aged for up to several weeks in order to lose their acidic content.
   (B) Farmers often put the wrong fertilizer on a crop.
   (C) Fertilizers contain compounds that are very toxic to many species.
   (D) Eager farmers are more likely than patient farmers to apply their fertilizers correctly.
   (E) Fertilizers derived from manure can harm crops if applied in excessive quantities.

5. Types of artificial sweeteners have been manufactured that do not include sugar. The absence of sugar allows people to make their foods sweet without also including calories that would lead to fat and obesity. However, many proponents of dieting, health, and fitness decry the use of artificial sweeteners. Instead, they recommend that people take the extra calories present in sugar.

Which of the following, if true, would explain why fitness experts do not advocate the use of artificial sweeteners?

(A) Fitness experts would be out of a job if everyone were suddenly to lose weight.
(B) Sugar has positive benefits for people in addition to the negative ones that most people realize.
(C) Artificial sweeteners replace sugar with compounds that are even more deleterious to the body.
(D) It has been proven that using artificial sweeteners can lead to obesity.
(E) Foods can be sweet, healthy, and tasty even though they have a remarkably high sugar content.

6. After seatbelts were introduced throughout America, national data showed that fatalities related to automobile accidents dramatically decreased. To get a better picture of the situation, an interest group went to hospitals around the country to review postcrash data regarding auto accidents where the survivors wore seatbelts. This group found that a huge percentage of these people suffered serious seatbelt-related injuries that would not have occurred had there been no seatbelts. Based on these findings, the interest group recommended banning the use of seatbelts in order to preclude seatbelt-related injuries.

Which of the following, if true, would be the best safety-related reason for keeping seatbelts even though they cause injury?

(A) Seatbelts can cause injuries that are completely unrelated to crashes.
(B) The total number of injuries on the highway has increased since the introduction of seatbelts.
(C) Experts in the automobile industry recommend using a seatbelt despite what interest groups claim.
(D) Even though seatbelts cause injury, they prevent still greater injuries from occurring.
(E) The government has imposed laws that require people to use seatbelts whenever they are riding in a car.

7. White tigers are majestic animals that are in danger of extinction. Because of the deforestation occurring in their natural habitats, white tigers have been forced to move into habitats that are less conducive to their type of hunting. The tigers' stark white coats, which allow them to blend into the snow of their natural habitats, now make them easy for prey animals to spot. However, it has been documented that white tigers are eating more prey in their new habitats than they did on average in their old ones.

Which of the following, if true, would explain the discrepancy in the claims noted above?

(A) White tigers have a genetic predisposition to hunt in certain types of forests.
(B) Prey animals have not yet realized that the new white beasts are tigers, so they do not flee from them.
(C) White tigers are hunting larger creatures in their new habitat than they hunted in their old one.
(D) The white coats that allowed tigers to blend into the snow also allow them to blend into some parts of the forest.
(E) Hunting skills are of fundamental importance to animals in the forest regardless of the color of their coats.

ANSWERS AND EXPLANATIONS

Question 1

Squib: A survey has shown that people in the United States like Marble Ice more than any other brand of ice cream. However, on a worldwide basis, Marble Ice lags behind its competitors.

Question stem: Explain why Marble Ice, which is so popular in the United States, is not a leading brand worldwide.

Correct answer: E. This explains why people in the United States might prefer an ice cream that is less popular in other nations.

(A) This piece of information does not explain the discrepancy in the facts.

(B) This fact contradicts the information in the problem and would lead you to think that Marble Ice is more dominant abroad than it apparently is.

(C) This fact does not relate to global sales figures in any way.

(D) The higher price is not necessarily the reason for slower sales worldwide. This information is not enough to resolve the discrepancy definitively.

Question 2

Squib: There are four important pieces of information in this squib. First, when *different* traits are cross-bred, they produce offspring that express the dominant trait. Second, there are long and short varieties of green beans. Third, the short trait is not dominant. Fourth, Sam's green beans are always short.

Question stem: It asks you to explain why Sam's beans are always short.

Correct answer: D. This is the only possible explanation for the continued production of short beans. Sam is cross-breeding short beans with other short beans. If he were cross-breeding short beans with long beans, the offspring would be long.

(A) This does not explain the situation since Sam *always* produces short beans, not just "sometimes."

(B) Sam's personal wishes are completely irrelevant to this problem.

(C) The traits of a different type of bean are irrelevant to the traits of green beans.

(E) What happened in Sam's garden 10 years ago is irrelevant to the breeding patterns that are occurring now.

Question 3

Squib: This passage tells you that parents who both have type O blood will always have children with type O blood. It then introduces a couple who are happily married. You know that the couple's previous children all have type O blood, which would lead you to believe that the couple has type O blood, but you do not know this for sure. Finally, you know that the next child will have type A blood.

Question stem: What would explain why a happily married couple who have three children with type O blood would produce a child with type A blood?

Correct answer: B. This is the best possible explanation. Just because an event is unlikely does not mean that it could not happen once, twice, or even three times.

(A) This answer, while perhaps comically appealing, it not the best choice. First, the couple are described as happily married. Second, even if an infidelity had occurred, the neighbor's type O blood would not explain why the new baby is type A.

(C) The squib does not state that the season of birth has anything to do with the blood type of the child.

(D) This genetic mutation evidence would be relevant if the fourth child had type B blood, but the child will have type A blood, so this fact tells us nothing.

(E) That certain scientific findings have been proven to be untrue does not explain this particular situation.

Question 4

Squib: You are confronted with the paradox: Organic fertilizers are beneficial to crops, but under certain conditions they can be harmful. The problem seems to be in the way in which they are applied.

Question stem: Why would crops sometimes die when a fertilizer that is normally good is applied to them?

Correct answer: A. Acid is well known to be detrimental to living things. If fresh fertilizer has a high acid content, then it makes sense that large applications of it would kill plants. The fertilizer is beneficial only once the acid is removed through aging.

(B) The fact that farmers often make mistakes with fertilizers does not explain this situation.

(C) Even if certain fertilizer compounds are toxic to some species, that does not mean that they are toxic to the species of plant for which they are intended.

(D) This idea just confuses the situation: If the eager farmers are applying the fertilizer correctly, then why are their crops dying?

(E) Almost anything that is applied in excessive quantities can be harmful. However, the squib does not state that the eager farmers apply the fertilizer in excessive quantities, and there is no reason to assume that they are doing so.

Question 5

Squib: This squib tells you that by using artificial sweeteners, people can avoid sugar, calories, fat, and obesity. However, many fitness experts still recommend against using these substances. You must find a good reason for their recommendation.

Question stem: Explain why fitness experts do not recommend artificial sweeteners.

Correct answer: C. This would be a good reason. If the drawbacks to using artificial sweeteners were greater than the benefits, then it would make perfect sense for fitness experts to recommend against them.

(A) While this is probably true, it is unreasonable to assume that fitness experts are lying to keep their jobs.

(B) This is true, but there are still reasons to want to avoid the negative effects of sugar. This is a good second-best choice, but it does not really address the reason why fitness experts do not recommend artificial sweeteners.

(D) Just because something can happen does not mean that it is likely to happen. If you eat enough vegetables, it has been proven that you will get fat. But this is not as likely as if you eat foods loaded with sugar.

(E) This fact is not relevant to the squib or to the paradox at issue.

Question 6

Squib: This squib says that after seatbelts were introduced, highway fatalities dramatically decreased. An interest group found that many people involved in accidents suffered seatbelt-related injuries that would not have occurred had there been no seatbelt. You are asked to find a reason why seatbelts should be retained even though they sometimes cause injury.

Question stem: It asks for a reason to keep seatbelts despite the incidence of seatbelt-related injuries.

Correct answer: D. If this is true, then the use of seatbelts is always beneficial since even when they cause harm, they actually prevent much worse harm from occurring.

(A) This would encourage people to ban seatbelts instead of keeping them in cars.

(B) This fact may or may not have anything at all to do with seatbelt use. In any case, you cannot use it as an argument for retaining seatbelts.

(C) "Expert opinion" is almost never the correct answer in this type of question. You are looking for an answer that makes logical sense; you are not looking for someone's opinion.

(E) The fact that seatbelts are required by law does not help you decide if they are still a good idea even if they sometimes cause injury.

Question 7

Squib: White tigers have been exiled from their old habitat into a new habitat where they have a hard time blending into the forests. This inability to hide or move stealthily has implications for their survival and hunting. But surprisingly, the tigers are thriving despite this disadvantage and are eating more prey now than they did before.

Question stem: You must choose the answer that explains why white tigers are able to catch and eat more prey in an environment in which they have a disadvantage.

Correct answer: B. If the prey animals have not yet identified the tigers as predators, then they can be caught and eaten more easily. This would account for the tigers' current hunting success.

(A) Just because the tigers have a certain genetic predisposition does not mean that their new habitat is more conducive to their hunting skills than their old one was.

(C) This change would not really explain why the tigers are more successful at hunting now than they were before. The answer choice would have to say that the prey animals were also slower and less intelligent in order for you to infer why the tigers are now more successful.

(D) Just because the tigers can blend into certain parts of the forest does not mean that they can blend into all or even most parts of the forest, which they would have to do if this were to explain why they are now more successful hunters.

(E) The truth of this statement is completely unrelated to the issue at hand.

3 "Strengthen" Questions

This type of question begins with a squib that is an argument leading to a conclusion or an explanation for a particular set of facts. There are two versions of this question type. We will call the first one the *"support" version*. In this version, the question stem asks for an answer choice that if true, would support the conclusion made in the argument. You should choose the answer choice that would make the argument most compelling, and you must choose an answer choice that would make the argument tenable no matter how preposterous the answer choice itself is. Remember, the question stem states "which of the following, *if true*," meaning that the test could require you to accept the truth of any statement for the purpose of the question. Here is an example of this type of question:

The rising temperatures of the ocean floor off the coast of Namibia have changed the aquatic environment drastically. A type of anemone that used to make its home in the warmer waters to the north has migrated to Namibia's southern waters and is proliferating at rapid rates. Currently the native species have not yet been disturbed by the new anemones' presence, but if the new anemones' rate of reproduction continues unchecked for nine more months, then the native anemone species will be overcome due to their inability to effectively compete for food or sunlight. The only way for us to reinstate the native anemones at the top of the cnidarian heirarchy would be to find a way to eradicate all new migratory anemones that are in Namibian waters before more time elapses.

Which one of the following, if true, supports the conclusion in the passage?

A number of answer choices could be correct for this question:

- In nine months' time, the population of migratory anemones will actually be three times what scientists have predicted if the anemones are not first eradicated.
- If left unchecked, the migratory anemones will completely cover the ocean floor within three months, edging out every other species of anemone.

- Each member of the migratory species of anemone releases a poison waste by-product that has the side effect of killing all neighboring cnidarian species within 100 miles.
- The migratory species of anemone carries a disease to which it is immune, but which will decimate the population of all neighboring anemones within a 1 mile radius.
- The native species of anemone will never be dominant again in Namibian waters if the migratory species of anemone is not eradicated.

Each of these answer choices, no matter how preposterous, could be the correct answer to this question. For this type of question, the correct answer always supports the argument in the squib. All the other answer choices will either be irrelevant or undermine the conclusion.

There is a second, more extreme form of this "strengthen" question type. We will call this the *"assumption" version*. It asks, "Which of the following is an *assumption*" that must be drawn in order for the argument to be valid. In other words, "This argument is flawed and unsupportable unless which of the following is definitely true?" Questions like this usually have a very limited number of possible answers. Here is an example:

A particular children's camp in the north woods of Georgia has two roads that enter the camp: a North road and an East road. Buses servicing the camp must use one or the other of the two roads. Off-roading is impossible due to the trees and ravines that border the campgrounds. On a particular day, a counselor named Sally decided that she wanted to take her campers to get ice cream in town. It is clear that Sally must have taken the East road.

For the argument to be logically correct, it must make which of the following assumptions?

There are only a few possible correct answers to this question. All of them must be reasons why Sally could not use the North road. Here are some possibilities:

- A tree fell across the North road last night, preventing its use.
- The camp director forbade using the North road to exit the camp this week.
- The bus that Sally drove is too wide to fit on the North road.
- Last week's mudslides carried away the pavement of the North road, rendering it completely impassable.

The following sample questions will help you understand more about the two versions of "strengthen" questions.

Sample "Strengthen" Questions

1. In a theocracy, politicians not only have to understand the laws of the land, but also the edicts of the god(s) or religion that their society follows. This type of understanding is difficult because it combines secular knowledge with the requisite of a more abstract and spiritual knowledge. Many people cannot adequately fulfill this dual requirement, which is why there are fewer total politicians in all the theocratic governments throughout the world than in all the democratic governments.

For the argument to be logically correct, it must make which of the following assumptions?

(A) There are not more democratic nations than theocratic nations in the world.
(B) Theocratic politicians need to assess the spirituality of their polity when making decisions.
(C) Theocratic nations satisfy the needs of their people better by using fewer politicians.
(D) Democratic nations require a larger number of politicians on average due to the numerous factions that their politicians represent.
(E) The edicts of any sort of god are not knowable or understandable as they apply to politics.

Squib: The argument claims that theocratic politicians have to understand both legal and spiritual rules. The argument further claims that this fact limits the number of people who have the potential to be theocratic politicians because so few have the ability to understand both kinds of rules. However, from there the argument makes a broad and unbased claim that, because a smaller percentage of people have the potential to be theocratic politicians, there must be fewer theocratic politicians in the world than democratic politicians. Without more information comparing democratic nations to theocratic nations, this logical leap is completely unfounded and therefore fallacious. In order to make this argument logical, there is something that you must assume about the relationship between democratic nations and theocratic nations.

Question stem: It asks you to find an assumption that would be necessary for the argument to be valid.

Correct answer: A. If the converse were true and there were more democratic nations in the world, then you might logically assume that this is the reason why there are more democratic politicians than theocratic politicians, not some limit on who is able to be a theocratic politician. However, if the number of democratic nations was the same as or less than the number of theocratic nations and there were still fewer theocratic politicians, then this fact would more likely be due to the reason given in the squib.

(B) While this is true, it does not affect the relationship between democratic and theocratic politicians, and so it cannot be the correct answer.

(C) This does not touch on the relationship between democratic and theocratic nations. The word *better* implies a comparison, not one between theocratic and democratic nations, but instead one between theocratic nations with more politicians and theocratic nations with fewer politicians.

(D) This choice offers a comparison between democratic nations and other kinds of nations, but there might still be fewer theocratic politicians simply because there are fewer theocratic nations.

(E) This is not really relevant because people strive to apply the rules regardless of whether they completely understand them. Furthermore, this choice has no bearing on the relative numbers of different kinds of politicians.

2. Daniel had a bad day yesterday and left the office without closing his door or turning his computer off the correct way. Unfortunately, the computer in Daniel's office controls the network of computers in the rest of the offices, and if it is not shut down in the proper way, then hackers are able to gain access to the rest of the company's computers. Last night, hackers gained access to Mary's computer, a computer in Daniel's office network. This occurrence must be partially Daniel's fault, since he did not turn his computer off properly.

Which of the following, if true, supports the conclusion in the passage?

(A) Daniel would not have left the office without turning off his computer properly if someone else in the office had not caused him to have a bad day.
(B) The network of computers in Daniel's office operates together in a cluster that has many access points.
(C) Hackers can enter into the office network by using any one of several widely available penetration techniques.
(D) A hacker could not access the office's computers unless Daniel failed to shut down his computer properly.
(E) Information about what the hacker did or saw in Mary's computer is available only to Daniel through his computer.

Squib: This squib tries to pin the guilt for a hacker break-in on Daniel, who forgot to shut off his computer properly because he had a bad day. As evidence for this conclusion, the squib says that hackers can gain access to the network if Daniel's computer is not shut down in the correct way. However, nothing is said about whether or not there are other ways for a hacker to enter the office network. Any correct answer that would support the conclusion must specify that a hacker break-in is possible *only* if Daniel fails to shut off his computer properly.

Question stem: It asks for a true statement that would support the conclusion that the hacker break-in was Daniel's fault.

Correct answer: D. This choice states the necessary condition that a hacker break-in is possible only if Daniel's computer is shut down improperly. The answer choice specifies that there would be no other way to gain access.

(A) This choice has no real meaning. It holds no implication for the hackers or their actions. It merely tries to spread the blame to other people.

(B) This would lead you to believe that there are numerous ways for a hacker to gain access to the network besides Daniel's computer. This is the opposite of what you are looking for.

(C) This choice says that hackers could access the office computers in many ways, so it does not support the argument that the break-in is exclusively Daniel's fault.

(E) This choice would lead you to believe that information about the break-in was recovered through Daniel's computer, but it does not provide enough information to pin the blame for the break-in on Daniel.

3. Any team that wins a championship must have practiced day in and day out throughout the entire season. Effective coaches are able to infuse their team with a desire for victory that is unrivaled. Therefore, in order to become champions, a team must have an effective coach.

In taking the position outlined, the author presupposes which of the following?

(A) Teams that are consistently victorious will win a championship at the end of the season.
(B) Effective coaches provide many benefits to a team besides getting them to practice more.
(C) Teams that do not have an effective coach will not practice day in and day out throughout the season.
(D) Desiring victory is the only motive that will make a team practice enough to win a championship.
(E) A team must practice harder than all other teams in its division in order to become champion for that season.

Squib: This squib sets up to sufficient-necessary statements that you must recognize in order to make a logical deduction. The first sentence makes one statement and the main conclusion makes another, and the correct answer choice is the one that will logically connect the two statements. Here are the statements diagrammed:

First sentence: Champion → Practice
Conclusion: Champion → Effective Coach

To connect the two statements, you must choose an answer that either states the main conclusion directly (Champion → Effective Coach) or that connects day-in,

day-out practicing with requiring an effective coach (Practice → Effective Coach).

Question stem: What is the author assuming in this argument?

Correct answer: C. This answer choice states that Practice → Effective Coach. This is exactly what you are looking for because it links the two chains and makes the main conclusion logical.

(A) This choice does not relate to either logical chain.

(B) This statement is irrelevant.

(D) This choice relates to one ability of effective coaches. However, this choice does not make the necessary link between having an effective coach and practicing enough to win a championship.

(E) This choice makes no reference to the link between a coach and team practice.

"Strengthen" Questions: Common Traits

Now that you have reviewed some sample "strengthen" questions, you should be able to recognize their common traits. These traits are listed in the following outline.

I. **General Format**
   1. Squib is three to seven sentences.
   2. Word count: 48–110.
   3. Questions may present an argument with a hole in it; you need to choose the answer choice that fills the hole.
   4. Questions may present a good argument; you need to pick the answer choice that supports the conclusion of the argument.

II. **Support Version**
   A. **Sample Question Stems**
      1. Which one of the following, if true, lends the most *support* to the position?
      2. Which of the following, if true, *supports the conclusion* in the passage?
   B. **Correct Answer**
      1. strengthens the argument in some way

   C. **Second-Best Choice**
      1. in some limited situations could strengthen the argument, but usually or does not always strengthen the argument
   D. **Clearly Wrong Answers**
      1. undermine the argument
      2. are true but irrelevant to the argument

III. **Assumption Version**
   A. **Sample Question Stems**
      1. Which one of the following is an *assumption* upon which the argument in the passage depends?
      2. Which one of the following is an *assumption* that would permit the conclusion above to be properly...?
   B. **Correct Answer**
      1. will be a fact that connects the facts in the squib to the conclusion
      2. is a piece of information that you must know in order to properly draw the conclusion
   C. **Second-Best Choice**
      1. provides more information about either the facts or the conclusion but does not relate the facts sufficiently to the conclusion
   D. **Clearly Wrong Answers**
      a. generally do not relate to either the facts or the conclusion
      b. generally provide a piece of information that relates to the subject matter of the squib but not to its logic

Now that you have seen some of the test makers' tricks, answer the following seven "strengthen" questions. Every correct answer and incorrect answer choice will match a particular point on the outline you just read. The same will be true for questions on the actual LSAT, so knowing the points on the outline will help you to identify correct answers quickly and consistently.

DRILL: "STRENGTHEN" QUESTIONS

1. A news flash went through city last year that police would begin to pay more attention to illegally parked vehicles. In fact, the police chief publicly stated that he was ordering a fourfold increase in the number of police patrols looking for illegally parked cars. But according to the city's fiscal statement for the past year, the money received from parking tickets was exactly the same as it had been the year before, while the money received from speeding tickets quadrupled. Therefore, it is evident that the police chief chose to increase the number of police scouting for speeders on the highway instead of increasing the number of police monitoring parking violations.

   Which of the following is an assumption on which the argument depends?

   (A) An increase in police officers monitoring parking violations would not lead to more tickets.
   (B) More people on average in the city speed than park their cars in illegal spaces.
   (C) People changed their parking habits based on the news flash about the parking violation crackdown.
   (D) The police do not have enough officers to cover both residential parking violations and highway speeding violations.
   (E) The money received for a violation is directly proportional to the number of police who monitor that violation.

2. Scientist: Ever since the price of gasoline rose sharply and then doubled at the end of last year, people have been consuming less gasoline. We are not sure how they achieved this reduction in consumption, but we have a good theory. To save gasoline, it is likely that fewer people have been taking cars to work and more people have been relying on means of public transportation like buses, trains, and airplanes.

   Which of the following, if true, would tend to support the scientist's theory?

   (A) There are no ways to save fuel besides taking public transportation.
   (B) Ticket sales on two major airlines have tripled to quadrupled over the past year.
   (C) Ticket sales for buses and trains did not vary from the levels that were considered normal in previous years.
   (D) No one during the past year has made any effort to conserve gasoline.
   (E) Next year, gas prices will return to the lower level of two years ago.

3. When French explorers first journeyed into Africa's interior in 1477, they noticed that the pygmy tribes did not use anything besides wooden spears to hunt. When English explorers first arrived in 1632, one of them noticed a young pygmy man hunting for a tiger with a sharp chiseled rock lashed to his wooden spear. Thus, we can be sure that pygmies first started hunting tigers between the years 1477 and 1632.

   The conclusion above depends on which of the following assumptions?

   (A) Pygmies now hunt many more types of animals than they did in 1477.
   (B) Pygmies did not hunt tigers with just wooden spears.
   (C) Pygmies did not use rocks for cooking in the era before the first French explorers arrived.
   (D) Pygmies hunt tigers for purposes that are different from the ceremonial purposes for which African Bushmen hunt elephants.
   (E) Pygmies made technological advances not related to hunting in the years between 1477 and 1632.

4. Active volcanoes can erupt with little to no warning. That is why it is never a good idea to live near a mountain that might be an active volcano. For homeowners everywhere, floods of lava are never a happy surprise. So if people can live in any geographic location they want, it is better to not live near any mountain because of the danger of eruption.

The argument will be logically drawn if we assume which of the following?

(A) It is a better idea to live on an earthquake fault line than near a volcano.
(B) Most people do not enjoy seeing floods of lava that are not near their house.
(C) Geographic location is an important factor in people's home-buying decisions.
(D) Active volcanoes and regular mountains are equally likely to produce eruptions.
(E) Scientists can predict with perfect certainty the date of any future volcanic activity in the world.

5. This political season, the most extensive political poll in history was taken in our nation. The question was simple: "Who do you think will win this year's election?" An impressive 80% of those surveyed returned the survey after choosing the incumbent with near-complete uniformity. Based on this survey, it is clear that Milton, the incumbent, will decisively win this election.

Which of the following, if true, would be the best evidence for the conclusion of the passage?

(A) The 20% who did not return the survey had the same opinion as the 80% who did return the survey.
(B) In general, incumbents win more elections than candidates who challenge them.
(C) Milton's only challenger is very unpopular with some political groups and factions of society.
(D) In a different country with different rules and a different voting scheme, the challenger would win an election against Milton.
(E) The vast majority of people will vote for the candidate who they feel has the best chance of winning the election.

6. Politicians use propaganda to bolster their campaigns instead of appealing to substantive issues on which they differ from their opponents. This propaganda trend makes a person's past and credibility more important in the election process than his or her political views or likely actions in office. This state of affairs is very unfortunate for our nation because candidates are elected on the basis of a series of 30-second commercials that focus on their personal character instead of on the quality of job that they will likely do in office.

Which of the following is an assumption that must be true in order for the conclusion to be logically formed?

(A) Propaganda reveals information not only about candidates' personalities but also about their policy positions and political views.
(B) People are able to look at information that is not propaganda and determine everything that a candidate will do while in office.
(C) The quality of a candidate's personal character and past is no indicator of the kind of job that he or she will do in office.
(D) Credibility and personal aspects of a candidate cannot be revealed by the propaganda circulated by an opposing party.
(E) Our nation would be better served by not allowing candidates to use television advertisements during the election process.

7. In preindustrial England, a certain species of moth was entirely white. Only genetic throwbacks of this species had colored wings. After the industrial revolution and 100 years had passed, researchers noticed that most members of this species of moth had developed gray wings. The white wings had allowed the moths to blend in with the pale rocks and white sand of the coast, but after the industrial revolution, white wings were not as good camouflage as they had been before. The change in wing color must be attributable to the soot of the industrial revolution, which caused the moths' habitat, the white rocks and sand, to turn gray.

Which of the following is an assumption that the conclusion of the argument depends upon?

(A) Gray moths can fly faster than white moths and are better able to avoid birds.
(B) The soot of the industrial revolution is the only reason why the rocks and sand turned gray.
(C) The rocks and sand were just as gray in preindustrial England as they are today.
(D) Moths that are best able to blend in with their habitats possess an evolutionary advantage.
(E) The presence or absence of factories in England held an implication for the diet of birds that lived on the coast.

ANSWERS AND EXPLANATIONS

Question 1

Squib: The police chief announced a fourfold increase in the number of police officers scouting for illegally parked cars. However, records show that there was no corresponding increase in parking tickets, but there was a fourfold increase in the money received from speeding tickets. As a result, the squib makes the assumption that (1) the number of police officers scouting for illegal parkers did not increase, and (2) the number of police officers on the highway increased.

Question stem: It asks for an assumption that is necessary for the argument to be logical.

Correct answer: E. If the money that is received for violations is directly proportional to the number of

police officers monitoring the violation, then the amount received would reveal any increase or decrease in the police force in certain areas. Since parking tickets did not change and speeding did, then no new police officers were assigned to parkers, but new police officers were assigned to speeders.

(A) This choice would mean that you would not be able to infer anything from the city's fiscal statement.

(B) The average number of people doing something does not matter when you are talking about an increase or decrease from the norm.

(C) This statement does not necessarily mean that people changed their parking habits enough for it to be significant. Furthermore, if this statement were true, it would undermine the argument since the same amount of money was collected for parking tickets even after people changed their parking habits.

(D) This assumption would be applicable to the argument and might even support the argument. However, it is not necessary for this statement to be true for the logic in the squib to be correct.

Question 2

Squib: The price of gasoline has increased and people have been consuming less of it. The scientist theorizes that people have achieved lower consumption levels by taking public transportation such as buses, trains, and airplanes.

Question stem: It asks for an answer choice that would support the scientist's conclusion.

Correct answer: A. It is stipulated that people have found ways to conserve gas. If the only ways to do so were those mentioned by the scientist, then the theory has to be correct.

(B) You cannot assume from this fact that people are relying less on cars. It may also be that while ticket sales for two airlines have increased, ticket sales for other airlines have declined, so the end result is a wash.

(C) This answer would tend to invalidate the scientist's conclusion.

(D) This answer would tend to undermine the scientist's conclusion.

(E) What gas prices will do in the future has no bearing on how people behaved during the past year in response to higher gas prices.

Question 3

Squib: Pygmies used only wooden spears for hunting before 1477. In 1632, a pygmy used a spear with a rock to kill a tiger. The squib argues that the pygmies started hunting tigers sometime between 1477 and 1632. For this to be true, there needs to be some link between pygmies hunting with rocks on their spears and pygmies first starting to hunt tigers. You must find an answer choice that makes that connection.

Question stem: The stem asks for an assumption that is necessary for the argument to be logical.

Correct answer: B. If the pygmies started hunting tigers only when they had developed spears with rocks, then you could be sure that they starting hunting tigers between 1477 and 1632.

(A) The fact that pygmies hunt more animals now than they did before does not mean that tigers were not hunted before 1477.

(C) What pygmies did with their cooking is irrelevant to the connection between their spears and tigers.

(D) This choice has no relevance at all.

(E) While this answer choice is excellent for the pygmies, it explicitly rules out any connection to hunting, so it is irrelevant to the relationship between hunting and tigers.

Question 4

Squib: The claim of this argument seems preposterous. It says that active volcanoes are very dangerous because they can erupt with no warning. From there, it recommends against living near volcanoes, because they could erupt. As a conclusion, the argument states that it is best not to live near any type of mountain at all because it might erupt. For this wild claim to be tenable, regular mountains must be liable to erupt just like volcanoes.

Question stem: It asks which assumption would be required for the argument to be logical.

Correct answer: D. If volcanoes and regular mountains are equally likely to erupt, then regular mountains would be just as dangerous as volcanoes. Therefore, it would be a bad idea to live near them.

(A) This choice does not refer to the relationship between volcanoes and mountains.

(B) This fact is true but irrelevant.

(C) People certainly do consider geographical location when choosing a home, but that does not mean that they refuse to live near any kind of mountain.

(E) If this statement were true, then it would not be dangerous to live near a volcano or any other kind of mountain because you would know if and when it was going to erupt. This predictability would actually encourage people to live near mountains.

Question 5

Squib: A political poll that had an 80% return rate had approximately 90 to 99% of respondents saying essentially, "I think the incumbent will win." Note that this is different from "I will vote for the incumbent." Based on this information, the author of the squib predicts that the incumbent will win the election. The only problem is that the poll did not ask respondents whom they will vote for, but only who they thought would win. Any correct answer choice will have to address this issue.

Question stem: The stem asks what assumption, if true, would support the conclusion.

Correct answer: E. If people actually vote for the candidate who they think will win the election, then, based on the poll, it is clear that Milton will win.

(A) If this statement were true, it would mean only that most people think that Milton will win. It says nothing about whether or not they will actually vote for him.

(B) This statement may be true, but it does not mean that you could make a prediction based on the results of this specific survey.

(C) This assertion is true of all politicians. Some people vehemently despise certain candidates and others admire them, depending on the voter's personal political views.

(D) It is impossible to extrapolate any conclusion from a country with a totally different voting scheme.

Question 6

Squib: This squib talks about how in today's political environment, elections are decided more on the basis of a person's past and credibility rather than on what policies he or she is likely to follow if elected. The squib assumes that this tendency is a bad thing. One particular assumption is needed to make this a tenable argument.

Question stem: It asks for an assumption that must be drawn for the squib to be logical.

Correct answer: C. This assumption is one of the few possible answers to this question. If a person's character and past are no indicators of what kind of job he or she will do in office, then commercials that address only these qualities would be completely worthless.

(A) This claim would undermine the argument because, if it were true, then commercials addressing character would give voters an idea about candidates' future job performance.

(B) This ability is irrelevant because, according to the squib, propaganda is all people have on which to base their views about a candidate.

(D) This choice would mean that the propaganda circulated by an opposing party is failing to achieve its intended effect. However, this does not mean that there is no link between the propaganda and a candidate's future job performance.

(E) Whether or not this statement is true, it does not address the lack of any connection between propaganda and a candidate's future job performance, so it cannot be the correct answer.

Question 7

Squib: This squib tells about a moth in England that used to have white wings before the start of the industrial revolution, but after the revolution began and 100 years passed, most members of the species had developed gray wings. The squib says that wing color helps the moths blend in with their environment, but it does not explain that good camouflage confers a genetic advantage. If it is, then the soot that turned the moths' habitat gray would be responsible for the change in the moths' wing color. But if it is not, then there is no logical reason why the moths' wings turned gray. The correct answer choice must address the idea that camouflage confers a genetic advantage.

Question stem: Choose an assumption that the argument depends upon.

Correct answer: D. This answer choice informs you that having good camouflage confers an evolutionary benefit to the moths: It helps them survive. Therefore, when the soot turned the rocks gray, moths that could best blend in with the new gray color were able to survive, and eventually the whole population had gray wings.

(A) This choice does not address the relationship between the gray soot and the moths' gray wings.

(B) This choice addresses the link between the soot and the color of the rocks, but it does not account for the moths' gray wings.

(C) This choice would actually undermine the conclusion of the argument because if this factor stayed constant, then the gray in the moths' wings would have to be the result of some other factor.

(E) This assertion does not necessarily mean that the birds' diet changed in regard to this particular moth species. There could have been several species of moths that developed better camouflage and therefore began making up a smaller share of the birds' diet.

4 "Weaken" Questions

This type of question is practically the opposite of the "strengthen" questions. Instead of asking for an answer choice that would strengthen the logic or conclusion of the argument, the question stem asks for an answer choice that would weaken the validity of the argument. Here is an example squib for a "weaken" question:

The term "generation X" is more of a concept present in the minds of the baby boom generation than a substantive description of the current youth of America. People growing up at different times have different experiences. These experiences give each new group certain idiosyncrasies that inevitably set them apart from prior generations. Labeling these characteristics with one overarching term does not aid in conceptualizing the multitudinous disparities that are actually present between generations. Due to these failings, we should hesitate to use generational labels because they provide no benefit to our society.

This paragraph is long and convoluted, but most correct answer choices will be very simple: They will undermine the conclusion of the paragraph. The conclusion was that people should avoid generational labels because they provide no benefit to our society. The following answer choices all undermine this conclusion:

- By utilizing generational labels, people gain insight about the background of members of the labeled generation.
- If society did not use generational labels, people would be generally worse off than they are now.
- Generational labels provide an excellent means of bolstering communication between young people and adults in America, thereby partially bridging the generation gap.

Each of these answer choices undermines the conclusion of the argument. Undermining the conclusion is the best way to weaken an argument. However, there are other ways of weakening arguments. A correct answer choice can undermine a fact that the conclusion relies upon. A correct answer choice can also

weaken supporting claims and subsidiary conclusions, thereby weakening the main conclusion. Here is an example of an answer choice that weakens a supporting claim of the conclusion:

- Labeling differences helps people conceptualize the disparities that exist between generations.

When faced with an answer choice that appears to weaken the evidence of an argument versus an answer choice that weakens the conclusion of the argument, you should always choose the answer choice that weakens the conclusion. That choice is the one that *most* undermines the argument as a whole.

Some "weaken" questions will ask you to pick the answer choice that weakens a specific part of the argument rather than the main conclusion. These questions are difficult because they oblige you to differentiate among the different parts of the argument and then decide which answer choice undermines the specified part.

Here are some sample questions to help you get acquainted with "weaken" questions.

Sample "Weaken" Questions

1. In the early 16th century, Copernicus proposed the novel idea that Earth revolves around the Sun. His ideas were disdained by the Church and monarchy who had always given credence to a geocentric model of the universe. Despite this contention, Copernicus rested his conclusions on geometry and mathematical models that all seemed to uphold his new heliocentric model. The Church sought to disprove his model by hiring its own mathematicians, who eventually reached the finding that the Sun still revolved around Earth.

   Which one of the following, if true, would most weaken Copernicus's and the Church's arguments?

   (A) Earth revolves around the Sun in an elliptical orbit that can only be modeled by trigonometry and geometry.

(B) The experimental mathematical techniques known in Copernicus's time were incapable of modeling data from space.

(C) Both Copernicus and the Church could have proved that the sun is not stationary in the sky but instead travels longitudinally through space at a constant speed.

(D) Both Copernicus and the Church strongly desired to demonstrate the accuracy of their views to the public.

(E) For many years, the geocentric model of the universe was considered correct, and it took until Copernicus's time for people to start giving credence to the heliocentric model.

Squib: This passage explains that Copernicus developed a mathematically based model to prove that the Earth revolves around the Sun (the heliocentric model). The Church and the king did not want to abandon their old beliefs, so the Church hired mathematicians who used a different mathematically based model to prove that the Sun revolves around Earth (the geocentric model).

Question stem: The stem asks which answer choice would undermine both Copernicus's and the Church's arguments.

Notice that this question stem specifies the *arguments* and not the conclusions that the model is either heliocentric or geocentric. Instead, the passage asks for an answer choice that would weaken both sides' methods of reaching their conclusions.

Correct answer: B. Both sides arrived at their conclusion through the use of mathematical techniques. If the techniques known at the time were incapable of modeling information from space, then neither the Church nor Copernicus would be able to make a supportable conclusion based on math.

(A) This choice would not undermine Copernicus's argument. Instead, it seems to explicitly agree with it.

(C) What could have been proved is irrelevant to the validity of both arguments.

(D) This is the second-best choice because it implies that both sides might have incorrectly interpreted data in order to support their conclusions. However, this is not the best answer choice because unethical behavior on Copernicus's part is unlikely.

(E) Other people's opinions do not really hold any implication for the ways in which the Church and Copernicus arrived at their conclusions.

2. Studies of retinal capacity and ocular degeneration in mice have demonstrated that a full 90% of the human population would go blind if humans were consistently able to live past the age of 175. Interestingly, the same is not true for chimps. Studies have shown that the older chimps get, the better their eyesight becomes. In fact, mother chimps almost always possess better eyesight than their young offspring. Based on these observations, it appears that if chimps were able to reach the age of 175, then the eyesight of most chimps passing this age mark would likely be quite good.

Which one of the following, if true, would tend to invalidate the conclusion?

(A) The studies done on humans and mice were conducted only with specimens that already had poor eyesight.

(B) Poor eyesight would be a greater detriment to a chimp living in a natural environment than to a human who enjoys the comforts of society.

(C) The life-extending hormones that would be needed to enable a chimp to live past 175 have not yet been designed.

(D) Chimp eyesight improves until sexual maturity around the age of 20, but then it begins to deteriorate rapidly.

(E) Ninety percent of chimps will have perfect eyesight for the whole of their natural lives.

Squib: The squib gives you a number of facts. If humans were to live past 175, then 90% would go blind. The squib then claims that the eyesight of chimps gets better as they age. In the last sentence, the squib makes the conclusion that because the average chimp's eyesight improves with age, then it is likely to continue to improve, or at least not worsen in chimps passing the 175-year mark.

Question stem: It asks for an answer choice that would undermine the conclusion.

Correct answer: D. This answer choice states that after sexual maturity at 20, the eyesight of chimps begins to deteriorate rapidly. Based on this data, you could reasonably infer that chimps reaching over eight times this age would have very poor to no eyesight.

(A) This choice might invalidate the applicability of the studies, but it would not invalidate the conclusion of the studies as well as choice D would. That is because the final conclusion is not really based on the studies, but on a separate observation—that the eyesight of chimps improves with age.

(B) This contention is completely unrelated to the conclusion of the argument or to any ancillary point of the argument.

(C) This is also true for humans, but since we are admittedly dealing with a hypothetical situation, this fact is not relevant.

(E) If anything, this choice would tend to support the conclusion. Even though living to age 175 might not be considered "natural life," it would still be compelling that chimp eyesight maintains itself this well.

3. Books should never be published before being proofread by the publisher, unless the author is very concerned about how his or her book is viewed by the public. This is because authors who are concerned about public perception will be sure to do their best to completely correct their book before even submitting it for publication. Therefore, there is never a reason to proofread a book whose author is concerned about public perception.

Which of the following would call the conclusion of the passage into question?

(A) Some authors who are concerned about public perception are not capable of proofreading their own work effectively.
(B) Authors in general care more about the public perception of themselves and their lives than their publishers do.
(C) If authors were always to proofread their books effectively, there would be no need for publishers.
(D) Publishers do not do as good a job of proofreading manuscripts as do authors who are concerned about public perception.
(E) The book industry standard is for publishers to correct and proofread a book even when an author is concerned about public perception.

Squib: This squib essentially states only one idea: Authors who are concerned about public perception will always do their best to proofread their book effectively before submitting it to their publisher. This leads to the conclusion that it is not necessary to proofread the works of these perfectionist authors.

Question stem: Choose an answer choice that undermines the conclusion that a publisher need not proofread all books before publication.

Correct answer: A. This would be a good reason to proofread all books, especially those by authors who are concerned about public perception, because some members of this group are incapable of removing all errors from their manuscripts.

(B) This claim is definitely true in general, but it does not relate to the merits of proofreading.

(C) This assertion does not deal with the reality that many authors do not effectively proofread their books, thereby creating a need for publishers to do so.

(D) If this statement were true, then it would support the conclusion because this group of authors proofreads manuscripts better than a publisher.

(E) Current industry standards are not a compelling reason to maintain the status quo when there is no demonstrable reason for doing so.

"Weaken" Questions: Common Traits

Now that you have reviewed some sample "weaken" questions, you should be able to recognize their common traits. These traits are listed in the following outline.

I. **General Format**
   1. Squib is three to seven sentences.
   2. Word count: 48–110.
   3. In general, the squib presents an argument that is fairly strong, so you will have a hard time picking an answer choice that weakens it.
   4. Be wary of question stems that ask you to select the choice that weakens a particular part of an argument.

II. **Sample Question Stems**
   1. Which one of the following *conflicts* with information in the passage?
   2. Which one of the following, if true, would *weaken* the argument?
   3. Which one of the following, if true, is the strongest *defense* against the argument?
   4. Which one of the following, if true, would *cast doubt* on the conclusion?

III. **Correct Answer**
   1. invalidates the main conclusion or the part of the argument that was specified by the question stem

IV. Second-Best Choice

1. undermines parts of the argument other than the conclusion or the specified part of the argument
2. undermines the general context of the argument, conclusion, or discussion without actually undermining the argument itself

V. Clearly Wrong Answers

1. **support** the squib
2. are **not relevant** to supporting or undermining the squib
3. refer to the **same subject matter** as the squib but do not specifically undermine any part of the argument
4. use a **moral outcry** or **appeal** to **authority** to undermine the argument

Now that you have seen some of the test makers' tricks, answer the following seven "weaken" questions. Every correct answer and incorrect answer choice will match a particular point on the outline you just read.

DRILL: "WEAKEN" QUESTIONS

1. The homecoming of American soldiers after World War II was supposedly followed by a dramatic increase in the birthrate commonly known as the "baby boom." But this "boom" has been overdramatized. Statistics for the average birthrate over the 10-year period encompassing the war and early postwar period show no unusual increase. Instead, the birthrate merely continued the slow, steady rise that had begun in the 1870s.

   Which of the following, if true, most seriously undermines this conclusion that the baby boom has been overstated?

   (A) Statistics for the 10-year period should have shown a drop in the birthrate, but they failed accurately to depict this trend.
   (B) The birthrate is only one aspect of the cultural phenomenon known as the baby boom.
   (C) Many women had children in the year or two following their husbands' return from the war.
   (D) The term *baby boom* has been in common use ever since the end of World War II.
   (E) The dramatic increase in the birthrate would have been evident in statistics covering just the five-year period following the war.

2. Critic: Since the late 1980s, many advances in automotive technology have made people nationwide feel safer in their cars and on the roads. The auto industry claims that airbags and antilock brakes decrease the chances that serious injury will result from a car crash, but I have yet to see statistics that support such claims. Quite the contrary, figures from the 1990s show that despite these new technologies, deaths and injuries on the highways continue to climb. This irrefutable trend makes it clear that there are no genuine benefits to airbags or antilock brakes.

   The following would undermine the critic's conclusion EXCEPT:

   (A) Feeling safer on the roadways causes people to drive more recklessly.
   (B) There were more drivers on the roads in the 1990s than in the 1980s.
   (C) People in the 1990s were on average more likely to drive while intoxicated or while using narcotics than people were in the 1980s.
   (D) No one throughout the nation drove a car with either antilock brakes or an airbag during the 1990s.
   (E) Head-on collision tests show that airbags frequently fail to inflate when needed.

3. Learning how to acquire food is an important part of a young lion cub's life, but hunting is a difficult skill for mother lionesses to teach. Cubs are unable to practice their hunting skills on the savannah because the grassland is filled with other savage animals that could easily kill a neophyte hunter. For this reason, lionesses encourage their cubs to engage in "play fighting," an activity that helps the young lions build up their defensive skills while still under their mother's protection. Some child psychologists make an analogy between the lion cubs' predicament and that of human children. On these grounds, they recommend that parents encourage their children to fight with one another at home in order to prepare them adequately for preschool.

Which of the following, if accurate, would most undermine the advisability of these psychologists' recommendation?

(A) Preschool is a tough place and children often get into fights, so they should be prepared.
(B) Fights in preschool are often won by the child who was best prepared at home in accordance with the recommendations of these psychologists.
(C) Children should not fight to solve their problems because there are other ways to find solutions.
(D) Children who are allowed to fight at home with their siblings cannot be considered to be adequately prepared for preschool.
(E) Human children are different from lion cubs and therefore have many different needs and requirements that need to be fulfilled in order to grow up properly.

4. A popular restaurant guide rates the quality of different restaurants according to how long it takes the cooks to prepare customers' food. The guide's authors say that their purpose is to give the average consumer the benefit of knowing which restaurants serve food of a superior quality.

Which of the following, if true, would most tend to invalidate the use of the guide's rating system?

(A) The quality of a restaurant's food is not necessarily tied to how long it takes a cook to prepare it.
(B) Culinary ratings tend to be so subjective that they never accurately depict the objective quality of any specific restaurant's food.
(C) It may take longer to prepare certain types of dishes than it does to prepare other types that are of a superior quality.
(D) The stopwatch broke during some of the time trials, but the authors of the guide still published the data.
(E) Restaurants should be given fair warning before their food preparation is timed in order for them to prepare for the challenge.

5. The principal at Ames Middle School hired a new math teacher, Mr. Jordan, after the former math teacher retired. After Mr. Jordan had worked for a year, the principal received some unsavory reviews of his performance. In fact, five letters were received from students, all stating that they hated Mr. Jordan. The principal took these statements to heart and fired Mr. Jordan, assuming that if a few students did not like Mr. Jordan, then most others felt the same way.

All of the following, if true, cast doubt on the advisability of the principal's decision to fire Mr. Jordan EXCEPT:

(A) Students who like a teacher are much less likely to tell anyone about it than students who dislike a teacher.
(B) Most students who took Mr. Jordan's class hated the subject matter.
(C) Principals throughout the state receive an average of 10 complaint letters about each math teacher every year.
(D) The five letters did not explicitly state the name of the disliked teacher, but the principal assumed that since there had never been complaints about anyone before, the students must have been referring to Mr. Jordan.
(E) All teachers throughout the state get at least five complaint letters in their first year of teaching at a new school.

6. Solar panels produce electric power through the use of two purified silicon plates. When the sun shines on the top silicon plate, electrons are bumped off negative ions and are forced to travel through a wire to the plate on the other side. However, this wire does not lead the electrons to the positive ions residing in the opposite silicon plate; instead, the wire diverts them away into a battery that stores the electrons in the form of potential energy. When the power goes out in a house that uses solar power, the average person assumes that this is because the battery has run out.

Which of the following, if true, would make this a faulty assumption?

(A) During inclement weather, solar cells do not receive enough light to provide adequate power to a battery to support a house.
(B) A wire that connects the battery to the house is frayed and is then snapped by the weather.
(C) Solar panels are more technologically advanced than batteries and are therefore less likely to break than batteries.
(D) Batteries for solar-powered homes tend to run out every night after the sun has been down for a couple of hours.
(E) Every five years, solar cells need to be cleaned and possibly replaced in order to capture energy from sunlight.

7. Scientist: Astrology's predictive methods are as novel as they are uncanny: Soothsayers use star signs and monthly formations of the constellations to read omens and foretell the future. For years the reality of astrology has been shrouded in myth, but my research conclusively demonstrates that some astrologers are able to predict the future. My evidence centers on the fact that some predictions by astrologers definitely do come true.

Which of the following, if true, would most undermine the persuasiveness of the scientist's evidence?

(A) There are so many astrologers predicting so many things that some predictions are bound to come true merely by the laws of chance.

(B) The predictive ability of star signs is directly related to the predictive ability of stellar formations.

(C) Some astrologers cannot predict the future even though they claim to.

(D) Some people who do not claim to be astrologers have been known to consistently and accurately predict future events.

(E) The predictions of most astrologers never come true when the specified future time arrives.

ANSWERS AND EXPLANATIONS

Question 1

Squib: The main point of this passage is that on average, there was no dramatic increase in the birthrate during the 10-year period covering World War II and the immediate postwar years, so the whole idea of the baby boom is a myth. However, this average includes statistics for the war years, when husbands were overseas and birthrates were very low. Consequently, it is no surprise that the average for this whole 10-year period does not show an unusual increase. If, on the other hand, the writer had calculated the average for just the immediate postwar years, the picture would likely be dramatically different.

Question stem: The stem asks for an answer choice that would undermine the argument that the baby boom was overstated.

Correct answer: E. According to this answer choice, the baby boom would be evident if you averaged the birthrates for just the five postwar years, not for the

10-year span that includes the war. This approach makes logical sense and greatly undermines the argument that the baby boom is a myth.

(A) This choice would not undermine the conclusion that there was no baby boom. In fact, it might even support it.

(B) This statement is irrelevant because you are considering the existence of the baby boom itself, not its many cultural aspects.

(C) This choice is definitely true, but it does not necessarily prove that more women than usual had children during those years.

(D) The fact that the term baby boom has long been in common use does not necessarily invalidate an argument based on statistics.

Question 2

Squib: According to this passage, there are now many new automobile safety features, yet paradoxically, there are more deaths and injuries on the highways than ever before. Based on this information, the critic claims that the new features do not make drivers any safer.

Question stem: The stem asks for the only choice that *does not* undermine the critic's conclusion. *Note:* This turns into a "strengthen" question because of the use of "EXCEPT."

Correct answer: E. This choice provides concrete evidence that airbags do not necessarily make drivers safer. This supports the critic's argument that airbags are not effective.

(A) This choice implies that highway injuries rose, not because safety features were ineffective, but because people were driving more recklessly. This claim undermines the critic's argument.

(B) This choice implies that highway injuries rose, not because safety features were ineffective, but because there were more drivers on the road. This assertion undermines the critic's argument.

(C) This choice implies that highway injuries rose, not because safety features were ineffective, but because more people were driving while intoxicated. This statement undermines the critic's argument.

(D) This choice implies that highway injuries rose, not because safety features were ineffective, but because no one had those features. This claim undermines the critic's argument.

Question 3

Squib: This passage tells how lion cubs learn survival skills by fighting with one another. Mother lionesses encourage this behavior because of the benefits that it entails. At the end of the squib, there is a huge leap from lion society to human society. Child psychologists recommend that parents allow their children to fight with one another at home so that the children will be prepared—in terms of combat skills—for preschool.

Question stem: Choose the answer choice that undermines the psychologists' recommendation that parents encourage their children to fight.

Correct answer: D. If children who fight with one another at home cannot be "considered to be adequately prepared" for preschool, then this assertion completely undermines the conclusion of the passage.

(A) This choice would support the conclusion of the passage and encourage parents to teach their children combat skills.

(B) This choice would support the conclusion of the passage, especially if you assume that winning fights constantly in preschool is a positive thing.

(C) This choice argues against fighting in general, but it does not rule out having children prepare for preschool by learning combat skills. Choice D is a better answer.

(E) This statement is true, but it does not mean that human children and lion cubs do not have similar needs in some situations.

Question 4

Squib: The quality of a restaurant's food is judged entirely by the speed at which it is prepared. More than likely this is not a good way to judge food, especially when it is the only criterion. A correct answer choice will likely point to this idea.

Question stem: Find the answer choice that invalidates the use of preparation speed to determine culinary quality.

Correct answer: A. This choice means that the whole premise of the survey is false. That would utterly invalidate the rating system used by the restaurant guide.

(B) The ratings in the guide are not subjective because they are made by a timer. Therefore, this answer choice does not apply to this scenario.

(C) This claim does not make a significant difference, because it is probable that at times the converse is also true.

(D) The fact that the stopwatch broke during the preparation trials does nothing to invalidate the underlying premise of the rating system.

(E) This is merely an emotional appeal to be fair to restaurants. It is irrelevant to the validity of the rating system.

Question 5

Squib: A new math teacher came to a certain school. At the end of his first year, the principal received five bad reviews about the teacher's performance, and then the principal fired him based on those reviews, assuming that most students disliked the new teacher because five people had reviewed him negatively.

Question stem: Choose the answer choice that *does not* cast doubt on the principal's decision to fire the new teacher. *Note*: This turns into a "strengthen" question because of the use of "EXCEPT."

Correct answer: B. The fact that most children hated the subject matter of the class is largely unrelated to the quality of the teacher. Therefore, this fact would not undermine the principal's decision.

(A) This assertion implies that there might be numerous students who liked the new teacher but did not state their opinion. This would cast doubt on the principal's decision to fire the new teacher based only on five negative reviews.

(C) This fact would mean that the new teacher did much better than the average math teacher and therefore should probably not be fired.

(D) This assumption might well be invalid, depending on the size of the school. It would not be a good idea to fire someone on the basis of five reviews that could all refer to different teachers.

(E) This statement implies that five negative reviews is about average for a new teacher—and definitely not grounds for him or her to be fired.

Question 6

Squib: This squib carries a large amount of technical information that is all irrelevant to the conclusion. This conclusion is merely that most people who live in solar-powered homes assume that when the power goes out, it is the fault of the battery.

Question stem: What would make the conclusion of these homeowners faulty?

Correct answer: B. If there were a break in the wire, the power outage would not be the fault of the battery, so the homeowners' conclusion would be invalid.

(A) This choice describes one reason a battery can fail, so it supports the homeowner's conclusion.

(C) This choice makes it more likely that the battery is the culprit, so it supports the homeowner's conclusion.

(D) This choice describes a reason a battery can fail, so it supports the homeowner's conclusion.

(E) This choice is irrelevant to any assertion about why the power might fail.

Question 7

Squib: In this passage, a scientist postulates that some astrologers can predict the future. The evidence offered in favor of this argument is exceptionally weak: The scientist merely says that some predictions by astrologers do, in fact, come true. You are asked to select a statement that undermines this weak evidence.

Question stem: What undermines the scientist's evidence?

Correct answer: A. This choice says that even some random predictions are bound to come true just by chance. That means that the scientist's evidence is too weak to support the stated conclusion.

(B) Even if true, this idea is completely unrelated to the argument in the passage.

(C) This choice would not undermine the argument, because the scientist claims only that some predictions (not all of them) come true.

(D) This choice would tend to be either irrelevant to the passage or that some predictions do come true.

(E) This claim does not mean that some astrologers cannot predict the future. It only means that most cannot.

5 Reasoning Strategy Questions

This type of logical reasoning question analyzes the argument's structure and asks about the method that the author utilizes to support his or her point. To respond correctly to this type of question, you need to have a good working knowledge of the parts of an argument. Review the explanation of argument parts in section 1 conclusion questions if you have trouble remembering which parts of an argument are which.

Reasoning strategy questions come in two versions. We call the most common version the "correct argument" version, because the squib presents an argument that appears to be tenable. Here is an example:

> Dave's dynamo shop has been in business for the past 20 years and he has become the major supplier of dynamos for Wichita County. Over the past couple of years, his shop has become so dominant that nobody in Wichita County ever orders dynamos from anyone but Dave. Dave has recognized this fact and has increased his prices threefold in order to take advantage of his monopoly. However, people do not like paying an unfair amount for their products and will stop frequenting shops that charge unfair prices for a product. Because Dave is charging an unfair amount for his major product, it is likely that he will lose some of his business to any competitors who emerge in his market area.
>
> The fact that people hate to pay an unfair amount for products plays which one of the following roles in the argument?

This argument is a valid one because people hate to pay too much and will look for other options if any are available. This would cause Dave to lose some business. The question stem could lead to the following possible answer choices:

> - It is a premise that supports the conclusion.
> - It is a piece of evidence that supports the idea that Dave will lose business due to his unfair prices.
> - It is a supporting claim.

Notice that the question stem indicates a particular part of the argument and asks about its function. To answer these questions correctly, you need to be able to determine the identity and function of each part of an argument.

The second version of reasoning strategy questions we will call the "flawed argument" version. In these questions, the squib contains logic that is flawed. Here is an example of a flawed argument and a corresponding question stem:

> Today Abraham set out to observe a flock of seagulls on the beach. As he was walking, he tripped and fell on the sand. The sand was very coarse and dry, and a couple of grains got in his eyes. As he was trying to wash the sand out of his eyes, he accidentally washed both of his contacts out. He tried to find them in the ocean, but success in doing so of course was impossible. He walked around for awhile after that, but eventually returned home. It is safe to say that Abraham did not get to do what he set out to do today.
>
> A flaw in the reasoning in the argument above is that this argument . . .

This argument makes the assumption that because Abraham did not have contacts in his eyes, he could not observe a flock of seagulls. This assumption is too broad to be supportable, so you need to find an answer choice that points out this fact. Here are some possibilities:

> - relies on an unsupportable assumption
> - assumes that Abraham did not observe a flock of seagulls before losing his contacts
> - assumes that Abraham did not go back home to replace his contacts and come back to the beach to observe the seagulls
> - takes it for granted that Abraham could not see the seagulls without his contacts

Logical arguments can have many different kinds of flaws. Identifying the flaws may take practice, but if you work through enough sample problems you can eventually develop a certain knack for it. If you think you need more practice with this question type than

is provided in this book, be sure to visit the Curve-breakers Web site ([www. curvebreakers.com](www.curvebreakers.com)) for supplementary materials.

Note that for many LSAT takers, reasoning strategy questions take a little longer to answer than other kinds of logical reasoning questions.

Sample Reasoning Strategy Questions

1. Creatine is a dietary supplement that has gained popularity with competitive athletes over the last decade. The short-term effects of this supplement are readily evident—athletes grow very strong in a short amount of time. Scientists have yet to determine the long-term ramifications of this supplement since there are no long-term data available. The chemical makeup of the supplement partly resembles ADP, which is a chemical that has existed safely in human bodies for millennia, so it is safe to assume that Creatine is entirely beneficial.

   A flaw in the argument is that the author

   (A) implies that there are health-related risks involved in not using Creatine.
   (B) appeals to scientific data and chemical structure to support the point that Creatine is safe.
   (C) makes a claim about popularity when people's tastes are difficult to determine.
   (D) assumes that Creatine is entirely beneficial without enough evidentiary support.
   (E) assumes that using Creatine for just a short period of time will produce some benefits.

Squib: This argument refers to a dietary supplement called Creatine. Questions as to the safety of Creatine have arisen, but the chemical makeup partly resembles ADP, which exists safely in the body in large amounts. Based on this similarity and on the safety of ADP, the author assumes that the whole chemical makeup of Creatine must be safe. This is a flawed assumption.

Question stem: It asks for a flaw in the argument.

Correct answer: D. There is not enough evidence to assume that Creatine is entirely safe. Just because part of the compound resembles a certain compound found naturally in the body does not mean that the entire supplement is safe.

(A) The author does not imply that there are risks involved in not taking Creatine. People have done this for centuries and survived well enough.

(B) This statement is true, but this part of the argument is well fashioned because scientific data are one of the few means available to determine whether Creatine is safe.

(C) The claim that is made about popularity is not related to the conclusion of the argument.

(E) The benefits are not assumed but instead are readily visible in athletes who "grow very strong in a short amount of time."

2. Religious fundamentalists ostentatiously exhibit the most extreme opinions espoused by adherents of their specific religious sect. However, examining these extreme views is useful in learning more about the views of the other, more moderate members of their religion because the belief systems of all members of a religion are in complete concordance.

   Which of the following is a flaw in the argument?

   (A) It assumes that all members of a particular religion espouse identical beliefs.
   (B) It assumes that it is easier to identify the opinions of religious extremists.
   (C) The author implies that there is some accord between a person's actions and beliefs.
   (D) A single religion can appeal to diverse sets of people.
   (E) The author ignores the fact that religious extremism is harmful to most people.

Squib: This passage states that fundamentalists hold the most extreme opinions of their particular religious groups. It goes on to state that analyzing extreme opinions helps you to learn about more moderate opinions within the religious group. This claim is supported by an assumption that is too far reaching: The belief systems of all members of a religion are the same.

Question stem: The stem asks for a flaw in the argument.

Correct answer: A. This is a restatement of the final assumption on which the conclusion is based. This has to be the correct answer, because all other parts of the squib are logically sound.

(B) This is probably a good assumption because extremists "ostentatiously" exhibit their opinions.

(C) This is a good assumption.

(D) If this statement is true, then it is not a flaw in the argument. Instead, it points out why the argument might be flawed.

(E) The author does ignore this idea, but it is not relevant to the conclusion of the passage.

3. Gene therapy is a new technology that has the potential of combating many forms of disease. However, legislation has been enacted categorically to prohibit the use of gene therapy in medical treatment. Voters are afraid that if society permits the manipulation of our genetic code through gene therapy, then society will stumble down a slippery slope and eventually tolerate the use of genomics to influence the characteristics of our children. Instead of placating voters by forbidding positive applications of gene therapy, we should strive to find a middle ground that permits beneficial uses of this new technology but also protects against its dangers.

The idea that society should find a middle ground plays which of the following roles in the argument?

(A) It is the conclusion of the argument.
(B) It is a general principle on which the conclusion rests.
(C) It is a piece of evidence that supports the conclusion.
(D) It is unachievable scenario inserted for the purpose of analogy.
(E) It is a particular example of the general proposition being examined.

Squib: This is a supportable argument. It claims that society is losing out on the many possible benefits of gene therapy because voters are afraid that allowing any kind of gene therapy will open the way to dangerous applications of genomics. The conclusion of the passage is that society should find a middle ground that would allow for beneficial uses of gene therapy while protecting against its dangers.

Question stem: What is the function of the sentence that states that society should find a middle ground?

Correct answer: A. This is the conclusion of the argument, because it is the idea that all points in the argument lead to and support.

(B) It is not a general principle.

(C) No piece of evidence is offered in this sentence.

(D) There is no reason to think that the scenario proposed in the sentence is unachievable.

(E) This is not an example of anything, and there is no general proposition that is outlined elsewhere in the squib.

Reasoning Strategy Questions: Common Traits

Now that you have reviewed some sample reasoning strategy questions, you should be able to recognize their common traits. These traits are listed in the following outline.

I. **General Format**
   1. Squib is three to seven sentences.
   2. Word count: 48–110.
   3. Presents an argument that is either correct or flawed and asks you to identify the parts of the argument or the flaw.

II. **"Correct Argument" Version**
   A. **Sample Question Stems**
      1. Which one of the following *argumentative strategies* is used above?
      2. In the passage, the author does which one of the following?
      3. A specific topic figures in the argument in which one of the following ways?
   B. **Correct Answer**
      1. correctly identifies the part of the argument to which the specified sentence belongs
      2. correctly identifies the strategy that the author uses to make his or her point
   C. **Second-Best Choice**
      1. describes the specified sentence, but not in a way that is as accurate as another answer choice does
      2. explains why the argument is well founded instead of identifying the strategy that is used to make the argument
   D. **Clearly Wrong Answers**
      1. identify the wrong part of the argument
      2. identify a nonexistent part of the argument
      3. mislabel the specified part of the argument

III. "Flawed Argument" Version

A. Sample Question Stems
1. A *flaw* in the argument is that the author . . .
2. Which one of the following indicates an *error* in the *reasoning* leading to the prediction above?

B. Correct Answer
1. accurately identifies the flaw in the argument.

C. Second-Best Choice
1. explains the reason why the argument is wrong instead of identifying the specific flaw
2. identifies a flaw in the argument that is not directly related to the conclusion of the argument

D. Clearly Wrong Answers
1. identify irrelevant parts of the passage
2. identify strong points of the argument
3. imply flaws that are not present in the argument

Now that you have seen some of the test makers' tricks, answer the following seven reasoning strategy questions. Every correct answer and incorrect answer choice will match a particular point on the outline you just read.

DRILL: REASONING STRATEGY QUESTIONS

1. Old man: Tales of ghosts and other spiritual phenomena that make the news are usually dreamed up by country bumpkins or other people with too much time on their hands. The ghost of the *Mississippi River Belle* supposedly plagued a number of riverboat captains on their trips down the Mississippi in the 1960s, but as with all these stories, it turned out that a couple of young hooligans were causing all the ruckus. The same is true for the crop circles that have been sprouting up in fields across Mississippi this year—I saw my son and a couple of his friends making the circles last night, trying to create a great "hoax." Any reasonable person would understand that tales of ghosts throughout the country are created in the same way, not by phantasmal creatures, but by juveniles looking to stir up some fun.

The assertion that the *Mississippi River Belle* ghost was a hoax serves which of the following functions in the argument?

(A) It is the argument's conclusion.
(B) It is a piece of evidence offered in support of the conclusion.
(C) It is a subsidiary conclusion on which the main conclusion is based.
(D) It is a reiteration of the main point for the purpose of emphasis.
(E) It is an inference from a general premise.

2. The current proposal to drill for oil in Alaska is not the answer to our nation's oil needs. The proposal's supporters are the notorious RefineCo and GasPump corporations that have been looking for new places to drill for the past half-century and have never been satisfied with the amount of oil they have been able to extract. Their dissatisfaction is likely to continue, so there is no reason to destroy another wildlife refuge to appease their greed.

A flaw in the argument is that the author

(A) supports the conclusion by relying entirely on a circular argument.
(B) avoids addressing the merits of the proposal by focusing on the proposal's supporters.
(C) uses emotionally charged words like *notorious* and *greed* that must never be used in an argument.
(D) assumes that there is no implication for the future in past events.
(E) fails to identify nonexistent evidence used to contradict the conclusion.

3. Pop stars are like shooting stars: their fame is brilliant for a number of minutes before they fall off into obscurity, never to be heard from again. If you want to achieve long-term fame in the music industry, then you must find a way to make your name known to as few people as possible, for otherwise you and your band will banished to the unknown within a year.

Which of the following is a flaw in the argument?

(A) It omits unfounded assertions.
(B) It mistakes a sufficient condition for a necessary condition.
(C) It mistakes a cause for an effect.
(D) It offers contradictory advice.
(E) It draws an analogy between ideas that are not comparable.

4. Mohandas Gandhi was an Indian holy man who advocated the use of nonviolent protests to defy the British colonial authorities. His methods earned respect from foreign leaders because he was able to take the moral high road, protesting abuse while transcending it, as opposed to giving in to anger and reciprocating the violence unleashed by the authorities. Gandhi's success set an example for many future leaders such as Martin Luther King, Jr., who brought Gandhi's method to America. Without Gandhi's thoughtful teachings, it is unlikely that the civil rights protests in America would have been largely nonviolent.

The statement that Martin Luther King, Jr., was influenced by Gandhi's teachings figures into the argument in which one of the following ways?

(A) It is a misconstrued syllogism that supports the conclusion.
(B) It is the main conclusion of the passage.
(C) It is a subsidiary conclusion of the passage.
(D) It supports two other claims in the argument and is supported by other claims.
(E) It is an assertion that cannot be valid for the conclusion to be correct.

5. At its point of foundation, a society has a number of choices to make. Which values does it want to incorporate into its legal doctrine? Which economic system would be most equitable for its people? Above and beyond these questions is the most important one: How should leaders be chosen? Creating a stable mechanism that ensures that good people will lead is of utmost importance. For no matter how well designed the system is, it will not bring about "good" when it is run by evil people.

The assertion that a system run by evil people will not bring about good serves which one of the following functions in the argument?

(A) It is a piece of supporting evidence.
(B) It represents a compromise between competing views.
(C) It is an instance of reasoning by analogy between premises.
(D) It is a proposition that supports the conclusion.
(E) It is the conclusion backed by the three questions as premises.

6. In August, by spending 10% more time fishing than in July, the fishing fleet caught 3 million more fish. In September, by spending 20% more time fishing than in July, the fleet will catch 6 million more fish.

Which of the following is a flaw in the reasoning of the passage?

(A) The author fails to provide a necessary distinction between attitudes regarding fishing.
(B) The passage fails to point out that fishing too much is harmful to the environment.
(C) The author relies on irrelevant data regarding July's fishing numbers.
(D) The author assumes that fish can always be caught at the same rate.
(E) The passage is based on imprecise time spans to determine fishing levels.

7. Atheism is tantamount to a religion. Many fervent believers in major religions feel that they will never know that God exists beyond a shadow of a doubt, but they still believe because their faith allow them to overcome the small doubts that act as barriers to their belief. In the same way, atheists can never know for certain that God does not exist. Possession of this type of knowledge is simply epistemologically impossible. People who profess to be atheists must also take a "leap of faith," and therefore their belief system is equivalent to a religion.

Which of the following characterizes the sentence that asserts that a type of knowledge is epistemologically impossible?

(A) It is a piece of evidence that is irrelevant to the passage's claims.
(B) It is a fact gained through the process of reasoning by analogy.
(C) It is an inference drawn from the premise that religions require "leaps of faith."
(D) It is a proposition that would have to be true for the main point to be true.
(E) It is an implicit conclusion that readers might draw when reading the passage.

Answers and Explanations

Question 1

Squib: This squib tells about a ghostly riverboat that turned out to be a hoax. It also tells of crop circles that people believe are created by extraterrestrials but that are undoubtedly hoaxes because the old man saw his son creating them. The old man draws the conclusion that all such supernatural stories are also hoaxes based on this evidence.

Question stem: The stem asks how the assertion that the *Mississippi River Belle* ghost was a hoax plays into the argument.

Correct answer: B. It was a piece of evidence that supports the old man's conclusion that all supernatural occurrences are really created by juveniles.

(A) This assertion is not the conclusion. Many points in the passage lead to a different conclusion.

(C) This is the second-best answer, but this assertion is not really a conclusion since no other sentence in the passage is designed to support it.

(D) This statement is not true. It does not restate the main point in any way. The main point comes after it in the passage, so it would be impossible to reiterate a main point that has not yet been stated.

(E) This assertion was not an inference but was instead stated as a fact.

Question 2

Squib: The argument is largely based on the author's ire for the RefineCo and GasPump corporations. This predisposition introduces a large flaw, because arguments need logical elements to support them, not strictly emotional ones.

Question stem: It asks for a flaw in the argument.

Correct answer: B. The argument focuses entirely on criticisms of RefineCo and GasPump rather than on the merits or drawbacks of the actual proposal.

(A) The argument is not circular; it is just based on inadequate evidence.

(C) The argument does use emotionally charged words like *notorious* and *greed*, but there is no rule that such words should never be used in an argument.

(D) The squib actually does just the opposite. The author assumes that RefineCo and GasPump will despoil Alaska just as they have other areas.

(E) This answer choice contains an apparent contradiction. How can you identify nonexistent evidence?

Question 3

Squib: This author advises musicians to avoid becoming pop stars if they wish to enjoy long careers in the music industry. To this end, the author advises musicians to allow as few people as possible to know their names. Of course, the contradiction here is that it is hard to be successful as an artist without making your name known to the general public.

Question stem: It asks for a flaw in the argument.

Correct answer: D. The advice is contradictory in that it recommends doing something that would prevent a person from becoming famous in order to achieve fame.

(A) Omitting unfounded assertions from arguments strengthens arguments instead of weakening them, so this is not the answer.

(B) This does not occur in any way that would relate to the strength of the squib.

(C) This does not happen.

(E) This is not an argument by analogy.

Question 4

Squib: This squib speaks of Mohandas Gandhi, the 20th-century Indian leader who was renowned for advocating nonviolent protest against British colonial rule. Gandhi's success inspired Dr. Martin Luther King, Jr., who used Gandhi's methods in civil rights protests in the United States. The conclusion of the passage is that without Gandhi's influence, civil rights protests in the United States would not have been largely nonviolent.

Question stem: How does the statement that Martin Luther King, Jr., was influenced by Gandhi figure into the passage?

Correct answer: C. This is a subsidiary conclusion. It is supported by the idea that Gandhi's methods earned worldwide respect and influenced many later leaders, of whom King was one. This point then supports the main conclusion that had King not heard of Gandhi, then the civil rights movement led by King and others would probably not have been largely nonviolent.

(A) Even if this were a syllogism, it certainly could hardly be misconstrued.

(B) The statement is not the main conclusion of the passage, because it is used to support another idea.

(D) The statement supports only one claim in the passage.

(E) This statement is not true, because other people besides King might have spread Gandhi's ideas to America.

Question 5

Squib: This squib presents a number of issues regarding the formation of a society. It says that the most important one is for people to create some mechanism to ensure that "good" people will lead them. The final sentence supports this statement by saying that no matter how well designed the system is, it will not bring about good if bad people control it.

Question stem: What part in the argument is played by the assertion that a system will not bring about good if it is not run by good people?

Correct answer: D. The statement is a claim that supports the main conclusion drawn in the previous sentence. This is one of the first squibs that you have seen where the main conclusion is not the final sentence of the squib.

(A) The statement is not really evidence. It is more of a claim that would actually need more supporting evidence to be complete and well founded.

(B) There are no competing views here to necessitate a compromise.

(C) Analogous reasoning is not used in the argument.

(E) Even if this were a conclusion, the questions still could not be considered its premises.

Question 6

Squib: The data showed that in August, when fishing time was increased by x over the fishing time in July, the number of fish caught increased by y. Based on this fact, the author assumes that in September, if fishing time is increased by $2x$, the number of fish caught will increase by $2y$. This reasoning assumes that there is a constant, linear correlation between time spent fishing and number of fish caught.

Question stem: The stem asks you to identify a flaw in the reasoning of the passage.

Correct answer: D. There is no logical reason to think that there is a linear relationship between time spent fishing and number of fish caught. In fact, if a great many fish were caught in one month, it would be possible for fewer fish to be caught in later months.

(A) There is no mention in the squib of any attitudes regarding fishing.

(B) This moral outcry to save the environment is ethically compelling but logically irrelevant to the passage.

(C) The data are quite relevant in projecting future fish catches.

(E) There is no reason to think that the time spans in the data are imprecise.

Question 7

Squib: This religiously charged squib claims that atheism is a religion because atheists are similar to religious people in one respect: They must take a "leap of faith" in order to believe in the rightness of their ideas. This could be a flawed argument because it assumes that two groups are the same based on a single similarity, but instead the squib asks you to identify the function of one part of the argument.

Question stem: What is the function of the sentence claiming that knowledge that there is not a God is epistemologically impossible?

Correct answer: D. If the sentence were not true, then atheists would not have to take a leap of faith to be certain that God does not exist. Thus, this proposition must be true in order for the conclusion to also be true.

(A) This is not a piece of evidence. It is a claim that is very relevant to the rest of the passage.

(B) There is no reasoning by analogy in the passage. The reasoning could be construed to be reasoning by comparison, but nothing more abstract than that.

(C) The idea in the sentence is related to the fact that religions require "leaps of faith," but it is not an inference drawn from that idea. The claim that it is impossible to know with certainty that there is no God is independent of claims about "leaps of faith."

(E) This is definitely not a conclusion that readers might draw for themselves while reading the passage.

6 Analogous Reasoning Questions

Analogous reasoning questions build on the knowledge that you acquired from working with reasoning strategy questions. But instead of asking you to choose a flaw in an argument or to analyze the parts of an argument, questions of this type ask you to choose an argument that is similar in its logical structure to the argument in the squib. These questions are the hardest ones in the whole Logical Reasoning section, so hard in fact that many test-preparation programs recommend skipping them entirely. However, this is not a good idea because, with a little work and study, you can learn how to answer these questions correctly and add points to your score. Keep in mind, though, that you will probably need more than twice as much time to answer each analogous reasoning question than you will need to answer any other kind of logical reasoning question.

Most analogous reasoning questions ask you to select the answer choice that has either a flaw similar to one in the squib or an argument similar in structure to one in the squib. Here is one that asks you to find a similar flaw:

> Would-be suitor: Brendan and Julie started dating just last week. But in this short span of seven days, I have never before heard Julie talk so positively about anyone. To me, it seems that their marriage is inevitable and that my dreams of Julie and me being together again will be shattered.
>
> Which one of the following exhibits a flaw similar to that of the argument presented in the passage?

To make an informed choice, we have to determine the flaw of the argument in the squib before even looking at the answer choices. It appears that the suitor is jumping to conclusions a little bit. Julie has been dating Brendan for a week and holds him in very high esteem after seven days, but more often than not, relationships do not last. The suitor's logical error is that he makes a long-term assumption on the basis of extremely short-term events. Each of the following answer choices makes this same error:

- Executive: The new phone system has been working great for the past month. I am convinced that our company will never again need a new phone system.
- The Ferris wheel drew the largest crowd of any attraction ever on opening day. Undoubtedly, the lure of the Ferris wheel will continue throughout the summer.
- The movie *Philip's Jeans* is the biggest hit ever. Ticket sales during its first two days swamped all previous sales records. This trend will surely continue and will make *Philip's Jeans* the highest-grossing movie of all time.
- Brad is unable to determine whether he will wear the blue socks or the pink socks. Since he has hesitated for so long, it is clear that Brad will not go out tonight because he cannot decide what to wear.
- Evan plans on working on his book for 10 weeks. He wrote 100 pages for the book in this last week. Extrapolating from this information, it is clear that Evan will write a 1000-page book.

Other analogous reasoning questions ask you to pick the answer choice that presents an argument with the same structure as the one in the squib. Here is an example:

> The Whigs were a well-known reformist party in 18th- and 19th-century England and America. They inspired a spirit of revolution, not only in the populace of both countries in their own time, but also in the hearts of today's exciting new Whig rock and roll band. Considering the success of the Whig party in revolutionary America, the party's namesake band is sure to be extremely successful and bring a welcome revolution to today's music scene.
>
> Which one of the following most closely parallels the reasoning in the argument presented in the passage?

The logic of this passage is fairly clear: It assumes that because one group with a particular name was successful and revolutionary long ago, a completely

different group today will also be successful and revolutionary just because it happens to have the same name. This could also be a flawed reasoning passage, but it is not, so you are looking for an argument that has the same structure as the one in the squib. Here are some possibilities:

> - William Jennings was a great preacher and defender of the right. His son, William Jennings, Jr., will also be a great orator and advocate of justice.
> - Lancelot was a knight of unparalleled success. He defeated his opponents in every competition that he entered, from jousting to dueling. Based on his success, it is clear that the new bug spray named "Lancelot" will also be extremely successful.
> - Green Bay sports teams are always very successful. A new dodgeball team has been formed taking the name "Green Bay." They will surely win the dodgeball tournament.

Before proceeding to the sample questions, take a look at the following chart. It lists four general rules that govern comparisons between arguments. These rules have some exceptions, but they are good general guidelines for understanding analogous reasoning problems and for quickly eliminating incorrect answer choices.

Guidelines for Comparing Logical Arguments

1. An argument that states that something *will* happen is not comparable to an argument that states that something *will not* happen.
2. An argument that states that something *might*, *may sometimes*, or *could possibly* happen is not comparable to an argument that says that something will *definitely* happen or not happen.
3. A flawed argument cannot be compared to a well-supported argument.
4. One type of sufficient-necessary chain is not comparable to a different type of sufficient-necessary logic chain.

Now look at some sample analogous reasoning questions, keeping these rules in mind. Be sure to determine the reasoning strategy that the squib applies before looking at any answer choices.

Sample Analogous Reasoning Questions

1. If Justine did not like children, then she would not volunteer every week to baby-sit my aunt's children. Since she does volunteer freely to do this, she must like children.

   The logical structure of the argument is most similar to the logical structure of which of the following?

   (A) If Johnny did not like cats, then he would purchase a dog for his pet. Since he did not purchase a dog, he must like cats.
   (B) If Gina did not like children, then she would not choose to be a teacher. Since she has chosen to be a teacher, she must like teaching.
   (C) If reagents could not combine to form smaller compounds, then chemical additions could not form strange compounds. Since strange compounds are formed, reagents can combine to form smaller compounds.
   (D) If ants could carry 50 times their own weight, then humans could carry at least 100 times their own weight. Since humans can carry several thousand times an ant's weight, ants must be able to carry 50 times their own weight.
   (E) If a pet is not housebroken, then it would have trouble maintaining proper household etiquette. Since Fido is not housebroken, it is clear that all dogs have trouble maintaining proper household etiquette.

Squib: This argument is nothing more than sufficient-necessary statements. You can diagram them to get a better understanding:

   A. ~~Justine likes children~~ → ~~Volunteer to baby-sit~~
   B. Volunteer to baby-sit → Justine likes children

This is a supportable argument since it concludes the truth of the contrapositive statement based on the truth of the original sufficient-necessary statement.

Question stem: Which of the following has similar argument structure?

Diagram each answer choice using the sufficient-necessary chain to view its structure.

Correct answer: C.

~~Reagents Combine~~ → ~~Chemical Additions Strange~~
Chemical Additions Strange → Reagents Combine
This is exactly the same structure. Two negative statements are used to form their contrapositive.

(A) ~~Johnny likes Cats~~ → Purchase Dog
~~Purchase Dog~~ → Johnny likes Cats
A conclusion is made based on the sufficient-necessary link, but there is an inverse relationship present here that is not present in answer choice C. This is why it is a good idea at least to scan all the possible answer choices and diagram all that you think might be pertinent.

(B) This is not even a connected sufficient-necessary deduction. It states that if Gina did not like children, then she would not be a teacher. However, she has chosen to be a teacher, so it leaps to the conclusion that she likes teaching. This is not a similar argument structure.

(D) This convoluted answer choice does not contain comparable sufficient-necessary chains and therefore cannot be the correct answer.

(E) This answer choice does not contain comparable sufficient-necessary chains and therefore cannot be the correct answer.

2. All people who volunteer at least 40 hours a year to charities are generous people. Some generous people give large sums of money to their favorite charity, so some people who volunteer at least 40 hours a year to charities also give large sums of money to their favorite charity.

Which of the following is flawed in a way most similar to the way in which the argument is flawed?

(A) All people who are omnivorous eat meat. Some people who eat meat also like hunting, so some people who are omnivorous eat vegetables.

(B) All people who are sociable like other people. Some people who like other people like hunting, so some people who like other people like hunting.

(C) All artists are able to express their emotions through paintings. Some other people are also able to express their emotions through painting, so these people are also artists.

(D) All veterinarians take care of animals every week. Some people who take care of animals every week have pets of their own, so some veterinarians must have pets.

(E) All people who are greedy want to make a lot of money. All people who want to make a lot of money are not greedy, so some people who are not greedy want to buy big houses.

Squib: You can diagram this squib as follows:

A. Volunteer 40 Hours per Year → Generous
B. Generous—(S)—Give Money

These chains can be combined to form:

C. Volunteer 40 Hours per Year → Generous—(S)—Give Money

The conclusion wants you to make the invalid assumption that some people who volunteer 40 hours per year give money. Think about the logic chain given above and realize why this assumption is not necessarily true. If you volunteer 40 hours per year, then you must be generous. However, if you are generous, you do not have to give money. Some volunteers who are generous people do not give money. You need to look for a similar mistake in an answer choice.

Question stem: Choose the answer choice that contains a similar logical flaw.

Correct answer: D. 1. Vet → Animals Every Week
2. Animals Every Week—(S)—Have Pets
3. Vet → Animals Every Week—(S)—Have Pets

The argument makes the conclusion that some vets must have personal pets. This is incorrect for the same reason as the squib.

(A) 1. Omnivorous → Eat Meat
2. Eat Meat—(S)—Hunting
3. Omnivorous → Eat Meat—(S)—Hunting

This answer choice reaches a flawed conclusion in a different way from the way the squib does. It talks about vegetables when an answer with the same structure as the squib would have talked about omnivores liking to hunt.

(B) 1. Sociable → Like People
2. Like People—(S)—Hunting
2. Sociable → Like People—(S)—Hunting

This is a logical argument. This answer choice holds that some people who like people like hunting.

(C) 1. Artists→ Express through Paintings
2. Other People—(S)—Express through Paintings
3. Artists→ Express through Paintings—(S)—Other People

The argument reaches the flawed conclusion that other people are artists. This is not true, and it is also not true in a different way from the correct answer choice. This conclusion states that *all* "other people" are "artists." An argument flawed in the same way as the squib would say that only *some* are.

(E) This answer choice contains a contradiction and an unrelated sufficient-necessary statement. It is incorrect.

3. People believe that those who watch sports on television tend to be more athletic than the average members of the population. Do people who watch soap operas tend to be more romantic than average?

In which one of the following does the logic most closely parallel the reasoning utilized in the argument?

(A) People who participate in sports tend to be relatively athletic. Do people who act in soap operas tend to be less romantic than the average members of the population?

(B) People who play violent videogames have a relatively high penchant for aggression. Do people who play videogames based on science fiction have, on average, a higher affinity for fantasy?

(C) People who are obese tend to eat more food than the average members of the population. Do people who eat more food than the average members of the population necessarily have to be obese?

(D) Runners tend to watch more sports than other parts of our population. Do football players on average watch more soap operas than the average players of other sports?

(E) Vegetarians eat more meat than the average members of the rest of our population. Do carnivores eat more vegetables relative to the vegetable consumption of the rest of our population?

Squib: This squib states an assumption about people who watch one type of TV program. The author of the squib then tries to extend the tenuous logic of the squib by posing a question about people who watch a different genre of TV program. We should look for a similar assumption and then question in an answer choice.

Question stem: Find an answer choice with logic parallel to that of the squib.

Correct answer: B. This answer states an assumption about people who play one type of videogame. It then extends that assumption to people who play a different genre of videogame.

(A) This choice tries to extend an assumption from sports participants to actors rather than from one kind of sports participant to another. Additionally, it switches the relationship by inserting "less romantic" into the sentence.

(C) This choice does not try to extend an assumption to another or different genre. Therefore, it is not similar to the squib.

(D) This is a convoluted answer choice that would just confuse any would-be diagrammer. It suffices to say that these logic chains do not relate in a way that is similar to those in the squib.

(E) The question asks about a different qualitative relationship from the one the assumption does. Additionally, this whole answer choice is probably false, claiming that vegetarians eat more meat than the average members of the population do. It is completely nonsensical.

Analogous Reasoning Questions: Common Traits

Now that you have reviewed some sample analogous reasoning questions, you should be able to recognize their common traits. These traits are listed in the following outline.

I. General Format
1. Squib is two to five sentences.
2. Word count: 25–73.
3. Questions present an argument that is either flawed or well made and ask you to identify the answer choice that contains an argument that is similarly flawed or well made.

II. Sample Question Stems
1. Which one of the following has a logical structure most like that of the argument above?
2. Which one of the following exhibits both of the *logical flaws* exhibited in the argument above?
3. Which one of the following most closely *parallels* the reasoning in the argument above?

III. Correct Answer
1. is the argument that is formed using the same method as the squib
2. is the argument that makes the same logical error as the squib

IV. Second-Best Choice
1. concludes with *possibly*, *sometimes*, or *might* when the squib reaches a definite conclusion
2. is logically correct according to sufficient-necessary chains, but the variables have an inverse or opposite relationship to those in the squib

V. Clearly Wrong Answers
1. arguments that have characteristics that are clearly different from those in the squib
2. arguments that are flawed when the squib is well founded

Now that you have seen some of the test makers' tricks, answer the following seven analogous reasoning questions. Every correct answer and incorrect answer choice will match a particular point on the outline you just read. The same will be true for questions on the actual LSAT, so knowing the points on the outline will help you to identify correct answers quickly and consistently.

DRILL: ANALOGOUS REASONING QUESTIONS

1. A major organized crime syndicate has found that all members who are involved in a bank robbery are captured immediately afterward if they do not have either a fast getaway car or a large amount of firepower. The group is planning a bank robbery for this weekend and is not bringing firepower, so all members who are involved in the robbery will be captured.

   Which of the following is most analogous to the reasoning used in the passage?

   (A) An exterminator has found that termites will reinfest a house if he does not spray compound 1 or 2. Since he has no compound 2 with him, termites will reinfest the house.
   (B) A biologist has found that biological equilibriums are upset when there are no predators. There are no predators in the Sahara, so the biological equilibrium has been upset.
   (C) A sociologist has found that people need both love and money to survive happily in this world. The lower portions of the socioeconomic strata do not have money, so they do not survive happily.
   (D) An Olympic jumper has found that her jumps will improve by her either running faster or jumping higher. This jump will be improved because she jumped higher and ran much faster.
   (E) A weightlifter has found that he does not need weights or lifting to continue getting stronger. Since he uses neither of these methods, he will continue getting stronger.

2. Well-adjusted teenagers all develop and consistently use exemplary social skills for the rest of their lives. Since this adult never utilizes exemplary social skills, she was not a well-adjusted teenager.

   Which one of the following has a logical structure most like that of the argument above?

   (A) Caring people are friendly people. Since this person is clearly not a caring person, she is not friendly.
   (B) Passionate people develop artistic habits that they follow for the rest of their lives. Since this person does not follow artistic habits, he is not an artist.
   (C) Well-adjusted adults use the social skills that they developed as teenagers. Since this person has poor social skills, she was a not a well-adjusted teenager.
   (D) Computers that are based on a binary system are the only type of computers in existence. Since this computer does not use a different type of system, there are computers that do not use the binary system in existence.
   (E) Penguins that have achieved evolutionary success always lay two eggs instead of one. Since this penguin laid only one egg last year, it has not achieved evolutionary success.

3. All entertaining people have a good sense of humor. I have great sense of humor. So I must be a comedian.

   Which of the following exhibits the same logical flaw as that exhibited in the argument above?

   (A) All sports players are aggressive. This person is exceptionally aggressive. So he must a boxer.
   (B) All gorillas are curious. This primate is exceptionally curious. So it must be a gorilla.
   (C) All good years bring wealth. This year did not bring poverty. So it was a good year.
   (D) All comedians stress interpersonal relationships. Since this person depends on an extensive personal network, she must be a comedian.
   (E) Professors talk a lot. This person talks all of the time. So he will be a philosophy professor in the future.

4. If you work hard all your life, then you will inevitably be successful. If you are successful, then you will be fulfilled. So if you work hard all your life, then you will eventually be fulfilled.

Which of the following most closely parallels the reasoning in the argument above?

(A) People who study religion are spiritual. People who are spiritual are less likely to commit crimes than criminals. Therefore, people who study religion are less likely to commit crimes than the average person.

(B) Mammals feed their young with milk. Creatures that feed their young with something other than milk all have gestation periods shorter than nine months. Therefore, mammals have gestation periods longer than nine months.

(C) Bees will fly around until they find honey. This insect has found honey. Therefore, this insect must be a kind of bee.

(D) Tigers that are trapped in the woods will all eat pigs. Animals that eat pigs will glean an essential protein from their diet. Therefore, all tigers trapped in the woods will glean an essential protein from their diet.

(E) Socialites try to be social butterflies. Social butterflies are the light of every party. Therefore, socialites are the light of every party.

5. If a primate is a gorilla, it can learn sign language. This primate did learn sign language. So it is a gorilla.

Which of the following exhibits a pattern of reasoning most similar to that in the argument above?

(A) Nature is beautiful. If it were not beautiful, then I would not be here. Since I am here, I am surrounded by nature.

(B) Sign language can be taught to some people who are deaf. This person is deaf. So this person can learn sign language.

(C) If cherubim call, then people listen. This angel called, and people listened. So the angel must have been a cherub.

(D) Elysian beach resorts bring in large amounts of money. This resort brings in a lot of money. Therefore, this beach resort is not Elysian.

(E) Able-minded people agree: To write is to fight. David, a social activist, is a writer. Therefore, he is also a fighter.

6. The high council forced all fighters who were not members of the Jartha contingent to enter the war zone. Thus, if a fighter was not forced into the war zone, then he was a member of the Jartha contingent.

Which of the following is an argument that contains a logical structure that is most similar to the argument above?

(A) People who collect rhinestones also get rhinoplasties. This person has gotten a rhinoplasty so he also collects rhinestones.

(B) All peas in this pod are green. If the pea is not green, then it is not a pea in this pod.

(C) Ignoring a problem often makes it worse. Thus, to cure a problem, you must pay attention to it.

(D) Paying lip service to a greater cause makes you a hypocrite. If you are a hypocrite, then you pay lip service to a greater cause.

(E) Fast-food restaurants produce only food with a high fat content. If the food does have a high fat content, then it was not produced in a fast-food restaurant.

7. If a president encourages peace and altruism, then his personal example will cause people within his country to engage in prosocial activities. When Abraham Lincoln was president, the U.S. population engaged in large amounts of prosocial activities. Therefore, Lincoln must have encouraged peace and altruism.

An error of reasoning of the same kind as one contained in the passage exists in all of the following EXCEPT:

(A) If a person asks for a hot dog and gets a hamburger, then he will be angry. This person is angry, so he must have asked for a hot dog and gotten a hamburger.

(B) Johnny is a person who has always liked refried beans. This person likes refried beans, so he must be Johnny.

(C) Governments that encourage good foreign relations enjoy safety for their citizens in other nations. The citizens of a certain nation are extremely safe in other nations, so their government must encourage good foreign relations.

(D) Impatience is a quality that should not be tolerated by civilized people. These people are civilized, so they encourage the virtue of patience.

(E) Lotus flowers are the pride of eastern Chinese farmers. This farmer prides himself on a lotus flower, so he must be an eastern Chinese farmer.

ANSWERS AND EXPLANATIONS

Question 1

Squib: The squib is a sufficient-necessary argument that says that if you don't have either a fast getaway car or firepower, then you will be captured. This can be diagrammed as follows:

1. ~~Fast Getaway~~ → Captured
2. ~~Firepower~~ → Captured

This weekend the group is planning a robbery and is not bringing firepower. Based on this evidence, the author of the squib assumes that the robbers will be captured without eliminating the variable of "fast getaway car." If the robbers have a fast getaway car, then they can avoid capture even without firepower. You need to find an answer choice that draws a conclusion without eliminating a variable that could cause a reversed outcome.

Question stem: Find the answer choice with an analogous argument structure.

Correct answer: A.

~~1~~ → Reinfest
~~2~~ → Reinfest

Termites will reinfest if the exterminator does not use either of theses two chemicals. We know that he does not have one, but just as the robbers could still make a fast getaway, he could still have the other chemical. Regardless of this fact, the author of the answer choice jumps to a conclusion.

(B) Predators → Equilibrium Upset
Based on this information, the author deduces that this will be true in a specific environment. This is a logical argument and therefore not similar.

(C) Survive → Love
Survive → Money
You need both of these things to survive, and the author of the answer choice correctly infers that since some people do not possess one, then they cannot survive.

(D) Run Faster → Jumps Improve
Jump Higher → Jumps Improve
The author of the answer choice correctly infers that because she has done both on this jump, it will be an improvement.

(E) In this case, there are no real variables specified, so there is not one specific one to neglect in favor of another, so this argument is not comparable.

Question 2

Squib: This is also a sufficient-necessary argument. It can be diagrammed as follows:

Well-adjusted Teenager → Exemplary Social Skills
~~Exemplary Social Skills~~ → ~~Well-Adjusted Teenager~~

Based on this information, the author of the squib infers that because this person never uses exemplary social skills, she was not a well-adjusted teenager. This is a logical inference since it is the contrapositive of a statement that is stated to be true in the squib.

Question stem: Identify the answer choice that uses the same type of supportable logic that was used in the squib.

Correct answer: E.

Evolutionary Success → Lay Two Eggs
~~Lay Two Eggs~~ → ~~Evolutionary Success~~

Based on this information, you can infer that this particular penguin will not achieve evolutionary success because last year it laid just one egg.

(A) Caring People → Friendly People
The answer choice makes the assumption that since this person is not caring, then she is not friendly. This is an unsupportable assumption.

(B) Passionate → Artistic Habits
The answer choice states that since this person does not follow artistic habits, he is not an artist. This contention is not linked to any sufficient-necessary statement and is therefore not analogous to the squib.

(C) Well-Adjusted Adult → Use Previously Developed Skills
This is a confusing answer choice, but it is clear that just because a person at times has poor social skills, it does not mean that she was not a well-adjusted teenager. In addition, the variable "well-adjusted teenager" is different from both variables in the sufficient-necessary statement. Therefore, you can infer nothing about this variable based on the sufficient-necessary statement. Beware of answer choices like this one that use the same subject matter as the squib, because they are almost always traps.

(D) This answer choice poses a contradiction that is not found in the logic of the squib.

Question 3

Squib: This is a flawed method of reasoning. The author makes this sufficient-necessary statement:

Entertaining People → Great Sense of Humor

Based on this fact, the person claims that since he has a great sense of humor, he must be a comedian. You need to find an answer choice that reverses the order of the logical chain and then raises the level of a variable in this same way.

Question stem: Find the argument that possesses a similar logical flaw.

Correct answer: A. Sports Player → Aggressive
The choice states that this person is aggressive, so he must be a particularly aggressive type of sports player. This is the answer choice that is closest to the squib.

(B) Gorilla → Curious
The inference is made that since this primate is curious, it must be a gorilla. This makes the same logical error as the squib in proceeding in the wrong direction in the sufficient-necessary chain, but it does not raise the level of the variable "gorilla."

(C) Good Years → Wealth
Just because this year did not bring one extreme (poverty) does not mean that it brought the other extreme (wealth).

(D) Comedians → Interpersonal Relationships
The inference is made that since this person depends on an extensive network of relationships (which is quite different from stressing them), then she must be a comedian. There is no raising of the level of the first variable, and the "depending on relationships" and "stressing relationships" are inconsistent.

(E) This argument makes a claim about the future. The squib does nothing like that, so this answer choice is not comparable to the squib.

Question 4

Squib: This argument contains a string of sufficient-necessary statements.

1. Work Hard → Successful
2. Successful → Fulfilled
3. Work Hard → Successful → Fulfilled

The argument is logical, so we need to find another argument that adds logical chains in the same way and then makes a similar inference.

Question stem: Find the method of reasoning that is similar to that of the squib.

Correct answer: D.

A. Tigers Trapped → Eat Pigs
B. Eat Pigs → Essential Protein
C. Tigers Trapped → Eat Pigs → Essential Protein

These inferences directly mirror those in the squib.

(A) 1. Study Religion → Spiritual
    2. Spiritual → Fewer Crimes than **Criminals**
    3. Study Religion → Spiritual → Less Likely to Commit Crimes than **Average Person**

The new variable of "Less Likely to Commit Crimes than Average Person" causes a break in similarity from the squib.

(B) 1. Mammals → Milk
    2. ~~Milk~~ → Gestation <9 months

Already, this answer choice is blatantly different from the squib. It then goes on to make an insupportable inference based on these claims.

(C) This answer choice makes several insupportable inferences. Comparable ones are not found in the squib.

(E) 1. Socialites → Try to Be Social Butterflies
    2. Social Butterflies → Light of Party

The author then tries to add the chains to infer that socialites are the light of every party. However, this addition is unsupportable because the variable "Try to Be Social Butterflies" is different from the variable "Social Butterflies."

Question 5

Squib: This squib makes an insupportable inference. Here is the fact that we know:

Gorilla → Sign Language Potential

The author then assumes that because this primate has learned sign language, then it must be a gorilla. However, human beings, the inventors of sign language, are also primates.

Question stem: Find a similar pattern of reasoning.

Correct answer: C.

Cherubim Call → People Listen

Based on this, the author assumes that because an angel called and people listened, then the angel must have been a cherub. But this neglects other kinds of angels (seraphim, perhaps) who might also call, just as the squib neglected human beings who are also able to learn sign language.

(A) This answer choice makes a series of loose and unconnected postulations. The squib does not do this, so this answer is not the correct one.

(B) Beware, since this answer choice refers to the same subject matter as the squib. These assertions are all unconnected and cannot be contained by a single sufficient-necessary statement as the variables in the squib are.

(D) Elysian Resort → Lots of Money

Based on this, the author assumes that since the resort brings in lots of money, then it is not Elysian. This is directly opposite to the way the squib concluded. An analogous answer based on these facts would claim that this beach resort brings in lots of money, so it is Elysian.

(E) The first statement tells us:

$$\text{Write} \rightarrow \text{Fight}$$

David is a writer. Therefore, David is a fighter. This sketchy inference is flawed in a different way from the squib.

Question 6

Squib: This passage makes a correct inference using sufficient-necessary chains. The statement that is given as fact is:

$$\text{~~Jartha Contingent~~} \rightarrow \text{War Zone}$$

Based on this fact, the author concludes the contrapositive of this fact:

$$\text{~~War Zone~~} \rightarrow \text{Jartha Contingent}$$

This is a true statement and makes a valid argument.

Question stem: Choose the most comparable argument.

Correct answer: B.

Fact:	In This Pod → Peas Green
Conclusion:	~~Peas Green~~ → ~~In this Pod~~

This uses the same type of reasoning as the squib to form the conclusion.

(A)
Fact:	Collect Rhinestones → Rhinoplasties
Conclusion:	Rhinoplasties → Collect Rhinestones

This answer choice makes an incorrect inference.

(C) This choice talks about what *often* happens. What often happens cannot be compared to what will *definitely* happen.

(D)
Fact:	Lip Service → Hypocrite
Conclusion:	Hypocrite → Lip Service

This answer choice makes an incorrect inference.

(E)
Fact:	Fast Food → High Fat
Conclusion:	High Fat → ~~Fast Food~~

This answer choice forms the contrapositive incorrectly.

Question 7

Squib: "President encourages peace and altruism" is written as PEPA. "People engage in prosocial activities" is written as EPSA.

Fact:	PEPA → EPSA
Conclusion:	EPSA → PEPA

This is a fallacious conclusion.

Question stem: You must find an answer choice that does NOT make the same kind of reasoning error as the one in the squib.

Correct answer: D. This statement does not make any real conclusion or inference. Therefore, it is impossible for it to make the same kind of error as the one in the squib.

(A)
Fact:	Ham Instead of Hot Dog → Mad
Conclusion:	Mad → Ham Instead of Hot Dog

This is the same kind of error as the one in the squib.

(B)
Fact:	Johnny → Likes Refried Beans
Conclusion:	Likes Refried Beans → Johnny

This is the same kind of error as the one in the squib.

(C)
Fact:	GEGFR → Safe Paths
Conclusion:	Safe Paths → GEGFR

This is the same kind of error as the one in the squib.

(E)
Fact:	Eastern Chinese Farmer → Lotus Flower Pride
Conclusion:	Lotus Flower Pride → Eastern Chinese Farmer

This is the same kind of error as the one in the squib.

7 Controversy Questions

Controversy questions are characterized by two speakers who argue about a specific issue. These questions come in many forms. Sometimes the question stem asks about the argument of only one of the two speakers, but most controversy questions ask about how one speaker's argument relates to that of the other speaker. Controversy questions may ask:

- What point are the speakers arguing about?
- What do they agree about?
- What do they disagree about?

The following sample squib can be used to illustrate the three types of questions.

> John: Tennis is the greatest sport throughout the land. I played since I was a child and have and will always consider tennis to be a better sport than basketball, football, soccer, croquet, Ping-Pong, and golf.
>
> Jennifer: Tennis is a great sport, but it is not better than soccer or football. I have played Ping-Pong since I was a little girl and agree that tennis is better than "table tennis." In addition, nobody really likes golf, so that is a moot point.
>
> Which of the following is the point at issue between John and Jennifer?

This question asks for the main point about which John and Jennifer are debating. In order to determine what this point is, it is necessary to identify the main points of the arguments of each person. John's main point is essentially that tennis is the greatest sport. Jennifer's main point is that tennis is not the greatest sport, even though it is a great sport. Based on this understanding, we need to determine what point they are arguing about. Any of the following answer choices would be correct:

- how tennis compares to other sports
- the greatness of tennis when compared to other sports
- the overall merits of tennis when compared to the overall merits of other types of sports

For the following two question stems, any point about which John and Jennifer specifically agree or disagree in the entire squib could be a correct answer choice. Incorrect answer choices offer points about which they have not overtly agreed or disagreed.

> Which of the following are John and Jennifer committed to agreeing about?

All the following are possible correct answers:

> - Tennis is a great sport.
> - Tennis is better than Ping-Pong.
> - Tennis is better than golf.
> - Tennis is better than Ping-Pong and golf, and it is a great sport.

> Which of the following are John and Jennifer committed to disagreeing about?

All the following are possible correct answers:

> - Tennis is the greatest sport.
> - Tennis is greater than soccer.
> - Tennis is greater than football.
> - Tennis is a greater sport than soccer and football, and it is the greatest sport.

Now you are ready to take a look at some sample controversy questions. Keep in mind that not all LSAT questions (and not all the sample questions in this book) that present arguments between two speakers are true controversy questions. Based on the kind of question asked in the question stem, some belong to the other types of questions that you have studied previously.

Sample Controversy Questions

1. Jamie: Hedonism is not a good methodology for living. It encourages people to be selfish and maintain a knowing disregard for the needs of other people that should never be present in modern society.

   John: You may be right about hedonism in general, but being selfish can be very positive. After all, if everyone were to behave unselfishly all of the time, then no one person would ever get what he or she wanted.

Which one of the following is a point at issue between Jamie and John?

(A) the merits of living life in a hedonistic fashion
(B) the value of people in our society behaving selfishly
(C) the need for altruistic people to set good examples for inherently selfish people
(D) the advisability of a certain code of conduct when it is not applied to people
(E) the value of people in society sometimes getting what they want

Squib: The point of Jamie's argument is that hedonism is not a good methodology for living because it encourages people to be selfish. John's point is that hedonism in general is not a good methodology for living but that being selfish sometimes is. So they agree that hedonism is bad, but they differ about whether being selfish is always bad. Any correct answer choice will deal with selfishness.

Question stem: Choose the answer choice that contains the point that John and Jamie are arguing about.

Correct answer: B. This answer choice deals with the merits of people acting selfishly, so it is correct.

(A) This choice solely deals with hedonism, which the two speakers agreed about so it cannot be a point at issue.

(C) Altruistic people are never mentioned in either speaker's argument so this cannot be the answer.

(D) This answer choice does not really make any sense.

(E) This choice has some relationship to people being selfish, but Jamie does not disagree that people getting what they want in a society is sometimes a good thing, so this is not a point at issue.

2. Electrician: The circuit in your fan has been destroyed by a surge in power that occurred last week. You should go to the department store and buy a new fan because there is no way to get this fan to work. In fact, it would be a good idea to go ahead and get a new house because the electrical wiring in this one is fairly poor.

   Homeowner: I take offense at your contentions and think that it is an awful idea to purchase a new house. The best way of solving this problem would be to get a new circuit for the

old fan at the department store. Furthermore, there were no power surges in the house last week, and finally, I did the wiring in this house myself, and it is of superior quality.

The electrician and the homeowner disagree about all the following EXCEPT:

(A) that the circuit in the fan was destroyed by a power surge last week
(B) that the current fan can be repaired in some way
(C) that the homeowner should go to the department store
(D) that the wiring in the house is of superior quality
(E) that it would be a good idea for the homeowner to get a new house

Squib: The speakers disagree about all the following: (1) getting a new house would be a good idea, (2) the best way to fix the problem would be to fix the fan, (3) the fan is fixable, (4) the fan was broken by last week's power surge, and (5) the wiring of this house is poor. Any one of these numerous items could be the correct answer to a disagreement question.

Question stem: What do the electrician and homeowner not disagree about?

Correct answer: C. Both speakers state that it would be a good idea for the homeowner to go to the department store in order to fix the problem.

(A) The speakers disagree about this.

(B) The speakers disagree about this.

(D) The speakers disagree about this.

(E) The speakers disagree about this.

3. Jane: Expensive clothing is a moral pitfall for people. Those who insist on wearing only expensive clothing must be trying to hide something they dislike about themselves underneath all of that fabric.

   Brian: There are so many things that $500 could buy a person besides a new suit. If people have an excess amount of money, they should be vigilant about not being morally whimsical with their uses of that money. Expensive clothing should never be purchased, because the money could be put to so many other uses to help people in our society.

Jane and Brian are committed to agreeing about which of the following?

(A) Expensive clothing should be purchased on occasion.
(B) People should never be morally whimsical when making purchases.
(C) People who buy expensive clothing are trying to hide something about themselves they dislike.
(D) A person who buys a $500 suit is engaging in a morally questionable action.
(E) Those who decide never to purchase expensive clothing are morally vigilant people.

Squib: Jane's main point is that expensive clothing is a moral pitfall for people and that those who wear expensive clothing must be trying to hide something about themselves. Brian's point is that expensive clothing should never be purchased because the money could be better spent on more virtuous causes.

Question stem: What are the speakers committed to agreeing about?

Correct answer: D. Both speakers claim that buying expensive clothing is a bad thing. Brian claims that expensive clothing should never be bought, and Jane declares that expensive clothing in general is a moral pitfall, so it is likely that both would agree with the contention of this answer choice.

(A) They would probably both disagree with this statement.

(B) Jane does not explicitly declare this about expensive clothing, and Brian states it only in regard to expensive clothing. It is not fair to infer that Brian holds this opinion for all other purchases or that Jane holds it for expensive clothing.

(C) Brian does not state this.

(E) This statement is not necessarily true based on the contentions of either person. They say that people who buy expensive clothing are immoral, but they do not proceed to make any conjectures about the morality of those who do not buy the clothing.

Controversy Questions: Common Traits

Now that you have reviewed some sample controversy questions, you should be able to recognize their common traits. These traits are listed in the following outline.

I. General Format
1. Squib is 4 to 10 sentences.
2. Word count: 53–110.
3. Questions present two speakers who are arguing about a particular point.

II. Sample Question Stems
1. Which one of the following is the *point at issue* between Alexander and Teresa?
2. The exchange between Bart and Anne most strongly supports the view that they *disagree* as to . . .
3. Which of the following are John and Joe committed to *agreeing* about?

III. Correct Answer
1. correctly identifies the point about which the speakers would agree or disagree
2. is the main point of agreement or disagreement between the speakers

IV. Second-Best Choice
1. point that speakers agree or disagree about but that is not the major point of agreement or disagreement
2. point that speakers might agree or disagree about, but this fact is not explicitly stated in the squib

V. Clearly Wrong Answers
1. points that are unrelated to the speakers' arguments
2. points that speakers would disagree about when the question stem asks what they would agree about, and vice versa (Many people choose these answer choices because they miss seeing a *not* or an *unless* that changes the meaning of the question stem.)

Now that you have seen some of the test makers' tricks, answer the following seven controversy questions. Every correct answer and incorrect answer choice will match a particular point on the outline you just read. The same will be true for questions on the actual LSAT, so knowing the points on the outline will help you to identify correct answers quickly and consistently.

DRILL: CONTROVERSY QUESTIONS

1. Government official: Right now, we do not have resources available to devote to looking for alternative energy sources. We must devote all our research resources to finding new ways to refine and drill for oil. If we were to halt this research, then humanity would have no energy supply.

    Environmentalist: The oil reserves that our country has stored up over the past decade would provide us with more than enough oil to power our energy needs without a lapse between the time when we divert research funds away from oil and the time when our research succeeds in endowing our society with a new power source.

    The environmentalist and the government official are committed to disagreeing about which of the following points?

    (A) Research into alternative energy sources will never bear fruit.
    (B) Our society should end its dependence on oil by switching to alternative energy sources.
    (C) It is impossible simultaneously to research oil technologies and alternative energy sources.
    (D) People are unable to function in a modern society without the use of power.
    (E) If research on oil technologies were ended, there would be a gap in energy supplies.

2. Byron: Looking in a mirror discomforts people every time they catch their reflection. All people have self-image issues that the mirror reminds them of, so people would be better off ignoring those issues by resolving to avoid mirrors whenever possible.

    Sally: All people have issues with their self-image—even me. A good way to deal with these issues is to address them and talk about them. Repressing them will lead to insecurity and fear about one's flaws, which is much more detrimental than acknowledging those flaws.

    Which of the following best expresses the point at issue between Byron and Sally?

    (A) the advisability of looking obsessively in a mirror
    (B) whether or not everyone has flaws in appearance that mirrors bring out
    (C) the merits of repressing one's self-image issues
    (D) the value of talking about one's issues with a psychiatrist
    (E) the question of whether people accurately view their reflection in a mirror

3. TV evangelist: If you send me money, then the work of God will be served. I am accepting donations of $100, $1000, and $1,000,000 to contribute to my efforts to build a new church for our community. Praise be to God and let His work be served by the building of this church.

TV watcher: This church is being built for you and not the community; your work will be served by people sending you money. Just because you allege a connection between you and some ephemeral spirit does not mean that a divine being's work will be served by your building a church.

The TV evangelist and TV watcher are committed to disagreeing about which of the following points?

(A) whether the church will serve both the community and the TV evangelist
(B) whether God's work will be served by people sending money to the TV evangelist
(C) whether people will be willing to send a million dollars to the TV evangelist
(D) whether alleged connections between people and spiritual beings are not always real
(E) whether people will praise God if a new church is built regardless of whom the church was built for

4. Zeke: Actresses and actors gain their positions by being very attractive people. There is no other single criterion in their profession that is even half as important as their physical features. Being the son or daughter of a famous actor comes close, but if you are not at least cute, then you do not have a chance of getting an acting job in Hollywood.

Amy: You make an interesting point, but what about Jonathan Smith? Most people feel that he is one of Hollywood's greatest actors, but no one thinks that he is the least bit attractive. He is the son of James Smith, the famous actor who starred in *Modern Eccentricities*.

Which of the following is the point at issue between Zeke and Amy?

(A) whether all people who star in Hollywood are either children of famous actors or are exceptionally attractive
(B) whether James Smith is a person who might be considered to be attractive by some people
(C) whether Amy is biased in her view of Jonathan Smith because she might have dated him previously
(D) whether a profession that selects its workers on such superficial criteria could produce work that is profound
(E) whether Jonathan Smith is attractive enough to be considered cute by most people

5. Billy Bob: Traditional Native American culture was infatuated with the use of mind-altering substances. Smoking the peace pipe was a cultural archetype. Medicine men would go on vision quests where they would see their spiritual animal through the use of peyote, a substance that contains some of the compounds currently found in a drug known as "acid."

Peggy Sue: You build an overblown case for cultural obsession through the use of limited examples. I would not say that our society is infatuated with the use of mind-altering substances, but I think that people use them more often than Native Americans once did. Drinking alcohol and smoking cigarettes at bars are more than cultural archetypes; they are staples of our time.

Which of the following best expresses the point at issue between Billy Bob and Peggy Sue?

(A) the value of using mind-altering substances to serve certain functions in traditional Native American culture versus their value in contemporary American society
(B) Billy Bob's possible vested interest in proving that Native Americans of long ago were infatuated with the use of mind-altering substances
(C) the advisability of any culture being obsessed with substances that impair normal functions enough to be considered mind-altering
(D) whether traditional Native American society was infatuated with the use of mind-altering substances when compared to our own society
(E) whether drinking alcohol and smoking cigarettes in bars, if done by Native Americans, would be equivalent to their traditional cultural practices

6. Dermatologist: Your skin is nearly perfect. However, it could be improved by applications of moisturizer every other night. If you do this, then it will not get rough and scaly. Additionally, your skin will breathe better, because the moisture will open up your pores to the environment.

Patient: I see what you are saying, but I feel that medicine would be more appropriate than moisturizer. I know that you think that moisturizer is medicine, but I feel that something more potent is in order.

Which of the following is the main point of the dermatologist's argument?

(A) The client should heed the advice of a doctor rather than the client's uninformed personal opinion.
(B) The client's skin is essentially perfect, but there are ways to improve it.
(C) The client's skin could be improved by applying moisturizer every other night.
(D) Medicine would be a better treatment than moisturizer.
(E) Skin breathes better when moisturizer is applied to it every other night.

7. Physicist: Travel at the speed of light will never be possible. When a massive entity gains speed, its mass increases so that it takes more and more energy to increase its speed.

Student: But what about particles and objects that are really small? Take, for example, this baseball. There will certainly be some method to propel it faster than the speed of light.

Which of the following characterizes the student's response to the professor?

(A) The student does not provide an alternative hypothesis regarding objects and speed.
(B) The student does not understand science as well as the professor.
(C) The student has misinterpreted a key term used by the professor.
(D) The student completely agrees with the professor's conclusion.
(E) The student surmises that something is always true when it is true only sometimes.

ANSWERS AND EXPLANATIONS

Question 1

Squib: The government official's main point is that if resources were devoted to looking for alternative energy sources instead of new oil technologies, then soon society would not have the power it needs. The environmentalist claims that resources can be devoted to looking for alternative energy sources even if searching for oil ceases because enough oil has been stored up to meet energy needs until the alternative sources come into use.

Question stem: It asks for a point about which the speakers are committed to disagreeing.

Correct answer: E. The government official says that there would be a gap in energy supplies, but the environmentalist claims that there is enough oil in storage to bridge the gap.

(A) The government official never makes this claim, and the environmentalist claims the opposite.

(B) No such idea is formulated in the passage.

(C) The speakers seem to agree about this point, even though the environmentalist does not explicitly state a position.

(D) Neither speaker discusses what might happen if energy supplies run out.

Question 2

Squib: Byron claims that people should avoid looking into mirrors in order to ignore and repress issues relating to their self-image. Sally never claims anything about mirrors but instead says that rather than ignoring self-image issues, people should address those issues and talk about them. So what the speakers disagree about is how to deal with self-image issues.

Question stem: Find the point at issue between the speakers.

Correct answer: C. The merits of repressing one's self-image issues is the topic that the speakers debate.

(A) Sally does not make a claim about mirrors, and we cannot infer her opinion based on the evidence provided.

(B) Sally does not make a claim about mirrors, so we cannot choose this answer choice.

(D) Sally would probably agree with this point, but we cannot really tell if Byron would disagree. He never says that issues in general should not be talked

about. He merely says that a specific category, self-image issues, should be repressed in some situations.

(E) Sally says nothing about mirrors.

Question 3

Squib: The evangelist's point is that God's work will be served by the evangelist building a church. The TV watcher's point is that the church is being built for the evangelist and not necessarily for any God, and certainly not for the community.

Question stem: What are the speakers committed to disagreeing about?

Correct answer: A. The evangelist claims that the church is being built "for our community." The TV watcher claims that the church is not being built for the community.

(B) This is a good second-best choice, but it is important to note that the TV watcher does not definitively claim that God will not be served by sending the evangelist money. He merely claims that it is not certain that God will be served. Therefore, he is not committed to disagreeing with the evangelist's contention that the work of God will be served by sending him money.

(C) This is not stated by either speaker.

(D) The evangelist would surely agree with the TV watcher about this claim.

(E) The speakers do not address this idea directly.

Question 4

Squib: Zeke claims that if you are not at least cute, then you do not have a job in Hollywood. Amy provides the counterexample of Jonathan Smith, who is a great Hollywood actor whom people would not consider to be cute. The truth of this example would invalidate Zeke's contention that if you are not cute, then you do not have a job in Hollywood.

Question stem: Determine the point at issue between the speakers.

Correct answer: E. If Zeke feels that Jonathan Smith is cute, then his previous claims would be valid. However, if Amy is correct and Jonathan is not cute, then Zeke's claims would be invalid. For these reasons, this is a point at issue between the characters.

(A) Both speakers agree that Jonathan Smith is a child of a famous actor even though he might not be personally attractive.

(B) Questions about the attractiveness of James Smith were not raised by Amy.

(C) This is not pointed out by Zeke or Amy.

(D) While this is an interesting thought, it is a little too profound for Zeke's and Amy's discussion.

Question 5

Squib: Billy claims that traditional Native American culture used drugs prolifically and was infatuated with mind-altering substances. Peggy claims that Billy draws his conclusion based on too few examples. She makes the counterclaim that modern society is not infatuated with mind-altering substances even though people today use them more than the Native Americans did.

Question stem: What is the point at issue?

Correct answer: D. Whether or not traditional Native American society was infatuated with mind-altering substances is the point at issue. Billy does not contend that Native Americans in times gone by were more infatuated with these substances than modern Americans in general, but this is still the best answer choice even though this comparison is included.

(A) Neither speaker makes a normative judgment about mind-altering substances.

(B) Neither speaker makes a claim that Billy has a vested interest in proving anything.

(C) The advisability of anything is never discussed.

(E) This hypothetical scenario is too drawn out and abstract to be put forward by either speaker. Neither speaker claims that this would be the case or that it would not be the case.

Question 6

Squib: This question is not a true controversy question, but instead is thrown in to demonstrate how these questions are sometimes tweaked to become a different type of question. This question is actually a conclusion question. The dermatologist's main point is that the patient's skin would be improved by applying moisturizer to it every other night.

Question stem: Find the main point of the dermatologist's argument.

Correct answer: C. This is the main point of the dermatologist's argument. Everything else that he states in his opinion leads up to and supports this contention.

(A) This is never stated by the dermatologist.

(B) This point is true, but it is too general to be the dermatologist's main point. He specifically recommends moisturizer and gives reasons why the patient should apply this specific treatment.

(D) This is the main point of the patient's argument.

(E) This is a supporting claim made by the dermatologist that would support the patient's applying the moisturizer.

Question 7

Squib: This is actually a reasoning strategy question because, even though there are two speakers arguing, the question asks how to characterize the student's response; that is, was the logic sound and what type of logic was used? The physicist claims that "massive bodies" will never be able to reach the speed of light. The student misinterprets "massive" to mean an object that is relatively large. The professor means any body that has mass, which would include the student's counterexamples.

Question stem: Characterize the student's response.

Correct answer: C. Misinterpreting the term *massive bodies* is what confuses the student.

(A) The student does do this.

(B) This is possibly true based on the student's remarks, but this does not characterize the logic of his response to the professor.

(D) The student disagrees and provides a counterexample to refute the professor's conclusion.

(E) The student does not do this.

LOGICAL REASONING: TIPS FOR FURTHER STUDY

1. Identify the question types that consistently give you trouble. Spend time practicing these types of questions. On the test, slow down when you reach these types of questions, and take some extra time to get them right.
2. Identify the question types that you consistently answer correctly. On the test, you can answer these questions more quickly and save time for question types that are more difficult for you.
3. Diagram the sufficient-necessary statements within squibs.
4. Use scholarly reading techniques to annotate important ideas in the squib.
5. Practice these questions, because the more that you practice, the more you will gain in speed and accuracy. Test takers have a huge potential for improvement on logical reasoning questions.

CHAPTER 5

READING COMPREHENSION

In this chapter you will learn:

- The six major types of LSAT reading comprehension questions

- Techniques for understanding and retaining information as you read

- Easy-to-follow solution methods for every kind of reading question

Reading comprehension is a question type that most test takers have been faced with since high school on standardized tests such as the PSAT, SSAT, SAT, and ACT, so this part of the LSAT should hold few surprises. Each LSAT reading comprehension section contains four passages, each of which is followed by six to eight questions.

The Technique of "Scholarly Reading"

To improve your ability to read these passages and retain the information, the best thing you can do is start practicing a technique called *scholarly reading*. The actual details of this technique will be different for each person, but in general, scholarly reading consists of underlining, starring, and bracketing parts of paragraphs that you think are important.

The importance of scholarly reading should not be underestimated because

1. It helps you to interact more with the passage while you read, thereby causing you pay closer attention to what is being said.
2. It enables you to turn a mass of words into a marked, noted, and organized parcel of information. (The actual amount of markup that

you do will depend on the passage and also on your own preferences, but organizing the passage to some degree will help you to find hidden information quickly and efficiently.)
3. It causes you to remember more of the passage as a whole, because you will be constantly asking yourself which parts are important so that you can underline or star them. By doing this, you will have already quizzed yourself on the information even before the questions ask you about particular ideas.

Reading the passages in a scholarly way is very important. Begin developing your own scholarly reading style as soon as you can. That way, interacting with what you read will become second nature to you, and that reading skill will raise your LSAT score.

Be careful that you do not overuse this technique. The point is to identify ideas that are important and remember them while filtering out the fluff. Underlining everything without discriminating between what is important and what is not is the functional equivalent of underlining nothing—and even worse, you will waste time doing it. Do not worry if, at first, you are not sure how much to note or underline. As you practice, you will develop whatever personal scholarly reading style is most helpful to you.

Here is a sample LSAT Reading Comprehension section passage. It has been underlined, starred, and annotated in ways that would help a test taker locate and remember important information.

As personifications of their respective nations, the United States and England, Uncle Sam and John Bull became popular caricatures during the nineteenth century. John Bull originated earlier, as
5 a character in John Arbuthnot's *The History of John Bull* (1712). He became widely known from cartoons by Sir John Tenniel published in the British humor magazine *Punch* during the middle and late nineteenth century. In those cartoons, he
10 was portrayed as an honest, solid, farmer figure, often in a Union Jack waistcoat, and accompanied by a bulldog. He became so familiar that his name frequently appeared in books, plays, periodical titles, and as a brand name or trademark. Although
15 frequently used through World War II, since the 1950s John Bull has been seen less often.
Uncle Sam originated in popular culture. His origins are disputed, but the name usually is associated with Sam Wilson, a businessman who
20 supplied the army during the War of 1812. His barrels were stamped "U.S." for the government, leading him to be nicknamed "Uncle Sam." The symbolic Uncle Sam's appearance evolved from that of Brother Jonathan, the most common earlier
25 symbol for the United States. The character Brother Jonathan had actually originated shortly after the American Revolution. Americans, united, despite their differences, in a new free Union, referred to each other as "Brother Jon" to express their
30 newfound fraternity as Americans. The two characters, Uncle Sam and Brother Jonathan, were used interchangeably from the 1830s through the 1860s.
As with John Bull, the cartoonists of *Punch*
35 helped develop the figure of Uncle Sam, showing him as a lean, whiskered man wearing a top hat and striped pants. The famous American cartoonist Thomas Nast crystallized the image with his cartoons beginning in the 1870s. By 1917, when
40 James Montgomery Flagg depicted him on the famous World War I recruiting poster, Uncle Sam was an icon, readily recognized around the globe. He was officially adopted as the national symbol of the United States in 1950.
45 John Bull and Uncle Sam have often been depicted interacting, as friends or antagonists, and thus have served as symbols of international relations as well as national caricatures. As the personifications of entire nations of people, Uncle
50 Sam and John Bull have both served as cultural stereotypes, national inspirations, and international icons for their respective countries, and, although fictional, both should be appreciated as important historical figures.

Handwritten margin notes (left): popular caricatures John Bull; Uncle Sam & Brother Jon origin; Cartoonists crystallize Uncle Sam; representations & symbols

All proper names, people, places, and other items that will play active roles in the passage should be circled the first time they appear. This is why Uncle Sam, John Bull, *Punch*, and Brother Jonathon are circled.

In the margin next to each paragraph, a three- to five-word synopsis of the paragraph should be written in order to jog your memory if you need to review the paragraph.

Facts that seem important should be underlined.

Whenever an important fact is stated about a specific character, the name should be bracketed so that you can easily tell to whom the information refers.

Facts that are particularly important should be starred. The fact that cartoonists from *Punch* had a hand in developing both national symbols is important.

Bracketing of facts may be faster than underlining, or you may wish to differentiate some material by bracketing it rather than underlining it.

PART II / SOLUTION STRATEGIES FOR EVERY LSAT QUESTION TYPE

The sample just shown illustrates one style of scholarly reading, but you should use whatever style works for you. Develop your own techniques to order and process the information in Reading Comprehension passages in whatever way suits you best.

Here is a sample Reading Comprehension passage with questions:

Taiwan's highest judicial organ is the Judicial *Yuan* (*Ssu-fa yuan*), which is responsible for supervising the administration of the various levels of the courts. It has the
(5) further responsibility of insuring the discipline of civil servants. The structure of the body is changing due to constitutional amendments; as of 2003, the Judicial *Yuan* will have 15 grand justices, of whom two will be appointed
(10) by the President to serve as president and vice-president of the *Yuan*.

Under the Judicial *Yuan* are the Supreme Court, the high courts, district courts, the Administrative Court, and the Commission on
(15) the Disciplinary Sanctions of Public Functionaries. In addition, there is a Council of Grand Justices, made up of the grand justices of the Judicial *Yuan*. Beginning in 2003, eight of the grand justices, including the
(20) president and vice-president of the *Yuan*, will serve four-year terms, and the remaining grand justices will serve eight-year terms. The function of the Council is to interpret the Constitution and unify the interpretation of
(25) laws and ordinances; it meets regularly and may hold oral proceedings when necessary. The interpretations are published, together with any dissenting opinions.

In 1993, a Constitutional Court was
(30) established to adjudicate cases concerning the dissolution of political parties that have violated the Constitution. It is composed of the grand justices. The Ministry of the Interior, which oversees political parties, may
(35) petition the Constitutional Court to consider dissolving any political party whose goals and actions are found to endanger the existence of the Republic of China or its democratic, constitutional order.
(40) Ordinary courts are arranged in a three-level hierarchy: district courts for cases of the first instance, high courts that hear appeals, and the Supreme Court, as the highest appellate level. Issues of fact are determined
(45) at the first and second instances; only issues of law are considered at the Supreme Court, the court of third instance. Criminal cases in which rebellion, treason, and offenses against friendly relations with other nations are
(50) alleged are handled by high courts as the courts of first instance, with appeals possible to the Supreme Court.

Although Taiwan is a civil law jurisdiction, and as such does not adopt the general concept
(55) of binding precedent, judicial authorizations are nonetheless widely consulted. In general, court decisions bind only the case in trial. Nevertheless, court decisions do become binding precedent when they are final
(60) judgments made by the Supreme Court or the Supreme Administrative Court and are selected as precedent based on decisions of the periodical symposiums of those two courts. The Supreme Court has jurisdiction
(65) over both civil and criminal cases; the Supreme Administrative Court, on the other hand, has jurisdiction over administrative lawsuits. As for decisions made by other general courts of first and second instance
(70) (called "district courts" and "high courts") or the first instance administrative courts (called "the high administrative court"), they will serve merely as references.

1. Which one of the following best states the purpose of the passage?

   (A) to explain the purpose of the Judicial *Yuan* in Taiwan
   (B) to make a case for changing a specific judicial court in Taiwan
   (C) to provide a general description of the judicial courts in Taiwan
   (D) to analyze the factors responsible for recent changes in the Taiwanese government
   (E) to placate the opposition that developed in 1993 after the Constitutional Court was established

2. Which court is a member of a three-level judicial hierarchy?

   (A) the Judicial *Yuan*
   (B) the constitutional court
   (C) the high court
   (D) commission on Disciplinary Sanctions
   (E) none of the above

3. Which would most undermine the author's claim that the Constitutional Court was established to adjudicate cases where political parties have violated the Constitution?

(A) The Taiwanese Constitution was created in 2002.
(B) In some cases, the court has ruled against certain political parties.
(C) The court mostly tries cases of civil disobedience unrelated to the Constitution.
(D) Most justices who sit on the court have never read the Taiwanese Constitution.
(E) There were never any Constitutional violations before the 1950s.

4. The author of the passage uses the term "precedent" in line 55 to refer to

(A) compelling opinions
(B) previous occurrences
(C) judicial contraventions
(D) accepted body of law
(E) previously documented facts

5. The author would most likely describe the role of the "Ministry of the Interior" in lines 33–34 as which of the following?

(A) petitioning for the dissolution of certain political parties
(B) monitoring the activity of political parties within Taiwan
(C) interacting closely with the Constitutional Court
(D) administering the land with sufficient precedent
(E) determining which political parties receive government subsidy

6. The passage provides support for all of the following claims about the Judicial *Yuan* EXCEPT:

(A) The council of Grand Justices is partly composed of members of the Judicial *Yuan*.
(B) All members of the Judicial *Yuan* serve eight-year terms.
(C) The Judicial *Yuan* has 15 grand justices.
(D) The Supreme Court is under the Judicial *Yuan*.
(E) The Judicial *Yuan* is responsible for supervising the administration of courts.

Reading Comprehension Question Types

Several different types of questions are commonly used with LSAT Reading Comprehension passages. Recognizing these question types and knowing what each one is asking will help you raise your Reading Comprehension score.

Here are the six main types of LSAT Reading Comprehension questions:

1. **Main Point:** These questions ask you to identify the main point of a particular paragraph or of the passage as a whole. They are similar to conclusion logical reasoning questions, and the same solution rules hold true. For instance, be sure to identify the main point and not a subsidiary point or supporting claim.
2. **Author's/Character's Opinion:** These questions ask you to identify the author's or a character's opinion about a particular issue presented in the passage. Opinions can support, oppose, or be neutral toward the issue.
3. **Claims:** These questions ask you to identify particular claims, ideas, or propositions formulated by the author or by characters in order to support a theory.
4. **Syntax:** These questions ask you to provide the meaning of a particular word. They also ask you what words refer to and why they are used.
5. **Inference:** These questions ask you to identify an inference made by the author or by characters within a passage. They may also ask you to make your own inference about a condition or event mentioned in the passage. These questions are similar to conclusion logical reasoning questions.
6. **Support/Undermine:** These questions are exactly the same as "strengthen" and "weaken" logical reasoning questions, except that they apply to a reading comprehension passage.

The best way to master LSAT Reading Comprehension questions is to practice question types one at a time. To that end, each of the following passages has been constructed to support just a single question type. (Note that this never happens on the actual LSAT!) Reading the passages and working through the accompanying questions can help you boost your LSAT Reading Comprehension score.

By their own accounts and those of their critics, the current generation of students is a video generation. They learned to read with Big Bird on *Sesame Street*, and their view of
(5) the world has been largely formed and shaped through visual culture. This familiarity can make film and video a powerful pedagogical tool. Visual media also address different learning modalities, making material more
(10) accessible to both visual and aural learners. Add to this the rich array of diverse videos and documentaries available, and it's easy to see why these formats represent the second most popular source used in social studies
(15) classes.

However, the very qualities that make film and video so popular present problems as well. For students raised on a steady diet of media consumption, film and documentary
(20) footage used in the classroom often becomes "edutainment." This does more than simply distort historical and social issues. It reinforces the passive viewing and unquestioning acceptance of received material
(25) that accompanies growing up in a video environment.

That passivity and lack of critical awareness is anathema to a democracy. An essential aspect of social studies education is
(30) the teaching of information and skills needed by people who are to participate actively as citizens in a democratic society. Thirty years ago this meant teaching students to read the newspaper critically, to identify bias there,
(35) and to distinguish between factual reporting and editorializing. Critical viewing skills must be added to this effort. One solution to the omnipotence of visual culture is to develop a critical awareness of that culture.

(40) The last 10 years have witnessed many efforts combining media literacy and pedagogy. It is important to understand that the same types of questions must be asked of film as of any other document. Firstly, this
(45) includes questions about the content of the piece. What is the composition trying to portray, and how do unique media techniques add to, take away from, or change the message? Secondly, what factors of
(50) production affect the final product? For example, if the director or writers have a background that disposes them to bias, it is important to be aware of it when critically analyzing the visual media. Finally, how was

(55) the document received at the time of its production? By researching the answers to these questions, students add a more critical element to the use of visual media in the classroom and, in turn, enhance it as an
(60) educational tool.

1. Which one of the following best states the main idea of the passage?

  (A) Passive viewing of visual media is just as dangerous as passive reading of educational literature.
  (B) "Edutainment" is increasingly encouraged by school administrators in America.
  (C) Film and video in the classroom do nothing but distort historical and social views.
  (D) Visual media can be a powerful educational tool if presented properly.
  (E) By learning to study any media critically, students become better prepared for participation in a democratic society.

2. The first paragraph primarily serves to

  (A) introduce the current generation as one that has been educated by visual media since it was very young
  (B) describe Big Bird as a educational icon of the current generation
  (C) present the educational potential of visual media for the current video generation
  (D) explain how video bridges the gap between visual and aural learners
  (E) formulate an argument that the current generation's view of the world has been shaped through a camera lens

3. The second paragraph primarily serves to

(A) bring up the social issues associated with the use of visual media in the classroom
(B) describe the greatest potential danger of using visual media in the classroom
(C) define the term *edutainment*
(D) present an argument for the use of visual media in the classroom
(E) propose edutainment as an alternative to the use of visual media in the classroom

4. The third paragraph primarily serves to

(A) present bias as a vice of democracy
(B) explain that critical awareness is a skill that should be learned early in education
(C) detail the problem of passive viewing and propose a solution
(D) summarize the problems associated with edutainment
(E) argue that critical cultural awareness can come only from viewing media in the classroom

5. The fourth paragraph primarily serves to

(A) explain how a film should be critically analyzed by students to comprehend its value
(B) ask questions about visual media that the reader is supposed to answer
(C) demonstrate that there are still many unanswered questions about edutainment
(D) present visual media as a great pedagogical tool
(E) summarize the rest of the passage through questions

6. Which one of the following best describes the content of the passage as a whole?

(A) There is a rich array of diverse film and documentary choices available for use in the classroom.
(B) Visual media in the classroom plant the seeds of passive viewing and apathy into our democratic society.
(C) Education in America is becoming digitized, and new critical thinking skills must be introduced to deal with this phenomenon.
(D) Visual media offer both a unique educational tool and an opportunity for the practice of critical analysis.
(E) Because the current generation is a television generation, edutainment can take place at home as well as in the classroom.

ANSWERS AND EXPLANATIONS

1. **D** The first paragraph introduces the use of visual media as a potentially ideal way to educate the current generation. The following two paragraphs bring up the possible problems associated with "edutainment," but the final paragraph concludes that if these problems can be resolved, visual media can be a powerful educational tool. Therefore, choice D is the correct answer.

(A and E) These are both points made in the passage, but neither is strong enough to be considered the main idea. The idea in choice E appears at only a single point in the passage. The idea in choice A appears at several points, but the passage as a whole is about both the good and positive and the negative aspects of visual media.
(B) Not only does the author present the term "edutainment" in a negative light, but also there is no mention of school administrators in the passage. This choice cannot be the main point of the passage.
(C) The author says that improper viewing of film in the classroom can distort historical and cultural views. However, this is a minor point, and as choice C is phrased, it is a misrepresentation of what the author actually wrote.

2. **C** In the first paragraph, the author introduces the current generation as a television generation, argues that education through visual media serves both visual and aural learners, and states that there is a huge array of visual media teaching materials available. Choice C is clearly the best summary of these ideas.

(A and D) Both these points are made in the paragraph, but they merely support the main idea encapsulated by choice C.
(B and E) These are both minor implications of statements made in the first paragraph. They are not the main focus of the paragraph.

3. **B** The second paragraph introduces the primary danger of visual media education: its potential for becoming "edutainment." The author supports this idea by saying that edutainment can distort historical and cultural views as well as reinforce passive viewing. Choice B clearly captures this point.

(A) The issues associated with the use of visual media that the second paragraph brings up are not social issues. They are more like pedagogical issues or educational dangers. Choice B is a better answer.

(C) The term *edutainment* is not actually defined at any point in the essay. Rather, readers understand its meaning through its context and its roots.

(D) If anything, the dangers presented in the second paragraph serve as a counterargument to the use of visual media in the classroom. However, the author overcomes this counterargument in the remainder of the passage.

(E) Again, edutainment is not presented as a positive term. Its negative connotations tell you that it is not something the author would offer as a good alternative to efficient use of visual media in the classroom.

4. **C** The third paragraph has five sentences: Two detail the dangers associated with passive viewing and three address the problem. Choice C is therefore the best answer.

(A) This statement is not a reasonable inference to make. "Bias" and "democracy" are not even mentioned in the same context.

(B) While the content of choice B may be true, age is not referred to in this paragraph or earlier in the passage. Therefore, this is not a good inference to make.

(D) The problems associated with edutainment were first presented in the second paragraph. The third paragraph serves more to do what choice C says: detail the problem and start to address it.

(E) This statement is not made, and it is too strong an inference to make from the information the passage gives you.

5. **A** The final paragraph essentially lists the general analytical questions that should be asked of any document used in class. It says that this analysis enhances the use of media as an educational tool. Choice A is the best answer.

(B) These questions are clearly not meant for readers to answer themselves. Rather, they are presented to give readers a clearer understanding of what critical awareness entails.

(C and E) Given the context of the paragraph and the content of the questions, neither of these is accurate.

(D) This has already been established from earlier in the essay. The final paragraph builds on this point, but given its content, it is by no means the paragraph's main idea.

6. **D** It is clear that this passage focuses on two things: using visual media as an educational tool and using critical analysis to combat the problems associated with visual media. Therefore, choice D is the only reasonable answer.

(A and B) Both these statements are very narrow views of what the passage is about. Statement A reflects a minor point from the first paragraph, while statement B offers a theme that, when taken alone, distorts the meaning of the passage as a whole.

(C) Choice C takes its analysis too far by using a more general term ("digitized"). The passage was not written about all forms of digitization but only about the use of visual media in the classroom.

(E) Choice E is an inference not directly supported by the passage, nor does it reflect the main idea.

It is a common saying that thought is free. A person can never be hindered from thinking whatever he chooses so long as he conceals what he thinks. The working of his mind is
(5) limited only by the bounds of his experience and the power of his imagination. But this natural liberty of private thinking is of little value. It is unsatisfactory and even painful to the thinker himself if he is not permitted to
(10) communicate his thoughts to others, and it is obviously of no value to his neighbors. Moreover, it is extremely difficult to hide thoughts that have any power over the mind. If a man's thinking leads him to call in
(15) question ideas and customs which regulate the behavior of those about him, to reject beliefs which they hold, or to see better ways of life than those they follow, it is almost impossible for him, if he is convinced of the truth of his
(20) own reasoning, not to betray by silence, chance words, or general attitude that he is different from them and does not share their opinions. Some have preferred, like Socrates, and some would prefer today, to face death
(25) rather than conceal their thoughts. Thus freedom of thought, in any valuable sense, includes freedom of speech.

At present, in the most civilized countries, freedom of speech is taken as a matter of
(30) course and seems a perfectly simple thing. We are so accustomed to it that we look on it as a natural right. But this right has been acquired only in quite recent times, and the way to its attainment has lain through lakes of blood. It
(35) has taken centuries to persuade the most enlightened peoples that liberty to publish one's opinions and to discuss all questions is a good and not a bad thing. Human societies in the past (there are some brilliant exceptions)
(40) have been generally opposed to freedom of thought, or, in other words, to new ideas, and it is easy to see why.

The average brain is naturally lazy and tends to take the line of least resistance. The
(45) mental world of the ordinary person consists of beliefs that she has accepted without questioning and to which she is firmly attached; she is instinctively hostile to anything that would upset the established order of this
(50) familiar world. A new idea, inconsistent with some of the beliefs that she holds, means the necessity of rearranging her mind; and this process is laborious, requiring a painful expenditure of brain energy. To his and her
(55) peers, who form the vast majority, new ideas and opinions that cast doubt on established beliefs and institutions seem evil because they are disagreeable.

The repugnance due to mere mental
(60) laziness is increased by a positive feeling of fear. The conservative instinct hardens into the conservative doctrine that the foundations of society are endangered by any alterations in its structure. It is only recently that people have
(65) been abandoning the belief that the welfare of a state depends on rigid stability and on the preservation of its traditions and institutions unchanged. However, wherever that belief prevails, novel opinions are felt to be
(70) dangerous as well as annoying, and anyone who asks inconvenient questions about the why and the wherefore of accepted principles is considered a pestilent person.

1. This passage is primarily concerned with

   (A) free thought and its continued social prominence
   (B) the customs that regulate the behavior of people in society
   (C) free speech, the relatively newfound right to express free thought openly in society
   (D) mental laziness, the abhorrence of new ideas
   (E) the attainment of natural rights in a lazy society

2. The main idea of the first paragraph is to

   (A) explain that the natural liberty of private thinking is particularly valuable to an individual or a society
   (B) present freedom of thought as a basic natural right
   (C) argue that it is worth dying rather than having to conceal all one's thoughts
   (D) suggest that the only limits on freedom of thought are the bounds of imagination
   (E) justify philosophically the natural link between freedom of thought and freedom of speech

3. The second paragraph primarily serves to

   (A) dramatize the subject through the mention of shed blood
   (B) introduce freedom of speech as an age-old right in most human societies
   (C) decry society's fight against all odds for freedom of thought and speech
   (D) explain that the attainment of freedom of speech was no simple task
   (E) illustrate the ongoing governmental resistance to freedom of speech

4. The goal of the third paragraph is to

   (A) debate whether or not free thought is evil

   (B) describe why people can feel threatened by new ideas, and in turn, free speech

   (C) explain why the majority in a society is typically politically conservative

   (D) argue against the introduction of new ideas into an accepted world of beliefs

   (E) offer a conservative alternative to the radicalism of free speech

5. The final paragraph is used to

   (A) express the author's hatred for mental laziness

   (B) link the conservative doctrine to the creation of novel opinions

   (C) relate the effect a belief in "rigid stability" has on the ability to speak freely in a society

   (D) enhance the reader's understanding of mental laziness through an explanation of the term "novel opinions"

   (E) argue that one who asks questions is a danger to modern society

6. What is the author's purpose in using Socrates in line 23?

   (A) As a famous martyr in the fight for freedom of private thought, Socrates exemplifies the importance of restraint in expression.

   (B) By using the name of a famous figure in history, the author personalizes for readers the argument that freedom of speech is a great gift.

   (C) The author uses Socrates' famous death to convey the real danger of self-expression.

   (D) The author uses Socrates as an example to give the argument a credible base in reality.

   (E) By mentioning a famous martyr in the fight for freedom of speech, the author seeks to convey the idea that the subject of the passage is very important.

ANSWERS AND EXPLANATIONS

1. **C** The author uses the first paragraph philosophically to define free speech as the right to express free thought openly in society. The rest of the passage describes why freedom of thought is important and why it has been a difficult right to attain. Choice C does the best job of encompassing all these ideas.

   (A) The first paragraph is the only paragraph directly focused on free thought. The rest of the passage is focused on free speech, and despite their clear correlation, this choice is not as good as choice C.

   (B) This choice is not a logical leap to make. It is merely an out-of-context quote from the text meant to confuse you.

   (D) This is the focus of the second half of the passage, but the passage is meant to do more than just discuss mental laziness. Choice C is a better answer.

   (E) This answer is not specific enough. The passage does not describe the attainment of all natural rights in a lazy society but only free speech.

2. **E** The author introduces free thought as the most basic of natural rights and carefully makes the link between free thought and free speech, which the author says should be considered an innate part of free thought. Clearly, the purpose of this paragraph is expressed well in choice E.

   (A, B, C, and D) Each of these choices is a point made in the first paragraph, but none explains the purpose of the paragraph as well as choice E. The passage as a whole is about free speech, so it is important that the author introduce this term in the first paragraph for use in the rest of the passage.

3. **D** A good way to summarize the second paragraph would be as follows: "Many people think we have always had free speech, but after many centuries of violent attempts at persuasion, it is actually a rather recent acquisition." Using this summary, choice D is the most accurate response.

   (A) Given the thoughtful tone of the passage, it seems unlikely that the author was trying to dramatize the subject matter in a manner such as this.

   (B) This is directly counter to what is stated in the paragraph.

   (C) The author does mention society's fight for freedom of speech over many centuries. However, he or she does not decry it, but rather, if anything, extols it.

   (E) The paragraph actually states that governmental resistance is no longer an ongoing problem; instead, in the most civilized countries, freedom of speech is now nearly a matter of course.

4. **B** Essentially, the third paragraph describes "mental laziness," the difficulty people often have in accepting new thoughts or opinions. The author clearly explains why new ideas often make people feel that their own beliefs are being threatened. Given the context, you can infer that the introduction of new ideas is a direct result of free speech.

(A) The tone of this paragraph is definitely that of a description of something the author sees as clear-cut. There is no debate or clash of opinions.

(C) The author mentions nothing about politics in this paragraph; that leap is made in the next paragraph. Here, she or he only explains why people are often ideologically conservative.

(D and E) Both of these choices include ideas that contradict the author's argument. The passage definitely presents free speech in a positive light, so it would be illogical for the author to present these contradictory ideas.

5. **C** "Rigid stability" is essentially the conservative doctrine that the only stable things in a society are those which will not change. The author concludes this paragraph by saying that where this doctrine still prevails, free speech is not safe. This idea is the point of the paragraph, so choice C is the best answer.

(A) The author presents mental laziness as a natural tendency that should be fought. Though it is described in a somewhat negative tone, it should not necessarily be assumed that the author hates it. Nor is this a reasonable description of the paragraph.

(B and E) Both of these choices offer statements that are counterintuitive to the information given in the passage.

(D) While this paragraph is written to enhance the reader's understanding of mental laziness in some ways, it is not also written to explain "novel opinions."

6. **E** The author uses Socrates' name to allude to the ancient philosopher's choice to die rather than conceal his thoughts. By reminding readers that real people have actually chosen to martyr themselves in the name of free speech, the author gives more weight to the subject matter.

(A) Not only was Socrates not a martyr for private thought (if his thoughts were kept private, he would not have been killed), but the author is also not trying to argue for restraint in expression of thought.

(B) The use of Socrates' name does not personalize any of the issues for readers. Since Socrates was an ancient philosopher, mentioning him might actually make the issues seem more distant.

(C) A portrayal like this would be counterintuitive to the rest of the author's argument.

(D) The author's argument is firmly grounded in reality, so there is no need to bring in Socrates merely to emphasize this point.

2 Author's/Character's Opinion Questions

More than 2400 years ago the father of medicine, Hippocrates, first recognized and described stroke as the sudden onset of paralysis. Until recently, modern medicine
(5) has had very little power over this disease, but the world of stroke medicine is changing, and new and better therapies are being developed every day. Today, some people who have a stroke can walk away
(10) from the attack with no or few disabilities if they are treated promptly. Doctors can finally offer stroke patients and their families the one thing that until now has been so hard to give: hope.
(15) In ancient times, stroke was called apoplexy, a general term that physicians applied to anyone suddenly struck down with paralysis. Because many conditions can lead to sudden paralysis, the term
(20) apoplexy did not indicate a specific diagnosis or cause. Physicians knew very little about the cause of stroke and the only established therapy was to feed and care for the patient until the attack ran its course.
(25) The first person to investigate the pathological signs of apoplexy was Johann Jacob Wepfer. Born in Schaffhausen, Switzerland, in 1620, Wepfer studied medicine and was the first to identify
(30) postmortem signs of bleeding in the brains of patients who died of apoplexy. From autopsy studies he gained knowledge of the carotid and vertebral arteries that supply the brain with blood. He also was the first
(35) person to suggest that apoplexy, in addition to being caused by bleeding in the brain, could be caused by a blockage of one of the main arteries supplying blood to the brain; thus, stroke became known as a
(40) cerebrovascular disease (*cerebro* refers to a part of the brain; *vascular* refers to the blood vessels and arteries).
Medical science would eventually confirm Wepfer's hypotheses, but until very
(45) recently doctors could offer little in the area of therapy. Over the last two decades, basic and clinical investigators have learned a great deal about stroke. They have identified major risk factors for the disease
(50) and have developed surgical techniques and drug treatments for the prevention of stroke.

But perhaps the most exciting new development in the field of stroke research is the recent approval of a drug treatment
(55) that can reverse the course of stroke if given during the first few hours after the onset of symptoms.
Studies with animals have shown that brain injury occurs within minutes of a
(60) stroke and can become irreversible within as little as an hour. In humans, brain damage begins from the moment the stroke starts and often continues for days afterward. Scientists now know that there is
(65) a very short window of opportunity for treatment of the most common form of stroke. Because of these and other advances in the field of cerebrovascular disease, stroke patients now have a growing chance
(70) for survival and recovery.

1. Based on the first paragraph, which of the following best characterizes the author's opinion of stroke?

   (A) Even as the world of medicine has changed, stroke has always stayed one step ahead of treatment options.
   (B) Stroke has been successfully treated since the time of Hippocrates, 2400 years ago.
   (C) Stroke must have a more specific definition to be treatable.
   (D) Until recent medical developments, stroke was a devastatingly hopeless disease.
   (E) Despite the development of better stroke therapies, it is doubtful that stroke will ever be fully treatable.

2. Which of the following best describes the opinion of the author of the passage with respect to Wepfer's work?

   (A) unique but directly antithetic
   (B) well-documented but radical
   (C) illuminating but initially ineffectual
   (D) thorough but specious
   (E) innovative but still insignificant

3. It can be inferred from the passage that the author most likely holds which of the following opinions about future cerebrovascular disease research?

   (A) It will focus only on developing new surgical techniques.
   (B) It will result in greater and greater chances for a full recovery from stroke.
   (C) It will focus more and more on autopsy studies due to their clinical reliability.
   (D) Its significance in application will dwindle from this point on.
   (E) It will eventually make apoplexy a completely preventable condition.

4. According to the author, Wepfer's work differed from Hippocrates' in that Wepfer

   (A) did much more field research than Hippocrates
   (B) identified major preliminary risk factors for the disease
   (C) was immediately credited with correctness in his research
   (D) came up with the first modern treatments for stroke
   (E) established the direct physical causes of apoplexy

5. Ancient physicians probably felt which of the following about apoplexy?

   (A) stoic indifference
   (B) reverent acceptance
   (C) cognizant appreciation
   (D) helpless befuddlement
   (E) subconscious denial

6. Based on statements in the passage, which of the following is probably true about the author?

   (A) He or she is grateful that all the apoplexy research efforts of the past are finally resulting in the useful treatments of today.
   (B) He or she has probably suffered a stroke.
   (C) He or she is an accomplished researcher enjoying success in the medical field.
   (D) He or she fears that lack of funding will unfortunately prevent scientists from ever completely preventing cerebrovascular disease.
   (E) He or she is hopeful that Wepfer's research will eventually bring an end to long-term stroke damage as we know it today.

ANSWERS AND EXPLANATIONS

1. **D** Based on lines 4 and 5, we know that "until recently, modern medicine has had very little power over [stroke]." This tells us that the author believes two things: First, in earlier times little could be done to treat stroke victims, and second, recently this situation has changed. Therefore, choice D is basically stated in the text.

   (A) This choice contradicts the phrase "until recently" in line 4, which lets the reader know that stroke is no longer as untreatable as it once was.
   (B) This choice is directly contradictory to the phrase "until recently, modern medicine has had very little power over [stroke]," which tells the reader that, for most of history, stroke has been basically untreatable.
   (C) This choice is not even alluded to in the first paragraph.
   (E) This choice is not inferable from the first paragraph. In fact, the author seems to believe that great advances are soon to come in the field of stroke victim treatment.

2. **C** Questions like this one are often more like a vocabulary test than a difficult analytical test. First, establish what you know from the passage: Wepfer's work was the first of its kind, it was very revealing, it was verified years later, and it was ahead of its time in terms of the ability to apply the knowledge. Therefore, it was *illuminating*, meaning revealing, though not initially *effectual*, meaning usable.

   (A) This choice translates into "one of a kind, but opposite former theories." Given that there were no former theories offered in the passage, this choice is illogical.
   (B) The vocabulary in this choice is simpler, but the choice is still incorrect. The passage says nothing about how Wepfer documented his research, nor does it tell the reader whether or not autopsies were a radical form of research at the time.
   (D) Specious means "seemingly correct, though actually false." The first sentence of the third paragraph tells the reader that Wepfer's findings were accurate.
   (E) This choice translates into "ahead of the times, but still unimportant." The author presents Wepfer's as the most important step in stroke research up to that point in history.

3. **B** Starting in the first paragraph, the tone of the whole passage is one of hope. In particular, the phrase "growing chance" in line 69 establishes choice B as the best answer.

(A and C) These two choices both have no support in the text. Choice A is discredited by its use of the word *only*, while choice C has no real foundation at all.

(D) This choice is counter to the tone and content of the passage. See "growing chance" (line 69).

(E) There is no way for the reader or the author to verify the truth in this statement. It is simply too strong an inference to make in the presence of a more reasonable answer B.

4. **E** The second paragraph tells how Wepfer developed the hypothesis that apoplexy was caused by bleeding in the brain or by blockage in one of the main arteries leading to the brain. It also says that Wepfer was the first to come up with these theories. The passage does not mention any thoughts of Hippocrates on the cause of stroke.

(A) Nothing is said about the amount of research that either Hippocrates or Wepfer undertook, even though it does describe the results of Wepfer's research. Therefore, choice A is not a valid inference.

(B) The passage attributes this to researchers long after Wepfer's time. See lines 46–51.

(C) The author's use of the word eventually in line 43 tells the reader that Wepfer's theories were not verified until sometime later.

(D) Based on lines 43–46 and the fact that the author does not attribute any developed treatments to Wepfer, this choice can be discounted.

5. **D** This is another vocabulary game. It is apparent that ancient physicians would have looked on apoplexy with confusion, hopelessness, and possibly fear. This fits best with choice D.

(A) It is doubtful that any physicians would ever be indifferent to a disease. It is their job to care.

(B) This choice translates into "respectful acceptance." This implies almost the same indifference as in choice A and is therefore equally unlikely.

(C) The word appreciation completely discredits this choice. No one appreciates a disease.

(E) There is no implication of denial from ancient physicians. They established a name for the disease and treated it as well as they could.

6. **A** The tone of the passage clearly indicates that the author is pleased with the new therapies for stroke patients. Choice A is a good summary of the theme of the passage. It is also a good analysis of the author's feelings.

(B and C) Both of these choices are inferences without any real textual base.

(D) There is nothing in the passage that references funding at all. This is also a baseless inference.

(E) Wepfer's research described only the direct physical causes of stroke. His findings no longer play any active role in the hunt for preventive measures. He has been dead for nearly 400 years.

In the American Civil War, the Union and the Confederacy were not well matched as opponents. The census of 1860 showed the North had a population of 20 million while the

(5) South had a population of 9 million, and of the Southern population, 3.5 million were slaves. The number of white males between the ages of 15 and 40 was about 4 million in the North, and only 1.1 million in the South. As Union

(10) General William Sherman had pointed out, the South also had a poor industrial and economic infrastructure. When the war started, only 10% of American goods were manufactured in the South. The North had 22,000 miles

(15) (35,400 kilometers) of railroad track, the South had only 9000 miles (14,500 kilometers), and these Southern lines tended to be local feeder routes, disconnected and based on different rail gauges. The Southern

(20) economy was based on cotton exports, which made it vulnerable to naval blockade, and the Confederacy suffered from a feeble financial infrastructure that would make funding a war difficult.

(25) However, the South also had its advantages. Much of the old U.S. Army high command had been from the South, and the Southern clique had in fact by accident or design driven promising Northern officers out

(30) of the prewar Army. The Confederacy began the war with superior military leadership. Furthermore, the South was fighting on the defensive, which would help even the odds against an attacker with superior numbers by

(35) forcing him to attack entrenchments and fortifications. An attacker would also be reliant on long supply lines that would stretch and become more vulnerable to a counterstrike the further the invader drove into

(40) Southern territory, while the Confederates would be able to move troops and supplies on shorter and more easily protected interior lines of communications.

The South, however, suffered from

(45) wartime disadvantages due to its political philosophy and social structure. In the first place, the Confederacy was based on the concept of states' rights, which entailed a certain degree of national disunity as a

(50) fundamental principle. Additionally, while Northern society could hardly be described as classless, Southern society resembled the social structure of serfdom that existed in the Middle Ages. The elite that led the

(55) Confederacy was only 0.5% of the population, and even outside of the institution of slavery, whose unstable state made it a liability in a class all its own, the South was riddled with class distinctions that hindered it from

(60) unifying as tightly as the North did for the war.

Relatively few Southerners owned slaves. The poor farmers who resided near the bottom of the Southern social order had no stake in

(65) the Confederacy and no interest in fighting to sustain the institution of slavery. But Southerners shared a common sense of independence, and many would still fight against the Union merely because they were

(70) confronted with an invader who threatened their homes and families. After the war was well under way, a captive rebel private was asked what he was fighting for. He simply replied: "I'm fighting because ya'll are down

(75) here."

1. Based on the passage, which of the following best describes the author's opinion of the Southerners in the Civil War?

    (A) The Southerners were underdogs, but they were still willing to fight.
    (B) Southerners' development of secret military weapons was the turning point in the war.
    (C) Southerners did not concern themselves with troublesome class distinctions.
    (D) While the Southerners suffered many setbacks, their many advantages over the North guaranteed ultimate victory.
    (E) The Southerners were at such a disadvantage that they could not offer any resistance.

2. Based on the passage, which of the following best describes the author's opinion of the Northerners in the Civil War?

    (A) Without General William Sherman, their economic and industrial strength would have been wasted.
    (B) They knew in advance how to overcome every Southern advantage.
    (C) Their society was more stable because it was classless and egalitarian.
    (D) Their superior numbers and infrastructure gave them an advantage over the South.
    (E) They were underdogs throughout the course of the war.

3. According to the author, which of the following best describes opinion in the South on the reasons for fighting?

   (A) All Southerners were utterly united around a single set of war aims.
   (B) Wealthy and poor Southerners believed it was more important to fight each other than to battle the Northern armies.
   (C) For upper-class and poor Southerners alike, the main issue was the Northern naval blockade.
   (D) Different social strata in the South shared some reasons for fighting but not others.
   (E) Southerners of different social strata agreed only on the need to fight to protect slavery.

4. The average Southerner probably felt which of these sentiments once the war was well underway?

   (A) stoic defensiveness
   (B) economic security
   (C) physical invulnerability
   (D) military superiority
   (E) terrified hopelessness

5. With which of the following would the author of the passage most likely disagree?

   (A) The Civil War turned out to be a much more difficult war than initially expected.
   (B) The North was more likely to win the Civil War from the beginning.
   (C) The South boasted no noticeable military advantage over the North.
   (D) The North's inferior military leadership was one of the South's major advantages.
   (E) Southerners feared for themselves and their families during the war.

6. Based on the passage, you can infer that the author

   (A) is an accomplished Civil War historian
   (B) pities the South for choosing to battle a superior enemy for a dubious cause
   (C) is a proud Northerner
   (D) fears the persistent effects of the Civil War on American society
   (E) is concerned to establish an unbiased historical perspective on the Civil War

ANSWERS AND EXPLANATIONS

1. **A** The passage describes the South's disadvantages in almost every category. However, Southerners were still willing to fight, particularly, as the war went on, to defend their homes and families against the Northern armies. Choice A best expresses these ideas.

   (B) There is no reference whatsoever to secret military weapons in the passage.
   (C) According to the passage, "the South was riddled with class distinctions." This directly contradicts choice C.
   (D) The passage is written in the past tense and definitely suggests that the author knows how the war ended. Since the South was ultimately defeated, choice D cannot be correct.
   (E) According to the passage the South had many disadvantages but also certain advantages, and at least at the start of the war, these encouraged Southerners to fight. Thus choice E cannot be correct.

2. **D** This passage is a comparison of the Northern and Southern sides as the Civil War began. From the start, the reader is told that the deck was stacked in the favor of the North; its much larger population and more advanced industrial infrastructure were huge advantages.

   (A) General Sherman is mentioned in line 10, but the author certainly does not hail him as the savior of the North.
   (B) There is no support for this idea in the passage. The South started the war with certain advantages, and the author never claims that Northern leaders knew in advance how to overcome them.
   (C) Lines 51–52 states "Northern society could hardly be described as classless."
   (E) This statement is contradicted by the passage, which details the many advantages the North held over the South.

3. **D** According to the passage, protecting slavery was surely important to upper-class slaveholders, but "the poor farmers who resided near the bottom of the Southern social order had no stake in the Confederacy and no interest in fighting to sustain the institution of slavery." At the same time, however, all classes cherished their independence and were willing to fight to retain it. Moreover, as the war went on and the Northern armies drew closer, this became an increasingly important reason for fighting. Thus Southerners shared some reasons for fighting but not others. This matches choice D.

(A) According to the passage, some Southerners fought to protect slavery, but for others (especially the poor farmers), slavery was not an important issue. Thus choice A cannot be correct.

(B) Wealthy and poor Southerners may have been at odds over many issues, but nothing in the passage suggests that they were interested in fighting each other, especially in the face of the approaching Northern armies.

(C) The passage mentions the naval blockade put in place by the North to clock Southern cotton exports, but nowhere does it describe how the various Southern social strata reacted to the blockade. It also never suggests that the blockade was the most important issue for anyone in the South.

(E) According to the passage, Southerners of every class agreed on the need to battle the Northern armies. Slavery, on the other hand, was important mostly to the upper classes and not to the large stratum of poor farmers.

4. **A** Once the war had been going on for some time and Northern armies were campaigning in the South, average Southerners felt that they were standing up to an invader. The final quote of the passage from a captive Southern soldier articulates this feeling. "Stoic defensiveness" is the best choice for describing what such people felt.

(B) Southerners were surely well aware of their economic dependence on cotton exports and the possibility that their ports would be blockaded.

(C) Southerners were aware that the Northern armies were approaching and that they faced actual physical attack.

(D) Despite having better military leaders, the South had a smaller population and no reason to consider itself militarily stronger than the North.

(E) Southerners were surely dismayed at the possibility of fighting against a more powerful enemy on their own soil, but as the author explains in the second and fourth paragraphs, they had no reason to feel hopeless—at least until the very end of the war.

5. **C** The author states that the South began the war with better military officers than those who fought for the North. See the second paragraph and lines 30–31.

(A) The passage says that both sides started the Civil War with certain advantages. It is therefore reasonable to think that the author would agree with the idea that the war turned out to be more difficult than expected.

(B) According to the passage, from the start of the war the North had huge advantages in population and economic strength. It is therefore reasonable to think that the author would agree with the idea that the North was more likely to be the victor.

(D) According to the passage, "the Confederacy began the war with superior military leadership." It is therefore reasonable to think that the author would agree with the idea that the North was at a disadvantage in this regard.

(E) The author makes this point clear in the final paragraph. See lines 66–71.

6. **E** This passage sticks strictly to the facts, and although it attributes an advantage to the North, it does so justifiably. The author does not pick philosophical or emotional sides but merely presents an unbiased view of the advantages and disadvantages of each side.

(A and C) Both of these options are unfounded assumptions that cannot be supported from the passage. They are not good choices.

(B) The tone of the passage is straightforward and unemotional. Consequently, there is no basis for assuming that the author feels pity for one side or the other.

(D) This is an unfounded claim. Nowhere in the passage is there any reference to the persisting effects of the war.

The nature and origins of words have long held a fascination for interested scholars and lay public, not only to satisfy intellectual curiosities but also because word knowledge
(5) has particular importance in literate societies. For the same reasons, scholarly interests have turned toward determining the nature of vocabulary development—that is, how and to what extent speakers and writers of English
(10) become masters of our lexical stock. The outcomes of these investigations are of more than passing interest to educators, for word knowledge contributes significantly to achievement in the subjects of the school
(15) curriculum as well as in formal and informal speaking and writing. In fact, a substantial body of research has been published in this century concerning the educational implications of these vocabulary studies.

(20) Languages are as vibrant and dynamic as the cultures of which they are a part, and the lexical stock of a language is a vivid example of this linguistic principle. Words are, after all, no more than labels for concepts about the
(25) world around us, and as new concepts emerge or old ones change, the lexical stock changes accordingly. It is a linguistic paradox that change is a constant when applied to vocabulary. Many words in common use 200
(30) years ago are now obsolete, just as many words in use today will be tomorrow's artifacts.

The English language is no exception, with a lexicon that reflects its many sources of
(35) origin and the effects of change over time. Besides the core stock of words rooted in Anglo-Saxon beginnings, English contains additional thousands of words borrowed from language communities with whom we have
(40) come in contact. Both of these sources have provided yet more words—those that have been derived from earlier word forms by addition of prefixes and suffixes or those that have been shifted to new grammatical
(45) functions. Still more words have emerged by the process of compounding, in which existing words are joined to form new combining parts of words, or simply by creating new words out of "whole cloth." The ingredients of our
(50) lexical stock are indeed rich and varied.

The vocabulary, or lexicon, of language encompasses the stock of words of that language which is at the disposal of a speaker or writer. Contained within this lexical

(55) storehouse is a core vocabulary of the words used to name common and fundamental concepts and situations of a culture, as well as subsets of words that result from one's personal, social, and occupational
(60) experiences. Probably the most important influence on one's speech is the simple circumstance of the language spoken in the country of one's birth. Each of us grows up interacting with and interpreting the world
(65) around us, to a large degree through the medium of language. Therefore, understanding vocabulary and language to the greatest capacity possible should be a fundamental tenet of anyone's education.

1. Which one of the following is a claim that the author of the passage makes about the English lexicon?

   (A) The lifespan of a word in common use is about 200 years.
   (B) Most of our language was developed in Roman times.
   (C) Many English words have nothing to do with the language's Anglo-Saxon core.
   (D) New words are rarely created anymore.
   (E) Change in our lexical stock is a relatively uncommon occurrence.

2. The passage supports which one of the following claims about word origins?

   (A) There are myriad possible origins for words.
   (B) Words are often derived from ancient languages but rarely from other cultures.
   (C) There are relatively few ways for a word to come into common usage.
   (D) Words are created only as often as they drop out of use.
   (E) Culture and history have little to do with the words that are currently in common use.

3. The information in the passage provides the LEAST support for which one of the following claims?

    (A) Studying a population's language can reveal much about its culture.

    (B) How a lexical stock changes is dependent on how concepts in the world around us change.

    (C) Without language, it would be much more difficult to interpret and interact with the world around us.

    (D) Old words can adopt new meanings as the concept they were meant to label evolves over time.

    (E) The least important influence on one's speech is which language we learn to speak first.

4. Based on the passage, the author would most likely claim that a good background in lexicology, the study of language, also includes which of the following?

    (A) cultural and historical education

    (B) religious and communications education

    (C) geographical and mathematical education

    (D) scientific and social education

    (E) technological and philosophical education

5. As stated in lines 12–15, the claim that "word knowledge contributes significantly to achievement in the subjects of the school curriculum" is best supported if which of the following is true?

    (A) Students who score better on vocabulary tests score better on all their tests.

    (B) The study of language fosters the development of such important learning skills as reading comprehension and critical thinking.

    (C) Students who concentrate on lexicology often also do well in physics.

    (D) The study of linguistics is similar to the study of math or computer science in that they all involve learning to communicate in a unique language.

    (E) Students who enjoy foreign language classes often develop a more eclectic perspective to apply in their other studies as well.

6. The author presents the example of the English language in order to illustrate which one of the following claims?

    (A) Because English is not a language native to America, it is a perfect example of how well language can adapt to its environment.

    (B) Our language is the single exception to the trend of varied word origins.

    (C) Few peoples have done as much to shape the English language in America as the Native Americans.

    (D) Our own language is a prime example of the diverse origins of a lexical stock.

    (E) Few people today can understand any of the English words that were in use more than 200 years ago.

Answers and Explanations

1. **C** Review lines 37–40, "English contains additional thousands of words borrowed from language communities with whom we have come in contact." These borrowed words are not related to the language's Anglo-Saxon core.

    (A) Although the author uses "200 years ago" as an example of the time period during which some words that were once common have dropped out of use, there is no claim that this is any special length of time or a common lifespan for language.

    (B) This choice has no support in the text. There is no mention of Roman times or when modern English language actually developed.

    (D and E) Both of these choices are directly contradicted by the passage. Lines 36–49 explain the creation of new words, and lines 27–29 explain how language changes often.

2. **A** Especially in the third paragraph, the author makes it clear that there are many, many paths by which a word can find its way into a lexicon.

    (B and C) Both of these choices contradict what is stated in the third paragraph. Choice B goes against what is said in lines 37–40, and choice C goes against the theme of the paragraph.

    (D) While the author makes the point that words are often created and often go out of use, there is no attempt to posit this kind of one-to-one relationship.

    (E) This is contradicted by lines 20–23 and by the first part of the third paragraph, which directly relates the origins of language to the influence of history.

3. **E** This choice directly contradicts what is stated in lines 60–63: "Probably the most important influence on one's speech is the simple circumstance of the language spoken in the country of one's birth." The passage therefore does not support this claim at all.

(A) Lines 20–23 and the third paragraph's explanation of word origins support this claim.
(B) This claim is supported by lines 23–27.
(C) This claim is supported in lines 63–65.
(D) This claim is supported by lines 23–27 and the explanation of new words being created from old words in lines 40–49.

4. **A** There is a clear theme in the passage that language has always been molded by both history and culture. With this in mind, one could claim that a strong background in lexicology should include these two subjects.

(B) Religion is not referred to in the passage. This choice would be an unfounded assumption.
(C) There is no mention of math in the passage. This choice would be an unfounded assumption.
(D) The author does not bring up science in the passage. This choice would be an unfounded assumption.
(E) There is no reference to technology in the passage. This choice would be an unfounded assumption.

5. **B** If choice B is true, then linguistic study could be an important tool in developing some of the building blocks of education. These skills would be applicable to many more subjects than just vocabulary, and students who had developed these skills would be at a distinct advantage in all their studies over those who had not. Choice B therefore supports the claim very well.

(A) This choice is not conclusive enough to support the claim. The relationship cannot be determined to be causal. Students might score high on all their tests because they score high on vocabulary tests, but the opposite could also be true: students might score high on vocabulary tests because they score high on all their tests.
(C) Like choice A, this choice is not innately conclusive and does not serve as good support for the claim.
(D) Just because subjects are similar to each other does not mean that they innately complement each other. This is not especially strong support for the claim.
(E) While this statement could be true, no direct causal relationship is specified between a more eclectic perspective and higher achievement in the classroom. Again, this is insufficient support.

6. **D** The sentence in which the example first appears states, "The English language is no exception, with a lexicon that reflects its many sources of origin and the effects of change over time" (lines 33–35). This is almost identical to the statement in choice D.

(A and C) Both these choices can be immediately discredited because there is no reference or allusion to America or the English language in America anywhere in the passage. Therefore, these cannot be the claims the author wished to illustrate.
(B) This is counter to what is stated in the text (lines 33–35).
(E) The statement referring to languages 200 years ago (lines 29–32) was made before this example was given (lines 33–35). Furthermore, this statement is too strong ("any") to be congruent with the passage.

Many people do not realize how easily criminals can obtain our personal data without having to break into our homes. In public places, for example, criminals may engage in "shoulder surfing," watching you from a nearby location as you punch in your telephone calling card number or credit card number or listen in on your conversation if you give your credit-card number over the telephone to a hotel or rental car company.

(5)

(10)

Even the area near your home or office may not be secure. Some criminals engage in "dumpster diving," going through your garbage cans or a communal dumpster or trash bin—to obtain copies of your checks, credit card or bank statements, or other records that typically bear your name, address, and even your telephone number. These types of records make it easier for criminals to get control over accounts in your name and assume your identity. If you receive applications for "pre-approved" credit cards in the mail but discard them without tearing up the enclosed materials, criminals may retrieve them and try to activate the cards for their use without your knowledge. (Some credit card companies, when sending credit cards, have adopted security measures that allow a card recipient to activate the card only from his or her home telephone number, but this is not yet a universal practice.) Also, if your mail is delivered to a place where others have ready access to it, criminals may simply intercept and redirect your mail to another location.

(15)

(20)

(25)

(30)

In recent years, the Internet has become an appealing place for criminals to obtain identifying data, such as passwords or even banking information. In their haste to explore the exciting features of the Internet, many people respond to "spam," unsolicited e-mail that promises them some benefit but requests identifying data, without realizing that in many cases the requester has no intention of keeping his promise. In some cases, criminals reportedly have used computer technology to obtain large amounts of personal data.

(35)

(40)

(45)

With enough identifying information about an individual, a criminal can take over that individual's identity to commit a wide range of crimes: for example, false applications for loans and credit cards, fraudulent withdrawals from bank accounts, fraudulent use of telephone calling cards, or obtaining other goods or privileges which the criminal might be denied if he were to use his real name. If the criminal takes steps to ensure that bills for the falsely obtained credit cards, or bank statements showing the unauthorized withdrawals, are sent

(50)

(55)

to an address other than the victim's, the victim may not become aware of what is happing until the criminal has already inflicted substantial damage on the victim's assets, credit, and reputation.

(60)

1. The passage supports which one of the following claims about identity theft?

   (A) Because identity theft is relatively easy, people must be careful to keep their personal information secure.
   (B) Identity theft is solely the result of a victim's poor judgment.
   (C) While relatively few crimes are associated with identity theft, all are very serious.
   (D) With enough of a victim's personal information at their disposal, identity thieves can even take over their victim's job.
   (E) Car theft is classified as identity theft in many legal circles.

2. Based on the passage, the author would most likely claim that good self-defense against identity theft includes all of the following EXCEPT

   (A) shredding any documents or letters before throwing them away
   (B) having mail delivered to a secure location
   (C) being very aware of one's surroundings when in public
   (D) making all personal phone calls from a cell phone
   (E) not responding to any unsolicited e-mail

3. Which one of the following is a claim that the author makes about "dumpster diving"?

   (A) It is the most common way for identity thieves to obtain information on a potential victim.
   (B) Sanitation services employees are most likely to engage in it.
   (C) It can be done without the victim realizing it until too late.
   (D) It is the easiest way for criminals to break into a victim's e-mail account.
   (E) Recently, many credit card companies have established programs to find criminals who have activated "pre-approved" cards in someone else's name.

4. The author brings up Internet fraud in order to draw attention to which one of the following claims?

   (A) The use of e-mail, instead of postal mail, allows people to exchange personal information more freely without the threat of fraudulent activity.
   (B) As new technology enters our everyday lives, we must learn to take precautions against new methods of victimization.
   (C) People who pay for their Internet services using a credit card run a huge risk of accidentally publicizing their account number.
   (D) Most of the new technology that is now part of our daily lives carries little risk of victimization by fraud.
   (E) Even e-mailing friends and family puts a person at potentially great risk of identity theft.

5. Which one of the following, if true, would most undermine the author's attempt to urge readers to be wary of identity theft?

   (A) Despite being a relatively serious crime, identity theft is usually not punished severely by the courts.
   (B) Fraud and identity theft are two of the least common crimes in America.
   (C) Identity theft is legal in Eastern Europe.
   (D) Insurance often does not cover financial losses due to credit card fraud.
   (E) The author was once convicted of fraud.

6. The information in the passage provides the LEAST support for which one of the following claims?

   (A) If criminals know what they are doing, they can get away with fraud for quite some time without even being noticed.
   (B) The Internet presents many new risks for the uninformed user.
   (C) There is no truly efficient way to combat fraud or identity theft.
   (D) Many identity thieves use other people's names to get things that they could otherwise not acquire.
   (E) Fraud can cost a victim as little as a few dollars to as much as many thousands of dollars.

ANSWERS AND EXPLANATIONS

1. **A** The passage describes various ways in which a criminal can assume someone else's identity using stolen personal information. This information supports the idea that a good way to avoid identity theft is to keep one's personal information carefully guarded.

   (B) While identity theft is relatively easy to prevent, victims cannot be blamed for crimes committed against them. Furthermore, even with precautions in place, it is still possible to experience identity theft.
   (C) Lines 46–54 describe the "wide range" of crimes an identity thief may commit.
   (D and E) There is no reference or allusion in this passage to the theft of anyone's job or anyone's car. These are unfounded statements.

2. **D** The author never makes a statement like this. In fact, if cell phones are used in public, then the information exchanged in personal phone calls is put at risk.

   (A) This would combat "dumpster diving" (lines 12–18).
   (B) This would combat mail interception (lines 30–34).
   (C) This would combat activities like "shoulder surfing" (lines 3–10).
   (E) This would combat e-mail fraud and "spam" (lines 37–44).

3. **C** In lines 54–62, the author says that a victim may not find out about identity theft until after substantial damage has been done. This easily fits in with fraud as a result of "dumpster diving" (i.e., using a discarded "pre-approved" credit card letter to get a credit card in the victim's name).

   (A) At no point in the passage does the author make any claim about which method of stealing personal information is the most common.
   (B) The author does not accuse any particular category of people of taking part in "dumpster diving."
   (D) This is an unfounded claim and not a logical inference to make.
   (E) This claim is not made in the passage. The statement about the precautionary measures some credit card companies are taking is explained in lines 25–30. However, that statement is not congruent with this claim.

4. **B** Even though the author does not go into much detail regarding fraud committed using new technology, the third paragraph best supports the claim made in choice B. The point of this paragraph is that even though new technology offers many conveniences, we should be wary of the opportunities it creates for fraud.

(A) This choice contradicts the author's point that the use of new technology such as e-mail does not provide protection from fraud. Instead, it provides new opportunities for fraudulent activity.

(C) The author makes no reference to Internet billing or payment in the passage.

(D) The author does not claim that new technology provides increased protection against fraud. Instead, the third paragraph points out that e-mail provides new opportunities to commit various kinds of fraud.

(E) The passage states that responding to "spam" e-mail messages may expose a person to identity theft. But this is very different from claiming that any e-mail communication carries this risk. The passage never makes this claim.

5. **B** In the passage, the author cautions readers that personal identity information can easily be stolen and that thieves can use this information to commit a wide range of crimes. However, if in fact such crimes were quite rare, that would certainly detract from the importance of the author's point.

(A) The severity (or lack thereof) of the punishment for identity theft has no bearing on the author's point, which is the need for people to protect themselves from this type of crime.

(C) Even if this statement were true, it would have no bearing on the author's point about the need for caution to protect against identity theft.

(D) If this statement were true, the potential cost of fraud would be even greater to the victim. That would reinforce the author's point, not undermine it.

(E) If this statement were true, it would only add weight to the author's argument, because the author would be explaining how frauds are perpetrated from the criminal's point of view.

6. **C** The passage warns that personal information is easy to steal if one is not cautious. From this, you can deduce that if you are cautious and take a few preventive measures, you can be relatively safe from this kind of crime. That is the exact opposite of the claim in choice C.

(A) This claim is supported fairly well in lines 58–62.

(B) The third paragraph is dedicated to supporting this claim.

(D) This claim is explicitly explained in lines 46–54.

(E) The author offers examples of fraud ranging from the theft of a telephone calling card (possibly worth only a few dollars) to a fake loan application (worth perhaps several thousand dollars). Thus, this claim is supported by the passage.

Of the nations that have contributed to the direct stream of Western civilization, Egypt and Mesopotamia are at present believed to be the oldest. The chronological

(5) dispute as to the relative antiquity of the two countries is of minor importance; for while in Babylonia the historical material is almost entirely inscriptional, in Egypt we know the handicrafts, the weapons, the arts,

(10) and, to a certain extent, the religious beliefs of the race back to a period when it was just emerging from the Stone Age. In a word, Egypt presents the most ancient race whose manner of life is known to humankind. From the

(15) beginning of its history—that is, from about 4500 B.C.—we can trace the development of a religion one of whose most prominent elements was a promise of a life after death. It was still a great religion when the

(20) Christian doctrine of immortality was enunciated. In the early centuries of the Christian era, it seemed almost possible that the worship of Osiris and Isis might become the religion of the classical world, and the

(25) last stand made by civilized paganism against Christianity was in the temple of Isis at Philae in the sixth century after Christ.

It is clear that a religion of such duration must have offered some of those

(30) consolations to humankind that have marked all great religions, chief of which is the faith in a spirit, in something that preserves the personality of the person and does not perish with the body. This faith was, in fact, one

(35) of the chief elements in the Egyptian religion—the element best known to us through the endless cemeteries that fill the desert from one end of Egypt to the other, and through the funerary inscriptions.

(40) It is necessary, however, to correct the prevailing impression that religion played the greatest part in Egyptian life or even a greater part than it does in Muslim Egypt. The mistaken belief that death and the well-

(45) being of the dead overshadowed the existence of the living is due to the fact that the physical character of the country has preserved for us the cemeteries and the funerary temples better than all the other

(50) monuments.

The narrow strip of fertile black land along the Nile produces generally three staple crops a year. It is much too valuable to use as a cemetery. But more than that, it

(55) is subject to periodic saturation with water during the inundation and is, therefore, unsuitable for the burials of a people who wished to preserve the contents of the graves. On the other hand, the desert,

(60) which bounds this fertile strip so closely that a dozen steps will usually carry one from the black land to the gray, offers a dry preserving soil with absolutely no value to the living. Thus all the funerary

(65) monuments were erected on the desert, and, except where intentionally destroyed, they are preserved to the present day. The palaces, the towns, the farms, and many of the great temples that were erected on the

(70) black soil have been pulled down for building material or buried deep under the steadily rising deposits of the Nile. However, the tombs of six thousand years of dead have accumulated on the desert

(75) edge as living testaments to the dead.

1. The author's attitude toward ancient Egyptian religion is most readily indicated by which of the following words or phrases?

   (A) "great" (line 19)
   (B) "minor importance" (line 6)
   (C) "intentionally destroyed" (line 66)
   (D) "overshadowed" (line 45)
   (E) "mistaken belief" (line 44)

2. The phrase "civilized paganism" (line 25) can best be interpreted as referring to which of the following?

   (A) any religion that did not offer "the faith in a spirit"
   (B) any religion that arose before the modern era
   (C) Christianity, as opposed to the worship of Isis and Osiris
   (D) any religion that believed in many gods and that dominated in an advanced civilization of the past
   (E) any religion supported by a national government

3. As used in line 8 of the passage, the meaning of "inscriptional" can best be explained by which of the following?

(A) discovered only recently
(B) poorly preserved
(C) consisting of written words
(D) of dubious authenticity
(E) known only from later Egyptian texts

4. In the context of the passage, which one of the following could best be substituted for "overshadowed" (line 45) without changing the author's meaning significantly?

(A) thoroughly confused
(B) cheered and brightened
(C) played no part in
(D) greatly upset
(E) took precedence over

5. The Egyptian tombs are "living testaments" (line 75) because

(A) they are a sign that Egypt is rapidly running out of space to bury the dead
(B) they remind foreign visitors of the ancient Egyptians' obsession with death
(C) they offer definite proof that there is life after death
(D) they are the remnants of great temples that have now disappeared
(E) they are reminders of the strong religious faith of the ancient Egyptians

6. The "physical character" (line 47) of Egypt is its

(A) religion
(B) population
(C) culture
(D) geography
(E) history

ANSWERS AND EXPLANATIONS

1. **A** According to the passage, the ancient Egyptian religion was powerful enough to attract believers for thousands of years, even vying for dominance throughout the classical world. In the light of this fact, it is not surprising that the author characterizes the religion as "great" (line 19).

(B) "Minor importance" (line 6) refers to the dispute over the relative antiquity of Egypt and Mesopotamia, not to ancient Egyptian religion.
(C) "Intentionally destroyed" (line 66) refers to funerary monuments that were demolished for one reason or another, not to the ancient Egyptians' religion itself.
(D) "Overshadowed" (line 45) refers to an idea that the author specifically says is mistaken: that the ancient Egyptians placed more emphasis on death than on life. That is not how the author characterizes their religion itself.
(E) "Mistaken belief" (line 44) refers to some people's erroneous idea that death was more important than life in ancient Egypt. The author specifically rejects this idea, and the phrase is not used to characterize the ancient Egyptians' religion itself.

2. **D** The phrase "civilized paganism" is used to describe the pre-Christian religion of the classical world. A pagan religion is one that believes in many gods, and the author uses the adjective *civilized* to emphasize the advanced nature of classical civilization.

(A) According to the passage, ancient Egyptian religion did indeed offer faith in the spirit (lines 28–34), so choice A cannot be correct.
(B) Several nonpagan religions, including Christianity, arose before the modern era, so choice B cannot be correct.
(C) In the passage, the phrase is used to refer to a religion that is in competition with Christianity, so choice C cannot be correct.
(E) Nonpagan religions, including Christianity, have often been supported by national governments, so choice E cannot be correct.

3. **C** In this passage, "inscriptional" material from ancient Mesopotamia is contrasted with the handicrafts, weapons, arts, and religious beliefs known from ancient Egypt. The implication is that almost all we know about ancient Mesopotamia comes only from words inscribed in stone or written on other materials.

(A, B, D, and E) Although some of these choices might seem to make sense when substituted for inscriptional in the passage, none of them is consistent with the actual meaning of inscriptional.

4. E In the passage, the author says that because most of the structures surviving from ancient Egypt happen to be funerary monuments, many people mistakenly believe that for the ancient Egyptians, death was far more important than life. Based on this argument, readers should be able to infer that "overshadowed" means something like "took precedence over."

(A, B, C, and D) None of these choices is consistent with the definition of "overshadowed" or with the context of the passage.

5. E The passage says that ancient Egyptian religion is "best known to us through the endless cemeteries that fill the desert from one end of Egypt to the other" (lines 36–38). In other words, the tombs in those cemeteries are "testaments" to the ancient Egyptians' strong religious faith.

(A) There is nothing in the passage to suggest that Egypt is running out of space in which to bury the dead.

(B) The clear implication of the passage is that the tombs are testaments to the strength of ancient Egyptians' religious faith, not to a supposed obsession with death that the author dismisses as nothing but a mistaken impression.

(C) The author makes no claims about whether there is or is not life after death.

(D) This choice is contradicted by the passage, which never connects the tombs with the "palaces, the towns, the farms, and many of the great temples" that were built in the Nile Valley but have now disappeared.

6. D The "physical character" of the country is its remarkable geography: the narrow, fertile river valley where food is produced versus the surrounding desert, useful only for cemeteries, which has preserved so many artifacts of ancient Egyptian civilization.

(A, B, C, and E) None of these choices is consistent with the meaning of the phrase or with the context of the passage.

About two-thirds of the Earth's surface lies beneath the oceans. Before the 19th century, the depths of the open ocean were largely a matter of speculation, and most
(5) people thought that the ocean floor was relatively flat and featureless. However, as early as the 16th century, a few intrepid navigators, by taking soundings with hand lines, found that the open ocean can differ
(10) considerably in depth, showing that the ocean floor was not as flat as generally believed. Oceanic exploration during the next centuries dramatically improved our knowledge of the ocean floor. We now
(15) know that most of the geologic processes occurring on land are linked, directly or indirectly, to the dynamics of the ocean floor.

"Modern" measurements of ocean depths
(20) greatly increased in the 19th century, when deep-sea line soundings (*bathymetric surveys*) were routinely made in the Atlantic Ocean and Caribbean Sea. In 1855, a bathymetric chart published by U.S. Navy
(25) Lieutenant Matthew Maury revealed the first evidence of underwater mountains in the central Atlantic. Survey ships laying the trans-Atlantic telegraph cable later confirmed this fact. Our picture of the ocean
(30) floor greatly sharpened again after World War I (1914–1918), when echo-sounding devices—primitive sonar systems—began to measure ocean depth by recording the time it took for a sound signal from the ship
(35) to bounce off the ocean floor and return. Time graphs of the returned signals revealed that the ocean floor was much more rugged than previously thought. Such echo-sounding measurements also clearly
(40) demonstrated the continuity and roughness of the submarine mountain chain in the central Atlantic (eventually named the *Mid-Atlantic Ridge*) suggested by the earlier bathymetric measurements.

(45) In 1947, seismologists on the U.S. research ship *Atlantis* also found that the sediment layer on the floor of the Atlantic was much thinner than originally thought. Scientists had previously believed that the
(50) oceans have existed for at least 4 billion years, so therefore the sediment layer should have been very thick. Why then was there so little accumulation of sedimentary rock and debris on the ocean floor? The
(55) answer to this question, which came after much further exploration, would prove to be vital in advancing the theory of plate tectonics.

In the 1950s, oceanic exploration greatly
(60) expanded again. Data gathered by
oceanographic surveys conducted by many
nations led to the discovery that a great
mountain range on the ocean floor virtually
encircled the entire Earth. Called the *global*
(65) *midocean ridge,* this immense submarine
mountain chain—more than 50,000
kilometers (km) long and, in places, more
than 800 km across—zig-zags between the
continents, winding its way around the
(70) globe like the seam on a baseball. Rising an
average of about 4500 meters (m) above the sea
floor, the midocean ridge overshadows all
the mountains in the United States except
for Mount McKinley in Alaska (6194 m). If
(75) the seas were drained, the global midocean
ridge system would be the most prominent
topographic feature on the surface of our planet.

1. Which one of the following excerpts best
   summarizes the ideas presented in the first
   paragraph?

   (A) "About two-thirds of the Earth's surface
        lies beneath the oceans."
   (B) "As early as the 16th century, a few intrepid
        [but poorly equipped] navigators … found
        that the open ocean can differ considerably
        in depth."
   (C) "Before the 19th century, the depths of
        the open ocean were largely a matter of
        speculation, and most people thought
        that the ocean floor was relatively flat."
   (D) "We now know that most of the geologic
        processes occurring on land are linked . . .
        to the dynamics of the ocean floor."
   (E) "Oceanic exploration during the 19th and
        20th centuries dramatically improved our
        [formerly speculative] knowledge of the
        ocean floor."

2. The author's use of the word *modern* (line 19)
   when referring to bathymetric measurements
   of the 19th century relates to the fact that

   (A) these were the first of many major
        advances in bathymetric science that
        have continued to today
   (B) these were the most advanced techniques
        that were ever developed for efficient
        measuring of the ocean floor
   (C) the techniques used at that time did not
        produce accurate measurements
   (D) these are the only methods still in use today
   (E) these were the first measurements made
        using echo-sounding devices

3. The author's interest in bathymetry is best
   indicated by which of the following pairs of
   words from the passage?

   (A) *flat* and *featureless*
   (B) *routinely* and *primitive*
   (C) *long* and *winding*
   (D) *early* and *considerably*
   (E) *dramatically* and *vital*

4. Which one of the following words most
   accurately expresses the meaning of the word
   virtually as it is used in line 63 of the passage?

   (A) fundamentally
   (B) perfectly
   (C) nearly
   (D) morally
   (E) intrinsically

5. As used in line 38 of the passage, the meaning
   of *rugged* can best be explained by which of
   the following pairs of words?

   (A) flat and featureless
   (B) precipitous and craggy
   (C) thin and muddy
   (D) turbulent and cloudy
   (E) gentle and smooth

6. In the context of the passage, which one of the
   following could best be substituted for
   prominent in line 76 without significantly
   changing the author's meaning?

   (A) pertinent
   (B) famous
   (C) conspicuous
   (D) attractive
   (E) convoluted

ANSWERS AND EXPLANATIONS

1. **E** Especially with the information in brackets, this
   excerpt perfectly summarizes the introductory
   paragraph. The main ideas of the paragraph are
   as follows: (1) our knowledge of the ocean floor
   was once only speculative, and (2) over the
   centuries, exploration has greatly improved our
   knowledge. Choice E captures both of these
   points.

   (A) This choice provides only a detail of the first
        paragraph.
   (B) This choice addresses only one of the two main
        ideas of the introductory paragraph. It is not as
        good an answer as choice E, which addresses
        both main ideas of the paragraph.

(C) This choice addresses only one of the two main ideas of the introductory paragraph. It is not as good an answer as choice E, which addresses both main ideas of the paragraph.

(D) This choice provides only a detail of the first paragraph.

2. **A** The author uses the word *modern* to differentiate the bathymetric methods of recent times from the primitive methods of the 16th century. The author is explaining that beginning in the 19th century modern bathymetric methods have greatly expanded our knowledge of the deep-sea floor.

(B) This choice must be incorrect because the passage describes many improvements in bathymetric methods that have been made since the first "modern" methods were introduced in the 19th century.

(C) A lack of accuracy in the 19th-century measurements would hardly be a reason to term them "modern." This choice cannot be correct.

(D) This choice must be incorrect because the passage describes many newer and more precise bathymetric methods that have superseded the 19th-century techniques.

(E) This choice must be incorrect because the 19th-century methods referred to were deep-sea line soundings, not echo soundings.

3. **E** An author who knows this much about the history of bathymetry evidently finds the subject quite compelling, as indicated by the use of the words *dramatically* (to describe the amount of scientific progress in this field) and *vital* (to describe the importance of knowledge about the ocean floor).

(A) The words flat and featureless are used in the passage to describe outdated conceptions of the ocean floor. These bland adjectives are definitely not appropriate to describe the author's evidently keen interest in bathymetry.

(B) The words routinely and primitive are used in the passage to describe certain aspects of early bathymetric research. Neither one is appropriate to describe the author's evidently keen interest in bathymetry.

(C) The words long and winding are used in the passage to describe the midocean ridge system. Neither one is appropriate to describe the author's evidently keen interest in bathymetry.

(D) The words early and considerably are used in the passage as part of the description of the very first attempts to measure the ocean depths. Neither one is appropriate to describe the author's evidently keen interest in bathymetry.

4. **C** Saying that the midocean ridge "virtually encircled the entire Earth" means that this mountain system makes a nearly complete circle around the globe. So *nearly* is the best synonym for *virtually*.

(A, B, D, and E) None of the other choices would be considered synonyms for virtually. Furthermore, none of them fits the context of line 63 of the passage.

5. **B** The passage states that at one time people thought that the ocean floor was flat and featureless, but once scientific studies were made, it was found to contain immense chains of underwater mountains. From this information, even if you did not know the meaning of *rugged*, you could infer that it means the opposite of *flat* or *smooth*. Choice B, "precipitous and craggy," is the best answer.

(A) Based on the passage, the ocean floor is not at all "flat and featureless," so these cannot be synonyms for rugged.

(C) The sediment on the ocean floor may be described as "thin and muddy," but these words do not describe the mountainous topography. So neither word can be a synonym for rugged.

(D) The deep ocean waters might be described as turbulent or cloudy, but these words do not describe the mountainous topography. So neither word can be a synonym for rugged.

(E) The ocean floor is described as mountainous, not gentle or smooth, so neither word can be a synonym for rugged.

6. **C** The passage says that if the seas were drained, the midocean ridge would be Earth's most prominent feature; that is, it would be the one that would stand out above all the others. Of the choices, the word that could most easily be substituted for *prominent* is *conspicuous*.

(A) Pertinent means "relevant" or "pertaining to the subject." It is not a synonym for prominent.

(B) The author is saying that the midocean ridge would be Earth's most visible feature, not its most famous or well-known one.

(D) The author is saying that the midocean ridge would be Earth's most visible feature, not its best-looking or most attractive one.

(E) The author is saying that the midocean ridge would be Earth's most visible feature, not its most convoluted or twisted one.

Fraudulent telemarketers usually sound no different from anyone else with whom you talk on the telephone. People who work in telemarketing schemes may be male or
(5) female, relatively young or middle-aged, and come from all areas of the country and many racial and ethnic backgrounds. In addition, many fraudulent telemarketers try to make their prospective victims believe
(10) that the telemarketers genuinely care about the welfare and interests of the victims. Often, it is common for fraudulent telemarketers to try to ingratiate themselves with the people they call, particularly with older people, and
(15) to persuade the victims to rely on the telemarketers to look out for them in carrying out the "transaction" for which they are to send money.

The reality is that in the experience of
(20) law-enforcement and regulatory authorities who have investigated telemarketing fraud, fraudulent telemarketers know, when they contact their victims, that neither they nor their company will do anything to protect a
(25) victim's interests or to conduct an honest business transaction with a victim. Indeed, they often express contempt for their victims, and use derogatory terms like "mooch" when they talk about a victim they
(30) have contacted.

For example, certain telemarketing schemes are devised to victimize people who have bad credit or whose income levels may be too low to allow them to
(35) amass substantial credit. In many credit card telemarketing schemes, telemarketers contact prospective victims and represent that those victims can obtain credit cards even if they have poor credit histories. The victim who
(40) pays the fee demanded by the telemarketer usually receives no card, or he or she receives only a credit-card application or some cheaply printed brochures or flyers that discuss credit cards. In a variant of these schemes,
(45) the credit card that some consumers are given, after paying the fee to the telemarketer, requires the consumer to pay a company located outside the United States $200 or $300 and limits the consumer's
(50) charges on that card to an amount no greater than the amount of money the consumer has paid to the offshore company.

A telemarketing scheme has only two objects: to obtain as much money as

(55) possible from its victims, preferably by the quickest possible means; and to retain as much money as possible from those victims if they later complain to the telemarketer or to the authorities. While larger
(60) telemarketing schemes have what they call "customer service departments," the real purpose of these departments is to resist returning any money to the customer for as long as possible. Some "customer service
(65) departments" will therefore offer the complaining victim another "gimme gift," or at best a partial refund, rather than cancel the transaction or return the victim's money. Usually, fraudulent telemarketers will make
(70) a full refund only if they determine that the victim has complained to a state attorney general or to the FBI or other criminal law-enforcement agency. Consumers therefore cannot rely solely on what they hear over
(75) the telephone in deciding whether a telemarketer who calls is legitimate.

1. It can be inferred that which of the following is a common part of a telemarketing fraud victim's experience?

(A) being content with the experience in the end
(B) receiving threats of physical force from the telemarketer
(C) refusing the telemarketer's offer to participate in fraudulent schemes
(D) receiving full compensation from insurance companies for any losses
(E) allowing the telemarketer to gain the victim's trust

2. It can be inferred from the second paragraph that

(A) fraudulent telemarketers often don't know their business is dishonest until informed by regulatory authorities
(B) telemarketing fraud is sometimes just an honest business transaction gone wrong
(C) fraudulent telemarketers almost always know that what they are doing is illegal and harms their victims
(D) many fraudulent telemarketers joke with their victims about being "mooched" before actually "mooching" them
(E) telemarketing fraud normally starts with the victim making the first phone call

3. From the third paragraph discussion of credit card scams, it can be inferred that which of the following makes someone more prone to becoming a target of telemarketing fraud?

(A) having bad credit or no credit at all
(B) allowing his or her phone number to be listed in the public directory
(C) being a very skeptical personality
(D) not having access to a working telephone
(E) possessing more credit cards than the average person

4. It can be inferred that the author's opinion of fraudulent telemarketers is closest to which of the following?

(A) They are the predators that drive the wheel of Social Darwinism.
(B) They are worse than murderers.
(C) They are just doing their best to get by.
(D) They are relatively harmless but clever criminals.
(E) They are malevolent social parasites.

5. It can be inferred that the best way to fight telemarketing frauds is which of the following?

(A) complain to the telemarketing company's customer service department
(B) report the incident to a law-enforcement agency
(C) keep demanding "gimme gifts" up to the value of the money owed
(D) threaten to report the telemarketers to the telephone company
(E) sue the fraudulent company for an amount equal to what was taken

6. Which of the following can be inferred from the information in the first paragraph?

(A) Very few fraudulent telemarketers are women.
(B) A fraudulent telemarketer sounds as legitimate as any other telemarketer.
(C) Fraudulent telemarketers typically use a "grab fast and hold fast" strategy with their victims' money.
(D) Most fraudulent telemarketers eventually regret their acts and go to work for legitimate companies.
(E) Fraudulent telemarketers genuinely care about most of their victims, but they take their money anyway.

ANSWERS AND EXPLANATIONS

1. **E** Lines 7–11 especially outline the point that, for telemarketing fraud to work, the victim must trust the criminal. Obviously, this is trust is undeserved.

(A) This is not a reasonable inference to make based on the information given. Certainly, being a victim of fraud is quite an unpleasant experience, and there is no reason to believe that a victim will feel contented.
(B) The author never implies that the telemarketers actually threaten physical violence.
(C) A person who successfully refuses to participate in a fraudulent scheme is not a victim. This choice is faulty.
(D) The author never refers to financial payments to telemarketing fraud victims by insurance companies, nor is there any reason to infer that such payments are common.

2. **C** The second paragraph states that "fraudulent telemarketers know, when they contact their victims, that neither they nor their company will do anything to protect a victim's interests or to conduct an honest business transaction with a victim." Clearly, business that is not honest is illegal and harms the victim involved.

(A and B) Both of these choices are contradicted by the passage. See the explanation for choice C for a more detailed reference to the text.
(D) Telemarketers are said to talk among themselves about their "mooch" victims, but there is no reason to infer that they use this term jokingly when speaking with the victims themselves.

(E) This inference is illogical in that any telemarketing starts with a call from a telemarketer. Telemarketing does not work the other way around.

3. **A** Lines 31–35 explicitly state "certain telemarketing schemes are devised to victimize people who have bad credit or whose income levels may be too low to allow them to amass substantial credit." Therefore, those with bad credit or no credit are definitely more prone to telemarketing fraud.

(B) This inference is not supported by anything in the passage.

(C) One can infer that people who are gullible are most prone to telemarketing fraud. Therefore, those who are the opposite (skeptical) are less, not more, prone to fraud.

(D) This choice is not logical. Telemarketing fraud cannot be committed if a criminal cannot connect with a victim via the telephone.

(E) Nothing in the passage supports this inference. Furthermore, it is illogical; someone who has many credit cards must already have substantial credit and is therefore less likely to fall victim to fraudulent telemarketers.

4. **E** While this language seems strong, choice E is the best one offered. The author clearly feels that fraudulent telemarketers mislead people (i.e., they are "malevolent"), and they take money from those who earned it honestly (i.e., they are "social parasites"). Of the choices, this inference is the safest.

(A) While the author does portray criminals as predators, he does not glorify them as nobly weeding out the weak from society in Social Darwinian terms. If anything, the author takes a tone of sympathy for fraud victims.

(B) Nothing in the passage supports the idea that the author holds this extreme view. This choice is neither safe nor justified.

(C) This choice implies that the author sympathizes with fraudulent telemarketers, but based on the passage, this attitude is certainly not the case.

(D) The author certainly portrays fraudulent telemarketers as fairly clever criminals, but there is no reason to think that he or she considers their frauds to be harmless.

5. **B** Refer to lines 69–73, "fraudulent telemarketers will make a full refund only if they determine that the victim has complained to a state attorney general or to the FBI or other criminal law-enforcement agency." Choice B clearly matches this text.

(A) The fourth paragraph explains that these "customer service departments" are just another part of the victimizing experience.

(C) Nothing in the passage supports this inference. The "gimme gifts" might help appease angry customers, but they do not have any real financial value.

(D) The telephone company is not mentioned in the passage, so there is nothing to support this inference.

(E) There is nothing in the passage to imply that suing fraudulent telemarketers is an effective tactic.

6. **B** The first paragraph explains that there is no such thing as typical fraudulent telemarketer. Fraudulent telemarketers can be of either gender, of any age, and of any race, ethnicity, and origin. Nothing in such persons' voices necessarily indicates fraud, so a fraudulent telemarketer sounds no different from a legitimate telemarketer on the phone.

(A) This choice directly contradicts lines 3–5: "People who work in telemarketing schemes may be male or female . . ."

(C) While this idea can be deduced from the first sentence of the fourth paragraph, there is nothing in the first paragraph on which to base such an inference.

(D) There is nothing anywhere in the passage to support this inference.

(E) This inference has no support in the passage. Indeed, it is contradicted by information in the second paragraph.

Books and news stories regularly focus popular attention on inequities within our educational system. In about one-third of our states, lawsuits have sought or are
(5) seeking to remedy funding disparities correlated with lower achievement for students from poor communities. Concerns about our changing school population, the plight of our cities, and the perceived
(10) failures of public education have all fueled cries for educational reform that meets the needs of all our children. Technology is routinely touted as a potentially powerful agent of that reform. For years, the
(15) computer was cited as the vehicle for overcoming a wide array of inequities. Today, distance education approaches like teleconferencing, interactive television, e-mail, and expanded telecommunications
(20) networks are promoted as avenues to improved resources for underserved students. But despite the promise of emerging technology, it is important to remember that technology and equity are
(25) not inevitable partners.

The literature on computer equity reveals that many students—not only minority, disadvantaged, and inner city but also female, handicapped, and rural—have been
(30) hampered by inequitable access to computers and by widespread patterns of inequitable distribution and use of computers within and across schools. Problems begin at the "counting" level, with
(35) wealthy districts having a 54:1 student-computer ratio and poor districts having a ratio of 73:1. Factors other than sheer numbers can also limit computer access to selected groups. Locating hardware in labs
(40) and classrooms restricted to advanced students and setting unnecessarily difficult prerequisites for computer courses can easily deprive average and slower students of computer opportunities. Handicapped
(45) students can be withheld from computer opportunities by lack of adaptive devices, special software, or information about how to adapt regular software.

Finally, software that incorporates
(50) stereotypes and uses of technology that reflect subtle biases can create the most pernicious inequities of all. "Drill and kill" programs heighten the "masculinity" of both math and computers, thus reinforcing girls'
(55) frequently negative attitudes toward both. Economically disadvantaged students, who often use the computer for remediation and basic skills, learn to do what the computer tells them, while more affluent students,

(60) who use it to learn programming and tool applications, learn to tell the computer what to do.

Technological equity is a complex issue that encompasses disparities in access to
(65) and uses of powerful learning tools because of differences in socioeconomic status, gender, ability level, racial and ethnic identification, geographic location, and handicapping condition. Each of these areas
(70) has its own problems, research community, and suggested solutions. What the areas share is a need for unremitting attention. Only when all students are routinely granted access to hardware and to appropriate
(75) software, and only when technology is used to help each student achieve his or her own personal best, can we speak of technology and equity as partners.

1. It can be inferred that a major difference between the author and most other educational reformers is that those reformers

   (A) lack the knowledge to have a real opinion on the matter of educational computing
   (B) think computers have no place in the classroom
   (C) consider computer science to be a necessary part of today's education
   (D) expect the simple presence of computers to increase equity in the classroom
   (E) understand that computers can produce the same inequities as any other unfairly distributed educational tool

2. It can be inferred from the passage that the author would most likely describe the current state of student access to computers in schools as

   (A) unequal and hampered by restrictive rules and issues of social inequity and gender bias.
   (B) generally equal, but poorer schools still need more computers.
   (C) unequal but improving as more rules are made about which students get access to computers
   (D) unequal, but only at the elementary "counting" level
   (E) equal in that nearly every student in America has access to a computer and the Internet.

3. It can be inferred from the passage that the author would most likely agree with which one of the following generalizations about computers in the classroom?

   (A) Economically disadvantaged students can often get more out of computers than more affluent students can.
   (B) Fast-access computers should be limited to select groups of students.
   (C) They have great potential as educational aids to students.
   (D) They are useful only for mathematical education.
   (E) Young female students often have limited access to computers because teachers feel it threatens those students' emotional well-being.

4. Which one of the following can be inferred from the second paragraph of the passage?

   (A) Rural schools are only slightly better off than inner-city schools in regard to technology education.
   (B) Schools in poorer districts have at most half the computers that those in wealthy districts have.
   (C) Wealthy districts are much more likely than poorer districts to misuse technology resources.
   (D) Classes in adaptive hardware are necessary to help economically disadvantaged children learn.
   (E) Inequities in computer access are partly the fault of teachers and administrators.

5. Based on the passage, which of the following would the author likely consider to be a good use of technology to remedy inequities?

   (A) Wealthy schools are given more computers so that their affluent students have better access.
   (B) More adaptive hardware and special software are made available to students with disabilities.
   (C) Computers are not introduced until after elementary school so that some students do not gain a technological advantage so early.
   (D) Female students are regularly coerced into using "drill and kill" programs as often as their male counterparts.
   (E) Students are taught about the inequitable distribution of technological materials between schools before being allowed access to the materials.

6. Which of the following CANNOT be reasonably inferred about the "drill and kill programs" that the author references in lines 52–53?

   (A) They are generally targeted toward male students.
   (B) By incidentally incorporating stereotypes, they reinforce inequity through gender bias.
   (C) They are most often associated with mathematical education software.
   (D) By making computers seem more "masculine," they unnecessarily alienate female students from technology and from the subject matter of the software.
   (E) They are the most common type of software used for classroom education.

ANSWERS AND EXPLANATIONS

1. **D** In the first paragraph, before arguing that simply introducing computers into classrooms is not enough to overcome inequities, the author first states the common belief held by many others: "For years, the computer was cited [by educational reformers] as the vehicle for overcoming a wide array of inequities [in the classroom]." Choice D best describes this belief that the author disputes.

   (A and C) These choices lack any strong support in the passage. The reader cannot reasonably infer either one based on the given information.
   (B) This inference is directly contradicted by the text. See the explanation for choice D.
   (E) This statement reflects the author's viewpoint more than it does that of the other educational reformers. In fact, it is the opposite of what the author says the others believe.

2. **A** It should be clear that the author sees the present state of computers in the classroom as rife with inequities. The second paragraph says that minority, disadvantaged, female, handicapped, and rural students are relatively deprived of computer access, and that restrictive rules make the situation worse. The third paragraph says that some classroom software also reflects gender bias. Clearly, choice A is the best answer.

   (B) The author clearly does not believe that the situation is nearly equal or that simply providing poorer schools with more computers would solve the equity issues. Instead, the passage describes a wide range of unresolved equity issues involving computers in the classroom.

(C) The author certainly does believe that students are unequal when it comes to computer access, but he or she argues against, rather than for, rules restricting that access.

(D) The author certainly does believe that students are unequal when it comes to computer access, but the passage does not support the idea that inequity exists only at the "counting" level (lines 34–37).

(E) The author's point throughout the passage is that students do not have equal access to computers in the classroom.

3. **C** In lines 17–22 the author supports the idea that new technology in the classroom has great educational potential. Thus he or she would definitely agree with choice C. Nevertheless, the author's point is that even though computers can be great teaching aids, they will not be truly successful tools until issues of unequal access are addressed.

(A) This statement is contradicted in lines 56–59.

(B) The author argues against this sort of restriction in lines 39–44. Selective access to hardware and software is a notable source of inequity.

(D) There is no support for this inference in the passage. While the author does mention math as a subject computers can help teach, there is no reason to infer that the author believes that math is the only such subject.

(E) There is no support for this inference in the passage. The author talks about gender bias in software in lines 52–55 but never mentions gender bias in computer access.

4. **E** Based on lines 39–48, teachers and administrators often foster unequal computer access (even if they do so inadvertently) by limiting computer access to advanced students or by simply not making special considerations for handicapped students.

(A) There is not enough information in the passage to support this inference. Both rural and inner-city schools are said to have less access to computers, but there is no comparison made or suggested between them.

(B) The passage includes comparative student-computer ratios for wealthy school districts and poorer districts, but no information is given about actual numbers of computers.

(C) There is not enough information in the passage to support this inference. The author seems to imply that there are inequities virtually everywhere computers are used.

(D) There is nothing in the passage to support this inference.

5. **B** In the second paragraph, the author says, "Handicapped students can be withheld from computer opportunities by lack of adaptive devices, special software, or lack of information about how to adapt regular software." It is therefore reasonable to infer that the author would consider providing such students with adaptive hardware and special software as a good use of technology to remedy an inequity.

(A) This choice contradicts the author's argument. See lines 34–37 for a specific reference to this point.

(C) The passage does not support this inference. The author clearly views computers as a promising education technology, and you can therefore assume that the author would prefer universal and equal access to computers, not restrictions on their use.

(D) No inequities would be solved by forcing students to use programs that are biased against them. If one group of students has to adapt more than another, inequity still prevails.

(E) This choice has no support in the passage. There is no reason to expect that teaching students about the inequities in computer access will solve those inequities.

6. **E** Nothing in the passage suggests that "drill and kill" programs are very popular, let alone the most common type of software used in classrooms. This is not a reasonable inference to make with the information given.

(A) Because the author states that these programs "heighten the 'masculinity' . . . of computers" (line 53), the author most likely believes they must be targeted at male students.

(B and D) These choices repeat ideas found in lines 49–55 of the passage. Therefore, they are both reasonable inferences to make.

(C) The author states, "'Drill and kill' programs heighten the 'masculinity' of both math and computers." You can therefore infer that "drill and kill" programs are used (at least the vast majority of the time) for mathematical education.

6 Support/Undermine Questions

When students have the opportunity to study artworks from the past, they begin to understand how art reflects the values of society and how the arts have been influenced by social, political, and
(5) economic beliefs of a society. An art object reflects the historic time and cultural context of its origin. Indeed, much of what is known or surmised of ancient cultures comes from art and architectural evidence. Artworks may record how people,
(10) places, and things looked. Materials and production techniques of past eras may give indications of geographic environment and societal structure. Aesthetic choices made in form and decoration may reveal philosophic or religious beliefs.

(15) Students can also recognize the power and potential of art for shaping contemporary attitudes and values. Advertisers, entertainers, politicians, and private interest groups bombard public audiences daily with visual messages that persuade,
(20) cajole, direct, entice, and seduce viewers to think and act in predetermined ways. Tyrants, who seek to control the hearts and minds of people, understand that artists may use symbols powerfully to convey feelings and ideas that speak to the
(25) deepest human emotions. Images can be used to lull viewers into complacency, urge patriotic fervor, enrage against injustice, or inspire spiritual devotion. The arts are a living expression, an empowered and empowering voice of
(30) contemporary society, urging and molding society as well as reflecting it.

A student's understanding of the meaning of an artwork increases when the student experiences working with the materials and processes that
(35) artists use to create art. Understanding also broadens with knowledge of when and where the work was made, the creator, the function it served in society, and what experts said about it. This approach to art education is called
(40) discipline-based art education (DBAE). The DBAE construct gives four components to the study of visual arts. These components—art history, art criticism, art production, and aesthetics—are comparable to areas of social
(45) studies concern. All dimensions of the history of humankind, like the history of art, include a description of when, where, and by whom. Historical criticism, like art criticism, requires analysis of the unique features or aspects of the
(50) event, interpretation of how the event influenced the world around it, and judgment about the importance of the event in the historic stream.

A society that would be democratic and free requires a public capable of deciphering and
(55) criticizing nonverbal messages. Understanding the visual message empowers viewers to accept or reject the message, or transform the message. Controversies concerning censorship, which voices will be allowed to be heard, the appropriateness of funding for
(60) divergent voices, and even questions of what does or does not constitute art are ongoing issues that require response from a visually literate, critically thoughtful society.

1. Which one of the following remarks, if true, would provide the most support for the author's conclusion that a responsible democratic society must be visually literate?

(A) People who are visually literate usually support censorship.
(B) People who are visually literate have a tendency to be easily manipulated by political messages.
(C) People who are not visually literate tend to have less of a basis for their political beliefs.
(D) People who are not visually literate are usually much more critical of the information they receive than those who are.
(E) Political cartoons are becoming less and less popular.

2. Which one of the following statements, if true, lends the most support to the argument that advertisements are most effective when they use visual messages?

(A) Visual messages are often potent tools for inspiring a predictable sentiment in their viewers.
(B) Advertising has always been a medium by which the visual arts have reached the public.
(C) Political television ads are meant to be very persuasive.
(D) The vast majority of professional advertisers received a Bachelor of Arts degree in college.
(E) Advertisements over the radio are usually the most expensive for advertisers.

3. Which one of the following, if true, would provide the most support for the author's argument for DBAE?

   (A) DBAE limits the number of people who can be considered visually literate.

   (B) DBAE parallels art studies with social studies.

   (C) Images can often be used to inspire political fervor near election time.

   (D) DBAE can greatly enhance the critical understanding of any visual message a person encounters.

   (E) Art history classes in America often use an approach like DBAE to analyze important works.

4. Which of the following, if true, would best reinforce the credibility of the passage as a whole?

   (A) The author is also a very popular artist whose pieces usually address political and social issues.

   (B) The passage is an excerpt from a full-length novel.

   (C) Social studies and art history are still considered two completely separate subjects in most American educational institutions.

   (D) The passage is excerpted from a European art magazine.

   (E) The author is a critically acclaimed authority on social art history.

5. Assuming each of following statements is true, which would best support the argument that religious beliefs can often be inferred from aesthetic choices?

   (A) Most popular religions of the present and past have integrated some unique visual components, such as symbols, icons, and artistic trends.

   (B) Religious icons rarely materialize into tangible artwork; rather, they are usually spiritual ideals in the minds of believers.

   (C) Ancient religions set very specific guidelines for the creation of poetry, prose, and song.

   (D) Some trends in artistic method are common to several different religious sects.

   (E) Very few religions have ever established a relationship with the art world.

6. Which of the following, if true, might support an argument for censorship based on the information in the passage?

   (A) Because visual messages have the potential to be so emotionally powerful, they can easily be misused to distort public opinion.

   (B) Artwork is rarely studied by art students in the context of the cultural and historical happenings of its time.

   (C) Political candidates often use photos of themselves in their electoral campaigns.

   (D) DBAE is strengthening the value of artwork in our society.

   (E) A biased public opinion often results in artwork that misrepresents people and ideas.

ANSWERS AND EXPLANATIONS

1. **C** Assuming statement C is true, people who are not visually literate are not able to support their political beliefs as well as people who are visually literate. A responsible democratic society is a critical society that is well informed and that can make empirical political decisions based on as much information as possible. Therefore, choice C is the best answer.

   (A) Generally, censorship is considered anathema to a democracy, in which free speech is an important right everyone enjoys. Choice A actually contradicts the author's conclusion.

   (B) If people are easily manipulated by visual messages, then they are likely to derive their political beliefs from those messages and not from their own personal ideas. This does not make for a responsible democracy. Choice B contradicts the author's conclusion.

   (D) This choice resembles choice B in that both suggest that those who are visually literate are actually less critical (more easily manipulated) than those who are not. Therefore, like choice B, this choice does not support the author's conclusion.

   (E) Even if true, this statement is basically irrelevant to the author's conclusion.

2. **A** The goal of an advertisement is to elicit a very specific response from the viewer: a purchase. According to choice A, visual messages are powerful tools for doing so. Therefore, choice A is very supportive of the argument.

(B) This choice expresses a consequence of the argument that visual advertisements are the most effective, not a supporting idea.

(C, D, and E) These choices are all relatively unrelated to the specific argument presented in the question. None is as strong a supporting idea as choice A.

3. **D** Especially in the context of the entire passage, in which the author repeatedly suggests that the ability to understand visual messages critically is important to a responsible society, choice D provides the most support for the author's argument.

(A) The author favors DBAE as a way to enlarge the kind of visually literate public that the author believes is essential to a functioning democracy. But if choice A were true, that would undercut, not support, the author's argument for DBAE.

(B) This choice is a fact in the passage; however, it does not serve to strengthen or weaken the author's argument. Choice D is a better answer.

(C) This choice is related to the ideas presented the second paragraph (before DBAE is even mentioned), and it is not really relevant to the author's argument for DBAE in the third paragraph.

(E) Throughout the passage, the author argues for viewing critically not just historically notable artwork but any visual message that we encounter. Thus choice D better supports the author's argument.

4. **E** Credentials as an authority on social art history would certainly enhance the credibility of an author writing on the subject of the passage. A reputation for critical acclaim would enhance credibility as well.

(A) Mere popularity does not necessarily guarantee intellectual credibility. Choice E is a better answer.

(B) The fact that a passage is excerpted from a work of fiction might decrease, not enhance, its intellectual credibility.

(C) The passage does not directly address the treatment of social studies and art history in American educational institutions, so this choice does little to support or undermine the credibility of the arguments in the passage.

(D) The passage does not specifically address European art at any point, so you can discount this choice as irrelevant

5. **A** Clearly, if many religions have unique symbols, icons, or artistic trends, it should be fairly easy to infer the specific religious connotations of some aesthetic choices. For example, if a painting includes a crucifix or the Virgin Mary, it conspicuously exhibits a Christian context. Furthermore, if the architecture of an ancient building includes a sculpture of Buddha, then it unmistakably suggests a Buddhist context. This choice fully supports the argument.

(B) If religious icons rarely materialized outside of the minds of believers, then there would be few aesthetic choices from which to infer religious beliefs. Choice A is stronger.

(C) This choice does not offer any support to the argument relating religion to aesthetic choices because it says nothing about aesthetic choices.

(D) If this were true, a viewer could tell that certain aesthetic choices were religious, but not which specific religion was implied.

(E) If this were true, it would undermine, not support, the argument. Religious beliefs definitely could not be inferred from aesthetic choices if there were no links.

6. **A** The passage says that visual messages can be very powerful, and choice A tells one way this power can be misused: in misleading or manipulative propaganda. This choice might therefore support an argument for at least enough censorship to protect the integrity of public opinion.

(B and D) Both of these choices are basically irrelevant to the subject of censorship in society.

(C) This choice does not imply that the photographs are used in a distorting or manipulative manner. Therefore, it is not nearly as strong an argument for censorship as choice A.

(E) This choice gets the causality backwards: Instead of misused visual messages distorting public opinion, it has distorted public opinion contaminating visual messages (such as artwork). Thus, this choice does not support the given argument.

The general acceptance of the hypothesis that craters on Earth were formed by ancient asteroid impacts has raised the awareness of the possibility of future Earth impacts with asteroids that cross (5) the Earth's orbit. A few hundred such *near-Earth asteroids* (*NEAs*) are known, ranging in size up to 4 kilometers. Tens of thousands probably exist, with estimates placing the number of NEAs larger than 1 kilometer in diameter at up to 2000.

(10) There are three families of NEAs. These include the Atens, which have average orbital diameters closer than 1 astronomical unit (the distance from the Earth to the Sun), placing them inside the orbit of Earth; the Apollos, which have average (15) orbital diameters greater than that of Earth; and the Amors, which have average orbital diameters in between the orbits of Earth and Mars. Amors often cross the orbit of Mars, but they do not cross the orbit of Earth. The two moons of Mars, (20) Deimos and Phobos, appear to be Amor asteroids that were captured by the Red Planet. Also, notice the important condition of "average" orbital diameters. Some Atens and Apollos have eccentric orbits that cross the orbit of Earth, making them (25) a potential threat to our planet.

Astronomers believe that NEAs only survive in their orbits for 10 million to 100 million years. They are eventually eliminated either by collisions with the inner planets, or by being ejected from the (30) solar system by near misses with the planets. Such processes should have eliminated them all long ago, but it appears they are resupplied on a regular basis. Some of the NEAs with highly eccentric orbits appear to actually be extinct "short-period" (35) comets that have lost all their volatiles, and in fact a few NEAs still show faint cometlike tails. These NEAs were likely derived from the *Kuiper Belt*, a repository of comets residing beyond the orbit of Neptune. The rest of the NEAs appear to be true (40) asteroids, driven out of the asteroid belt by gravitational interactions with Jupiter.

There is also a threat of impacts by comets falling into the inner Solar System after having been disturbed from their orbits in the *Oort* (45) *Cloud*, a huge, tenuous sphere of comets surrounding the Solar System. Such "long-period" comets are only infrequent visitors into the inner Solar System, and they do not generally fall in orbits in the same plane as that of Earth, but (50) there is nothing to rule out the possibility that one might collide with Earth. The impact velocity of a long-period comet would likely be several times greater than that of an NEA, making it much more destructive.

(55) The threat of an Earth impact was emphasized by the collision of the comet Shoemaker-Levy 9 with Jupiter on 16 July 1994, resulting in explosive impacts that would have been catastrophic on Earth. To be sure, Jupiter is far larger and more (60) massive than Earth and so undergoes far more impacts, but the event still provided an illustration that such things do happen and can be unimaginably destructive. For that specific reason, it is important that the scientific community begin (65) tracking as many NEAs as possible and preparing possible action plans if an impact were to be judged inevitable.

1. Which one of the following, if true, would cast the most doubt on the proposed danger of an asteroid-Earth collision?

    (A) Increased amounts of air pollution have greatly decreased the odds that even a large asteroid could make it through the atmosphere without disintegrating.
    (B) Any collision involving an asteroid larger than 1 kilometer in diameter would almost certainly destroy all existing life on Earth.
    (C) Most NEAs survive in their orbits for nearly 100 million years.
    (D) Earth's gravitational field is actually far too weak to pull asteroids out of the asteroid belt.
    (E) NEAs are sometimes derived from what at one time were "near-Earth comets," which have lost their tails.

2. Which one of the following statements, if true, would most seriously undermine the author's suggestion in the last sentence of the passage?

    (A) It is difficult to prepare a foolproof action plan for an event as calamitous as an asteroid impact.
    (B) Earth is so small, especially compared to Jupiter, that the chances of impact are truly negligible.
    (C) We do not currently have the technology to track every NEA in our solar system.
    (D) All three families of NEAs are much more easily tracked than any kind of comet.
    (E) Most of the scientific community does not have the relevant educational background necessary for this task.

3. Which one of the following, if true, would most seriously undermine the author's explanation of the evolution of NEAs from the Kuiper Belt?

(A) Most of the NEAs with highly eccentric orbits did not originate in the Kuiper Belt.
(B) The Kuiper Belt is too far away from Jupiter to be affected by its gravitational field.
(C) It often takes a comet nearly 2 million years to give off all of its volatiles.
(D) All comets from the Kuiper Belt are made up strictly of volatile materials.
(E) Most comets are not large enough to do any damage in the event of an Earth collision.

4. Which one of the following, if true, most clearly weakens the Earth crater hypothesis as it is described in the first paragraph of the passage?

(A) Recent evidence indicates that craters can be formed by any number of natural geological processes.
(B) Several of these craters are older than 100 million years, the lifespan of asteroids in our solar system.
(C) Most of the ancient craters on Earth have either been filled by accumulating sediment or completely deformed by physical weathering.
(D) Near-Earth asteroids are the only asteroids that can potentially impact Earth.
(E) Rarely is any piece of the actual colliding asteroid discovered in these ancient craters.

5. Which one of the following, if true, would most undermine the author's description of the threat of long-period comets that originate in the Oort Cloud?

(A) Comets in the inner Solar System that originated in the Oort Cloud probably were gravitationally perturbed by a passing star.
(B) Their incredible velocity greatly reduces the amount of time they spend crossing Earth's orbit.
(C) While huge, the Oort Cloud is relatively sparsely populated by comets.
(D) Some of these comets orbit in a plane perpendicular to that of Earth's orbit.
(E) Comets that originate in the Oort Cloud generally have very few volatiles.

6. Which one of the following, if true, would most seriously undermine the comparison of the Shoemaker-Levy 9 collision with Jupiter and a possible Earth collision?

(A) Jupiter is farther away from Earth than Earth is from the Sun.
(B) Jupiter's completely gaseous composition caused the Shoemaker-Levy 9 collision to appear far more powerful than it actually was.
(C) The Shoemaker-Levy 9 comet was larger than any asteroid that has ever collided with Earth.
(D) The Shoemaker-Levy 9 comet had not yet lost all of its volatiles when it impacted with Jupiter.
(E) The Shoemaker-Levy 9 collision was the last collision of an approximate four-year streak of almost daily asteroid collisions on Jupiter.

ANSWERS AND EXPLANATIONS

1. **A** If this statement were true, then even a large asteroid would not survive through the collision to the point when it poses a real danger, when it impacts Earth's surface. Therefore, choice A casts real doubt on the idea that asteroids are a threat to the well-being of Earth and its inhabitants.

(B) This choice, if true, supports the idea that a collision would be not just dangerous but truly catastrophic.
(C) If true, this choice would imply a greater number of NEAs in current existence and therefore an increased likelihood of an asteroid-Earth collision.
(D) According to the passage, it is Jupiter's gravitational interaction with the asteroid belt, not Earth's, that is responsible for the origin of NEAs. Therefore, this choice does nothing to cast doubt on the danger of an asteroid-Earth collision.
(E) This choice does not imply that there are many fewer asteroids than the author mentions or that an impact would be less destructive. It does not address the threat of collision at all, and therefore does not cast any doubt on the danger of an asteroid-Earth collision.

2. **B** If the chances of impact are "truly negligible," then a collision is so unlikely that it is not worth worrying about. If asteroids pose so little threat to Earth, then there would be no need to track them or create action plans. Choice B best undermines the author's suggestion.

(A) Even though it might be difficult to concoct a foolproof plan, if the danger of an asteroid-Earth collision is real, then the difficulty is worth it. This choice does not undermine the author's suggestion.

(C and D) These choices offer information regarding the ease or difficulty of tracking NEAs. However, if the collision danger is real, that ease or difficulty has no real bearing on the need to follow the author's suggested plan.

(E) It is certainly true that most of the people in the scientific community are not astrophysicists. However, this does not mean that the astrophysicists are not up to task. Therefore, this choice does nothing to undermine the author's suggestion.

3. **D** The author explains that some NEAs are comets from the Kuiper Belt that have lost all their volatiles. But if all comets in the Kuiper Belt were composed only of volatile materials (as statement D suggests) and lost all their volatiles, then they would no longer exist—and could not become asteroids. Choice D undermines the author's explanation.

(A) Choice A is just another way of saying the following statement from the passage: "Some of the NEAs with highly eccentric orbits appear to actually be . . . derived from the 'Kuiper Belt.'"

(B) The author makes no causal link between the NEAs from the Kuiper Belt and Jupiter's gravitational pull. Therefore, choice B does not undermine the author's explanation.

(C) This choice does not contradict the author's explanation. Rather, it simply adds a detail to it: The loss of all volatiles (as described in the passage) takes about 2 million years (as described in choice C). Statement C then does not undermine the author's explanation in any way.

(E) The evolution of NEAs from comets in the Kuiper Belt does not include a collision with Earth. This choice should be immediately discounted because of its irrelevance.

4. **A** If choice A is true, then Earth craters could have formed naturally rather than being created by collisions with asteroids. This would then discount the hypothesis that asteroids formed Earth craters.

(B) The faulty reasoning in this choice is analogous to saying that humans could not have discovered America 500 years ago because the human lifespan is only about 80 years. This choice therefore does not weaken the author's hypothesis.

(C) The hypothesis is concerned with explaining how the craters were formed. This choice makes no reference to origin and therefore can be discounted.

(D) This choice does not address the truth or falsity of the hypothesis. It merely restricts the class of asteroids that could have caused the craters.

(E) The fact is that a collision as powerful as an Earth-asteroid impact would release so much energy the asteroid would instantly liquefy and mix with the Earth rock (which would also be melted by the intense heat). Even if you did not know this, choice E is still not as good an answer as choice A because lack of evidence is not as strong as counterevidence.

5. **B** The author suggests that because the comets' velocities are so great, a collision with Earth would be especially devastating. However, if statement B were true, then the increased threat in the event of collision would be counterbalanced by decreased odds of collision (the comets would spend less time crossing Earth's orbital path). Thus this choice does undermine the author's description of the threat.

(A, C, and E) All these choices have little relevance to the question because they do not specifically address impact or the threat of impact. Therefore, they do not undermine the author's description.

(D) As long as the comets do cross the Earth's orbital path, then they have at least a remote chance of colliding with it. Thus, this choice does not undermine the author's description.

6. **B** If choice B were true, then the comparison drawn between Jupiter and Earth would lose much of its relevance. Earth's solid composition would react differently from Jupiter's gaseous composition, and comparing the two would not be valid.

(A, D, and E) None of these choices really relates to the comparison made between a collision with Jupiter and a collision with Earth. Without positing a discrepancy in measurements or any significant difference in collision events or conditions, they do not serve to undermine the comparison.

(C) Even if this choice were true, it would not discredit the parallel between collisions with Jupiter and with Earth. First, Jupiter is much larger than Earth, so proportionally the comparison could still be relevant. Furthermore, the possibility would still exist that something that large could strike the Earth, and the comparison would thus be relevant.

READING COMPREHENSION: TIPS FOR FURTHER STUDY

1. Always read the passages in scholarly fashion, marking important points and processing important information as you read. Remember, however, that too much annotation can be detrimental.
2. Learn to pace yourself so that when you take the LSAT, you don't wind up having just 2 or 3 minutes to read the whole last passage and answer the final batch of questions.
3. Practice answering this type of question to build your test-taking stamina.
4. Keep in mind that Reading Comprehension is the last section that you should spend your time studying, since it's harder to improve reading comprehension skills over a short time than it is to improve the skills you'll need in order to do well on the other sections of the LSAT.

CHAPTER 6

THE LSAT WRITING SAMPLE

In this chapter you will learn:

- How law schools evaluate the LSAT writing sample

- Guidelines for writing a first-rate writing sample

The LSAT writing sample is used to give law schools an idea of your ability to forge a compelling argument based on a scenario or set of facts. Making arguments is what law school is all about, so schools would like to get an idea of how skilled you are at it before they admit you. The writing sample is not scored or calculated into your final LSAT grade, and many schools do not even read the writing samples of their applicants. Some schools read the writing sample only when they do not get a good enough idea of how well you write from your personal statement. Other schools look at writing samples all the time. You are better safe than sorry, so even though the writing sample comes at the end of three hours of stressful testing, you would be well served to focus for a final 30 minutes on writing a good essay.

The writing sample presents you with a one- or two-paragraph scenario in which a person or entity has to choose between two equally compelling courses of action. You are required to choose a side and defend it based on the evidence presented in the scenario. The space that you have to write your essay is minimal—usually only about three-quarters of a page with 25 blank lines—so you must choose your words carefully and make your points quickly.

Here are some guidelines for writing an excellent essay:

Choose a Side. Do not worry about choosing the "right" course of action for the person or entity in the scenario. The test writers construct the scenario so that either course is equally valid. The point is not which course you choose but how well you make your argument. So choose the side of the argument that you think you can best support based on the facts in the scenario.

Make an Outline. Spend some time outlining your argument before you begin to write. This will enable you to organize your ideas in a logical fashion that will be convincing. People who rush into writing without first outlining their thoughts tend to forget important facts and alternatives until it is too late to include them in a well-organized essay. It is best to read the scenario and then quickly sketch out the important facts on a piece of scratch paper while the information is still fresh on your mind. (Note that when you take the writing sample portion of the LSAT, scratch paper will be provided.)

Structure Your Argument. The LSAT writing sample is a test of how well you can structure and organize an argument. So focus on constructing and presenting your argument in a logical fashion. For instance, it would be a good idea to have one paragraph that presents the strengths of the side you chose, a second paragraph that points out the weaknesses of the other side, and finally a concluding sentence or short paragraph that sums up the strengths of your side when compared to the alternative.

Writing sample scenarios often ask you to make a recommendation based on two specific considerations or two specific criteria. Usually those considerations or

criteria are presented in the form of a bulleted list. When you are constructing your argument, make sure that you address both those bulleted items. Take both items into account when you are presenting the strengths and weaknesses of each side of the argument. An essay that focuses on just one of the two considerations will be weak by definition.

Don't Repeat Facts. There is no need to waste time and effort by merely repeating facts from the scenario. Space on the essay page is too valuable for doing so, and a reader will already know those facts anyway. Instead, devote the space you have to making your arguments and strengthening your points. When you mention the given facts, do so only to support your reasoning. Keep your references short and to the point.

Use Your Time Wisely. Keep track of the time allotted and use it wisely. Thirty minutes may seem like a lot, but your brain will be tired after three hours of test taking. Concentrate when reading the scenario, choose a side as quickly as possible, start outlining, and, once your outline is finished, start writing. You should have plenty of time to write much more than the space provided allows, so focus on organizing your thoughts, hitting all the main points of your argument, and writing as well as you possibly can.

Pay Attention to Grammar, Spelling, and Punctuation. It is unfortunate, but some law schools judge a candidate's essay solely on the mechanics of grammar, spelling, and punctuation. Remember, schools have been known to reject otherwise worthy candidates because of a single typographical or grammar error in the application. Standards for the writing sample are not necessarily so stringent, but schools do pay attention to mistakes in mechanics. They do this because they know that your writing sample (unlike your carefully edited personal statement) illustrates the kind of "unrefined" writing that you are capable of doing on the spot, without the luxury of later rounds of editing and reviewing. As such, the sample reveals a great deal about your real writing abilities and your knowledge of the rules of standard written English. So be aware that readers will be looking for errors, and do your best to avoid mistakes of grammar, spelling, and punctuation.

Sample Topic

Gary is a college student who is interested in a career in film. He will graduate in approximately one year and realizes that it is very difficult to get a good entry-level position in the film industry. In order to help his chances, Gary is looking to improve his résumé. With the following two considerations in mind, write an argument in support of one of Gary's two possible projects.

1. He wants to engage in work that will improve his reputation as an artist.
2. He wants to engage in work that could potentially lead to more work.

Gary is friends with a local rock band named "the Whigs," which is rapidly gaining popularity. The Whigs have asked him to film their live shows in order to create a concert DVD. Gary will earn royalties for every DVD that is sold, and if he works with the Whigs now, then chances are good that they will hire him in the future when they are famous. Also, if Gary films the Whigs' concerts, then he is likely to meet other musicians, and some of these musicians will probably want to hire Gary to make DVDs for them. The only problem is that Gary knows that filming concerts does not involve a lot of creativity.

Gary has also written a film script, and his favorite film teacher thinks the script is very promising. The teacher will lend him the camera equipment he needs to film it, but Gary doesn't have much money, so it will be difficult to hire actors. In addition, since the project will be so low budget, it is unlikely that any network, producer, or other film-industry member will buy it. However, if the project is artistically successful, then Gary may impress someone in the film industry with his talents.

Sample Essay

Think about taking a side of the issue. Pay special attention to the two considerations that Gary has when choosing a project (future work and artistic reputation) because your answer will be analyzed on the basis of its relevance to those considerations.

Here is a sample essay advocating one of Gary's choices:

> Gary should choose to film the script that he wrote. By creating a film from a script that he wrote personally, he would establish his reputation as a serious artist, and this would help fulfill his first consideration. The film will probably not make money, but it is important to note that money is not currently one of Gary's considerations. The film has the potential of impressing people in the film industry because it would showcase Gary's artistic talents as not only a writer but also as a director and a film producer. It is very likely that someone from the film industry who sees Gary's movie would be impressed enough with at least one of Gary's three artistic talents, not to mention the sheer industriousness that enabled him to film a full movie while still in college, to hire him for a future project that will allow Gary to bolster his artistic reputation even further.
>
> It is important to note that filming concerts would do very little for Gary's reputation as an artist. The talents and skills that are displayed and the experience that is gained in making a concert DVD have almost nothing to do with anything in the film industry. Making a concert DVD would bring Gary more money in the short term, but Gary does not now see this as important. Gary is definitely interested in finding projects that will lead to still more projects, and filming a concert DVD would probably help him land other, similar jobs with the Whigs or another band. However, such jobs would be equally lacking in artistic content, and they would not really help Gary to gain entrance into the film industry.
>
> Based on these considerations, it is clear that Gary should choose to film the movie based on his script. That project will help him gain a reputation as an artist and increase his chances of finding work in the film industry.

This essay is 322 words, which is about as long as a full LSAT writing sample essay should be. There isn't room for a lot of detailed explanation, which is why you should stick to highlighting the main points of your argument. Be sure to end your essay with a sentence that states your conclusion and recaps your argument.

PART III

FIVE PRACTICE TESTS

PRACTICE TEST 1

ANSWER SHEET

SECTION 1	SECTION 2	SECTION 3	SECTION 4
1. A B C D E	1. A B C D E	1. A B C D E	1. A B C D E
2. A B C D E	2. A B C D E	2. A B C D E	2. A B C D E
3. A B C D E	3. A B C D E	3. A B C D E	3. A B C D E
4. A B C D E	4. A B C D E	4. A B C D E	4. A B C D E
5. A B C D E	5. A B C D E	5. A B C D E	5. A B C D E
6. A B C D E	6. A B C D E	6. A B C D E	6. A B C D E
7. A B C D E	7. A B C D E	7. A B C D E	7. A B C D E
8. A B C D E	8. A B C D E	8. A B C D E	8. A B C D E
9. A B C D E	9. A B C D E	9. A B C D E	9. A B C D E
10. A B C D E	10. A B C D E	10. A B C D E	10. A B C D E
11. A B C D E	11. A B C D E	11. A B C D E	11. A B C D E
12. A B C D E	12. A B C D E	12. A B C D E	12. A B C D E
13. A B C D E	13. A B C D E	13. A B C D E	13. A B C D E
14. A B C D E	14. A B C D E	14. A B C D E	14. A B C D E
15. A B C D E	15. A B C D E	15. A B C D E	15. A B C D E
16. A B C D E	16. A B C D E	16. A B C D E	16. A B C D E
17. A B C D E	17. A B C D E	17. A B C D E	17. A B C D E
18. A B C D E	18. A B C D E	18. A B C D E	18. A B C D E
19. A B C D E	19. A B C D E	19. A B C D E	19. A B C D E
20. A B C D E	20. A B C D E	20. A B C D E	20. A B C D E
21. A B C D E	21. A B C D E	21. A B C D E	21. A B C D E
22. A B C D E	22. A B C D E	22. A B C D E	22. A B C D E
23. A B C D E	23. A B C D E	23. A B C D E	23. A B C D E
24. A B C D E	24. A B C D E	24. A B C D E	24. A B C D E
25. A B C D E	25. A B C D E	25. A B C D E	25. A B C D E
26. A B C D E	26. A B C D E	26. A B C D E	26. A B C D E
27. A B C D E	27. A B C D E	27. A B C D E	27. A B C D E
28. A B C D E	28. A B C D E	28. A B C D E	28. A B C D E
29. A B C D E	29. A B C D E	29. A B C D E	29. A B C D E
30. A B C D E	30. A B C D E	30. A B C D E	30. A B C D E

SECTION 1
Time—35 minutes
24 questions

<u>Directions for Logic Games Questions:</u> The questions in this section are divided into groups. Each group is based on a set of conditions. For each question, choose the answer that is most accurate and complete. For some questions, you may wish to draw a rough diagram to help you select your response. Mark the corresponding space on your Answer Sheet.

<u>Questions 1–6</u>

A squash league has seven members: A, B, C, D, E, F, and G. In order to accommodate everyone's schedule, players are divided into two groups to play. The makeup of the groups is determined by the following constraints:

Group 2 has four people, and group 1 has three people.
A is not in a group with F or E.
G is in a group with B.
If A is in group 2, then C is in group 1.

1. If B is in group 1, then which of the following must be true?

    (A) E is in group 1.
    (B) G is in group 2.
    (C) C is in group 1.
    (D) F is in group 2.
    (E) D is in group 1.

2. If A is in group 2, then which of the following could be true?

    (A) G is in group 1.
    (B) C is not in group 1.
    (C) D is in group 2.
    (D) F is not in group 1.
    (E) E is in group 2.

3. If C and D are both in group 1, then which of the following must be true?

    (A) F shares a group with A.
    (B) E shares a group with C.
    (C) G shares a group with D.
    (D) B shares a group with C.
    (E) B shares a group with F.

4. Which of the following can NEVER be true?

    (A) F and E do not share a group.
    (B) B and A share a group.
    (C) C and D do not share a group.
    (D) F and C share a group.
    (E) G and E share a group.

5. If C and D do not share a group, then which of the following people must NOT be in the same group?

    (A) G, B
    (B) B, A
    (C) F, C
    (D) E, G
    (E) A, D

6. How many different configurations are possible for this game?

    (A) 3
    (B) 4
    (C) 5
    (D) 6
    (E) 7

GO ON TO THE NEXT PAGE

Questions 7–12

Eight ice cream enthusiasts meet to visit a new ice cream shop and sample different flavors. The group consisting of A, B, C, D, E, F, G, and H get kind of pushy around their favorite sweets, so beforehand they drew straws to determine the order in which people are allowed to buy ice cream when they visit the shop. The order is determined by the following:

B goes before E.
A goes after B.
C goes after B.
F goes after E.
G goes after H, F, C, and A.

7. Which one of the following could be an order in which the members of the group get their ice cream, from first to last?

(A) D, H, B, E, F, A, C, G
(B) B, E, F, C, A, G, H, D
(C) B, C, A, F, E, H, D, G
(D) D, B, E, F, C, A, G, H
(E) H, G, F, C, A, B, D, E

8. How many different people could get their ice cream third?

(A) 3
(B) 4
(C) 5
(D) 6
(E) 7

9. If F is third and G is not last, then which of the following must be true?

(A) A and C get their ice cream consecutively.
(B) F and D get their ice cream consecutively.
(C) G and A get their ice cream consecutively.
(D) E and B get their ice cream consecutively.
(E) D and G do not eat their ice cream consecutively.

10. If none of F, C, H, or A is third or fourth, then which of the following could be true?

(A) G is seventh.
(B) D is eighth.
(C) E is first.
(D) C is fourth.
(E) H is second.

11. If B is third, then which of the following must NOT be true?

(A) F is fourth.
(B) D is second.
(C) G is eighth.
(D) A is seventh.
(E) H is first.

12. Which person could potentially buy ice cream consecutively with any person in the group?

(A) B
(B) C
(C) E
(D) F
(E) G

GO ON TO THE NEXT PAGE

Questions 13–18

Four fishermen named A, B, C, and D will fish on one day from Monday through Thursday. Each fisherman will catch one of four fish, R, S, T, and U. Each fisherman will catch only one fish, and each fish will be caught. Each fisherman will fish on only one day, and no fisherman will fish on the same day as any other fisherman. Who catches what is governed by the following constraints:

A catches fish S.
R is caught on the day immediately before the day when S is caught.
B catches U.
D fishes on a day that is later in the week than the day B fishes.

13. If R is caught on Monday, then which of the following must be true?

(A) A fishes after B.
(B) S and U are caught on the same day.
(C) C fishes on Wednesday.
(D) U is caught by C.
(E) T is caught by D.

14. If S is caught on Thursday and B fishes on Tuesday, then which of the following must be true?

(A) D fishes on Monday.
(B) U is caught on Wednesday.
(C) U is caught before T.
(D) D and C fish on consecutive days.
(E) C catches T.

15. If A fishes on Wednesday, then which of the following could be true?

(A) A fishes before C and D.
(B) R and T are caught on consecutive days.
(C) U is the last fish caught.
(D) D catches R on Tuesday.
(E) B fishes on Thursday.

16. If T is caught on Tuesday, then which of the following must be true?

(A) C catches R.
(B) D catches T.
(C) U is caught on Monday.
(D) R is caught on Thursday.
(E) D fishes before C.

17. If S is caught before U, then which of the following is the order in which the fish are caught?

(A) S, R, U, T
(B) T, R, S, U
(C) R, S, U, T
(D) S, U, R, T
(E) R, U, S, T

18. If R is caught on Wednesday, then which of the following is NOT possible?

(A) U is caught on Tuesday.
(B) C catches R on Wednesday.
(C) D catches T on Monday.
(D) T is caught on the day before U is caught.
(E) B catches U on Monday.

GO ON TO THE NEXT PAGE

<u>Questions 19–24</u>

An exclusive New York City club is trying very hard to pick its members from the social elite. An exact selection mechanism has been agreed upon that will ensure the entrance of only the most suave members from the group A, B, C, D, E, F, G, and H. Being "in" or "out" of the club is determined by the following rules:

If A is in, then G is out.
If H is out, then B is in.
If D is out, then E is out.
If H is in, then C is in.
If B is out, then G and D are out.

19. Which of the following is a complete group of people who could be "in"?

   (A) A, F, G
   (B) F, G, H, C, E, D
   (C) E, D, H, C, B
   (D) G, D, F, E
   (E) B, F, G, D, A

20. If B is out, then who must be in?

   (A) A
   (B) C
   (C) D
   (D) E
   (E) F

21. If E and G are in the club, then what other two people must also be in the club?

   (A) B, A
   (B) G, H
   (C) C, F
   (D) H, D
   (E) D, B

22. If B and D are out of the club, then which of the following must be true?

   (A) At least two people are in the club.
   (B) At least three people are in the club.
   (C) At most four people are out of the club.
   (D) At most five people are out of the club.
   (E) Exactly three people are out of the club.

23. If seven people are in the club, then who could be out?

   (A) A
   (B) B
   (C) E
   (D) C
   (E) H

24. Who could be the only person in the club?

   (A) A
   (B) B
   (C) C
   (D) F
   (E) G

S T O P

IF YOU FINISH BEFORE TIME RUNS OUT, CHECK YOUR WORK ON THIS SECTION ONLY.
DO NOT GO ON TO ANY OTHER TEST SECTION.

SECTION 2
Time—35 minutes
25 questions

<u>Directions for Logical Reasoning Questions:</u> The questions in this section are based on brief statements or passages. Choose your answers based on the reasoning in each passage. Do not make assumptions that are not supported by the passage or by common sense. For some questions, more than one answer choice may be possible, so choose the *best* answer to each question, that is, the one that is most accurate and complete. After you have chosen your answer, mark the corresponding space on the Answer Sheet.

1. MP3 players are revolutionizing the music industry. It is no longer necessary to buy CDs; you can just purchase songs online and download them to your computer. After that, you can upload your tunes to your MP3 player and have them available for selection at any time you want. Carting around a case of CDs is no longer necessary or even advisable, since you can carry the same number of songs on 1,000 CDs in a 5-inch by 3-inch electronic device that can be hooked up to any speaker and plugged in anywhere. CDs are fast becoming vestigial components and within a couple of years will no longer be circulated.

Which of the following, if true, would most support the conclusion of the passage?

(A) After the introduction of the CD, the tape lost popularity and eventually was phased out of the music industry.
(B) MP3 devices will become more reasonably priced and better products as more people buy them.
(C) Any new invention in the music industry will eventually preclude the circulation of previous competing inventions.
(D) Tape decks will come back into style after the CD begins to lose dominance as a method of music storage.
(E) The MP3 player will dominate the music storage industry until the introduction of the REV player in five years time.

2. A recent survey was conducted among the passengers of overseas airline flights. The results of the survey revealed that a full 50% of the people who took stress-related medication for the flight had higher levels of stress in flight than people who did not take any medication for stress. These results conclusively demonstrate that stress-related medication is beneficial because the medication causes a group of normally stressed-out people to exhibit an average stress level.

Which of the following, if true, would most weaken the conclusion of the survey?

(A) 100% of the stressed group were statistically distributed along a "stress bell curve."
(B) The study had a control group of passengers receiving no medication, and this group yielded the same stress-level results.
(C) People in general are more stressed out on plane flights when they know that a survey or scientific test is being conducted.
(D) The stressed-out people were given the strongest stress-related medication on the market in order to exaggerate the effectiveness of these medications in general.
(E) Some people who were onboard the flight were asked to participate in the survey but chose not to.

GO ON TO THE NEXT PAGE

3. Historical records show that in the 1400s there were 10% more wars between countries than there were in the 1300s. The almanacs would also suggest that there were 10% more countries in existence in the 1400s. These statistics show that countries were not more likely to be violent toward each other during the 1400s; there were just more of them around, which accounts for this 10% increase in the incidence of war.

Which of the following, if true, would cast the most doubt on a claim of the argument?

(A) The almanacs were mistaken, and there was actually a 15% increase in the number of countries in the 1400s.
(B) In general, national chroniclers chose to underreport wars in order to make their countries appear more virtuous and peaceful.
(C) In the 1400s, countries tended to act violently toward their neighbors using various means short of war.
(D) Warring nations tended to have a broader reach in the 1300s than in the 1400s.
(E) The 1500s had a 20% increase in the number of wars fought but did not show a corresponding increase in the number of countries.

4. Birthday parties for children are times when parents want to demonstrate their appreciation and love. Birthday balloons are a common staple of children's birthday parties, but parents should be careful about giving helium-filled balloons to their children under any circumstance. Many children like to inhale the helium from balloons to make their voices change into high-pitched tones. Surely, this makes people laugh for a minute or two, but children who try to be too funny and inhale too much helium are prone to asphyxiation and brain damage.

Which of the following is the main point of the passage?

(A) Balloons should never be given to children at birthday parties.
(B) Inhaling too much helium can cause asphyxiation and brain damage.
(C) Parties should be given only to children whose parents appreciate them.
(D) Parents should take care when helium balloons are present at birthday parties.
(E) Birthday balloons should be filled with inert argon gas instead of helium.

GO ON TO THE NEXT PAGE

5. Pirate: Our ships incite fear in everyone because people see the black skull and crossbones on our flags. This insignia of disaster taunts our soon-to-be captives, categorically unnerves them, and tells them that their corporal extinguishment is near.

Captive: I first saw the cannons on board the pirate ship and immediately grew fearful that we would be taken over. I was truly scared to death. I looked up the mast just to make sure the skull and crossbones were there. They were, so I knew it was a pirate ship. This sign calmed me as I prepared for battle.

The pirate and the captive are committed to disagreeing about which of the following points?

(A) Pirate ships incite fear in everyone.
(B) The flag is the first thing people see that informs them that the ship is a pirate ship.
(C) The sight of the skull and crossbones unnerves all soon-to-be captives.
(D) Some people who see the pirate flag feel that it is old-fashioned and outdated.
(E) The pirate flag's insignia informs people that their death is near.

6. In ancient armies archers were often brought to the front before battles to shoot a volley of arrows into the ranks of the opposing army. Generals believed that this action would incite fear in the enemy and weed out some soldiers before the hand-to-hand combat occurred. During the battle, archers would be moved to the back, where they would try to aim at commanders of the enemy forces. Eventually in the 15th century, opposing armies began to realize that if they sent soldiers on horseback to circle around behind the archers of the other army, then they would be able to kill off 100 archers for every 15 horsemen sent.

Which of the following can be concluded based on the information above?

(A) Armies began to discontinue their use of archers in the 15th century.
(B) Archers were less effective in the 15th century.
(C) Horsemen were effective in killing archers.
(D) Archers were able to incite fear in opposing armies.
(E) Archers were generally less athletic than other members of the army.

GO ON TO THE NEXT PAGE

7. Soft drinks have been around for a number of years, but the effects of drinking them have not been adequately analyzed until recently. Children who drink at least two soft drinks a day tend to have a blood-sugar level that is three times the level that is considered healthy for a child. Additionally, children who drink this many soft drinks tend to have behavioral problems that cause them to run into trouble with the authority figures at their schools. Therefore, parents who want a child to succeed in school must prohibit the child from drinking soft drinks.

Which of the following is an assumption on which the argument most depends?

(A) Behavioral problems do not cause children to be more inclined to drink soft drinks.
(B) Soft drinks cause children to have behavioral problems.
(C) Heightened blood-sugar levels cause children to have behavioral problems that get them into trouble at school.
(D) Schools should develop programs that warn parents of the risk involved in allowing their children to drink soft drinks.
(E) Children should be allowed to drink only one soft drink or less per day to avoid a drastic effect on their blood-sugar levels.

8. Training for their particular sport is the only way for athletes to excel. Natural talent is one thing, and certainly it is great, but it will not take someone very far unless it is combined with rigorous training and long hours of dedicated practice. In fact, some athletes have shown that people with supreme natural athletic abilities can be far outstripped by people who have trained themselves in a particular sport. Based on these assertions, it is clear that innate natural talent is never enough to take someone to the top of the sports world.

Which the following, if true, would tend to support the conclusion?

(A) James Avery is a famous baseball player who never trained a day in his life.
(B) All athletes train and practice for their sport without exception.
(C) Julio Ibaniz is a famous swimmer who trained with unparalleled dedication.
(D) Only people who train hard can rise to the top of the sports world.
(E) There have been chess players who have never studied the game of chess but still became world champions.

GO ON TO THE NEXT PAGE

9. Innovative people tend to function without a care for the accepted standards and mores of their time. Einstein was such a genius because his mind deviated from the ordinary to create theories that were new and provocative. Spaceships were designed by engineers, and several spacecraft reached the moon shortly after Einstein's death. Einstein was able to elucidate his theory of relativity by teaching people to follow his extraordinary pattern of thinking. Only when people departed from their habitual, mundane, and traditional interpretations of physics could their minds embrace the innovation that was Einstein's formula.

Which of the following is the function of the sentence about spacecraft?

(A) It is a partial conclusion of the passage.
(B) It is a piece of evidence that supports the main point.
(C) It represents a competing interpretation of a key term.
(D) It is a piece of evidence unrelated to the passage.
(E) It is a premise that, if accepted, would tend to validate the conclusion.

10. Reformist: With the passage of the new tort reform laws, the average cost of a doctor's insurance premium will decrease by $300 per month. Clearly, the savings from tort reform are in the interest of both doctors and patients.

Which of the following, if true, would most seriously call into question the conclusion of the reformist's argument?

(A) If tort reform laws are enacted, doctors will be more likely to make costly errors that will harm patients.
(B) Tort reform laws will enable doctors and patients to pay less per medical transaction.
(C) Insurance companies will not respond to tort reform laws by charging more money for other types of insurance.
(D) Healthcare, a major insurance provider, will pass along this $300 benefit to patients.
(E) Doctors and patients will behave differently toward each other if tort reform laws are passed.

11. Under-the-cap games boost the sales of all soft drink manufacturers. People who are not excited about the potential taste of a beverage are excited about the possibility of winning a game. If the prizes are huge, then even more people will buy beverages. This fact is why it is necessary for companies to look carefully at sales statistics to determine what size prize will maximize their beverage sales while minimizing the amount that the company has to give away. Usually a prize bordering the $1 million mark will be most profitable because it will attract a large number of buyers to the beverage without creating a payout that is too high for a large company to bear.

Which of the following could be concluded on the basis of the passage?

(A) More people will buy beverages offering a $5 million prize than beverages offering a $1 million prize.
(B) Prizes that are $1 million will always be the most profitable for soft drink companies.
(C) Under-the-cap games boost sales of cookies and crackers in addition to soft drinks.
(D) People's chances of winning the prize are greater when the prize is $1 million than when it is $10 million.
(E) Companies that want to promote their product should never make an under-the-cap game with a prize less than $1 million.

GO ON TO THE NEXT PAGE

12. Travelers wandering through desert regions have a hard time finding water because there is so little of it present on the surface of the land. A scientist examined the water level in the containers carried by a nomadic tribe that sometimes travels through the desert and sometimes travels near the seashore. Surprisingly, the water level in the nomads' water containers was consistently several levels higher when they were traveling in the desert than it was at any time when they were traveling by the seashore.

Which of the following would explain why the water levels were higher in a drier place like the desert?

(A) Nomads like to drink water more in the desert than they do near the seashore.

(B) Nomads prepare for traveling in the desert by filling up water containers near the sea.

(C) Water evaporates from the water containers faster in the desert.

(D) No water near the seashore is potable.

(E) The scientist made miscalculations regarding the sleeping habits of the nomads.

13. It is better to have a simple system of taxation that focuses solely on the sale of goods rather than an intricate and confusing set of tax laws with rules pertaining to consumers, workers, and businesses. Having a taxation scheme that lumps all current taxes into an increased sales tax would eliminate the need for the yearly hassle people go through to figure out their tax bracket and what they owe. Instead, merchants would pay the government a percentage of their revenue from each transaction. This simplified system would be more efficient and beneficial to our society than the current scheme.

Which of the following, if true, would undermine the argument?

(A) A set of tax laws that lumps all taxes into the sales tax would relieve the average person from having to fill out unnecessary tax forms.

(B) A set of tax laws that lumps all taxes into the sales tax would discourage people from buying goods.

(C) A system that enables people readily to understand the tax amount that the government receives would increase peoples' trust in the government.

(D) The government might be able to take in more money under this new taxation scheme than it does under the current scheme.

(E) Governments would refuse to implement this new and simplified taxation scheme.

GO ON TO THE NEXT PAGE

14. Dietitian: Weight loss pills are dangerous to the health of their users. People who use them should take precautions, especially when all the benefits gained from the pills are negligible. These pills cause a person to lose weight by acting as a diuretic that purges water completely from one's system.

Weight loss expert: Weight loss pills should be used cautiously by those who are overweight, but they help models shave off worrisome extra pounds by eliminating excessive water from their systems.

Which of the following is a point of disagreement between the dietitian and the weight loss expert?

(A) Some people who use weight loss pills do not have to use them cautiously.
(B) The loss of water weight due to the pills is of negligible benefit.
(C) Weight loss pills should not be used in any situation.
(D) Exercise is no safer than diet pills as a way to lose weight.
(E) Those who are not overweight should never use diet pills.

15. A major factor in determining how much people like living in a particular apartment is the strength of the water pressure in the shower and the number of minutes that the water heater can provide hot water to the shower. However, when looking at new apartments most people do not even turn on the shower, much less see how long it produces hot water. If people want to get a more accurate picture of how much they will like an apartment they are considering, they should always take a shower before signing the lease.

Which of the following can be concluded from the passage?

(A) People should always take showers in their apartments.
(B) There are variations in water pressure and heat between apartments.
(C) New apartments tend to have water pressure problems.
(D) People are concerned more about the water pressure than about other issues with their new apartments.
(E) Signing the lease for an apartment makes the contract final.

GO ON TO THE NEXT PAGE

16. Reginald never lost a baseball game. I believe that it was because he would wear his hat backwards while pitching. The sort of bold, brazen attitude that was manifested by his backwards hat seemed to fluster his opponents. I remember how the children in that little league would wither under his gaze even before he threw his pitches. However, it could also have been his baggy pants that signaled his rebel attitude. I have never really been sure myself, but regardless, those children must have been intimidated by his attitude, because he never lost a game that he pitched.

Which of the following if true would tend to support the conclusion of the passage?

(A) Baggy pants signaled Reginald's rebellious attitude just as much as the backwards cap did.
(B) In terms of pitching mechanics, talent, and skills, Reginald was the worst pitcher in the little league.
(C) No pitchers in the little league won all their games except those who wore their hats backwards.
(D) Baseball games are not affected by the style or even the attitude of the pitcher.
(E) Reginald was drafted last year by the Detroit Apples, an upcoming professional baseball team.

17. Evan: Paying bills online is truly the new wave of technology. Now instead of sending bills in letters like a common Neanderthal, I can click two buttons on a Web page to have a certain amount paid out from my bank account each month. I have already done this for all my bills, so I never have to think about paying a bill again.

Which of the following is necessary to assume for the argument to be logically drawn?

(A) Evan will think about paying bills even though he does not actively do so each month.
(B) Evan will never receive a bill from a company to which he has not previously made a payment.
(C) Evan will have a dispute about a bill with a company to which he is already paying bills.
(D) Companies try to cheat people who are so trusting as to allow automatic debits from their bank accounts.
(E) All companies everywhere accept the new technology of paying bills online.

GO ON TO THE NEXT PAGE

18. Water skiing is a great way to spend your time on the lake. When the water is smooth and not choppy, water skiing is great fun. It is also good exercise, because you are required to use your legs to balance yourself across the waves while you use your arms to hold onto a boat that is traveling at high speeds across the water. Skiing is also a great way to get a tan so long as you do not wear a life jacket that leaves tan marks, which all of them do. However, you should always wear a life jacket because water skiing is too dangerous without one.

Which of the following can be inferred from the passage?

(A) Water skiing is a good way to enjoy the lake without actually touching it.
(B) Ski boats can go faster than a water skier can keep up with.
(C) You get more exercise water skiing than you do swimming across the lake.
(D) Life jackets should be used only by inexperienced water skiers.
(E) It is too dangerous to get a perfect tan while water skiing.

19. If 2 people sit on a lawn in the spring for an hour, each will receive an average of 9 mosquito bites. Under the same conditions, 3 people will receive 6 mosquito bites each on average. However, 6 people sitting under the same conditions will receive 3 mosquito bites each on average.

Which of the following, if true, would explain why the people in different groups receive different numbers of bites on average?

(A) More people attract more mosquitoes, but only to a certain point when the mosquitoes become full.
(B) Mosquitoes are frightened by groups and tend to avoid collections of people in favor of attacking individuals.
(C) When a group of people is present, the total number of mosquito bites is distributed evenly among the people in the group.
(D) Mosquitoes are attracted to the CO_2 released by breathing, and the more people in a group, the more CO_2 is released to attract nearby mosquitoes.
(E) Mosquitoes tend to attack in summer as opposed to the spring, but even then, the numbers would be fairly similar to the ones given.

GO ON TO THE NEXT PAGE

20. All puppies who live with their mothers for more than a year either become larger than their mother and not submissive to her or they become submissive to her. In the past two years at the Rockingham kennel, all puppies that lived with their mother for more than a year and that were larger than her were also submissive to her. Therefore, all puppies that lived with their mother for more than a year were submissive to their mother.

The logic present in the previous argument is most similar to the logic in which of the following?

(A) All fishermen who have been at sea for more than a month get homesick. This fisherman has been at sea for two months, so he is definitely homesick.
(B) All children who are in preschool are either intelligent or they are well dressed. Some children in preschool who are well dressed are also intelligent. Therefore, all children in preschool are intelligent.
(C) All lemons are either sour or they are green in color. The lemons on this tree are sour and green in color. Therefore, all lemons are sour and green in color.
(D) All car drivers who have driven for more than two years are either careless or careful on the roads. Everyone in this driver's training class has been careless before. Therefore, everyone in the class who was careless is now careful.
(E) All purple eggs in the yard are either hardboiled or striped. All striped eggs are hardboiled. Therefore all purple eggs in the yard are hardboiled.

21. Robin has to sing in order to be noticed. Jared has to dance in order to be noticed. I have to run quickly in order to be noticed. If you are noticed, then you will be happy. Happiness will cause you to be satisfied.

Which of the following must be assumed in order to make the conclusion that Robin is happy?

(A) Robin has sung.
(B) Robin has sung, danced, and run quickly
(C) Robin was noticed.
(D) Robin is satisfied.
(E) Robin is satisfied and has sung.

22. Naturalist: I have examined all alternative interpretations and have concluded that baby whales form bonds with their mothers solely by following the mother throughout the ocean. My reasoning is based on the fact that baby whales do not form any noticeable bond with their fathers. Implicit in this realization is that baby whales do not follow their fathers through the ocean.

Oceanologist: You omit the fact that baby whales are fed by their mothers and not their fathers. Milk is a product of the mother. I think it evident that even if a baby whale were to follow its father through the ocean, the baby would still form a stronger bond with its food provider, the mother.

The naturalist and the oceanologist are committed to disagreeing about which of the following?

(A) The naturalist does not have the requisite credentials to make claims about whales that refute those of the oceanologist.
(B) A baby whale would follow its mother through the ocean even if she did not provide milk.
(C) Bonds would not be formed if the baby whale did not follow the mother in the ocean.
(D) The naturalist underplays the role of milk in the whale bonding process.
(E) There are alternatives to the theory that milk is responsible for the bond.

GO ON TO THE NEXT PAGE

23. Morally derelict people always seem to be the ones who make the news. Either people do not want to hear about people who are doing good things in the world or the news agencies do not want to promote the activities of these people. I personally think that the sensationalistic nature of news in today's society is horrendous and that it fosters an atmosphere of paranoia. If constantly televising horrible acts and people has the effect of creating paranoia, then televising great acts of people doing good in our society would result in a wave of optimism. The fact that news agencies choose to ignore this idea and continue to televise evil acts shows that networks are more concerned about ratings than social good.

    Which of the following would strengthen the conclusion of the argument?

    (A) If televising acts of goodness would result in higher ratings, then networks would not televise these acts.
    (B) If networks realized the implications of their behavior, then they would change their behavior.
    (C) If morally neutral acts drew the highest ratings, networks would continue to televise other kinds of acts as well.
    (D) If actions had "social goodness" ratings, networks would still use viewer ratings to decide whether to televise them.
    (E) If networks could determine the ratings that certain acts would draw before televising them, then they would never televise certain types of acts.

24. Food shopper: People love chocolate for its sweet and creamy taste, but chocolate also has many hidden benefits. The cocoa bean contains antioxidant compounds that deter aging, debilitating illnesses, and emaciation. Doctors recommend ingesting these antioxidants once a week for good health. Therefore, I will eat several bars of chocolate every day to make sure I get the antioxidants I need to stay healthy.

    The major flaw in the argument is that it

    (A) ignores a prominent reason why people choose to pursue a certain action
    (B) mistakes a condition necessary for an outcome with a condition that causes that outcome
    (C) draws a conclusion based on evidence that is obviously fallacious
    (D) assumes that something that is beneficial in small amounts will be even more beneficial in large amounts.
    (E) appeals to the opinions of scientists to support a personal decision

GO ON TO THE NEXT PAGE

25. To a pessimist, the upholstery business is a very shifty one. After all, it is almost completely concerned with covering up items, places, and things from view. Optimists would say that this is not the true aim of upholsterers; instead, their aim is to promote beauty with the fabric that they use to cover furniture. If you ask upholsterers about the nature of their job, they will respond much like the optimist, but how can one trust their response? They have too much invested in their jobs to agree with the pessimist.

Which of the following can be inferred from the passage?

(A) Upholsterers cannot offer truthful opinions about the nature of their work.
(B) Upholsterers do not offer truthful opinions about the nature of their work.
(C) Optimists see the true nature of the upholstery business.
(D) Pessimists disagree with most upholsterers about the nature of upholstery work.
(E) In general, the upholstery business promotes beauty.

S T O P

IF YOU FINISH BEFORE TIME RUNS OUT, CHECK YOUR WORK ON THIS SECTION ONLY.
DO NOT GO ON TO ANY OTHER TEST SECTION.

Section 3
Time—35 minutes
27 questions

<u>Directions for Logical Reasoning Questions:</u> The questions in this section are based on brief statements or passages. Choose your answers based on the reasoning in each passage. Do not make assumptions that are not supported by the passage or by common sense. For some questions, more than one answer choice may be possible, so choose the *best* answer to each question, that is, the one that is, most accurate and complete. After you have chosen your answer, mark the corresponding space on the Answer Sheet.

1. Football has been an American pastime since the early 19th century. The rules of the sport have evolved over the years into their present form, but the heart and soul of the game have remained the same—an artwork of brute physicality and unadulterated passion clashing on a canvas of green grass. Since our passion for this sport is grounded in the constant and unchanging nature of our beings, football will be played for thousands of years by passionate members of future generations.

   A flaw in the argument is that it

   (A) appeals to subjective emotional evidence instead of substantive evidence to support the conclusion
   (B) assumes that there will be an unchanging relationship between the past and the present
   (C) assumes the very thing that it sets out to prove
   (D) distorts the point that is the basic premise of the argument
   (E) ignores the fact that two different elements of the passage contradict each other

2. Australia is home to some very diverse creatures, animals that are difficult to classify as either mammals or reptiles. Take for instance the platypus. It lays eggs like a reptile, and it has fur like a mammal—but no other reptile or mammal has both traits. How should we classify this divisively idiosyncratic animal? It is strange in fact that an animal like the platypus ever developed, because on all other continents no mammal gained an evolutionary advantage by laying eggs, and no reptile gained an evolutionary advantage by having fur. The existence of the platypus must mean that the constraints imposed on the species by its environment were completely different from the constraints imposed on reptiles and mammals in all other parts of the world.

   Which of the following, if true, would most support the conclusion of the passage?

   (A) Australia has environmental factors that are different from those in all other parts of the world.
   (B) Platypuses are not the only type of animal in Australia that lays eggs and has fur.
   (C) Kangaroos are another type of Australian animal that many zoologists have a hard time classifying as a mammal.
   (D) Species that are codependent upon one another in Australia and other places will tend to merge into a conjoined species.
   (E) People who live in Australia tend to have a resting heart rate that is 40 beats below the average for the rest of the world.

GO ON TO THE NEXT PAGE

3. The level at which a CEO should be compensated is a pivotal decision for any company to make. CEOs can lead a company to prominence, and newly founded companies always try to attract talented CEOs to come to work for them. However, when a CEO's compensation level rises too high, other members of the company start to lose out on corporate profits and the company's level of capital can begin to decline. A decline in capital jeopardizes a company's future; therefore, it is often not a good idea for a company to risk its financial base in order to compensate a talented CEO.

Which of the following, if true, would cast the most doubt on the argument?

(A) Talented CEOs are resourceful and can find many ways for a company to expand and profit.

(B) Companies with smaller capital bases are exposed to a much higher risk of bankruptcy compared to their well-funded counterparts.

(C) At times, CEOs recommend decreasing their personal salaries when they see that their company is in dire financial straits.

(D) There are other ways of attracting talented people to a company besides offering high salaries.

(E) Talented CEOs will find ways to increase their company's capital far beyond the level of their personal compensation.

4. Window washer: Window washing on skyscrapers is one of the most thrilling jobs available. I have to be honest—I don't really care about the social value of keeping things clean. I am more interested in the thrill of heights. After work ends, our supervisor lets us race our trolleys all the way to the ground. The brush of wind against my hair and the competition inherent in the race as we tempt gravity is exhilarating. I have really never experienced anything like it besides whitewater rafting, but this I can do every day.

Which of the following can be concluded from the passage?

(A) Whitewater rafting can be exhilarating.

(B) Window washers live for danger.

(C) Window washing has more aspects to it than thrills, races, and cleanliness.

(D) Skyscrapers need the services of window washers in order to stay clean.

(E) The thrill of heights is enough to make many people desire to be window washers.

GO ON TO THE NEXT PAGE

5. A number of government officials have voted to conserve the boundary areas of a local park instead of allowing developers to use the land for building projects. The developers claim that the boundary portions reserved by the officials are essentially useless to park visitors and to everyone else if they are left undeveloped. All the government officials secretly concede this notion, yet they still choose to bar the developers from developing the useless areas along the park boundaries.

Which of the following would explain the actions of the government officials?

(A) They only like development that either enhances the inherent beauty of nature or makes something commercially viable out of the developed land.

(B) Because of past conflicts, they are all angry at one particular developer in the county.

(C) They feel that if the boundary areas are developed, then there will be heavy pressure to develop the rest of the park.

(D) The park's boundary areas have been left pristine and untouched since the pre–Civil War era, when the park was first established.

(E) In general, government officials and developers have different goals, because officials want to promote urbanization and modernization.

6. Shoes come in many different shapes and sizes. However, the most important characteristic of a shoe is its durability. Running shoes will not last when used to play tennis because they are not designed to support lateral movements. Tennis shoes will not last as long as running shoes, because they are designed to resist the strain of a multitude of diverse movements but not the one consistent forward motion that running involves. Based on this information, it makes sense to conclude that walking shoes would not make good tennis shoes.

The argument would be logically drawn if you assumed which of the following?

(A) Walking shoes will resist the same kinds of movements as running shoes.

(B) Walking shoes would perform adequately for badminton, a sport similar to tennis.

(C) Tennis shoes would perform well as walking shoes for short distances.

(D) Walking shoes and running shoes both stand up poorly to the same kind of movements.

(E) Running shoes are made of the same materials as walking shoes.

GO ON TO THE NEXT PAGE

7. TV stations are concerned with little besides the bottom line—their profits. After all, TV commercials are nothing more than 30-second blips of propaganda that are intent on brainwashing consumers in order to sell products. These commercials do nothing except manipulate people, bore them with repetitiveness, and waste their time. There is nothing prosocial about commercials or the TV stations that air them besides the questionable and capitalistic dream of making money.

A flaw in the reasoning of the passage is that it

(A) attacks the righteousness of an activity by focusing on the motives of the entities that engage in the activity

(B) appeals to the opinion of the majority of the population when the opinion of the minority is more relevant

(C) uses evidence against one group as evidence against another group to which the evidence does not really apply.

(D) provides relevant evidence in partial support of one of its conclusions

(E) assumes that what is true of the whole group is true of every member of that group

8. Toasters and microwaves can cook food very quickly. This is why many people prefer using a microwave or toaster to cook their breakfast. The reason is simple: In the morning people do not generally allow themselves enough time to wait for a meal that needs to be cooked for more than a couple of minutes. However, many people like to have hot food in the morning. Food could be heated in an oven or on a stove, but the truth is that most people do not have the patience or time to wait for these slower cooking methods. They prefer the speed of a microwave or toaster for cooking breakfast.

Which of the following is the main point of the passage?

(A) Toasters and microwaves cook breakfast food quickly.

(B) People do not use stoves or ovens to cook breakfast.

(C) Many people prefer to use a microwave or toaster to cook breakfast food.

(D) Food can be heated only with a microwave, an oven, a toaster, or a stove.

(E) People would rather have hot food than cold food for breakfast.

GO ON TO THE NEXT PAGE

9. Johnny Appleseed wandered the United States planting apple trees. He hoped that these trees would provide shade, habitats, nourishment, and beautiful scenery for all of America's inhabitants. In fact, animals loved the trees. They provided good shade, habitats, and food every spring once the trees had blossomed and then ripened with apples. People enjoyed these trees, too, because they provided food and shady places to sit. Johnny Appleseed's purpose would have been served equally well if he had planted pecan trees instead of apple trees.

Which of the following is assumed by the argument in reaching its conclusion?

(A) People would have enjoyed the pecan trees that Johnny planted.
(B) Pecan trees could have been planted in every region of America.
(C) Apple trees and pecan trees grow equally well in the majority of environments.
(D) Johnny was partial to planting apple trees because his last name was Appleseed.
(E) Pecan trees provide habitats for animals equivalent to those provided by apple trees.

10. Legal property rights are considered a "bundle of rights," and this complex multivariate amalgamation applies to every piece of property in existence. The bundle of rights confers numerous powers on the owner of any particular piece of property and offers the owner protection from theft, trespass, and much other harm that can be wreaked upon someone due to property ownership. The sum total of this property protection is carried out by the state, which is why positivists postulate that without an enforcing body like the state, there would be no such thing as property rights.

Which of the following, if true, would undermine the positivists' claim?

(A) The concept of a bundle of rights was formed long after states came into existence.
(B) Rights can be defined and actualized based solely on their potential to be enforced.
(C) The state does not enforce the property rights of many individuals.
(D) People regard property as their possession, not as a realizable object with an attached bundle of rights.
(E) People enjoyed ownership of what we now call property long before states ever came into existence.

GO ON TO THE NEXT PAGE

11. Advertisement: The job market is highly competitive, and good positions are getting scarce. The average college graduate earns $25,000 more than the average high school graduate. Dtech University offers a complete college education at an unbeatable price. After graduating from Dtech, you will earn at least $25,000 more than high school graduates.

Which of the following roles does the first line that mentions the job market play in the advertisement?

(A) It is a general principle upon which everything else is founded.
(B) It is a piece of evidence that supports the conclusion.
(C) It is a subsidiary conclusion that must be true if the main conclusion is true.
(D) It is an inference that will be drawn from facts later in the argument.
(E) It is an assertion that is largely unrelated to the rest of the argument.

12. Trees planted near houses can provide shade and beautiful scenery for people occupying the house. However, trees planted near houses also have the potential of falling over onto the house. Residents should be aware of this danger and keep in mind that if they live in a storm-prone area where lightning can strike down trees or if a tree is old and likely to fall over, then they should probably have the tree professionally chopped down. That way, the tree will not fall through the roof of the house and injure a resident. So long as the house is not in a storm-prone area and so long as the trees are not too old, it is a good idea to have a large number of trees planted around a house.

Which of the following is the main point of the passage?

(A) Planting trees around houses is beneficial.
(B) Trees that are old or in areas prone to storms can be dangerous.
(C) Trees that are old or in areas prone to storms should be chopped down.
(D) Subject to certain exceptions, it is good to have trees planted around a house.
(E) Large numbers of trees should be planted around houses for their shade and beauty.

13. Only people who are over 18 can serve in the military. You must be in the military in order for your case to be tried in a military court. Your case must also relate to military affairs for it to be tried in a military court. Brian is over 18 and in the military, and his case relates to military affairs, so his case will be tried in a military court.

The argument is flawed because it

(A) equates a condition necessary for an outcome with a condition that causes that outcome
(B) relates by cause and effect a series of variables that are only tenuously related
(C) mistakes evidence of a correlation for a cause-and-effect relationship
(D) treats an outcome that is possible as though it were entirely impossible
(E) assumes that there is an agreement of supporting terms where there is no overt agreement

GO ON TO THE NEXT PAGE

14. Doctor: Going to concerts is a fun-filled pastime for the majority of Americans. I wish only to encourage this activity, but I would also like to alert participants to the dangers of engaging in it too often. Most rock bands play their music so loudly that the noise vibrations will cause permanent hearing damage in all listeners within a 100-meter radius. Now I know this sobering dose of reality is not "cool" or is kind of "lame," but being cognizant of the dangers to our bodies that are inherent in any particular situation is incredibly important. The only way for fervent concert-goers to protect their hearing is to purchase headphones or some other sort of noise-dampening device that will soften the vibrations reaching their ears.

Which of the following, if true, would strengthen the doctor's conclusion?

(A) Sound quality can be just as high when the sound is filtered through a noise-dampening device.
(B) Musicians who play numerous concerts without noise-dampening devices do not suffer hearing loss.
(C) People would not go to concerts if they knew that doing so might damage their ears.
(D) Bands will not lower the volume of the music they make during their concerts.
(E) You should not do something that is not "cool" if you wish to maintain a reputation for urbanity and style.

15. A zoologist told Amelia that people cannot touch any member of the darter frog species without being badly hurt because the darter frog is very poisonous. However, Amelia knows that the babies of most poisonous frogs are not yet poisonous and thus will not hurt people who touch them. Therefore, Amelia reasons that what the zoologist told her is incorrect.

Which of the following most resembles the reasoning used by Amelia in the argument?

(A) John heard from an aircraft designer that planes can fly only when their wings receive lift. However, John knows that some planes fly using jet thrusters. Therefore, John assumes that the aircraft designer is wrong.
(B) Nancy was told by her teacher that speaking out of turn in class is bad. However, Nancy knows that some people who speak out of turn in class have interesting things to say. Therefore, Nancy reasons that her teacher is correct.
(C) Matt's chemistry teacher told him that acetone will not evaporate. However, Matt knows that acetone is a ketone, a family of molecules whose members evaporate quickly. Therefore, Matt assumes that his teacher is incorrect.
(D) Wanda tells her students that gasoline is bad because it harms the environment. However, gasoline also does many good things for the environment. Therefore, Wanda is both wrong and right.
(E) In history class Tammy was taught that the D-Day invasion was necessary. However, she knows that violence is sometimes not necessary. Therefore, she reasons that the D-Day invasion should not have occurred.

GO ON TO THE NEXT PAGE

16. The soaring prices of magazines have forced many doctors to stop offering all but a few types of magazines in their waiting rooms. Magazine suppliers claim that the average threefold increase in subscription prices is the result of a bad economy that has forced them to increase the prices of individual magazines in order to turn a profit and stay in business.

Which of the following, if true, would undermine the argument of the magazine suppliers?

(A) A bad economy cannot force a business to do anything; the business chooses its course of action.
(B) Magazine subscription prices are really not "excessive" when you consider that people are still paying them.
(C) Trends in the economy have no effect on the number or cost of magazines that are purchased each year.
(D) Magazine subscribers are now realizing that price increases will likely continue into the future.
(E) If the suppliers had kept the magazine prices at a reasonable level, they would have sold more magazines.

17. Today, when so many people are looking to combat problems like obesity with quick fixes like low-carbohydrate diets and diet pills, it is still clear that none of these quick fixes is the answer. Exercise is the only way to keep in good shape and lose weight. People can try all of the quick fixes they like, but without exercise, no one will lose weight. Quick fixes are popular only because salespeople and advertisements encourage people to believe that being lazy is okay so long as they take a certain pill every day. Advertisers spend billions each year to promote quick fixes, but the payoff is huge because people believe the advertisers' claims.

Which of the following can be inferred from the passage?

(A) All salespeople want people to be obese.
(B) Exercise is required for a person to lose weight.
(C) Diet pills and exercise do not work together to promote weight loss.
(D) People who are lazy will never lose weight.
(E) Low-carbohydrate diet books earn billions each year.

GO ON TO THE NEXT PAGE

18. Using well-thought-out political arguments does not help candidates to win a campaign. Therefore, candidates who replace well-thought-out political arguments with propaganda will be most likely to win an election.

The logic in the previous argument is most similar to the logic in which of the following?

(A) When teachers grade systematically, students are no less likely to be bored by schoolwork. Therefore, when teachers grade randomly, students are more likely to be interested in schoolwork.
(B) Managers who encourage their employees are liked more than other managers. Therefore, managers who do not encourage employees are liked least.
(C) Workers who are dedicated to high achievement get promoted more quickly than other workers. Therefore, workers who are very dedicated are more likely to be promoted quickly.
(D) Players who hate a game are more likely to be caught up in the game. Therefore, players who love a game are more likely to own the game.
(E) Fishermen who use certain methods to catch fish are not as successful as they would like to be. Therefore, fishermen who do not use these methods will be more satisfied than other fishermen.

19. Guidance counselors for troubled children recommend that parents of such children discuss drugs with their child early on, because troubled children have a higher proclivity for drug use, on average, during their high school years. This is because children who are maladjusted may look for any available way to make themselves look cool or feel a little happier. Drugs can satisfy these urges for both maladjusted and normal children, but maladjusted children feel a heightened pressure to do something to change their environment because they are overtly unsatisfied with it. This is why it is so important for parents of troubled children to tell these children that drugs are not a good route to take.

Which of the following is an assumption on which the argument relies?

(A) Normal children do not feel pressure to experiment with drugs in their teenage years.
(B) More maladjusted children use drugs than normal children do.
(C) Parents who talk to their drug-addicted child can dissuade the child from being involved with drugs.
(D) Maladjusted children are more likely to turn to drugs than are normal children.
(E) Parents are the only remedy available to help teenagers in the fight against drugs.

GO ON TO THE NEXT PAGE

20. Ornithologist: Hummingbirds are the only birds that can fly while remaining completely stationary in the air, motionless except for the high-speed fluttering of their wings. Their ability to achieve this evolutionary marvel is largely due to a diet that consists entirely of sugar. Hummingbirds acquire sugar in the same way that bees do, by traveling from flower to flower in search of nectar. To carry out this pursuit, hummingbirds have all of the essential flight-related attributes of the quintessential harvesters of nectar—bees. Birds that eat low-energy foods like grain do not need to fly in this way; they can eat while perched on branches. But hummingbirds must hang in midair like bees while delicately collecting nectar.

The final sentence that notes that hummingbirds and bees acquire sugar in the same way fulfills which of the following functions in the passage?

(A) It is an illustration of the conclusion.
(B) It sets up a comparison that is never referred to during the argument.
(C) It eliminates a well-known competing possibility.
(D) It reconciles the main conclusion with a series of ancillary conclusions.
(E) It is a metaphor.

21. The game of chess originated in either India or China many centuries ago. Its purpose in most cases was entertainment, but in the military, chess was used to train the minds of generals and prepare them for battle. Each piece was a regiment of soldiers that could be deployed to the square of the player's choice. The king represented the emperor and homeland; it was a piece that had to be protected at all costs. Emperors would watch prospective generals train with this game and identify the general with the most tactical skill so that they could give him charge of their army.

The sentence noting that each piece was a regiment plays which one of the following roles in the argument?

(A) It supports another claim in the argument.
(B) It explains the nature of the term *emperor*.
(C) It is a subsidiary conclusion that supports the main conclusion.
(D) It is the main point of the argument.
(E) It misunderstands the nature of the game of chess.

GO ON TO THE NEXT PAGE

22. Standardized testing is a misnomer. Instead of making a test that aptly equilibrates a pool of test applicants around a standard score, the test makers strive to make a test that will exaggerate the variations among test takers and draw them out along a score curve. The goal of test takers is to achieve a positive nonstandard result from a test that aims at differentiating between relatively homogenous and standard groups of people. My quandary is immense; I want to beat the standard score, but I am a standard person.

Which of the following is true of the first line of the argument?

(A) It illuminates the problems arising from different interpretations of the key term *testing*.
(B) It is a claim that lacks support in the rest of the argument.
(C) It is the conclusion of the passage.
(D) It is a principle that the rest of the argument strives to live up to.
(E) It is an adjacent claim made to compromise between two styles of thought.

23. Industrialist: Our capitalist economy proffers many advantages for the average citizen. This citizen, who in other countries is relegated to demeaning jobs, is given the opportunity to forge his or her own path. Many ultimately find the way to become multimillionaires.

Humanist: Many people who work in this society and are considered to be average citizens do find their way to become millionaires. The average citizen cannot do this in other societies, but that citizen is not consigned to jobs that are undignified.

Which of the following is the point at issue between the Industrialist and the Humanist?

(A) whether average citizens who work hard in this society can become multimillionaires
(B) whether the average citizen in other countries is relegated to demeaning jobs
(C) whether people in other countries who are not average citizens can become multimillionaires
(D) whether the average person in this country who is not a citizen can become a multimillionaire
(E) whether citizens on average do not become multimillionaires in any society

GO ON TO THE NEXT PAGE

24. Dennis: Action figures are good for kids to play with so long as no one plays with me. That's because my action figures are the greatest, and I don't want other kids to feel bad because their action figures aren't as good. All this year in preschool, my figures have never met their rivals. The figures of that cartoon cat were pretty close, I guess, but if you think about it, they were really more goofy and funny than cool. Next year, a new action figure will be introduced, and I will be the first in my class to buy it.

Which of the following can be inferred from the passage if Dennis's comments are presumed to be true?

(A) No one else in Dennis's class will buy the new action figure.
(B) Despite having cool action figures, Dennis is widely disliked by most members of his preschool class.
(C) Dennis will have trouble coping after it is no longer cool to play with action figures.
(D) Children can feel bad when their action figures are inferior to those of other children.
(E) The action figure of the cartoon cat was funnier than any action figure possessed by Dennis.

25. Internet connections are quite adaptable these days. Computers have become so intelligent that they respond immediately when an Internet connection is plugged into them. Computers with wireless cards can be programmed to beep when they sense a wireless network. More than likely in the next 10 years there will be no more wired Internet connections: All Internet data transmissions will be transmitted by satellite to the wireless card on your computer. Connection speeds will increase until the speed at which data are displayed on your screen is equal to the speed of the radio waves from the satellite—which travel at the speed of light.

Which of the following is an assumption that is made by the argument?

(A) The rate at which the computer displays the data on screen is not a limiting constant.
(B) Satellites are unable to facilitate Internet connections by using radio waves.
(C) All wired connections will be phased out after wireless connections begin gaining speed.
(D) People want to have Internet connections that are as fast as the speed of light.
(E) Radio waves will be able to transmit both neural signals and Internet signals.

GO ON TO THE NEXT PAGE

26. Local government officials planned out the construction of a new ice skating rink within a park. They projected that the total cost of construction of the rink would be $5 million. This projected cost caused some members of the government to vote against going forward with the project, but most voted for it regardless of the price. A major construction company offered to build the rink for $2 million, and the government accepted the company's bid.

Which of the following explains why there was such a large discrepancy between the projected cost of the ice skating rink and the company's bid?

(A) The bidding company offered to build a rink that was twice as large as the previously planned rink.
(B) The bidding company has had years of experience in building ice skating rinks.
(C) The bidding company expected the raw materials and labor to cost one-fifth of the amount projected by the government.
(D) The bidding company outbid its nearest competitor by $1.23 million.
(E) Government officials had planned to build the ice skating rink during the winter when labor costs were higher, but the rink was built during the summer.

27. If unregulated whaling were resumed, whale populations could drop. Whale specialists predict that if the current population were to decline by half, given the whales' low reproduction rate, the whale population will never regain its preindustrial age size.

Which of the following, if true, undermines the whale specialists' belief?

(A) Whale food sources such as krill were extraordinarily abundant in preindustrial times but are now unavailable.
(B) Whale specialists often exaggerate their predictions in order to gain public sympathy for a problem that has not yet developed.
(C) At a lower population density, there would be more food available to the whales, thereby encouraging them to reproduce at a faster rate.
(D) The whaling industry would benefit from a higher rate of whale reproduction.
(E) There will more than likely never be a time when the current whale population decreases by one-quarter of its current size.

S T O P

IF YOU FINISH BEFORE TIME RUNS OUT, CHECK YOUR WORK ON THIS SECTION ONLY.
DO NOT GO ON TO ANY OTHER TEST SECTION.

SECTION 4
Time—35 minutes
25 questions

<u>Directions for Reading Comprehension Questions:</u> Each passage in this section is followed by a group of questions. Answer each question based on what is stated or implied in the passage. For some questions, more than one answer choice may be possible, so choose the *best* answer to each question. After you have chosen your answer, mark the corresponding space on the Answer Sheet.

Seizing the opportunity of Berlin's distraction with the European War and wanting to expand its sphere of influence in China, Japan entered World War I by declaring war on Germany in
(5) August 1914 and quickly occupying German-leased territories in China's Shandong Province and the Mariana, Caroline, and Marshall islands in the Pacific. With its Western allies heavily involved in the war in Europe, Japan sought further to
(10) consolidate its position in China by presenting the Twenty-One Demands to China in January 1915. Besides expanding its control over the German holdings, Manchuria, and Inner Mongolia, Japan also sought joint ownership of a major
(15) mining and metallurgical complex in central China, prohibitions on China's ceding or leasing any coastal areas to a third power, and miscellaneous other political, economic, and military controls, which, if achieved, would have reduced China to
(20) a Japanese protectorate. In the face of slow negotiations with the Chinese government, widespread anti-Japanese sentiments in China, and international condemnation, Japan withdrew the final group of demands, and treaties were
(25) signed in May 1915.

Japan's hegemony in northern China and other parts of Asia was facilitated through other international agreements. One with Russia in 1916 helped further secure Japan's influence in
(30) Manchuria and Inner Mongolia, and agreements with France, Britain, and the United States in 1917 recognized Japan's territorial gains in China and the Pacific. The Nishihara Loans of 1917 and 1918, while aiding the Chinese government, put
(35) China still deeper into Japan's debt. Toward the end of the war, Japan increasingly filled orders for its European allies' needed war material, thus helping to diversify the country's industry, increase its exports, and transform Japan from a debtor to
(40) a creditor nation for the first time.

Japan's power in Asia grew with the demise of the tsarist regime in Russia and the disorder the 1917 Bolshevik Revolution left in Siberia. Wanting to seize the opportunity, the Japanese
(45) army planned to occupy Siberia as far west as Lake Baikal. To do so, Japan had to negotiate an agreement with China that allowed the transit of Japanese troops through Chinese territory. Although the force was scaled back to avoid antagonizing the
(50) United States, more than 70,000 Japanese troops joined the much smaller units of the Allied Expeditionary Force sent to Siberia in 1918.

The year 1919 saw Japan sitting among the "Big Five" powers at the Versailles Peace
(55) Conference. Tokyo was granted a permanent seat on the Council of the League of Nations, and the peace treaty confirmed the transfer to Japan of Germany's rights in Shandong, a provision that led to anti-Japanese riots and a mass political
(60) movement throughout China. Similarly, Germany's former Pacific islands were put under a Japanese mandate. Despite its small role in World War I (and the Western powers' rejection of its bid for a racial equality clause in the peace treaty), Japan
(65) emerged as a major actor in international politics at the close of the war.

GO ON TO THE NEXT PAGE

1. Based on the passage, which of the following was NOT a reason why Japan entered World War I in August 1914?

   (A) Its opponents' distraction with battles on other continents opened a window of opportunity for relatively unchallenged expansion.
   (B) It coveted a major mining and metallurgical complex in central China.
   (C) It feared anti-Japanese sentiments and international condemnation for not coming to the aid of its allies.
   (D) It wished to obtain more political influence in neighboring China, where some territories were leased to Germany.
   (E) It sought control of many German holdings in the Eastern Hemisphere, not just those in China.

2. Following imperialistic logic, a proponent of the Japanese occupation of Siberia would most likely have argued for which one of the following as well?

   (A) transforming Japan from a debtor to a creditor nation
   (B) taking financial advantage of Japan's allies' weaknesses after World War I
   (C) relinquishing Chinese territory seized during World War I
   (D) reverting to strict isolationism after World War I ended
   (E) seizing Chinese and Pacific territories at the first opportunity.

3. According to the passage, the evolution of the modern Japanese economy was based on the

   (A) opportunity to export vast amounts of war materials to allied countries in Europe during World War I
   (B) spoils gained from the territories Japan occupied during World War I
   (C) Nishihara Loans of 1917, which secured Chinese payments to Japan for years to come
   (D) acquisition of Lake Baikal, a huge gateway for Asian trade
   (E) quick recovery from the destruction suffered during World War II

4. It can be inferred from the passage that the author would most likely describe the Japanese role in the Versailles Peace Conference (line 54) as

   (A) inappropriate, though required for diplomatic reasons
   (B) intentionally misleading but ingenious nonetheless
   (C) strikingly ineffectual and historically trivial
   (D) minimal in practical terms but politically significant.
   (E) forced to submit to mandates of the other powers

5. Which of the following words can best replace the word "hegemony" in line 26 without significantly altering the author's meaning?

   (A) tyranny
   (B) misfortune
   (C) sovereignty
   (D) wealth
   (E) brutality

6. In the passage, the author is primarily concerned with

   (A) outlining the rise of Japan's international influence as a result of the country's involvement in World War I
   (B) offering an alternative explanation for post-World War I Japanese economic and military power
   (C) chronicling the brutality of the Japanese army in dealing with innocent civilians in World War I
   (D) analyzing Japan's decision to enter World War I in the historical context of the era
   (E) arguing that Japan's methods in dealing with China during World War I were backhanded and unjustified

GO ON TO THE NEXT PAGE

The Anglo-Saxons doubtless brought with them from the Continent the rude beginnings of poetry, such as come first in the literature of every people and consist largely of brief magical charms and
(5) of rough "popular ballads" (ballads of the people). The charms explain themselves as an inevitable product of primitive superstition; however, the ballads probably first sprang up and developed, among all races, in much the following way.

(10) At the very beginning of human society, long before the commencement of history, the primitive groups of savages who then constituted humankind were instinctively led to express their emotions together, communally, in rhythmical fashion.
(15) Perhaps after an achievement in hunting or war the village-group would mechanically fall into a dance, sometimes, it might be, around their village fire. Suddenly from among the inarticulate cries of the crowd, some excited individual would
(20) shout out a fairly distinct rhythmical expression. This expression, which may be called a line, was taken up and repeated by the crowd; others might be added to it, and thus gradually, over the course of generations, arose the regular habit of communal
(25) composition, composition of something like complete ballads by the throng as a whole. This procedure ceased to be important everywhere long before the literary period, but it led to the frequent composition by humble versifiers of more deliberate
(30) poems which were still "popular" because they circulated by word of mouth only, from generation to generation among the common people and formed one of the best expressions of their feeling.

Much later on, but still at an early period,
(35) professional minstrels, called by the Anglo-Saxons "scops" or "gleemen," disengaged themselves from the crowd and began to gain their living by wandering from village to village or tribe to tribe chanting to the harp either the popular ballads
(40) or more formal poetry of their own composition. Among all races, when a certain stage of social development is reached, at least one such minstrel is to be found as a regular retainer at the court of every barbarous chief or king, ready to entertain
(45) the warriors at their feasts, with chants of heroes and battles and of the exploits of their present lord. All the earliest products of these processes of "popular" and minstrel composition are everywhere lost long before recorded literature begins, but the
(50) processes themselves, in their less formal stages, continue among some people even down to the present time.

7. Which one of the following best states the purpose of the passage?

(A) to denigrate the savage lifestyle of prehistoric peoples
(B) to describe the rapid development of poetry from barbarism to modernism
(C) to hypothesize the likely origin and evolution of poetry
(D) to glorify the roles of professional minstrels in medieval society
(E) to argue that Anglo-Saxons were the sole source of modern poetry

8. Of the following hypothetical contributors to the creation of poetry, which one would the author most likely consider to be the most influential?

(A) minstrel composers
(B) victorious warriors
(C) primitive hunters
(D) communal composers
(E) barbarous chiefs

9. Which one of the following assertions, if true, would provide the most support for the author's explanation of the origin of communal composition in the second paragraph?

(A) The discovery of drums dating from that ancient era proves that these primitive groups did engage in rhythmic expression.
(B) Communally composed poetry is often referred to as a chant or a rune in modern society.
(C) Archeologists often find cryptic poetry carved into rock near the sites of these ancient primitive villages.
(D) In modern society, little connection is considered to exist between primitive hunters or warriors and poetic composition.
(E) Scottish "gleemen" never performed the popular ballads of previous eras; instead, they were only allowed to chant poetry of their own composition.

GO ON TO THE NEXT PAGE

10. The author of the passage uses the term *deliberate* in line 29 to refer to

   (A) the argumentative aspect of communal poetry composition
   (B) the composers' consideration of various alternatives to writing poetry
   (C) the fact that poems were no longer being composed accidentally
   (D) the forceful demeanor of barbarous chiefs and kings in dealing with wandering minstrels
   (E) the idea that the composer was giving careful consideration to each part of a poem

11. The author would most likely describe the role of early "communal composition" (lines 24–25) in the evolution of poetry as which of the following?

   (A) detrimental and strikingly unjustified
   (B) unrefined, yet fundamentally necessary
   (C) collaborative, but conspicuously insincere
   (D) unorganized and shamefully gratuitous
   (E) intriguing, but relatively insignificant

12. Which of the following generalizations about poetry in early society is NOT supported by the passage?

   (A) The harp was often used to accompany "popular ballads" in the time of professional minstrels.
   (B) Early poetry was relatively primitive compared to contemporary poetry, which is much more meticulously composed.
   (C) "Popular ballads" were a purely Anglo-Saxon phenomenon that then spread into other cultures.
   (D) Modern poetry evolved from a fairly barbaric and unorganized form of communal expression.
   (E) Professional minstrels were very popular entertainers in earlier societies.

GO ON TO THE NEXT PAGE

In the mid-1800s, the small town of Springfield, Missouri, was truly a part of the Wild West. The first recorded shootout in American history took place on the town square between "Wild Bill"
(5) Hickok and Dave Tutt (Hickok won). Springfield was a stop on the Butterfield Overland Mail stagecoach, the preferred method of travel for passengers wishing to go west to California. That town has changed since those days in many ways.
(10) Now a city of 156,000 people, Springfield has become decidedly more gentle. It has made quality of life a top priority to attract and retain residents. Its public library system has more than 450,000 volumes, its 42 parks attract residents and visitors
(15) alike, and the city works hard to keep its citizens informed about—and involved in—their government.

For people with disabilities living in the Springfield area, being fully involved in the
(20) community hasn't always been easy. Many barriers to access existed and had the unintended effect of keeping people with disabilities out of the mainstream, unable to access services, and unable to participate in all that Springfield has to offer its
(25) residents. Claudia Engram, a long-time Springfield resident and wheelchair user, recalls that, prior to the Americans with Disabilities Act (ADA), the only recourse she and others felt they had to increase access to city facilities was working to
(30) modify the city's building codes. "Changes then were few and far between."

But things have changed for people with disabilities in Springfield. In 1998, a complaint was filed with the Department of Justice alleging that
(35) the city's facilities, the city utilities' main office building, and the Springfield-Greene County Library were not accessible to people with disabilities. City officials began to take a look at their facilities and services, identify barriers, and
(40) develop a plan to remove those barriers. From the outset, the city demonstrated a sincere commitment to comply with the ADA and energetically worked to find creative, cost-effective solutions to provide access for all people with disabilities.
(45) The city and the Department of Justice reached agreements that apply to virtually everything the city does: from providing an accessible entrance and parking at the Midtown Library, to lowering the service counter at the city utilities' building, to
(50) installing accessible restrooms at the Busch Municipal Building. The city also agreed to remove barriers for people who have communication disabilities by installing Braille and raised-letter signage, to provide sign language interpreters, and

(55) to work to increase the accessibility of the city's Web page. The city entities combined their resources and worked closely with local disability rights groups to develop an ADA and disability awareness-training program, which has already
(60) been conducted throughout the city. The resulting agreements have already changed, and will continue to positively change, life for Springfield's residents with disabilities.

13. According to the passage, which of the following changes has occurred in the city of Springfield since 1998?

(A) The city finally made public shootouts illegal.
(B) The service counter in the city utilities' building was raised to enhance access by the disabled.
(C) "Changes have been few and far between."
(D) The city made many changes to remove barriers for the physically handicapped, but it generally neglected the mentally handicapped.
(E) Municipal events have become more likely to use sign language interpreters for the aurally impaired.

14. The author's opinion of the Springfield government's efforts can best be inferred from which of the following words or phrases?

(A) "sincere," in line 41
(B) "resulting agreements," in line 60–61
(C) "accessible," in line 47
(D) "easy," in line 20
(E) "unintended effect," in line 21

GO ON TO THE NEXT PAGE

15. The primary purpose of the passage is to

   (A) explain why a community with a past like the Wild West is unlikely to make the proper accommodations for its disabled members
   (B) describe the transition of Springfield to an increasingly ADA-compliant community thanks to the diligent efforts of city officials
   (C) tell why it is the responsibility of the citizens to enact changes they wish to see in their community
   (D) reveal the hidden agenda of the Springfield Utilities Department
   (E) argue that the ADA can be ineffective in a community without a determined disabled population and sincere commitment from the community leaders

16. The author's mention of Claudia Engram (line 25) primarily serves to

   (A) identify one of the government officials who had refused to abide by the ADA
   (B) support the author's argument that the disabled could help themselves as much as the government could help them
   (C) introduce the biggest proponent of the ADA in Springfield
   (D) justify the author's uncertainty regarding the viewpoint of the passage
   (E) add a personal element to the author's argument to further draw in the reader

17. Which one of the following best states the main idea of the first paragraph?

   (A) Despite its Wild West roots, Springfield has become a more civil and democratic city.
   (B) "Wild Bill" Hickok was decidedly the best gunfighter in the history of the Wild West.
   (C) Springfield's parks and libraries make it a huge beacon of tourism.
   (D) Springfield is still an important stop on the road to California from the East.
   (E) Modern-day Springfield is a long way from its historical persona as a gunfight and stagecoach town.

18. It can be inferred that the author of the passage regards governmental compliance with the ADA as

   (A) increasingly peripheral
   (B) mostly unnecessary
   (C) unjustifiably coercive
   (D) totally superfluous
   (E) morally obligatory

GO ON TO THE NEXT PAGE

European men learned about other strange lands to the East through a Venetian traveler, Marco Polo, who wrote accounts of his wonderful journeys to the court of the Grand Khan, or Emperor of the

(5) Mongols, of his travels through China, and of his return to Persia by sea. Many men in the Middle Ages had believed that east of Asia was a great marsh, and that because of it, even if they succeeded in sailing around Africa, it would be

(10) impossible to reach the region of the spices and silks and jewels which they so much desired. They also thought that the heat in the tropics was so intense that at a certain distance down the coast of Africa they would find the water of the ocean

(15) boiling. These things together with the tales of strange monsters that inhabited the deep sea had terrified them. The news that Marco Polo brought changed this feeling.

The way Marco Polo happened to visit the court

(20) of the Mongol emperor was this. The Mongol Tartars were great conquerors, and they not only subdued the Chinese but also marched further westward, overrunning most of Russia and stopping only when they reached the frontiers of Italy. For a

(25) long time, all of southern Russia remained under their rule. The capital of this vast Mongolian Empire was just north of the Great Wall of China. Even as a conqueror, the Mongol emperor bore no harsh feelings toward the Europeans. He even

(30) requested missionaries from the pope to teach his people.

While on a trading expedition, Marco Polo's father and uncle had found their way to the emperor's court, and on a second journey, in 1271,

(35) they took with them Marco, a lad of 17 years. The emperor was much interested in his western visitors and took young Marco into his service. Marco Polo traveled over China on official errands, while his father and uncle were gathering

(40) wealth by trade. After many years, the Polos desired to return to Italy, but the Grand Khan was unwilling to lose such able servants. At that time, however, it happened that the Khan wished to send a princess as a bride to the Emperor of Persia, also a Mongol

(45) sovereign, and the three Polos, who were known to be trustworthy seamen, were selected to escort the princess to her royal husband. After doing this, they did not return to China, but instead went on to Italy.

They had been absent 24 years, and

(50) they found that their relatives had given them up for dead and did not recognize them. It was much like the old story of Odysseus (Ulysses), who, when he returned to his native Ithaca after his wanderings, was recognized by nobody. The Polos proved the

(55) truth of their accounts by showing the great treasures that had been sewn into their dress had been done so in a Tartar pattern. They displayed jewels of the greatest value: diamonds, emeralds, rubies, and sapphires, and recovered their identities

(60) thus.

19. Which one of the following, if true, would most seriously have undermined the evidence that the Polos showed their relatives (lines 56–60)?

(A) The jewels were far too expensive for any of their relatives to purchase or trade for.
(B) The Tartar culture existed solely in Western Europe.
(C) People of that time were very skeptical by nature.
(D) The Tartar patterns at the time were very similar to other culture-specific artistic patterns of Eastern Asia.
(E) The Polos also brought back spices and silks from their travels to East Asia.

20. Based on the first paragraph, the author would most likely describe the European perception of East Asia at the time of the Polos as

(A) outdated
(B) unreliable
(C) infallible
(D) facetious
(E) exhaustive

GO ON TO THE NEXT PAGE

21. The author mentions that the Mongol emperor "requested missionaries from the pope to teach his people" (lines 29–31) primarily in order to

    (A) relate the Mongol emperor's great interest in the Catholic religion
    (B) explicate the emperor's desire to send a Mongol princess as a bride to the Persian emperor
    (C) demonstrate that, though the Mongols were a conquering people, they were not necessarily a barbaric people
    (D) represent the Mongols as a holy people and their wars as holy crusades
    (E) describe some of the errands that the Polos were asked to perform by the Mongol emperor

22. The author most likely compares Marco Polo to Odysseus in line 52 for which of the following reasons?

    (A) to make Marco Polo's journey seem as epic as that of the mythical hero
    (B) to point out the geographic proximity of Ithaca and Venetia
    (C) to incite nostalgia in the reader
    (D) to test the reader's knowledge of ancient Greek literature
    (E) to add credibility to his account by citing an instance of a similar occurrence

23. All of the following can reasonably be inferred about the Polos' roles as servants to the Mongol emperor EXCEPT that

    (A) they performed tasks involving both land travel and sea travel
    (B) they were able to communicate with the emperor
    (C) they did well with most of the tasks they were given to perform
    (D) they were still in touch with each other throughout their tenure as servants
    (E) they were some of the best-paid servants in the Mongol empire

24. Which one of the following best describes the function of the first paragraph within the passage?

    (A) It fully explicates the author's primary thesis.
    (B) It prefaces the author's full account by first offering opposite opinions.
    (C) It introduces all of the characters described at length later in the passage.
    (D) It justifies the significance of the content of the passage.
    (E) It presents contrasting views to be expanded upon later.

25. Which of the following is NOT mentioned by the author as characteristic of the Mongol empire in Marco Polo's time?

    (A) The Mongol Tartars were great subjugators of other peoples.
    (B) The Mongol empire held most of Russia in its thrall for a period.
    (C) The Mongols traded with the French instead of invading their land.
    (D) The capital of the Mongol empire was located near the Great Wall of China.
    (E) The Mongols, in general, did not possess harsh feelings toward Europeans.

S T O P

IF YOU FINISH BEFORE TIME RUNS OUT, CHECK YOUR WORK ON THIS SECTION ONLY.

DO NOT GO ON TO ANY OTHER TEST SECTION.

ANSWER KEY

Section 1	Section 2	Section 3	Section 4
1. D	1. C	1. A	1. C
2. C	2. B	2. A	2. E
3. E	3. C	3. E	3. A
4. A	4. D	4. A	4. D
5. D	5. C	5. C	5. C
6. A	6. C	6. D	6. A
7. A	7. B	7. C	7. C
8. E	8. D	8. C	8. A
9. D	9. D	9. E	9. A
10. E	10. A	10. E	10. E
11. A	11. A	11. E	11. B
12. B	12. D	12. D	12. C
13. E	13. B	13. A	13. E
14. E	14. B	14. D	14. A
15. D	15. B	15. C	15. B
16. C	16. B	16. C	16. E
17. C	17. B	17. B	17. A
18. C	18. E	18. A	18. E
19. C	19. C	19. D	19. B
20. B	20. E	20. A	20. B
21. E	21. C	21. A	21. C
22. A	22. D	22. C	22. A
23. A	23. D	23. B	23. E
24. B	24. D	24. D	24. D
	25. D	25. A	25. C
		26. C	
		27. A	

<u>Scoring Instructions:</u> To calculate your score on this Practice Test, follow the instructions on the next page.

CALCULATING YOUR SCORE

Now that you have completed Practice Test 1, use the instructions on this page to calculate your score. Start by checking the Answer Key to count up the number of questions you answered correctly. Then fill in the table below.

Raw Score Calculator

Section Number	Question Type	Number of Questions	Number Correct
1	Logic Games	24	_____
2	Logic Reasoning	25	_____
3	Logical Reasoning	27	_____
4	Reading Comprehension	25	_____
		(Raw Score) Total:	_____

On the real LSAT, a statistical process will be used to convert your raw score to a scaled score ranging from 120 to 180. The table below will give you an approximate idea of the scaled score that matches your raw score. For statistical reasons, on real forms of the LSAT the scaled score that matches a given raw score can vary by several points above or below the scaled score shown in the table.

Write your scaled score on this test here:

Practice Test 1 scaled score: _____

Raw Score	Scaled Score	Raw Score	Scaled Score	Raw Score	Scaled Score
0	120	22	125	44	143
1	120	23	126	45	144
2	120	24	127	46	145
3	120	25	128	47	145
4	120	26	128	48	146
5	120	27	129	49	147
6	120	28	130	50	147
7	120	29	131	51	148
8	120	30	132	52	148
9	120	31	133	53	149
10	120	32	133	54	150
11	120	33	134	55	151
12	120	34	135	56	151
13	120	35	136	57	152
14	120	36	137	58	153
15	120	37	137	59	153
16	120	38	138	60	154
17	120	39	139	61	154
18	121	40	140	62	155
19	122	41	140	63	155
20	123	42	141	64	156
21	124	43	142	65	157

Raw Score	Scaled Score	Raw Score	Scaled Score	Raw Score	Scaled Score
66	158	79	165	92	175
67	158	80	166	93	175
68	159	81	166	94	176
69	159	82	167	95	177
70	160	83	167	96	178
71	160	84	168	97	179
72	161	85	169	98	180
73	161	86	170	99	180
74	162	87	170	100	180
75	162	88	171	101	180
76	163	89	172		
77	163	90	173		
78	164	91	174		

ANSWERS AND EXPLANATIONS

Section I—Logic Games

Game 1: Grouping

Initial Setup:

$$
\begin{array}{ccc}
1 & 2 & A \neq F, E \\
* & * & \boxed{\begin{array}{c} G \\ B \end{array}} \\
\underline{\quad} & \underline{\quad} & \\
\underline{\quad} & \underline{\quad} & A_2 \to C_1 \,;\, C_2 \to A_1 \\
& \underline{\quad} &
\end{array}
$$

There are actually only three possible configurations for the variables in this game. It is not necessary for you to notice this initially, but the first three questions each refer to different possibilities. Here are the possible configurations:

$$
\begin{array}{cc|cc|cc}
1\ B & F & 2\ C & A & 3\ C & G \\
G & E & F & G & D & B \\
A & C & E & B & A & F \\
D & & D & & & E \\
\end{array}
$$

1. Correct answer: **D.** This refers to scenario 1.

2. Correct answer: **C.** This refers to scenario 2.

3. Correct answer: **E.** This refers to scenario 3.

4. Correct answer: **A.** It would be impossible for F and E not to share a group because neither can share a group with A. There is only one group that can go to in order to avoid A, so they must be in the same group.

5. Correct answer: **D.** This refers to scenario 2.

6. Correct answer: **A.** As you can see, there are only three scenarios possible.

Game 2: Sequential

Initial Setup:

$$
\begin{array}{c}
E < F \quad H \\
\swarrow \quad \nwarrow \quad \wedge \\
B < C < G \\
\nwarrow \quad \swarrow \\
A \\
D?
\end{array}
$$

7. Correct answer: **A.** This is a possible order.

   (B) G has to go after H.

   (C) E has to go before F.

   (D) H has to go before G.

   (E) A is the correct answer

8. Correct answer: **E.** The people who could do this are: H, D, F, E, C, A, and B. This is a total of 7 people.

9. Correct answer: **D.**

   $$\underline{B}\ \ \underline{E}\ \ \underline{F}\ \ \underline{\quad}\ \ \underline{\quad}\ \ \underline{G}\ \ \underline{D}$$

   B and E have to eat their ice cream consecutively.

10. Correct answer: **E.**

$$
\underline{\quad}\ \underline{\quad}\ \underline{\quad}\ \underline{\quad}\ \underline{\quad}\ \underline{\quad}\ \underline{\quad}
$$
$$
\begin{array}{cc}
\cancel{F} & \cancel{F} \\
\cancel{C} & \cancel{C} \\
\cancel{A} & \cancel{A}
\end{array}
$$

This figure does not help much, so you must analyze each answer choice independently. H could eat second.

(A and B) G could not be seventh, because then D would have to be eighth. This would make B first, E second, and then you would be forced to put F, C, or A in the fourth slot.

(C) E can never be first.

(D) The rules of the question disallow this.

11. Correct answer: **A.**

<u>D/H</u>   <u>H/D</u>   <u>B</u>   <u>   </u>   <u>   </u>   <u>   </u>   <u>   </u>   <u>G</u>

F cannot be fourth, because then E could not precede F.

(B and C) This can occur as shown by the diagram.

(D) This can occur.

(E) A is the correct answer.

12. Correct answer: **B.** The people who can do this are C, D, H, and A.

Game 3: Complex Linear

Initial Setup:

	Mon	Tues	Wed	Thur
A B C D				
R S T U				

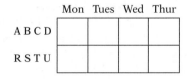

$B < D$

13. Correct answer: **E.** B must catch U and B must fish before D, so you can determine that D catches T.

Mon	Tues	Wed	Thur
C	A	B	D
R	S	U	T

14. Correct answer: **E.**

Mon	Tues	Wed	Thur
C	B	D	A
T	U	R	S

15. Correct answer: **D.**

Mon	Tues	Wed	Thur
B		A	
U	R	S	

16. Correct answer: **C.**

Mon	Tues	Wed	Thur
B	C/D	D/C	A
U	T	R	S

17. Correct answer: **C.** This is the same diagram as used in question 13. You can see that the order is R, S, U, and T.

18. Correct answer: **C.** Here are the two possibilities for the situation:

Mon	Tues	Wed	Thur
B	D/C	C/D	A
U	T	R	S

Mon	Tues	Wed	Thur
C	B	D	A
T	U	R	S

Game 4: Formal Logic

Initial Setup:

$$\cancel{B} \to H \to C$$
$$\cancel{C} \to \cancel{H} \to B$$
$$A \to \cancel{G} \qquad\qquad G \to \cancel{A}$$
$$\cancel{D} \to \cancel{E} \qquad\qquad E \to D$$
$$\cancel{B} \to \cancel{G} \qquad\qquad G \to B$$
$$\cancel{B} \to \cancel{D} \qquad\qquad D \to B$$

This is a list of all of the sufficient-necessary statements that act upon the game. The game can be solved completely using this list of statements. The best way to answer the questions is by going down the list of constraints in order to see which rules are violated.

19. Correct answer: **C.** E, D, H, C, and B could all be in together.

(A) A cannot be in with G

(B) B is out, so G must be out.

(D) If G is in, then B must be in.

(E) C is the correct answer.

20. Correct answer: **B.** If B is out, then H and C must be in.

21. Correct answer: **E.** If E is in the club, then D and B must be in the club. If G is in the club, then B must be in the club.

22. Correct answer: **A.** If B and D are out of the club, then H and C must be in the club. E and G must be out of the club. You can see that at least two people must be in the club.

23. Correct answer: **A.** If seven people are in the club, then the group must be E, D, B, H, F, and C. A or G must be the person left out.

24. Correct answer: **B.** B must be the only person in, because if B were out, then H and C must be in the club.

SECTION 2—LOGICAL REASONING

1. This squib concerns the technological frontiers of the music industry, specifically the MP3 player. It claims that the MP3 player will become so dominant and widespread that soon CDs will no longer be used.

   Question Type: "Strengthen"

   Correct answer: **C.** If this were true, then the MP3 would automatically outcompete the CD and eventually CDs would no longer circulate.

   (A) While this might seem convincing, it does not necessarily mean that the CD player and MP3 player will bear the same relationship.

   (B) This assertion is true of almost everything.

   (D) This statement would undermine the conclusion of the squib.

   (E) This prediction does not mean that CDs will not circulate anymore.

2. The squib says that 50% of people taking stress medication had higher stress levels than people taking no medication. That means that 50% of the people taking the medication had lower stress levels than people taking no medication. If this was the case, then the group as a whole exhibited a mean stress level that was about average. Therefore, it would appear that if there were a control group that yielded the same results, then the medication would be shown to not really do anything.

   Question Type: "Weaken"

   Correct answer: **B.** Here is the control group answer choice. Since this group has the same statistics as the group that used the medication, then it appears that the medicine did nothing at all.

   (A) This distribution is true of almost any population.

   (C) This tendency would affect all people in the same way.

   (D) This fact does not change the fact that 50% were still more stressed out than normal. This does not really undermine the conclusion that the medicine is effective.

   (E) This fact is irrelevant.

3. This squib tries to refute a claim that countries were 10% more aggressive during the 1400s by showing that there were 10% more countries in the 1400s. This could account for the added aggression since there were more entities capable of attacking.

   Question Type: "Weaken"

   Correct answer: **C.** If this tendency were true, then it would weaken the conclusion because countries would indeed have been more likely to be violent toward each other in the 1400s, they just would have stopped short of war. The 10% increase in the incidence of wars could be accounted for by the increase in number of countries, but there was also more lower-level violence that was not included in the war statistics.

   (A) This choice would support the argument.

   (B) This answer would tend to support the argument or be irrelevant.

   (D) This fact is not significant, because countries could just as easily declare war against countries on their borders.

   (E) What happened in the 1500s is not relevant to the 1400s.

4. This squib addresses the dangers of inhaling helium from balloons and recommends that parents be careful about giving helium-filled balloons to their children.

   Question Type: Conclusion

   Correct answer: **D.** This answer choice sums up the passage—parents should be careful when there are helium balloons around.

(A) The passage does not say this. This answer choice is too extreme.

(B) This is a subsidiary point of the passage.

(C) This statement is not true.

(E) There is no mention of argon gas in the passage.

5. The pirate claims that the sight of the skull and crossbones incites fear in all who see it. The captain claims that seeing the skull and crossbones calmed him as he prepared for battle.

Question Type: Controversy

Correct answer: **C.** The emotional response to the sight of the skull and crossbones is the issue to be addressed here.

(A) This point is not what either speaker argues.

(B) This point is not argued by the speakers.

(D) While this statement might possibly be true, it is not argued by the passage.

(E) The captain did not comment on this point, so it is impossible to tell whether he would disagree with it.

6. This squib talks about the use of archers in ancient battles. The pertinent part of the squib is that 15 soldiers on horseback could take out 100 archers.

Question Type: Conclusion

Correct answer: **C.** If 15 horsemen could kill 100 archers, then this killing appears to be effective.

(A) This point cannot be assumed from the information in the squib.

(B) This statement is not true. Just because the horsemen could take out the archers, it does not mean that there were not sharper arrows and stronger bows in the 15th century.

(D) There is no support for this statement.

(E) The passage has nothing to say about this idea.

7. This squib offers figures that try to link soft drinks, blood-sugar levels, and behavioral problems. The claim is that the more soft drinks children drink, the higher their blood-sugar level and the more behavioral problems they have.

Question Type: "Strengthen"

Correct answer: **B.** This point would need to be assumed in order to make the assumption that prohibiting children from drinking soft drinks would cure behavioral problems.

(A) This statement would not mean that parents should not prohibit these children from drinking soft drinks.

(C) While this point might be true, it is not necessary to make this assumption because choice (B) is a more direct assumption that points the finger directly at soft drinks. There is no proof that all soft drinks cause high blood-sugar levels.

(D and E) While these points might be true, they do not support the argument.

8. This squib claims that practice makes perfect and is almost always more important than athletic ability in determining one's success in a sport. The squib ends with a claim that no one could ever make it to the top of the sports world with just natural talent.

Question Type: "Strengthen"

Correct answer: **D.** If this statement were true, then the conclusion of the squib would be validated because no one could ever rise to the top on the basis of natural ability alone.

(A) This answer would undermine the squib.

(B) This choice might support the conclusion, but really, it could just be happenstance that this is the way that things are.

(C) This one person is not enough to support a global conclusion.

(E) Chess is not a sport.

9. This squib provides a series of comments about Einstein, innovation, and creativity. Then, out of nowhere, it throws in a line about spacecraft.

Question Type: Reasoning strategy

Correct answer: **D.** The line about spacecraft is unrelated to the rest of the passage and does not support the conclusion in anyway.

(A–C) These statements are not true.

(E) This choice is not true.

10. The reformist declares that when tort reform laws are enacted, doctors will save $300 per month on insurance premiums. He then claims that these savings will be beneficial to doctors *and patients*.

Question Type: "Weaken"

Correct answer: **A.** If this statement were true, then it would be clear that the tort reform laws would tend to harm patients.

(B) This choice would support the conclusion.

(C) This answer is irrelevant, but it might possibly be construed to weaken the conclusion. In any case, it is not convincing enough to be the correct answer.

(D) This statement would support the conclusion.

(E) This statement is true due to almost any change in any system.

11. This squib tells why soft drink manufacturers use under-the-cap games. More buyers are attracted by larger prizes, but larger prizes cost the company more. Therefore, companies should find the point at which the profit from sales minus the cost of paying out the prize is greatest.

Question Type: Conclusion

Correct answer: **A.** It is explicitly stated in the squib that more people will play under-the-cap games if the games have larger prizes.

(B) This answer is not necessarily true.

(C) While more than likely this statement is true, it is not something that can be concluded on the basis of the information in this passage

(D) This point is irrelevant.

(E) This conclusion cannot be reached because the squib states that all prizes attract more buyers.

12. A study was conducted of nomads who traveled at the seashore and in the desert. The water levels in their containers were found to be higher when the tribe was in the desert.

Question Type: "Resolve"

Correct answer: **D.** This answer would mean that the tribe would have no way of obtaining water near the seashore. As a result they would have to find water in the desert.

(A) This choice would suggest that water levels in the containers would be lower when the tribe was in the desert.

(B) This answer would mean that water-level measures taken when the tribe was near the sea would reflect this added water.

(C) This fact would not explain anything.

(E) Sleeping habits are unrelated to water levels.

13. This squib argues for a tax system based on a single sales tax. The current system is confusing, because many different transactions from many different people are taxed, and the author of the squib argues that society would be better served if the government taxed only the sale of goods.

Question Type: "Weaken"

Correct answer: **B.** This would cause the economy to slow and would be bad for society.

(A and C) These points would be beneficial and support the argument.

(D) This ability could be either good or bad, depending on your point of view.

(E) This is irrelevant when determining its normative value.

14. The dietitian claims that weight loss pills have no significant benefits. The weight loss expert claims that the pills help models to shave off worrisome extra pounds.

Question Type: Controversy

Correct answer: **B.** This is the crux of the issue: The weight loss expert sees these lost pounds as beneficial whereas the dietitian does not.

(A) This point is irrelevant.

(C) The dietitian never recommends that people not take weight loss pills, just that they exercise caution when using the pills.

(D) Exercise is not mentioned in the squib.

(E) The weight loss expert disagrees with this, and there is no mention of the dietitian's position regarding this statement.

15. This squib recommends that people take a shower before renting an apartment in order to determine the water pressure and amount of hot water available.

Question Type: Conclusion

Correct answer: **B.** For testing the shower to be a worthwhile idea, water pressure and heat levels would have to be different in different apartments.

(A) This point is not stated by the squib.

(C) It cannot be determined whether this statement is true.

(D) Water pressure is a concern, but the squib does not claim that it is the major concern.

(E) The truth or falsity of this claim cannot be determined on the basis of the squib.

16. This squib claims that Reginald never lost a game he pitched because of his attitude. An obvious competing reason that might explain why he never lost a game is that Reginald could have been a very good pitcher.

Question Type: "Strengthen"

Correct answer: **B.** If Reginald was a terrible pitcher, then something about his attitude would be necessary to explain his success.

(A) This statement does not really support the fact that Reginald's attitude won games for him.

(C) This choice does not necessarily mean that there were any other pitchers besides Reginald who wore their hats backwards.

(D) This answer would undermine the contentions of the squib.

(E) This information is irrelevant.

17. Evan claims that paying bills online automatically each month is better than mailing checks because when you pay bills electronically, you do not have to think about any future transactions. You could forget about bills entirely, because you have already instructed the computer to pay them for you.

Question Type: "Strengthen"

Correct answer: **B.** If Evan received a bill from a company to which he had never before made a payment, then he would have to think about paying this bill because the computer would not have been instructed to pay it.

(A and C) These answers would undermine the conclusion.

(D) This point does not mean that Evan will realize that he is being cheated or that a company will cheat him specifically.

(E) This point would support the argument, but it is not necessary for the argument to be logically drawn.

18. The squib promotes the value of water skiing as great exercise and a good way to get a tan. The squib then states that getting a "perfect tan" requires not wearing a life jacket, and not wearing a life jacket while water skiing is extremely dangerous. Thus you can infer that trying to get a perfect tan while water skiing is dangerous.

Question Type: Conclusion

Correct answer: **E.** This is the conclusion that can be made on the basis of what is stated in the squib.

(A) It is impossible to water ski on a lake without touching the water.

(B) There is no information to support this statement in the squib.

(C) This answer cannot be determined on the basis of the information given.

(D) The passage claims quite the opposite.

19. Different groups are described, each receiving a total of 18 mosquito bites. Since there are different numbers of people in each group, the number of bites per person is different.

Question Type: "Resolve"

Correct answer: **C.** This would explain the fact that when each group receives the same number of bites, the people in different groups receive different numbers of bites on average.

(A) This answer is not supported by the evidence in the squib.

(B) This choice would tend to support the idea that the group of 6 people would receive fewer bites than the groups of 2 or 3 people.

(D) If this were so, the group of 6 people would receive more bites than the groups of 2 or 3 people.

(E) This information is irrelevant.

20. Two categories are presented:

1. Puppies who are larger than their mother and not submissive to her.

2. Puppies who are either smaller than their mother and therefore automatically submissive and puppies who are larger than their mother and submissive.

The squib claims that there were none in the first category, so it makes sense that all puppies had to be in the second category.

Question Type: Analogous reasoning

Correct answer: **E.** Since there are two categories and all of one category also belongs in the second category, then we know that all purple eggs are hardboiled.

(A) This logic is completely different.

(B) This logic is similar, but it says that *some* children are well dressed and intelligent. This is not comparable because "some" is different from the "all" present in the squib.

(C) This logic is similar, but here there is an extrapolation on the basis of a single tree to a group of trees. There is no comparison between groups in the squib. *All* are the puppies in the kennel.

(D) This logic is completely different after the two categories are stated.

21. This question asks about Robin being happy, so you should diagram the portion of the squib related to Robin.

    1. Robin Noticed→Robin Must Sing

    2. Robin Noticed→Robin Happiness

    3. Happiness→Satisfied   (This is actually not necessary.)

    It is clear that if Robin is noticed, then she will be happy.

    Question Type: "Strengthen"

    Correct answer: **C.** This is the assumption that you are looking for.

    (A) This answer is not correct, because if Robin sings, then you do not know for sure that she will be noticed.

    (B) This choice is not true, for the same reasons as choice A.

    (D) This is the necessary condition, not the sufficient condition.

    (E) This answer is not correct, for the same reasons that choices A and D are not correct.

22. The naturalist claims that baby whales bond with their mothers because the babies follow their mothers throughout the ocean. The oceanologist claims that the bond is formed because the mother is the food provider.

    Question Type: Controversy

    Correct answer: **D.** The naturalist would disagree with this statement, and the oceanologist would endorse it.

    (A) Credentials are not mentioned in the squib.

    (B) This claim is not made by either speaker.

    (C) Both speakers would agree with this statement, because if the baby did not follow the mother, then the baby would be alone in the middle of a big, dark sea.

    (E) Both speakers would agree that there are several alternative theories to explain the bonding process.

23. This squib claims that televising the evil actions of evil people fosters paranoia in our society. Therefore, the assumption is made that televising

good acts would foster optimism in society. Finally, the conclusion is made that since networks choose not to televise good acts, the networks must be most concerned with their ratings.

Question Type: "Strengthen"

Correct answer: **D.** This statement directly supports the conclusion that ratings are more important than social goodness to networks.

(A) This statement does not strengthen the argument.

(B) This answer would undermine the argument, because it would show that networks care about things besides ratings.

(C) This answer choice would undermine the contentions of the squib, because the networks would be televising acts other than those that receive the highest ratings.

(E) This point does not mean that networks always defer solely to ratings.

24. This speaker rationalizes a steady diet of chocolate bars as a way of getting enough of several antioxidants, thereby completely ignoring the harmful effects of too many sweets.

Question Type: Reasoning strategy

Correct answer: **D.** The steady consumption of chocolate by the speaker is not likely to lead to good health.

(A–C) These answers do not apply.

(E) This is not an error. It is often an advisable thing to do.

25. Pessimists claim that upholsterers are a shifty lot. Optimists claim that they promote beauty. Upholsterers agree with the optimists.

Question Type: Conclusion

Correct answer: **D.** Since upholsterers agree with optimists and optimists disagree with pessimists, it makes sense (due to the transitive property) that pessimists disagree with upholsterers.

(A) This is too great an inference to be made from the squib.

(B) This choice is not necessarily true—even if upholsterers lie about the metanature of upholstery work, it does not mean that all opinions are lies.

(C and E) There is not enough information given to determine if these answers are so.

SECTION 3—LOGICAL REASONING

1. This argument assumes that because people today are so emotionally involved in football, the sport will forever remain popular in our society. However, if someday people's natures change, then they might not be so enamored of football.

Question Type: Reasoning strategy

Correct answer: **A.** The evidence within the passage is largely based on highly abstract and emotional appeals. Arguments that do not base their claims in reality are often not supportable.

(B) This statement is definitely true. The relationship between the past and the present cannot change, so it is not fallacious to assume that it won't change.

(C) The argument does not assume its conclusion, which is that football will continue to be played far into the future. Instead, it tries to base that conclusion on weak evidence.

(D) This distortion does not occur.

(E) No contradictory evidence is presented in this passage.

2. The squib notes that the platypus is a very idiosyncratic animal. The author points to the unusual environmental constraints found in Australia to explain this fact since nowhere else do mammals lay eggs or do reptiles have fur.

Question Type: "Strengthen"

Correct answer: **A.** Australia's idiosyncratic environment would affect the natural selection of platypuses, thereby endowing the species with idiosyncratic characteristics.

(B and C) This information is not really relevant to the squib, nor does it support the conclusion.

(D) This is a strange idea, and because it is impossible to determine exactly what it means based on the information in the squib, it will probably not be the answer.

(E) This choice is completely irrelevant to the fact that platypuses have fur and lay eggs.

3. This squib first describes the benefits of having a good CEO, but then cautions that paying a CEO too much could jeopardize a company's finances. Based on this situation, the author warns that a company should not risk its finances by paying too much to attract a talented CEO.

Question Type: "Weaken"

Correct answer: **E.** If this answer were true, then it would always be a good idea to hire a talented CEO, whatever the cost.

(A) Even though this statement is true, it does not mean that paying the CEO a very high salary might not endanger the company.

(B) This is an irrelevant true statement.

(C) This recommendation is a good thing, but it does not necessarily mean that the CEO's salary might not still jeopardize the company.

(D) This answer choice would cast a little doubt on the argument, but it does not state that such tactics work with CEOs.

4. This squib recounts the thrills of window washing on a skyscraper. The excitement of racing trolleys up and down the side of a building is compared to the excitement of whitewater rafting.

Question Type: Conclusion

Correct answer: **A.** You can infer that if this thrill-seeking individual claims that whitewater rafting is like racing trolleys up and down skyscrapers, then whitewater rafting must be fairly exhilarating.

(B) Not all window washers live for danger, just this particular one.

(C) This is all that the squib details.

(D) This informatin is not something that can be inferred based on the details of the squib.

(E) This statement is not true.

5. According to the squib, government officials have barred development in the boundary areas of a park despite appeals from developers to allow construction projects on these unused lands.

Question Type: "Resolve"

Correct answer: **C.** If this statement were true, that would explain why the government officials would refuse to allow the developers to build on any part of the park.

(A) The proposed development would enhance the commercial viability of the land, so this answer choice does not explain anything.

(B) This fact does not mean that the officials are angry at the particular developers who are lobbying to build in the park's boundary areas.

(D) This fact does not mean that the park's boundary areas should never be developed.

(E) This does not mean that the two groups necessarily hold divergent views in regard to this specific project.

6. This squib asserts that running shoes are not fit for tennis and tennis shoes are not fit for running. The conclusion claims that following this logic, walking shoes would not be fit for tennis.

Question Type: "Strengthen"

Correct answer: **D.** This answer would mean that if running shoes did not stand up under the pressure of tennis, then neither would walking shoes.

(A) This information would be irrelevant, because walking shoes might be designed to resist additional movements when compared to running shoes.

(B) This choice would undermine the contentions of the passage.

(C) This passage doesn't say anything about tennis shoes performing as walking shoes.

(E) This answer does not mean that the shoes are not built in different ways, or even that tennis shoes are not also made from these same materials.

7. This squib claims that TV stations are concerned solely with profits. The basis of this claim is the fact that they consistently air repetitious and boring commercials.

Question Type: Reasoning strategy

Correct answer: **C.** Evidence that is true of commercials is used to convict TV stations of focusing solely on profits. This reasoning is definitely a flaw of the squib.

(A) This attack does not occur in the squib. And even if it did, this would not be a bad way of fashioning an argument.

(B) This type of appeal does not occur.

(D) This evidence does not occur, and if it did, the passage would not be flawed because of it.

(E) This assumption does not occur.

8. This squib claims that in the morning people want their meals cooked quickly, and that is why so many people use the toaster and microwave to cook breakfast food.

Question Type: Conclusion

Correct answer: **C.** This is the conclusion of the passage.

(A) This is a subsidiary point that explains why people use toasters and microwaves in the morning.

(B) This point is not necessarily always true, nor is it a main point.

(D) This answer is not true.

(E) This is a claim of the squib, but not the main claim.

9. Johnny Appleseed's apple trees were designed to provide shade, habitats, pleasant scenery, and food. These purposes would be served only if pecan trees provided the same benefits.

Question Type: "Strengthen"

Correct answer: **E.** This would make pecan trees and apple trees interchangeable.

(A) This information does not mean that they would have enjoyed them as much as apple trees.

(B and C) This information is irrelevant.

(D) This answer would tend to undermine the argument.

10. This squib makes a number of claims about property rights, but it concludes that positivists claim that there would not be any property rights without the existence of the state to enforce the rights.

Question Type: "Weaken"

Correct answer: **E.** If this statement were true, then it would appear that the existence of a state is not necessarily required for people to enjoy some property rights. This conclusion would undermine the conclusion of the positivists.

(A) This answer would support the positivist argument.

(B) If this statement were true, then it would not matter, because property rights are enforced—their potential is actualized by the power of the state.

(C) This fact does not mean that the state does not enforce the rights of all individuals.

(D) It does not matter what people regard property to be for the purposes of this argument.

11. This squib states that college graduates on average will earn $25,000 more than people who do not graduate from college. Dtech claims that if you graduate from Dtech, then you will make at least the average increase of $25,000 more than people who do not graduate from college.

Question Type: Reasoning strategy

Correct answer: **E.** The assertion does not relate to the argument that you will earn more after graduating from college or from Dtech.

(A) Nothing is founded upon this statement.

(B) This piece of evidence is irrelevant to the conclusion.

(C) This answer is not correct.

(D) This choice is not accurate.

12. This squib outlines the benefits of having trees planted around a house so long as the house is not in a storm-prone area and so long as the trees are not too old.

Question Type: Conclusion

Correct answer: **D.** This is the general conclusion of the squib.

(A) This is part of the main point, but this statement does not include the idea that there are some exceptions to this rule.

(B and C) These are subsidiary conclusions.

(E) This is one claim of the squib.

13. This argument claims three things:

1. In Military → Over 18

2. Military Court → In Military

3. Military Court → Cause Related to Military Affairs

The argument assumes that because Brian meets all the necessary conditions, his case will be heard in military court. This, of course, is an invalid assumption.

Question Type: Reasoning strategy

Correct answer: **A.** This is the mistake. The conditions would allow Brian's case to be heard in military court but would not ensure that it would be heard in such a court.

(B) These variables are all directly related.

(C) There is no correlative relationship that is present here.

(D and E) These do not occur.

14. The doctor does not seek to prevent people from attending concerts. He merely is interested in alerting people to the dangers of listening to the loud music that is played at concerts. He claims that the only way to protect listeners' ears at concerts is by using headphones or some other noise-dampening device.

Question Type: "Strengthen"

Correct answer: **D.** This would show that concertgoers have no alternative to the doctor's recommendation, if they wish to save their hearing.

(A) This statement does not strengthen the doctor's conclusion.

(B) This fact would tend to undermine the doctor's conclusion.

(C) This information is irrelevant to the doctor's claim that the only way to protect ears at concerts is through noise-dampening devices.

(E) This answer is irrelevant to ear protection.

15. Amelia reasons that the zoologist is wrong to warn her against touching any member of the darter frog species because she knows that the babies of some types of poisonous frogs are not poisonous. However, Amelia does not know if this is true specifically of darter frogs.

Question Type: Analogous reasoning

Correct answer: **C.** Matt makes the same mistake as Amelia. The teacher says that acetone will not evaporate, but Matt knows that acetone is a member of the ketone family, and that other members of that family do evaporate quickly. Therefore, Matt makes the generalization that Amelia also makes—that acetone will have the same properties as all others in its family.

(A) Planes with jet thrusters also rely on lift.

(B) In the squib, Amelia reasons that an authority figure was wrong, but, here, Nancy reasons that an authority figure is correct.

(D and E) These are not comparable to the squib.

16. Magazine prices have increased threefold, and magazine suppliers claim that the bad economy has forced them to raise prices in order to continue to turn a profit.

Question Type: "Weaken"

Correct answer: **C.** This answer would directly contradict the claim of the magazine suppliers.

(A) This statement is true, but it is unrelated to the suppliers' claim about the role of the economy in this situation.

(B and D) Neither statement is relevant to the conclusion of the squib.

(E) This statement implies that the suppliers might have raised magazine prices for some other reason besides the drop in sales. This implication might strengthen the claim of the magazine suppliers.

17. This squib claims that a mentality of laziness is bred into the population by advertisers but that creating this mentality is very profitable because it motivates people to buy the advertisers' products.

Question Type: Conclusion

Correct answer: **B.** The claim is made in this passage that exercise is the sole way to lose weight or maintain a proper weight.

(A) This choice is not necessarily true of all salespeople.

(C) This statement might be true, but it cannot be inferred from the passage.

(D) It is not possible to make the inference that all lazy people will never lose weight.

(E) It is impossible to tell exactly how much is made from such products each year.

18. This passage claims that political campaigns based on substance are not effective. Based on this knowledge, it claims that campaigns based on nonsubstantive issues will be successful.

Question Type: Analogous reasoning

Correct answer: **A.** Teachers who grade systematically do not increase student interest. Based on this information, the answer choice claims that teachers who grade randomly will increase student interest. This reasoning is unsupportable in the same way the squib is.

(B) This is a relatively supportable argument and therefore not comparable with the completely fallacious argument in the squib.

(C) This does not compare.

(D) Owning the game and being caught up in the game are not the same variable.

(E) This compares one group of fishermen to another group. There is no comparable comparison made between candidates in the squib.

19. This argument refers to the lure of drugs for troubled youngsters. The squib states that drug use may appeal to any child, but drugs are especially dangerous and attractive to maladjusted children because these children are unhappy with their environment. That is why parents of these children must be especially vigilant in protecting their children against drugs.

Question Type: "Strengthen"

Correct answer: **D.** This is the crux of the squib. If this were not the case, then it would not be any more necessary for parents of such children to talk to their children about drugs than it would be for parents of normal children to do so.

(A) This point is not assumed.

(B) This is not explicitly stated by the squib even though it is probably true.

(C) Nothing is stated about a parent's prospective success when talking to a drug-addicted child.

(E) The squib does not claim that there are not other remedies for drug problems besides parents.

20. The ornithologist differentiates hummingbirds from other birds by claiming that the diet of the hummingbird requires it to obtain food in a different way. Because of this difference, hummingbirds are in some ways like bees when they acquire nectar from flowers.

Question Type: Reasoning strategy

Correct answer: **A.** The conclusion is that hummingbirds and bees collect nectar in similar ways. This final sentence illustrates that idea.

(B) The comparison between hummingbirds and bees is not set up in the final sentence.

(C–E) These statements are not the case.

21. This squib reviews the origins and original purposes of chess. Watched by the emperor, prospective generals used to train for war by using the chessboard as a battlefield. The emperor would then choose the most successful chess player to lead his army.

Question Type: Reasoning strategy

Correct answer: **A.** The sentence supports the idea that generals used to use games of chess to train for war.

(B) The emperor is not a chesspiece.

(C) It is not a conclusion; it is more of a claim.

(D) This is certainly not the main point of the argument.

(E) This statement is not true, since supposedly this was the nature of the game (at least according to the squib).

22. The writer of this squib mistakes the meaning of *standardized* in the term *standardized testing*, which actually means merely that the tests are all basically the same. Instead, the writer's point is that standardized testing produces anything but standard scores.

   Question Type: Reasoning strategy

   Correct answer: **C.** The passage claims in various ways that standardized testing is not an appropriate name for these tests.

   (A) Most interpretations of testing are the same.

   (B) This claim is well supported.

   (D) This is not a principle.

   (E) There is no compromise made in or about the argument.

23. The industrialist claims that average people are relegated to demeaning jobs in other societies. The humanist claims that in other societies average people are not forced into demeaning jobs.

   Question Type: Controversy

   Correct answer: **B.** This is the essence of their disagreement.

   (A) Both speakers agree with this claim.

   (C) This statement is not made by either speaker.

   (D and E) These points are not addressed by either speaker.

24. Dennis claims that his action figures are so superior that other children should not play with him because they will feel bad on account of their inferior action figures.

   Question Type: Conclusion

   Correct answer: **D.** If Dennis's statements are taken to be true, then his claim that children can feel bad when they play with inferior action figures must also be true.

   (A) Dennis claims only that he will be the first to buy the figure.

   (B) This point might be true, but there is not enough evidence to make this inference.

   (C) This inference is probably true, but it cannot be determined based on the squib.

   (E) This sentence is a misinterpretation of what Dennis says.

25. This squib claims that Internet connections will get faster and faster until the speed at which the data are displayed on your screen is equivalent to the speed of light.

   Question Type: "Strengthen"

   Correct answer: **A.** If this were a limiting constant, then the data from the satellite might have to slow up when they reach the electronic network inside the computer.

   (B) The exact opposite is assumed by the squib.

   (C) This occurence is not necessarily going to happen immediately after the wireless connections begin gaining speed.

   (D) This assumption is irrelevant.

   (E) What occurs with neural signals is unrelated to what will happen with internet signals.

26. Government officials wanted to build an ice skating rink, but the price seemed prohibitive until a construction company offered to build the rink for $2 million—$3 million less than the projected price tag.

   Question Type: "Resolve"

   Correct answer: **C.** This lower cost would allow the construction company to offer a much lower price than government officials had expected.

   (A) This statement adds to the confusion.

   (B) This explanation does not mean that they would easily be able to save $3 million.

   (D) This point is irrelevant.

   (E) It is highly unlikely that labor costs would be $3 million higher during the winter.

27. This squib states that if the whale population were to decrease dramatically, then more than likely there will never again be as many whales as there were in preindustrial times.

   Question Type: "Weaken"

   Correct answer: **A.** This statement would imply that the whale population might have been extraordinarily large during the preindustrial age. It was probably unusual for it to be that big back then, and it is unlikely that it will ever be that big again in the future.

   (B) This answer does not mean that the specialists are exaggerating in this particular case.

   (C–E) These points are irrelevant.

SECTION 4—READING COMPREHENSION

1. Correct answer: **C.** Japan's entrance into the war is described in the first paragraph. There is never any indication that Japan was criticized for not aiding its allies.

    (A) The passage states this (line 9).

    (B) The passage states this (lines 13–15).

    (D) The passage states this (lines 11–13).

    (E) The passage states this (lines 5–7).

2. Correct answer: **E.** If you follow imperialistic logic, you would want to take advantage of every opportunity to occupy or control as much territory as possible.

    (A and B) Financial benefits do not relate as closely to imperialism as does occupation of territory.

    (C) Relinquishing territory would not really be on the agenda of most imperialists.

    (D) This advice may or may not be something that an imperialist would offer.

3. Correct answer: **A.** This occurred when Japan turned from a debtor to a creditor for the first time at the end of World War I (lines 39–42).

    (B) Nothing is mentioned about spoils aiding the Japanese economy.

    (C) This is the second-best answer, but the passage does not point to these loans in the same way as the transition from debtor to creditor.

    (D) Nothing is mentioned about Lake Baikal being a huge gateway for trade. Additionally, this acquisition occurred after the economic transition.

    (E) World War II is not mentioned in the passage.

4. Correct answer: **D.** The passage is concerned with detailing the growth of Japan's political power. The final paragraph tells how the Japanese gained political ground by taking part in this international conference.

    (A) There is no hint that the role is inappropriate.

    (B) There was no reason for their presence to be misleading.

    (C) This was definitely a historically significant event.

    (E) This statement is not true, because it appears that Japan achieved many of its aims at the conference.

5. Correct answer: **C.** *Hegemony* means superiority or dominance, so *sovereignty*, which has a similar meaning, is the correct answer.

    (A) *Tyranny* is close but it does not match exactly.

    (B) *Misfortune* has an entirely different meaning.

    (D and E) These words would change the meaning.

6. Correct answer: **A.** The author primarily tracks the rise of Japanese influence during and after World War I.

    (B) The passage never offers any alternative explanations.

    (C) There is no mention of brutality.

    (D) Only the beginning of the passage analyzes the decision to enter the war. The rest is concerned with the effects on Japan of the country's participation in World War I.

    (E) This argument might be implied, but it is not such an overriding theme that it could be considered the primary concern of the passage.

7. Correct answer: **C.** The passage offers a hypothesis about the development of rhythmic chants among prehistoric peoples. These chants eventually evolved into poetry and songs that were sung by minstrels in the Middle Ages.

    (A) Nothing negative is said about prehistoric peoples.

    (B) The passage does not characterize the development of poetry as "rapid."

    (D) The role of minstrels is described, but the main point of the passage is not to glorify such people.

    (E) No claim is made that the Anglo-Saxons were the sole source of the chanting that turned eventually into poetry and song.

8. Correct answer: **A.** The main purpose of people in this group was to recite and spread poetry. Minstrel composers developed poetry from the randomly produced utterances made by savages into an art form that was enjoyed and prized by all society.

    (B) These warriors might have chanted at times, but they were not really responsible for any contribution.

    (C) These hunters may have chanted around the fire, but their major purpose was not artistic in nature.

(D) "Communal composers" were essentially the same as the groups that chanted by the fire.

(E) In the passage, barbarous chiefs are mentioned as employers of minstrels but not as composers of poetry themselves.

9. Correct answer: **A.** If this statement were true, then it would prove that groups did collect around the fire to engage in communal chant and dance.

(B) What such poetry is called today is irrelevant to its development in prehistoric times.

(C) This written form of poetry might imply that individuals, not groups, developed poetry and that it did not first develop in a spoken form.

(D) This statement would undermine the author's argument.

(E) This point is irrelevant.

10. Correct answer: **E.** At first it seemed that poetry was created only communally and largely in random chants. More "deliberate" poems were ones created with more attention paid to each part of the poem.

(A) This explanation is not what the word means.

(B) Alternatives to writing poetry are never discussed in the passage.

(C) The poems were never composed completely accidentally; they were just performed in random sequence.

(D) Minstrels and barbarous chiefs are not mentioned until the paragraph following the one containing the word *deliberate*.

11. Correct answer: **B.** The author claims that communal chants were a necessary precursor to modern poetry.

(A) The opposite is stated.

(C) The sincerity (or insincerity) of communal composition is never mentioned.

(D) This statement is too extreme.

(E) The significance of these acts is emphasized.

12. Correct answer: **C.** The passage never makes any claim that the Anglo-Saxons were the exclusive originators of popular ballads.

(A) This point is made in the passage (line 40).

(B and D) These statements are true, because early poetry was a communal composition created by primitive hunters.

(E) This generalization is true, as stated in the final paragraph.

13. Correct answer: **E.** The passage mentions this change (line 54).

(A) More than likely this practice was already illegal.

(B) This service counter was lowered, not raised.

(C) This statement was true prior to 1998 (see lines 30–31).

(D) Nothing is said about neglecting the mentally handicapped.

14. Correct answer: **A.** The author describes the city's efforts as sincere.

(B–E) The author uses all of these words or phrases to describe things other than the city's efforts.

15. Correct answer: **B.** The purpose of the passage is to track the development of Springfield as a city from a place where shootouts occurred to one that conscientiously provides for ADA-protected individuals.

(A) This conundrum is not mentioned.

(C) This point is true, but it is not the purpose of the passage to express this idea.

(D) No Springfield department is said to have a hidden agenda.

(E) This argument is implied, but it is not the primary purpose of the passage to promote this idea.

16. Correct answer: **E.** The mention of Claudia Engram adds human interest to the passage by providing a personal recollection from someone with a disability.

(A) Engram was not a government official.

(B) This is not an argument that the author is trying to advance.

(C) It is not claimed that Engram was the city's biggest proponent of the ADA.

(D) This answer is nonsensical.

17. Correct answer: **A.** The purpose of the passage is to track Springfield's progression from a city known for its shootouts to one in which quality of life for its citizens is a top priority. From this progression, you can see that this answer choice is correct.

(B) No assessments are made about "Wild Bill" Hickok's gunfighting abilities.

(C and D) These statements are true but are not the main thrust of the passage.

(E) This is the second-best choice, but answer choice A best encapsulates the full nature of Springfield's progression.

18. Correct answer: **E.** The author writes about the progress made in Springfield and claims that it is laudable, so more than likely the author feels that governmental compliance with the ADA is a moral duty.

(A–D) The opposite of these choices is stressed.

19. Correct answer: **B.** If the Tartar culture existed only in Western Europe, then there would be no reason to believe that the robes were from the East.

(A) This choice would bolster their story.

(C) This point is irrelevant.

(D) This statement would strengthen their claims.

(E) This answer would not undermine the evidence; it would be additional evidence.

20. Correct answer: **B.** The opposite of the Europeans' opinions was true about Asia, so those opinions could be considered to be unreliable.

(A) There was not yet any evidence available to change the opinions, so they could not be considered to be outdated.

(C) The opinions were very fallible.

(D) The opinions were sincere, not sarcastic.

(E) The opinions were more superficial than exhaustive.

21. Correct answer: **C.** This fact was included in the passage in order to show that the Mongols did not destroy what they conquered; instead, they sought to learn from foreign nations, even concepts as abstract as spirituality.

(A) This is the second-best answer, but the main purpose of mentioning this point is not to demonstrate the emperor's interest in Catholicism but to show that the emperor bore no hard feelings toward the conquered Europeans.

(B) This point is not mentioned until much later in the passage.

(D) This statement is just not true.

(E) The Polos were not said to have been asked to perform this errand.

22. Correct answer: **A.** The purpose of mentioning Odysseus was to embellish the story of the Polos by comparing it to the story of the great Greek hero.

(B) Geography was not a consideration.

(C) It is unlikely that nostalgia was the purpose of this allusion to Greek mythology. What would readers have to be nostalgic about? The last time they read the *Odyssey*?

(D) This passage is not a test of the reader's knowledge.

(E) This choice might sound plausible at first. But it is not logical to try to add credibility to one outlandish story by comparing it to a more outlandish story.

23. Correct answer: **E.** There is no mention of the Polos' pay except to say that at the time of their escape from the emperor they possessed nice robes and jewels.

(A) The Polos traveled by land and also were known to be consummate sailors.

(B) This point must be true if the emperor so strongly relied on them to perform government business.

(C) This reason is why the emperor did not wish to release them from duty.

(D) This statement must be true if the Polos were able to escape together.

24. Correct answer: **D.** Europeans' misperceptions were corrected by the Polos' stories. This choice shows how important these stories were.

(A) The passage does not completely explicate the thesis in the first paragraph.

(B) The passage does not offer opposing opinions about the Polos, who are the central characters and focus of the passage.

(C) The author does not express the opinion that the characters in the passage are embellished in any way.

(E) The passage does present contrasting views about Asia, but these views are never really expanded later. Actually, the views are contradicted later.

25. Correct answer: **C.** The passage never really talks about the French. It talks about Europeans in general, but does not explicitly state that the Mongols traded with any European country besides Italy.

(A) This statement is made in the first line of the second paragraph.

(B) This point is made in the second paragraph, where it is noted that the Mongols moved through Russia to Italy.

(D) It is stated that the Mongol capital was just north of the Great Wall of China.

(E) This point is made and supported by the fact that the Mongols requested missionaries to teach them.

PRACTICE TEST 2

ANSWER SHEET

SECTION 1	SECTION 2	SECTION 3	SECTION 4
1. A B C D E	1. A B C D E	1. A B C D E	1. A B C D E
2. A B C D E	2. A B C D E	2. A B C D E	2. A B C D E
3. A B C D E	3. A B C D E	3. A B C D E	3. A B C D E
4. A B C D E	4. A B C D E	4. A B C D E	4. A B C D E
5. A B C D E	5. A B C D E	5. A B C D E	5. A B C D E
6. A B C D E	6. A B C D E	6. A B C D E	6. A B C D E
7. A B C D E	7. A B C D E	7. A B C D E	7. A B C D E
8. A B C D E	8. A B C D E	8. A B C D E	8. A B C D E
9. A B C D E	9. A B C D E	9. A B C D E	9. A B C D E
10. A B C D E	10. A B C D E	10. A B C D E	10. A B C D E
11. A B C D E	11. A B C D E	11. A B C D E	11. A B C D E
12. A B C D E	12. A B C D E	12. A B C D E	12. A B C D E
13. A B C D E	13. A B C D E	13. A B C D E	13. A B C D E
14. A B C D E	14. A B C D E	14. A B C D E	14. A B C D E
15. A B C D E	15. A B C D E	15. A B C D E	15. A B C D E
16. A B C D E	16. A B C D E	16. A B C D E	16. A B C D E
17. A B C D E	17. A B C D E	17. A B C D E	17. A B C D E
18. A B C D E	18. A B C D E	18. A B C D E	18. A B C D E
19. A B C D E	19. A B C D E	19. A B C D E	19. A B C D E
20. A B C D E	20. A B C D E	20. A B C D E	20. A B C D E
21. A B C D E	21. A B C D E	21. A B C D E	21. A B C D E
22. A B C D E	22. A B C D E	22. A B C D E	22. A B C D E
23. A B C D E	23. A B C D E	23. A B C D E	23. A B C D E
24. A B C D E	24. A B C D E	24. A B C D E	24. A B C D E
25. A B C D E	25. A B C D E	25. A B C D E	25. A B C D E
26. A B C D E	26. A B C D E	26. A B C D E	26. A B C D E
27. A B C D E	27. A B C D E	27. A B C D E	27. A B C D E
28. A B C D E	28. A B C D E	28. A B C D E	28. A B C D E
29. A B C D E	29. A B C D E	29. A B C D E	29. A B C D E
30. A B C D E	30. A B C D E	30. A B C D E	30. A B C D E

SECTION 1
Time—35 minutes
25 questions

<u>Directions for Reading Comprehension Questions:</u> Each passage in this section is followed by a group of questions. Answer each question based on what is stated or implied in the passage. For some questions, more than one answer choice may be possible, so choose the *best* answer to each question. After you have chosen your answer, mark the corresponding space on the Answer Sheet.

The stored communication portion of the Electronic Communications Privacy Act (ECPA) creates statutory privacy rights for customers of and subscribers to computer
(5) network service providers. In a broad sense, ECPA "fills in the gaps" left by the uncertain application of Fourth Amendment protections to cyberspace. To understand these gaps, consider the legal
(10) protections we have in our homes. The Fourth Amendment clearly protects our homes in the physical world: Absent special circumstances, the government must first obtain a warrant before it searches there.
(15) When we use a computer network such as the Internet, however, we do not have a physical "home." Instead, we typically have a network account consisting of a block of computer storage that is owned by
(20) a network service provider, such as America Online. If law-enforcement investigators want to obtain the contents of a network account or information about its use, they do not need to go to the user to
(25) get that information. Instead, the government can obtain the information directly from the provider.
    Although the Fourth Amendment generally requires the government to
(30) obtain a warrant to search a home, it does not require the government to obtain a warrant to obtain the stored contents of a network account. Instead, the Fourth Amendment generally permits the
(35) government to issue a subpoena to a network provider that orders the provider to divulge the contents of an account. ECPA addresses this imbalance by offering network account holders a range of
(40) statutory privacy rights against access to stored account information held by network service providers.
    Because ECPA is an unusually complicated statute, it is helpful when

(45) approaching the statute to understand the intent of its drafters. The structure of ECPA reflects a series of classifications that indicate the drafters' judgments about what kinds of information implicate
(50) greater or lesser privacy interests. For example, the drafters saw greater privacy interests in stored e-mails than in subscriber account information. Similarly, the drafters believed that computing
(55) services available "to the public" required more strict regulation than services not available to the public. (Perhaps this judgment reflects the view that providers available to the public are not likely to
(60) have close relationships with their customers, and therefore might have less incentive to protect their customers' privacy.) To protect the array of privacy interests identified by its drafters, ECPA
(65) offers varying degrees of legal protection, depending on the perceived importance of the privacy interest involved. Some information can be obtained from providers with a mere subpoena; other
(70) information requires a special court order; and still other information requires a search warrant. In general, the greater the privacy interest, the greater the privacy protection.

GO ON TO THE NEXT PAGE

1. The primary purpose of the passage is to

   (A) qualify and explain the purpose of the ECPA
   (B) argue that the Fourth Amendment alone is not enough protection in our age of technology
   (C) exalt the brilliance of the drafters of the ECPA
   (D) describe the difficulty of obtaining a search warrant for information in cyberspace
   (E) debate the ethicality of network service provision

2. Using inferences from the passage, the author would be most likely to describe the attitudes of the public network service providers referenced in line 41 as

   (A) ignoble
   (B) impious
   (C) pompous
   (D) clandestine
   (E) indifferent

3. The author argues that the ECPA is an important reinterpretation of our right to privacy because

   (A) subpoenas are extremely easy to obtain
   (B) public network service providers have very little incentive to protect their customers' rights, especially if the providers can make a profit
   (C) the greater the need for privacy, the more protections the ECPA tends to provide
   (D) as our personal information becomes more likely to be stored in a nonphysical realm, the Fourth Amendment alone has a decreasing power to protect it
   (E) the complicated nature of the statute allows it to be interpreted in many different ways, depending on who wants to use it in their favor

4. According to the author, the Fourth Amendment had what kind of effect on cyberspace privacy rights before the ECPA?

   (A) momentous
   (B) ambiguous
   (C) incendiary
   (D) progressive
   (E) adverse

5. The author most likely mentions that "our homes [are] in the physical world" (lines 11–12) in order to

   (A) offer a place where there are gaps to be filled in the Fourth Amendment by the ECPA
   (B) remind the reader of the difference between a real home and a "cyber" home
   (C) explain why there is less incentive for government officials to pursue obtaining personal data from computer memory when it is far easier to get a search warrant for a physical home
   (D) address the contrast between the relative simplicity of protecting a physical object as opposed to the uncertain protection of computer memory
   (E) distinguish our homes from the homes of government workers

6. The passage provides support for which of the following claims?

   (A) The drafters of the ECPA were some of the most popular legislators in America.
   (B) Personal e-mails are legally considered more private than personal account information.
   (C) It is considered less important to protect privacy in computing services available "to the public" than in those that are "private."
   (D) In our modern age, the Fourth Amendment is outdated and could be generally disregarded without effect.
   (E) Network service providers have given the government a great deal of legal trouble with reference to privacy rights over the past several years.

GO ON TO THE NEXT PAGE

Russia is the largest of the 15 geopolitical entities that emerged in 1991 from the Soviet Union. Covering more than 17 million square kilometers in
(5) Europe and Asia, Russia succeeded the Soviet Union as the largest country in the world. As was the case in the Soviet and tsarist eras, the center of Russia's population and economic activity is the
(10) European sector, which occupies about one-quarter of the country's territory. Vast tracts of land in Asian Russia are virtually unoccupied. Although numerous Soviet programs had attempted to populate and
(15) exploit resources in Siberia and the Arctic regions of the Russian Republic, the population of Russia's remote areas decreased in the 1990s. Thirty-nine percent of Russia's territory but only 6 percent of
(20) its population in 1996 was located east of Lake Baikal, the geographical landmark in south-central Siberia. The territorial extent of the country constitutes a major economic and political problem for
(25) Russian governments lacking the far-reaching authoritarian clout of their Soviet predecessors.

In the Soviet political system, which was self-described as a democratic
(30) federation of republics, the center of authority for almost all actions of consequence was Moscow, the capital of the Russian Republic. After the breakup of the Soviet Union in 1991, that long-
(35) standing concentration of power meant that many of the other 14 republics faced independence without any experience at self-governance. For Russia, the end of the Soviet Union meant facing the world
(40) without the considerable buffer zone of Soviet republics that had protected and nurtured it in various ways since the 1920s; the change required complete reorganization of what had become a
(45) thoroughly corrupt and ineffectual socialist system.

In a history-making year, the regime of President Mikhail Gorbachev of the Soviet Union was mortally injured by an
(50) unsuccessful coup in August 1991. After all the constituent republics, including Russia, had voted for independence in the months that followed the coup, Gorbachev announced in December 1991 that the

(55) nation would cease to exist. In place of the monolithic union, there remained the Commonwealth of Independent States (CIS), a loose confederation of 11 of the former Soviet republics, which now
(60) were independent states with an indefinite mandate of mutual cooperation. By late 1991, the Communist Party of the Soviet Union (CPSU) and the Communist Party of the Russian Republic had been banned
(65) in Russia, and Boris Yeltsin, who had been elected president of the Russian Republic in June 1991, had become the leader of the new Russian Federation.

Under those circumstances, Russia has
(70) undergone an agonizing process of self-analysis and refocusing of national goals. That process, which seemingly had only begun in the mid-1990s, has been observed and commented upon with more analytic
(75) energy than any similar transformation in the history of the world. As information pours out past the ruins of the Iron Curtain, a new, more reliable portrait of Russia emerges, but substantial mystery remains.

7. Which of the following best describes the main idea of the passage?

(A) In its transition to self-governance, Russia, unlike the other 14 republics, has been shaken by controversy, political failure, and stubborn remnants of the corrupt Soviet regime.
(B) Corruption among the Communist leadership was the sole problem in Soviet politics, but in the end it was enough to dissolve the Union.
(C) Russia's strength relies on the full exploitation of its resources, and the Soviet Union's inability to tap into Siberian riches led to its downfall.
(D) Russia's political remodeling since late 1991 has been one of the most studied transformations in history.
(E) Over the past several years, Russia's rapid emergence from a corrupt socialist system has required political transformations on a colossal scale.

GO ON TO THE NEXT PAGE

8. Which one of the following would Russian politicians probably deem the most detrimental contributor to Russian politics before 1991?

   (A) the Russian Federation
   (B) Boris Yeltsin
   (C) Europe
   (D) Communism
   (E) self-governance

9. The phrase "monolithic union" in line 56 most likely to refers to

   (A) a metaphor comparing the Soviet Union to obdurate stone
   (B) the massiveness and perceived indestructibility of the Soviet Union in late 1991
   (C) the way that the republics together comprised a single association and acted as a uniform block
   (D) the Soviet leaders' tradition of demonstrating their power by building huge statues that were displayed around the republics
   (E) a popular nickname the stalwart Mikhail Gorbachev acquired due to his physical build and political obstinacy

10. The second paragraph primarily serves to

   (A) explain why the effects of the breakup of the Soviet Union meant that the new republics would need to entirely reconstruct their political systems and attitudes
   (B) offer several reasons why the 15 republics were better off in the long term as part of the Soviet Union
   (C) describe the short-term goals of most of the republics just after the breakup of the Soviet Union
   (D) blame the collapse of the Soviet Union on Communism
   (E) argue that the 15 republics were far better off when the center of authority was in Moscow

11. It can be inferred that most Russian citizens view Siberia as which of the following?

   (A) intolerably inhospitable
   (B) politically overwhelmed
   (C) unfairly exploited
   (D) favorably desolate
   (E) uncomfortably overpopulated

12. According to the passage, all the following are true of Russia since its emergence from the Soviet Union EXCEPT

   (A) it has had to deal with the loss of control of the satellite republics that constituted its buffer zone
   (B) it banned Communist parties from the country
   (C) it has attracted the attention of many social scientists, historians, and cultural analysts
   (D) it underwent a very difficult political transformation
   (E) it has developed into a corruption-free, benevolent political entity

GO ON TO THE NEXT PAGE

Stem cells have recently become an important focus for scientific research around the world. They have two important characteristics that distinguish
(5) them from other types of cells. First, they are unspecialized cells that renew themselves for long periods through cell division. Also, under certain physiologic or experimental conditions, they can be
(10) induced to become cells with special functions such as the beating cells of the heart muscle or the insulin-producing cells of the pancreas.

Scientists primarily work with two
(15) kinds of stem cells from animals and humans: embryonic stem cells and adult stem cells, which each have different functions and characteristics. Scientists discovered ways to obtain or derive stem
(20) cells from early mouse embryos more than 20 years ago. Many years of detailed study of the biology of mouse stem cells led to the discovery, in 1998, of a means to isolate stem cells from human embryos and
(25) grow the cells in the laboratory. These are called human embryonic stem cells. The embryos used in these studies were created for infertility purposes through in vitro fertilization procedures, and when they
(30) were no longer needed for that purpose, they were donated for research with the informed consent of the donor.

Stem cells are important for living organisms for many reasons. In the three- to five-
(35) day old embryo, called a blastocyst, a small group of about 30 cells called the inner cell mass gives rise to the hundreds of highly specialized cells needed to make up an adult organism. In the developing
(40) fetus, stem cells in developing tissues give rise to the multiple specialized cell types that make up the heart, lung, skin, and other tissues. In some adult tissues, such as bone marrow, muscle, and brain, discrete
(45) populations of adult stem cells generate replacements for cells that are lost through normal wear and tear, injury, or disease. It has even been hypothesized that stem cells may someday become the basis for treating
(50) diseases such as Parkinson's disease, diabetes, and heart disease.

Scientists want to study stem cells in the laboratory so they can learn about their essential properties and what makes them

(55) different from specialized cell types. As scientists learn more about stem cells, it may become possible to use the cells not just in cell-based therapies but also for screening new drugs and toxins and
(60) understanding birth defects. Current research goals include both determining precisely how stem cells remain unspecialized and self-renewing for so long and identifying the signals that cause
(65) stem cells to become specialized cells.

13. The author's primary purpose in writing this passage was to

(A) argue the necessity for an effective diabetes treatment and oppose the use of mouse embryonic stem cell research
(B) aggressively defend the ethicality of gathering embryonic stem cells from human embryos
(C) hesitantly debate the role stem cells will most certainly play in future medicine
(D) offer a relatively new-age alternative medicine therapy as a possible treatment for several persistent diseases
(E) explain stem cell research in relatively basic terms and point out its greatly untapped potential

14. According to the passage, the hypothesis, given in the end of the third paragraph, that stem cells hold the key to treating some of the most troublesome diseases of our time would suggest which of the following?

(A) Stem cell research will provide the means for several preventive therapies, which could be put in place in a developing fetus.
(B) Research in the field of stem cells is rapidly nearing its limit of applicability.
(C) Cells that have already become specialized are of little use when it comes to disease treatment.
(D) Many more stem cell donors will be needed to supply the cells needed for all the upcoming research.
(E) Stem cell research could prove more important in the medical world than anyone could have possibly anticipated.

GO ON TO THE NEXT PAGE

15. Which one of the following statements is best supported by the properties of stem cells listed by the author?

(A) A single cell may originate as a stem cell, but it could still live the majority of its lifespan as a muscle tissue cell.
(B) Stem cells embody the peak of evolutionary achievement.
(C) Embryo donors are vastly decreasing in numbers as legislation is passed against these sorts of infertility procedures.
(D) Birth defects are most often caused by improper differentiation of cells from stem cells.
(E) Stem cells can be gathered from only embryos or cadavers.

16. Which one of the following statements, if true, lends the most support to the author's argument that stem cell treatments will become a valuable staple in the medical world in years to come?

(A) Currently, stem cells are considered relative mysteries of science, but many researchers still believe in their promise.
(B) Stem cells multiply without any contact inhibition, much like cancer cells.
(C) Though stem cells have much potential as a new form of medical treatment, there is doubt whether we will ever be able to efficiently manipulate them.
(D) By inducing stem cells to differentiate into the tissue of choice, doctors can use healthy new cells to replace an afflicted patient's damaged or diseased cells.
(E) There is no need for any more embryo donors for the harvesting of stem cells because they renew themselves indefinitely.

17. Which one of the following can replace the word *essential* in line 54 without significantly changing the author's intended meaning?

(A) auxiliary
(B) fundamental
(C) necessary
(D) superfluous
(E) unique

18. Which one of the following best describes the organization of the passage?

(A) A topical theory is offered, the author supports the theory with mundane evidence, and then he or she concludes by calling the reader to action using emotional persuasion.
(B) Clashing hypotheses are produced, the merits of each side are debated, and then the hypotheses are merged into a single, more accurate theory.
(C) A topic is introduced, its known features and its mystery are discussed, and then future goals and applications are proposed.
(D) A scientific enigma is explained, its history is chronicled, and then certain applications are attacked for their simplicity.
(E) A point of view is presented, several hypotheses regarding the point of view materialize, and then the future of the point of view is predicted in the author's conclusion.

GO ON TO THE NEXT PAGE

Around the middle of the 17th century, the evolution of a sugar-plantation society based on slave labor marked an important watershed in Caribbean history.

(5) Introduced by the Dutch when they were expelled from Brazil in 1640, the sugar-plantation system arrived at an opportune time for the fledgling non-Spanish colonists with their precarious economies.

(10) The English yeoman farming economy based mainly on cultivation of tobacco was facing a severe crisis. Caribbean tobacco could compete neither in quality nor in quantity with tobacco produced in the mid-

(15) Atlantic colonies. Because tobacco farming had been the basis of the economy, its end threatened the economic viability of the islands. As a result, the colonies were losing population to the

(20) mainland. Economic salvation came from what has been called in historical literature the Caribbean "sugar revolutions," a series of interrelated changes that altered the entire agriculture, demography, society,

(25) and culture of the Caribbean, thereby transforming the political and economic importance of the region.

In terms of agriculture, the islands changed from small farms producing cash

(30) crops of tobacco and cotton with the labor of a few servants and slaves—often indistinguishable—to large plantations requiring vast expanses of land and enormous capital outlays to create

(35) sugarcane fields and factories. Sugar, which had become increasingly popular on the European market throughout the 17th century, provided an efficacious balance between bulk and

(40) value—a relationship of great importance in the days of relatively small sailing ships and distant sea voyages. Hence, the conversion to sugar transformed the landholding pattern of the islands.

(45) The case of Barbados illustrates the point. In 1640 this island of 430 square kilometers had about 10,000 settlers, predominantly white; 764 of them owned 4 or more hectares of land, and virtually

(50) every white was a landholder. By 1680, when the sugar revolution was underway, the wealthiest 175 planters owned 54% of the land and an equal proportion of the servants and slaves. More important,

(55) Barbados had a population of about 38,000 African slaves and more than 2000 English servants who owned no land. Fortunes, however, depended on access to land and slaves.

(60) The sugar revolutions were both cause and consequence of the demographic revolution. Sugar production required a greater labor supply than was available through the importation of European

(65) servants and irregularly supplied African slaves. At first, the Dutch supplied the slaves, as well as the credit, capital, technological expertise, and marketing arrangements; but as the transformation

(70) pushed on, the supply still failed to meet the demand, and all types of private traders eventually entered into the transatlantic commerce. This ensured the persistence of the Caribbean islands as important economic footholds in the New World for many European countries.

19. The author's primary purpose in writing this passage was to

(A) explain the importance of balancing bulk and value in the days when ships were much smaller
(B) reveal the importance of the Dutch to Caribbean economic development
(C) present today's political attitude toward the Caribbean islands as a direct result of the "sugar revolutions" of the 17th century
(D) chronicle the transition of Caribbean society to an economic foundation of sugar production
(E) relate the mid-Atlantic tobacco industry to the Caribbean sugar industry

20. The author's explanation of the development of a sugar-plantation based Caribbean economy is strengthened by using all of the following EXCEPT

(A) a debated historical theory
(B) statistics
(C) historical background information
(D) a contrast
(E) a specific example

GO ON TO THE NEXT PAGE

21. Which of the following claims is best supported by information given in the passage?

    (A) Fewer than 200 planters actually owned slaves in Barbados, despite their huge economic reliance on slave labor.
    (B) The majority of the "sugar revolutions" took place within a single decade.
    (C) The Spanish were the main contributors to the evolution of a sugar-plantation society in the Caribbean.
    (D) The term "sugar revolutions" applies only to the agricultural and economic shifts that took place outside the Caribbean.
    (E) Without the existence of slave labor, it is doubtful that sugar plantations would have evolved in the Caribbean.

22. The word *watershed* used in line 4 could best be replaced by which of the following without significantly changing the author's intended meaning?

    (A) economic highlight
    (B) cultural transition
    (C) anticlimactic emergency
    (D) water management problem
    (E) demographic transaction

23. Using evidence from the passage, which one of the following can best be described as a change that occurred in the Caribbean market from around 1640 to 1680?

    (A) While almost no one owned slaves in 1640, by 1680 nearly every English family in the Caribbean owned at least one slave.
    (B) The concentration of family-operated businesses was rapidly decreasing.
    (C) Natives were developing special skills to challenge colonists for their jobs.
    (D) More people owned land in the Caribbean than ever before.
    (E) There was an increasing demand for labor from a decreasing number of employers.

24. Inferences from the passage would suggest that the author would most likely refer to which of the following as the LEAST important element in the evolution of the Caribbean sugar-plantation society?

    (A) the English yeoman farming economy
    (B) access to slave labor
    (C) sugar's popularity in the European market
    (D) thriving mid-Atlantic tobacco plantations
    (E) sugar's quality of being valuable without being bulky

25. According to the author, in the decade beginning in the year 1680, people were emigrating from the Caribbean colonies to the mainland primarily for which reason?

    (A) The weather and frequent tropical storms had intensified in the 1650s.
    (B) People were more successful growing sugar on the mainland.
    (C) Tobacco farming was becoming less economically viable.
    (D) Democracy in the United States was flourishing and attractive to settlers.
    (E) The disparate allocation of wealth encouraged people to leave the country.

S T O P

IF YOU FINISH BEFORE TIME RUNS OUT, CHECK YOUR WORK ON THIS SECTION ONLY.

DO NOT GO ON TO ANY OTHER TEST SECTION.

SECTION 2
Time—35 minutes
26 questions

Directions for Logical Reasoning Questions: The questions in this section are based on brief statements or passages. Choose your answers based on the reasoning in each passage. Do not make assumptions that are not supported by the passage or by common sense. For some questions, more than one answer choice may be possible, so choose the *best* answer to each question, that is, the one that is most accurate and complete. After you have chosen your answer, mark the corresponding space on the Answer Sheet.

1. Somnambulism is a habit that should be discouraged in any way possible. People have been known to get into dangerous situations by opening their doors and leaving their rooms while sleepwalking. To prevent this risk, people who have had previous sleepwalking episodes should make sure to securely fasten and lock their doors at night. Even though people can unlock their doors easily when awake, for some reason people have a hard time doing so while sleepwalking.

   Which of the following can be inferred from the passage?

   (A) Sleepwalkers will be unable to unlock the door of the room they are in.
   (B) Sleepwalkers could endanger themselves if they exit the room.
   (C) A room full of people will be sleepwalkers if they are not somnambulistic.
   (D) Doors that are securely fastened have different properties from doors that are used by sleepwalkers.
   (E) Experts recommend that sleepwalkers sleep in rooms that are locked.

2. The postal service not only provides a method of transferring letters and trinkets but also serves as a conduit for thoughts, love, and feelings. Just as sound waves carry our spoken words during conversation, the postal service carries our written words to people with whom we are connected in some way. By working well and intricately throughout the world, the postal service strengthens interpersonal connections and makes us a more tight-knit and loving society. Without the strand of connection that the postal service has provided for our nation throughout the decades, we would never have been able to maintain the high levels of patriotism, national pride, and social cohesion that have held Americans together through the years.

   Which of the following, if true, would tend to support the argument?

   (A) Russia had no international postal service and eventually dissolved in civil war.
   (B) Americans would have a lower level of national pride if the postal service had never existed.
   (C) E-mail is not replacing the postal service as the favored form of transmitting writings.
   (D) Postal services of many different types have existed in many successful countries throughout the ages.
   (E) With a more organized postal service, Americans would be even more tightly knit together than they are.

GO ON TO THE NEXT PAGE

3. Bodybuilder: I have been working out since I was 10 and have found that every year I get stronger. The stronger I get, the more muscles I have. The more muscles that I have, the more romances that I have have. I should work out even more to get more romances.

   Woman friend: When a guy has too much muscle, he becomes unattractive. The more a guy works out past a certain point, the more unattractive he becomes. I believe that you should stop working out and realize that you have had more romances because you are older and more time has passed, not because you are more muscular.

   The bodybuilder and his woman friend are committed to disagreeing about the following?

   (A) The more years that the bodybuilder works out, the more romances he will have had.
   (B) In general, women find muscular men repellent rather than attractive.
   (C) Romances can hinder a bodybuilder from getting stronger, because there is no added incentive.
   (D) Women prefer men who are too skinny to men who are overly muscular.
   (E) The more muscles a man has, the more women and romance he will attract.

4. Driving teacher: Cars should be driven and not aimed. You have to take into account both road conditions and weather conditions when you drive. You are most likely to be involved in a traffic accident when you are not paying close attention to the road or when you are not prepared for the unexpected. To prevent accidents from occurring you must anticipate them, thus protecting yourself and others from the dangers of a collision.

   Which of the following is assumed by the argument?

   (A) The unexpected can be prepared for.
   (B) No person wants to get into a collision.
   (C) Accidents occur when people are paying attention.
   (D) Cars that are aimed can be deemed to be driven well.
   (E) Driving teachers drive better than most of their students do.

GO ON TO THE NEXT PAGE

5. Water runoff from one yard can be damaging to other yards. Different states have different laws regulating who is liable for water runoff. In some states, the person whose land the water came from is liable. In other states, the person whose land is hurt has no remedy because he is expected to personally protect himself from any impending rains or excess runoff. Ethically, it is not clear who should be responsible. Water is difficult to control, and, just as people do not want water runoff to come onto their land, they also do not want to keep it on their land or be responsible if it leaves.

Which of the following can be inferred from the passage?

(A) Water should be controlled and maintained on a person's land.
(B) Water runoff is always harmful to the land onto which it spills.
(C) People with swimming pools like to get water runoff onto their land to fill the pool.
(D) In some states, a person can be liable for water that runs off his or her land.
(E) The person whose land initially collects water can sue people whose land drains the water.

6. Doctor: Your sonogram reveals only that you will give birth to a girl or to a boy. We cannot yet conclusively determine which. In fact, based on our current knowledge, you are as likely to give birth to a boy as to a girl, but by next Tuesday, we will be able to tell you with at least 30% certainty that your baby is a girl.

Which of the following is an assumption that the argument makes?

(A) The mother is not giving birth to a boy.
(B) Next Tuesday the doctor will not be unsure about the sex of the baby.
(C) The mother will not give birth next Tuesday after her appointment with the doctor.
(D) The mother will not give birth to twins.
(E) The father does not have a premonition about the sex of his child.

7. Bottle rockets are toys that many children like. The rockets are filled with water. Then a pump is attached to the rocket, and the pump is used to increase the pressure inside the rocket. After the bottle is pumped to the required level, the pressure is released through the rocket's tail, producing a plume of water that propels the rocket into the sky.

Which of the following can be inferred from the passage?

(A) Without pressure the rocket would not be propelled.
(B) The bottle rocket must not use apple juice to fly.
(C) Adults do not play with bottle rockets.
(D) Pumps are needed to make all rockets fly.
(E) Bottles of water can be made to fly in the same way as bottle rockets.

8. A nation convinced of the value of fulfilling its manifest destiny created the railroads. Railroads made it possible to transport people and goods over long distances, thereby creating a mass-transaction economy. The mass-transaction economy created wealth for many people and enforced the capitalistic nature of our society. Undoubtedly, capitalism would never have taken hold had our nation rejected the commercial mechanism of the mass-transaction economy. This is why it is clear that without the railroads, the United States would surely have become socialist.

Which of the following, if true, would cast the most doubt on this conclusion?

(A) The United States could have chosen from many other economic systems besides socialism if it did not choose capitalism.
(B) It is clear that capitalism led to the creation of the railroads and not the other way around.
(C) A mass-transaction economy will always lead to the building of railroads.
(D) Other nations that developed in a similar fashion to the United States did not embrace capitalism or socialism.
(E) The founders of the United States would never have embraced socialism for our nation.

GO ON TO THE NEXT PAGE

9. Forest ranger: Quicksand is a very dangerous natural trap in some parts of the park. In fact, quicksand kills more animals in this park than anything else. Keep in mind that if you fall into quicksand, you should remain still and not struggle, for struggling will only make you sink further. Also, never jump in to try to save a friend who has fallen into quicksand. Such an action will only result in you, too, becoming embroiled in the muck. The only way to rescue a person from quicksand effectively is to find a branch or some rope to throw to your friend so that you can pull your friend out from the safety of dry ground.

Which of the following is an assumption made by the argument?

(A) When bears fall into quicksand, their friends have no effective recourse to save them.

(B) A person must be in a safe place in order to save a person from an unsafe position.

(C) The forest ranger has had personal experience with quicksand and its dangers.

(D) If you cannot obtain rope or a branch, there is no effective way to save someone from quicksand.

(E) Some Olympic-class swimmers can swim through the trap of quicksand.

10. The circus comes to town every year with some new and interesting marvel. Last year, it was the man who swam with alligators. The year before, it was the man who drove his motorcycle around in a circle encapsulated by a ball of flame. Two years ago, it was a contortionist who performed on the trapeze. They have not announced the new crowd pleaser for this year, but still, there will be all the exciting attractions that come back year after year. There are always the lion tamers with their impressive show of courage and the enormous elephants who do tricks to please the crowd.

Which of the following can be concluded from the passage?

(A) All children enjoy watching the circus.

(B) Lion tamers are never unable to attend a circus.

(C) Every year the circus has a new attraction.

(D) Elephants that do tricks were a marvel, but now they are a staple of the circus.

(E) The ringmaster is the least entertaining part of the circus.

11. Ben: My antipathy toward John is unbearable. His personality is the absolute antithesis of mine. When he walks into the room, I exit. When John laughs, I grumble. When he talks in class, I retreat to the corner, quietly mulling my thoughts. If only I could extricate myself completely from him and his surroundings, then perhaps I could be free of this burden, but I cannot, for I am John and he is me.

Which of the following, if true, would tend to support the final contention of the passage?

(A) John just started dating Ben's girlfriend of three years, and Ben does not like it.

(B) All people in the world are inseparable members of the same universal being.

(C) Ben does not have multiple personality disorder or any type of schizophrenia.

(D) John and Ben have known each other for many years, and John hates Ben with the same sort of ire.

(E) John and Ben are brothers who have a hard time with sibling rivalry.

GO ON TO THE NEXT PAGE

12. Because of the commercialization of music that occurred in the United States in the 1990s, many talented singers left the United States in the hope of finding greater appreciation for their talents in other countries. Therefore, it is safe to assume that the talented singers who stayed in the United States now enjoy a heightened demand for their performances.

Which of the following, if true, would most undermine the conclusion of the passage?

(A) There is significantly less demand for talented singers now than there was before the 1990s.
(B) There has been a significant increase in the demand for untalented singers since the 1990s.
(C) Singing talent is so subjective that it is hard to determine whether a singer is talented or not.
(D) Untalented singers on average made more money than talented singers did before the 1990s, and they do so again today.
(E) Most singers, regardless of their talent, have left the United States in search of better places to perform.

13. The vast majority of predictions made by psychics are undeniably false. Therefore, it is unreasonable to impute extrasensory perception to a self-proclaimed psychic on the grounds that one or two of her predictions came true.

Which of the following exhibits reasoning that is analogous to the reasoning in the argument?

(A) Most people who cry wolf are not really in danger. Therefore, it is unreasonable to believe that a person who cries wolf is ever in danger.
(B) The vast majority of politicians are swindlers. Therefore, it is unreasonable to impute immorality to a politician on the basis on one or two bad acts.
(C) Vulgar people use more vulgarities than polite comments in their speech. Therefore, it is unreasonable to classify a vulgar person as low class on the basis of numerous polite comments.
(D) Generally, the claims of liars are untrue. Therefore, it is unreasonable to give credence to a liar on the basis of the fact that a couple of his or her statements have been true.
(E) Ski resorts attract many more people who are rich than people who are poor. Therefore, it is unreasonable to force a ski resort to lower its prices to accommodate the few skiers who have lower incomes.

GO ON TO THE NEXT PAGE

14. Onscreen Television Company introduced its new line of televisions to the market this year. The quality of the new Onscreen television is undeniably worse than that of all its competitors, but still Onscreen's marketing director felt certain that the new television line would be financially successful. Remarkably, his predictions came true. This year's recession that hurt most other television companies actually boosted sales of Onscreen's new television line.

Which of the following would explain why Onscreen's new televisions sold well during the recession compared to the competing products?

(A) Onscreen's competitors did not point out the inferior quality of Onscreen's televisions even though most purchasers knew of this fact.

(B) Onscreen televisions were attractive to a particular segment of the population because of the ethnicity of the company's founder.

(C) Onscreen's televisions were easier to carry than one competing brand, easier to use than one competing brand, and had better screen quality than one competing brand.

(D) Despite the recession, more television sets were sold during this past year than in any previous year.

(E) The poor quality of Onscreen's televisions allowed the company to sell them at a low price, which was attractive to buyers during the recession.

15. A recent science experiment revealed that when a yellow dye is mixed with a blue dye, the result is a dye with a green color. Preschool students repeat this experiment in class on a daily basis and consistently deliver the same results— yellow dyes mix with blue dyes to make one green dye. These consistent results led a budding scientist named Tommy to exclaim, "If something blue mixes with something yellow, then it will always make green!"

Which of the following, if true, would undermine Tommy's analysis?

(A) Yesterday Tommy's playmate Sarah mixed a purple dye and a red dye and formed a green dye.

(B) Some preschool dye experiments offer results different from the results arrived at in a science lab.

(C) One hundred years ago, when atmospheric conditions were different, adding a blue dye to a yellow dye consistently made a red dye.

(D) Different-colored paints mixed at temperatures below freezing always form an orange-colored paint.

(E) Dye experiments are important only to preschoolers, and the results of the experiments are generally not green.

GO ON TO THE NEXT PAGE

16. Cashier: If you give me $10, then I will give you the purse. It is a simple transaction that is carried out several times a minute throughout the world. You cannot just walk out of the store without paying, because that is dishonest.

    Store clerk: My contract states that I am entitled to one free item from the store per month. I have not taken anything this month, so I would like to take this purse without paying for it.

    On which of the following would the store clerk and cashier disagree?

    (A) A store clerk with no contract who had not taken an item from the store that month would not be dishonest in taking a purse home.
    (B) A store clerk with an equivalent contract who had not taken an item from the store that month would not be dishonest in taking a purse home.
    (C) A store clerk with a directly comparable contract who had taken an item from the store that month would be dishonest in taking a purse home.
    (D) A store clerk with a directly comparable contract who had taken an item from the store that month would not be dishonest in taking a purse home if it were first paid for.
    (E) A store clerk with no contract who had taken an item from the store that month would not be dishonest in taking this purse home if it were first paid for.

17. Columnist: It is a well-known fact that girls reach puberty long before boys do. To account for this gender discrepancy, we should educate children about the implications of their maturity at different ages. Girls should receive this education several years before boys do, but regardless of the age differential, the classes should send the same message across the gender gap: Growing up is normal, and it is something that should be embraced, not feared.

    Which of the following, if true, would eliminate any gain from following the columnist's advice?

    (A) In general, it is best to teach a child a message as soon as the child is capable of understanding the message.
    (B) Age has no bearing on the good or bad effects of education.
    (C) Boys are not responsible enough to handle lessons about growing up at whatever age they are educated.
    (D) Girls would benefit from learning about the maturational process several years before boys have access to similar information.
    (E) Maturational education is not in the least bit helpful to many people.

    GO ON TO THE NEXT PAGE

18. Ornithologists heatedly debate whether birds evolved from a type of dinosaur or whether they are direct descendants from a genus that predated dinosaurs on the evolutionary tree. Dr. Spock notes that certain dinosaurs, called pterodactyls, had wings and flew through the air using the same hollow bone structure that birds employ today. However, Dr. Jones disagrees with Dr. Spock's contentions regarding the existence of a dinosaur-bird link and argues that birds and pterodactyls evolved in a parallel fashion that was not directly related. Dr. Jones believes that birds developed long before the dinosaur age from a small birdlike creature that was indigenous to Antarctica and used feathers to keep warm.

Which of the following, if true, would disprove Dr. Jones's theory?

(A) The birdlike creatures populating the Antarctic did not have any wings.
(B) Birds are not descended from pterodactyls, because pterodactyls were cold blooded and had reptilian skin flaps.
(C) An ice age came and eradicated all of the small birdlike creatures that Dr. Jones refers to.
(D) Dr. Spock has demonstrated that some types of dinosaurs are actually descended from the tiny birdlike creatures in Antarctica.
(E) Immediately before the dinosaur age, all species that were not dinosaurs were completely wiped out by an ice age.

19. Running a marathon takes an extraordinary level of dedication and preparation. Most people do not easily travel 26.2 miles on foot, so it makes sense that many people spend months preparing their bodies to travel such a great distance. What does not make sense is that the winners of this sport make only about $15,000 to $80,000 per race. In general, marathon runners face as many as 20,000 competitors in each race, and yet, the compensation they receive for winning does not compare even to that of professional tennis players.

Which of the following can be concluded from the passage?

(A) The average tennis player is paid more than the average runner.
(B) Professional runners have never won more than a million dollars for winning a race.
(C) No one could run 26.2 miles without training for it.
(D) The best tennis player is paid more than the best marathon runner.
(E) Runners do not get large numbers of endorsements that increase their compensation.

GO ON TO THE NEXT PAGE

20. Manhattan socialite: Going out to bars at night is the only way to meet new friends. Previous acquaintances are great, but after I have interacted with them for a while, they offer no new surprises or exciting interchanges. By going with acquaintances into bars at night, I am able to provide myself with a stable base from which to reach out to new people. So yes, acquaintances serve a purpose in the same way that new friends do. However, acquaintances are only valuable insofar as they help to procure new friends.

If all of the socialite's words are true, which of the following can be concluded from the passage?

(A) Old friends are not tired of the socialite in the same way that the socialite is tired of them.

(B) The socialite is able to meet new friends by going out to bars at night with old acquaintances.

(C) New friends will not eventually become valueless when they have been known long enough to become old acquaintances.

(D) There are other ways to meet people besides going out to bars at night with acquaintances.

(E) The stable base that acquaintances provide is worthless if it does not help gain new friends.

21. Medical malpractice insurance has become very costly over the past decade. Compared to private medical malpractice insurance providers, comprehensive insurance plans for self-insuring hospitals require smaller initial investments, take no profits away from the medical industry, and are more sympathetic to doctors' needs. Based on these unquestionable facts, it is clear that all hospitals should self-insure instead of relying on outside companies for their insurance needs.

Which of the following, if true, would call into question the recommendation of the passage?

(A) Doctors dislike the insurance industry and would prefer not to work with private insurance companies if at all possible.

(B) Patients do not receive any benefit when their doctor belongs to a self-insuring hospital.

(C) Self-insuring hospitals and their doctors spend more total money paying for insurance than hospitals that do not self-insure.

(D) Average premiums for medical malpractice insurance will continue to rise no matter what the health-care industry does.

(E) Insurance companies strive to foresee the risk of providing coverage to doctors and then make a cost-benefit analysis to determine their prices for premiums.

GO ON TO THE NEXT PAGE

22. Primatologist: Gorillas can understand human language. The famous gorilla Koko could create art, interact with people, and communicate with them through the use of sign language. By allowing gorillas to teach sign language to their young, we can indirectly teach English to a whole species of gorillas.

Psychologist: Gorillas will never be able to speak English audibly because of lingual physical constraints. Additionally, the creation of art requires a part of the brain that gorillas do not have. Finally, a gorilla cannot really interact with people in the same way that humans can interact with each other. Nor will any gorilla ever be able to do so.

Which if the following is the point at issue between the primatologist and the psychologist?

(A) Gorillas will never be able to speak English audibly.
(B) A whole species of gorillas will never be able to learn English.
(C) Gorillas are unable to create anything that is truly art.
(D) Even gorillas who cannot sign can understand human language.
(E) A gorilla could evolve into a different species that would be able to speak English.

23. Geologist: Humankind's conception of the essence of what is "living" versus that which is characterized as "nonliving" is erroneous. I have dedicated my life to the study of rocks and have determined that they are, in actuality, living beings. Rocks do not breathe, reproduce, or consume, but they morph into many different forms, shapes, and creations over a lifetime that encompasses millions of years. People cannot understand the living nature of rocks because the lifespan of the average human is miniscule in comparison to the lifespan of a rock. No human who has lived for fewer than several million years is able to postulate that rocks are living things, but if someone did live this long, then this fact would be clear to that person.

A flaw in the preceding argument is that it

(A) argues for a conclusion that is unreasonable to the majority of the population
(B) unfairly redefines a key term that is pivotal for the interpretation of the words *living* and *nonliving*
(C) assumes that independently insufficient factors cannot be sufficient to produce an outcome when present together
(D) undermines a central issue that defines the people who would interpret the thesis of this passage
(E) bases its conclusion upon a premise that invokes an apparent contradiction

GO ON TO THE NEXT PAGE

24. Herbivores eat plants. Plants need sunlight to survive. We are still not certain what the sun consumes in order to keep burning, but we are reasonably sure that it is nothing. Basically, we believe that the sun is cannibalizing itself: creating heat by creating new fusion and fission reactions inside its hot, molten core. Eventually, the sun will consume all of its resources and will begin to die out. Light will be lost for the plants, and then plants will be lost to the herbivores. At this point, we are sure the carnivores will also die out, because they will not have herbivores to consume.

Which of the following is an assumption that is made by the argument?

(A) When the sun consumes all of its reserves, all life on Earth will not die out.
(B) Herbivores would consume the rays of the sun if they were biologically advanced enough.
(C) Nuclear fusion and fission would not take place on the Earth if it did not take place on the sun.
(D) Carnivores will not be able to create energy to sustain their life on the planet.
(E) Humans will not have moved to other planetary systems by the time the sun dies out.

25. Running in hot weather is more dangerous than running in cooler weather and requires large amounts of hydration. In hot weather the body produces more perspiration in order to cool off. As a result, the body requires more hydration so that it can continue to break down energy and make more perspiration. People who run in the cold should also take certain precautions in order to prevent injury. Stretching is necessary before exercising because it warms up muscles. If cold muscles are not warmed up, they are subject to tearing or being pulled.

Which of the following is the main point of the passage?

(A) Stretching is necessary before running in order to prevent muscle pulls or tears.
(B) There are precautions that should be taken when running in hot or cold weather.
(C) Hydration is not important in cool weather running because the body does not perspire as much.
(D) Inclement weather can cause injury.
(E) Runners run faster in the cold weather than in warm weather.

GO ON TO THE NEXT PAGE

26. Ben and Raul are professional weightlifters who qualified for the 1996 Olympics. Raul can lift up to 500 pounds at a time, and Ben can lift 425 pounds. While both are working out in the weight room, a weight machine weighing 1500 pounds falls across the door, completely blocking the exit of the room. Ben and Raul are the only two people inside the room and they will be unable to clear the machine from the doorway since even together they are unable to lift 1500 pounds.

A flaw in the reasoning of the passage is that it

(A) assumes that independently insufficient factors cannot be sufficient when added together
(B) treats one possible solution to a problem as the only viable solution to that problem
(C) appeals to past evidence about a certain activity when future implications of that evidence are analyzed
(D) mistakenly equates a specific number to an amount that is indeterminable
(E) treats something that is definite as though it were probable

S T O P

IF YOU FINISH BEFORE TIME RUNS OUT, CHECK YOUR WORK ON THIS SECTION ONLY.
DO NOT GO ON TO ANY OTHER TEST SECTION.

SECTION 3
Time—35 minutes
25 questions

Directions for Logic Games Questions: The questions in this section are divided into groups. Each group is based on a set of conditions. For each questions, choose the answer that is most accurate and complete. For some questions, you may wish to draw a rough diagram to help you select your response. Mark the corresponding space on your Answer Sheet.

Questions 1–6

A dentist will see patients in two different hospitals from Monday to Friday of next week. Patients A, B, C, D, and E are in hospital 1, and patients R, S, T, U, and V are in hospital 2. The dentist sees only one patient from each hospital per day, but the dentist sees two patients per day. The order in which the dentist sees patients is governed by the following:

A is seen on the same day that R is seen.
C is seen on the same day as T.
V is not seen on the same day as D or E.
A is seen before C
S is seen after C.

1. If A is seen on Wednesday, then which of the following could be true?

    (A) D is seen on Monday with V.
    (B) V is seen after S.
    (C) B is seen on the same day as U.
    (D) D is seen on Friday with S.
    (E) T is seen on a day before V.

2. If B is seen on Wednesday, then which of the following must be true?

    (A) A is seen on Tuesday or Monday.
    (B) D is seen before B.
    (C) E is seen on the same day as S.
    (D) D is seen on the same day as U.
    (E) A and B are seen on consecutive days.

3. If B is seen on Friday, then which of the following must NOT be true?

    (A) D is seen on the same day as V.
    (B) A is seen on Monday with R.
    (C) V is seen on Friday with B.
    (D) R is seen after the day that U is seen.
    (E) C and T are seen on Wednesday.

4. If C is seen on Tuesday, then which of the following could be true?

    (A) D is seen with V on Wednesday.
    (B) S is seen on Monday or Tuesday.
    (C) B is seen on Friday with S.
    (D) Neither D nor E is seen on the same day as S.
    (E) E is seen on Friday with U.

5. If V is seen on Tuesday and D is seen on Wednesday, then which of the following must be true?

    (A) E is seen on Friday with S.
    (B) D is seen with S on Wednesday.
    (C) A, B, and C are seen on consecutive days.
    (D) A is seen on Tuesday.
    (E) U and S are seen on consecutive days.

6. If B is seen the day after the day that S is seen, then which of the following could NOT be true?

    (A) V is seen the day after E is seen.
    (B) U is seen the day after D is seen.
    (C) E is seen the day after A is seen.
    (D) D is seen the day before A is seen.
    (E) T is seen the day before U is seen.

GO ON TO THE NEXT PAGE

Questions 7–13

Eight players—A, B, C, D, E, F, G, and H—come to a basketball court and split into two teams. Four people are on team 1, and four people are on team 2. Their grouping is governed by the following constraints:

If A is on team 1, then B is on team 2.
If D is on team 1, then F is on team 2.
If B is on team 2, then D is on team 1.
E is not on a team with F.

7. Which of the following is a group that could comprise team 1?

(A) A, D, F, G
(B) E, G, H, C
(C) H, C, G, D
(D) G, D, E, A
(E) A, D, B, E

8. If B is on team 2 with A, then which of the following could be true?

(A) E is on team 2.
(B) A is on team 1.
(C) C is on team 1.
(D) D is on team 2.
(E) G, H, and C are all on the same team.

9. If A and F are on the same team, then which of the following must be true?

(A) E is on team 1.
(B) B is on team 2.
(C) C is on team 1.
(D) D is not on a team.
(E) F is on the same team as H.

10. If D and B are on the same team, then which of the following must be true?

(A) C shares a team with G.
(B) G shares a team with E.
(C) B shares a team with F.
(D) D shares a team with H.
(E) A shares a team with F.

11. Which of the following people can never be on the same team as F?

(A) A
(B) B
(C) C
(D) D
(E) E

12. If F is on team 1, then how many different configurations are possible for the people on the teams?

(A) one
(B) two
(C) three
(D) four
(E) five

13. If D and A are on separate teams, then which of the following must NOT be true?

(A) E is on team 2.
(B) B is on team 1.
(C) G is on team 2 with H.
(D) B is on team 2.
(E) D is on team 1.

GO ON TO THE NEXT PAGE

Questions 14–18

The first step in planning a new building is to determine whether to build revolving doors or double doors at each of its eight entrances. The entrances are in the following places on the building:

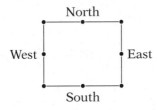

Whether an entrance will have revolving doors or double doors is determined by the following constraints:

Every revolving door is next to at least one revolving door and one double door.
The South door is a revolving door.
The Northwest door is a double door.
Exactly two corner doors are revolving doors.

14. Which of the following must be true?

   (A) The North door is a double door.
   (B) The Southwest door is a revolving door.
   (C) The West door is a double door.
   (D) The Northeast door is not a revolving door.
   (E) The East door is a revolving door.

15. If the Southwest door is revolving, then which of the following must be true?

   (A) There are five double doors.
   (B) There are four revolving doors.
   (C) There are three double doors.
   (D) There are three revolving doors.
   (E) There are nine entrances.

16. Which of the following must be true when the East door is a revolving door?

   (A) The Southwest door is a revolving door.
   (B) The North door is a revolving door.
   (C) The Southeast door is a revolving door.
   (D) The West door is a revolving door.
   (E) There are five revolving doors.

17. Which of the following is NOT a possible list of doors that could all be revolving doors at the same time?

   (A) South, Northeast, North, Southwest
   (B) South, Northeast, East, Southwest
   (C) South, Northeast, North, Southeast
   (D) South, Northeast, East, Southeast
   (E) South, Northeast, Southwest, East

18. How many different door configurations are possible?

   (A) one
   (B) two
   (C) three
   (D) four
   (E) five

GO ON TO THE NEXT PAGE

Questions 19–25

A lonely ornithologist maintains a number of birds in cages in his house. In his favorite cage, eight parakeets sit in a row along a perch. Their names are A, B, C, D, E, F, G, and H. The order in which the parakeets sit on the perch is governed by the following constraints:

> H sits third.
> C sits after D but before F.
> H sits after D but before A and E.
> B sits after A
> E sits before G.
> If F or A sits fifth, then E sits seventh.

19. Which of the following could be the order of the birds from first to last?

    (A) D, C, H, F, A, E, B, G
    (B) D, C, F, H, A, B, E, G
    (C) D, C, H, A, F, B, E, G
    (D) D, H, C, F, E, G, A, B
    (E) D, H, C, F, A, E, B, G

20. Which of the following must be true?

    (A) F sits fourth.
    (B) E sits seventh.
    (C) C sits second.
    (D) F sits before A.
    (E) E sits before B.

21. Which of the following must NOT be true?

    (A) A sits sixth.
    (B) G sits before F.
    (C) B sits immediately next to H.
    (D) B sits after H.
    (E) F and A sit next to each other.

22. If A does not sit fourth, sixth, or seventh, then which of the following must be true?

    (A) E sits fifth.
    (B) F sits fourth.
    (C) G sits seventh.
    (D) A sits eighth.
    (E) B sits fifth.

23. If E sits sixth, then which of the following must NOT be true?

    (A) F sits after A.
    (B) B sits before G.
    (C) G sits next to F.
    (D) B sits seventh.
    (E) F sits eighth.

24. If E and G do not sit next to each other, then which of the following could be true?

    (A) B sits sixth.
    (B) C sits third.
    (C) A sits fifth.
    (D) E sits seventh.
    (E) A sits seventh.

25. If A sits immediately before F, then which of the following must NOT be true?

    (A) B sits eighth.
    (B) F sits fifth.
    (C) E sits fourth.
    (D) G sits sixth.
    (E) E sits seventh.

S T O P

IF YOU FINISH BEFORE TIME RUNS OUT, CHECK YOUR WORK ON THIS SECTION ONLY.
DO NOT GO ON TO ANY OTHER TEST SECTION.

SECTION 4
Time—35 minutes
25 questions

<u>Directions for Logical Reasoning Questions:</u> The questions in this section are based on brief statements or passages. Choose your answers based on the reasoning in each passage. Do not make assumptions that are not supported by the passage or by common sense. For some questions, more than one answer choice may be possible, so choose the *best* answer to each question, that is, the one that is most accurate and complete. After you have chosen your answer, mark the corresponding space on the Answer Sheet.

1. A recent news story featured a runner whose shoes caught fire just as the runner completed a 100-meter dash. An attendant near the track quickly put out the fire with a fire extinguisher. The story indicated that the friction of the shoes on the track had sparked the fire, but after thinking about it, I questioned why someone would be ready with a fire extinguisher near a track. It must have been a publicity stunt because the runner claimed that this had never happened before.

   Which of the following is the main point of the passage?

   (A) The friction from the track did not cause the runner's shoes to catch fire.
   (B) The fact that the running shoes caught fire was nothing more than a publicity stunt.
   (C) Runners faster than this runner have never had their shoes catch fire after a race.
   (D) The news network did not reveal the publicity stunt because it attracted more viewers.
   (E) The runner's feet were not burned by the fire.

2. All trees in the Gaghan forest are hardwoods. All squirrels living in hardwood trees have fluffy tails or matted tails, but not both. All squirrels in the Gaghan forest live in hardwood trees in Gaghan forest.

   Which of the following can be concluded from this passage?

   (A) All squirrels have fluffy or matted tails.
   (B) Squirrels who live in Gaghan forest never climb softwood trees.
   (C) Squirrels without tails are present in the Gaghan forest.
   (D) No trees in the Gaghan forest are softwoods.
   (E) All shrubs in the Gaghan forest are hardwoods.

3. John: Moving is an incredibly exhausting process. Surely all of my energy is not sapped just by moving boxes. I feel as though I am forcefully extricating myself from a past life every time I move. I am probably as emotionally tired as I am physically exhausted.

   Wanda: Extracting yourself from your previous home is hard and tiresome. It is just as much an emotional venture as it is a physical one.

   What is the main point of John's argument?

   (A) Moving is an exhausting process.
   (B) Moving is emotionally and physically tiring.
   (C) Moving boxes is the most tiring aspect of moving.
   (D) John is moving from a good point to a worse point.
   (E) Wanda should have been helping John to move instead of watching television.

GO ON TO THE NEXT PAGE

4. City elections are a trying time for all candidates. Voters peruse the life histories, opinions, and personalities of the candidates in order to determine who is best suited for office. Knowing that they have been so carefully scrutinized by the public, candidates can be extremely disheartened if they lose. Some candidates never get over the sense of rejection that comes with losing the race. However, candidates should understand that, in most cases, they are competing with equally qualified and worthy opponents. Recognizing the strength of the competition, candidates should not feel rejected when they lose.

Which of the following is the main point of the passage?

(A) City elections should be decided based on the strength of the candidate pool instead of a person's subjective opinions.
(B) City elections are places where voters choose between several credible candidates in order to determine who is best suited to govern their city.
(C) Candidates should be less competitive because they are all trying to do the same thing: elect the person who would best serve the interests of the city.
(D) Mature candidates realize that getting elected is difficult, and they are not disappointed if they happen to lose.
(E) Elections are difficult times for candidates, and losers should use perspective when interpreting their losses.

5. Beer commercials are famous for appealing to wit and humor in order to sell their products. Beer brands try to associate themselves with a carefree nature that takes on the world and then laughs at it after the world has been won over. This illusion of dominance is something that all men crave, so a beer that appeals to this attitude is bound to be successful. Beer marketers understand this fact, acknowledge it, and use it to produce some of the most compelling advertisements on TV.

If the claims of the passage are true, then which of the following can be concluded?

(A) Commercials that appeal to males' illusion of dominance are generally successful.
(B) Less beer would be purchased if beer was not so heavily advertised.
(C) Humor is a good way to market all products.
(D) Beer marketers can also make commercials that cater to women's illusions.
(E) An advertisement's success is determined by the number of products it sells.

GO ON TO THE NEXT PAGE

6. Even though the brain patterns of infants are qualitatively different from the patterns common to adults, it is helpful to study infant brain patterns because they give insight into how adult brain patterns develop. Additionally, research on infant brains makes evident a sort of neural progression that accompanies the process of maturing. Specific infants have unusual brain patterns that do not resemble the normal infant pattern, and while these infants do receive some attention from scientists, they do not receive nearly as much attention as the groups of infants with normal infant brain patterns.

Which of the following, if true, would explain why infants with idiosyncratic brain patterns do not receive a lot of attention?

(A) Nothing can be determined about neural development by studying infants with unusual brain patterns.
(B) Infants with normal brain patterns and normal development schemes tend to be much cuter than infants with abnormal patterns.
(C) Abnormal brain patterns hold the key to understanding the brain pattern progression extending from childhood to adulthood.
(D) Scientists tend to look for idiosyncrasies when studying groups of infants, but not when studying adults.
(E) Not enough research money is devoted to studying infants with idiosyncratic brain patterns.

7. I. Freezers produced by French companies tend to be more durable than freezers produced by American companies.
II. The average life of a freezer made by an American company is about five years longer than the average life of a freezer made by a French company.

Which of the following, if true, would explain the discrepancy noted in the passage above?

(A) Freezers produced by French companies tend to have longer lifetimes than they do in France or in the northern parts of America.
(B) Freezer specialists would prefer to use a French refrigerator in their offices and an American freezer in their homes.
(C) French freezers are made from more durable parts than American freezers.
(D) People buy only freezers made by companies in their country, and the French subject their freezers to greater levels of stress than Americans do.
(E) Certain people would like to falsify records regarding average freezer life in order to gain an edge for national trade.

GO ON TO THE NEXT PAGE

8. Scientists have found that disorders of the immune system are not caused by psychological factors; instead they are caused almost entirely by physiological factors. Yet numerous statistical accounts support the fact that people being treated for stress by psychologists are much more likely to have immunological disorders than are members of the general population.

Which of the following, if true, would resolve the paradox presented in the argument?

(A) A psychological problem that causes stress is not generally known to contribute to immunological disorders.
(B) Immunological disorders cause many psychological problems, one of them being stress.
(C) The presence of doctors tends to dramatically increase the level of stress in a person who is being measured for stress level.
(D) People without immunological disorders tend to be more stressed during the times when they believe that they have a disorder than during the times when they do not believe this.
(E) Numerous rare elements have been discovered that would contribute not only to a person's stress level but also to diseases affecting the immune system.

9. Koi ponds are an excellent addition to any backyard. Koi can grow to about 3 feet in length, and in a large enough pond, they will spawn more koi. Each individual Koi has vibrant color patterns and can live for decades, if taken care of properly. If you have a pond that is big enough, all of your koi will live to be at least 15 years old.

Which of the following must be assumed in order to properly draw the conclusion?

(A) Koi are better pets for children than dogs are because most children are unable to swim with their dogs.
(B) Koi keep their color patterns until they are at least 15 years old.
(C) If your pond is big enough, a heron will not eat one of your koi when it is 5 years old.
(D) Koi cannot live in a pond that is big enough in some environments.
(E) Koi will not eat each other when they reach the age of 25.

GO ON TO THE NEXT PAGE

10. Billy: Karate movies are the best movies to watch with a date. Think of it this way: If your date can't enjoy a dumb movie, then you probably do not want to continue hanging out with her. But, if your date is cool enough to like a karate movie, then she would probably like other, more meaningful movies too. Either way, going to a karate movie will allow you to tell immediately if your date is someone you want to hang out with.

Which of the following must be assumed for this argument to be logically drawn?

(A) Determining whether a date is someone you want to hang out with is something most boys like to do.
(B) Girls in general do not like karate movies because the movies are silly, violent, and boring.
(C) Most boys would sit through a karate movie in order to determine whether a date is someone they want to hang out with.
(D) The movie differentiation mechanism would work just as well with a movie about jujitsu.
(E) If a date does not like at least one type of dumb movie, she is not someone you want to hang out with.

11. Westerbrook Academy requires the donations of many generous patrons in order to continue operating. Generous patrons need good financial prospects or tax breaks in order to donate to Westerbrook. The government needs a surplus or a negligent executive in order to give tax breaks to people in the economic bracket of Westerbrook's patrons. The executive of the government is never negligent.

If Westerbrook Academy gets donations and there is no governmental surplus, then which of the following must be assumed?

(A) Tax breaks were given to Westerbrook Academy's patrons.
(B) A negligent executive was one of Westerbrook Academy's patrons.
(C) Westerbrook Academy received funding in addition to that given by generous patrons.
(D) Westerbrook Academy's generous patrons have good financial prospects.
(E) Westerbrook Academy relies on government contributions to sustain itself.

12. Valentine's Day is the most difficult day of the year for people who are not in love. A holiday that was maniacally crafted by candy makers, card makers, and florists to sell their products has exacerbated feelings of loneliness in all the single members of our society. To change this situation, we must unite to refuse to buy candy or send cards to anyone this Valentine's Day. By doing so, we serve the greater good of eliminating this holiday once and for all.

Which of the following is an assumption upon which this argument relies?

(A) Valentine's Day is a holiday that serves no purpose besides making people feel lonely.
(B) The government would be served by eliminating Valentine's Day as a holiday.
(C) Holidays cannot be unmade by people in the same way that they were made by corporations.
(D) The negative effects associated with Valentine's Day outweigh any positive effects of the day.
(E) Valentine's Day will not be eliminated as a holiday by any effort made by anyone.

GO ON TO THE NEXT PAGE

13. I hear beautiful music coming from far off in the orchard. Chords that sound this mellow must have been made by a stringed instrument. Also, I hear someone singing as the music plays. People who play any stringed instrument besides guitar do not sing while they are playing. Based on these facts, I can deduce that there is a guitar player singing and playing in the orchard.

The argument makes which one of the following assumptions when drawing its conclusion?

(A) The same person is playing the instrument and singing.
(B) Guitar players are the only musicians who sing while playing their instruments.
(C) The person making music is making it on the speaker's land.
(D) Any instrument that makes chords cannot be a violin or viola.
(E) Mellow sounds are not made by instruments other than stringed instruments.

14. In a study of centenarians, it was shown that there were several commonalities among people in the group. First, each person exercised moderately, going on walks of at least an hour five times a week. Second, none of them consistently used any mind-altering substances like alcohol, tobacco, or any other more serious drug. Lastly, many people gardened. Scientists are uncertain of the effect of gardening on a person's longevity, but apparently it is profound, because otherwise the centenarians as a group would not have been doing it so consistently. To increase my chances at living past 100, I will begin gardening today.

Which one of the following is an assumption on which the conclusion is based?

(A) Taking long walks and abstaining from harmful substances promote good health, and gardening is an inspirational activity.
(B) Moderate exercise combined with gardening and abstinence from harmful substances will cause a person to become a centenarian.
(C) Old age was not the sole reason why so many in the centenarian group were gardeners.
(D) Scientists will not be able to develop a pill that can confer on people the positive effects of gardening.
(E) There are no factors that contribute to a person's longevity besides those listed.

GO ON TO THE NEXT PAGE

15. Psychologist: There has been a long-standing debate concerning the implications of nurture versus nature in a person's development. A person's "nature" refers to the set of genes inherited from the person's parents, and a person's "nurture" corresponds to the environment in which a person lived while growing up. More than likely this debate will never cease, because it is impossible to separate the effects of nature from those of nurture on a person's development. But someday this argument will end, not because a solution has been found or a consensus reached, but solely because people are without exception tired of arguing about it.

Which of the following, if true, most undermines the conclusion of the passage?

(A) Although the nature-versus-nurture debate has raged for years, the leaders of each camp have never come to an agreement.

(B) Ten years after the psychologist wrote this passage, a solution to the debate was found by a premier German biologist.

(C) The truth is that both nature and nurture influence development in a synergistic rather than unilateral fashion.

(D) In 50 years, 75 percent of society will believe that nurture is the factor that is mostly responsible for a person's development.

(E) Most people are already tired of the nature-versus-nurture debate, and more than likely this unconcerned percentage will increase in future years.

16. Millions of people throughout the years have relied on the assumption that in winter the weather gets colder and in summer it gets warmer. It appears, however, that this assumption is wholly unfounded. Dr. Spock, a noted climatologist, stated in a speech earlier this year that the climate change associated with changing seasons is nothing more than an illusion. It makes sense, therefore that there is really no such thing as a discrepancy in the average temperatures between the different seasons.

The major flaw in the reasoning of the passage is that it

(A) assumes that a traditional view is incorrect on the basis of an appeal to a unilateral authority in that field

(B) ignores the possibility that there will be no correlation between the past and the future

(C) relies merely on the opinion of millions of people over many years.

(D) engages in a type of syllogistic reasoning that is uncommon and not in accord with clear scientific tradition

(E) confuses evidence in support of a certain conclusion with evidence in support of a different conclusion

GO ON TO THE NEXT PAGE

17. Brain surgeon: The feeling of nostalgia is triggered by a portion of the brain that does not trigger any other type of emotion. Most emotional responses result from the activation of synapses in one particular cranial region, but nostalgia is activated by synapses in an isolated subdorsal cranial region. Searching for a reason that accounts for this discrepancy has led me to hypothesize that nostalgia is not a real emotion, that it is an emotion that develops later in life than any other emotion, or that it is the result of something unexplained in our evolutionary history. Since nostalgia has to be a real emotion, it follows that it must develop later in people's lives than all other emotions.

A flaw in the passage is that it

(A) assumes that a temporal sequence in the evidence implies a causal relationship
(B) draws a conclusion without first eliminating all possible competing solutions
(C) misinterprets the key term *emotion* when formulating the conclusion of the passage
(D) appeals completely to emotion when a scientific theory is evaluated
(E) provides no evidence in support of an obvious contention that would disprove the conclusion

18. Miriam: Scientists claim that dogs can hear high-pitched noises better than all other mammals. This is certainly true in respect to cats. Yesterday I blew my high-pitched dog whistle right next to my cat, but she did not twitch a muscle. However, this contention does not apply to bats. Last night, I blew the same whistle outside when a group of bats was eating bugs near the streetlamp. The bats heard the whistle, started shrieking, and flew away.

The argumentative technique Miriam employs to refute the opinion of the scientists is to

(A) use the scientific method to determine whether dogs hear high-pitched noises better than bats
(B) elucidate an implicit contradiction in the scientists' logic
(C) supply clear evidence that would refute the scientists' claim
(D) misinterpret the meaning of the key term *hear* when testing the scientists' theory
(E) point out the existence of a group that scientists might not have examined

GO ON TO THE NEXT PAGE

19. Jane: Eighty years ago, the Potomac River was the most pristine natural habitat in the known world. The river boasted a multitude of flora and fauna that other rivers in the United States were too polluted to maintain. These flora and fauna still survive today in other parts of the world where the water remains clean and clear. Surely the flora and fauna still populate the Potomac River, since they also populate other rivers in the United States.

The argumentative technique Jane uses to form her conclusion is to

(A) assume that there is continuity between conditions in the past and present
(B) make a comparison that will prove her conclusion
(C) assert that the evidence she cites in support of her conclusion is false
(D) provide an alternative reason for accepting that only the fauna remain in the Potomac
(E) stop short of describing the minimal implications of agreeing with her position

20. The price of computer printers in stores generally does not accurately reflect the overall quality of the printer. Companies that make printers derive most of their profits from the sales of ink cartridges that replace the printer's original cartridges. Potential profits from these replacement cartridges are so great that companies will sell printers at a loss in order to hook a customer into buying a type of printer that requires their particular ink cartridge. Therefore, no accurate comparisons can be made between computer printers in a store based on price.

The argument uses which of the following argumentative methods?

(A) It claims that accurate comparisons can be based only on prices that are discounted in relatively similar ways.
(B) It provides support for another, rarely contemplated explanation besides quality that determines a printer's price.
(C) It argues that computer printer manufacturers never profit immediately from the sale of their printers.
(D) It proposes that over a printer's lifetime, buying expensive ink cartridges would cost more than the printer.
(E) It contradicts the contention that the number of printers in a store does not accurately reflect the overall quality of the printers.

GO ON TO THE NEXT PAGE

21. People who treat others worse than they would like to be treated tend to incur the fury and disdain of the person who has been badly treated. People who treat others better than they like to be treated tend to be taken for granted and eventually rejected. Based on these findings, it appears that a person should follow the Golden Rule: Treat others as you would like to be treated. The application of this age-old rule will facilitate positive interactions in our society. Children should be taught this rule in preschool so that they will unerringly adhere to its wisdom as adults.

The argument makes use of which of the following argumentative methods?

(A) It makes a conclusion that is completely unrelated to the passage.
(B) It supports a contention by negating a premise that rejects that contention.
(C) It derives a general principle from supporting claims.
(D) It forges a conclusion based on an appeal to morality without a correlative appeal to logic.
(E) It constricts the application of a rule that should be implemented.

22. Wireless networking has changed the electronic format of college campuses. Computers can access the Internet from more places, making it more reasonable for students to have laptop computers. Students can log on to the Internet when they are bored in class. Networks can be built that exchange files between computers within a certain distance of each other. As wireless networking gains ground, it will continue to mold our college campuses.

The argument makes use of which of the following argumentative methods?

(A) It makes a conclusion that is dramatically broader than is warranted.
(B) It offers contradictory evidence in support of a singular premise.
(C) It makes an assumption based on a nonrepresentative group of people.
(D) It delineates examples to support a specific claim.
(E) It eliminates several competing premises in favor of a superior premise.

23. A well-known histamine blocker is known to decrease the incidence of allergies in its users by 10%. The incidence of allergies in a local nursing home has been decreased by 10%, so patients there must be using the histamine blocker.

Which of the following contains the same flawed reasoning as the passage above?

(A) Whaling has been determined to decrease the population of whales by 15% each year. The whale population has decreased by 15% this year, so whaling must be the culprit.
(B) Weightlifting has been determined to increase the performance of individuals up to 15%. The performance of a high school basketball team has increased by 15%, so players must have started weightlifting.
(C) Injury is likely to decrease a joint's effectiveness by 15%. John's joint is 15% less effective than it was before, so he must have injured it.
(D) Heart attacks strike 15% of people in their old age. Therefore, 15% of people in this nursing home will have a heart attack.
(E) Watching sports is a pastime that 15% of American households engage in all day Sunday. People in this household have watched television all Sunday, so they must have been watching sports.

GO ON TO THE NEXT PAGE

24. The coach should have realized that making his son captain of the team was immoral. It is wrong to let a child make decisions for a team just because he is the coach's son, so it is also wrong for a large group of team members that includes the coach's son to make decisions for the team.

Which of the following contains reasoning that is flawed in the same way as is the reasoning in the argument?

(A) Actors should not be allowed to be in movies solely because they are attractive people. People who are spontaneous should be in movies in addition to actors who are attractive.

(B) Sports players should not be allowed to gain commercial sponsorships solely because of their natural athletic abilities. Therefore, it is wrong for a large group of people to gain commercial sponsorship when a sports player is not included in the group.

(C) The coach's sons are the two captains of the team, and this situation is wrong because other people wanted to be captains. Therefore, other people should be captains besides the coach's sons.

(D) Animals should not be relegated to the outskirts of our society solely because they are not human. Therefore, impoverished people in our society should not be relegated to the outskirts of our society.

(E) The rich should not be allowed to make all political decisions solely because of their wealth. Therefore, it is wrong to include any rich people in the governmental body that makes political decisions.

25. Stuntman: I prefer car crashes to motorcycle crashes, because in a car crash, I have a shield of metal protecting me from the ground and other vehicles. Motorcycle crashes are more dangerous because there is nothing to protect me. Jumping out of burning buildings is the worst, though, because then I don't even have a bike—only a trampoline cushions my fall.

Daredevil: I like jumping out of burning buildings best because it makes me look cool. After that, I like motorcycle stunts because they increase the likelihood of getting into an accident that will really test my body's limits. Car crashes are too dangerous since there are so many other people and vehicles involved.

The daredevil and the stuntman are committed to disagreeing about which of the following?

(A) Car crashes are more dangerous than motorcycle crashes.

(B) Jumping out of burning buildings makes people look cool.

(C) The more vehicles involved in an accident, the more dangerous it is.

(D) The less metal to shield a person's body in an accident, the more dangerous it is.

(E) Stuntmen often do not use trampolines to cushion their falls from burning buildings.

S T O P

IF YOU FINISH BEFORE TIME RUNS OUT, CHECK YOUR WORK ON THIS SECTION ONLY.
DO NOT GO ON TO ANY OTHER TEST SECTION.

ANSWER KEY

Section 1	Section 2	Section 3	Section 4
1. A	1. B	1. D	1. B
2. E	2. B	2. A	2. D
3. D	3. E	3. A	3. B
4. B	4. A	4. E	4. E
5. D	5. D	5. A	5. A
6. B	6. D	6. B	6. A
7. E	7. A	7. D	7. D
8. D	8. A	8. C	8. B
9. C	9. D	9. A	9. C
10. A	10. C	10. E	10. E
11. A	11. B	11. E	11. D
12. E	12. A	12. C	12. D
13. E	13. D	13. A	13. A
14. E	14. E	14. C	14. C
15. A	15. D	15. B	15. B
16. D	16. B	16. A	16. A
17. B	17. B	17. D	17. B
18. C	18. E	18. C	18. E
19. D	19. D	19. C	19. A
20. A	20. E	20. C	20. B
21. E	21. C	21. C	21. C
22. B	22. C	22. B	22. D
23. E	23. E	23. D	23. B
24. A	24. D	24. A	24. E
25. C	25. B	25. D	25. A
	26. B		

<u>Scoring Instructions:</u> To calculate your score on this Practice Test, follow the instructions on the next page.

CALCULATING YOUR SCORE

Now that you have completed Practice Test 2, use the instructions on this page to calculate your score. Start by checking the Answer Key to count up the number of questions you answered correctly. Then fill in the table below.

Raw Score Calculator

Section Number	Question Type	Number of Questions	Number Correct
1	Reading Comprehension	25	_____
2	Logical Reasoning	26	_____
3	Logic Games	25	_____
4	Logical Reasoning	25	_____
		(Raw Score) Total:	_____

On the real LSAT, a statistical process will be used to convert your raw score to a scaled score ranging from 120 to 180. The table below will give you an approximate idea of the scaled score that matches your raw score. For statistical reasons, on real forms of the LSAT the scaled score that matches a given raw score can vary by several points above or below the scaled score shown in the table.

Write your scaled score on this test here:

Practice Test 2 scaled score: _____

Raw Score	Scaled Score	Raw Score	Scaled Score	Raw Score	Scaled Score	Raw Score	Scaled Score
0	120	26	128	52	148	78	164
1	120	27	129	53	149	79	165
2	120	28	130	54	150	80	166
3	120	29	131	55	151	81	166
4	120	30	132	56	151	82	167
5	120	31	133	57	152	83	167
6	120	32	133	58	153	84	168
7	120	33	134	59	153	85	169
8	120	34	135	60	154	86	170
9	120	35	136	61	154	87	170
10	120	36	137	62	155	88	171
11	120	37	137	63	155	89	172
12	120	38	138	64	156	90	173
13	120	39	139	65	157	91	174
14	120	40	140	66	158	92	175
15	120	41	140	67	158	93	175
16	120	42	141	68	159	94	176
17	120	43	142	69	159	95	177
18	121	44	143	70	160	96	178
19	122	45	144	71	160	97	179
20	123	46	145	72	161	98	180
21	124	47	145	73	161	99	180
22	125	48	146	74	162	100	180
23	126	49	147	75	162	101	180
24	127	50	147	76	163		
25	128	51	148	77	163		

SECTION I—READING COMPREHENSION

1. Correct answer: **A.** The purpose of the passage is to discuss the ECPA and why it was enacted.

   (A) This is an issue that is addressed in the passage, but it is not the major issue of the passage.

   (C) The brilliance of the drafters cannot be said to have been exalted. Instead, the ECPA is said to be confusing and unusually complicated.

   (D) This statement is not made by the passage.

   (E) This point is tangentially related to the passage, but not explicitly discussed.

2. Correct answer: **E.** Public network service providers are said to be indifferent to the rights of their users because the providers are so tenuously connected to the users.

   (A) This word is not an accurate description.

   (B) The service providers do not completely ignore the rights of their users; they are just disinclined to jump through legal hoops to protect those rights.

   (C) This word is not an accurate description.

   (D) This word is not an accurate description.

3. Correct answer: **D.** The author describes how the added importance and growth of cyberspace has created legal issues regarding privacy that are not covered by the Fourth Amendment. In order to protect the spirit of the Constitution, the EPCA was drafted to outline the rights of Internet users.

   (A) This statement was not made in the passage. It was merely said that they are easier to gain than search warrants.

   (B) The passage does not say that service providers protect no rights, just that they do not protect the rights of privacy zealously.

   (C) This statement is not really supported by the passage; the EPCA protects rights where they deserve to be protected, not where there is a "need for privacy."

   (E) This statement is not true; the statute is interpreted based on the intent of the drafters.

4. Correct answer: **B.** It was hard to tell what the Fourth Amendment would and would not allow in cyberspace.

(A) The opposite was stated.

(C–E) These words do not describe the effects of the Fourth Amendment.

5. Correct answer: **D.** The purpose was to contrast that which the Fourth Amendment was designed to protect with that which it is currently being used to protect, namely computers on the Internet.

   (A) This statement is partially true, but this is not a place where the gaps would be filled in.

   (B) There is no mention of cyber homes in the passage.

   (C) This is not the case.

   (E) This is not the case.

6. Correct answer: **B.** This is stated explicitly in lines 50–53.

   (A) This point is not stated or implied by the passage.

   (C) The opposite is stated to be true.

   (D) This statement is not true. The Fourth Amendment still applies to our homes.

   (E) It cannot be determined whether this sentence is true. More than likely it is not true, since the passage claimed that providers were indifferent to handing over information.

7. Correct answer: **E.** The passage relates the facts surrounding the dissolution of the U.S.S.R, and Russia's reemergence onto the global scene. It goes on to tell how Russia has had to change in order to adapt to the new system of government.

   (A) This description was true of the other governments also.

   (B) It was never stated that this was the only thing wrong with Russian politics.

   (C) It was not stated that the inability to tap into Siberian resources hurt the Soviet Union in any way.

   (D) This statement is true, but it is not the main idea of the passage.

8. Correct answer: **D.** Support for this idea is found in the lines 61–65.

(A) The Russian Federation came into existence after 1991.

(B) According to the passage, Yeltsin came onto the scene after 1991.

(C) Europe did not break up the Soviet Union. The Soviet Union was destroyed in an internal coup.

(E) There was no self-governance, as stated in lines 37–38.

9. Correct answer: **C.** The "monolithic union" refers to the unified states under the Soviet Union.

(A) The word *monolithic* is used to describe "unwieldy" and "large" instead of "stone."

(B) This could be correct if the date preceded 1991, but afterward there was no sense of indestructibility.

(D) This point is not mentioned in the passage.

(E) This point is not mentioned in the passage.

10. Correct answer: **A.** This passage explains the implications of the breakup of the Soviet Union.

(B) The passage makes no such claim.

(C) There is no explanation of the short-term goals of the smaller republics.

(D) This point was hinted at by the paragraph, but the purpose of the paragraph is to explain how the states would need to reorganize, not to cast blame.

(E) There is no normative judgment made regarding the location of the capital in Moscow.

11. Correct answer: **A.** This view was shown by their preference to avoid living in Siberia.

(B) This statement is not true. There is thought to be almost a vacuum of power in the region since the fall of the Soviet Union.

(C) This inference is not accurate.

(D) This is a contradiction in terms. Favorably desolate?

(E) The opposite of this description is stated.

12. Correct answer: **E.** Nothing is said about Russia currently being benevolent or corruption-free.

(A) The passage makes this point (lines 38–43).

(B) The passage makes this point (lines 61–65).

(C) The passage makes this point (lines 69–71).

(D) This is the main point of the passage.

13. Correct answer: **E.** The primary purpose of the passage is to introduce and describe stem cells. Additionally, the passage emphasizes the potential importance of stem cell research to our society.

(A) Diabetes is not mentioned in the passage.

(B) This issue is touched upon, but its ethicality is not aggressively discussed.

(C) The passage merely offers a hypothesis about the effects stem cell research may have in medicine. Additionally, the potential effects are not "hesitantly" discussed.

(D) Stem cells are not considered "alternative medicine."

14. Correct answer: **E.** The importance of the research is unknown, but the potential that stem cells hold may be greater than anyone can imagine based on the small amount of research that has been conducted.

(A) Putting cures into a developing fetus is not an issue that is discussed.

(B) The opposite of this sentence is stated in the passage.

(C) The passage never makes this claim.

(D) This statement is probably true, but the passage never suggests that more donors would be needed.

15. Correct answer: **A.** This answer is correct, since stem cells can originate in undifferentiated form and then turn into a specific type of cell.

(B) Nothing about evolutionary achievement is discussed in the passage.

(C) The legislature is not mentioned in the passage.

(D) The passage does not offer enough information to make this assumption.

(E) The passage does not suggest that stem cells can be gathered from cadavers.

16. Correct answer: **D.** If this statement were true, then stem cells could potentially cure any disease. This potential would certainly cause them to become a valuable staple of the medical community.

(A) This is not convincing support that stem cells will eventually become highly beneficial in medicine.

(B) This statement does not imply much of anything about the usefulness of stem cells.

(C) This statement would undermine the contention that stem cells will prove to be extremely valuable to the medical community.

(E) This lack of need is a good thing, but it is not relevant to how beneficial stem cells will be.

17. Correct answer: **B.** Scientists want to learn the basics about stem cells, which is why they want to understand their essential or fundamental properties.

(A) *Auxiliary* means "secondary." The passage implies that scientists are looking for the basic or central qualities of the stem cells.

(C) This word does not fit the meaning of the sentence.

(D) This word does not fit the meaning of the sentence.

(E) *Unique* is a good second choice, but the word *different* (or *unique*) is used next in the sentence, so it makes sense that *essential* refers to something besides *unique* properties.

18. Correct answer: **C.** The first paragraph introduces the topic of stem cells. The second and third paragraphs discuss the features and mysteries of stem cells. Finally, the fourth paragraph discusses the future goals of the research.

(A) The author does not try to call the reader to any action. The purpose of this passage is completely informative.

(B) There is really only one hypothesis outlined for every claim. There is never a debate between clashing theories.

(D) Nothing is attacked because of its simplicity.

(E) A point of view is not discussed. A scientific frontier is analyzed.

19. Correct answer: **D.** The purpose of the passage is to discuss the economic and social effects of the "sugar revolutions" in the Caribbean islands.

(A) This is a small point that is discussed.

(B) Although this issue runs through the entire passage, a higher focus is placed on the Caribbean islands themselves.

(C) Today's political attitude toward the Caribbean is never presented.

(E) This is the purpose of the first paragraph, but not of the whole passage.

20. Correct answer: **A.** No theory is ever presented to be contradicted or debated in the passage.

(B) This point is stated in lines 45–59.

(C) This history is frequently mentioned in the first and second paragraphs.

(D) Contrasts are consistently made between the times during which Caribbean people grew tobacco and when they grew sugarcane.

(E) The specific example of Barbados is used in the third paragraph.

21. Correct answer: **E.** This fact is stated in lines 58–59.

(A) The passage states that 175 people owned 54% of the slaves. This means that more than likely more than 200 people owned slaves.

(B) The passage discusses a 40-year time period from 1640 to 1680.

(C) The Dutch were mainly responsible.

(D) There were revolutions in the Caribbean; they are the subject matter of the passage.

22. Correct answer: **B.** *Watershed* could be replaced with *cultural transition*, and the sentence would still have the same meaning.

(A–E) All these phrases would completely change the meaning of the sentence.

23. Correct answer: **E.** Lines 60–73 support this point.

(A) The opposite occurred. The resources were more evenly distributed in the 1640s as opposed to being held mainly by the wealthy in the 1680s.

(B) Family-operated businesses are different from farms, and the passage does not mention them.

(C) This point is not stated in the passage.

(D) The passage does not state that more people owned land. It states that a smaller proportion of people owned more of the land in the 1680s.

24. Correct answer: **A.** This type of farming economy is described as outdated and in severe crisis in the Caribbean. It was used only for tobacco farming. However, it was not the reason why the Caribbean islands moved away from tobacco farming. Competition from the mid-Atlantic colonies was the reason for the start of the sugar revolutions.

(B) This was a very important issue that is frequently stressed in the passage.

(C) This element was important because it gave a market for the produce of the islands.

(D) This development forced the Caribbean islands into the sugar market and away from their unsuccessful attempts at competing in the tobacco market.

(E) This point is important in terms of shipping it to European markets.

25. Correct answer: **C.** The passage states succinctly that people were moving out of the Caribbean colonies because the tobacco farms were being outcompeted by the farms in the mid-Atlantic colonies.

(A) This point is not mentioned.

(B) It is stated that people were more successful growing tobacco on the mainland, not sugar.

(D) This reason is never mentioned in the passage.

(E) This point is hinted at toward the end of the passage, but it is never explicitly stated that it was a reason that caused people to leave the colonies.

SECTION 2—LOGICAL REASONING

1. Somnambulism is a bad habit because people can put themselves in grave danger if they get outside while sleepwalking. To prevent this risk, known somnambulists should lock their doors at night.

Question Type: Conclusion

Correct answer: **B.** This choice essentially states that somnambulism is dangerous for the same reasons that the squib does.

(A) The squib claims that the people could not open the door.

(C) This answer choice is nonsensical.

(D) This inference is not necessarily true, since some sleepwalkers securely fasten their doors.

(E) This is a good second choice, but it is impossible to know what numerous experts might recommend from the information in the squib.

2. This squib claims that the postal service is responsible for forging the ties that bind our society. Without the connections that the postal service has provided, Americans would not be as patriotic.

Question Type: "Strengthen"

Correct answer: **B.** If this point were true, then the conclusion of the sentence would be validated.

(A) This answer does not mean that the lack of a postal service was responsible for Russia's civil war.

(C) This point is irrelevant.

(D) This statement might support the squib, but there is really not enough information to select this answer.

(E) This answer does not mean that the current level of organization is making Americans closer.

3. The bodybuilder claims that the more he works out, the more muscles he has and the more women he attracts. To attract more women, he claims that he should work out more. The woman friend claims that working out too much makes a man unattractive. She further claims that the bodybuilder has had more romances simply because he is older.

Question Type: Controversy

Correct answer: **E.** This is the thesis of the bodybuilder that the woman friend rejects.

(A) This point is agreed upon by both people.

(B) The woman friend does not say this. She says that after a certain point woman become disgusted.

(C) This statement is not made by either person.

(D) This determination cannot be made based on either person's contentions.

4. This driving teacher stresses the need to know both road conditions and weather conditions when you are driving. The teacher claims that if you know the conditions, then you will be able to prevent accidents from occurring.

Question Type: "Strengthen"

Correct answer: **A.** If this were not true, then there would be no reason to take account of the unexpected.

(B) This determination cannot be made on the basis of the squib.

(C) This answer would not support the argument.

(D) This is not an assumption of the argument.

(E) This is not an assumption of the argument.

5. This passage states that laws regarding water runoff differ from state to state. It says that it is not easy to assign responsibility for runoff since no one wants it to come onto their land, no one wants it to stay on their land, and no one wants to be responsible for it when it drains away to someone else's land.

Question Type: Conclusion

Correct answer: **D.** This point is explicitly stated in the passage.

(A) The passage makes no ethical determination on this idea.

(B) This answer cannot be determined from the passage. Some people might have ponds that need filling.

(C) People with swimming pools do not like muddy runoff rainwater to come into their pool.

(E) The passage states that in some states this option is not possible.

6. The doctor states that the baby will either be a boy or girl. Additionally, there is at least a 30% chance that the baby will be a girl.

Question Type: "Strengthen"

Correct answer: **D.** This point must be assumed, otherwise the mother could be giving birth to a girl *and* a boy.

(A) The percentage would indicate that she is.

(B) The doctor states that she or he will probably not be able to tell for sure next Tuesday what the sex of the baby is.

(C) This point cannot be determined

(E) This point cannot be determined.

7. This squib details the mechanics of a bottle rocket. The rocket is pumped up to increase the pressure that will later launch the rocket into the sky.

Question Type: Conclusion

Correct answer: **A.** The squib states that an increase in pressure is required to make the rocket fly.

(B) This point cannot be determined.

(C) Just because children play with bottle rockets does not mean that adults cannot play with them too.

(D) This point is certainly not true of space rockets.

(E) This point could be true, but it cannot be determined on the basis of the information in the squib.

8. This squib states that our population created the railroads, which led to a mass-transaction economy, which enforced capitalism. However, it then makes the claim that without the railroads, Americans would have become socialists. This conclusion is a real jump in logic.

Question Type: "Weaken"

Correct answer: **A.** More than likely this answer is true, and if so, it would completely undermine the conclusion of the argument.

(B) This choice does not address the issue of socialism.

(C) This statement does not address the issue of socialism.

(D) This answer does not state whether or not the United States would not still have embraced socialism.

(E) Nevertheless, the founders of the United States were no longer in power by the time the railroads reached the West.

9. The forest ranger says that quicksand is incredibly dangerous. The ranger then says that no one should jump into quicksand in an attempt to save a friend. The only way to save someone who is mired in quicksand is to use a branch or rope to pull the person out.

Question Type: "Strengthen"

Correct answer: **D.** This is the conclusion of the passage. Since there is no other way to save people, if these means were not available, then the person would be doomed.

(A) They wouldn't—unless they can be handed a rope or branch. It cannot be assumed that neither people nor other bears would refrain from using these methods for a bear.

(B) This statement is probably true, but it is not assumed by the argument.

(C) This answer cannot be determined from the information in the squib.

(E) This choice would undermine the argument, so it is definitely not assumed.

10. The circus comes to town every year with some exciting new attraction. The squib details several new attractions from previous years and then describes some of the exhibits that do not change from year to year.

Question Type: Conclusion

Correct answer: **C.** This point is explicitly stated in the first sentence of the squib.

(A) From the information in the squib, it cannot be determined whether or not all children love the circus.

(B) This statement is not true, according to the squib.

(D) It cannot be determined whether elephants were ever a marvel.

(E) Some people may like the ringmaster better than the dancers or trapeze artists.

11. This is a very strange squib, but it is resolved when Ben claims that he is John. In other words he either has multiple personality disorder or some unique oneness with all creatures in the world.

Question Type: "Strengthen"

Correct answer: **B.** If this statement were true, then Ben could claim to be an inextricable part of John without it being a complete falsehood.

(A) This answer would not mean that John is a part of Ben.

(C) This choice would undermine the argument.

(D) This point is irrelevant to the conclusion of the passage.

(E) Even if Ben and John are brothers, it cannot be concluded that they are the same person.

12. The squib states that many talented singers have left the United States because their talents were not appreciated. Based on this information, the squib claims that the talented singers who have stayed must be in higher demand even though the passage makes it clear that many singers left initially because the demand was so low.

Question Type: "Weaken"

Correct answer: **A.** If there were no demand and this was the reason why many singers left, then it would make sense that the remaining singers are not in more demand.

(B) This answer does not mean that there is not also a greater demand for talented singers.

(C) This point would be irrelevant.

(D) This point would be irrelevant.

(E) This choice does not mean that the ones who stayed are receiving any added publicity.

13. This squib claims that since most predictions are false, it is unreasonable to claim that a psychic has extrasensory perception simply because one or two of her many predictions has come true.

Question Type: Analogous reasoning

Correct answer: **D.** Most of a liar's claims are false, so it would be unreasonable to give full credence to a liar just because the liar told the truth once or twice.

(A) This answer is very dissimilar to the reasoning in the argument.

(B) This answer is very dissimilar to the reasoning in the argument.

(C) This choice would be closer to the reasoning in the argument if the vulgar person were to be classified as "high class" instead of "low class."

(E) This reasoning is much different from that in the passage.

14. Onscreen televisions are lower in quality than most other televisions, but because of the recession, Onscreen televisions have sold very well.

Question Type: "Resolve"

Correct answer: **E.** During a recession people would be more inclined to purchase cheaper sets even if they are of a lower quality.

(A) If most purchasers knew that Onscreen televisions were of low quality, then it would not matter that the competitors did not point it out.

(B) This is not a compelling enough reason to explain why the televisions sold so well compared to the competition. The sales of the Onscreen televisions would still be hurt by the recession despite this fact.

(C) There are many competing brands. Even if Onscreen televisions were better at a few things than some of their competitors, they could still be worse than competitive brands on average.

(D) This answer would still not explain why Onscreen televisions sold well compared to their competitors.

15. Tommy claims that, on the basis of dye experiments, whenever something yellow is mixed with something blue, something green will result. However, this result has been tested only with dyes.

Question Type: "Weaken"

Correct answer: **D.** This answer would mean that blue mixed with yellow will sometimes result in an orange color.

(A) This statement does not mean that the mixing of yellow and blue will not still make green.

(B) This choice does not mean that this particular experiment is different.

(C) Tommy uses the future tense. It cannot be assumed that the atmosphere will revert to its past state.

(E) This answer does not mean that the implications of the experiments are not valid.

16. The cashier claims that the store clerk cannot walk out of the store without paying for the purse, because it would be dishonest. The store clerk claims that her contract states that she is entitled to take one free item each month and that her choice for the month is the purse.

Question Type: Controversy

Correct answer: **B.** The cashier is committed to disagreeing with this statement, based on her claims. The store clerk would claim that this person's contract would allow her to take the purse.

(A) This person has no contract, so the situation would be different.

(C) Both people would probably agree with this statement.

(D) Both people would probably agree with this statement.

(E) Both people would probably agree with this statement.

17. Girls mature before boys do, so they should be given classes about maturity before boys are. The question stem asks what, if true, would eliminate any positive gains from doing this.

Question Type: "Weaken"

Correct answer: **B.** This answer would mean that teaching girls earlier than boys would not matter.

(A) This choice would support the columnist's ideas.

(C) This point is irrelevant to what should happen with girls.

(D) This statement would support the columnist's ideas.

(E) This answer does not mean that it is not helpful to some people.

18. Spock and Jones are disagreeing about the ancestry of birds. Dr. Jones claims that birds evolved from small creatures that used to leap around in Antarctica.

Question Type: "Weaken"

Correct answer: **E.** If this statement were true, then the species that Dr. Jones points to would have been eradicated by an ice age, thereby disproving his theory.

(A) This answer does not mean that they could not have subsequently evolved wings.

(B) This fact would only strengthen theories competing with Dr. Spock's.

(C) This answer does not mean that some of these birdlike creatures could not have evolved into a new and different species before the old species was eradicated.

(D) This statement would strengthen Dr. Jones's theory.

19. This squib relates the difficulty of preparing for and running a marathon and then questions why compensation levels for this sport are so low, considering that the winners have to compete with up the 20,000 people at one time.

Question Type: Conclusion

Correct answer: **D.** The best runner and the best tennis player are likely to be professionals. The final sentence states that professional runners are not nearly as well compensated as are professional tennis players.

(A) It cannot be assumed that the average member of either group would be a professional in the sport. Therefore, this conclusion is not valid.

(B) This point cannot be assumed, based on the squib.

(C) The squib says that most people train for a marathon, but it does not claim that all do.

(E) There is no information to support this statement.

20. The socialite claims that old acquaintances are valuable only insofar as they are able to lead to new friends.

    Question Type: Conclusion

    Correct answer: **E.** The socialite claims that this stable base provided by acquaintances is worthless unless it helps to find new friends.

    (A) This determination cannot be made.

    (B) It cannot be determined whether the socialite is successful in her ventures.

    (C) This answer is probably not the case.

    (D) The truth of this statement cannot be assumed on the basis of the information in the squib.

21. This squib recommends that hospitals use self-insuring regimes in order to curb medical malpractice expenses that are driven up by private insurers.

    Question Type: "Weaken"

    Correct answer: **C.** If this statement were true, then insurance would be more expensive for self-insuring hospitals. Therefore, it would not be a good idea for these hospitals to self-insure.

    (A) This answer would support the recommendation of the passage.

    (B) If this statement were true, it would not mean that doctors did not receive some sort of benefit.

    (D) This answer does not mean that the self-insurance premiums will not rise at a slower rate than private ones.

    (E) This point is irrelevant, because self-insuring hospitals do the same.

22. The primatologist claims that gorillas can do these three things: create art, interact with people, and use sign language. The psychologist claims that gorillas cannot do these three things: speak English, create art, and interact with people in the same way that people interact with people.

    Question Type: Controversy

    Correct answer: **C.** The point about which both disagree is whether gorillas can be said to create art.

    (A) The primatologist does not claim that gorillas will one day be speaking English audibly.

    (B) The psychologist does not claim that gorillas cannot learn English through sign language.

(D) This point is not stated.

(E) This point is not stated.

23. The geologist claims that rocks are living things and that humans cannot realize this fact because our lifespans are so miniscule when compared to the lifespans of rocks.

    Question Type: Reasoning strategy

    Correct answer: **E.** The geologist claims that rocks are living things while concurrently claiming that only a person who has lived for several million years would be able to make this claim. This is a contradiction.

    (A) This answer does not mean that the argument is logically flawed.

    (B) There is no key term upon which the definitions of these terms depend.

    (C) This answer is not the case.

    (D) This answer is not the case.

24. This squib claims that the sun feeds plants that feed herbivores that feed carnivores. The squib then claims that if the sun lost its energy, then this whole chain would starve and eventually would be wiped out.

    Question Type: "Strengthen"

    Correct answer: **D.** If carnivores were able to do this, then their lives would not end when the sun ended.

    (A) The opposite is assumed by the squib.

    (B) This is not a claim that is made by the squib.

    (C) This point is irrelevant.

    (E) This answer has nothing to do with what will happen on Earth.

25. This passage claims that running in hot weather is more dangerous than running in cold weather. Furthermore, it claims that running in hot and cold weather have different dangers that require different precautions to be taken.

    Question Type: Conclusion

    Correct answer: **B.** This is the purpose of the passage: to point out the dangers and recommend ways to avoid them.

    (A) This is not the main point. It is a subsidiary point.

    (C) This point is not even stated in the passage.

(D) Hot weather and cold weather cannot really be described as inclement weather. Even if they were, this choice is too narrow to cover the whole passage.

(E) This point is not stated in the passage.

26. Two weightlifters are trapped in a room with a 1500-pound obstacle blocking the door. Together they cannot lift 1500 pounds, so the passage assumes that they will be unable to exit the room.

Question Type: Reasoning strategy

Correct answer: **B.** It is possible that the weightlifters could roll something that is 1500 pounds out of the way of the door. Maybe they could find an alternate exit or people from the outside could help push the machine.

(A) This uses calculation to determine the factors that will not be sufficient when added. There is no assumption made here.

(C) This is not a flawed way of making conclusions.

(D) This does not occur.

(E) This does not occur.

SECTION 3—LOGIC GAMES

Game 1: Complex Linear

Initial Setup:

	Mon	Tue	Wed	Thur	Fri
A, B, C, D, E					
R, S, T, U, V					

A	C	B
R	T	V

A < C < S

1. Correct answer: **D.** Notice that B must be with V, so the only possibility is for D to be seen on Friday with S:

		A	C	
U/V	V/U	R	T	S

2. Correct answer: **A.** Because A < C < S, if B is seen on Wednesday, then A must be seen on Monday or Tuesday.

3. Correct answer: **A.** B is seen with V, so D can never be seen on the same day as V.

4. Correct answer: **E.** None of the previous four possibilities could occur. However, E could be seen on Friday with U:

A	C		
R	T		

5. Correct answer: **A.** In this scenario, we can figure out the entire configuration of the game. The A < C < S relationship is pivotal in these deductions:

A	B	D	C	E
R	V	U	T	S

6. Correct answer: **B.** S is paired with either D or E. These two variables could go on any day except immediately after S or immediately before V. U could go before or after any variable except immediately after S or immediately before V.

Game 2: Grouping

Initial Setup:

___*	___*	E ≠ F
___	___	$A_1 \rightarrow B_2$
___	___	$B_2 \rightarrow D_1$
E/F	F/E	$D_1 \rightarrow F_2$

7. Correct answer: **D.** G, D, E, and A is a possible group.

(A) If A is on team 1, then F must be on team 2.

(B) If B is on team 2, then D must be on team 1.

(C) E cannot be on team 2 with F.

(E) If A is on team 1, then B is on team 2.

8. Correct answer: **C:**

$$\frac{D}{E} \quad \frac{B}{A}$$
$$\frac{}{} \quad \frac{F}{}$$
$$\frac{}{} \quad \frac{}{}$$

9. Correct answer: **A.**

$$\frac{D}{E} \quad \frac{B}{A}$$
$$\frac{}{} \quad \frac{F}{}$$
$$\frac{}{} \quad \frac{}{}$$

10. Correct answer: **E.**

$$\frac{D}{B} \quad \frac{A}{F}$$
$$\frac{E}{} \quad \frac{}{}$$

11. Correct answer: **E.** This question is very easy, since the last constraint states that E can never be with F.

12. Correct answer: **C.** Three players who could go on team 2: C, G, and H.

$$\frac{F}{B} \quad \frac{A}{D}$$
$$\frac{}{} \quad \frac{E}{}$$
$$\frac{}{} \quad \frac{}{}$$

13. Correct answer: **A.** For D and A not to be required to be on the same team, then A has to be on team 2, Since we know that D is on a different team, we know that D is on team 1. D's presence on team 1 requires F to be present on team 2. F cannot be in the same group as E, so E is on team 1. Therefore, we know the answer: E must not be on team 2.

Game 3: Mapping

Initial Setup:

1
```
  D     R     R
  •     •     •

D •           • D

  •     •     •
  D     R     R
```

2
```
  D    R/D    R
  •     •     •

D •           • R/D

  •     •     •
  R     R     D
```

Getting the initial setup is hard, but if done correctly, you will see that there are only two main configurations for the game. First, you can deduce that the Northeast door must be a revolving door because otherwise the South revolving door would be next to two revolving doors on the corners. Based on this, you can draw one arrangement where the final corner revolving door is on the Southwest corner, and another where the final revolving door goes on the Southeast corner. In both arrangements, it appears that the West door is always a double door.

14. Correct answer: **C.** This is evident in both diagrams.

15. Correct answer: **B.** This is shown in diagram 2. There cannot be only three double doors, because one must also be next to the Northeast revolving door.

16. Correct answer: **A.** This must be diagram 2 because in diagram 1 the East door must be a double door. According to diagram 2, the Southwest door must be a revolving door.

17. Correct answer: **D.** The South and the Northeast doors are always revolving. The East and the Southeast doors could not be revolving in the same diagram.

18. Correct answer: **C.** There is one configuration for diagram 1. There are two configurations for diagram 2. This makes a total of three for the game.

Game 4: Sequential

Initial Setup:

$$\begin{array}{c} {}_{\angle} C {}^{\angle} F \\ D < H < A < B \\ {}_{\llcorner} \\ E < G \end{array}$$

$$H = 3$$

$$F_5 \text{ or } A_5 \rightarrow E_7 \;;\; \cancel{E}_7 \rightarrow \cancel{F}_5 \text{ and } \cancel{A}_5$$

$$\frac{D}{1} \quad \frac{C}{2} \quad \frac{H}{3} \quad \frac{}{4} \quad \frac{}{5} \quad \frac{}{6} \quad \frac{}{7} \quad \frac{}{8}$$

Since H is third, then C and D must be second and first, respectively.

19. Correct answer: **C.** The initial order must be D, C, and H, so you can eliminate choices (B), (D), and (E). Choice (A) is not correct because if A is fifth, then E must be seventh.

20. Correct answer: **C.** You know that this is true from the initial diagram.

21. Correct answer: **C.** It would be impossible for B to sit fourth because A must precede B.

22. Correct answer: **B.** This means that A must sit fifth, because A cannot sit last since B must sit after A. If A is fifth, then E is seventh, which would make G eighth. This makes B sixth and F fourth:

$$\underline{D}\ \ \underline{C}\ \ \underline{H}\ \ \underline{F}\ \ \underline{A}\ \ \underline{B}\ \ \underline{E}\ \ \underline{G}$$

23. Correct answer: **D.** If E sits sixth, then neither F nor A can sit fifth. A cannot sit fifth nor can A sit after E, because then B would have to sit after E also, and that would leave no space for G after E. Therefore, A must sit forth and B must sit fifth:

$$\underline{D}\ \ \underline{C}\ \ \underline{H}\ \ \underline{A}\ \ \underline{B}\ \ \underline{E}\ \ \underline{F/G}\ \ \underline{G/F}$$
$$\underline{\cancel{F}}$$
$$\underline{\cancel{A}}$$

24. Correct answer: **A.** If F or A sits fifth, then E would sit seventh and G would sit eighth. This is impossible under the conditions of the question; therefore, neither F nor A can sit fifth:

$$\underline{D}\ \ \underline{C}\ \ \underline{H}\ \ \underline{}\ \ \underline{}\ \ \underline{}\ \ \underline{}\ \ \underline{}$$
$$\underline{\cancel{F}}$$
$$\underline{\cancel{A}}$$

(B) C never can sit third.

(C) This is not possible. If A sits fifth, then E and G would have to be next to each other in seventh and eighth places.

(D) This would require G to sit eighth, which is impossible.

(E) If A sits seventh, then B sits last. G would have to sit sixth, and E would have to sit fourth. However, this would force F to sit fifth, which would be impossible since it would force E to sit seventh.

25. Correct answer: **D.** The sufficient-necessary constraint here confines where A and F can sit. There are two possible scenarios where A could sit immediately before F:

$$1\quad \underline{D}\ \ \underline{C}\ \ \underline{H}\ \ \underline{A}\ \ \underline{F}\ \ \underline{B}\ \ \underline{E}\ \ \underline{G}$$
$$2\quad \underline{D}\ \ \underline{C}\ \ \underline{H}\ \ \underline{E}\ \ \underline{G}\ \ \underline{A}\ \ \underline{F}\ \ \underline{B}$$

SECTION 4—LOGICAL REASONING

1. A fire started in a sprinter's shoes after a race. At first, the author attributes the fire to friction, but upon further reflection the author decides that it was just a publicity stunt.

Question Type: Conclusion

Correct answer: **B.** This is the conclusion the author comes to.

(A) This point cannot be determined on the basis of the passage. The author claims only that whatever happened was a publicity stunt.

(C) This point is not stated in the passage.

(D) This point is not stated in the passage.

(E) This point is not stated in the passage.

2. This is a sufficient-necessary question:
   1. Gaghan Tree → Hardwood
   2. Hardwood Squirrel → Tail Is Fluffy or Matted

   The conclusion is:
   3. Gaghan Squirrel → Gaghan Tree → Hardwoods

   Question Type: Conclusion

   Correct answer: **D.** This is true, as shown by the first sufficient-necessary statement.

   (A) This statement is true only of squirrels living in hardwood trees.

   (B) This point cannot be determined, because squirrels could exit the forest to climb a softwood tree.

   (C) This point cannot be determined because squirrels that do not live in the forest could enter it.

   (E) Nothing in the passage relates to Gaghan shrubs.

3. John states that moving is physically and emotionally exhausting. He says that he has been moving, so he is physically and emotionally exhausted.

   Question Type: Conclusion

   Correct answer: **B.** This answer restates his major thesis.

   (A) This point curtly states his thesis without giving enough details.

   (C) This is a subsidiary point of his argument.

   (D) This point cannot be determined on the basis of the information provided.

(E) This point cannot be determined on the basis of the information provided.

4. This squib describes the intensity of the election process. Since candidates put so much into running for office, it is not surprising that they are very disappointed when they lose. However, all candidates should recognize the high caliber of the competition and should not feel rejected if they lose.

Question Type: Conclusion

Correct answer: **E.** This answer essentially sums up the squib.

(A) This point is not addressed in the squib.

(B) This point is part of the squib, but it leaves out a major part of the story: how losing candidates should interpret and deal with their losses.

(C) Being more or less competitive is not an issue addressed in the squib.

(D) There is nothing said about losing candidates not being disappointed.

5. This squib claims that beer commercials are extremely compelling because they appeal to the male illusion of dominance.

Question Type: Conclusion

Correct answer: **A.** This conclusion would make sense, because the squib claims that beer commercials are incredibly successful only because they appeal to this illusion.

(B) This point cannot be determined from the squib. There might be fewer purchases of a particular brand of beer, but it is unlikely that the frequency with which beer as a whole is purchased would drop if the number of advertisements dropped.

(C) This conclusion is too extreme to be drawn from the squib. Would humor be good to market caskets?

(D) This point cannot be determined from the information provided.

(E) This statement is probably true, but the passage does not mention whether this is the case.

6. This passage states that the major reason why infants' brains are studied is to understand how their brain processes mature into adult brain processes. It would make sense that idiosyncratic infants would not give a lot of insight into the normal maturational process of the brain, and therefore doctors might not be as interested in studying these infants.

Question Type: "Resolve"

Correct answer: **A.** If this were the case, then it would be pointless for doctors interested in development to study infants with abnormal brain patterns.

(B) This answer does not mean that doctors dedicated to science would ignore the other infants because they are not cute enough.

(C) This point would further confuse the situation.

(D) This point undermines the conclusion of the passage.

(E) This statement does not explain why there is not enough research money devoted to studying these infants.

7. Freezers made by French companies are more durable than freezers made by U.S. companies. However, freezers made by U.S. companies have an average life that is five years longer than that of French-made freezers. Maybe the French are much harder on their freezers than Americans are.

Question Type: "Resolve"

Correct answer: **D.** If this statement were true, then French freezers would be destroyed more quickly even though they are more durable.

(A) This statement makes a comparison between two things and nothing. It is nonsensical and therefore is not the answer.

(B) This choice is unrelated to the squib and does not really explain anything.

(C) This answer does not explain the discrepancy between durability and lifetime.

(E) This point is irrelevant.

8. The scientists claim that immunological disorders arise from physiological conditions, not psychological ones. Yet, it is noted that many people being treated for stress have immunological conditions. This would lead one to believe the opposite. However, it is also possible that immunological disorders lead to stress.

Question Type: "Resolve"

Correct answer: **B.** This statement would explain why many people with immunological disorders are also being treated for stress.

(A) This answer would not explain anything.

(C) This statement does not mean that the people who are going to psychiatrists were not stressed out before they went to the doctor.

(D) People without immunological disorders are not relevant to a discussion of people with the disorders.

(E) Just because some elements have been discovered that affect both things does not mean that these rare elements act consistently to link these problems.

9. This squib talks about koi ponds. It claims that if you have a pond that is big enough, then all your koi will live to be at least 15 years old.

   Question Type: "Strengthen"

   Correct answer: **C.** This point must be assumed, or the conclusion of the squib would be invalid.

   (A) Nothing is said about the quality of koi as pets.

   (B) Koi could lose their vibrant colors patterns so long as the fish stay alive.

   (D) This answer choice is nonsensical.

   (E) Nothing is stated about what happens when koi pass the age of 15.

10. Billy claims that a date who is not cool enough to enjoy a dumb movie is not someone he wishes to hang out with.

    Question Type: "Strengthen"

    Correct answer: **E.** If this were not the case, then Billy's statement would be invalidated.

    (A) This statement may or may not be true, but the passage only offers ways to do this. It does not claim that all boys like to do this.

    (B) The passage says nothing about what girls think about karate movies.

    (C) What most boys are expected to do cannot be determined from the squib.

    (D) Assumptions were made only about dumb movies and karate movies. It cannot be inferred that jujitsu is a form of karate based on the syntax of the answer choice.

11. This is a sufficient-necessary question:

    1. Westerbrook Operating → Donations from Patrons

    2. Donations from Patrons → Good Financial Prospects **or** Tax Breaks

    3. Tax Breaks → Surplus **or** Negligent Executive

    Since there is never a negligent executive, we can say:

    3. Tax Breaks → Surplus

    Question Type: "Strengthen"

    Correct answer: **D.** If there were no surplus, then there would be no tax breaks. This would mean that the only source of donations for Westerbrook Academy would be from patrons who have good financial prospects.

    (A) This is impossible.

    (B) This would not be helpful.

    (C) This does not change the fact that Westerbrook *requires* donations from generous patrons to continue operating.

    (E) This is not a necessary assumption.

12. The author claims that the negative implications that Valentine's Day has for single people are huge. It cannot be determined whether the author is single, but the author neglects the positive benefits that Valentine's Day might bring to couples. To justify the elimination of Valentine's Day, the author would have to show that the benefits of Valentine's Day to couples do not outweigh the harmful effects of Valentine's Day to singles.

    Question Type: "Strengthen"

    Correct answer: **D.** This is the calculation upon which the argument depends.

    (A) The purpose of selling candy is also mentioned.

    (B) This determination cannot be made from the squib.

    (C) The opposite is assumed.

    (E) The opposite is assumed.

13. The speaker claims that there is a stringed instrument playing mellow chords far off in the orchard. He additionally claims that the instrument must be a guitar because he hears singing and the only stringed instrument that a person sings with is the guitar.

    Question Type: "Strengthen"

    Correct answer: **A.** This point would have to be assumed for it to be logical to infer that the instrument is a guitar.

(B) This was stated only of stringed instruments, not all instruments.

(C) It cannot be determined that the orchard is owned by the speaker.

(D) This point is not stated or assumed.

(E) The speaker assumes that an instrument that makes mellow sounds at this distance must be a stringed instrument.

14. This squib lists several commonalities among centenarians in a group. These are exercise, abstinence from drugs, and gardening. The speaker assumes that if she begins to garden, then she will also become a centenarian.

Question Type: "Strengthen"

Correct answer: **C.** If old age caused people to garden instead of gardening increasing the likelihood of living to an old age, then there would be no reason for the author to begin gardening.

(A) It cannot be determined that the author believes gardening to be an inspirational activity; healthy, maybe, but not inspirational.

(B) The passage does not assume that these are the sole factors responsible for living to a ripe old age.

(D) This is not assumed by the passage.

(E) This is not assumed by the passage.

15. The psychologist claims that a nature-versus-nurture debate is raging. Furthermore, the psychologist claims that people will not reach a consensus in the debate, but eventually they will stop talking about it because it is boring.

Question Type: "Weaken"

Correct answer: **B.** If a solution to the debate were found, then the psychologist's claims would be contradicted.

(A) This answer would support the argument.

(C) It does not matter what the truth is if people never find it or stop arguing about it.

(D) There is still no consensus evident here.

(E) This statement would support the claims made in the squib.

16. This squib introduces Dr. Spock, who makes the wild claim that there is no such thing as climate change from winter to summer. Based on this claim, the author claims that there is no discrepancy in the temperature between the seasons.

Question Type: Reasoning strategy

Correct answer: **A.** It is not a good or logical idea to allow the opinion of one person to change your mind about something that you know occurs repeatedly throughout the years, especially when there is no added support for this person's claims.

(B) This assumption does not occur.

(C) It does not rely on the opinions of these people; it contradicts them.

(D) This is not the case.

(E) This is not the case.

17. This doctor explains that nostalgia is triggered in a part of the brain that is different from the part where other emotions are triggered. For this reason, the doctor claims that nostalgia must satisfy one of these three conditions: (1) It develops later in life than other emotions. (2) It is not a real emotion. (3) It is the result of something unexplained in evolutionary history. The doctor rules out the idea that nostalgia is not a real emotion, so he or she assumes that it develops later in life than other emotions and completely ignores the third possibility.

Question Type: Reasoning strategy

Correct answer: **B.** The doctor does not eliminate the possibility that the emotion is due to something unexplained in evolutionary history.

(A) This is not true.

(C) This is not true.

(D) This is not true.

(E) The evidence in support of the idea that nostalgia arose from an unexplained part of evolutionary history would not necessarily disprove the doctor's claims.

18. Miriam agrees that dogs hear high-pitched noises better than some other mammals, but she also identifies another mammal, the bat, on which to test the theory. Observing that bats are extremely disturbed by the high-pitched whistle, she concludes that bats have an even greater response to high-pitched noises than dogs do.

Question Type: Reasoning strategy

Correct answer: **E.** She finds a group that the scientists probably did not think about and uses it to disprove their theory.

(A) Miriam certainly does not use the scientific method. She merely guesses based on a one-time observation that dogs don't hear high-pitched noises as well as bats.

(B) This is not true.

(C) It is not clear that the bats were more disturbed by the noise than a dog would be. Nor is it clear that the bats could hear it better.

(D) This is not true.

19. This passage assumes that since the Potomac River was once pristine, it is still pristine. However, much has happened in the past 80 years that could—and does—make this an invalid assumption.

    Question Type: Reasoning strategy

    Correct answer: **A.** Jane assumes that what was once true of the Potomac will still be true.

    (B) This does not occur.

    (C) This does not occur.

    (D) This does not occur.

    (E) This does not occur.

20. This squib claims that the prices of computer printers in stores do not really reflect the overall quality of the printers because the manufacturers want to lock customers in to buying their particular type of expensive ink cartridges.

    Question Type: Reasoning strategy

    Correct answer: **B.** This is exactly what occurs. The author claims that the prices are lower because the companies are looking to sell their ink.

    (A) The squib claims that no accurate comparison can be made based on the price of the printers.

    (C) This claim is too extreme.

    (D) This statement is not necessarily true. Although the squib claims that selling ink cartridges is more profitable than selling printers, it never claims that the cost of replacement ink cartridges will exceed the cost of the printer.

    (E) The opposite occurs.

21. Based upon two examples of behavior that will not elicit positive treatment from other people, this passage recommends the golden rule. Then, it recommends that this rule be taught to preschoolers.

Question Type: Reasoning strategy

Correct answer: **C.** The principle of the Golden Rule is derived from two supporting claims about failed methods for treating people.

(A) This is not true.

(B) This is not true.

(D) There is an appeal made to logic.

(E) This does not occur.

22. This passage discusses ways in which wireless networking has affected college campuses. It claims that the full effects have not yet been felt and that as wireless networking improves and more people "go wireless," campuses will continue to change.

    Question Type: Reasoning strategy

    Correct answer: **D.** Many examples are given showing how college campuses have changed because of wireless networking.

    (A) The conclusion follows intuitively from the introduction.

    (B) This does not occur

    (C) This does not occur.

    (E) No competing premises are offered in the squib.

23. This histamine blocker decreases allergies by 10%. A 10% decrease in allergies is noted in a nursing home, so the assumption is made that the nursing home just started using the histamine blocker.

    Question Type: Analogous reasoning

    Correct answer: **B.** Weightlifting increases performance by 15%, so it is assumed that a basketball team that has improved its performance by 15% is now lifting weights. This corresponds exactly to the squib.

    (A) This is a logical statement.

    (C) This is different, because it states that injury is *likely to* decrease effectiveness by 15%. It does not say that it does.

    (D) This reasoning is completely different.

    (E) This reasoning is completely different.

24. This squib assumes that because it is wrong to make the coach's son solely responsible for decisions affecting the team, it is wrong to allow the son any voice in decisions affecting the team.

Question Type: Analogous reasoning

Correct answer: **E.** This answer is directly analogous, because it claims that it is wrong to allow rich people to make all decisions. Therefore, it also assumes that it would be wrong to allow rich people to make any decisions.

(A) This answer is completely different.

(B) This answer is completely different.

(C) This answer is completely different.

(D) This answer is completely different.

25. The stuntman claims that car crashes are more dangerous than motorcycle crashes. The daredevil claims that motorcycle crashes are more dangerous than car crashes.

Question Type: Controversy

Correct answer: **A.** This is their point of disagreement.

(B) The stuntman does not comment on this idea.

(C) The stuntman does not comment on this idea.

(D) This is not necessarily always going to be a point of disagreement. What about plane crashes and car crashes? Probably the stuntman and the daredevil would both agree that even though plane crashes have more metal shielding a person's body, they are more dangerous than car crashes, which have less metal shielding a person's body.

(E) The stuntman and daredevil would not disagree with each other regarding this idea.

PRACTICE TEST 3

ANSWER SHEET

Directions for Test

- Before beginning the test, photocopy this Answer Sheet or remove it from the book. Mark your answer to each question in the space provided. If a section has fewer questions than answer spaces, leave the extra spaces blank.
- When you have finished the test, you may check your answers against the Answer Key on page 411. Explanations for each question begin on page 413. To calculate your raw score and scaled score, use the chart on pages 412–413.
- *Note:* If you have purchased the book-CD version of *McGraw-Hill's LSAT,* you may enter your answers directly on your computer rather than on this Answer Sheet. The CD program will automatically calculate your score, provide explanations for every question, and show you which question types were easiest for you and which ones were most difficult.

SECTION 1	SECTION 2	SECTION 3	SECTION 4
1. A B C D E	1. A B C D E	1. A B C D E	1. A B C D E
2. A B C D E	2. A B C D E	2. A B C D E	2. A B C D E
3. A B C D E	3. A B C D E	3. A B C D E	3. A B C D E
4. A B C D E	4. A B C D E	4. A B C D E	4. A B C D E
5. A B C D E	5. A B C D E	5. A B C D E	5. A B C D E
6. A B C D E	6. A B C D E	6. A B C D E	6. A B C D E
7. A B C D E	7. A B C D E	7. A B C D E	7. A B C D E
8. A B C D E	8. A B C D E	8. A B C D E	8. A B C D E
9. A B C D E	9. A B C D E	9. A B C D E	9. A B C D E
10. A B C D E	10. A B C D E	10. A B C D E	10. A B C D E
11. A B C D E	11. A B C D E	11. A B C D E	11. A B C D E
12. A B C D E	12. A B C D E	12. A B C D E	12. A B C D E
13. A B C D E	13. A B C D E	13. A B C D E	13. A B C D E
14. A B C D E	14. A B C D E	14. A B C D E	14. A B C D E
15. A B C D E	15. A B C D E	15. A B C D E	15. A B C D E
16. A B C D E	16. A B C D E	16. A B C D E	16. A B C D E
17. A B C D E	17. A B C D E	17. A B C D E	17. A B C D E
18. A B C D E	18. A B C D E	18. A B C D E	18. A B C D E
19. A B C D E	19. A B C D E	19. A B C D E	19. A B C D E
20. A B C D E	20. A B C D E	20. A B C D E	20. A B C D E
21. A B C D E	21. A B C D E	21. A B C D E	21. A B C D E
22. A B C D E	22. A B C D E	22. A B C D E	22. A B C D E
23. A B C D E	23. A B C D E	23. A B C D E	23. A B C D E
24. A B C D E	24. A B C D E	24. A B C D E	24. A B C D E
25. A B C D E	25. A B C D E	25. A B C D E	25. A B C D E
26. A B C D E	26. A B C D E	26. A B C D E	26. A B C D E
27. A B C D E	27. A B C D E	27. A B C D E	27. A B C D E
28. A B C D E	28. A B C D E	28. A B C D E	28. A B C D E
29. A B C D E	29. A B C D E	29. A B C D E	29. A B C D E
30. A B C D E	30. A B C D E	30. A B C D E	30. A B C D E

SECTION 1
Time—35 minutes
24 questions

<u>Directions for Reading Comprehension Section:</u> Each passage in this section is followed by a group of questions. Answer each question based on what is stated or implied in the passage For some questions, more than one answer choice may be possible, so choose the *best* answer to each question. After you have chosen your answer, mark the corresponding space on the Answer Sheet.

Simply stated, bibliotherapy can be generally defined as the use of books to help people solve problems. Another, more precise definition is that bibliotherapy is a family of techniques used for
(5) structuring interaction between a facilitator and a participant based on mutual sharing of literature. The idea of healing through books is certainly not a new one—it can be traced far back in history, from the days of the first libraries in Greece. The use of
(10) books in healing, however, has been interpreted differently by classical scholars, physicians, psychologists, social workers, nurses, parents, teachers, librarians, and counselors. There is, in fact, confusion in determining the dividing line
(15) between what is simply "reading guidance" and what is actually bibliotherapy. And every piece of professional literature that is available on bibliotherapy naturally mirrors the point of view of the helping professional who wrote it and the field
(20) in which he or she is an expert.

Riordan and Wilson, two notable psychological researchers, in a review of the literature of the effects of bibliotherapy, found that a majority of the studies show mixed results for the efficacy of
(25) bibliotherapy as a separate treatment for the solving of problems. They concluded that bibliotherapy generally appears to be more successful as an adjunctive therapy. Despite such mixed research results, however, interest in the use of bibliotherapy

(30) appears to have increased in the past few years. This most likely reflects the increase of societal and familial problems in the United States—rise in divorce, alienation of young people, excessive peer group pressure, alcohol and drug abuse, and so on.
(35) Educators have also begun to recognize the increasingly critical need for delivering literacy instruction to at-risk and homeless children and their families.

In addition, researchers Riordan and Wilson
(40) concluded that the explosion of self-help programs during the past decade has contributed to the rise in the use of bibliotherapy, in the form of popular self-help books, such as *What Color Is Your Parachute?* and *The Relaxation Response*. Books
(45) such as these are the prescriptive choice of most mental health professionals for their clients, rather than fiction or poetry, according to the two researchers. Is self-help (even directed self-help) really bibliotherapy? This popular practice
(50) underscores the confusion about defining the actual technique of bibliotherapy mentioned at the beginning of this essay. Despite the increased interest in bibliotherapy over the past several years, it seems that until a clearer definition is agreed
(55) upon, inconsistent methods of therapy will lead to inconsistent results in studies on the efficacy of bibliotherapy.

GO ON TO THE NEXT PAGE

1. Which one of the following best expresses the main idea of the passage?

   (A) Although Greek in origin, bibliotherapy is currently considered an American psychological tradition due to its prevalence in America.

   (B) Bibliotherapy is becoming a very powerful psychological treatment for Americans.

   (C) Riordan and Wilson's review of the studies of bibliotherapy found mixed results regarding its efficacy as a psychological treatment.

   (D) Although professionals cannot seem to distinguish between what is "reading guidance" and what is bibliotherapy, they are both commonly considered effective as psychological treatments.

   (E) Despite an increased national interest, the confusion regarding the exact definition of bibliotherapy has led to inconsistent theories about its actual effectiveness.

2. Which one of the following statements about bibliotherapy is best supported by information found in the passage?

   (A) Bibliotherapy is most effective when practiced in conjunction with other treatments.

   (B) Ancient Greek scholars had a much different interpretation from Americans of what bibliotherapy actually is.

   (C) Bibliotherapy is most commonly practiced with children and teenagers.

   (D) Poetry is typically heralded as the best medium for bibliotherapy.

   (E) At-risk children have the most potential for being helped by bibliotherapy.

3. Based on the passage, the author would most likely agree with which one of the following generalizations about bibliotherapy?

   (A) It will likely become one of the more common treatments in America as societal and familial problems continue to rise.

   (B) The most powerful form of bibliotherapy is in directed self-help.

   (C) Its tendency to receive mixed reviews is a direct result of its ambiguous definition.

   (D) Its history has been long and diverse, and its eclecticism is one of its greatest strengths.

   (E) Its sole proponents so far have been Riordan and Wilson.

4. In the first paragraph, the author's primary purpose is to

   (A) provide a basic understanding of bibliotherapy and introduce the controversy relating to its exact definition

   (B) suggest that, while bibliotherapy does not yet have a precise definition, its interpretation is consistent throughout several different disciplines

   (C) build a framework by telling what bibliotherapy is and prepare a debate about each of its components

   (D) offer an alternative to bibliotherapy in what is known as "reading guidance"

   (E) introduce bibliotherapy as a recovering psychological treatment from ancient Greece

GO ON TO THE NEXT PAGE

5. Which one of the following, if true, would most undermine the theory that concludes the passage?

    (A) Bibliotherapy, if used correctly, has the potential to be one of the most effective psychological treatments in years.

    (B) Every current interpretation of bibliotherapy tends to yield relatively predictable results.

    (C) Ancient Greek philosophers had similar difficulties in defining bibliotherapy in an effective manner.

    (D) Interest in bibliotherapy is expected to begin decreasing again over the next few years.

    (E) It will be difficult for proponents of bibliotherapy from so many different disciplines to agree upon a single definition.

6. The author's opinion of Riordan and Wilson is most accurately inferable from which of the following excerpted words?

    (A) adjunctive
    (B) inconsistent
    (C) prescriptive
    (D) notable
    (E) popular

GO ON TO THE NEXT PAGE

In early 1949, North Korea seemed to be on a war footing. Dictator Kim Il Sung's New Year's speech was bellicose and excoriated South Korea as a puppet state. The army expanded rapidly, soldiers
(5) drilled in war maneuvers, and bond drives began to amass the necessary funds to purchase Soviet weaponry. The 38th Parallel was fortified, and border incidents began breaking out. Neither South nor North Korea recognized the parallel as a
(10) permanent legitimate boundary.

Although many aspects of the Korean War remained murky, it seemed that the beginning of conventional war in June 1950 was mainly Kim's decision, and that the key enabling factor was the
(15) existence of as many as 100,000 troops with battle experience in China. When the South Korean regime, with help from United States military advisers, severely reduced the guerrilla threat in the winter of 1949–1950, the civil war moved into a
(20) conventional phase. Kim sought Stalin's backing for his assault, but documents from Soviet and Chinese sources suggested that he got more support from China.

Beginning on June 25, 1950, North Korean
(25) forces fought their way south through the South Korean capital of Seoul. South Korean resistance collapsed as the roads south of Seoul became blocked with refugees, who were fleeing North Korean columns spearheaded with tanks supplied
(30) by the Soviet Union. Task Force Smith, the first United States troops to enter the war, made a futile stand at Suwn, a town some 30 miles south of Seoul. Within a month of the start of the invasion, North Korean forces had seized all but a small
(35) corner of southeastern Korea anchored by the port city of Pusan. Repeated North Korean efforts, blunted by heavy United States Air Force bombing and stubborn resistance by the combined United States and South Korean forces on the Pusan
(40) perimeter, denied Kim Il Sung forceful reunification of the peninsula. The fortunes of war reversed abruptly in early September when General MacArthur boldly landed his forces at Inch'n, the port city for Seoul in west-central Korea. This
(45) action severed the lines of communication and supply between the North Korean army and its base in the north. The army quickly collapsed, and combined United States and South Korean forces drove Kim Il Sung's units northward and into
(50) complete defeat.

The United States thrust in the fall of 1950, however, motivated China to bring its forces in on the northern side; these "volunteers" and the North Korean army pushed United States and South

(55) Korean forces out of North Korea within a month. Although the war lasted another two years, until the summer of 1953, the outcome of early 1951 was definitive: both a stalemate and a United States commitment to containment that accepted the de
(60) facto reality of two Koreas. By the time the armistice was signed in 1953, North Korea had been devastated by three years of bombing attacks that had left almost no modern buildings standing. Both Koreas had watched as their country was
(65) ravaged and their prewar expectations were turned into nightmares.

7. The author's primary purpose is to

(A) argue against some common public misconceptions
(B) analyze a historical event
(C) address bias in historical interpretation
(D) back a controversial theory of foreign social science
(E) connect well-known events that naturally seem incongruous

8. Which of the following is NOT referenced as a prewar condition or event?

(A) the North Korean dictator becoming increasingly belligerent
(B) the preparing of the North Korean military for conflict
(C) the insulting and taunting of the South Korean government by the North Korean dictator
(D) the North Korean repudiation of American negotiation efforts
(E) the fortifying of the North Korean and South Korean border

GO ON TO THE NEXT PAGE

9. Which of the following statements regarding the Korean War is best supported by information given in the passage?

(A) Though it began as a relatively contained civil war, the Korean War played out as an obstinate battle of internationally entangled political powers.
(B) Although both Koreas were nearly destroyed by the war, postwar aid from each Korea's respective allies quickly rebuilt the countries and brought them both into a new age of economic prosperity and political reform.
(C) Even if other countries had not gotten involved, the Korean War would likely have ended very similarly to the way it did.
(D) The Korean War was rather one-sided from the beginning, but it ended in huge losses for the aggressor only.
(E) Although the United States Air Force played an important role in the war, the United States Navy's embargo on North Korea was truly decisive.

10. The quotation marks around the word *volunteers* in line 53 are used to imply which of the following?

(A) The Chinese assistance to North Korea was entirely composed of citizen volunteers sympathetic to the North Korean cause.
(B) These military personnel were volunteered by the Chinese government to North Korea without any North Korean petition.
(C) The Chinese government does not pay its military for their service; rather, military service in China is completely voluntary.
(D) The forces brought into the Korean War by China were mobilized completely in response to United States aid that strengthened South Korea.
(E) Although the Chinese diplomatically masked this military operation as a spontaneous effort by individual volunteers, the forces were most likely sent by the Chinese government.

11. It can be inferred from the passage that the author would most likely describe the results of the Korean War as

(A) regrettably devastating to both Koreas
(B) unforeseeable from prior events in the war
(C) justified with respect to North Korea's groundless aggression
(D) ambiguous, in that no treaty or armistice was ever proposed
(E) abominable, considering America's relative lack of political malleability coupled with its postwar indifference

12. Which of the following would the author describe as a turning point in the Korean War?

(A) North Korean soldiers drilling in combat maneuvers
(B) the United States Air Force bombing North Korean forces on the Pusan perimeter.
(C) General MacArthur landing his forces at the port city of Inch'n
(D) North Korea's fortification of the 38th Parallel.
(E) the arrival of Soviet-supplied tanks to bolster the assault southward

13. Which of the following would most aptly characterize the author's opinion of the Korean War?

(A) pointless and harmful
(B) regrettable and poetic
(C) unavoidable and hard-fought
(D) grateful and diplomatic
(E) avoidable and serene

GO ON TO THE NEXT PAGE

In 1998, the United States sued Microsoft, alleging violations of Sections 1 and 2 of the Sherman Antitrust Act. After trial, the court found Microsoft had violated Section 2 by unlawfully maintaining

(5) its monopoly in the market for Intel-compatible PC operating systems ("OSs") and by unlawfully attempting to monopolize the market for Internet browsers, and that it had violated Section 1 by illegally tying its Windows operating system and its

(10) Internet Explorer ("IE") browser. The court ordered Microsoft to submit a plan of divestiture that would split the company into an OS business and an applications business, and ordered interim conduct restrictions.

(15)   On appeal, the Supreme Court affirmed that Microsoft unlawfully maintained its OS monopoly through specific acts impeding the emergence of two nascent middleware threats to that monopoly. However, it rejected 8 of 20 findings that particular

(20) acts constituted exclusionary conduct and held that Microsoft's general course of conduct was not an additional basis for liability. The Court reversed the determination that Microsoft had attempted to monopolize the browser market in violation of

(25) Section 2. The Court also vacated the judgment on the Section 1 tying claim, remanding it for reconsideration under the rule of reason with specific limits on the government's theories and proof on remand.

(30)   The Court vacated the remedial order and remanded for further proceedings, because, notably, it had "drastically" altered the district court's conclusions on liability, and found that an evidentiary hearing on remedy was necessary.

(35) Recognizing that "as a general matter, a district court is afforded broad discretion to enter that relief it calculates will best remedy the conduct it has found to be unlawful," the Court directed the district court to "reconsider whether the use of the

(40) structural remedy of divestiture is appropriate." Finally, the Court directed the district court to "consider whether plaintiffs have established a sufficient causal connection between Microsoft's anticompetitive conduct and its dominant position

(45) in the operating system market." Absent "clear" indication of a "significant causal connection between the conduct and creation or maintenance of the market power," Microsoft's unlawful behavior "should be remedied by an injunction

(50) against continuation of that conduct." The Court emphasized that it had "found a causal connection between Microsoft's exclusionary conduct and its continuing position in the operating systems market only through inference," and that the district court

(55) "expressly did not adopt the position that Microsoft would have lost its position in the operating system market but for its anticompetitive behavior." The remedy should be "tailored to fit the wrong creating the occasion for the remedy," the Court instructed,

(60) thus leaving both the scope and the particulars of remedy to be addressed in district court.

14. The primary purpose of the third paragraph is to

(A) explain why the Supreme Court remanded the case to the district court
(B) define the term *liability* as applied to this specific case
(C) describe at full length the directions the district court gave the Supreme Court for further proceedings
(D) praise the Supreme Court's decision to vacate the remedial order and remand it for more consideration
(E) specify the parts of the original ruling that were reversed by the Supreme Court

15. The phrase "the scope and the particulars," as used in line 60, could be replaced by which of the following without significantly altering the author's intended meaning?

(A) the range and the depth
(B) the focus and the appropriateness
(C) the extent and the specifications
(D) the documentation and the legality
(E) the pervasiveness and the leniency

GO ON TO THE NEXT PAGE

16. According to the passage, the Supreme Court sent the case back to the district court primarily to

(A) relieve itself of the political pressure of one of the world's richest and most influential corporations

(B) seek an explanation from the district court concerning its first opinion about Microsoft's liability

(C) allow the district court to prepare a written compromise between the various decisions regarding the liability of Microsoft in the antitrust suit

(D) order the district court's reconsideration of what would be an appropriate remedy in the light of the Supreme Court's revision of Microsoft's liability

(E) follow the tradition that cases originating in a district court also terminate in a district court

17. Which one of the following, if true, would most seriously undermine the inference that Microsoft's exclusionary behavior was causally related to its dominant position in the OS market?

(A) Private companies rarely have the financial resources to dominate a market.

(B) Microsoft's domination of the market has resulted directly from its ability to intimidate or buy out potential competitors.

(C) Microsoft's competitors have generally been small companies with unique products, unable to compete with such a well-known and rich corporation.

(D) Other than this single antitrust suit, Microsoft has never been accused of any other illegitimate dealings.

(E) Microsoft's superior products and customer service are of unsurpassable quality and value.

18. Which one of the following statements about Microsoft's antitrust suit is best supported by information given in the passage?

(A) It was the first antitrust case addressed in America in years.

(B) Its conclusion included decisions made by two different courts.

(C) The final remedy decided upon by the district court had little effect on Microsoft other than a substantial fine.

(D) It was the unfortunate result of an outdated law that has not appropriately been repealed.

(E) Little was changed from the district court's original ruling in the Supreme Court's ruling.

GO ON TO THE NEXT PAGE

Mexico's military claims a rich heritage dating back to the pre-Columbian era. As early as the beginning of the 15th century, the Aztec army had achieved a high degree of military organization that
(5) included formal education and training, weapons production, war planning, and the execution of coordinated operations. The importance of military service was impressed upon each young male in the ritual of declaring to him, shortly after birth, that
(10) his destiny was to be a warrior and to die in combat, the most honorable death in Aztec culture. The powers of the Triple Alliance, formed by the urban centers of Tenochtitlán, Texcoco, and Tlacopán —all three of which are in the area of
(15) present-day Mexico City—reportedly could assemble a force of between 16,000 and 18,000 combatants on an hour's notice. Evidence of this indigenous influence on the modern military is found in the profile of an eagle warrior, the name
(20) given Aztec society's fighting elite, on the insignia of the Superior War College in Mexico.

At the beginning of the 16th century, the forces of the Triple Alliance were at the peak of their military development. Nevertheless, when the
(25) Spanish conquistadors under Hernán Cortes arrived in 1519, the native warriors put up little resistance. The two decisive factors in the Spanish victories were the conquistadors' possession of firearms and the mobility they gained from horses, elements of
(30) battle hitherto unknown to the Aztec. The cruelty of the Spanish induced the Aztec to rebel in 1520, and Cortes was forced to abandon the Aztec capital of Tenochtitlán. After launching a new offensive, the Spanish regained control, destroying the
(35) magnificent city. A Spanish alliance with indigenous peoples opposed to the Aztecs, the belief of the Aztec ruler, Montezuma, that Cortes was an Aztec god (whose return was predicted by legend), and the rapid spread of smallpox (carried
(40) from Europe by the Spanish) all contributed to the Spanish victory as well. Despite the Aztecs' continued subterfuge, the Spanish succeeded in superimposing their own theocratic-militaristic traditions on the conquered society.
(45) The Spanish organized the new colony as the Viceroyalty of New Spain and established an army there in the latter part of the 18th century. By 1800 the army's main components were four infantry regiments and two dragoon regiments,
(50) rotated periodically from Spain. These were supported by 10 militia regiments of infantry and 9 regiments of dragoons recruited locally. In all, the army numbered about 30,000 members.

After Mexico gained independence from Spain,
(55) the Mexican armed forces gradually eliminated many practices of the Spanish colonial army. The practice of granting military officers special rights or inappropriate privileges was abolished in 1855. The military also phased out the 19th-century
(60) practice of forced conscription, which often filled the ranks with criminals or other social undesirables whom local leaders wished to be rid of. Two legacies still remain from the years of colonial rule, however: the use of the original Spanish military
(65) ranks and the high prestige traditionally accorded to cavalry units.

19. The primary purpose of the passage is to

(A) debate whether the Aztecs or the Spanish were more influential culturally on the modern Mexican army
(B) explain Mexico's military history through myths of social changes in Mexican history
(C) describe the origins of Mexico's rich military heritage
(D) impress the reader with the advanced military organization of the ancient Aztecs
(E) chronicle the gradual elimination of colonial Spanish practices from the Mexican military

20. According to the passage, which one of the following accounts for the prevalence of theocracy in the modern Mexican military?

(A) The Aztecs considered religious justification a moral necessity for going into battle.
(B) The Viceroyalty of New Spain could assemble a force almost twice as large as the Aztec force that came before.
(C) The colonial Spanish impressed their religion-based military traditions upon the conquered Aztecs in the 16th century.
(D) Cortes was thought to be an Aztec god upon his arrival in Mexico.
(E) Forced conscription in the 19th century drew many religious men into military service.

GO ON TO THE NEXT PAGE

21. The author asserts that Cortes's relatively easy victory over the Aztecs was a result of all of the following EXCEPT

    (A) the Spaniards' superior numbers of servicemen
    (B) the Aztecs' inferior weaponry and defenses
    (C) the Spaniards' alliances with Aztec enemies
    (D) the Aztecs' vulnerability to European disease
    (E) the Spaniards' mobility gained from horses

22. The author's use of the word *subterfuge* in line 42 primarily refers to

    (A) the expression of gratitude for the conquistadors who brought the Aztecs freedom
    (B) Aztecan attempts to revolt against their Spanish conquerors
    (C) the Aztecan tradition of separating religion and military
    (D) strategies devised by the Aztecs to avoid assimilation with the Spanish
    (E) positive attitudes the Aztecs had about various European cultures

23. The author would most likely agree with which of the following statements regarding the practices of the Spanish colonial army?

    (A) Most of the practices would be considered dignified and respectable even under the majority of modern moral codes.
    (B) Because the Spanish colonial army was considered a distinguished organization, most of its regular practices deserved commendation.
    (C) In many ways, practices of the colonial Spanish army were riddled with haughtiness and indifference.
    (D) The natives over whom the colonial army ruled considered the practices unpleasant at times, though generally necessary.
    (E) The prestige awarded to cavalry units was quickly stripped away in the wake of 20th-century technology.

24. Which of the following points about Mexican history is LEAST important to its rich military heritage?

    (A) The Aztecan Empire was conquered by theocratic Spanish conquistadors.
    (B) Many of the colonial Spanish military practices were immoral and inhumane.
    (C) Gunpowder was introduced in Mexico around the time of the arrival of the first Spanish forces.
    (D) The Spanish brought horses with them to the New World.
    (E) The Aztecs had an advanced and proud military tradition, far ahead of their time.

S T O P

IF YOU FINISH BEFORE TIME RUNS OUT, CHECK YOUR WORK ON THIS SECTION ONLY.
DO NOT GO ON TO ANY OTHER TEST SECTION.

SECTION 2
Time—35 minutes
26 questions

<u>Directions for Logic Games Questions:</u> The questions in this section are divided into groups. Each group is based on a set of conditions. For each question, choose the answer that is most accurate and complete. For some questions, you may wish to draw a rough diagram to help you select your response. Mark the corresponding space on your Answer Sheet.

<u>Questions 1–6</u>

Joe the cook has three very particular customers: Sharon, Tom, and Violet. Sharon likes meals with exactly two ingredients, while Tom and Violet like meals with exactly three ingredients. To satisfy his hungry customers, Joe keeps in stock apples, bacon, eggs, and flour, and he spices his meals with curry, dill, and ginger. Joe makes a meal for each customer every morning with the following conditions:

Sharon eats only ingredients that no one else is eating that day.
Tom insists on having curry in every meal.
No one will eat a meal containing only spices.
Joe uses every ingredient in at least one of the meals each day.
Sharon never eats apples with any spices.
Violet will eat flour only when it is spiced with dill.

1. If Sharon has apples and Violet has eggs and flour, what could Tom eat?

(A) apples, curry, and eggs
(B) apples, curry, and ginger
(C) bacon, dill, and flour
(D) curry, dill, and ginger
(E) curry, eggs, and ginger

2. If Violet refuses to eat spices one day, what could Sharon order?

(A) apples and dill
(B) bacon and flour
(C) curry and flour
(D) eggs and ginger
(E) flour and ginger

3. Tom orders bacon, curry, and eggs. What can Violet NOT order?

(A) apples
(B) bacon
(C) curry
(D) flour
(E) ginger

4. Tom orders curry, flour, and ginger. What can Violet order?

(A) apples, dill, and eggs
(B) apples, dill, and flour
(C) bacon, curry, and eggs
(D) bacon, eggs, and ginger
(E) bacon, flour, and curry

5. Tom and Violet both order flour. What can Sharon NOT order?

(A) apples and bacon
(B) apples and ginger
(C) bacon and eggs
(D) bacon and ginger
(E) eggs and ginger

6. One day Joe runs out of eggs and flour. What must Sharon order?

(A) apples
(B) bacon
(C) curry
(D) dill
(E) ginger

GO ON TO THE NEXT PAGE

Questions 7–12

At a dancing contest, there are seven stalls, numbered from 1 to 7, available for changing into costume. However, the dancers are very particular about who is in the stalls near them. No dancer shares a stall and all dancers R, S, T, U, V, W, and X use a stall concurrently with the other dancers. The arrangement of the stalls is governed by the following conditions:

T is always in a lower-numbered stall than R.
If S is in stall 4, then U is in stall 5.
If U is in stall 6, then S is in stall 7.
V cannot be in a stall with a number consecutive to the number of W's stall.

7. Which of the following could NOT be an order of the dancers in the stalls from least to greatest?

(A) T, R, S, U, V, X, W
(B) T, X, S, U, V, R, W
(C) X, S, U, V, T, W, R
(D) V, U, T, S, X, R, W
(E) T, X, V, R, W, U, S

8. If V and W are placed in stalls 5 and 7, respectively, then which of the following is a pair of people, NEITHER of whom could be placed in stall 6?

(A) R, S
(B) S, T
(C) T, U
(D) X, R
(E) U, X

9. If T goes in stall 3 and S goes in stall 4, then which of the following must be true?

(A) X goes in stall 1 or 2.
(B) R is in a lower-numbered stall than V.
(C) W is in a lower-numbered stall than T.
(D) X and T are in consecutive stalls.
(E) R and W are in consecutive stalls.

10. If five stalls are in between V and W, then which of the following must NOT be true?

(A) T and R are before W.
(B) T is in stall 5.
(C) R is not in a lower-numbered stall than S.
(D) U is in stall 6.
(E) W and X are in consecutive stalls.

11. If S goes in stall 4 and T goes in stall 6, then we know the position of how many dancers total, including T and S?

(A) one
(B) two
(C) three
(D) four
(E) five

12. If T goes in stall 5 and U is not in stall 7, then which of the following must NOT be true?

(A) V and W are in lower-numbered stalls than T.
(B) X is not in a higher-numbered stall than T.
(C) R and U are in consecutive stalls.
(D) T is not in a consecutive stall with X or V.
(E) U is in stall consecutive with S and T.

GO ON TO THE NEXT PAGE

<u>Questions 13–19</u>

In the log ride at a local theme park, there are eight seats per log. The seats are composed of four rows and two columns that resemble the following diagram (1–2 being the front of the log):

1   2
3   4
5   6
7   8

Eight people, A, B, C, D, E, F, G, and H, ride the ride and are seated according to the following constraints:

B sits in the same row as C.
A sits in the same row on the left of D.
E sits immediately in front of D.
A sits two seats behind F.

13. If G sits in seat 4, then which of the following must be true?

(A) H sits in seat 5.
(B) C sits in seat 1.
(C) B sits in seat 1.
(D) D sits in seat 6.
(E) A sits in seat 2.

14. If E does not sit in the third row, then which of the following must be true?

(A) H sits in the first row.
(B) A sits in the second row.
(C) B sits in the fourth row.
(D) C sits on the left.
(E) A sits on the right.

15. Which person could potentially sit in the greatest number of rows?

(A) A
(B) B
(C) F
(D) H
(E) C

16. Who could never sit in the same row?

(A) H, E
(B) G, F
(C) A, D
(D) G, H
(E) B, C

17. If A sits in a lower-numbered seat than B, then which of the following must NOT be true?

(A) G shares a row with E.
(B) B sits immediately behind D.
(C) D sits in the same column as H.
(D) F shares a row with C.
(E) A shares a row with D.

18. Who could never sit next to or immediately behind B?

(A) C
(B) D
(C) F
(D) G
(E) H

19. How many different seating configurations are possible for this game?

(A) six
(B) eight
(C) ten
(D) twelve
(E) fourteen

GO ON TO THE NEXT PAGE

A veterinarian will see seven cats each day of this week, starting Monday and ending Sunday. Only one cat will be seen each day, and the vet's medical charts refer to the cats as A, B, C, D, E, F, and G. The order that the cats will be seen in is governed by the following:

Cat D will be seen before cat G.
Cat G will be seen before cat B.
If cat A is seen on either Monday or Tuesday, then cat D will be seen on Friday.
If cat D is seen on Monday or Tuesday, then cat A will be seen later in the week than Friday.
Cat A is seen before cat E.

20. Which of the following could be the order in which the cats are seen, from Monday to Sunday?

   (A) D, C, F, B, G, A, E
   (B) G, A, E, B, D, C, F
   (C) A, C, F, E, D, G, B
   (D) D, A, E, C, F, G, B
   (E) C, A, F, D, E, G, B

21. If neither D nor A is scheduled for Monday or Tuesday, then we know the exact position of how many cats?

   (A) none
   (B) one
   (C) two
   (D) three
   (E) four

22. If neither D nor A is scheduled for Monday or Tuesday, then which of the following must be true?

   (A) Cat A is seen before cat D.
   (B) Cat B is seen on Sunday.
   (C) Cats C and F are seen on consecutive days.
   (D) Cat D is seen on Wednesday.
   (E) Cats B and E are seen on consecutive days.

23. If Cat A is seen on Tuesday, then which of the following must be true?

   (A) F is seen on a day consecutive with either A or D.
   (B) F is seen on a day later than D.
   (C) C is seen on a day later than A.
   (D) A is seen on a day consecutive with E.
   (E) We know the exact positions of exactly five cats.

24. If cat F is seen on Tuesday, cat G is seen on Thursday, and cat C is seen on Wednesday, then which of the following must NOT be true?

   (A) Cat G is seen after cat C.
   (B) Cat D is seen before cat F.
   (C) Cat G is seen before cats B and A.
   (D) Cat B is seen after cat A.
   (E) Cat E is seen on Sunday.

25. If cat D is seen on Tuesday and cat F is seen after cat G, then we know the exact position of how many cats?

   (A) three
   (B) four
   (C) five
   (D) six
   (E) seven

26. If cat A is seen on Friday and cat G is seen on Thursday, then which of the following must be true?

   (A) Cat F is seen on Monday.
   (B) Cat E is seen on Sunday.
   (C) Cat D is seen on Wednesday.
   (D) Cat B is seen on Sunday.
   (E) Cat C is seen on Tuesday.

S T O P

IF YOU FINISH BEFORE TIME RUNS OUT, CHECK YOUR WORK ON THIS SECTION ONLY.
DO NOT GO ON ANY OTHER TEST SECTION.

SECTION 3
Time—35 minutes
26 questions

<u>Directions for Logical Reasoning Questions:</u> The question in this section are based on brief statements or passages. Choose your answers based on the reasoning in each passage. Do not make assumptions the are not supported by the passage or by common sense. For some questions, more than one answer choice may be possible, so choose the *best* answer to each question, that is, the one that is most accurate and complete. After you have chosen your answer, mark the corresponding space on the Answer Sheet.

1. Global positioning systems ("GPSs") are widely used to help people navigate through unknown areas. In the wilderness, if people can find an open spot that is not blocked by mountains or by trees, their handheld GPSs can inform them of their exact position and the direction that they need to travel in order to reach their destination. Recently, GPSs have been added to cars and combined with road map data to create a system that tells drivers to turn when they should in order to drive to their particular destination.

   Which of the following can be concluded from the passage?

   (A) GPSs in cars do not work when under bridges or near mountains.
   (B) All cars will soon be equipped with GPSs.
   (C) Global positioning systems never lead people to the incorrect place.
   (D) GPSs can be used in areas with little satellite coverage.
   (E) A person's destination can be input into the GPS.

2. Alligators normally do not go very far from their natural habitats. Over the course of an alligator's entire lifetime, it will usually travel only between 15 and 25 miles from where it was born. However, there are some "explorer" alligators that unwittingly "sign up" for the circus and are carted thousands of miles away from their homes and birthplaces. Even though it is probable that these alligators experience great adventures and see things that they would never have seen had they not been hijacked into the circus, they never would have traveled so far away from their homes had humans not intervened in their lives.

   Which of the following is an assumption that would make this argument logical?

   (A) An alligator could never travel more than 25 miles outside of its home without the help of another creature.
   (B) Alligators can sometimes be caught in oceanic squalls that will transport them to the other side of the ocean unharmed.
   (C) No alligator has ever traveled as far and wide as the alligators that are in the circus.
   (D) Only an alligator in the circus could travel thousands of miles from its original home.
   (E) No other creatures can interfere in the lives of animals to the extent that humans can.

GO ON TO THE NEXT PAGE

3. People who have risen to the top of the governmental hierarchy in our country are extremely intelligent. Most politicians have attended not only college but also some sort of graduate school. Without this academic background, they would not have the requisite brainpower to impress the populace enough to gain its vote. It is counterintuitive, therefore, that highly intelligent people searching for honest solutions to our nation's problems should need to group themselves into disagreeing factions. We can only conclude that while getting into office is directly tied to a person's intelligence, his or her political opinions are not.

Which one of the following most accurately identifies an error in the author's conclusion?

(A) The author ignores the fact that people who are not intelligent or did not go to college vie for political office.
(B) The author mistakenly assumes that a person's level of brainpower helps him or her get elected.
(C) The author makes an assumption that all politicians are equally intelligent.
(D) The author omits the fact that people hold different opinions due to their ethics and religious convictions.
(E) The author contends that people disagree about solutions to national issues without articulating specific problems.

4. Child: Mom, I took the dog outside this morning before we left. There is no way that he could have gotten inside during the day and eaten up the furniture. I left him in the yard.

Parent: The dog must have gotten inside somehow. I hesitate to believe your story that your little brother chewed up our couch.

Which one of the following, if true, most helps to reconcile the child's story with the parent's opinion?

(A) Whenever the dog gets the chance, he gnaws on every available piece of furniture in the house.
(B) The child forgot to lock the doggy door, which the dog can use to enter the house.
(C) The child's little brother has a penchant for gnawing on his pacifier while he's sleeping.
(D) The dog has never before touched a piece of furniture in the house.
(E) The child's older brother came home at midday and did not let the dog in from outside.

GO ON TO THE NEXT PAGE

5. Cell phones are slowly changing the world and merging people with computers. Anytime and anyplace, people can receive electrical signals that connect them with others and allow them to communicate, gain knowledge, and interact with the rest of the world. People enjoy this situation so much that many have already become effectively conjoined with their cell phones. In a few decades human implants will replace cell phones as scientists find ways to allow biological neurons to interact and communicate with computer chips.

Which of the following, if true, would tend to support the argument?

(A) Electronic cell phones will never be able to interact with biological neurons.
(B) Scientists have already found ways to merge artificial limbs with neurons in an amputee's body.
(C) The government will not disallow people from permanently conjoining their physical bodies with computer chips.
(D) In the future, people will find it increasingly inconvenient not to house electronic implements within their bodies.
(E) The technology will be present one day to make a half-person/half-machine sentient humanoid figure.

6. Environmentalist: Oil consumers decry the probability that the earth will be unable to provide enough oil to sustain the operation of twice as many petroleum-dependent cars as are driven today. But there are many benefits to this limit. Our population will be forced to find a different method of producing energy. We will not pump any more oil-related pollutants into our air or rivers. We will also reduce our dependence on foreign nations that currently sell oil to our nation.

The environmentalist uses which of the following argumentative methods to advance the passage's point?

(A) Chooses one alternative from several by using the process of elimination.
(B) Shows that a consideration often cited only as a limitation can produce many positives.
(C) Attacks the proponents of a particular view rather than the substantive portions of their view.
(D) Exposes a particular group's position as morally derelict and devoid of any potential positive gain.
(E) Mischaracterizes the opinion of a particular group in order to better prove her or his own point.

GO ON TO THE NEXT PAGE

7. Tom: Area 51 was an army base where aliens landed several decades ago. Many people believe that the aliens crash-landed, but I was there and I know the truth: They intentionally landed in order to begin their takeover. Unfortunately for them, they found that we humans are not to be trifled with, especially those of us who are in the army. We routed their attack and captured their leader. After the firefight subsided, the CIA was contacted and it flew down special agents in order to cover up the entire debacle. This cover-up was only partially successful, which is why so many people have heard tiny details about the affair.

Which of the following can be concluded, if the information supplied by Tom is correct?

(A) Extraterrestrials have tried to invade the United States.
(B) Aliens can be killed with the use of conventional bullets.
(C) The current CIA director knows all the facts surrounding the Area 51 invasion.
(D) There have not been alien invasions since Area 51.
(E) No one will ever know the truth about what took place at Area 51.

8. Dodgeball has been played since the early 16th century, when it was first invented by noblemen in the English court. These knights compared the dodgeball to a cannonball and reasoned that if they could dodge a light metal ball being hurled at them from a couple of yards away, then they would easily be able to dodge a spear or cannonball that was shot at them from a long distance. Many attempts at proving the effectiveness of their theories failed, but nevertheless, the game gained in popularity with the children of the nation and was played in schoolyards daily for the next five centuries.

Which of the following, if true, would tend to support the contentions of the argument?

(A) Dodgeball was never played before the early 16th century.
(B) Children were encouraged to play dodgeball by their teachers.
(C) Knights who tried to dodge cannonballs almost always died.
(D) Being hit by light metal balls hurts much worse than being hit by a plastic ball.
(E) English soldiers were killed less often by arrows shot at them after the 15th century than before.

GO ON TO THE NEXT PAGE

9. Cell phones used to be utilized only for talking to friends and family. Now, technological advances have added entirely new capabilities to cellular phones. There are phones that can take pictures, phones that can shoot movie clips, phones that allow you to surf the Internet, and phones that enable you to determine your location based on a Global Positioning System, or GPS. Future technological advances are likely to yield even more gadgets that will be absorbed into the body of a cellular phone, making this device serve more and more functions as time goes on.

Which of the following can you infer from the passage?

(A) GPS was put into the cellular phone after the capability to surf the Internet.
(B) Cell phones will get more and more expensive as time passes and more technological advances occur.
(C) The total number of functions able to be included in a cellular phone has not yet been exceeded.
(D) Cell phones are just as capable of performing functions as devices that are dedicated solely to these functions.
(E) Cell phones are no longer used to make calls between family and friends.

10. June and Betty are trying to sell their house but they have been having problems finding buyers because the house is infested with termites. They called the company TermExterm to treat their house for termites, hoping that spraying would fix their problem. Little did they know, however, that TermExterm covertly released more bugs into the woodwork of their house. Betty discovered the new bugs the next day and decided that TermExterm released the bugs in hopes that she and June would rehire the company to exterminate again. In fact, TermExterm did not spray for bugs at all when they came to visit, so it logically follows that the woodwork in June and Betty's house is still being slowly destroyed.

Which of the following, if true, would undermine the conclusion of the passage?

(A) TermExterm has been around for 42 years and has never before been cited for a bad business practice.
(B) The woodwork in the houses of 97% of the customers of TermExterm is not being slowly destroyed after the company leaves.
(C) June and Betty will be forced to spray for termites on their own if TermExterm does not return to spray for them.
(D) TermExterm utilizes the most technologically advanced spraying techniques to eradicate termites.
(E) The bugs that TermExterm released are natural predators of termites.

GO ON TO THE NEXT PAGE

11. If the law punishes speeding, then the city has an obligation to put up speed limit signs. But Mohegan County does not punish speeders, so its cities have no obligation to post speed limit signs.

    Which one of the following contains the same type of flawed reasoning as the argument above?

    (A) If the law punishes gambling, then it has an obligation to create other ways for people to make money. Las Vegas does not punish people for gambling, so it has no obligation to create other ways for people to make money.

    (B) If the college does not punish cheating, then it has no obligation to monitor people taking exams. Since it does not monitor people taking exams, the college must not punish cheating.

    (C) If the law punishes tax evasion, then it is obligated to provide easy ways for people to do their taxes. Since the law does punish tax evasion, it must provide people with easy ways of doing their taxes.

    (D) If a team cannot function well communally, then it has an obligation to promote interpersonal relationships. However, team A functions well communally, so its members have good interpersonal relationships.

    (E) If a parent punishes children for swearing, then the parent is obligated to teach the children cleaner words with which to express themselves. Since the Browns don't punish their children for swearing, they aren't obligated to teach their children cleaner words.

12. Truck drivers are more inclined than vacationing drivers to stop at rest stops. It is hard to determine whether this is because truck drivers have been on the road for more hours than vacationing drivers or because vacationing drivers actually enjoy being on the road for longer periods of time because they do not normally drive for so many hours in succession. Either way, when vacationing drivers visit a rest stop, they are likely to see more vacationing drivers than truck drivers.

    Which of the following is an assumption that could be made in order for the argument's conclusion to be logically drawn?

    (A) Rest stops do not meet the same needs of vacationing drivers and truckers.

    (B) Truckers are most likely to stop at rest stops at the same times of day as other truckers.

    (C) Truckers sleep in their trucks more often than vacationing drivers sleep in their cars.

    (D) There are more vacationing drivers on the road than truck drivers.

    (E) Rest stops charge truck drivers more for their purchases than they charge vacationing drivers.

GO ON TO THE NEXT PAGE

13. Gambler: The overall lottery payout keeps increasing every time someone does not win. When people do not win, they are more likely not to play again in the near future. So to have the best chances of winning the money, all I have to do is wait until the payout gets very large before buying my tickets.

Which of the following, if true, calls into question the validity of the gambler's argument?

(A) Large payouts are often split between several winners who have played a lottery in the past.

(B) Advertisements of large payouts cause droves of people who have not played the lottery in the recent past to buy tickets.

(C) People who win the lottery are more likely to play the lottery in the near future than are people who lose the lottery.

(D) Some people consistently lose the lottery but continue to play it regardless of whether the prospective payout is large or small.

(E) The lottery is a massive wealth reallocating scheme, and anyone not seeking huge payouts will soon be restricted from taking part.

14. There are two different types of muscles: slow twitch and fast twitch. People with mostly slow-twitch muscles are very good at long-distance running, whereas people with predominantly fast-twitch muscles are good at sprinting. People with predominantly fast-twitch muscles can train to become superior marathon runners, but people with mostly slow-twitch muscles are incapable of becoming consummate sprinters.

Which of the following would explain this discrepancy?

(A) People can train their slow-twitch muscles to twitch faster than fast-twitch muscles.

(B) A property of fast-twitch muscles allows them to assume the attributes of slow-twitch muscles.

(C) Most people who are world-class marathon runners have predominantly fast-twitch muscles.

(D) Muscles cannot change their type; i.e., slow-twitch muscles cannot become fast-twitch muscles.

(E) A scientist claims that fast-twitch muscles are more capable of long-distance running than slow-twitch muscles are.

GO ON TO THE NEXT PAGE

15. To reach the nearest star system, astronauts have only two possible courses of action. One is to make a wormhole near the edge of our own solar system that would transport us immediately into the space occupied by the nearest star system. The only other potential course of action would be to create a ship capable of speeds that can approximate the speed of light. Our scientists have determined that creating a spaceship able to travel at even a quarter of the speed of light is practically impossible. Therefore, to travel to the nearest solar system, astronauts will have to find a way to create a wormhole.

To reach the conclusion, the author employs which of the following methods of reasoning?

(A) Generalizes a controlling principle on the basis of two competing observations that are found within the passage.

(B) Offers evidence that is relevant to neither of the competing alternatives given in the passage's opening lines.

(C) Indirectly establishes the validity of a certain conclusion by arguing that the alternative is impossible.

(D) Creates a hypothetical proposition by eliminating several possibilities in favor of a specific possibility.

(E) Strongly advocates undertaking a specific course of action on the premise that an alternative course of action is theoretically impossible.

16. A ghostwritten manuscript generally gains more attention than would a similar book published by the author under his or her own name. However, the attention is meaningless to the ghostwriter because all the fame surrounding the book will be focused directly on the titular writer of the book. So basically, the ghostwriter goes through laborious efforts to write an entire manuscript for which he or she will never receive any credit from the public. It is always a better idea for ghostwriters to go ahead and publish their books under their own names, thereby beginning to gain fame for themselves.

Which of the following is an assumption that must be made for the argument to be logically drawn?

(A) Authors who use ghostwriters are generally more popular than authors who have ghostwritten themselves.

(B) Publishers encourage ghostwriters to write books for famous people because these books tend to make more money than books written by unknowns.

(C) Fame is the major and singularly compelling issue associated with writing a manuscript.

(D) Ghostwriters engage in morally dubious behavior when they allow someone to lie about the creation of their manuscript.

(E) Famous people would almost always be better served by publishing books written by themselves rather than by ghostwriters.

GO ON TO THE NEXT PAGE

17. Insecticides are dangerous chemicals. The insects that these chemicals are designed to kill are some of the hardiest creatures on the planet. Therefore, it takes some very potent poisons to kill them. For this reason, trace amounts of insecticides are enough to make humans very sick, but some people do not realize this fact and spray insecticides indiscriminately around their houses. Care should be taken to understand the potential effects of the active and inactive ingredients in insecticides, because then people will be able to avoid using them improperly.

Which of the following, if true, would tend to support the conclusion?

(A) Bugs in general are a hardier form of life than human beings are.

(B) The potent chemicals in insecticides could kill a person if they were imbibed.

(C) When people understand the effects of ingredients in products, they use these products in safer ways.

(D) Insecticides should never be used in a household with children who like to crawl around searching for things in the corners.

(E) Insecticides are not the only way for a person to eradicate arthropodan pests from an infested household.

18. Linguist: People who speak several languages fluently are able to learn an additional language more quickly than other students. This is because by learning another language, you are able to view the idiosyncrasies of your native tongue. All people should learn a second language so that they will be more proficient at learning a third, if the need ever arises.

Student: A more realistic solution would be to encourage people to give more thought to the type of second language that they would like to learn so that they will never need or desire to learn a third.

Which is the inference most supported by the argument of the linguist?

(A) The average American takes more time to learn Chinese than English.

(B) The average bilingual person will learn another language more slowly than the average trilingual person.

(C) The average Japanese person learning a second language will take less time learning Chinese than learning English.

(D) A Spaniard who knows English and Spanish fluently will learn Chinese in less time than it took to learn Spanish.

(E) The average English person will learn his or her first language faster than the average Chinese person.

GO ON TO THE NEXT PAGE

19. Astronauts have sent probes to Mars in an effort to find out whether life has existed on the red planet. The last series of probes found water but no life-forms or biological traces. Satellite imagery of the planet surface also has not revealed any evidence of life. Thus, there is clearly no life on Mars.

The reasoning in the passage is flawed because it

(A) treats evidence that is necessary to draw a conclusion as evidence that is not sufficient to support a conclusion
(B) confuses an absence of evidence for a hypothesis with the existence of evidence against the hypothesis
(C) interprets a disagreement over a theoretical postulation as a disproof of that postulation
(D) makes a decision regarding a theoretical impossibility by using a full complement of facts that support a possibility.
(E) assumes that a characteristic applies to an entire group when it applies only to a specific part of the group

20. Sibling rivalries should not be discounted because they are often the basis of future behavior. Some boys who are athletic but who have brothers taking part in several sports will choose to play different sports from the ones in which their siblings compete—merely in order not to have to vie with their older brothers. If a younger brother excels in a certain field, then often an older brother will not want to go into that field, thereby avoiding the possibility of feeling inferior to his younger sibling. On the other hand, there are brothers who seek competition. These brothers try to dominate and outcompete each other. Their relationships only result in feelings of subjugation or superiority and actions that are not even remotely supportive. It is better for sibling rivalry to cause dispersion rather than competition.

Which of the following, if true, would best support the conclusion of the passage?

(A) Brothers who engage in noncompetitive behavior have a hard time achieving superiority in their fields.
(B) Competitive brothers tend to be less happy than brothers who do not seek to compete.
(C) Sisters who compete tend to display positive social and personal effects because of this competition.
(D) Brothers who compete together without feeling inferior are better off than those who do feel inferior.
(E) Universal notions of "brotherly love" lead us to believe that it results from competition.

GO ON TO THE NEXT PAGE

21. Being a pizza delivery person must be one of the most interesting jobs in the world. You get to travel all day long and meet lots of different people. More than anything else, though, you never know who or what is going to open the door when you knock. This type of variety is not present in your normal Wall Street or legal job—or any other job, for that matter. Therefore, being a pizza delivery person is the best job in the world.

Which of the following must be assumed to make this a logical argument?

(A) Variety is the sole characteristic that determines the greatness of a job.
(B) Wall Street traders do not get to travel around the world and meet lots of people.
(C) Legal jobs are not as interesting as the job of pizza delivery.
(D) Pizza delivery persons do not receive as much compensation as workers in other jobs, because the intrinsic fun of the job pays for itself.
(E) Good jobs are determined by how interesting they are, their variety, and how many new people they allow you to meet.

22. People should stop watching TV because they never benefit when they do. Undoubtedly, there are entertaining shows on TV and people have fun while watching, but people who watch a great amount of TV are generally more boring than those who do not. People who would rather watch TV than do anything else allow TV to become detrimental to their overall well-being. Therefore, I can only conclude that TV watchers either have masochistic tendencies or want to be boring.

The argument is flawed because it

(A) attacks the merits of a claim by attacking the proponents of that claim
(B) accepts that a conclusion is true when it is clear that those who support the conclusion benefit from that conclusion being true
(C) concludes that a particular piece of data is inapplicable because another piece of data is less applicable than most of the others
(D) conveniently overlooks evidence that offers more convincing support for an alternate conclusion
(E) makes a misleading assumption due to the misinterpretation of the key term *detrimental*

GO ON TO THE NEXT PAGE

23. Tattoos are a very enigmatic trend of juvenile life. In general, young adults have a very hard time committing to anything: jobs, relationships, and even places to live. However, many have no trouble at all committing to a long-term relationship with a tattoo. Some get tattooed on a night of revelry and are sorry about it for many years, but others do it purposefully. These people rationalize their commitment by labeling the tattoo as a piece of art or a pronouncement of love for a girlfriend or boyfriend. This reasoning is strange, because you do not see teenagers buying houses, or even furniture, with their sweethearts.

Which of the following is the main point of the argument?

(A) It is strange that some teenagers get tattoos when they refuse to make commitments in most other areas of their lives.
(B) Teenagers should think twice before getting a tattoo.
(C) There are better ways of declaring love to a significant other than by tattooing that person's name on a body part.
(D) Juveniles should refrain from making only one specific kind of commitment when they are afraid of making all other kinds of commitments.
(E) Tattoo artists should not tattoo people who are obviously partying so much that they may not have good judgment.

24. For every person entering a poker tournament, it is a reasonable belief that he or she will lose. Therefore, it is reasonable to believe that no one will win a poker tournament.

Which one of the following exhibits the same logical flaw as the argument above?

(A) Generally, no employees at company X are promoted to manager. Therefore, it makes sense that no one will be promoted.
(B) Usually, no one soccer team has a good probability to win the championships. Therefore, it makes sense that only one team will win.
(C) More than likely, any horse that enters a horse race will lose, so it makes sense to believe that no horse will win the race.
(D) Except under exceptional circumstances, no new band will become famous, so it is logical to believe that no new band has ever become famous.
(E) For every dime that is spent on taxes, 99 percent of it goes to "bureaucratic shuffling," so it makes sense to assume that little of our tax dollars is used well.

GO ON TO THE NEXT PAGE

25. Salesperson: Mailboxes come in all shapes and size, all colors and configurations. However, there are several functional considerations that should be taken into account when you are selecting a mailbox. First, would anyone want to take your mail before you see it? Second, are there teenagers in your subdivision who could vandalize your mailbox, if given the opportunity? If you answered yes to both of these questions, then MailRight 2000 is the product for you. It is the premier mailbox on the market, disallowing unauthorized keyless entry and able to withstand many kinds of vandalism, even a battering by bats. If your mail is susceptible to risks, then only by purchasing MailRight 2000 can you keep your mail safe.

Which of the following is an assumption required by the argument?

(A) MailRight 2000 is able to sustain the security of your mail under all kinds of attacks.
(B) Your subdivision is the only place where MailRight 2000 can be used effectively.
(C) Houses without MailRight 2000 will be broken into by hooligans who want to steal the mail inside.
(D) Your postal carrier will not give you mail if he or she does not have the key to open your mailbox.
(E) If people have the ability to negatively affect the safety of your mail, then they will.

26. Medical doctors have demonstrated that having low levels of calcium in one's diet correlates inversely with the incidence of a condition of the bones called *osteoporosis*. The characteristics of this condition are brittle bones, which are more susceptible to injury than normal, healthy bones. A recent study has shown that the concentration of calcium in bones of people with osteoporosis is lower than the concentration of calcium in normal bones. Therefore, in order to decrease a person's chance of getting osteoporosis, he or she should increase the dietary intake of calcium.

The argument of this passage is flawed for which one of the following reasons?

(A) It fails to identify alternate characteristics that are associated with a lack of calcium in a person's daily diet.
(B) It ignores the fact that low levels of calcium in bones can lead to many other problems besides osteoporosis.
(C) It assumes that because people have osteoporosis, they will also have a low concentration of calcium in their bones.
(D) Its proposition that lower calcium levels correlate with osteoporosis implies that calcium intake could alleviate the condition.
(E) It fails to demonstrate that a low calcium level in the bones causes osteoporosis.

STOP

IF YOU FINISH BEFORE TIME RUNS OUT, CHECK YOUR WORK ON THIS SECTION ONLY.
DO NOT GO ON ANY OTHER TEST SECTION.

SECTION 4
Time—35 minutes
25 questions

<u>Directions for Logical Reasoning Questions:</u> The question in this section are based on brief statements or passages. Choose your answers based on the reasoning in each passage. Do not make assumptions that are not supported by the passage or by common sense. For some questions, more than one answer choice may be possible, so choose the *best* answer to each question, that is, the one that is most accurate and complete. After you have chosen your answer, mark the corresponding space on the Answer Sheet.

1. Referee: I am sorry, but your last shot was out. When a tennis ball lands outside of the court boundaries without touching the line, then it is out.

    Tennis Player: But my ball was not out. It seems that your calls are unfairly favoring the other player. If my last ball was out, then all of her shots that you called in over the past couple of games must have been out.

    For the tennis player's argument to be logically correct, which of the following assumptions must be made?

    (A) The referee is unfairly siding with her opponent.
    (B) Tennis is a game where it is impossible post facto to determine whether a ball landed out.
    (C) The referee was watching while the last point occurred.
    (D) Her opponent is currently beating her in the match.
    (E) Her last shot either hit the line or was within the court's boundaries.

2. The Great Wall of China was built in order to prevent nomads and wandering warrior bands from entering the Chinese countryside in order to ravage and pillage the towns. However, the ranging warrior bands could climb over the wall, and numerous Chinese soldiers were required to guard the wall in order to ensure that no one climbed over. Since the wall required numerous soldiers, it seems that the emperor of China could have saved a lot of money by not building the wall at all; instead, he could have deployed to the individual cities those members of the army who would have guarded the wall. This deployment would have had the same effect as the wall, and the emperor would not have wasted so much money on building a huge stone structure across his countryside.

    Which of the following, if true, would support the argument above?

    (A) China was plagued by warrior bands inside of the wall in addition to those outside.
    (B) The emperor built the wall more as a monument to his greatness than for any other reason.
    (C) Villagers could have been taught by soldiers to more adequately defend themselves.
    (D) The countryside of China was not safe for builders of the Great Wall to traverse without accompaniment.
    (E) There was no added defensive advantage to guarding a wall as opposed to a town.

GO ON TO THE NEXT PAGE

3. Salesperson: Packages that are shipped around December 10 should be wrapped extra carefully because of the high volume of packages that are sent during that time of the year. Hanukkah and Christmas gifts flood the mail during December, and because of the excessive numbers of packages, handlers at the post office are more careless in their treatment of the packages. Parcels are more likely than they normally are to be thrown, stored underneath mounds of boxes, and even lost. Bubble wrapping items inside packages will protect against many of these dangers, which is why it is so important to buy large quantities of bubble wrap now, before everyone rushes to purchase it during December.

Which of the following could be concluded from the passage?

(A) The same risks associated with shipping in December because of Hanukkah and Christmas are present in November around Thanksgiving.
(B) It would be better to avoid shipping packages at all during December because of the risks involved.
(C) Post offices are unable to protect most packages that are delivered to them from being harmed by the shipping process.
(D) Bubble wrap cannot protect gifts from all dangers that threaten them when they are shipped in December.
(E) Styrofoam buttons provide just as much protection for packages as bubble wrap does.

4. Many fast-food chains have spread throughout the nation, creating veritable monopolies on restaurant food production in our country. This would not be such a large concern except for the fact that fast food is often not very healthy and these large organized fast-food chains have a lot of vested interest in selling their unhealthy food. To better sell their products, fast-food companies make advertisements that strive to put a positive spin on the value of the food. These ads and propaganda effectively brainwash the nation's populace, creating a situation in which the public spends billions of dollars that ultimately go toward encouraging people to persist in their unhealthy eating habits. Congress should put a stop to this horrible situation by breaking up the fast-food chain monopolies.

For the conclusion to be effective, which of the following must be a correct assumption?

(A) Brainwashing the nation can never be healthy, even if advertising told of the benefits of going to health-food restaurants rather than fast-food chains.
(B) The advertising efforts of more numerous but smaller fast-food companies would not be as effective as the advertising campaigns launched today by the large chains.
(C) Congress has the potential to correct most social problems it faces by taking specific actions to change the existing state of affairs.
(D) Fast-food chains are unlikely to acknowledge the negative effects that they are having on the population or to change their behavior voluntarily.
(E) Propaganda is just as widely used in electing political officials as it is used in selling food, so members of Congress intimately understand the transgressions of fast-food companies.

GO ON TO THE NEXT PAGE

5. Plumber: Your sink must have been stopped up for several days to create this amount of drainage. If rice was the cause of the stoppage, then normally, after several days, the stoppage would have disappeared because, given this much standing water, the rice would usually have decomposed within a day.

Homeowner: We haven't used the sink since several days ago when we cooked a meal that had rice in it. In fact, I started noticing problems right after that dinner. I guess the leftovers of that meal found their way down the drain and caused the problem.

Which of the following, if true, would support the homeowner's conclusion?

(A) The leftovers of that night's meal contained other substances in addition to rice.
(B) They used the sink for other things in between that meal and today.
(C) The sink would not be stopped up with just rice for this length of time.
(D) The plumber was unable to fix the sink because of the excessive amount of water in the drain.
(E) The homeowner had never had a sink get stopped up before.

6. All very young girls in Interstate Preschool have red hair or brown hair. Tommy's sister is a child who has red hair. All older boys in Interstate Preschool have brown hair. Therefore, Tommy's sister is in Interstate Preschool.

Which of the following is an assumption that could be made for the argument to be logically correct?

(A) All very young girls with red hair are in Interstate Preschool.
(B) No girls without red hair are in Interstate Preschool.
(C) Boys are the only children with red hair outside of Interstate Preschool.
(D) No girls with any hair color besides red are outside of Interstate Preschool.
(E) All red-haired girls are not in Interstate Preschool.

7. The average member of a hunter-gatherer society worked fewer hours per day than the average member of a farming society. Extra free time is often associated with increased happiness, so it would appear that hunter-gatherer societies were happier in general than farming societies. This logic can be extrapolated to apply to the capitalistic society of today, in which the average person works 1.5 times the number of hours worked by the average member of a farming society. Through this analysis, it becomes clear that the more advanced a society is, the less happy the average person will be.

Which of the following, if true, would most undermine the analysis presented in the passage?

(A) People in farming communities were more susceptible to disease than people in hunter-gatherer societies.
(B) People in capitalistic societies are on average less happy than people who lived in farming societies.
(C) Many people who live in advanced societies wish that they had the opportunity to live in a society that required fewer working hours.
(D) People in more advanced societies derive more additional happiness from their work than the amount of happiness they lose because of having less free time.
(E) Members of hunter-gatherer societies would, without exception, refuse to work the long hours that people work in capitalistic societies.

GO ON TO THE NEXT PAGE

8. Increased rainfall is associated with an increased rate of plant growth in the rainforest. This past decade has shown an increase in rainfall that is relatively dramatic, and scientists claim that there has been a correspondingly dramatic increase in rainforest plant growth. However, looking at the rainforest, we can clearly see that its borders are shrinking rapidly.

Which of the following would account for the increased rate of plant growth coupled with the decreased border size?

(A) There were years in the past decade that produced lower levels of rain than average.
(B) Companies have destroyed small parts of the rainforests in the past decade.
(C) People harvest much of what is determined to be an increase in plant growth.
(D) Throughout the past decade, the rate of deforestation exceeded the rate of plant growth.
(E) The increased rainfall did not affect only specific areas of the rainforest.

9. Oil lobbyist: Environmentalists overstate the problems associated with drilling for oil in natural wildlife preserves. The entire purpose of most of these groups is to follow oil companies around, no matter what those companies are doing, and complain. Literally, environmentalists are never satisfied with any activity that our companies undertake. If environmentalists had the perspective necessary to view the big picture, then they would understand that we as a society need to drill everywhere that oil can be found.

The argument uses which of the following questionable methods of reasoning?

(A) Attacking the proponents of a view rather than the merits of the view.
(B) Drawing a conclusion on the basis that there is no possible evidence to refute it.
(C) Generalizing from a particular group with certain characteristics to another group with questionably similar characteristics.
(D) Inferring that a group of people sharing beliefs in a particular domain will continue to share congruent beliefs in a different domain.
(E) Making a claim based on case studies rather than statistical evidence.

GO ON TO THE NEXT PAGE

10. The importance to a society of knowing the correct time is very telling about the nature of that society. In America, people find it important to know the time, often down to the exact second. In Spain, however, time is relative and looser, and people think it is more important to be aware of the hour of a scheduled meeting, for instance, than its precise starting minute. When people switch societies, it is difficult for them to get used to a different attitude about time's importance.

Which of the following can be inferred from the passage?

(A) There are societies that acknowledge the importance of even milliseconds.
(B) There are societies that only use time based on the day of the week.
(C) Spanish people are more relaxed than people in America.
(D) An American is more likely to be punctual in America than a newly arrived Spaniard.
(E) Societies that place a higher importance on smaller units of time are generally more technologically advanced than other societies.

11. Ecologist: The status quo of our economy provides disincentives to corporations that would like to be pro-environmental. If a company chooses to buy goods made from materials that are not grown in ill-used rainforests, then it inevitably finds that these alternate goods are more expensive, because the very cheapest raw materials are always found in rainforests. Therefore, whenever a consumer buys a cheap product, he or she has contributed to the destruction of the world's forestry resources. We need to educate corporations about ways to make cheap products without having to devastate rainforests.

A flaw of the argument is that it

(A) makes a conclusion without first offering a piece of evidence in support of that conclusion
(B) contributes to a subject that is often the center of heated debate without offering a way to stem the problem
(C) makes an ethical appeal to a group that can exert no control over its practices
(D) relies on a generalization about a subset of one group that is not necessarily inherent in another group
(E) makes an argument that is tautological and completely circular

GO ON TO THE NEXT PAGE

12. Male blue jays are some of the most territorial birds in existence. If a male blue jay is within two yards of another male's nest, then the two are likely to fight to the death before the breeding season ends. Some males are so aggressive that they will attack anything that moves in the yard close to their nests. Cats, dogs, and people mowing their grass are all likely to bear the brunt of a blue jay's fury. There must be some kind of evolutionary reason for this heightened aggression, so I hypothesize that if the male blue jay of a mating pair died during breeding season, the female blue jay would become just as aggressive as the male had been.

Which of the following, if true, would tend to support the conclusion of the argument?

(A) During breeding season, when a female wren's mate is not in or around the nest, it can become just as aggressive as a male blue jay.

(B) Dogs, cats, and people have all been attacked by female blue jays whose partners have died.

(C) When her partner dies, the female blue jay's neural gland, which controls levels of aggression, changes so as to mirror a male's.

(D) Because of their duties warming their eggs, female birds are incapable of aggression equal to their male counterparts.

(E) Blue jay eggs that have aggressive parents are more likely to hatch, and the hatchlings are more likely to reproduce successfully when they reach maturity.

13. The industry standard is for computer programmers to be paid for a certain project on an hourly basis even though they are commissioned to finish the entire project regardless of the number of hours they work on it. For example, if a project is commissioned to one programmer, then the programmer can set the rate at $100 per hour for as many hours as he can make his client believe that he worked on the project. So it appears that the programmer decides how much money he will receive from a specific project. However, despite the open-endedness of programmers' fees, client companies always have a good idea about how much a specific project will cost them.

Which of the following resolves the paradox present in the argument above?

(A) Programmers are a very honest group of people when it comes to product quality, but they are not as honest when it comes to their fees.

(B) Representatives of client companies sometimes know the programmers they hire, both personally and through previous business relationships.

(C) Programmers never claim that they have worked on a project for more hours than the number a client company recommends they spend.

(D) It is impossible to determine how long it will take a person to complete a project that involves computer programming.

(E) Programmers paid an hourly rate tend to spend more time on a project than they would have spent if they were being paid a flat fee for the completed project.

GO ON TO THE NEXT PAGE

14. Celebrities who commit crimes are best served by acknowledging their mistakes and immediately apologizing. It is amazing what fans will forgive if they receive an apology. They do so is because people generally understand that we all, even celebrities, are flawed and make mistakes. The public is usually willing to forgive those celebrities who confess their transgressions, but it persecutes those celebrities who try to cover up their culpability.

Which of the following can be inferred from the passage?

(A) A celebrity who does not commit a crime will not be persecuted by the public.
(B) Celebrities will be forgiven for any transgressions for which they apologize.
(C) Tennis stars who shoplift would be best advised to apologize for their actions.
(D) Celebrities usually apologize for transgressions that are not flagrant.
(E) People who doubt the morality of a celebrity are still often enamored of him or her.

15. People who say that there is a drought in Maraland County are clearly incorrect. People who are living through a drought do not build artificial ponds to store water. Several people on farms in Maraland County are building ponds. Therefore, Maraland County has no drought problem.

Which of the following has a flaw in reasoning similar to that present above?

(A) People who say Green Acres is not windy are wrong. People who do not receive enough wind do not build wind farms. The people in Green Acres are building wind farms, so they must be getting enough wind.
(B) People who say that Earth is completely polluted are incorrect. A world that is completely polluted does not support life. There is plenty of life supported by Earth. Therefore, Earth must not be completely polluted.
(C) People who say that Marble Road doesn't get enough sunlight are wrong. Farmers without sunlight do not plant fruits and vegetables to sell. Some farmers living on Marble Road have planted fruits and vegetables. Therefore Marble Road gets enough sunlight.
(D) People who say that Maryland is one big eyesore are wrong. Tourists would not visit a place that is an eyesore, and they would not ride through Maryland. Therefore, Maryland is not an eyesore.
(E) People who say that aliens have visited Earth are incorrect. Aliens would not haphazardly visit a place like Earth. Therefore, since no aliens have visited Earth yet, they will never visit.

GO ON TO THE NEXT PAGE

16. The modern fascination with celebrity has grown to the level of an epidemic. A seemingly harmless guilty pleasure has expanded into such a widespread mania that it is infringing not only upon the rights of the celebrities but also upon their safety. Something must be done, indeed, to protect these people, although any substantive action on the part of the government would necessarily restrict the public's First Amendment freedoms. Therefore, a governmental response is clearly not the answer. A solution might be effectuated, however, by the media, the fans, and the celebrities themselves.

Which one of the following is most strongly supported by the argument above?

(A) The solution to this problem lies in changing the attitudes of the fans, who, in order to eliminate this "epidemic," should no longer patronize tabloid newspapers.

(B) In some cases, the government should forgo the protections of the First Amendment for the sake of a practical outcome.

(C) Everyone is to blame for this phenomenon.

(D) The answer to the problem lies in changing the habits of the media, the celebrities, their fans, or some combination thereof.

(E) Celebrities are putting themselves at risk by allowing their lives to become public domain.

17. The lottery and the world series of poker tournament are essentially massive wealth-transferring mechanisms. Both require people to purchase an "entry"—a ticket or a seat to play, respectively—and the winner is able to collect a large portion of the accumulated entry fees. Generally, when someone loses, he or she gets nothing. But sometimes, if a person almost wins, he or she may be given a small portion of the "take," greater than the amount of the entry fee. These mechanisms of wealth transfer are so similar that it would appear that since the lottery does not require any skill to win, neither does poker. Regardless, whoever comes out of the lottery or poker tournament as the victor still wins a pile of money.

The argument utilizes which of the following argumentative methods?

(A) illuminating the contrasts between two different but similar domains

(B) overly relying on the conclusion that when someone loses, he or she get no money

(C) calling into question the moral sustainability of the subject matter of the passage

(D) identifying the similarities between the three major wealth-transferring mechanisms

(E) inferring that because two institutions are similar in several respects, they will be similar in another

GO ON TO THE NEXT PAGE

18. A recent study regarding childhood eating habits demonstrated that preadolescent children who are messy eaters are more likely to grow up to be disorganized adults. On the other hand, preadolescents who are taught to be clean and to chew their food without spilling it all over themselves normally grow up to be organized adults. The study also found that those children who are sometimes messy eaters and sometimes clean eaters normally grow up to be organized adults, because they were at least sometimes clean as children.

Which of the following can be inferred from the passage?

(A) Children who are messy eaters never grow up to be organized adults.
(B) Unorganized adults were messy eaters when they were children.
(C) Children's eating habits show their predilection for organization as adults.
(D) Teenagers who are messy eaters are more than likely going to be disorganized adults.
(E) Recent studies about children's eating habits have been debunked.

19. Flexibility is an important aspect of one's physical routine. Increased flexibility is associated with lower injury risks and increased speed. Long-distance running is a sport that involves many repeated movements, but the same is not true of dancing. Studies have shown that dancers tend to be more flexible during their dance routines than when they warm up beforehand. Additional studies have revealed that long-distance runners are less flexible while running races than they were prior to the race.

Which of the following would explain the difference in performance flexibility between groups of runners and groups of dancers?

(A) Dancers are more likely to hurt themselves during a routine than long-distance runners are during a race.
(B) If dancers ran a long-distance race, then they would also tighten up during the race.
(C) When specific muscle movements are repeated, they cause the body to tighten up in order to conserve energy.
(D) If long-distance runners engaged in a dance routine, they would be less flexible during the routine than during the warm-ups.
(E) Muscle movements that are not geared toward achieving a specific goal tend to have little implication for a person's flexibility.

GO ON TO THE NEXT PAGE

20. In the past decade, corporate tax evasion and corporate stealing have become gigantic problems for companies that employ over 500 people. These problems are now so rife in today's corporate world that the average shareholder's portfolio shows the negative effects of at least one kind of corporate abuse. Generally, this abuse stems from the dishonesty of one person sitting in a position of power in the company. For this reason, the legislature should mandate that all corporations employing more than 500 people be required to hire accounting firms to audit their books to ensure accuracy.

Which of the following, if true, would cast doubt on the conclusion of the passage?

(A) Generally, it is good for a company to have an audit done because audits help companies streamline their financial operations.

(B) Companies that employ fewer than 500 people or more than 2000 people never have any problems with dishonesty.

(C) Accounting firms sometimes help corporations exploit methods to abuse the system.

(D) The majority of people distrust accounting firms much more than they are distrust big corporations.

(E) When corporate crime is perpetrated by more than one person in a company, it is harder to track and to stop.

21. Motivator: People really have no excuse for being bored. In fact, only boring people get bored, and they do is because they can't entertain themselves. A person who can entertain himself or herself can usually entertain others. In fact, most of us are attracted only to people who entertain us, and we strive, in turn, to entertain them. Therefore, if you are bored, then you are boring, and you are lonely.

Which of the following is implied by the passage?

(A) People have no excuse for loneliness except boredom.

(B) Entertainment is the greatest gift a person can bestow on another.

(C) There is a connection between loneliness and boredom.

(D) People who are unable to entertain themselves are not able to entertain others.

(E) Boredom is something that can be cured by hard work and dedication.

GO ON TO THE NEXT PAGE

22. Statistically, the guns that a family keeps inside its house for protection are more often used in an intrafamilial incident than on an intruder. This fact has led many supporters of gun control to lobby for laws that outlaw guns in homes. They conclude that if there is no gun in a house, then it is less likely that a family member will be hurt while growing up.

Which of the following, if true, would most call the conclusion of the passage into question?

(A) Owning guns is an inalienable Second Amendment right that should not be waived because of superficial concerns of a minority of the population.

(B) A much higher percentage of burglars possess, and are intent on using, guns than the percentage of homeowners who are the victims of these burglars.

(C) Free speech rights could not be protected if there were no guns in our society.

(D) The government would gain power and turn into a totalitarian regime if its citizens did not maintain guns in their homes to protect themselves from this change.

(E) Houses that have guns are less likely to have a family member hurt during a robbery than houses that do not have guns.

23. There is simply no reason not to have telephone wires and electrical wires buried underground instead of hanging over the streets. When these wires are buried, the neighborhood is a lot more aesthetically pleasing to residents and visitors. Also, there is a far lower likelihood that a storm will damage the lines and cause a power outage. Our city has all of its power lines aboveground, so it is clear that there was some very poor planning going on at city hall when the location of these wires was decided.

Which of the following can be inferred from the argument?

(A) Electrical wires that are underground can put people who are digging in their yards in danger of electrocution.

(B) Lower cost is not a reason that would encourage a city to build power lines aboveground.

(C) Cities are always concerned about making the best decisions for their residents and visitors.

(D) There are good reasons that city planners might choose not to build power lines underground.

(E) Numerous people have been hurt by telephone wires falling onto their cars.

GO ON TO THE NEXT PAGE

24. A ski slope requires all patrons to sign a waiver releasing the proprietors from liability in the event that the skier gets hurt on the premises. This waiver covers situations in which the negligent behavior of the ski slope's employees has led to an injury that might have been preventable. Many times, waivers of liability for negligent behavior are found to be unenforceable by courts because they run counter to public policy—it is never a good idea to give a company an incentive to be negligent. Mary was skiing the other day and broke her leg on the ski slope. Her lawyer reviews the waiver she signed and tells her that she has no case.

Which of the following, if true, would cast the most doubt on the lawyer's contention?

(A) Mary's lawyer almost flunked out of law school and is now in financial trouble.
(B) Mary did not break her leg because of the negligence of an employee of the ski slope.
(C) The case will be tried in a jurisdiction where the courts do not enforce waivers for any kind of liability.
(D) The ski slope manager told Mary that she should be careful before trying to ski down a black diamond.
(E) Most people who sue the ski slope that Mary would like to sue end up winning.

25. Picasso was a man of great zeal. His passionate flair shined through paintings that depicted such subjects as the scenic beauty of nature, the frenzied lives of people, and the gore and glory of the Spanish bullfight. It is no small wonder that his passion also found expression in a romantic relationship, a bond so important to him that he wanted to give his love something of himself to keep forever.

Which of the following, if true, would undermine a contention of the passage?

(A) People of Picasso's time felt that he was a very sedate man and that his paintings were trivialities.
(B) Picasso's girlfriend spurned his love because she could not understand the source of his passion.
(C) Picasso was incapable of expressing passion through his art or through relationships.
(D) Bullfights were the main subject that captivated Picasso throughout the years of adolescence.
(E) Picasso did not become truly passionate until after his short and unremarkable relationship with his first girlfriend.

STOP

IF YOU FINISH BEFORE TIME RUNS OUT, CHECK YOUR WORK ON THIS SECTION ONLY.
DO NOT GO ON ANY OTHER SECTION IN THE TEST.

ANSWER KEY

Section 1	Section 2	Section 3	Section 4
1. E	1. E	1. E	1. E
2. A	2. E	2. D	2. E
3. C	3. D	3. C	3. D
4. A	4. B	4. B	4. B
5. B	5. B	5. D	5. A
6. D	6. B	6. B	6. C
7. B	7. D	7. A	7. D
8. D	8. C	8. A	8. D
9. A	9. A	9. C	9. A
10. E	10. D	10. E	10. D
11. A	11. E	11. E	11. D
12. C	12. C	12. D	12. C
13. A	13. A	13. B	13. C
14. A	14. C	14. B	14. C
15. C	15. D	15. C	15. C
16. D	16. D	16. C	16. D
17. E	17. D	17. C	17. E
18. B	18. B	18. D	18. C
19. C	19. B	19. B	19. C
20. C	20. C	20. B	20. C
21. A	21. A	21. A	21. C
22. D	22. C	22. D	22. E
23. C	23. A	23. A	23. B
24. B	24. D	24. C	24. C
	25. C	25. E	25. C
	26. C	26. E	

<u>Scoring Instructions:</u> To calculate your score on this Practice Test, follow the instructions on the next page.

CALCULATING YOUR SCORE

Now that you have completed Practice Test 3, use the instructions on this page to calculate your score. Start by checking the Answer Key to count up the number of questions you answered correctly. Then fill in the table below.

Raw Score Calculator

Section Number	Question Type	Number of Questions	Number Correct
1	Reading Comprehension	24	_____
2	Logic Games	26	_____
3	Logical Reasoning	26	_____
4	Logical Reasoning	25	_____
		(Raw Score) Total:	_____

On the real LSAT, a statistical process will be used to convert your raw score to a scaled score ranging from 120 to 180. The table below will give you an approximate idea of the scaled score that matches your raw score. For statistical reasons, on real forms of the LSAT the scaled score that matches a given raw score can vary by several points above or below the scaled score shown in the table.

Write your scaled score on this test here:

Practice Test 3 scaled score: _____

Raw Score	Scaled Score	Raw Score	Scaled Score	Raw Score	Scaled Score
0	120	23	126	46	145
1	120	24	127	47	145
2	120	25	128	48	146
3	120	26	128	49	147
4	120	27	129	50	147
5	120	28	130	51	148
6	120	29	131	52	148
7	120	30	132	53	149
8	120	31	133	54	150
9	120	32	133	55	151
10	120	33	134	56	151
11	120	34	135	57	152
12	120	35	136	58	153
13	120	36	137	59	153
14	120	37	137	60	154
15	120	38	138	61	154
16	120	39	139	62	155
17	120	40	140	63	155
18	121	41	140	64	156
19	122	42	141	65	157
20	123	43	142	66	158
21	124	44	143	67	158
22	125	45	144	68	159

Raw Score	Scaled Score	Raw Score	Scaled Score	Raw Score	Scaled Score
69	159	80	166	91	174
70	160	81	166	92	175
71	160	82	167	93	175
72	161	83	167	94	176
73	161	84	168	95	177
74	162	85	169	96	178
75	162	86	170	97	179
76	163	87	170	98	180
77	163	88	171	99	180
78	164	89	172	100	180
79	165	90	173	101	180

ANSWERS AND EXPLANATIONS

SECTION I—READING COMPREHENSION

1. Correct answer: **E.** This passage repeatedly addresses the problem that since there is not a universal definition of *bibliotherapy*, there will not be consistent results in studies regarding its effectiveness.

   (A) There is no mention of bibliotherapy as an American psychological tradition.

   (B) This statement is one idea of the passage, but not its main idea. The passage focuses on the difficulties in defining the term.

   (C) This statement mentions a single point made in the passage, but it does not zero in on the main idea.

   (D) This statement is a minor point in the passage.

2. Correct answer: **A.** Line 28 stresses that bibliotherapy is most effective as an adjunctive treatment.

   (B) We are unable to determine whether this statement is true. It is said that healing through books has been interpreted differently by different groups of professionals, but the interpretation of the ancient Greeks is not described.

   (C and D) These statements cannot be supported by details in the passage.

   (E) It is said that at-risk children have the potential to be helped by bibliotherapy, but the passage does not claim that they have the greatest potential.

3. Correct answer: **C.** This generalization ties in with the main point of the passage.

(A) The author does not claim a future dominance of bibliotherapy.

(B) Directed self-help is mentioned, but no claim is made that it is the most powerful kind of bibliotherapy.

(D) Being eclectic is never praised.

(E) Riordan and Wilson reviewed the literature of bibliotherapy, but they are not its sole proponents.

4. Correct answer: **A.** The first paragraph introduces the concept of bibliotherapy and notes that there are several different interpretations of the practice. Toward the end of the paragraph, the questionable definition is discussed.

   (B) It is never stated that the interpretation of bibliotherapy is consistent across several disciplines. In fact, this choice contradicts lines 21–26.

   (C) The components are not debated, because the paragraph does not successfully elucidate its components.

   (D) The paragraph offers no alternatives.

   (E) Bibliotherapy is not introduced in this way.

5. Correct answer: **B.** The final theory is that mixed results will be produced until a singular definition of bibliotherapy is developed. If consistent results were already being produced, then this theory would be invalidated.

   (A) This statement is unrelated to the theory concluding the passage.

   (C and D) These statements are irrelevant.

(E) The author does not argue that it would necessarily be difficult to agree on a single definition, nor does this statement undermine the conclusion of the passage.

6. Correct answer: **D.** Right after introducing Riordan and Wilson, the author characterizes them as notable.

    (A) This word was used to describe an application of bibliotherapy.

    (B) The author's opinion is not inconsistent about Riordan and Wilson.

    (C and E) These words are not used in the passage.

7. Correct answer: **B.** The author's purpose is to describe and analyze the Korean War.

    (A) The passage does not mention any misconceptions.

    (C–E) These answers cannot be supported by the content of the passage.

8. Correct answer: **D.** It was never stated that the Americans ever strove to negotiate peace between the Koreas.

    (A) This event is mentioned in the passage (line 3).

    (B) This event is mentioned in the passage (line 5).

    (C) This event is mentioned in the passage (lines 3–4).

    (E) This event is mentioned in the passage (lines 7–8).

9. Correct answer: **A.** The Korean War began as a civil war, but conditions enticed the United States, China, and the Soviet Union to each take some part in the conflict.

    (B) There is never any mention of postwar aid.

    (C) Based on information in the passage, we are unable to determine whether this would have been the case. It seems that the North would have won.

    (D) The war ended in a stalemate.

    (E) The passage does not mention the United States Navy.

10. Correct answer: **E.** The soldiers from China were clearly not volunteers, but instead they were placed there by the Chinese government in a strategic effort designed to overcome South Korea.

(A) If the word *volunteer* were meant to have its literal meaning, the author would not have enclosed it in quotation marks.

(B and C) These answers require too many doubtful inferences.

(D) We are unable to determine if this implication is true based on the information in the passage.

11. Correct answer: **A.** This inference can be supported by lines 62–66.

    (B) The devastation was foreseeable, given the involvement of superpowers on both sides.

    (C) It's unlikely that the author would find the results justified in any way.

    (D) An armistice was signed in 1953.

    (E) Neither "lack of political malleability" nor "postwar indifference" is implied by the passage.

12. Correct answer: **C.** By landing at Inch'n, General MacArthur was able to cut off the supply lines of the North Korean army, causing it rapidly to disband. Then the United States, which had been cornered in South Korea, pressed rapidly forward and occupied parts of North Korea.

    (A) The drilling started the war, so it was not the turning point.

    (B) This event almost ended the war for the South Koreans and United States. It was not a turning point.

    (D) The fortification was a cause that contributed to starting the war.

    (E) This event was a contributory factor in starting the war.

13. Correct answer: **A.** The author stresses the war's pointlessness by emphasizing that after the war the political alignment on the Korean peninsula returned to its prewar state. The author stresses the harmful nature of the war by emphasizing the destruction it caused in both Koreas.

    (B) The war was regrettable, but the author never claims that it was "poetic."

    (C) The war was clearly hard-fought, but the author does not characterize it as unavoidable.

    (D) The exact opposite of this opinion is stressed.

    (E) The war is never characterized as serene.

14. Correct answer: **A.** The first sentence of the third paragraph contains the word *because*—a clue that the paragraph explains the Supreme Court's reasoning for the remand.

(B) *Liability* is not defined in the third paragraph.

(C) The Supreme Court instructs the district court, not the other way around.

(D) The passage makes no judgment, positive or otherwise, about the Supreme Court's decision.

(E) The second paragraph, not the third, tells which parts of the ruling were reversed and which were affirmed.

15. Correct answer: **C.** The scope is the extent of the remedy, and the particulars are the specifications for that remedy.

(A) *Range* is synonymous with *scope*, but *depth* is not synonymous with *particulars*.

(B) *Appropriateness* cannot replace either "scope" or "particulars."

(D) *Legality* is comparable neither to "the scope" nor "the particulars."

(E) *Leniency* is irrelevant.

16. Correct answer: **D.** After the case was remanded, the issue that the district court had to resolve was the remedy (line 61).

(A) The passage includes no information showing that the Supreme Court acted as a result of political pressure.

(B) The district court's first opinion did not have to be explained, because it was rejected by the Supreme Court.

(C) There is no mention of a written compromise.

(E) This is not a tradition; cases often end in the Supreme Court.

17. Correct answer: **E.** This statement would offer an alternative explanation for the dominance of Microsoft, rather than its anticompetitive behavior.

(A) Microsoft had those resources. Therefore, this statement is irrelevant.

(B) This statement would support, not undermine, the inference.

(C) This statement would be irrelevant since it says nothing about Microsoft's exclusionary behavior.

(D) This statement does not mean that the inference is unsupportable now.

18. Correct answer: **B.** The Supreme Court gave its ruling, and the district court was left alone to determine the remedy.

(A) This fact is not mentioned.

(C) We are not told what the remedy was.

(D) This statement cannot be supported by the details.

(E) The opposite of this statement seems to be true.

19. Correct answer: **C.** The purpose of the passage is to describe the military history of Mexico, starting with information about Aztec warriors and their conquerors.

(A) The passage contains no debate about which culture had more influence.

(B) No myths are described in the passage, only documented historical facts.

(D) The description of the Aztecs' military organization supports the purpose, but is not, itself, the purpose.

(E) The gradual elimination of colonial Spanish practices is mentioned only in the last paragraph, as a side note.

20. Correct answer: **C.** The Spanish imposed their theocratic-militaristic tradition on the Aztecs (lines 42–44).

(A) We are unable to determine how often religion enticed the Aztecs to go to war.

(B) This statement is probably not true, because if the Triple Alliance could muster a force of 18,000 in an hour, then it probably could have mustered many more fighters from outlying cities in the span of several hours.

(D) This statement does not account for the presence of the theocratic-militaristic tendencies of the Mexican army.

(E) Forced conscription in the 19th century is not responsible for the prevalence of theocracy in the Mexican military today.

21. Correct answer: **A.** You are repeatedly told that this was not the case.

    (B) The passage makes this statement. (The Spanish had guns, line 28.)

    (C) The passage makes this statement (line 36).

    (D) The passage makes this statement (line 39).

    (E) The passage makes this statement (line 29).

22. Correct answer: **D.** *Subterfuge* is meant to convey the idea that the Aztecs actively resisted the Spanish imposition of their theocratic-militaristic traditions.

    (A) The conquistadors did not bring the Aztecs freedom.

    (B) *Subterfuge* does not mean "revolts."

    (C) We do not know whether the Aztecs separated religion and military service, but lines 7–11 make it appear unlikely that they did.

    (E) The Aztecs did not have a positive attitude about the Spanish culture, which is the only European culture mentioned.

23. Correct answer: **C.** The facts in the second and third paragraphs show that the Spanish were both haughty and indifferent toward the conquered people.

    (A) Given the Spanish history of conscription and "special rights," the exact opposite of this statement is implied.

    (B) The author seems to imply that the Spanish army's practices were not commendable.

    (D) The conquered natives were unlikely to believe that the practices were necessary.

    (E) The last sentence says that the cavalry units are accorded high prestige.

24. Correct answer: **B.** A history of immoral and inhumane treatment would not be considered part of a "rich military heritage."

    (A) A major part of the passage describes the Spanish conquest of the Aztecs.

    (C and D) Both these facts were important factors leading to the Spanish conquest of Mexico.

    (E) In other words, the rich military tradition goes back farther historically than the Spanish conquest.

Section 2—Logic Games

Game I: Grouping

Initial Setup:

S	T	V
*	C	___
___	___	___
	___	___

A, B, E, F = Food
C, D, G = Spices
S ≠ T
S ≠ V
A_S → ~~Spice~~
F_V → D_V

1. Correct answer: **E.** Tom cannot have apples or bacon, or all three spices. Since Joe uses all ingredients, Tom must have ginger.

S	T	V
A	C	E
B	___	F
	___	D
	~~A~~	

2. Correct answer: **E.**

S	T	V
F	C	A
D/G	___	B
~~A~~	___	E
		~~F~~

3. Correct answer: **D.** If Violet ate flour, then Sharon would have to have an ingredient that was also eaten by someone else:

S	T	V
F	C	A
D/G	___	B
~~A~~	___	E

4. Correct answer: **B.** This is a very difficult question. You should solve this type of question by going through and eliminating the answer choices instead of drawing out the possible scenarios, but here are the three possibilities for this scenario:

B/E	C	A
D	F	E/B
	G	C/G

B/E	C	A
E/B/D	F	D/B/E
	G	C/F/G

A	C	E/B
B/E	F	D
	G	F/G/C

5. Correct answer: **B.** This answer is very easy. Sharon can never order a spice when she orders apples.

$$
\begin{array}{ccc}
\boxed{S} & \boxed{T} & \boxed{V} \\
\underline{} & C & F \\
\underline{} & F & D \\
\\
\underline{} & \underline{} &
\end{array}
$$

6. Correct answer: **B.** In order for Sharon not to share any ingredient with another person, she would have to eat bacon (since no one can eat a meal containing only spices).

Game 2: Linear

Initial Setup:

$T < R$

$S_4 \rightarrow U_5$

$U_6 \rightarrow S_7$

$\boxed{V/W}$

$$
\underline{} \;\; \underline{} \;\; \underline{} \;\; \underline{\overset{*}{}} \;\; \underline{} \;\; \underline{\overset{*}{}} \;\; \underline{}
$$

7. Correct answer: **D.** If S is in stall 4, then U must be in stall 5.

8. Correct answer: **C.** If U is in stall 6, then S has to be in stall 7. Neither T nor U could be in stall 6:

$$
\underline{} \;\; \underline{} \;\; \underline{} \;\; \underline{} \;\; \underline{V} \;\; \underline{} \;\; \underline{W}
$$
$$
 \cancel{T}
$$
$$
 \cancel{U}
$$

9. Correct answer: **A.** R must be in stall 6 or 7, and either V or W must also be in stall 6 or 7:

$$
\underline{V/W/X} \;\; \underline{V/W/X} \;\; \underline{T} \;\; \underline{S} \;\; \underline{U} \;\; \underline{R/V/W} \;\; \underline{R/U/W}
$$

10. Correct answer: **D.** If U were in stall 6, then S would have to be in stall 7:

$$
\underline{V/W} \;\; \underline{} \;\; \underline{} \;\; \underline{} \;\; \underline{} \;\; \underline{} \;\; \underline{V/W}
$$

11. Correct answer: **E.** We know the exact position of five dancers:

$$
\underline{V/W} \;\; \underline{X} \;\; \underline{W/V} \;\; \underline{S} \;\; \underline{U} \;\; \underline{T} \;\; \underline{R}
$$

12. Correct answer: **C.** If T were in stall 5, then R would have to be in stall 6 or 7. If R were in stall

6, U cannot be in stall 6 (by the description of the scenario). If R were in stall 7, U cannot be in stall 6, because then S would have to go in stall 7.

Game 3: Mapping

Initial Setup: Notice that there is a large constraining box that fully dictates this game:

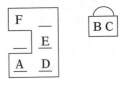

There are only two places that this box can go in the game:

$$
\begin{array}{cccc}
\underline{B/C} & \underline{C/B} & \underline{F} & \underline{H/G} \\
\underline{F} & \underline{G/H} & \underline{G/H} & \underline{E} \\
\underline{H/G} & \underline{E} & \underline{A} & \underline{D} \\
\underline{A} & \underline{D} & \underline{B/C} & \underline{C/B}
\end{array}
$$

13. Correct answer: **A.** This refers to scenario 1. It would make H sit in seat 5.

14. Correct answer: **C.** This refers to scenario 2. B and C have to sit in the fourth row.

15. Correct answer: **D.** H and G could sit in three rows.

16. Correct answer: **D.** G and H could never sit in the same rows.

17. Correct answer: **D.** This puts us in scenario 2. F cannot share a row with C.

18. Correct answer: **B.** C, F, G, and H could all sit either next to or immediately behind B. Therefore, D is a possible answer.

19. Correct answer: **B.** In scenario 1, there are four possible configurations. In scenario 2, there are four more possible configurations. This makes a total of eight.

Game 4: Linear

Initial Setup:

$$
\underline{\overset{*}{}} \;\; \underline{\overset{*}{}} \;\; \underline{} \;\; \underline{} \;\; \underline{} \;\; \underline{} \;\; \underline{}
$$

$C, F?$ $\qquad A_{M \text{ or } T} \rightarrow D_F$

$A < E$ $\qquad D_{M \text{ or } T} \rightarrow A_{Sat \text{ or } Sun}$

$D < G < B$

20. Correct answer: **C.** This could be an order.

    (A) G has to go before B.

    (B) D has to go before G.

    (D and E) If A is seen on Monday or Tuesday, then D must be seen on Friday.

21. Correct answer: **A.** The scenario does not reveal the exact position of any cat.

22. Correct answer: **C.** Only cats C and F could be seen, in some order, on Monday and Tuesday:

    <u>C/F</u> <u>F/C</u> <u>   </u> <u>   </u> <u>   </u> <u>   </u> <u>   </u>

23. Correct answer: **A.** F is seen on Monday, Wednesday, or Thursday:

    <u>C/F</u> <u>A</u> <u>   </u> <u>   </u> <u>D</u> <u>G</u> <u>B</u>

24. Correct answer: **D:**

    <u>D</u> <u>F</u> <u>C</u> <u>G</u> <u>B</u> <u>A</u> <u>F</u>

25. Correct answer: **C.** We would know the position of five cats:

    <u>C</u> <u>D</u> <u>G</u> <u>F/B</u> <u>B/F</u> <u>A</u> <u>E</u>

26. Correct answer: **C.** If A goes on Friday and G goes on Thursday, then we know that E and B must go at some point on either Saturday or Sunday. This means that D must go on Wednesday, because if D went before then, the sufficient-necessary rule would cause A to go on Saturday.

SECTION 3—LOGICAL REASONING

1. GPS is described and several of its uses are listed. The last sentence of the squib mentions a new technology that allows people to use GPS in their cars to tell them which turns to make on a road.

Question Type: Conclusion

Correct answer: **E.** For a GPS in a car to be able to tell a driver to turn at a particular place, the GPS would have to "know" the driver's destination. Obviously, that destination would have to be input.

(A) GPSs will work near mountains as long as the mountains do not completely block it.

(B and C) You are unable to determine whether these statements are true or not.

(D) From what you have read in the passage, you do not know the effects of satellites on GPSs.

2. This passage explains that alligators rarely stray farther than 25 miles from their birthplaces. Then the passage describes circus alligators that stray up to several thousand miles from their homes.

Question Type: "Strengthen"

Correct answer: **D.** If this statement were true, it would strengthen the idea that for an alligator to travel as far as a circus alligator does, people must have intervened.

(A) This answer choice is very convincing, but a "creature" does not necessarily have to be a human being.

(B) This statement would undermine the contentions of the squib.

(C) This statement refers to alligators' actions in the past, but it does not necessarily refer to their actions in the future.

(E) This statement is irrelevant.

3. This squib states that politicians have all been educated very well. Despite this education, they all seem to disagree about political topics. At this point, the squib assumes that since all politicians are intelligent, intelligence must not be tied to political views. However, this is a faulty assumption, because there is no compelling reason to believe that all politicians have the same level of intelligence.

Question Type: Reasoning strategy

Correct answer: **C.** This error is the one discussed above.

(A) Following the author's argument, he or she would probably claim that unintelligent and uneducated people never get elected. This claim would likely be an error, but it does not relate to the author's conclusion.

(B) It is probably a sound assumption that brainpower helps politicians get elected.

(D) Even if the author had not omitted the fact that people's ethical and religious backgrounds lead them to endorse different positions, the same conclusion could have been arrived at. Ethical and religious convictions are not a function of intelligence.

(E) The author's conclusion has nothing to do with specific problems.

4. The child claims that she took the dog outside, so it could not have gotten inside during the day. The mother claims that the dog must have gotten inside, because the little brother probably would not have chewed up the couch.

Question Type: "Resolve"

Correct answer: **B.** If this statement were true, then the dog would have been able to reenter the house after the child took it outside.

(A) According to the child's story, though, the dog did not have a chance to gnaw the furniture that day.

(C) This statement does not mean that the little brother would have gnawed on the couch if given the opportunity.

(D and E) Neither of these facts would reconcile the child's story with the parent's opinion.

5. This squib claims that because cell phones have so quickly been adopted in our society, people will eventually want to have phones implanted within their bodies. Without any supporting evidence, we may not necessarily believe that people will want to do this.

Question Type: "Strengthen"

Correct answer: **D.** If this statement were true, then people would probably want to use neural implants rather than cell phones.

(A) This statement would undermine the argument.

(B) This does not mean that the trend will continue for cell phones or that people will want their legs electronically optimized.

(C) This statement does not mean that people will want to do so.

(E) However, nonhumanoids (ordinary people) may not want to make use of this technology.

6. The environmentalist tries to show that people will actually be well served if oil supplies run out.

Question Type: Reasoning strategy

Correct answer: **B.** This is exactly the method the environmentalist uses. The fact that oil supplies could run out is an oft-cited limitation on the production of new cars, but the environmentalist reveals this situation to be very positive.

(A, C–E) These are not argumentative methods used by the environmentalist.

7. Tom claims that he was in Area 51 when it was invaded by aliens. He claims that the army routed their attack and captured their leader.

Question Type: Conclusion

Correct answer: **A.** This fact was stated by Tom in his second sentence. The aliens landed to begin their takeover.

(B) We are not told that the army used bullets at all or that any aliens were killed.

(C) We are not sure about the information passing into the top ranks of the CIA or remaining there for a number of years.

(D) We do not know this fact.

(E) It seems that several people, including Tom, do know the truth about area 51.

8. This passage tells of the (fictional) evolution of dodgeball as a sport. The knights supposedly used the game to prepare them to dodge objects during war. Eventually, the game was taken over by to English children.

Question Type: "Strengthen"

Correct answer: **A.** If dodgeball was invented in the 16th century, then it would not have been impossible to play it before.

(B–D) These statements would not strengthen the contentions of the argument.

(E) This fact might only be due to the technological advances in armor that occurred after the 15th century.

9. Cell phones have grown in use as technology has increased their capabilities. The squib claims that this trend will continue indefinitely.

Question Type: Conclusion

Correct answer: **C.** If the statements of the squib are true, then this statement would also have to be true—otherwise no more functions could be placed into cell phones.

(A) We are unable to infer the timeline for the introduction of various innovations into cell phones.

(B and D) We are unable to infer this contention.

(E) Obviously, this statement is not true.

10. This squib relates how, after TermExterm was called to get rid of termites in a house owned by June and Betty, it released new bugs rather than

exterminating the termites already there. Betty reasons that the company did so to be rehired to treat for bugs again.

Question Type: "Weaken"

Correct answer: **E.** If TermExterm released termite-eating bugs, it may not need to be to rehired.

(A) This statement is irrelevant. Maybe they just started releasing bugs recently, or perhaps no one had noticed this practice previously.

(B) What happens to other houses is not relevant to what will happen to this house.

(C) This statement would strengthen Betty's argument.

(D) The spraying techniques that TermExterm uses are not relevant to whether or not the company got rid of the termites.

11. This squib states that if speeding is punished, then the government needs to post speed limit signs. Conversely, it claims that if the government does not punish speeding, then there is no obligation to post signs. Clearly, this is not true; safety concerns (as well as other concerns) call for the presence of speed limit signs.

Question Type: Analogous Reasoning

Correct answer: **E.** Parents should be teaching their children cleaner words regardless of whether or not they punish their children for swearing. This reasoning relates directly to how the idea that the government should post speed limit signs regardless of whether or not speeders are punished.

(A) Gambling is not really a tenable way of making money, so governments need not find an alternative. The first premise in this answer choice is nonsensical, whereas the squib's first premise makes sense.

(B) Unlike the squib, this choice does not transition from a general principle to a specific instance, since it focuses on only one college. Additionally, this is a syllogistic argument, instead of one based on moral premises.

(C) The law does punish something (tax evasion) in this choice, so it is not related to the squib, in which the law does not punish something (speeding).

(D) This choice does not emulate the reasoning in the squib.

12. Truck drivers stop more often at rest stops than vacationing drivers, and yet, when vacationing drivers visit a rest stop, they are more likely to see other vacationing drivers. This is either because truck drivers stop at different rest stops than vacationers or because there are more vacationers on the road.

Question Type: "Strengthen."

Correct answer: **D.** This choice offers one of the alternative explanations mentioned above.

(A) Each group has different needs, but this assumption does not help us to draw the logical conclusion in the squib.

(B) This assumption does not relate to the times during which vacationing drivers stop.

(C and E) These assumptions are irrelevant.

13. The gambler claims that the chances of winning the jackpot increase as the jackpot increases, because people who previously played and lost are less likely to play again. However, the gambler neglects to mention that the larger jackpot would create incentive to play, even for those people who have not played before.

Question Type: "Weaken"

Correct answer: **B.** People who have not played recently *will* play the lottery this time, thereby negating the gambler's argument.

(A) This statement does not mean that the winners have played this particular lottery recently. The gambler may still be correct about the odds.

(C) This statement would support the gambler's argument.

(D) This statement does not mean that the majority of the recent losers continue to play.

(E) Since most people playing the lottery are seeking huge payouts, this statement is not relevant.

14. Fast-twitch muscles can perform well in activities that are normally suited for slow-twitch muscles. However, the converse is not true: slow-twitch muscles cannot be trained to sprint well. What would allow fast-twitch muscles to be so adaptable?

Question Type: "Resolve"

Correct answer: **B.** If this statement were true, it would mean that fast-twitch muscles could be able to perform all activities for which slow-twitch muscles are normally used.

(A) This statement would undermine the contentions of the passage.

(C and D) Neither of these statements explains the discrepancy.

(E) This statement would not explain why fast-twitch muscles, normally good for sprinting, can be used for long-distance running. Additionally, what one scientist claims is not compelling enough to be an answer choice.

15. The author states that there are two possibilities for traveling to other star systems: (1) Create a wormhole or (2) create a ship that can travel at approximately the speed of light. The author rules out the second possibility and therefore claims that our only hope is creating a wormhole. This is a logical argument.

Question Type: Reasoning strategy

Correct answer: **C.** Traveling at the speed of light is impossible, so the author argues for the alternative, creating a wormhole.

(A and B) Neither of these methods of reasoning are employed by the author, who neither generalizes nor offers irrelevant evidence.

(D) This choice could be construed to be correct if we don't think about it sufficiently. The author does not eliminate several possibilities, only one of two alternatives.

(E) The author does not "strongly advocate" creating a wormhole. He or she merely states that doing so would be the only way to travel to other galaxies.

16. Ghostwriters never gain fame from the books that they pen for other people. Therefore, the squib claims, ghostwriters should always write their books under their own names and begin to gain fame for themselves, rather than writing books for other people. This squib neglects to mention money, as well as fame, as a consideration for writing a book.

Question Type: "Strengthen"

Correct answer: **C.** If this were true, then monetary considerations would not be as important, and there would be no reason ever to publish a book that would not bring fame to a writer.

(A) This tangential fact does not need to be assumed.

(B) This assumption would undermine the conclusion, because it brings the consideration of money into the mix.

(D) This assumption is irrelevant.

(E) The squib does not pertain to what famous people should do. It concerns what ghostwriters should do.

17. Insecticides are dangerous because the bugs that they are designed to kill are very hardy creatures. Potent poisons must be used. Therefore, humans should make themselves aware of the potential dangers associated with these chemicals.

Question Type: "Strengthen"

Correct answer: **C.** This statement would validate the conclusion. When people know about products, they use these products safely.

(A) This statement does not support the conclusion that people should become more knowledgeable about bug poisons and so are improper use.

(B) Regardless of their specific knowledge about a chemical, most people realize that drinking a chemical would be a bad idea. This statement would not support the conclusion.

(D and E) These statements are irrelevant.

18. The linguist claims that if a person speaks two or more languages, then he or she will be more proficient than other students at learning an additional language.

Question Type: Conclusion

Correct answer: **D.** If the person is a Spaniard, then Spanish will probably have been his or her first language. The person has also learned English. So learning a third language (Chinese) would take less time than was taken in learning either of the other two.

(A) The linguist does not claim that a person will be more proficient at learning a first language than at learning a second.

(B) The linguist does not claim that a person's learning speed increases indefinitely with each new language learned.

(C) The linguist does not make any claims about the speed of learning a second language, regardless of a person's first language.

(E) This inference cannot be supported.

19. This reasoning assumes that just because we have not found traces of life on Mars, there must never have been life there.

Question Type: Reasoning strategy

Correct answer: **B.** The squib uses the lack of evidence for life on Mars to draw an erroneous conclusion.

(A, C–E) These choices do not describe the squib's reasoning.

20. This squib claims that sibling rivalry results either in dispersion (brothers avoiding competition by choosing different things in which to show an interest) or in competition (brothers seeking to do the same things and outcompete one another). The author then claims that dispersion is better than competition, because the latter prevents siblings from being mutually supportive.

Question Type: "Strengthen"

Correct answer: **B.** This statement, which says that sibling competition negatively affects a child's happiness, would bolster the author's conclusion.

(A) This statement would undermine the author's conclusion.

(C) The squib focused on sibling rivalry between brothers, not sisters.

(D) This statement is irrelevant to the author's conclusion.

(E) This statement would undermine the author's conclusion.

21. Based on only one criterion (variety), this squib claims that being a pizza delivery person is the greatest job.

Question Type: "Strengthen"

Correct answer: **A.** If this assumption were made, then delivering pizzas would be the greatest job if it truly had more variety than any other jobs.

(B) This assumption says nothing about legal or pizza delivery jobs (or any other jobs, for that matter), so it does not support the argument.

(C) This statement does not mean that legal jobs are not qualitatively better than pizza delivery.

(D) However, people work for compensation, so it cannot be said, based on this assumption, that pizza delivery would be the best job.

(E) But good jobs may be determined by other criteria, as well.

22. The squib admits that TV is entertaining, but it claims that TV has detrimental effects for some of its watchers: Either they become boring or their well-being is harmed. The squib concludes that all TV watchers are either masochistic or boring. However, this conclusion neglects the previously stated idea that people watch TV to gain pleasure.

Question Type: Reasoning strategy

Correct answer: **D.** This conclusion overlooks the statements regarding how entertaining TV is.

Instead, it just abruptly concludes that TV watchers are masochists or boring. The conclusion overlooks some important details mentioned in the squib.

(A) The squib does not mention a claim or its proponents.

(B, C, E) These strategies do not occur in the argument.

23. The purpose of this passage is to question why youngsters are so quick to get permanent tattoos when they shy away from all other kinds of commitments.

Question Type: Conclusion

Correct answer: **A.** This statement sums up the squib beautifully.

(B) Although this warning is an underlying point of the argument, it is not the main point.

(C) This statement is not implied by the squib.

(D) The squib does not make a judgment regarding young people getting tattoos. It just says that it is strange that teenagers are so willing to commit to tattoos when they are averse to making any other kinds of commitments.

(E) Most people would agree with this statement, but it is not the main point of the passage.

24. The squib claims that because the probability of any entrant winning a poker tournament is small, no entrant will win the tournament. This outcome, of course, is impossible.

Question Type: Analogous reasoning

Correct answer: **C.** This argument uses exactly the same logic as the squib.

(A) This argument would be analogous to the squib if it stated that no employee will be promoted to manager. Instead, it says merely that no one will be promoted at all.

(B) Unlike the squib, this argument's conclusion is rational.

(D) The flaw in this argument is different from the flaw in the squib's. (It is not logical to believe that exceptional circumstances have never occurred.)

(E) If the premise of this argument were true, it would be a logical argument.

25. The salesperson claims that there are two dangers that MailRight 2000 prevents: vandalizing teenagers and mail thieves. The salesperson claims that you can prevent these disasters only by purchasing MailRight 2000.

Question Type: "Strengthen"

Correct answer: **E.** This squib claims that any risks to which your mail is susceptible will be actualized. Of course, that claim is not true. There are many people who choose not to exploit the openness of you mailbox, so we would need to assume the truth of this answer choice for the squib to be logical.

(A) The squib never claims that MailRight 2000 would be able to withstand a hacksaw or a bomb.

(B) This assumption is not necessarily true.

(C) The squib is about an outdoor mailbox. Nothing need be assumed about houses.

(D) This assumption would undermine the argument for using MailRight 2000.

26. This squib states that a low calcium level in the diet correlates with osteoporosis. Additionally, the squib states that osteoporosis correlates with a lower calcium level in the bones.

Question Type: Reasoning strategy

Correct answer: **E.** Causation is left out of the squib completely. If osteoporosis causes lower levels of calcium in the bones, a person's diet of calcium would not be sufficient to cure the problem.

(A) These characteristics would be irrelevant to the passage.

(B) This choice is irrelevant. The passage is specifically about osteoporosis.

(C and D) These choices are both valid assumptions, based on the data given in the squib.

Section 4—Logical Reasoning

1. The tennis player claims that her ball was in. For the ball to have been in, it would have had to have been within the boundaries of the court or hit the line.

Question Type: Reasoning strategy

Correct answer: **E.** If her ball was not out, this assumption must be true.

(A) The tennis player did not claim that the referee was siding with the opponent; she merely claimed that it seemed as if this were so.

(B–D) These assumptions would all be irrelevant.

2. This squib claims that since soldiers were required to protect the Great Wall, the emperor would have been better served by avoiding the expense of the wall, instead just sending soldiers to the individual towns that needed defending.

Question Type: "Strengthen"

Correct answer: **E.** This statement means that there would have been no reason defensively to have the wall. Placing the soldiers in the cities, instead of at the wall, would have had the same results.

(A) The squib relates only to preventing attacks from outside the wall.

(B) This statement would undermine the conclusion.

(C) This statement does not mean that the wall would not have been more beneficial than deploying soldiers to individual towns.

(D) This choice is irrelevant to the squib.

3. The salesperson states that packages shipped during the month of December are prone to being thrown, crushed, or lost. The salesperson states that bubble wrap mitigates the former two dangers, but clearly bubble wrap would not prevent a package from being lost.

Question Type: Conclusion

Correct answer: **D.** Bubble wrap cannot protect packages from the dangers of being lost.

(A) Thanksgiving is irrelevant.

(B) A complete proscription from shipping packages during December would not be a reasonable solution to the slight added risk of damage.

(C) This conclusion cannot be drawn from the details.

(E) We are unable to determine whether this fact is true.

4. This squib states that fast-food chains can be considered monopolies. The squib further claims that even though fast food is unhealthy, the chains use advertising to get people to eat it. To solve this problem, the squib recommends breaking up the fast-food monopolies.

Question Type: "Strengthen"

Correct answer: **B.** This assumption must be true for the conclusion to be effective. Otherwise, the breakup of the fast food monopolies would have no positive effect on advertising.

(A) Brainwashing the nation to go to health-food restaurants would increase the health of the public.

(C) Even if Congress has the ability to correct most social problems, we are still unsure whether or not it would be able to cure the fast-food problem.

(D and E) These statements are irrelevant.

5. The homeowner acknowledges the plumber's claim that rice will usually decompose after several days in a sink. He or she then goes on to state that the stoppage occurred after a meal that included rice. The homeowner believes that this meal was the problem even though we know that rice will decompose. Therefore, there must have been elements in the meal besides rice that would have stopped up the sink.

Question Type: Conclusion

Correct answer: **A.** If this statement were true, it would strengthen the homeowner's conclusion that the specific meal of a few days ago was the one that caused the stoppage.

(B) This statement does not mean that they poured anything down the sink that would have stopped it up. They could have used the sink only to get water from the tap.

(C) This statement would not support the conclusion.

(D and E) These facts are both irrelevant.

6. This is a sufficient-necessary question:

1. Interstate Preschool Girl → Red Hair or Brown Hair
2. Tommy's Sister → Red Hair
3. Interstate Older Boys → Brown Hair

Conclusion = Tommy's Sister → Interstate Preschool

We need to find an assumption that would link the conclusion with one of the sufficient-necessary statements or facts.

Question Type: "Strengthen"

Correct answer: **C.** If this assumption were true, then all red-haired girls would have to go to Interstate Preschool.

(A) We do not know that Tommy's sister is a very young girl.

(B) This statement would just mean that all girls in Interstate Preschool have red hair.

(D and E) These two statements just mean that there are redheads outside the preschool.

7. This squib claims that as we have progressed as a society, we have devoted a larger and larger portion of our days to work. Based on the idea that time spent working makes us unhappy, the squib further claims that we have become increasingly unhappy as we have progressed. The squib then makes the unfounded assumption that all these trends will be continued into the future.

Question Type: "Weaken"

Correct answer: **D.** In other words, the net happiness gained from working would exceed the happiness lost because of less free time. The total happiness, therefore, would be greater.

(A) This choice is irrelevant.

(B and C) These statements would support the analysis in the squib.

(E) This choice is irrelevant, since it does not refer to happiness.

8. Rainfall is associated with additional plant growth. However, even though there has been a huge surplus of rainfall, there was not a corresponding increase in plant growth.

Question Type: "Resolve"

Correct answer: **D.** Deforestation might have caused the surplus in plant growth to be negatively offset by the loss of trees due to lumbering.

(A) This fact would not resolve the apparent logical problem.

(B) This statement does not mean that companies destroyed a large enough portion of the rainforest to offset the additional growth due to increased rainfall.

(C) This fact does not mean that people harvest all of the extra plants.

(E) This fact would not resolve anything.

9. The oil lobbyist never makes a substantive point when putting forth the argument. All the lobbyist talks about is the character of environmentalists.

Question Type: Reasoning strategy

Correct answer: **A.** All the lobbyist does is address the character of environmentalist groups rather than the merits of their views.

(B–E) These methods of reasoning are not used.

10. This squib claims that different societies attach different importance to knowing the exact time. The squib notes the difference between American and Spanish attitudes about time, and it then claims that it is hard for people to accustom themselves to new ideas about time when they move from one place to another.

Question Type: Conclusion

Correct answer: **D.** This statement has to be true because the passage states that Spanish people are less concerned about punctuality than Americans are. Additionally, the statement claims that people have a hard time adapting to a new society's attitudes about time.

(A and B) These inferences cannot be made from the details in the squib.

(C) The Spanish general attitude cannot be determined just on the basis of their relaxed view of time.

(E) Although this statement might be true when comparing America and Spain, we are unable to determine from the information within the passage that this is always the case.

11. The ecologist claims that it is difficult for corporations not to use "the very cheapest raw materials," found only in rainforests. The ecologist goes on to claim that by buying cheap goods, the consumer is inadvertently supporting the destruction of the rainforests.

Question Type: Reasoning strategy

Correct answer: **D.** The very cheapest raw materials are not necessarily always to be found in cheap products. Conversely, cheap products are not always made from the very cheapest raw materials.

(A) There is evidence offered to support the conclusions of the passage.

(B) The squib does offer a way to stem the problem.

(C) It is possible for companies to exert control over their practices.

(E) The argument in the squib is neither tautological nor circular.

12. The author notes that male blue jays are incredibly aggressive during laying season and claims that there must be some sort of benefit to this aggression. The author then hypothesizes that if a male blue jay died, the female would become extremely aggressive in order to reap the supposed benefits of this heightened aggression.

Question Type: "Strengthen"

Correct answer: **C.** If the gland that controls aggression in a female mirrors a male's, then it is likely that the female would assume the aggressive tendencies of a male.

(A) What happens to wrens is irrelevant to what happens to blue jays.

(B) This fact does not mean that the female was being as aggressive when she attacked as the male might have been.

(D) This fact would undermine the squib's conclusion.

(E) This statement would strengthen the contention of the passage that having an aggressive father is beneficial to blue jay eggs. However, the statement does not relate to the conclusion of the squib that a female blue jay would assume the aggression levels of her dead mate.

13. This squib claims that computer programmers get paid by the hour instead of per project. The programmer, then, could charge for more hours worked than there really were. However, despite this fact, the squib declares that companies have a good idea of how much they will have to pay for a given project, even though they set no limits on a programmer's hours.

Question Type: "Resolve"

Correct answer: **C.** If this statement were true, then client companies would always know the maximum they would have to pay to a programmer, and thus they would be able to figure out what they will have to pay for a program.

(A) This statement would confuse the situation.

(B) This statement does not help resolve the paradox.

(D) This fact would confuse the situation.

(E) This statement does not mean that client companies would be able to guess how many hours it would take a programmer to complete a project.

14. This squib says that celebrities benefit by apologizing for mistakes, because the public will tend to forgive these mistakes. If celebrities do not apologize, the public will persecute them.

Question Type: Conclusion

Correct answer: **C.** This conclusion follows from the premises in the squib.

(A) This conclusion cannot be drawn. The public might persecute a celebrity for something other than failing to admit a mistake.

(B) The squib said only that the public will usually forgive them.

(D) This choice is irrelevant.

(E) This statement seems to contradict the contentions of the passage.

15. The squib claims that no one builds artificial ponds to store water when there is a drought. Since people are building ponds in Maraland County, the author claims that there is no drought. The flaw in the reasoning is that maybe they are building ponds for reasons besides storing water.

Question Type: Analogous reasoning

Correct answer: **C.** This squib is analogous because it claims that farmers who don't get enough sunlight don't plant fruits and vegetables to sell. The farmers on Marble Road have planted fruits and vegetables, so the author assumes that the farmers get enough sunlight. However, they could be planting fruits and vegetables to eat themselves, not to sell.

(A and B) These arguments are not flawed.

(D and E) These arguments are flawed in different ways from the squib.

16. This squib tells about America's fascination with celebrities, and claims that this fascination has become a problem. The squib states that an answer to this problem might be found and acted upon by the media, the fans, and the celebrities themselves.

Question Type: Conclusion

Correct answer: **D.** This choice essentially restates the final sentence.

(A) Nothing is specifically implied about the effectiveness of not patronizing the tabloids.

(B) This suggestion is not advocated by the squib.

(C) The squib blames three distinct groups of people, not everyone.

(E) This claim is not stated or supported by the squib.

17. This squib draws a comparison between the lottery and the world series of poker. They are clearly distinct entities, but the author claims that because they are so similar, almost all their characteristics must be similar. The author uses this faulty reasoning to infer that since the lottery requires no skill, neither does poker.

Question Type: Reasoning strategy

Correct answer: **E.** The author assumes that since there are so many similarities, poker success must not depend on a person's skill any more than does lottery success.

(A) The squib does just the opposite.

(B–D) These are not argumentative methods used in the squib.

18. This study shows that preadolescents who are consistently messy eaters are likely to grow up to be disorganized. Clean eaters and eaters who are only sometimes clean are both likely to become organized adults.

Question Type: Conclusion

Correct answer: **C.** This claim is true based on the results of the study.

(A) The study said that messy eaters usually grow up to be disorganized, but not always.

(B) Sometimes clean eaters become disorganized adults.

(D) Nothing is stated about teenagers.

(E) This statement is irrelevant.

19. This squib relates that dancers need more flexibility during their routines, and it also claims that they are more flexible during the routines. However, the squib claims that runners do not need flexibility while running and indeed are less flexible while doing so.

Question Type: "Resolve"

Correct answer: **C.** The repetitive movements in running would cause people to become tighter, not more flexible, but the varied movements of dance would not induce tightness.

(A–B, D–E) These statements do not explain the differences in performance flexibility.

20. According to the squib, corporate crimes have been heavily felt by today's shareholders. To remedy this situation, the author argues for a government mandate that orders corporations to hire accounting firms to audit their books. One problem with this recommendation is that most corporations already do hire accounting firms to

audit their books, and it has been demonstrated that some accounting firms have criminally collaborated with corporate officers.

Question Type: "Weaken"

Correct answer: **C.** In other words, hiring accounting firms will sometimes worsen the problem of corporate crime.

(A) This statement would support the conclusion, not weaken it.

(B) But the author's solution might be effective for the companies not falling within these ranges.

(D) The emotions of the public are irrelevant.

(E) This statement is irrelevant.

21. This squib states that boredom occurs because a person is unable to entertain himself or herself. People who can entertain themselves can also entertain others. People who cannot entertain themselves cannot entertain others, and they will not be attractive. Therefore, loneliness is connected to boredom.

Question Type: Conclusion

Correct answer: **C.** The passage implies this statement, as the above reasoning shows.

(A) Surely, there are other excuses available.

(B) "The greatest" is a little extreme. The squib does not make this claim.

(D) The squib does not make this claim.

(E) We are unable to make this assumption based only on the squib.

22. This squib states that guns in houses are more likely to be used on a family member than an intruder. Therefore, lobbyists have tried to ban guns in homes, thinking that this ban will result in lower rates of injury to members of a household.

Question Type: "Weaken"

Correct answer: **E.** This statement completely contradicts the conclusion.

(A) As explained in the squib, the concerns are not superficial.

(B) These percentages are irrelevant.

(C) The author does not argue for no guns in society, only for no guns in homes.

(D) Even if true, this statement does not undermine the conclusion that fewer family members would be hurt growing up.

23. This squib claims that there is no reason not to build power lines underground.

Question Type: Conclusion

Correct answer: **B.** If cost were a factor, then the first premise in the passage would be untrue.

(A) This inference cannot be made based on the statements in the squib.

(C) This statement is irrelevant and cannot be inferred.

(D) This inference contradicts the first statement in the squib.

(E) This statement is irrelevant and cannot be inferred.

24. The squib states that waivers of ski slope liability are sometimes not enforceable in court. Mary's lawyer reviewed her waiver and told her that she did not have a case. However, if the state does not accept her waiver, then she would have a case.

Question Type: "Weaken"

Correct answer: **C.** If the courts do not enforce waivers, Mary might have a case.

(A) These facts would weaken the lawyer's credibility, but they would not necessarily mean that the lawyer is incorrect about Mary's situation.

(B) Since there was no negligence involved, she would almost definitely not have a case. The lawyer's contention is therefore probably correct.

(D) This choice is irrelevant.

(E) The people might have sued the ski slope for bad business practices rather than for an accident covered in their waivers.

25. The passage says that Picasso was an extremely passionate man. He expressed this passion in his paintings and also in a romantic relationship.

Question Type: "Weaken"

Correct answer: **C.** If this statement were true, then it would undermine the idea that his "passionate zeal" showed through his paintings.

(A) It does not matter what the contemporaries of Picasso thought.

(B, D–E) These statements are irrelevant.

PRACTICE TEST 4

ANSWER SHEET

SECTION 1	SECTION 2	SECTION 3	SECTION 4
1. Ⓐ Ⓑ Ⓒ Ⓓ Ⓔ	1. Ⓐ Ⓑ Ⓒ Ⓓ Ⓔ	1. Ⓐ Ⓑ Ⓒ Ⓓ Ⓔ	1. Ⓐ Ⓑ Ⓒ Ⓓ Ⓔ
2. Ⓐ Ⓑ Ⓒ Ⓓ Ⓔ	2. Ⓐ Ⓑ Ⓒ Ⓓ Ⓔ	2. Ⓐ Ⓑ Ⓒ Ⓓ Ⓔ	2. Ⓐ Ⓑ Ⓒ Ⓓ Ⓔ
3. Ⓐ Ⓑ Ⓒ Ⓓ Ⓔ	3. Ⓐ Ⓑ Ⓒ Ⓓ Ⓔ	3. Ⓐ Ⓑ Ⓒ Ⓓ Ⓔ	3. Ⓐ Ⓑ Ⓒ Ⓓ Ⓔ
4. Ⓐ Ⓑ Ⓒ Ⓓ Ⓔ	4. Ⓐ Ⓑ Ⓒ Ⓓ Ⓔ	4. Ⓐ Ⓑ Ⓒ Ⓓ Ⓔ	4. Ⓐ Ⓑ Ⓒ Ⓓ Ⓔ
5. Ⓐ Ⓑ Ⓒ Ⓓ Ⓔ	5. Ⓐ Ⓑ Ⓒ Ⓓ Ⓔ	5. Ⓐ Ⓑ Ⓒ Ⓓ Ⓔ	5. Ⓐ Ⓑ Ⓒ Ⓓ Ⓔ
6. Ⓐ Ⓑ Ⓒ Ⓓ Ⓔ	6. Ⓐ Ⓑ Ⓒ Ⓓ Ⓔ	6. Ⓐ Ⓑ Ⓒ Ⓓ Ⓔ	6. Ⓐ Ⓑ Ⓒ Ⓓ Ⓔ
7. Ⓐ Ⓑ Ⓒ Ⓓ Ⓔ	7. Ⓐ Ⓑ Ⓒ Ⓓ Ⓔ	7. Ⓐ Ⓑ Ⓒ Ⓓ Ⓔ	7. Ⓐ Ⓑ Ⓒ Ⓓ Ⓔ
8. Ⓐ Ⓑ Ⓒ Ⓓ Ⓔ	8. Ⓐ Ⓑ Ⓒ Ⓓ Ⓔ	8. Ⓐ Ⓑ Ⓒ Ⓓ Ⓔ	8. Ⓐ Ⓑ Ⓒ Ⓓ Ⓔ
9. Ⓐ Ⓑ Ⓒ Ⓓ Ⓔ	9. Ⓐ Ⓑ Ⓒ Ⓓ Ⓔ	9. Ⓐ Ⓑ Ⓒ Ⓓ Ⓔ	9. Ⓐ Ⓑ Ⓒ Ⓓ Ⓔ
10. Ⓐ Ⓑ Ⓒ Ⓓ Ⓔ	10. Ⓐ Ⓑ Ⓒ Ⓓ Ⓔ	10. Ⓐ Ⓑ Ⓒ Ⓓ Ⓔ	10. Ⓐ Ⓑ Ⓒ Ⓓ Ⓔ
11. Ⓐ Ⓑ Ⓒ Ⓓ Ⓔ	11. Ⓐ Ⓑ Ⓒ Ⓓ Ⓔ	11. Ⓐ Ⓑ Ⓒ Ⓓ Ⓔ	11. Ⓐ Ⓑ Ⓒ Ⓓ Ⓔ
12. Ⓐ Ⓑ Ⓒ Ⓓ Ⓔ	12. Ⓐ Ⓑ Ⓒ Ⓓ Ⓔ	12. Ⓐ Ⓑ Ⓒ Ⓓ Ⓔ	12. Ⓐ Ⓑ Ⓒ Ⓓ Ⓔ
13. Ⓐ Ⓑ Ⓒ Ⓓ Ⓔ	13. Ⓐ Ⓑ Ⓒ Ⓓ Ⓔ	13. Ⓐ Ⓑ Ⓒ Ⓓ Ⓔ	13. Ⓐ Ⓑ Ⓒ Ⓓ Ⓔ
14. Ⓐ Ⓑ Ⓒ Ⓓ Ⓔ	14. Ⓐ Ⓑ Ⓒ Ⓓ Ⓔ	14. Ⓐ Ⓑ Ⓒ Ⓓ Ⓔ	14. Ⓐ Ⓑ Ⓒ Ⓓ Ⓔ
15. Ⓐ Ⓑ Ⓒ Ⓓ Ⓔ	15. Ⓐ Ⓑ Ⓒ Ⓓ Ⓔ	15. Ⓐ Ⓑ Ⓒ Ⓓ Ⓔ	15. Ⓐ Ⓑ Ⓒ Ⓓ Ⓔ
16. Ⓐ Ⓑ Ⓒ Ⓓ Ⓔ	16. Ⓐ Ⓑ Ⓒ Ⓓ Ⓔ	16. Ⓐ Ⓑ Ⓒ Ⓓ Ⓔ	16. Ⓐ Ⓑ Ⓒ Ⓓ Ⓔ
17. Ⓐ Ⓑ Ⓒ Ⓓ Ⓔ	17. Ⓐ Ⓑ Ⓒ Ⓓ Ⓔ	17. Ⓐ Ⓑ Ⓒ Ⓓ Ⓔ	17. Ⓐ Ⓑ Ⓒ Ⓓ Ⓔ
18. Ⓐ Ⓑ Ⓒ Ⓓ Ⓔ	18. Ⓐ Ⓑ Ⓒ Ⓓ Ⓔ	18. Ⓐ Ⓑ Ⓒ Ⓓ Ⓔ	18. Ⓐ Ⓑ Ⓒ Ⓓ Ⓔ
19. Ⓐ Ⓑ Ⓒ Ⓓ Ⓔ	19. Ⓐ Ⓑ Ⓒ Ⓓ Ⓔ	19. Ⓐ Ⓑ Ⓒ Ⓓ Ⓔ	19. Ⓐ Ⓑ Ⓒ Ⓓ Ⓔ
20. Ⓐ Ⓑ Ⓒ Ⓓ Ⓣ	20. Ⓐ Ⓑ Ⓒ Ⓓ Ⓔ	20. Ⓐ Ⓑ Ⓒ Ⓓ Ⓔ	20. Ⓐ Ⓑ Ⓒ Ⓓ Ⓔ
21. Ⓐ Ⓑ Ⓒ Ⓓ Ⓔ	21. Ⓐ Ⓑ Ⓒ Ⓓ Ⓔ	21. Ⓐ Ⓑ Ⓒ Ⓓ Ⓔ	21. Ⓐ Ⓑ Ⓒ Ⓓ Ⓔ
22. Ⓐ Ⓑ Ⓒ Ⓓ Ⓔ	22. Ⓐ Ⓑ Ⓒ Ⓓ Ⓔ	22. Ⓐ Ⓑ Ⓒ Ⓓ Ⓔ	22. Ⓐ Ⓑ Ⓒ Ⓓ Ⓔ
23. Ⓐ Ⓑ Ⓒ Ⓓ Ⓔ	23. Ⓐ Ⓑ Ⓒ Ⓓ Ⓔ	23. Ⓐ Ⓑ Ⓒ Ⓓ Ⓔ	23. Ⓐ Ⓑ Ⓒ Ⓓ Ⓔ
24. Ⓐ Ⓑ Ⓒ Ⓓ Ⓔ	24. Ⓐ Ⓑ Ⓒ Ⓓ Ⓔ	24. Ⓐ Ⓑ Ⓒ Ⓓ Ⓔ	24. Ⓐ Ⓑ Ⓒ Ⓓ Ⓔ
25. Ⓐ Ⓑ Ⓒ Ⓓ Ⓔ	25. Ⓐ Ⓑ Ⓒ Ⓓ Ⓔ	25. Ⓐ Ⓑ Ⓒ Ⓓ Ⓔ	25. Ⓐ Ⓑ Ⓒ Ⓓ Ⓔ
26. Ⓐ Ⓑ Ⓒ Ⓓ Ⓔ	26. Ⓐ Ⓑ Ⓒ Ⓓ Ⓔ	26. Ⓐ Ⓑ Ⓒ Ⓓ Ⓔ	26. Ⓐ Ⓑ Ⓒ Ⓓ Ⓔ
27. Ⓐ Ⓑ Ⓒ Ⓓ Ⓔ	27. Ⓐ Ⓑ Ⓒ Ⓓ Ⓔ	27. Ⓐ Ⓑ Ⓒ Ⓓ Ⓔ	27. Ⓐ Ⓑ Ⓒ Ⓓ Ⓔ
28. Ⓐ Ⓑ Ⓒ Ⓓ Ⓔ	28. Ⓐ Ⓑ Ⓒ Ⓓ Ⓔ	28. Ⓐ Ⓑ Ⓒ Ⓓ Ⓔ	28. Ⓐ Ⓑ Ⓒ Ⓓ Ⓔ
29. Ⓐ Ⓑ Ⓒ Ⓓ Ⓔ	29. Ⓐ Ⓑ Ⓒ Ⓓ Ⓔ	29. Ⓐ Ⓑ Ⓒ Ⓓ Ⓔ	29. Ⓐ Ⓑ Ⓒ Ⓓ Ⓔ
30. Ⓐ Ⓑ Ⓒ Ⓓ Ⓔ	30. Ⓐ Ⓑ Ⓒ Ⓓ Ⓔ	30. Ⓐ Ⓑ Ⓒ Ⓓ Ⓔ	30. Ⓐ Ⓑ Ⓒ Ⓓ Ⓔ

SECTION 1
Time—35 minutes
26 questions

<u>Directions for Logical Reasoning Questions:</u> The questions in this section are based on brief statements or passages. Choose your answers based on the reasoning in each passage. Do not make assumptions that are not supported by the passage or by common sense. For some questions, more than one answer choice may be possible, so choose the *best* answer to each question, that is, the one that is most accurate and complete. After you have chosen your answer, mark the corresponding space on the Answer Sheet.

1. Switch-hitting is the ability to bat both right-handed and left-handed. Most players are naturally inclined to bat a certain way, and only at an older age devote the time and practice to acquiring the ability to hit from the other side of the plate. Interestingly enough, quite often the hitter who chooses to learn to switch-hit will become more technically proficient at the new batting style than at the method to which he or she is naturally inclined. Observing this phenomenon in the distant but comparable milieu of literature, it is apparent that many foreign-born writers—Nabokov and Conrad quickly come to mind—have demonstrated a mastery of the English language that surpasses fluency and even their own respective grips on their own respective native tongues.

   If the statements above are true, it can be concluded on the basis of them that:

   (A) Nabokov is a better writer in English than he is in Russian, his native language.
   (B) Baseball and writing are not as different as one might think.
   (C) Human beings, no matter what they pursue, possess astounding powers of adaptability.
   (D) Nabokov and Conrad devoted countless hours to studying the English language.
   (E) Just as switch-hitting helps a baseball player, the ability to write in two languages greatly benefits a writer.

2. Julio: The tower rising in the east is surely being built by Solomon the Great. Only he could muster an army and regiment great enough to build a tower of that size.

   Marcos: That tower is being built by my brother! He recruited the army a year ago and is finally putting it to work on the tower. Do not worry; you have nothing to fear from him.

   Which of the following would best resolve the apparent discrepancy in opinions regarding who is building the tower without contravening anyone's opinion?

   (A) The tower is not being built by Marcos's brother, but it is not being built by Solomon the Great either.
   (B) Solomon the Great only builds towers in the east so long as people are to the west of him.
   (C) The army of Marco's brother would be able to decimate the army of Solomon the Great if they ever were to meet in battle.
   (D) Solomon the Great has also built temples to the east along with the castles that have been built by Marcos's brother.
   (E) Marcos's father is married to the mother of Solomon the Great.

GO ON TO THE NEXT PAGE

3. Statesperson: Professional athletes have trained their whole lives to excel in purely physical domains. Practicing all day in order to dominate the competition in their specific sport, these athletes do not have the time to study, to read, or to pursue any real intellectual endeavor. Therefore, when I hear about a country that consistently elects leaders who have been professional athletes, or even worse, professional actors, I immediately become disgusted. For it is quite clear that neither actors nor athletes possess the requisite learning that is necessary to effectively lead a country.

Which of the following, if true, would undermine the statesperson's conclusion?

(A) Many of the world's largest and most powerful countries consistently elect leaders who were professional athletes or actors.

(B) A professional athlete or actor can take the time to master the knowledge necessary to become an effective leader.

(C) It is very myopic to let personal views about the characteristics of professional athletes or actors bias your view toward an entire country.

(D) Actors and professional athletes are often very successful in other careers after they finish their stint as actors or athletes.

(E) The statesperson was once a professional poker player, but he is now a brilliant intellectual and excellent politician.

4. A current advertisement claims that grapes will dramatically increase one's life span. This advertisement first entered the marketplace about a year ago, and when contacted, the scientists whose work provides the backing for this claim admit that they have conducted research regarding the claim for only about two years. It is impossible to determine whether something can "increase one's life span dramatically" in just two years' time, so it is obvious that this is a clear-cut case of false advertising.

The argument utilizes which of the following methods to advance its point?

(A) It analogizes the scientists' fact-based claim to a previous case regarding false advertising.

(B) It infers that the originators of a claim did not encourage the misleading use made of it in the advertisement.

(C) It addresses the issue that certain scientific data must be collected before conclusions can be negated.

(D) It asssumes, on the basis of a competing theory, that the scientists' theory regarding the benefits of grapes is flawed.

(E) It undermines a postulation on the grounds that it is impossible to confirm it based on current evidence.

GO ON TO THE NEXT PAGE

5. Grapes are left out in the sun to make raisins because the sugar from the grape will interact with sunlight to caramelize and form a raisin. This is the reason why there is such a difference in taste between grapes and raisins. But this explanation does not make complete sense, because grapes were left in the sun for many months while they were growing on the vine and they did not turn into raisins. Only after they were removed from the vine did they turn into raisins. In order to make raisins, it must be necessary not only to put the grapes in the sun but also to remove them from the vine.

Which of the following, if true, would most support the conclusion of the passage?

(A) Grapes that are left on the vine past the point that they are normally picked will rot before morphing out of their grape state.

(B) Sunlight will caramelize cranberries if the cranberries are taken off the vine and placed in a dry, sunlit area.

(C) Grapes do not become raisins if they are grown in an environment where there is not enough sunlight for the sugar to caramelize.

(D) Sugar can turn into caramel only with the mixture of heat, light, and complex natural sugars that are present in certain fruits.

(E) Raisins will turn back into grapes if they are grafted back onto the vine through use of high-tech botanical techniques.

6. When paper is littered, it will be an eyesore for a period of time but eventually it will decompose. When plastic is littered, it will not decompose into the surrounding environment for thousands of years. This fact is why choosing between paper and plastic grocery bags is such an important decision. Choosing paper encourages companies to cut down more forests, but choosing plastic creates refuse that will almost never decompose. One particular environmental agency believes that it has solved this problem and recommends that its members choose plastic bags.

Which of the following, if true, would resolve the seeming discrepancy between the agency's opinion and the facts of the argument?

(A) Agency members have been instructed to recycle the plastic bags, so that they will be reused instead of littered.

(B) If everyone used paper bags, then there is a small chance that America's forestlands could eventually be decimated.

(C) When plastic bags are littered, certain chemicals can be poured on them to make them decompose more quickly.

(D) Plastic bags compress more easily than paper bags, and after several years in a landfill, they compress to one-half their original size.

(E) Some agency members use plastic bags that they get from the grocery store for additional purposes besides carrying home their groceries.

GO ON TO THE NEXT PAGE

7. Guidance counselor: Teen movies are an excellent source of entertainment for growing teenagers and adults alike. The movies are fast-paced, comical, and relatively devoid of nuanced plot. Apart from their entertainment value, the movies provide examples of social behavior for teenagers to view and compare to their own lives. Teenagers learn the consequences of being the anti-intellectual jock, the domineering bully, or the class clown. After reviewing the trials and tribulations of movie characters, teenagers will strive to avoid resembling the high school social archetypes that they see caricatured in these films.

Which of the following, if true, would most support the conclusion?

(A) Action movies provide teenagers with role models who are different from the high school archetypes they see in teen movies.

(B) Teachers in teen movies encourage their students to depart from the traditional roles that students assume in a high school.

(C) Domineering bullies always change their ways after seeing a movie that depicts a domineering bully in a bad light.

(D) After students from several high schools saw a certain teen movie, they reversed their normal social roles for a number of weeks.

(E) The lunch room is always a more peaceful place after groups of students have seen a teen movie.

8. Organic chemistry is the most important class on a premed applicant's transcript. Medical schools feel that the rigorous learning process required to do well in an organic chemistry class is very similar to the rigorous learning process required for the majority of classes in medical school. Therefore, medical schools believe that students who do not achieve high marks in organic chemistry will not be capable of performing well in medical school classes.

Which of the following, if true, would question the appropriateness of the assumption of the medical schools?

(A) Because the subject matter is so difficult, organic chemistry is much more taxing for students than any medical school course would be.

(B) Because the subject matter is so uninteresting, many students who would excel in medical school classes do not achieve high marks in organic chemistry.

(C) Because there is a shortage of organic chemistry teachers, the course is not taught at some universities, so medical schools look at the biochemistry scores of applicants from these schools.

(D) Because organic chemistry is so different from the subjects taught in medical school, a much better test of an applicant's future success in medical school would be performance in a medical school class.

(E) Because organic chemistry is so different from other college subjects, organic chemistry scores are no indicator of an applicant's undergraduate academic performance.

GO ON TO THE NEXT PAGE

9. When a parent who regularly exceeds the speed limit when driving tells a child not to speed, the advice is almost never heeded. However, when a child is told not to speed by a parent who never speeds, then the advice is sometimes heeded.

Which of the following has a logical structure similar to the argument above?

(A) When a country with a nuclear program tells another country not to develop a nuclear program, the directive is almost never accepted. However, when a country without a nuclear program advises a country not to develop a nuclear program, the advice is accepted.

(B) When a teacher who is mean advises a student to play well with others, the advice is almost never accepted. However, when a teacher who is nice advises a student to play well with others, the advice is sometimes accepted.

(C) When parents who are intelligent advise their child to study harder, the child almost always studies harder. However, when parents who are not intelligent advise their child to study harder, the child almost never studies harder.

(D) When a rocket scientist develops an engine that will go to the moon, the government almost never accepts it. However, when a NASA scientist develops an engine that will go to the moon, the government sometimes accepts it.

(E) When tobacco lobbyists ask a politician for tax breaks, they almost always get them. However, when raw-materials lobbyists ask for similar tax breaks, they almost never get them.

10. Executive: Internet banking is clearly the wave of the future, and in anticipation of this change, our company must examine the opportunities involved. More and more companies are downsizing their accounting departments for the sake of online services that accomplish the same thing far more efficiently. Soon enough, this trend will extend into the home, as individual bill payers and account holders realize that instead of taking the time to write out and mail a check, with the risk that the check might be lost in the mail, they have the option of simply clicking on a Web site that provides this service, choosing the appropriate payee, and typing in the amount they wish to pay.

Which of the following best summarizes the executive's main point?

(A) The executive's company should look into opportunities in online banking.

(B) Online banking and bill paying is far superior to its offline equivalent.

(C) Not only businesses but also individuals will pay their bills offline.

(D) One risk of paying bills without an online service is that the mailed check may get lost.

(E) Internet banking is the wave of the future.

GO ON TO THE NEXT PAGE

11. Secret agencies like the NSA, CIA, and even some college fraternal orders are relatively interesting to outsiders. The allure of secrecy and exclusivity attracts the attention and respect of all sorts of people. People assume that if information is closely guarded, then it must be exciting and important. The same phenomenon is present in certain nightclubs that stop people from entering into certain spaces through the ingenious use of velvet ropes. The clubs have VIP rooms, then VIP rooms in the VIP rooms, and then an upper level for the most VIP of the VIPs. Essentially, these clubs get rich by selling elitism. People really seem to buy into it, but it has a horrible effect on society by promoting a class system that breeds separatism and jealousy.

Which of the following, if true, would most support the argument?

(A) Nightclubs that do not promote elitism are socially beneficial because they allow people to sit down and have drinks together.
(B) VIP rooms do not allow people to move around easily and speak to other people in different VIP rooms.
(C) People in societies that promote elitism are on average far less satisfied with their lives than are people in societies that do not promote elitism.
(D) Secret agencies like the CIA and NSA are not necessary for the safety or security of our country.
(E) College fraternal orders that promote elitism always make freshmen's lives more unpleasant.

12. At Stanley Carpets, all shags are dark cherry colored, and all throws are light cherry colored. Some shags are manufactured by the premium carpet maker Bowden, Inc. Bowden, Inc. manufactures carpets only in colors that are approved by its Director of Colors, Mrs. Bowden. Mrs. Bowden prefers light cherry to dark cherry, and she prefers shags to all other types of carpet, although her company provides all of Stanley Carpets' throws.

If the information provided is true, which of the following can be concluded?

(A) At Stanley Carpets, some shags are light cherry colored.
(B) At Stanley Carpets, none of the dark cherry shags are provided by Bowden, Inc.
(C) Bowden, Inc. provides Stanley Carpets with light cherry colored throws.
(D) All of Bowden, Inc.'s shags are dark cherry colored.
(E) Bowden, Inc. only manufactures throws that are light cherry colored.

GO ON TO THE NEXT PAGE

13. High school student: Semester grades are counterproductive. Students who love to learn should be commended by their knowledge instead of a piece of paper. If grades were not an issue, then people who did not want to come to class would not come. The classroom would be filled only with students who love learning, thereby creating an academic environment imbued with a thirst for knowledge that is not often found in high school. Furthermore, I feel that my fellow teens who dislike learning agree with my view. They feel that their time would be better spent playing video games than learning the riddles of trigonometry. It is clear that the students have reached a consensus, so semester grades will be abolished.

Which of the following, if true, would contradict the validity of this student's conclusion?

(A) High school students' opinions about semester grades are irrelevant in the determination as to whether there will continue to be semester grades.

(B) All students feel that a new system to monitor student progress should be implemented if semester grades are to be abolished.

(C) A very small minority of high school students actually like semester grades and do not feel that they should be abolished.

(D) If principals and teachers also felt that semester grades should be abolished, then grades would be abolished.

(E) Most teachers hate the grading system because it increases the likelihood that they will have counterproductive grade-grubbers in their class.

14. One of the most fundamental theorems of geometry is the Pythagorean theorem. It holds that the sum of the squares of the two sides of a right triangle is equal to the square of the hypotenuse of the triangle. The recently discovered Juilliard theorem has been gaining ground with math students. This theorem holds that the sum of the squares of the two sides of a right triangle is equal to the square root of the hypotenuse. The head of the math team cannot decide which theorem to choose when asked a question in the local math bowl, but it would be advisable for her to choose the traditionally accepted theory.

The argument utilizes which of the following methods to advance its point?

(A) It recommends a specific course of action on the grounds that it has been traditionally accepted.

(B) It argues for a certain alternative by claiming that an opposing alternative is incorrect.

(C) It delineates three specific options and advises a student to choose a specific option in a certain case.

(D) It infers that because a theory is innovative and new, it is probably more correct than theories propounded earlier.

(E) It argues that the premise of a particular theory contradicts the more correct premise of the competing theory.

GO ON TO THE NEXT PAGE

15. John: Many people believe that ghosts are nothing more than figments of peoples' imaginations. After all, it is strange that a person who is a little more nervous or paranoid than the rest of us always seems to be the one crying "ghost" and creating a scare for us normal people.

Mary: It is true that nervous people are always the ones who see ghosts. Thank goodness that someone does it so that they do not float around unnoticed!

Which of the following would resolve the two opinions by explaining why it is nervous people who see ghosts?

(A) Nervous people dislike being alone and tend to call attention to themselves in order to avoid feeling lonely.
(B) Nervous people want to keep other people from feeling as nervous as they do.
(C) Nervous people are naturally more attuned to the spiritual world than normal people are.
(D) Normal people do not generally believe the claims of nervous people except when they are about ghosts.
(E) Normal people generally identify just as many ghosts as nervous people do.

16. Jillian: Painting a house bright blue is a good way to alienate your neighbors. If you are interested in maintaining good relations with those living close to you, then it is a good idea to paint all portions of your house in colors that are more conservative than bright blue or electric orange. In addition to painting your house a bright color, having a dog that barks or a burglar alarm that sounds constantly in the night while people are sleeping are also good ways to make everyone mad. I myself had a rooster that liked to crow at sunup every morning. Everyone loved him because he was the perfect wake-up call. Some people even said that they saved money on buying an alarm clock.

Which of the following is assumed by Jillian?

(A) Everyone in the neighborhood will love a rooster that crows at nighttime.
(B) A dog that barked at sunup every morning would be as widely loved as a rooster that did so.
(C) People respond differently to loud noises at night and loud noises in the morning.
(D) Bright house colors upset people just as much as a rooster crowing each morning at sunup.
(E) Saving money on alarm clocks is more important to people than sleeping a couple of extra hours.

GO ON TO THE NEXT PAGE

17. Hedge clipper: Cutting hedgerows into specific designs and shapes is one of the most difficult forms of art to maintain. I liken my work to that of a master chef, toiling over his dish, his masterpiece, only to have it eaten and destroyed by people who could never appreciate the work as much as he could himself. Everyday he goes into work to make beautiful culinary opuses, only to have them destroyed immediately after their creation. What a difficult job his must be. In the same way, I go and clip a set of bushes to resemble a portrait, a racecar, or anything. However, the bushes inevitably continue to grow and by growing destroy the art that I created with their branches.

Which of the following is assumed by the hedge clipper?

(A) Master chefs and hedge clippers are of equal artistic merit.
(B) Food is comparable to bushes in every way that is artistically important.
(C) All bushes grow after hedge clippers shape them into artistic formations.
(D) A culinary specialist could never appreciate the art of a master chef.
(E) Homeowners cannot appreciate the work of the hedge clipper as much as he can.

18. Politician: There has been incendiary controversy abounding about last year's budget report. Claims have been made that my office skimmed funds off the top of statewide tax revenues and generated incorrect figures for the budget report, but the data simply do not support these conjectures. As proof of my innocence, I have provided my opponents with the four financial statements that were used to make last year's budget report. My opponents will review the figures in last year's report based on these statements, and through this review, they will be able to conclusively demonstrate that I deserve to be exonerated from all allegations of graft.

Which of the following is an implicit flaw in the reasoning of the argument?

(A) It ignores the fact that the politician might still deserve to be accused of gambling and intemperance.
(B) It assumes that the figures offered in the four financial statements are completely accurate.
(C) It fails to recognize that politicians would never allow a budget report to show that they skimmed funds off the tax revenue.
(D) It confuses the phrase "incendiary controversy" with the phrase "allegations of graft."
(E) It embraces the fact that epistemologically there is no way to offer convincing proof of anything with reports and statements.

GO ON TO THE NEXT PAGE

19. Retiree: Now that I have quit my job, I am going to enjoy the fat life. I have no work to do, I have nowhere to go, and I have plenty of money to spend and keep me happy until I die.

Investment adviser: I am not so sure about that, John. Looking at your portfolio and the recent trends in the stock market, it appears that you will have to return to work in five years to support yourself.

Which of the following, if true, would undermine the conclusion of the investment adviser?

(A) Recent trends indicate that the stock market will start going up sometime in the next five years.
(B) The investment adviser is always correct in his predictions about the need to return to work.
(C) John's friends who are also retired will not need to return to work, despite the stock market trends.
(D) John will return to work again 10 years from now after having quit another job.
(E) John has many excellent nonstock investments that the adviser doesn't know about.

20. Existentialist: The weather is a valid indicator of my attitude. I am so connected to the natural forces that if it is rainy, then I too am sad. If it is sunny and bright, then I am happy. If it is windy, then I am pensive and contemplative. If it is snowing lightly, then I am tranquil and pristine. Today, it is foggy, and for some reason, I cannot decide my emotional content at the moment. Therefore, I am unsure whether or not all of my emotions are connected to the natural forces.

Which of the following would support the idea that the existentialist's emotions are completely connected to the weather?

(A) When it is foggy, the existentialist's emotions are not tied to the weather.
(B) When viewing a rainbow, the existentialist experiences transcendental happiness.
(C) Foggy weather causes the existentialist to become confused.
(D) Foggy weather induces a feeling of isolation in most people.
(E) Weather forecasters who try to predict foggy weather sometimes frustrate the existentialist.

GO ON TO THE NEXT PAGE

21. Airline executive: The recent trend in the airline industry to minimize or, in some cases, eliminate altogether any in-flight amenities or extras, such as complementary meals and entertainment, will open up myriad opportunities for our company to win customers away from our competitors. This newly popular no-frills strategy, which saves each ticket buyer only a few dollars, will prove less satisfactory to passengers than our competitors believe, since recent satisfaction surveys indicate that 63 percent of airline passengers feel, at some point during their flights, either hungry or bored.

Which of the following, if true, would most seriously damage the airline executive's argument?

(A) The napkins the executive's company provides are generally considered by airline passengers to be "unsatisfactory."

(B) Airline passengers, responding to a survey, indicate that cost is by far their primary consideration when they book a flight, even if the cost difference between two flights is quite small.

(C) Fifty-four percent of airline passengers report feeling hungry, while only 9 percent report feeling bored.

(D) Other airlines allow their passengers to bring their own food aboard their planes.

(E) Other airlines still plan to offer meals and entertainment, but they will charge for both.

22. Politician: Poverty levels around the globe are on the rise. Due to overpopulation, many countries are unable to provide their impoverished citizens with enough food to sustain their lives. Something must be done about this problem in the United States. We will mandate that all farmers must sell all of their stores of grain this year, including the amount that they normally save in order to seed next year's crop. This will create a surplus of food that will curb hunger in our nation until we can find additional ways to help alleviate the problem.

Which of the following illuminates a major flaw in the politician's argument?

(A) Poverty and hunger are separate problems that require very different solutions.

(B) The only way to solve the hunger problem is to teach the poor to grow enough food for themselves.

(C) There is no reason to believe that feeding people more grain will adequately fulfill their dietary requirements.

(D) Consuming all grain stores will be likely to aggravate future hunger problems instead of alleviating them.

(E) The argument assumes what it set out to prove, that by providing more food to the poor, the poor will receive food.

GO ON TO THE NEXT PAGE

23. The digital guitar amplifier, introduced in the early 1990s by a number of manufacturers, presented an alternative to tube amps by providing a lighter body and myriad features and effects unavailable in the classic Vox or Boogie tube models. Though these new amps could not quite match the sound quality and richness of tone provided by their tube-style predecessors, some of the best models came quite close, while at the same time offering a wide array of extra features never before seen on an amplifier. And yet, most serious guitarists continue to play through tube amps.

Which of the following is the main point of the passage?

(A) The digital amp has not had the effect on the amplifier market among serious guitarists that its manufacturers hoped that it would.
(B) Most serious guitarists prefer richness of tone to lightness of body and a plethora of features and effects.
(C) Although serious guitarists tend to prefer tube amps, more amateur guitarists might enjoy all that digital amps have to offer.
(D) Digital amps are in many ways better than tube amps.
(E) Though digital amps rival the sound quality of tube amps while offering additional features, they have not overcome tube amps' popularity among serious guitarists.

24. The first concern of all political candidates should be that their supporters go out and vote on election day. Good speeches, heart-felt handshakes, and campaign promises make no difference if your supporters do not go out and vote.

Which of the following possesses a logic structure most similar to that of the argument above?

(A) Teachers' primary concern should be teaching their students well, because if students are not taught well, then they will not do well on tests.
(B) Politicians' first concern should be utilizing their governmental position to bring about good for the community. If they are elected and do not bring about good for the community, then the support that was given to them on election day makes no difference.
(C) Coaches' first priority should be getting the team members to the games on time. Because if the team members do not arrive at the games, everything done at practice will be meaningless.
(D) Physicians should be most concerned with making their patients healthy. For if this is not their first concern, then there is no reason for them to be physicians and patients would be better served by being treated by someone else.
(E) Sports players should be most concerned with being athletic. They should be because if they are not athletic, then all of their sports drink endorsements will soon dry up and not be offered anymore.

GO ON TO THE NEXT PAGE

25. Fisherman: The best way to catch fish is to creep up behind them and throw your bait at them while they are not looking.

Philip: Are you serious? That sounds like the way that people are supposed to hunt deer, not catch fish. Fish don't care whether you sneak up behind them or drive your boat right on top of them, so long as your hook has a worm on it.

Which of the following, if true, would cast doubt on Philip's conclusion regarding fish?

(A) When fish do not realize that a boat is nearby, they are more likely to eat worms.
(B) Sneaking up on deer is not an effective hunting method.
(C) Forty-two years of experience has led the fisherman to be right in almost all of his conclusions.
(D) Philip has never gone fishing before, even though he is an avid deer hunter.
(E) Fishermen who sneak up on their prey encounter fewer sharks than those who do not.

26. Recent extrapolative computer-generated models have suggested that if and when Earth enters another ice age, the mammal best suited to withstand and survive the extreme climate change will be, surprisingly, the aardvark. Clearly, this is because the aardvark possesses not only an insulated, thick epidermal layer but also a self-regulating internal thermometer that, in cases of extreme cold, allows its system to shut down to an almost reptilian level of body fuel efficiency.

Which one of the following best identifies the flawed reasoning in the passage above?

(A) The information about the aardvark upon which it is based is not faulty.
(B) Scientific theory cannot rely solely upon computer-generated simulations.
(C) The aardvark exists primarily only in the southwestern United States, an area that would be one of the last to be affected by another ice age.
(D) More is required for survival in extreme climates than a thick epidermal layer and a self-regulating internal thermometer.
(E) Earth is unlikely to enter another ice age until the aardvark has evolved into several new species.

STOP

IF YOU FINISH BEFORE TIME RUNS OUT, CHECK YOUR WORK ON THIS SECTION ONLY.
DO NOT GO ON TO ANY OTHER TEST SECTION.

SECTION 2
Time—35 minutes
24 questions

<u>Directions for Logic Games Questions:</u> The questions in this section are divided into groups. Each group is based on a set of conditions. For each question, choose the answer that is most accurate and complete. For some questions, you may wish to draw a rough diagram to help you select your response. Mark the corresponding space on your Answer Sheet.

<u>Questions 1–6</u>

John, Frank, and Stan all go into a pet store one day to buy fish A, B, C, D, E, F, G, and H. John buys two fish, Frank buys three, and Stan buys three. Certain fish cannot live in the same tank together and some like living together, so they are purchased according to the following constraints:

> A is bought along with two other fish.
> Frank buys B.
> D and F are not bought together.
> If A is bought by Frank, then F and G are bought by John.
> If C is bought by John, then E, F, and G are bought together.

1. Which of the following pairs of fish could have been bought by John?

   (A) B, C
   (B) F, D
   (C) A, G
   (D) G, H
   (E) B, A

2. Which pair of fish can Frank NOT buy?

   (A) A and G
   (B) E and B
   (C) B and D
   (D) C and G
   (E) D and A

3. Which of the following is a list of the fish that Stan could buy?

   (A) B, A, D
   (B) F, G, C
   (C) E, C, H
   (D) B, H, G
   (E) E, F, D

4. If John buys E and G, then which of the following must be true?

   (A) D is bought by John.
   (B) H is bought by Stan.
   (C) A is bought by Stan.
   (D) D is bought by Stan.
   (E) H is bought by Frank.

5. If Frank buys A, then which of the following could be true?

   (A) G is bought with A.
   (B) B is not bought with A.
   (C) E is bought with F.
   (D) C is bought with H.
   (E) E is not bought with A, H, or D.

6. If D is bought by John and E is bought by Frank, then which of the following must NOT be true?

   (A) E is bought by Frank.
   (B) A is bought by Stan.
   (C) H is bought by John.
   (D) G is bought by Frank.
   (E) C is bought by John.

GO ON TO THE NEXT PAGE

Questions 7–12

A pet store puts pairs of animals together in four cages. Animals A, B, C, and D from group 1 will each be paired with one animal R, S, T, or U from group 2 in cages labeled from 1 to 4. Only one pair of animals goes in each cage. There are two animals in each cage and only one animal from each group in each cage.

D is in cage 2.
A does not share a cage with U.
There is exactly one cage in between the cages of R and T.
D shares a cage with either S or R.

7. If D shares a cage with S, then which of the following must be true?

(A) T is in cage 3.
(B) U is in cage 4.
(C) A is not in cage 1 or cage 3.
(D) D is in a lower-numbered cage than A.
(E) U shares a cage with B.

8. If S is in cage 1, then which of the following could NOT be true?

(A) A is in cage 3.
(B) B shares a cage with T.
(C) C shares a cage with S.
(D) S is in a lower-numbered cage than U.
(E) U and T are in consecutive cages.

9. If A is in cage 4, then which of the following must be true?

(A) S is in a lower-numbered cage than U.
(B) S shares a cage with no other animal.
(C) B and C are in consecutive cages.
(D) D is in a higher-numbered cage than A.
(E) U is in a lower-numbered cage than T.

10. If B is in cage 3 and C is in cage 4, then which of the following could be true?

(A) C shares a cage with S.
(B) D shares a cage with T.
(C) U shares a cage with D.
(D) A shares a cage with R.
(E) B shares a cage with S.

11. If T is in a lower-numbered cage than S, then which of the following must NOT be true?

(A) T shares a cage with C.
(B) B shares a cage with R.
(C) R shares a cage with D.
(D) B is in a lower-numbered cage than D.
(E) A is in a higher-numbered cage than C.

12. If which two variables are in cage 1, then we know the positions of all the other variables in the game?

(A) A and R
(B) S and A
(C) U and B
(D) C and S
(E) R and D

GO ON TO THE NEXT PAGE

Questions 13–18

At a local dog show, four judges have chosen their top two picks for the prizewinning dogs. Strangely, eight different dogs, A, B, C, D, E, F, G, and H, have been chosen for awards, manifesting complete disagreement among the judges. The judges' top two picks can be partially determined by the following constraints:

> The judge that chooses D chooses G.
> The judge that chooses H chooses A.
> If judge 3 chooses D, H, or F, then judge 2 chooses B.
> F cannot be chosen with B or C.
> Judge 3 cannot choose C.
> If E is chosen by judge 1, then H is not chosen by judge 3.

13. If H is chosen by judge 3, then which of the following must be true?

    (A) C is chosen by judge 1.
    (B) E is chosen by judge 1.
    (C) F is chosen by judge 4.
    (D) A is chosen by judge 1.
    (E) B is not chosen by judge 2.

14. If B and E are not chosen by consecutively numbered judges, then which of the following could NOT be true?

    (A) B and A are chosen by consecutively numbered judges.
    (B) C is chosen with B.
    (C) D is chosen with G.
    (D) G is chosen by a lower-numbered judge than A.
    (E) H and D are chosen by consecutively numbered judges.

15. If F is chosen by judge 3, then which of the following must be true?

    (A) H is chosen by judge 1.
    (B) A is chosen by judge 4.
    (C) E is chosen by judge 3.
    (D) D is chosen by judge 2.
    (E) G is chosen by judge 3.

16. If H is chosen by a lower-numbered judge than E, then which of the following could be true?

    (A) G is chosen by judge 4, and A is chosen by judge 1.
    (B) D is chosen by judge 3, and G is chosen by judge 1.
    (C) F is chosen by judge 1, and H is chosen by judge 3.
    (D) C is chosen by judge 1, and A is chosen by judge 1.
    (E) E is chosen by judge 4, and E is chosen by judge 3.

17. If E and B are chosen by consecutively numbered judges, then which of the following must NOT be true?

    (A) H is chosen by judge 1.
    (B) A is chosen by judge 3.
    (C) D is chosen by judge 4.
    (D) F is chosen by judge 1.
    (E) E is chosen by judge 3.

18. How many different configurations of the variables are possible?

    (A) one
    (B) two
    (C) three
    (D) four
    (E) five

GO ON TO THE NEXT PAGE

Questions 19–24

Little Joey is a bit obsessive compulsive and likes his action figures to be in specific drawers within his closet. No action figure can share a drawer with another action figure, and each of six action figures occupies one of the six drawers that Joey's mother has meticulously labeled from 1 to 6 because she likes to keep things ordered herself. The occupation of each drawer is subject to the following constraints:

Figure D is in a drawer numbered one greater than figure F's drawer.

Figure C is in a lower-numbered drawer than figure F.

Exactly one drawer is in between figure C's drawer and figure F's drawer.

Figure A is in a lower-numbered drawer than figure D.

Figure B is in a higher-numbered drawer than figure C.

19. Which of the following could be an order of the action figures from the lowest-numbered drawer to the highest-numbered drawer?

    (A) A, F, C, B, E, D
    (B) C, A, F, E, D, B
    (C) E, C, B, F, D, A
    (D) A, C, E, F, D, B
    (E) F, A, C, D, E, B

20. If figure B goes in drawer 4, then which of the following must be true?

    (A) B is in a higher-numbered drawer than F.
    (B) D does not go in the highest-numbered drawer.
    (C) A and E are in consecutively numbered drawers.
    (D) B is not in a lower-numbered drawer than F.
    (E) C is in a lower-numbered drawer than E.

21. If figure A is in a higher-numbered drawer than figure C, then which of the following must NOT be true?

    (A) E is in a lower-numbered drawer than C.
    (B) B is in a higher-numbered drawer than D.
    (C) A does not go in drawer 1, 2, or 3.
    (D) F goes in the drawer numbered one lower than D's drawer.
    (E) C is not in drawer 2.

22. If D goes in the highest-numbered drawer, then which of the following could be true?

    (A) Neither A nor E is in a drawer consecutively numbered with C's drawer.
    (B) B is in higher-numbered drawer than E.
    (C) E is in drawer 6.
    (D) A is in the drawer numbered one lower than F's drawer.
    (E) E and A are not in consecutive drawers.

23. Which is a complete list of the figures that could be in drawer 3?

    (A) A, B, E
    (B) B, E, F
    (C) C, A, B, E
    (D) A, B, C, E, F
    (E) A, B, C, D, E, F

24. Which action figure could NOT be in drawer 5?

    (A) B
    (B) C
    (C) D
    (D) E
    (E) F

S T O P

IF YOU FINISH BEFORE TIME RUNS OUT, CHECK YOUR WORK ON THIS SECTION ONLY.

DO NOT GO ON TO ANY OTHER TEST SECTION.

SECTION 3
Time—35 minutes
27 questions

<u>Directions for Reading Comprehension Questions:</u> Each passage in this section is followed by a group of questions. Answer each question based on what is stated or implied in the passage. For some questions, more than one answer choice may be possible, so choose the *best* answer to each question. After you have chosen your answer, mark the corresponding space on the Answer Sheet.

Article I, Section 7, of the Constitution provides in part that "every Bill which shall have passed the House of Representatives and the Senate, shall, before it becomes a Law, be presented to the
(5) President of the United States." In actual practice, the Clerk, or the Secretary of the Senate when the bill originated in that body, delivers the original enrolled bill to a clerk at the White House and obtains a receipt. The fact of the delivery is then
(10) reported to the House by the Clerk. Delivery to a White House clerk has customarily been regarded as presentation to the President and as commencing the 10-day constitutional period for presidential action. Copies of the enrolled bill usually are
(15) transmitted by the White House to the various departments interested in the subject matter so that they may advise the President on the issues surrounding the bill. If the President approves the bill, he signs it and usually writes the word
(20) *approved* and the date. However, the Constitution requires only that the President sign it.

The bill may become law without the President's signature by virtue of the constitutional provision that if the President does not return a bill with
(25) objections within 10 days (excluding Sundays) after it has been presented to the President, it becomes law as if the President had signed it. However, if Congress by their adjournment prevent its return, it does not become law. This is known as a "pocket
(30) veto"; that is, the bill does not become law even though the President has not sent his objections to the Congress. The Congress has interpreted the President's ability to pocket-veto a bill to be limited to final adjournment "sine die" of a Congress,
(35) where Congress has finally prevented return by the originating House and not to interim adjournments or first-session adjournments where the originating House of Congress through its agents is able to receive a veto message for subsequent
(40) reconsideration by that Congress when it reconvenes. The extent of pocket veto authority has not been definitively decided by the courts.

Notice of the signing of a bill by the President is sent by message to the House in which it originated,
(45) and that House informs the other, although this action is not necessary for the act to be valid. The action is also noted in the *Congressional Record*. A bill becomes law on the date of approval or passage over the President's veto, unless it expressly
(50) provides a different effective date.

1. The author's primary purpose in this passage is to

(A) point out some of the formalities the government engages in despite a lack of Constitutional necessity
(B) summarize how Congress amends the Constitution
(C) describe a legislative process
(D) explain the "pocket veto"
(E) interpret the legislative provisions of the Constitution

2. According to the passage, which one of the following situations may best account for the existence of the "pocket veto?"

(A) The President is out of the country for more than 10 days, but Congress is in session.
(B) The President has objections to a proposed bill, but Congress is not in session to discuss any potential changes.
(C) The President wishes to sign a bill within the last 10 days Congress is in session.
(D) The President wishes to sign a bill on a Sunday, a day Congress is not in session.
(E) The President has objections to only certain provisions of a proposed bill, but Congress seems weary of changing them.

GO ON TO THE NEXT PAGE

3. Which of the following CANNOT be reasonably inferred about the legislative process described in this passage?

  (A) It is a complex process, though the rules are specifically defined.

  (B) Congress sometimes adjourns for short periods of time.

  (C) Once a bill is received by a White House clerk, it is then typically passed on to the President and his advisers.

  (D) Once the 10-day period of presidential action passes without objection or a President signs a bill into law within the 10 days, nothing can be done to change it.

  (E) Sundays are traditionally considered days on which work will not be done.

4. Which one of the following, if true, would best support the appropriateness of a White House clerk's ability to receive a proposed bill in the stead of the President?

  (A) Most White House clerks do not have the authorization to communicate directly with the President himself, but only with a few of the Cabinet members.

  (B) The clerk often can minimize the number of bills the President has to review by simply withholding them until their 10-day period has passed without objection.

  (C) Clerks hold the only position in the White House that is allowed to do official work on Sundays.

  (D) The clerk has the authority to sign for the President in matters pertaining to business or community.

  (E) The clerk saves the President time and energy by outlining the bill and sending copies to the appropriate presidential advisers.

5. The reader can infer that the Latin phrase "sine die" (line 34) means closest to which of the following within the context of the passage?

  (A) proximate
  (B) indefinite
  (C) previous
  (D) eternal
  (E) prompt

6. Based on the author's assertions, if a bill is delivered to a White House clerk and is then neglected for more than 10 days, what happens?

  (A) The Secretary of the Senate redelivers the bill.

  (B) The President signs the bill and it passes into law.

  (C) The bill becomes law if Congress is still in session.

  (D) The veto of the President causes the bill to be void.

  (E) The President attends to the bill when an opening appears in the presidential schedule.

7. According to the author, which is tantamount to presenting a bill to the President?

  (A) the Secretary of the Senate presenting the newly drafted bill to the President

  (B) giving the bill to a White House clerk in exchange for a receipt

  (C) the President reading the bill after reviewing the minutes of the last Senate meeting

  (D) the President receiving the bill and then writing "approve" on it

  (E) the President inducing a pocket veto by waiting 10 days to review the bill

GO ON TO THE NEXT PAGE

One of the enduring small mysteries in science is that of ball lightning, glowing balls of light that exhibit bizarre behavior. They were known during World War II as "foo fighters" by bomber crews
(5) who observed them "in escort" off their wingtips. There have been plenty of sightings on the ground as well, going back at least two centuries. In recent times, a British housewife, for example, saw a ball of violet light floating over her stove during a
(10) thunderstorm. Rattling faintly, the ball floated over to her, touched her, and disappeared with a boom, burning a hole in her dress but otherwise leaving her unharmed. In general, ball lightning will occur during thunderstorms. The ball will be about the
(15) size of a grapefruit, normally colored red to yellow, will meander around, unaffected by gravity or wind, and then vanish with a pop or boom after a few seconds, causing no serious damage. Witnesses in close contact with ball lightning report feeling no
(20) heat, but it will melt holes in glass. There are tales of them floating down the aisles of airliners.

Nobody has any idea what ball lightning really is. It's clearly associated with electrical storms, but suggestions as to what it might be have ranged from
(25) as far-fetched as a clump of antimatter to as overly simplistic as just a ball of luminescent air. One of the more plausible theories is that it is just glowing plasma (ionized gas) generated by a lightning strike. This doesn't in itself explain why the ball
(30) would retain its form, or seem cool. In addition, the hot plasma would be expected to rise, not hug the ground.

Further speculation along this line, however, shows that while the plasma would contain ions
(35) that quickly recombine to generate heat and light, it would also contain three relatively stable ions: positively charged hydrogen and negatively charged nitrites and nitrates. As these ions diffuse out of the hot core into cooler air, they attract water
(40) molecules, which are electrically polarized due to their asymmetric organization, that condense to form water droplets. The condensation of the water and the reaction of the nitrites with hydrogen to form nitrous acid both release heat to keep the
(45) interior of the ball hot. At the same time, nitrites on the very exterior of the ball could accumulate so much water that it requires an input of energy to convert them into nitrous acid, making the ball feel cool to the touch. If the nitrates were to keep
(50) accumulating water, it would both make the skin watery and make the ball heavy enough to keep close to the ground. In addition, nitrogen and oxygen migrating into the ball to sustain the reactions would keep the ball spherical. The

(55) hydrogen ions would provide a strong net positive charge that causes the ball to wander erratically, until it either loses enough energy to fade out or it is physically disrupted, resulting in an explosive reaction.

(60) Whatever the theories, in the absence of good observations, they remain speculative and unsubstantiated, no matter how viable they seem. Researchers encourage would-be ball-lightning hunters to be keen-eyed and, if at all possible, see if
(65) they can get a good picture of the phenomenon. Nobody has yet succeeded in doing so.

8. Which of the following CANNOT be inferred from this author's passage about ball lightning?

(A) The author wants to give curious readers an idea of what ball lightning looks like.
(B) The author is British.
(C) The author has decided to dramatize the mystery of ball lightning to enrapture readers.
(D) The author is able to reference stories about ball lightning sightings in history.
(E) The author wants to give readers a rational explanation for ball lightning.

9. Which one of the following is a claim that the author of the passage makes about ball lightning in the "glowing plasma" theory?

(A) The formation of nitrous acid in the ball generates the heat that would be necessary to melt rock.
(B) The constant influx of reactants into the ball lightning is the precise reason for its shape.
(C) Ball lightning could not exist in the absence of the abundant hydrogen, nitrogen, oxygen, and water vapor in Earth's atmosphere.
(D) Ball lightning is strongly polarized, causing its seemingly random meandering.
(E) Physical disruption is the most placid manner in which ball lightning is usually terminated.

GO ON TO THE NEXT PAGE

10. Using the passage, which of the following phrases would the author most likely use to describe ball lightning?

    (A) permanently inexplicable
    (B) mysterious, but not supernatural
    (C) unworthy of scientific speculation
    (D) water-saturated and asymmetric
    (E) curious, though not perplexing

11. Which following most accurately expresses the meaning of the word *plausible* as it is used in line 27 of the passage?

    (A) studied
    (B) worldly
    (C) reasonable
    (D) inconclusive
    (E) empirical

12. Which of the following, if true, would most seriously undermine the glowing plasma theory, as presented by the author?

    (A) Some areas where ball lightning has been spotted in the past have lower levels of the atmospheric reactants necessary for the reaction described in this theory.
    (B) No one has ever taken a photograph of ball lightning before.
    (C) Nitrous acid, a weak acid, would not dissolve completely in the water on the exterior of the ball.
    (D) Atmospheric conditions must be uncommonly ideal for the formation of the ball of chemical reactants described in this theory.
    (E) The slight positive charge of the surface of the earth causes all groups of charged ions in the vicinity of the surface to dissociate immediately.

13. The author uses the final paragraph primarily to

    (A) recapitulate the theory described in the third paragraph
    (B) convince readers that a single photograph could solve the mystery behind ball lightning
    (C) explain why the glowing plasma theory is just as speculative as any other
    (D) debate whether ball lightning is even common enough to permit experimental observation
    (E) reemphasize the idea that ball lightning remains a mystery

14. The author's attitude toward the nature of ball lightning can be best described as

    (A) repugnant
    (B) scientific
    (C) invested
    (D) speculative
    (E) disaffected

15. The author would most likely characterize the "ionized gas" theory (line 28) as

    (A) a theory that many scientists would be inclined to believe, regardless of their spiritual opinions
    (B) undermined by the idea that spiritual entities create ball lightning
    (C) the most scientifically supportable theory available, but one that is largely bereft of statistical support
    (D) the most plausible theory available except for the idea that ball lightning is created by phantasms
    (E) the only available theory that could adequately explain the existence of ball lightning

GO ON TO THE NEXT PAGE

"Official sources" are documents taken from locations prescribed by the government as the best evidence of law, and their retrieval and consultation is the most accurate and reliable form and content
(5) of the law. These sources, when available, are the preferred or required citations to be used by lawyers in court. What is and what is not an official source is one of the more complex and confusing aspects of the United States legal system.

(10)   For example, the true official sources for federal statutes are the slip laws, which are incorporated in the session laws contained in volumes designated as the United States Statutes at large. This is a chronological listing of the statutes enacted in each
(15) Congress. These statutes are then consolidated and codified into the United States Code. There are 50 broad subject titles in the United States Code; however, because many of the general and permanent laws that are required to be incorporated
(20) into this Code are inconsistent, redundant, and obsolete, the Office of the Law Revision Counsel of the House of Representatives has been engaged in a continuing, comprehensive project authorized by law to revise and codify each title of the United
(25) States Code, for enactment into positive law. When that project is completed, all the titles of that Code will be legal evidence of the general and permanent laws, and recourse to the numerous volumes of the United States Statutes at large for this purpose will
(30) no longer be necessary. Presently, only about half of the titles have been enacted into positive law. The matter contained in the other titles of the Code is merely prima facie evidence of the laws.

    Traditionally in the United States, the courts
(35) have issued written opinions, which are also considered official sources. Official reporters publish the opinions based upon the official texts supplied by the courts and are technically the only authoritative texts. For example, the decisions of
(40) the United States Supreme Court are found in an official reporter, the United States Reports.

    Unofficial sources include all other media reproductions of a document from an official source, or any published version when no actual
(45) pronounced official source exists; they are usually published by a private, commercial entity. No accuracy and reliability are guaranteed, but unofficial sources may contain additional or cross-referenced material that might make their use easier
(50) and more informative than the official source. Unofficial sources are cited when no official source is available and may even be cited as an additional reference after an official source citation.

16. This passage was written primarily to

(A) explain from a historian's perspective the necessity for distinguishing between official and unofficial sources
(B) define official sources and distinguish them from unofficial sources
(C) describe Congress's role in the legislative process
(D) compare and contrast the reasons why a lawyer would use either an official or an unofficial source in court
(E) support the legality of official sources using the Constitution

17. The passage supports which one of the following claims about official sources?

(A) Only revised portions of the United States Code are currently eligible for use as official sources.
(B) The Law Revision Counsel is the main determining body of the rules pertaining to official sources.
(C) Some official sources are media reproductions of other official sources.
(D) Congress generates more official sources than any other governmental body.
(E) Official sources are documents of several different origins, but all are from within the United States government.

18. The phrase "prima facie" (line 33) can best be interpreted as referring to which of the following qualities of the "of the laws" (line 33)?

(A) their authenticity
(B) their inimicality
(C) their extensibility
(D) their lenience
(E) their immediacy

GO ON TO THE NEXT PAGE

19. It can be inferred from the final paragraph that

   (A) unofficial sources can be as helpful or even more helpful than official sources at times
   (B) there is a large commercial market for unofficial reproductions of official sources
   (C) unofficial sources tend to contain far fewer details than official sources
   (D) citations of several unofficial sources can weaken an author's argument
   (E) except in rare cases, unofficial sources typically are inaccurate and unreliable

20. In the context of the passage, which one of the following could best be substituted for the word *pronounced* in line 45 without considerably changing the author's meaning?

   (A) spoken
   (B) figurative
   (C) certified
   (D) straightforward
   (E) well-known

GO ON TO THE NEXT PAGE

Investigators are working diligently to sequence and assemble the genomes of various organisms, including the mouse and human, for a number of important reasons. Although important goals of any (5) sequencing project may be to obtain a genomic sequence and identify a complete set of genes, the ultimate goal is to gain an understanding of when, where, and how a gene is turned on, a process commonly referred to as *gene expression*. Once we (10) begin to understand where and how a gene is expressed under normal circumstances, we can then study what happens in an altered state, such as in disease. To accomplish the latter goal, however, researchers must identify and study the protein, or (15) proteins, coded for by a gene.

As one can imagine, finding a gene that codes for a protein, or proteins, is not easy. Traditionally, scientists would start their search by defining a biological problem and developing a strategy for (20) researching the problem. Oftentimes, a search of the scientific literature provided various clues about how to proceed. For example, other laboratories may have published data that established a link between a particular protein and a disease of (25) interest. Researchers would then work to isolate that protein, determine its function, and locate the gene that coded for the protein. Alternatively, scientists could conduct what is referred to as linkage studies to determine the chromosomal (30) location of a particular gene. Once the chromosomal location was determined, scientists would use biochemical methods to isolate the gene and its corresponding protein. Either way, these methods took a great deal of time—years in some (35) cases—and yielded the location and description of only a small percentage of the genes found in the human genome.

Now, however, the time required to locate and fully describe a gene is rapidly decreasing, thanks (40) to the development of, and access to, a technology used to generate what are called Expressed Sequence Tags, or ESTs. An EST is a tiny portion of an entire gene that can be used to help identify unknown genes and to map their positions within (45) a genome. ESTs provide researchers with a quick and inexpensive route for discovering new genes, for obtaining data on gene expression and regulation, and for constructing genome maps. Today, researchers using ESTs to study the human genome (50) find themselves riding the crest of a wave of scientific discovery the likes of which have never been seen before.

21. Which one of the following best states the main idea of the passage?

(A) Researchers have found through the use of ESTs that the mouse genome and the human genome are surprisingly similar.
(B) In a time of rapidly emerging technology, former methods of genome research, such as linkage studies, have quickly become outdated.
(C) Although EST-based research is not as quick as some other methods, it is by far the most reliable method available.
(D) Despite ingenious traditional methods, the development of EST-based gene research has greatly increased the rate of genome sequencing.
(E) ESTs are the most valuable new research technology available on the market.

22. It can be inferred from the passage that the author would most likely describe the current genetic research situation as

(A) too caught up in using only the best technology
(B) at an all-time level of excellence
(C) immobilized by an extremely daunting task
(D) unsurpassable
(E) regressing from perfection

23. As used in the passage, the words *sequence* and *sequencing* refer to which of the following?

(A) the mapping out of the components and the order of genes in a genome
(B) the huge number of steps required to properly perform a linkage study
(C) the succession of research efforts aimed at unraveling the mystery of the genome
(D) the sheer length of the chromosomal genetic information
(E) the repetitive trends of genes in the genome

GO ON TO THE NEXT PAGE

24. Sufficient-inferential or direct support CANNOT be gathered from the passage for which of the following claims?

(A) ESTs are a relatively recent technological development.
(B) Genetic research is an extremely complex field.
(C) A specific protein is coded for by only one gene.
(D) It would be impossible to sequence the whole human genome without the help of EST-research technology.
(E) Mouse and human genomes are currently being sequenced.

25. The second paragraph primarily serves to

(A) specifically describe the traditional methods of genome research
(B) promote linkage studies as the next-best option for sequencing the genome
(C) explain the complication of sequencing the genome using traditional methods
(D) reveal the natural connection between traditional research methods and ESTs
(E) argue for a return to traditional sequencing methods due to their elevated levels of accuracy

26. According the author, what is the ultimate goal of any sequencing project?

(A) to isolate the protein that codes for the selected gene
(B) to identify the behavior of a gene during sickness
(C) to obtain a genomic sequence and identify a complete set of genes
(D) to map the line of DNA surrounding the gene
(E) to understand how a gene is expressed

27. Which of the following does the author claim is the role of scientific literature in this process?

(A) Literature explicates the method for carrying out genetic discoveries.
(B) Literature gives researchers insight about the course that their research should take.
(C) Literature is devoid of materials that new scientists will find useful.
(D) Literature gives an edge to well-read scientists over those scientists who use ESTs.
(E) Reading the relevant literature is essential if scientists wish to succeed in their experiments.

S T O P

IF YOU FINISH BEFORE TIME RUNS OUT, CHECK YOUR WORK ON THIS SECTION ONLY.
DO NOT GO ON TO ANY OTHER TEST SECTION.

SECTION 4
Time—35 minutes
24 questions

<u>Directions for Logical Reasoning Questions:</u> The questions in this section are based on brief statements or passages. Choose your answers based on the reasoning in each passage. Do not make assumptions that are not supported by the passage or by common sense. For some questions, more than one answer choice may be possible, so choose the *best* answer to each question, that is, the one that is most accurate and complete. After you have chosen your answer, mark the corresponding space on the Answer Sheet.

1. Neurologist: The synapses in your brain do not fire at times when you consciously attempt to activate them. Instead, it appears that they fire at random according to a pattern.

   Patient: I do not agree with your contentions. The synapses in my brain seem to be relatively under my control, and it is impossible for them to fire in a random pattern.

   The patient responds to the neurologist in which one of the following ways?

   (A) By discounting the neurologist's idea that the synapses in people's brains fire according to a certain pattern.
   (B) By pointing out a seeming contradiction in the terms in the neurologist's conclusion.
   (C) By agreeing with part of the neurologist's argument and by then making a contention not relevant to it.
   (D) By arguing against the neurologist solely because the neurologist's conclusion has negative implications.
   (E) By omitting to address the first and most prominent point in the neurologist's argument.

2. Since cinema is such a relatively young art form, critics tend not to agree about which *auteurs* will, for future generations, comprise the so-called filmic canon of our time. Whereas literature and visual art may be assessed and valued within a broader time framework by virtue of the fact that their respective histories are far longer than the mere century of motion pictures, two works that may very well be, in future years, considered filmic art of the same generic mold might today, for instance, be categorized as very opposites. In fact, we truly know very little about which films and filmmakers will stand the test of time. Ed Wood, for example, may very well be remembered more fondly than Fellini or Hitchcock.

   What is the main point of the passage?

   (A) Cinema will, in future years, change dramatically.
   (B) Ed Wood will probably be remembered as one of the greatest filmmakers of the 20th century.
   (C) Visual and literary art are more credible forms of expression than is filmic art since they have stood the test of time and will continue to do so.
   (D) Film is too young an art form for one to accurately predict the opinion future generations will hold of its early works.
   (E) Hitchcock and Fellini, though now highly regarded, may become less so over time.

GO ON TO THE NEXT PAGE

3. All great actors are method actors. Many great actors have studied under acting teaching legend Alice Smithee. She herself was taught under the Stanislavsky method, but didn't internalize it sufficiently to ever become a great actor herself, so she turned to teaching instead. Smithee didn't in fact teach method acting, but instead a technique wherein an actor imagines himself or herself spending time with the character he or she will be playing, and then examining the ways in which spending time with that character made the actor feel about himself or herself. A method actor, on the other hand, is defined as an actor who has been trained under and practices the Stanislavsky method. This is a technique Smithee herself never teaches.

If the information above is accepted as true, which of the following can be concluded?

(A) Some actors who studied under Alice Smithee learned method acting elsewhere.
(B) Smithee's method revolutionized the way acting is taught.
(C) Smithee's method developed as a result of the Stanislavsky method and therefore has produced many great actors.
(D) Smithee's and Stanislavsky's methods are essentially the same thing, at least in end result.
(E) One way to teach an actor to be great is to teach that actor the way Smithee teaches acting.

4. Citizen: The city government's proposed regulation requiring, at the car owner's expense, biannual emissions inspections on all two-axle vehicles over five years of age is excessive and unnecessary—it is, indeed, yet another basic example of underhanded overtaxation, intended not as a protection of our air quality and consequent health and safety, but in reality, as sheer governmental extortion of the populace.

Which of the following, if true, most strengthens the citizen's claim?

(A) A poll of citizens shows that a majority agrees with this assertion.
(B) The city government has a reputation for underhanded dealings.
(C) A study has shown that at least 90 percent of the city's population list clean air as merely a "minor" concern.
(D) A study shows that very few two-axle vehicles over five years old display a marked change in emissions rating over a six-month period, though the percentage greatly increases when the time span in question is one year.
(E) None of the legislative committee members owns a vehicle over five years old.

5. Patrick must choose a Halloween costume. He wants to wear a monster costume, but there is some confusion. In his mind, all goblins are monsters, but only some ghosts are monsters. Trolls are goblins if and only if the troll is green. Some ghosts are also trolls. All blue and green ghosts are, respectively, blue and green trolls. Patrick will not be satisfied unless he wears a monster costume for Halloween.

Based on the information above, which of the following costumes is sure to satisfy Patrick?

(A) a blue ghost
(B) a green banshee
(C) a red troll
(D) a blue troll
(E) a green ghost

GO ON TO THE NEXT PAGE

6. Art historian: Marrying art and commerce is necessarily either restrictive or compromising at best. The true artist is the one who creates not to sell, but merely and fundamentally to create, ergo, art for art's sake. Any piece of art that was made for the purpose of material gain is necessarily commercial and therefore invalidated as art. As proof, we look to the purest rendering of humanity's inherent instinct for self-expression: the earliest cave paintings. What gain did the Neanderthals acquire from their simple, beautiful scribbling? The answer is: none.

Which of the following is a weakness in the art historian's argument?

(A) The conclusion is based on art created according to standards that are not those of modern times.
(B) Cave paintings are not the purest of all art forms.
(C) Many great artists have sold their work; in fact, great art is sold all the time.
(D) Cave artists did indeed receive compensation for their work.
(E) The term *marrying* is used incorrectly.

7. People who are good at math often excel in musical activities. Experts claim that this is because many of the skills that are required for making and playing music are also required of mathematicians. Matthew refutes this claim by stating that someone could just as easily say that all artists often excel in music, because many of the skills that are required to make good art, such as creativity, are required for a person to be a good musician.

Which of the following, if true, would resolve this discrepancy in favor of the opinion of the experts?

(A) Matthew has a vested interest in this debate because he is an aspiring musician and a promising artist.
(B) The experts rely on largely numerical data, whereas Matthew is relying simply on his own ideas and personal experience.
(C) Skills that math and music have in common are more important musically than skills that music has in common with any other domain.
(D) Artists are more often musicians than mathematicians, because they are looking for additional fields in which to express their creativity.
(E) The skills of an artist are the most important in selling records, because the artwork on an album cover is the first thing that catches a buyer's eye.

GO ON TO THE NEXT PAGE

8. Spelling bee participants are a very quirky bunch. In fact, it is hard to believe that any child would ever be so innately interested in the dictionary as to want to spend hours each day studying it. And not studying it to learn the definitions of the words, but instead studying it to learn to spell them—a function that my word processing program has consummately perfected. In fact, I do not even have to type in most words correctly and it will proceed to respell them for me in the correct way. These children would be better served by devoting their time to skills that will eventually aid them in the real world.

Which of the following, if true, would support the conclusion of the passage?

(A) Spelling bee participants are not disadvantaged when compared to the average child of their intelligence.

(B) Children who participate in spelling bees often go on to have extremely successful lives as scholars.

(C) Spelling skills are vestigial components of the skill set that children are traditionally encouraged to develop.

(D) Parents of children in spelling bees often want their children to win more than their children want to win.

(E) Spelling bee participants would all be exceptional math students if they put similar efforts into their mathematical studies.

9. Animals will never be able to speak, not because they are not intelligent enough to comprehend aural symbols that are metaphors for real-world constructs but because they lack the lingual flexibility to move their tongues in order to produce an intricate variety of sounds. Take dogs, for instance. Clearly they understand verbal commands like "sit," "stay," "roll over," "shake," "speak," "fetch," and many others, but they are completely unable to reproduce these commands. It would make sense to assume that if they have the mental capacity to understand verbal commands, then they could also reproduce them. However, their tonal limitations constrain them to the default vocality of a "woof" sound. Deviations from woofing noises are impossible for dogs, so they will never be able to engage in aural language reproduction.

Which of the following is an assumption necessary for the argument to be drawn logically?

(A) Dogs are unable to deviate tonally from the "woof" noise enough to form discernible phonemes.

(B) Coyotes, animals that resembles dogs, will never be able to communicate orally because they too unintelligent.

(C) Some dogs make noises that sound like certain words in the English language, such as "bark," for instance.

(D) Parrots are able to reproduce all the different sounds in the English language, but they are not intelligent enough to form cohesive sentences.

(E) Gorillas are able to understand sign language and use it in order to make a language that passes between gorilla groups.

GO ON TO THE NEXT PAGE

10. Don Juan: Serenades are a great way to encourage a lady to fall in love with you. Just choose a night where the moon is right and the stars are out, and then go and take your accordion beneath your lady's window to sing to her about your love. In Spain, this worked for me like a charm, but for some reason in America, ladies feel that it is not classy or not cool. I have tried professing my love to four different ladies on this street tonight, and they have all turned me down. Clearly, serenades never work in America.

Which of the following is an assumption that Don Juan makes in his argument?

(A) Americans in general have a value set that is very different from that of Western Europeans.
(B) Accordions are the best instrument to use when serenading someone.
(C) American fathers are not more protective of their daughters than Spanish fathers are.
(D) Each of the ladies did not hear him serenading the previous lady.
(E) A serenade does not have to be sincere in order to work properly.

11. Standardized testing is said to be a way to determine a student's potential for future success in school. However, this type of testing in general is not a very good indicator of future success because people can skew their performance on the test by studying for it. People who study hard always do better on standardized tests, thereby evading having their raw intellect measured. Because people can study for standardized tests, these tests are ineffective in predicting a person's future success in school.

The argument assumes which of the following?

(A) Standardized testing is not the only way to determine a person's native intellectual capacity.
(B) People who tend to study more for a standardized test are unlikely to do better in school in the future.
(C) People who do not study for a standardized test but score high on it anyway will always do well in school in the future.
(D) Test results that are skewed are completely incapable of predicting future success in school.
(E) Schools are interested in knowing about a person's willingness to study before admitting that person.

GO ON TO THE NEXT PAGE

12. Students with school lockers should be very careful how they use them. Students may believe that they have a right to privacy in their lockers, but technically, they do not own the lockers and therefore cannot reasonably expect privacy in an area in which they do not have a proprietary interest. Students should realize that their unjustified expectations will be abrogated if they do not place their own locks on their lockers. However, they will get into trouble if they do not use the locks provided by their school. The principal may decide on a whim to open any locker that does not use a school lock. Therefore, any student who uses a locker will get into trouble.

Which of the following is assumed by the argument?

(A) Some students do not choose to avoid using their lockers.
(B) Students should have the same right to privacy for their school locker that they have for their wallets.
(C) School officials other than the principal have no desire to open student lockers.
(D) Students do not use their lockers to store school books and supplies.
(E) Whenever lockers are used, students use them for prohibited purposes.

13. Visceral turbulence is often the sign of impending danger. There are numerous documented cases of a person's stomach turning before an accident occurs, and it is believed that these visceral actions are incontrovertible proof of extrasensory perception (ESP). ESP has also been manifested in people's brows, which sometimes become furled before a person gets into an accident. To help people avoid getting into accidents, we simply need to teach them how to recognize these manifestations of ESP.

Which of the following is assumed by the argument?

(A) Visceral turbulence and furling brows are the only manifestations of ESP.
(B) A person can be taught to recognize ESP manifestations and the nature of the impending accidents that they signal.
(C) Extrasensory perception has been documented and is an effective way for all primates to ward off danger.
(D) Manifestations of ESP occur long enough before an accident for the person to avoid that accident.
(E) Visceral turbulence is not caused by anything other than ESP.

GO ON TO THE NEXT PAGE

14. Average lap times for NASCAR drivers have shortened dramatically ever since Global Motors introduced the new nitroglycerine-burning engine six months ago. This engine partially increases turbine efficiency by increasing the engine-environment heat differential. In the past without exception, the NASCAR rookie of the year used the most technologically advanced engine on the market. Jim Johnson will be the rookie of the year and has won more NASCAR races this year than any other competitor. Therefore, he must be using the new nitroglycerine engine.

Which of the following, if true, would cast the most doubt on the conclusion of the passage?

(A) Jim Johnson has stated publicly that he hates the nitroglycerine engine and thinks it should be banned from NASCAR.

(B) The nitroglycerine engine was developed specifically to help Global Motors cars, and Jim's car was not made by Global Motors.

(C) The frame of Jim Johnson's car is incompatible with any product released by Global Motors in the past year.

(D) NASCAR times are largely dependent on the weather, and the weather over the past six months has been very conducive to fast times.

(E) Global Motors' nitroglycerine engine is the most technologically advanced engine on the market.

15. All linguistics professors at the University of Ames have the hobby of fishing. Anyone who fishes also keeps a pet cat. Some people who have pet cats do not keep dogs, because cats and dogs tend to fight when kept together in the same house. It follows that no linguistics professors at the University of Ames keeps dogs.

Which of the following is the best counter to the passage's conclusion?

(A) Some people who fish do not keep cats.
(B) Not all professors at Ames University fish.
(C) Some people who keep dogs also keep cats.
(D) All linguistics professors keep cats.
(E) Some people who teach linguistics keep dogs.

GO ON TO THE NEXT PAGE

16. Keeping an aquarium is an excellent way to teach children responsibility. Children enjoy watching fish swim around in aquariums and therefore feel motivated to sustain their pets' lives by ensuring that the aquarium environment is healthy. Children learn that their pets' lives depend on their fulfilling duties such as feeding, changing the water, and checking on the filtration equipment. Acknowledgment of this codependent relationship will help children grow and understand that if they act responsibly, their behavior will foster all sorts of relationships, and not only of the aquatic kind.

Which of the following, if true, would tend to cast doubt on the conclusion of the passage?

(A) The link between responsible aquarium keeping and other responsible behavior is too abstract for a child to grasp on any level.

(B) Most children will enjoy taking care of their fish regardless of any sense of responsibility that their behavior creates.

(C) The abstract nature of responsibility is barely comprehensible to children, yet most of them are still able to make a logical connection.

(D) Children who tend to be careless aquarium keepers tend to be careless with relationships and responsibilities for the rest of their lives.

(E) Children who are taught to take care of cats develop a sense of responsibility just like that of children who take care of aquariums.

17. Bicycle riders face extremely hazardous road conditions, such oil spills, car exhaust, and the danger of being run over by cars. In addition to these external stressors, cyclists also face many internal obstacles. Forcing their bodies to toil for many hours and miles on the roadway requires willpower strong enough to overcome any obstacle, internal or external. It would make sense that this mental fortitude would transfer to other sports and enable cyclists to excel at any sport that they tried.

Which of the following, if true, would undermine the conclusion that cyclists would excel at any sport they tried?

(A) Cyclists do not initially do very well at sports that require any type of dexterity.

(B) Cyclists refuse to try any sport besides cycling because they are convinced that their talents would not transfer to other sports.

(C) Qualified cyclists often easily make the transition between long-distance running and cycling, regardless of the skill of their runner competitors.

(D) Cyclists possess a unique muscular makeup that is useless for any sport besides cycling.

(E) Cyclists have tried many other sports besides cycling but have never achieved greatness in any other sport.

GO ON TO THE NEXT PAGE

18. Manatee populations in Florida waters have been decimated by the huge numbers of speedboats now in use. The Florida manatee population peaked in 1996 at 1.4 million, but in early 1997 a manatee disease rippled through the state's waterways and infected hundreds of thousands of manatees. The effects of this disease still reverberate through the manatee community, and the disease infects newborn manatees that have not yet gained immunity to it. If there were some way to curb this disease, then we would be able to save the diminishing manatee population and return the population to 1996 levels.

Which of the following is the major flaw of the argument?

(A) It ignores the responsibility of a major alternate cause for the decline from 1996 population levels.
(B) It fails to examine the origin of the disease that hit the manatee population in 1997.
(C) It describes several problems associated with the declining manatee population but offers no solution.
(D) It undermines the contention that some third cause besides speedboats or the disease might be largely responsible for the manatee population decline.
(E) It confuses the fact that populations were once at a certain level with the idea that population size could regain that level.

19. People who constantly engage in self-aggrandizing behavior do so because they are insecure. This is because people who are insecure feel the need to boast to others about their personal merits in order to bolster their own feelings of self-worth. It follows that many successful professionals such as great authors, actors, and musicians are dreadfully insecure because they center their entire careers around aggrandizing every facet of their personality and its output—their "art."

The argument is flawed for which of the following reasons?

(A) It lumps three diverse groups of consistently self-aggrandizing people into one category—"successful professionals."
(B) It accepts the idea that there is some connection between a person's actions and that person's psyche.
(C) It relies on a fallacious assumption centering on a misinterpretation of the word *bolster*.
(D) It fails to recognize that actors do not make "art"; directors and producers make art.
(E) It ignores other compelling motives for the self-aggrandizing behavior of successful professionals.

GO ON TO THE NEXT PAGE

20. Total yield per acre of pinto beans farmed in Bolivia is about a quarter of the current per-acre yield of the most technologically advanced farms in the United States. Bolivian farmers do not have the up-front capital necessary to invest in the expensive machines that would bolster their per-acre crop yield, and neither do they have banks that would finance these investments. It is a sad state of affairs since the per-acre crop yield of Bolivian farmers could be salvaged and brought up to a level commensurate with that achieved by the most advanced United States farmers if the Bolivians only had more technologically advanced equipment.

Which of the following is a flaw in the argument?

(A) It ignores the possibility that the Bolivian climate might be less amenable to pinto bean farming than the United States climate.

(B) It confuses the sufficient condition of "advanced technology" with the necessary condition of "total per-acre yield."

(C) It describes a hypothetical state of affairs based on illusory past trends and statistical data.

(D) It fails to examine the total yield per acre of other types of Bolivian bean farmers.

(E) It concludes that more technology is needed without making a claim that would support this contention.

21. Many claim that what makes great literature "great" is the impressive literary skill of its writers, but I would argue that this proposition is flawed. Much that is considered to be great literature was written by people who would not be able to survive as writers in our time. Writing from long ago is considered great no matter who wrote it, solely because there were so few people back then who had the ability to read or write. Before the Gutenberg printing press, many who did write were not interested in spending their time handwriting a book that would be distributed to only one or two other people.

The argument utilizes which of the following methods to advance its point?

(A) It infers that because characteristics of a certain group are different from what is anticipated, no claims can be made about that group.

(B) It offers numerical data for a new theory that is more compelling than a traditionally accepted theory.

(C) It undermines a particular claim by demonstrating that the artists making that claim use logic that is consistently flawed.

(D) It shows that a presumption is flawed because it does not apply to a group to which it is said to apply.

(E) It argues that literary greatness has nothing to do with the time period when a work was created.

GO ON TO THE NEXT PAGE

22. Farmers claim that the weather, specifically the amount of rain in a season, is a determinative factor in the yield of corn for that season. However, data from the Agriculture Department suggest that corn crops deliver the same average yield regardless of whether the growing season is characterized by flooding, drought, or moderate rains. Bill the farmer notes that this growing season has been plagued by numerous floods, so he predicts lower yields for his crops. However, based on the scientific and statistical data from the Agriculture Department, it appears that his assumption is invalid.

The argument utilizes which of the following methods to advance its point?

(A) A claim is undermined by implying a lack of education on the part of a proponent of that claim.

(B) A proposition is undermined by showing that there have been as many instances in which it was false as when it held true.

(C) A conclusion is reached by examining scientific data that tend to refute that specific conclusion.

(D) Two incompatible assertions are demonstrated to have no implications for the seasonal crop yield of corn.

(E) An inference is made based on an inadequate database that supports a particular conclusion.

23. Anna: I will be asked to the dance by the most popular boy in school. I am sure that we will have a great time and that my daydreams will come true.

Jane: Rick, the most popular boy in school, already asked me to the dance. I am sorry, but it is impossible for you to go with him, since he has already committed to going with me.

Which one of the following, if true, most helps to resolve the apparent discrepancy described above?

(A) Anna is extremely realistic in her expectations regarding the dance and her daydreams.

(B) Jane does not like Anna because Anna went to the prom with Rick around this time last year.

(C) There is no way for a boy to take two dates to the dance or to renege on a date that he has already made.

(D) A different boy will be the most popular boy in school by the time that Anna is asked to the dance.

(E) The dance will be cancelled by thunderstorms created by the upcoming hurricane season.

GO ON TO THE NEXT PAGE

24. Pollster: Elections are lost and won based on
the percentage of a candidate's
constituency that actually decides to get
out and vote on a particular day. My
candidate lost, so it is clear that my
candidate's supporters are more reticent
than his opponent's supporters.

Which of the following identifies the logical
error present in the pollster's argument?

(A) He bases his argument on a percentage
that is irrelevant to his conclusion.
(B) He claims that a candidate's victory is
partially determined by voter turnout.
(C) He eliminates the possibility that one
candidate might be substantively better
than the other.
(D) He fails to take into account the relative
size of each candidate's constituency.
(E) He neglects to account for the percentage
by which his candidate lost.

S T O P

IF YOU FINISH BEFORE TIME RUNS OUT, CHECK YOUR WORK ON THIS SECTION ONLY.
DO NOT GO ON TO ANY OTHER TEST SECTION.

ANSWER KEY

Section 1	Section 2	Section 3	Section 4
1. A	1. D	1. C	1. B
2. E	2. A	2. B	2. D
3. B	3. C	3. D	3. A
4. E	4. C	4. E	4. D
5. A	5. D	5. B	5. E
6. A	6. E	6. C	6. A
7. D	7. B	7. B	7. C
8. B	8. A	8. B	8. C
9. B	9. E	9. B	9. A
10. A	10. D	10. B	10. D
11. C	11. C	11. C	11. B
12. C	12. D	12. E	12. E
13. A	13. C	13. E	13. D
14. A	14. E	14. D	14. C
15. C	15. C	15. C	15. C
16. C	16. A	16. B	16. A
17. C	17. B	17. E	17. D
18. B	18. E	18. A	18. A
19. E	19. D	19. A	19. E
20. C	20. C	20. C	20. A
21. B	21. C	21. D	21. D
22. D	22. B	22. B	22. B
23. E	23. D	23. A	23. D
24. C	24. B	24. D	24. D
25. A		25. C	
26. D		26. E	
		27. B	

Scoring Instructions: To calculate your score on this Practice Test, follow the instructions on the next page.

CALCULATING YOUR SCORE

Now that you have completed Practice Test 4, use the instructions on this page to calculate your score. Start by checking the Answer Key to count up the number of questions you answered correctly. Then fill in the table below.

Raw Score Calculator

Section Number	Question Type	Number of Questions	Number Correct
1	Logical Reasoning	26	_____
2	Logic Games	24	_____
3	Reading Comprehension	27	_____
4	Logical Reasoning	24	_____
		(Raw Score) Total:	_____

On the real LSAT, a statistical process will be used to convert your raw score to a scaled score ranging from 120 to 180. The table below will give you an approximate idea of the scaled score that matches your raw score. For statistical reasons, on real forms of the LSAT the scaled score that matches a given raw score can vary by several points above or below the scaled score shown in the table.

Write your scaled score on this test here:

Practice Test 4 scaled score: _____

Raw Score	Scaled Score	Raw Score	Scaled Score	Raw Score	Scaled Score
0	120	22	125	44	143
1	120	23	126	45	144
2	120	24	127	46	145
3	120	25	128	47	145
4	120	26	128	48	146
5	120	27	129	49	147
6	120	28	130	50	147
7	120	29	131	51	148
8	120	30	132	52	148
9	120	31	133	53	149
10	120	32	133	54	150
11	120	33	134	55	151
12	120	34	135	56	151
13	120	35	136	57	152
14	120	36	137	58	153
15	120	37	137	59	153
16	120	38	138	60	154
17	120	39	139	61	154
18	121	40	140	62	155
19	122	41	140	63	155
20	123	42	141	64	156
21	124	43	142	65	157

Raw Score	Scaled Score	Raw Score	Scaled Score	Raw Score	Scaled Score
66	158	79	165	92	175
67	158	80	166	93	175
68	159	81	166	94	176
69	159	82	167	95	177
70	160	83	167	96	178
71	160	84	168	97	179
72	161	85	169	98	180
73	161	86	170	99	180
74	162	87	170	100	180
75	162	88	171	101	180
76	163	89	172		
77	163	90	173		
78	164	91	174		

ANSWERS AND EXPLANATIONS

SECTION I—LOGICAL REASONING

1. This squib says that switch-hitters are able to achieve a technical mastery of their new batting stance that surpasses their mastery of their original stance. This situation is likened to that of certain writers—Nabokov and Conrad—whose native language was not English. The squib claims that these two writers achieved a mastery of English that surpassed their mastery of their native tongue.

Question Type : Conclusion

Correct answer: **A.** If Nabokov is a better writer in English than in his native language, then you can conclude the truth of this answer choice.

(B) This statement is not really something that can be concluded. Just because baseball players and some writers are comparable in one regard does not mean that baseball and writing are comparable.

(C) We are told about a power of learning, not one of adaptability.

(D) This statement is probably true, but on the basis of the passage there is no way of telling how much they studied.

(E) There is no way of telling if this ability benefits a writer to the same degree that it would benefit a baseball player.

2. Julio claims that Solomon the Great is building the tower. Marcos claims that his brother is building the tower.

Question Type: "Resolve"

Correct answer: **E.** This answer choice would make Julio the brother of Solomon the Great. This fact would reconcile the statements of the speakers.

(A) This information would just add to the confusion.

(B) This answer is intuitive.

(C) This point is irrelevant.

(D) This does not resolve the identity of the person building that specific tower.

3. The statesperson claims that athletes and actors never have the time to devote to any sort of real intellectual learning. Therefore, he is disgusted by countries that elect people to power who were professional athletes or actors, since these people do not have the requisite intellect for the job.

Question Type: "Weaken"

Correct answer: **B.** If this statement were true, then the whole of the statesman's contentions would be rejected.

(A) This point is irrelevant.

(C) This opinion does not mean that the statesman's views are not true.

(D) This statement does not mean that they are successful in the intellectual sphere.

(E) Poker is different from sports and acting.

4. A scientist conducting a study on the relationship between grapes and one's life span admitted that his research is based on only two years' worth of data. It would seem to be difficult to prove that anything increased the human life span based on data from such a limited amount of time.

Question Type: Reasoning strategy

Correct answer: **E.** The claim of the scientist is undermined because the evidence on which it is based is so weak.

(A) Nothing is mentioned about false advertising.

(B) You cannot tell if the scientists purposely encouraged the misleading claim or if the advertising company and grape producers did so.

(C) This statement is almost true, but it actually claims that certain scientific data must be collected before conclusions can be supported.

(D) This statement is not true.

5. The squib postulates that there is some connection between removing a grape from the vine and putting it in the sun in order to make a raisin.

Question Type: "Strengthen"

Correct answer: **A.** This would mean that grapes would never turn into raisins even if they were left on the vine. This would support the conclusion of the squib.

(B) Cranberries are a completely different kind of fruit.

(C) This statement has nothing to do with removing grapes from the vine.

(D) This information is irrelevant aside from informing you that grapes need sunlight to caramelize.

(E) This statement does not say whether the grapes became raisins after they were initially removed from the vine. The squib's conclusion relates only to whether the grapes must be removed from the vine before they turn into raisins.

6. This squib presents the negatives of choosing plastic and paper grocery bags. Paper bags require trees to be cut down, but plastic bags do not decompose for thousands of years. The environmental agency claims it has solved the problem by advising people to use plastic bags.

Question Type: "Resolve"

Correct answer: **A.** This would completely eliminate the negatives involved with using plastic bags.

(B) The likelihood that forestlands will be decimated is remote and in the far future, so it is improbable that the agency is basing its solution on this idea.

(C) This point does not mean that the chemicals are safe or that people would take the time to find each piece of litter.

(D) One-half is not a compelling compression rate, especially because paper bags will degrade hundreds of times faster than plastic bags.

(E) This point is irrelevant.

7. This squib claims that by watching teen movies, teenagers will learn the negatives of common high school archetypes and steer clear of acting in stereotypical ways.

Question Type: "Strengthen"

Correct answer: **D.** If this outcome occurred, then it would be likely that the claims of the squib were true—the movie caused people to steer clear of stereotypical roles.

(A) This point is true, but the passage is about teen movies and normal high school social roles.

(B) This point is irrelevant.

(C) This behavior does not mean that people in all social roles will do this.

(E) This result might be because the students are happy and entertained instead of determined to reject stereotypical social roles.

8. The assumption here is that if a student can do well in organic chemistry classes, then the student will undoubtedly do well in medical school classes. The problem is that this assumption neglects students who do not do well in organic chemistry for whatever reason but who would definitely do well in the entirely unrelated subjects that are taught in medical school.

Question Type: "Weaken"

Correct answer: **B.** This choice describes a group that the author of the passage omitted from consideration.

(A and C) This information is irrelevant.

(D) This point is true, but it is often not practical to teach this medical school class at an undergraduate level. Additionally, this answer does not contradict the author's conclusion.

(E) This answer does not mean that the grade does not accurately reflect the student's aptitude for medical subjects.

9. This squib states that parents who do not practice what they preach are often not heeded. However, parents who do practice what they preach are sometimes heeded.

Question Type: Analogous reasoning

Correct answer: **B.** The first teacher is a hypocrite, so the student does not heed the advice. The second teacher is not a hypocrite, so the student sometimes follows the advice.

(A) This switches the absolute statements for possible statements. In the squib, the advice is sometimes accepted. In this answer choice, the advice is always accepted.

(C) The relationship between parental orders and the child's acquiescence is completely different in this situation.

(D and E) These situations are completely different.

10. This squib presents information about the new wave of Internet banking. The executive claims that the company should examine opportunities in this new field because Internet banking is likely to increase.

Question Type: Conclusion

Correct answer: **A.** This is the best choice for the main point of the squib. The executive is presenting information in order to compel the company to enter the field of Internet banking.

(B) There is no normative statement in the passage.

(C) This statement is probably true, and it has been the case for years that people pay their bills offline.

(D and E) These are a subsidiary points of the argument.

11. This squib claims that there is an allure about secret societies and places that permit entry only to a select few. While allure incentivizes people to try to gain entrance to these places, it also increases the potential for rejection. The squib claims that this is a negative for society because it breeds separatism and jealousy.

Question Type: "Strengthen"

Correct answer: **C.** If this statement were true, then it would be true that people in societies promoting these elitist structures are less happy on average than people in more egalitarian societies.

(A) This point is irrelevant to the societal implications of elitist clubs.

(B) This information is irrelevant.

(D) This answer would mean that these agencies are worthless, but we are still not sure that these secret agencies are a source of negative elitism.

(E) This answer does not mean that over four years' time the fraternal orders do not bring a sum total of happiness to students.

12. Stanley Carpets has shags that are dark cherry color and throws that are light cherry in color. Bowden, Inc. provides all the throws for Stanley Carpets. Therefore, Bowden, Inc. must provide Stanley Carpets with light cherry colored throws.

Question Type: Conclusion

Correct answer: **C.** This point can be concluded.

(A and B) You cannot be sure of these points.

(D and E) Just because she prefers some colors to other colors does not mean that Mrs. Bowden would not approve of all colors.

13. The student claims that since no students like grades, grades will be abolished at school. The only problem with this logic is that students do not have any control whatsoever regarding the decision to grade their work.

Question Type: "Weaken"

Correct answer: **A.** If this answer were true, then the opinions of the students would be meaningless.

(B) This information is irrelevant.

(C) This answer does not mean that the majority of students who want to abolish grades would not drown out the contrary voices of a couple of individuals.

(D) This answer is irrelevant because teachers do not feel this way.

(E) This argument does not mean that the system is likely to be abolished, especially on the whim of students.

14. This squib describes the nature of the Pythagorean theorem. It then presents the faulty Juilliard theorem and claims that students in the math bowl should choose the former theory to solve the problem.

Question Type: Analogous reasoning

Correct answer: **A.** The main reason that the Pythagorean theorem is recommended is that it has been traditionally used, not because the theory is correct.

(B) This argument is not made, even though it would have been a supportable argument if the author chose to use it.

(C) There are only two options delineated.

(D) The opposite assumption is made.

(E) This argument is not made.

15. John seems to claim that nervous people are overreacting because it is always they who see ghosts. Mary agrees that nervous people always are the ones seeing ghosts, but she seems to thank them for their vigilance.

Question Type: "Resolve"

Correct answer: **C.** The question stem asks for a reason why nervous people report seeing ghosts. If this answer choice were true, then it would be a good reason why these people do report seeing ghosts.

(A) This tendency does not mean that they would lie consistently about spiritual occurrences.

(B) This answer would tend to contradict the contentions of the squib.

(D) This point is irrelevant.

(E) This answer would contradict the squib.

16. Jillian goes on tangents about how bright colors and loud noises alienate neighbors, but then she assumes that her rooster that crowed each morning ingratiated her with her neighbors. This seems an unlikely turn of events, and it is probable that the neighbors were sarcastic when they thanked her for the natural alarm clock.

Question Type: "Strengthen"

Correct answer: **C.** Jillian's rooster crowed in the morning, and she claims that people loved it. She also stated that people hate noises at night. Therefore, she would have to assume that people respond differently to loud noises at different times of the day.

(A) This rooster crowed in the morning.

(B) Jillian does not assume anything about dogs.

(D) Jillian claims the opposite.

(E) You cannot tell if her neighbors wanted to sleep for a couple of extra hours.

17. The hedge clipper likens his work to that of a master chef. He claims that he clips bushes and that they inevitably grow back and destroy his art.

Question Type: "Strengthen"

Correct answer: **C.** He claims that bushes "inevitably" grow, so this point is assumed by the hedge clipper.

(A) This assumption is not made. It is just assumed that their work has a couple of similar traits.

(B) This assumption is not made.

(D) This point is not stated. It is just said that they could not appreciate the food as much as the master chef could.

(E) You cannot determine whether or not this statement is true.

18. The politician has offered four forms to prove that he did not lie on the budget reports. He states that people will review the reports and exonerate him. However, if he lied about the budget, then it makes sense to assume that he lied in the reports he submitted regarding the budget.

Question Type: Reasoning strategy

Correct answer: **B.** This is not a good assumption if the politician might be guilty of graft.

(A) This is not a flaw in the reasoning.

(C) This point is acknowledged.

(D) This answer is not true.

(E) While this might be true, it is certainly not embraced by the passage.

19. The investment adviser tells John, a retiree, that based on his stock portfolio and on recent stock market trends, John will need to return to work in five years in order to support himself.

Question Type: "Weaken"

Correct answer: **E.** If this answer is true, then John can continue to feel confident that he has enough money to support himself without working.

(A) This indication does not mean that the market will go up enough to make it unnecessary for John to go back to work. Nor does it mean that the market will not start going up until 4 years and 364 days have passed.

(B) This answer would strengthen the contentions of the squib.

(C) What happens to John's friends is irrelevant.

(D) This point is irrelevant and would strengthen the contentions of the investment adviser.

20. The existentialist claims that his emotions directly reflect the weather. However, when it is foggy, he cannot decide what his emotions are, so he cannot decide whether they are all tied to the weather. It appears that the existentialist is confused.

Question Type: "Strengthen"

Correct answer: **C.** This would mean that the existentialist is experiencing an emotion due to the foggy weather.

(A) This answer would not support the idea that the existentialist's emotions are all tied to the weather.

(B) This point is irrelevant to what happens in the fog.

(D) What happens to the rest of the population is irrelevant to what happens to the existentialist.

(E) This point is irrelevant.

21. This executive claims that other airlines are cutting costs by reducing the number of amenities offered to passengers and that these passengers are becoming less satisfied with their flights. The executive claims that this dissatisfaction opens the door for his company to provide these services and gain an advantage.

Question Type: "Weaken"

Correct answer: **B.** This would mean that passengers would happily sacrifice these amenities for the "no frills" approach to airline transport.

(A) This does not mean that the food and entertainment provided are unsatisfactory.

(C) This does not matter.

(D and E) This is irrelevant.

22. If farmers sold every single seed that they had, then they would have nothing left with which to plant next year's crop. So this short-term solution to the problem would cause immense long-term problems.

Question Type: Reasoning strategy

Correct answer: **D.** This answer encompasses the flaw perfectly.

(A) This statement is not true.

(B) This solution is an unrealistic way of doing things for the poor who live in the city and don't own land.

(C) But feeding more grain would definitely fulfill most of the dietary requirements.

(E) The argument does not assume what it set out to prove.

23. This squib relates the history of guitar amplifiers.

Question Type: Conclusion

Correct answer: **E.** This answer states just about everything important that was stated in the passage.

(A) You cannot be sure of the target market that the manufacturers of the digital amp were aiming for.

(B) Lightness of body is not mentioned in the squib.

(C) There is no mention of amateur guitarists in the squib.

(D) This is only a subsidiary point of the squib.

24. The squib states that politicians not only have to convince people that they are the best candidate but also they have to convince people to vote for them.

Question Type: Analogous reasoning

Correct answer: **C.** This structure is directly comparable, because if players do not arrive at the game, the fact that they are better skilled than those on the other team does not matter.

(A–E) These logic structure are completely different.

25. Philip claims that fish do not care whether the boat sneaks up on them or whether it drives on top of them so long as a fisherman's hook has a worm on it.

Question Type: "Weaken"

Correct answer: **A.** If this statement is true, then it would not be true that driving on top of fish would be a good idea.

(B) This point is irrelevant.

(C) This answer would support his conclusion.

(D) This answer does not mean that he is not correct in his postulations.

(E) This point is completely unrelated to the squib.

26. This squib claims that the aardvark will be the only creature to survive the next ice age for two reasons: (1) a thick epidermal layer and (2) a self-regulating internal thermometer.

    Question Type: Reasoning strategy

    Correct answer: **D.** This answer is more than likely true, and if so, then it would be a flaw in the reasoning of the squib.

    (A) You cannot determine whether or not this statement is true.

    (B) This point is true but irrelevant.

    (C and E) These points are irrelevant.

SECTION 2—LOGIC GAMES

Game 1: Grouping

Initial Setup:

J	F	S
	B	
—	—	—
A̸	—	—

$D \neq F$

$A_F \rightarrow F_J$ and G_J

$C_J \rightarrow E_S, F_S, G_S$

1. Correct answer: **C.** A must be purchased by Stan, because if Frank were to purchase A, then John would have to purchase F and G.

2. Correct answer: **A.** If Frank buys A, then G must be bought by John.

3. Correct answer: **C.** E, C, and H could be bought by Stan.

   (A and D) Frank buys B.

   (B and E) This means that Frank would buy A, which would mean that F and G have to be bought by John.

4. Correct answer: **C.** A must be bought by Stan, otherwise F and G would have to be bought by John, which would contradict the question stem.

5. Correct answer: **D.** It is possible for C to be bought with H:

J	F	S
F	B	
G	A	
—	—	

6. Correct answer: **E.** C cannot be bought by John because that would force E, F, and G to be bought by Stan, which is impossible because A must be bought by Stan:

J	F	S
D	B	A
	E	
A̸		
F̸	—	—
C̸	A̸	

Game 2: Complex Linear

Initial Setup:

A, B, C, D		D		
R, S, T, U		R/S		

$$D \rightarrow Z$$

A
N̸
U

[R __ T]

D   D
‖   ‖
S or R

You can deduce that there are two main configurations for the game:

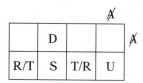

	D		
R/T	S	T/R	U

	D		
U/S	R	S/U	T

7. Correct answer: **B.** This would put you in scenario 1, and you would know that U has to be in cage 4.

8. Correct answer: **A.** A could not be in cage 3 because A cannot share a cage with U:

	D		
S	R	U	T

9. Correct answer: **E.** T would have to go last in this scenario, so U would have to precede T:

	D		A
S/U	R	U/S	T

10. Correct answer: **D.** A could share a cage with R:

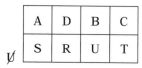

A	D	B	C
R/T	S	H/R	U

A	D	B	C
S	R	U	T

11. Correct answer: **C.** R cannot share a cage with D since R has to be in cage 3:

	D		C/B
T	S	R	U

---

12. Correct answer: **D.** The answer is C and S, as we can see by drawing out the scenarios:

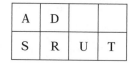

A	D		
R	S	T	

A	D		
S	R	U	T

C	D	B	A
S	R	U	T

B	D		
U	R	S	T

Game 3: Grouping

Initial Setup:

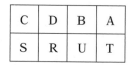

$$E_1 \rightarrow H/3$$

Since F cannot be paired with B or C, then F and E have to go together and B and C have to go together. If C cannot be picked by 3 and when D, H, or F are picked by 3, then B and C must always be chosen by judge 2.

13. Correct answer: **C.** E cannot go first in this situation, because H cannot go third:

D	B	H	F
G	C	A	E

14. Correct answer: **E.** H and D must be chosen by judges 1 and 3:

	B		F
	C		E

15. Correct answer: **C.** Since E goes with F, E must be chosen by judge 3:

$$\frac{\underline{\ \ \ }\quad \underline{B}\quad \underline{F}\quad \underline{\ \ \ }}{\underline{\ \ \ }\quad \underline{C}\quad \underline{E}\quad \underline{\ \ \ }}$$

16. Correct answer: **A.** There are two main scenarios for this corresponding to the following:

$$\frac{\underline{D/H}\quad \underline{B}\quad \underline{H/D}\quad \underline{F}}{\underline{G/A}\quad \underline{C}\quad \underline{A/G}\quad \underline{E}}$$

$$\frac{\underline{H}\quad \underline{B}\quad \underline{F}\quad \underline{D}}{\underline{A}\quad \underline{C}\quad \underline{E}\quad \underline{G}}$$

In the second scenario, G is chosen by judge 4 and A is chosen by judge 1.

17. Correct answer: **B.** A cannot be chosen by judge 3 because when E goes first, H and A cannot go third:

$$\frac{\underline{F}\quad \underline{B}\quad \underline{D}\quad \underline{H}}{\underline{E}\quad \underline{C}\quad \underline{G}\quad \underline{A}}$$

$$\frac{\underline{\ \ \ }\quad \underline{\cancel{D}}\quad \underline{F}\quad \underline{\ \ \ }}{\underline{\ \ \ }\quad \underline{C}\quad \underline{E}\quad \underline{\ \ \ }}$$

18. Correct answer: **E.** There are a total of five possibilities:

$$\frac{\underline{F}\quad \underline{B}\quad \underline{D}\quad \underline{H}}{\underline{E}\quad \underline{C}\quad \underline{G}\quad \underline{A}}\times 1$$

$$\frac{\underline{G/E}\quad \underline{B}\quad \underline{F}\quad \underline{E/G}}{\underline{D/F}\quad \underline{C}\quad \underline{E}\quad \underline{F/D}}\times 2$$

$$\frac{\underline{\ \ \ }\quad \underline{B}\quad \underline{\ \ \ }\quad \underline{F}}{\underline{\ \ \ }\quad \underline{C}\quad \underline{\ \ \ }\quad \underline{E}}\times 2$$

Game 4: Linear

Initial Setup:

$$\boxed{\underline{C}\quad \underline{\ \ \ }\quad \underline{F}\ \underline{D}}\qquad A < D$$
$$C < B$$

$$\underline{\ \ \ }\quad \underline{\ \ \ }\quad \underline{\ \ \ }\quad \underline{\ \ \ }\quad \underline{\ \ \ }\quad \underline{\ \ \ }$$

When there is a box rule that is this constraining, it is good to write out the possibilities. Here, there are only three places where the box can go:

1	C	A	F	D	B/E	E/B
2	A/E	C		F	D	B/E
3	A/E	E/A	C	B	F	D

19. Correct answer: **D.** A, C, E, F, D, and B would work in scenario 1.

20. Correct answer: **C.** This is scenario 3. A and E must be in drawers 1 and 2.

21. Correct answer: **C.** This relates to scenarios 2 and 1. In these scenarios, A must go in drawers 1, 2, or 3.

22. Correct answer: **B.** This is scenario 3. B must be in a higher-numbered drawer than E.

23. Correct answer: **D.** A, B, E, F, and C could go in drawer 3.

24. Correct answer: **B.** A and C could not go in drawer 5.

SECTION 3—READING COMPREHENSION

1. Correct Answer: **C.** The main point is to describe the President's part in making new laws.

   (A) There is a constitutional necessity behind the actions in the passage.

   (B) This is about laws, not amending the Constitution.

   (D) This is part of the purpose, but not the overarching purpose.

   (E) There is only one legislative provision interpreted.

2. Correct Answer: **B.** If this situation occurred, then it would make sense to allow the President to wait until the next legislative session to amend the bill.

   (A) Bills can still be given to the White House and are still transmitted through the appropriate channels despite the President's presence.

   (C) This would not be a veto.

   (D) This would not account for the situation.

   (E) A normal veto would be able to overcome this situation.

3. Correct answer: **D.** There is nothing said about there being no way to change a bill that has been passed into law. In actuality, bills can be repealed.

(A) There are numerous checks and balances that are evident by virtue of this passage.

(B) This inference is clear due to the existence of the pocket veto.

(C) This scenario is described in paragraph 2.

(E) This is presumable because Sundays are not counted in the days that the President has to examine the bill.

4. Correct answer: **E.** It seems that the clerk would receive the bill in order to save time for the President. The clerk would know which advisers to send the bill to so that the President's time would not be wasted determining whom the bill should go to.

(A) It seems that this statement is not true.

(B) This withholding would not be advisable and a clerk who did this would surely be fired.

(C) This statement is doubtful and not supported by the passage.

(D) This statement would not mean that the President would not still want to see the bills and would not explain why all bills go to the clerk.

5. Correct answer: **B.** It seems that this phrase relates to the adjournment of the legislature. We know that the adjournment will not be "eternal" but that it will be for some time if the President uses his pocket veto. Therefore, the word *indefinite* is the best choice.

(A, C–E) These choices are not appropriate.

6. Correct answer: **C.** If the bill is not signed in 10 days and Congress is not out of session, then the bill will pass into law.

(A) This redelivery would not occur. *Neglected* does not mean "lost" or "misplaced" in this context.

(B) It would be too late for the President's action to cause the bill to become law. A presidential signature would be meaningless at this point.

(D) This veto would be effective only if Congress goes out of session during the 10 days. You cannot be sure if this event will occur.

(E) This statement is not necessarily true, especially since this attention would not be relevant to whether the bill becomes law.

7. Correct answer: **B.** This action is stated to be the functional equivalent of actually presenting the bill to the President.

(A) This action is actually presenting the bill to the President—it is not tantamount to this action.

(C) This action is unrelated to the specific methods for presenting the bill to the President.

(D) This is a different stage of the process.

(E) This is a different stage of the process.

8. Correct answer: **B.** The author's nationality cannot be inferred from the passage.

(A) A description is given in lines 14–15.

(C) This dramatization is made throughout the passage.

(D) The author talks about ball lightning in airplanes, in World War II, and in the home of a British housewife.

(E) This explanation occurs in the scientific explanation in paragraph 3.

9. Correct answer: **B.** This claim is made in lines 53–54. The oxygen and nitrogen coming into the ball allow it to maintain its spherical shape.

(A) We are unsure if ball lightning could melt rock.

(C) The author does not make this claim.

(D) The ball is strongly charged, not polarized. (*Polarized* means having a charge on one end and an opposite charge on the other end.)

(E) This disruption results in an explosion (lines 58–59).

10. Correct answer: **B.** The point of the passage is to explain the mystery of ball lightning in a way that is scientific and not supernatural.

(A) This negative outlook is not assumed by the author.

(C) The opposite claim is made.

(D) Spheres are not asymmetric.

(E) It seems that ball lightning is very perplexing.

11. Correct answer: **C.** This word is a synonym for *plausible*. The author is relating reasonable explanations.

(A) Nothing about ball lightning has been given enough study.

(B and D) These statements are not accurate.

(E) No empirical study is referenced by the passage.

12. Correct answer: **E.** This charge would cause the group of positively charged ions that are said to be in ball lightning to dissociate, instead of meandering around until the ball loses energy.

   (A) This statement does not mean that the ball lightning was unable to use the reactants that were there.

   (B) This statement does not undermine any theory about ball lightning.

   (C) This would be a good second-best answer, but there is no reason to believe that all ions of acids in ball lightning would have to dissolve to sustain the reaction.

   (D) This statement might account for why ball lightning is so rare.

13. Correct answer: **E.** The main purpose of the final paragraph is to reemphasize the mystery of ball lightning after trying for a paragraph and a half to explain it.

   (A) This recapitulation does not occur.

   (B) He just said that a photograph would be nice, not that it would explain anything.

   (C) This explanation does not occur.

   (D) This point might be implied by the paragraph, but it is not the main purpose of the paragraph.

14. Correct answer: **D.** The author is entirely speculative about the existence of ball lightning. The whole essay is made up of speculations regarding theories that could explain its existence.

   (A) The exact opposite is true.

   (B) The author goes through many nonscientific explanations for ball lightning, so his attitude cannot be entirely "scientific."

   (C) It is not clear how the author's attitude would be "invested" in ball lightning.

   (E) The exact opposite is true.

15. Correct answer: **C.** This statement exactly summarizes the author's opinion toward the ionized gas theory.

(A) The author does not claim that most scientists would ignore their spiritual opinions when choosing a theory.

(B) This inference is something that you could make, but the author does not explicitly state it. Additionally, this tangential idea would not fully encompass the author's perspective on the ionized gas theory.

(D) The author refers to other "plausible theories" that would probably be more supportable than the phantasm theory.

(E) The author says that there are many "plausible theories."

16. Correct answer: **B.** This passage was written to describe "official sources" and "unofficial sources." Additionally, it relates the types of documents that make up each type of sources.

   (A) The perspective is a legal one, not a historian's. Additionally, the main purpose of the passage is not to explain why there needs to be a distinction between official and unofficial sources.

   (C) Congress's role in the legislative process is only the background of this passage.

   (D) This does not occur.

   (E) The Constitution is not mentioned in the passage.

17. Correct answer: **E.** This claim is true. Hence the name "the United States Code."

   (A) Both are eligible. One is positive law, and the other is prima facie.

   (B) They are engaged in recodifying the titles, but the passage does not state that they are responsible for all rules pertaining to official sources.

   (C) These are unofficial sources.

   (D) We are unable to determine the veracity of this postulation.

18. Correct answer: **A.** The best answer here is authenticity. A law is determined to be prima facie law if it is in the title. If there is a contradiction with this law somewhere else in the title, then the law is not necessarily applicable or authentic. This is compared to positive law, where there are no contradictions within the titles.

   (B–E) These answers do not apply.

19. Correct answer: **A.** This interpretation is backed up by lines 48–50.

    (B) There is nothing said about there being a "large" market for this sort of thing.

    (C) You are unable to make this inference.

    (D) The opposite is claimed.

    (E) This claim is not made. It is merely stated that their accuracy and reliability is not guaranteed.

20. Correct answer: **C.** *Certified* would be the best choice here.

    (A) *Pronounced* does not mean "spoken" in this context.

    (B) This substitution is not the same.

    (D) *Pronounced* is different from *straightforward*.

    (E) This substitution is not the same.

21. Correct answer: **D.** The passage describes the technology of gene sequencing and the introduction of the new technology called EST-based gene research.

    (A) This statement is not made in the passage.

    (B) The passage does not claim that linkage studies are completely outdated.

    (C) The EST-based approach is praised for its quickness, not reliability.

    (E) You cannot be sure of the truth of this statement.

22. Correct answer: **B.** The author describes those using EST-based research to be "riding the crest of a wave . . . the likes of which has never been seen before."

    (A) This claim is not made. The author stresses that the best technology should be used.

    (C–E) These statements are not how the author would describe things.

23. Correct answer: **A.** These terms refer to the scientists' efforts to map out particular genes in the order that they are placed in a strand of DNA.

    (B) This answer choice misinterprets *sequence* to mean the number of steps in a scientific procedure.

    (C) Something more specific is meant by these words.

    (D) This is the full sequence of genes, but these two words refer to the mapping process, not the entire chromosome.

    (E) The procedure of mapping the genes is what is referred to, not the repetitive trends in the genes.

24. Correct answer: **D.** It was never stated that this sequencing would be impossible, just that it would take a longer period of time without EST research technology.

    (A) This claim is made in the third paragraph.

    (B) It is prolifically evident throughout the passage that genetic research is profound.

    (C) This claim is made in lines 25–28.

    (E) This claim is made in lines 1–3.

25. Correct answer: **C.** This paragraph describes the difficulty of the way that genes are normally sequenced. It outlines the methods that were available for doing so before the release of EST-based technologies.

    (A) More than a description is provided. The purpose of this paragraph is to impress upon the reader how long these technologies took to produce usable information. This paragraph sets up the introduction of the faster EST-based technology.

    (B) This is not espoused by the paragraph.

    (D) No real connection is revealed between EST-based research and traditional research. EST-based research is not even mentioned in the second paragraph.

    (E) This is definitely not the purpose of the passage.

26. Correct answer: **E.** The author states word for word that "the ultimate goal is to gain an understanding of . . . a process commonly referred to as gene expression."

    (A) This is a subsidiary goal.

    (B) This is the goal that directs the research, but it is not the ultimate goal of the specific sequencing project.

    (C) These are subsidiary goals.

    (D) This is only a goal in certain circumstances.

27. Correct answer: **B.** The author claims that scientific literature gives hints about where to proceed and which course to take.

(A) This occurs sometimes, but the author claims that it gives hints, not that it outlines the entire process.

(C) The opposite is claimed by the author.

(D) No comparison is ever made between these two groups of scientists.

(E) This claim is implied, but it is not stated that they will never succeed.

SECTION 4—LOGICAL REASONING

1. The neurologist claims that the synapses in the patient's brain fire in a random pattern. The patient claims that it is impossible for things to fire at random while being in a pattern. The patient points out a contradiction made by the neurologist.

Question Type: Reasoning strategy

Correct answer: **B.** This responce is what occurs.

(A) Nothing is stated about people in general.

(C and D) These responses do not occur.

(E) The opposite response is what occurs.

2. The point of the squib is that since cinema is so new, it is almost impossible to determine which directors will be remembered.

Question Type: Conclusion

Correct answer: **D.** This is the crux of the squib.

(A) This point is implied by the squib, but it is not the main one.

(B) You cannot be sure about this point.

(C) This point is true of renowned artists in these art forms, but it is not doubted that cinema itself will stand the test of time.

(E) This is a subsidiary point of the squib.

3. The squib says that Smithee did not teach method acting. It further claims that all great actors are method actors. It says that Smithee has taught some great actors. Therefore, these great actors must have learned method acting somewhere besides from Smithee.

Question Type: Conclusion

Correct answer: **A.** This point must be true for her to have taught many great actors.

(B–E) You cannot determine these things.

4. The citizen claims that the real purpose of the government-imposed emissions tests is to collect more taxes, not to protect the environment.

Question Type: "Strengthen"

Correct answer: **D.** This answer would mean that having two emissions tests in a year is unnecessary.

(A) A majority opinion that is not supported with facts cannot be an answer.

(B) Their past misdeeds probably do not relate to emissions testing.

(C) This answer shows that the people are not concerned about air pollution.

(E) This point is irrelevant.

5. This squib is very complicated. It states the following [symbol (S) means "some"] :

1. Pat wants to wear a monster costume.
2. Goblin → Monster
3. Ghost—(S)—Monster
4. Green Troll → Goblin
5. ~~Green Troll → Goblin~~
6. Blue Ghost → Blue Troll
7. Green Ghost → Green Troll

Question Type: Conclusion

Correct answer: **E.** A green ghost would definitely be a good costume, since it would also be a green troll, which would be a goblin, which would be a monster.

(A) You cannot be sure if blue ghosts are monsters.

(B) You know nothing about banshees.

(C) You know nothing about red trolls.

(D) You cannot be sure if blue trolls are monsters

6. The art historian makes an unsound argument on the basis of the very first form of art in existence. This approch does not seem like a good way to fashion an argument.

Question Type: "Weaken"

Correct answer: **A.** The art made by Neanderthals can have no real implications for the modern artist or for the difference between commercial art and "art for art's sake."

(B–D) These points would be irrelevant.

(E) This answer is not true.

7. Experts claim that mathematicians are often talented in music because many of the core talents needed for musical excellence are necessary for math. Matthew claims that this is a preposterous claim because artists' talents could also be compared to the talents of musicians.

Question Type: "Resolve"

Correct answer: **C.** If this answer were true, then artists' creativity would not be as useful as mathematical skills for playing music.

(A) This answer does not resolve the issue in favor of anyone.

(B and D) These points are irrelevant.

(E) This answer does not mean that a person's musical skills have anything to do with artistic talent.

8. This squib claims that children who are in spelling bees would be better served by spending their time doing something else. The author claims that word processing programs have minimized the importance of good spelling.

Question Type: "Strengthen"

Correct answer: **C.** If they are *vestigial,* that means that they are outdated and useless. Therefore the children should spend their time developing more worthwhile skills.

(A and B) This answer do not mean that the children are aided or hurt by their pursuit.

(D) This point is irrelevant to whether children should spend time engaged in the activity.

(E) This answer does not mean that math is a better pursuit than spelling.

9. This squib claims that animals can understand language but are unable to reproduce it. Specifically, dogs will never be able to reproduce language because they are unable to alter their guttural utterances from the default noise of "woof."

Question Type: "Strengthen"

Correct answer: **A.** If this answer were true, then it would mean that dogs could never make an aural sound of speech.

(B) This assumption does not mean that dogs are not intelligent enough to communicate.

(C) This answer does not mean that they are intentionally trying to speak. Also, it does not mean that they would be able to form other words besides these particular ones.

(D) This answer does not mean that dogs would not be able to do so.

(E) This point is irrelevant to dogs' potential.

10. Don Juan claims that serenades always work in Spain but for some reason they are not working for him in America. Therefore, he assumes that serenades in America never work.

Question Type: "Strengthen"

Correct answer: **D.** If one lady heard Don Juan serenade the previous lady, then it is more likely that his serenades do not work because the ladies do not believe him rather than because serenades are ineffective in general.

(A) Nothing is assumed about Americans' value set.

(B) This assumption is not made.

(C) While this point might be true, Don Juan does not make this assumption.

(E) You cannot tell if Don Juan is being sincere in his professions of love. He could be a very loving man.

11. This argument assumes that because people can improve their scores on standardized tests by studying, standardized tests are poor predictors of future success in school. However, if high scores on standardized tests indicate who is likely to study, then the opposite of the author's opinion would be true, since good study habits correlate with future success in school.

Question Type: "Strengthen"

Correct answer: **B.** This point is assumed, because otherwise standardized tests for which people study would be good predictors of how well these people will do in school in the future.

(A) You cannot be sure of this point.

(C) The squib implies that most people will do well, but not that they will *always* do well.

(D) The squib does not say that they are completely incapable, just that they do not work as well.

(E) The opposite point is assumed by the squib.

12. This squib claims that students have no privacy in their school lockers. Furthermore, it states that they could obtain privacy by placing their own locks on the lockers, but they will get in trouble if they do so. Therefore, the squib assumes that students who use lockers will always get in trouble.

Question Type: "Strengthen"

Correct answer: **E.** This squib makes the broad assumption that all students using lockers have something to hide that can get them into trouble.

(A) The usage habits of students are not assumed.

(B) The squib says nothing about whether schools respect students' right to privacy in their wallets.

(C and D) You are unable to determine these points.

13. This squib gives a couple of pieces of evidence to support the existence of ESP. Then it states that if people were taught to recognize their ESP, they would be able to avoid accidents.

Question Type: "Strengthen"

Correct answer: **D.** If the opposite point were true, then people would never be able to avoid accidents despite their ESP.

(A) This assumption is not made by the argument. These manifestations are just the only two listed.

(B) It was not claimed that people are able to recognize the nature of the accident before it occurs.

(C) You cannot be sure if ESP is effective for monkeys.

(E) This claim was not made.

14. This squib assumes that because all past NASCAR rookies of the year have used the most technologically advanced engine, this year's rookie of the year must have used the most technologically advanced engine.

Question Type: "Weaken"

Correct answer: **C.** This answer would mean that his car was unable to use the nitroglycerine engine created by Global Motors.

(A) This answer does not mean that he has not used it knowing that it would give him an advantage.

(B) This answer does not mean that the engine does not work for other cars besides those produced by Global Motors.

(D) This point is irrelevant.

(E) This answer would only strengthen the claims of the squib.

15. This is a sufficient-necessary question [symbol (S) means some]:

1. Linguistics Professor → Fishing

2. Fishing → Cats

3. Cats—(S)— ~~Dogs~~

These can be combined to form:

Linguistics Professor → Fishing → Cats —(S)— ~~Dogs~~

The conclusion claims that no linguistics professor at the university keeps a dog.

Question Type: "Weaken"

Correct answer: **C.** This answer restates the fact that some people who keep cats also keep dogs.

(A) This point is impossible, according to the squib.

(B) But all linguist professors do fish.

(D) This point does not have any influence on the conclusion.

(E) This answer does not mean that professors teaching linguistics at the university keep dogs.

16. This squib claims that when a child keeps an aquarium, she or he learns the benefits that come from acting responsibly. Furthermore, it claims that children will understand that if they act responsibly in other types of relationships, then they will gain similar benefits in those relationships as well.

Question Type: "Weaken"

Correct answer: **A.** If children cannot grasp the link, then it is likely that they will not realize that they should act responsibly in other areas besides fish keeping.

(B) This answer does not mean that children do not learn from the experience.

(C) This answer would support the conclusion of the squib.

(D) This point is irrelevant.

(E) This answer does not mean that the children's understanding of the value of responsibility will transfer to other areas besides taking care of cats or fish.

17. The squib claims that bicyclists have to overcome numerous obstacles to excel in their sport. Based on this idea, the author claims that bicyclists would excel at any sport they attempted solely because of their mental fortitude.

Question Type: "Weaken"

Correct answer: **D.** This answer would mean that the natural abilities of cyclists would be applicable only to cycling.

(A) This answer does not mean that they do not excel eventually.

(B) This point is irrelevant.

(C) This answer would only strengthen the argument.

(E) This answer does not mean that they have not become great or excelled in those sports.

18. The squib offers two causes for the decimation of the manatee population. The first is the proliferation of speedboats, and second is the disease. The squib claims that if the disease were cured, then the manatee population would rebound to the levels that existed before either problem began.

Question Type: Reasoning strategy

Correct answer: **A.** The conclusion ignores the effects that speedboat accidents have on the manatee population.

(B) This point is not important.

(C) A solution is indeed offered.

(D) This is not an apparent flaw of the argument.

(E) This is a reasonable assumption.

19. The squib claims that people who are self-aggrandizing are insecure and need to offset their insecurity by boasting to others of their talents. The squib then focuses on professional actors, authors, and musicians who are constantly engaging in self-promotion. The squib makes the assumption that these particular people must be very insecure because of their constant self-aggrandizement.

Question Type: Reasoning strategy

Correct answer: **E.** This group of people must engage in self-aggrandizing behavior in order to entice people to buy their products. This is a more compelling reason than self-image issues for these people to act as they do.

(A) This action is not inappropriate.

(B) This is a sound connection.

(C) This action does not occur.

(D) Actors also make art.

20. This squib states that Bolivian pinto bean farmers do not have the technology that would allow them to bring their production levels up to par with that of United States farmers. The conclusion states that if Bolivian farmers had the technology, they could match the yields achieved by the most advanced United States farmers. (This reasoning is a jump from average to best.)

Question Type: Reasoning strategy

Correct answer: **A.** If this point were true, then regardless of technology, the Bolivian farmers would not be able to compete with the most advanced United States farmers.

(B) This confusion does not occur.

(C) The past trends are not said to be illusory.

(D) This examination would not be appropriate, if it occurred.

(E) A claim is used to support this conclusion.

21. According to the author, many claim that what makes great literature "great" is the skill of the writer. However, the author claims that greatness has less to do with the writer's skill than it does with the time when the work was written, because many so-called "great" books of the past would not even be considered so by today's publishers.

Question Type: Reasoning strategy

Correct answer: **D.** The presumption that what makes great literature "great" is the author's talent is shown to be false by the author's reference to what is considered to be great literature of the past.

(A) There is nothing unanticipated here. The claims are still the same, but the truth might be different from traditional claims.

(B) No numerical data are offered.

(C) The squib makes no mention of artists making a claim.

(E) The exact opposite of this argument is made.

22. The argument looks at statistical data to note that rain does not influence the yield of corn in a particular season. Based on this information, the author claims that Bill is incorrect in his analysis.

Question Type: Reasoning strategy

Correct answer: **B.** The statistical evidence shows that too much rain hurts crops just as often as it helps them. Therefore, Bill's analysis would be incorrect.

(A) Nothing is implied about a lack of education.

(C) The conclusion is reached by examining evidence that supports it, not evidence that refutes it.

(D) There is no demonstration of two incompatible assertions.

(E) An inference is made on adequate data (statistical agricultural data related to crop yields).

23. Anna claims that the most popular boy in school will ask her to the dance. Jane claims that the most popular boy in school has already asked her to the dance.

Question Type: "Resolve"

Correct answer: **D.** If this outcome were to occur, then the most popular boy in school could ask Anna to the dance and the most popular boy in school could have asked Jane to the dance.

(A) This point is irrelevant to resolution of the problem.

(B) This point is irrelevant.

(C) This answer would further confuse the situation.

(E) This answer would contradict Jane's statements.

24. This pollster talks about elections and claims that a candidate's ultimate success is based on the percentage of voters that support the candidate who actually get out and vote. This point is true, but the variable of the overall number of voters who support each candidate is neglected.

Question Type: Reasoning strategy

Correct answer: **D.** This answer choice gets directly to the fact that constituency size is an important element in an election.

(A) Voter turnout is very relevant.

(B) This claim is correct and therefore is not a problem with the argument.

(C) Even if this is the case, the relative worth of a candidate is often ignored in popular elections.

(E) This specific occurrence is irrelevant.

PRACTICE TEST 5

ANSWER SHEET

SECTION 1	SECTION 2	SECTION 3	SECTION 4
1. A B C D E	1. A B C D E	1. A B C D E	1. A B C D E
2. A B C D E	2. A B C D E	2. A B C D E	2. A B C D E
3. A B C D E	3. A B C D E	3. A B C D E	3. A B C D E
4. A B C D E	4. A B C D E	4. A B C D E	4. A B C D E
5. A B C D E	5. A B C D E	5. A B C D E	5. A B C D E
6. A B C D E	6. A B C D E	6. A B C D E	6. A B C D E
7. A B C D E	7. A B C D E	7. A B C D E	7. A B C D E
8. A B C D E	8. A B C D E	8. A B C D E	8. A B C D E
9. A B C D E	9. A B C D E	9. A B C D E	9. A B C D E
10. A B C D E	10. A B C D E	10. A B C D E	10. A B C D E
11. A B C D E	11. A B C D E	11. A B C D E	11. A B C D E
12. A B C D E	12. A B C D E	12. A B C D E	12. A B C D E
13. A B C D E	13. A B C D E	13. A B C D E	13. A B C D E
14. A B C D E	14. A B C D E	14. A B C D E	14. A B C D E
15. A B C D E	15. A B C D E	15. A B C D E	15. A B C D E
16. A B C D E	16. A B C D E	16. A B C D E	16. A B C D E
17. A B C D E	17. A B C D E	17. A B C D E	17. A B C D E
18. A B C D E	18. A B C D E	18. A B C D E	18. A B C D E
19. A B C D E	19. A B C D E	19. A B C D E	19. A B C D E
20. A B C D E	20. A B C D E	20. A B C D E	20. A B C D E
21. A B C D E	21. A B C D E	21. A B C D E	21. A B C D E
22. A B C D E	22. A B C D E	22. A B C D E	22. A B C D E
23. A B C D E	23. A B C D E	23. A B C D E	23. A B C D E
24. A B C D E	24. A B C D E	24. A B C D E	24. A B C D E
25. A B C D E	25. A B C D E	25. A B C D E	25. A B C D E
26. A B C D E	26. A B C D E	26. A B C D E	26. A B C D E
27. A B C D E	27. A B C D E	27. A B C D E	27. A B C D E
28. A B C D E	28. A B C D E	28. A B C D E	28. A B C D E
29. A B C D E	29. A B C D E	29. A B C D E	29. A B C D E
30. A B C D E	30. A B C D E	30. A B C D E	30. A B C D E

SECTION 1
Time—35 minutes
25 questions

<u>Directions for Logical Reasoning Questions:</u> The questions in this section are based on brief statements or passages. Choose your answers based on the reasoning in each passage. Do not make assumptions that are not supported by the passage or by common sense. For some questions, more than one answer choice may be possible, so choose the *best* answer to each question, that is, the one that is most accurate and complete. After you have chosen your answer, mark the corresponding space on the Answer Sheet.

1. In an alphabet soup, each of the letters is of one of three different flavors: chicken, beef, or pork. All Ps are pork. No Fs are beef. Half of the Rs are chicken, the other half are pork. The rest of the letters from A to M in the alphabet, with the exception of J, are chicken. No letter from N through Z in the alphabet is chicken.

    Which of the following words could you spell with alphabet noodles from this soup by using only letters that are definitely not beef-flavored?

    (A) PAGE
    (B) DOPE
    (C) RATS
    (D) PHAT
    (E) ZANY

2. People who like animals tend to dislike zoos because the animals there are caged and kept in an area that is tiny compared to their natural habitat. However, large numbers of people who like animals tend to work in zoos.

    Which of the following would explain why people will work in a place that they dislike?

    (A) A large percentage of people who work in zoos dislike the zoos.
    (B) No one who dislikes animals will work in a zoo.
    (C) A large portion of the animals in zoos love their attendants.
    (D) Many people who dislike animals also dislike zoos.
    (E) A large percentage of people who like animals do not like to work with animals.

3. Soft drink advertisements do not have the outcome that soft drink producers desire. Instead, the advertisements, which feature interactions between families and adolescent couples, tend to encourage people to engage in communal behavior. This communal behavior is great for a community because it builds stronger bonds between individual members, but it is totally inconsistent with the overt purpose of the advertising campaign: to impel people to buy more soft drinks.

    Which of the following, if true, would cast doubt on the accuracy of the passage's conclusion?

    (A) People who do not participate in communal behavior, regardless of the commercials, tend not to buy soft drinks.
    (B) Soft drink commercials are intended to increase communal behavior instead of selling soft drinks.
    (C) Advertising firms, through extensive market research, discovered that commercials promoting communal behavior would improve the public's opinion of soft drink companies.
    (D) Chemical compounds found in soft drinks are known to cause people to reduce their communal behavior.
    (E) By increasing the incidence of communal behavior, soft drink producers know they will increase their sales.

GO ON TO THE NEXT PAGE

4. Garage doors are necessary to allow a car to enter and exit without compromising the safety of the entire household. If there were no garage doors, then a person could enter your house and take everything as easily as entering your garage. We need all need automatic door closers that will close the garage door after our car leaves the garage. That way, burglars will not be able to enter our houses through the garage after a car leaves.

Which of the following is assumed by the argument?

(A) Burglars can see when there is no car in the garage and thereby tell that no one is home to guard the house.
(B) Automatic door closers will be able to prevent someone from entering the car when it is still parked inside the garage.
(C) People dislike having anyone enter their house through their garage.
(D) People without garage doors have no security measures in place to protect their house.
(E) Garages should not be added to houses that do not already have them solely for security reasons.

5. John says that, as a politician, he knows that most politicians are moral. And since most politicians are intelligent, at least some people who are immoral are unintelligent.

Which of the following has a flawed argumentative structure most like the one in the argument above?

(A) Bill says that, as an aardvark expert, he knows that most aardvarks have stubby arms. And since most aardvarks are also ill-tempered, most aardvarks are stubby armed and ill-tempered.
(B) Anna says that, as a driver, she knows that most drivers are courteous. And since most drivers drive well, at least some drivers who drive well are not courteous.
(C) Andy says that, as a pilot, you need to have good eyes. And since most pilots do have good eyes, at least some people who are not pilots have bad eyes.
(D) Julio says that, as a teacher, he knows that most teachers care about students. And since most teachers are well educated, at least some people who do not care about students are uneducated.
(E) Claire says that, as a stylist, she knows that most stylists love their job. And since most stylists are also artists, at least some people who do not love their job are stylists.

GO ON TO THE NEXT PAGE

6. People who are naturally poor spellers can use computer programs to turn in papers that are spelled well. However, regardless of the effectiveness of these programs, people who are naturally good spellers will always turn in papers that are spelled better than the papers turned in by poor spellers.

Which of the following, if true, would explain the situation in the passage above?

(A) People who spell well will not know when words that are approved by the program are not spelled correctly.
(B) People who use programs to correct their spelling are less likely to be good spellers than people who do not use them.
(C) People who turn in papers tend to care more about the content of their papers than about the fine points of spelling.
(D) No computer program can spell as well as people who are categorized as good spellers.
(E) Computer programmers in general cannot spell as well as the worst spellers who hand in papers.

7. Green and blue Martians are from Jupiter. Green Martians have pointy tails and blue eyes. Blue Martians have round tails and yellow eyes. All Martians on the landing ship do not have tails.

Which of the following must be assumed to reach the conclusion that the Martians on the ship are from Mars?

(A) All Martians without tails are from Jupiter or Mars.
(B) All Martians on the landing ship have pointy tails and blue eyes.
(C) All Martians that are not from Mars have tails, no tails, or half tails.
(D) All Martians that are not green or blue are from Mars.
(E) All Martians that are not from Jupiter have no tails.

8. Billy and Philip have fairly similar tastes in music. Two new CDs came out yesterday, and Billy went to the store to buy one of them. Philip asked Billy which one he bought, but Billy refused to tell him. Philip knows that one of the CDs released yesterday was a compilation of songs by Jane Singleton, a singer that Philip hates. Based on his personal music tastes, he concludes that Billy purchased the other CD.

Which of the following is a logic error made by Billy?

(A) He makes a fatal logic error by inappropriately applying the transitive property.
(B) He treats evidence that the conclusion is probably true as establishing that it is certainly true.
(C) He treats a sufficient condition as if it were completely necessary for an outcome to occur.
(D) He ignores obvious evidence indicating that either logical conclusion is false.
(E) He treats a failure to prove a certain theory as direct proof of evidence against that theory.

GO ON TO THE NEXT PAGE

9. Teacher: No grading system should be imposed on our students. Those who want to learn will learn, and those who do not, will not. There is no reason to impose external pressures on students to do something that they do not want to do naturally.

Principal: I agree with you in idealistic terms, but pragmatically, applying external pressures on students to learn causes them to study harder and learn more. This is why the grading system is a positive.

Which of the following are the principal and the teacher committed to disagreeing about?

(A) The grading system should be applied to teachers in order to determine who is doing their job.
(B) The grading system has some negative implications for students.
(C) Students who are subjected to external pressures tend to succumb to those pressures.
(D) The grading system will remain in place and unchanged in the next academic year.
(E) There is a reason to apply external pressures on students who do not want to do something naturally.

10. Investment banking is certainly a profitable career, but is that how people should spend their whole life? Most investment bankers work until their early thirties and then retire with the huge sums of money that they have made. When all things are considered, these people have probably worked about the same number of hours in 10 years as most other people do in 20 years. So when viewed in that light, it would seem that their early retirement is justified. Also, who would not want to retire when they have the means to do so and pursue personal goals and activities?

Which of the following is assumed by the author?

(A) Investment bankers work more than 100 hours a week, on average.
(B) Few investment bankers who are 40 years old want to retire.
(C) Investment banking is the nation's highest paying profession.
(D) Investment bankers' work is harder than that of average workers in today's economy.
(E) Few investment bankers in their early thirties do not want to retire.

GO ON TO THE NEXT PAGE

11. Social philosopher: There exists in our society a largely undiagnosed but deeply troubling disease, if I may be so bold as to call it that, which is manifested by our haphazard, blasé views toward the law and respect for the law. Consider this example: We are told that jaywalking, in many towns and cities, is a crime, and yet we do it anyway, and with little or no fear of punishment. We are told the speed limit is 55 miles per hour, and what do we do? We drive at 70, and lives are lost on our freeways every day. This attitude of disregard has permeated our culture so deeply that I fear a future of slippage and, eventually, revolt.

Which of the following most accurately expresses the philosopher's main point?

(A) Jaywalking is illegal, and because it is, it should be punished.
(B) Speed limit violations, even more so than jaywalking, have a serious and tangible consequence and therefore must be stopped.
(C) Where there is a social disease, we must find a social cure.
(D) Disregard for insignificant laws indicates a dangerous attitude of lawlessness.
(E) In the future, jaywalking and speeding will lead to a revolution of sorts.

12. Booklets on safety are the first things that are given to new employees. There is really only one reason for this, because after all, any person with an IQ above 2 already knows all of the information in such booklets. The reason is that companies want to place the burden of avoiding dangerous situations on the shoulders of their employees. That way, if an accident happens, the company can claim that it is not liable for damages. Instead, the company will claim that its employee is independently liable.

Which of the following, if true, would tend to support the statements of the passage?

(A) Companies that give their new employees booklets on safety are less likely to be sued than other companies.
(B) Legal rulings allow companies to waive responsibility for employee behavior only when employees have explicitly been instructed not to do something.
(C) People who do not follow the instructions in the safety booklets are often given one warning and then are fired.
(D) The booklets have at some point informed people of issues that they had not thought about previously.
(E) Booklets on safety are often accompanied by handbooks delineating expected modes of worker conduct.

GO ON TO THE NEXT PAGE

13. Even though daycare centers charge hefty prices, daycare center operators reap unremarkable profits from their daycare-related businesses. This situation is generally due to the lofty per-hour salaries that daycare workers receive. Market analysts find it surprising that daycare jobs, which require relatively unskilled labor, compensate people so generously, because this is certainly not the trend for salaries in the rest of the labor market. Analysts theorize that the powerful daycare workers' union is responsible for daycare worker's seemingly excessive compensation.

Which of the following, if true, would most undermine the conclusion of the argument?

(A) Individual daycare workers tend not to belong to the union even though they benefit from its effects.
(B) There is an exceedingly small supply of daycare workers when compared to the high demand.
(C) Parents are willing to pay lavish daycare costs because they believe that a large portion of their expenses will benefit their children.
(D) Daycare center operators could streamline their businesses in ways that would increase their profits without requiring them to combat the union.
(E) More of the hefty price paid for daycare is spent providing children with lunches and toys than on the salaries of the workers.

14. Brad: Football players are the best athletes. They are stronger, faster, and tougher than basketball players, baseball players, tennis players, or golfers—in fact, they could pound any of them into the ground if they so chose. Plus many football players possess incredible hand-eye coordination and fine motor skills—just look at place kickers who can kick the ball through narrow goal posts from 50 yards away.

Evan: That's a ridiculous argument, for a number of reasons. For one, even though a linebacker or a running back could measure up to the most strenuous of physical tests, this hardly holds true for most place kickers or punters. And you can hardly say that most linemen possess "incredible hand-eye coordination."

Which of the following argumentative tactics does Evan use to challenge Brad's assertion?

(A) He alters Brad's definition of the term *athlete*.
(B) He challenges the extent of Brad's claims regarding the term *football player*.
(C) He inverts Brad's conclusion in order to undermine his evidence.
(D) He contradicts Brad's appeal to personal emotion in place of logic.
(E) He attacks Brad's point of view by focusing on the proponents of that point of view.

GO ON TO THE NEXT PAGE

15. Ben and Sally are college students at the University of Ames. Ben asks Sally to go to the beach with him this coming weekend. Sally refuses, saying that she cannot afford to miss a weekend of studying in exchange for a weekend of leisure at the beach. Ben suspects that study time is not the real reason that Sally refuses to go to the beach with him because she makes the same excuse every time he asks her to take a weekend trip with him.

Which of the following is an error in Ben's reasoning?

(A) He fails to acknowledge that for most people, studying is more important than a weekend of leisure.

(B) He assumes that if Sally's proffered reason is her only reason, then it cannot be her real reason at all.

(C) He does not examine the possibility that Sally's behavior is adequately explained by the reason she gives for it.

(D) He ignores the idea that Sally is probably not romantically interested in him and is therefore using studying as an excuse.

(E) He fallaciously correlates a person's penchant for study to that person's dislike of leisure activities.

16. Lissy: I love dancing at the May parade. I have been to every parade this season and will continue to go to every future parade that has dancing. I feel that dancing is a calling of mine.

Robert: I hate dancing, and your love of it makes me feel inferior. I am not sure if I will be able to dance with you any more tonight and retain any sense of pride.

If Lissy's words are true, then which of the following is an inference that you can make based on her claims?

(A) Lissy has been to every parade that occurred in this past year.

(B) If there is a parade in June with dancing, then Lissy will attend it.

(C) Lissy will be a professional dancer.

(D) Robert will not dance with Lissy any longer during this parade.

(E) Lissy is a better dancer than Robert.

17. Fox Farm Vineyards produces three varietals of wine: chardonnay, Riesling, and zinfandel. Swan Song Vineyards produces three varietals as well: merlot, chardonnay, and cabernet. All Swan Song merlots are heavy. All Fox Farm varietals are dry except for its Riesling. The only nondry wines Swan Song offers are its chardonnay and its cabernet. Fox Farm's chardonnay is not heavy, nor is its zinfandel.

Rita wants a heavy, dry wine. Which should she choose?

(A) Fox Farm chardonnay
(B) Swan Song cabernet
(C) Swan Song merlot
(D) Fox Farm zinfandel
(E) Swan Song chardonnay

GO ON TO THE NEXT PAGE

18. Professor: A recent study has auspiciously confirmed my conclusions. People who have iguanas as pets tend to suffer from fewer allergies than other people. Dog owners actually suffer from 16% more types of allergies than cat owners, who suffer from 32% more allergies than iguana owners. People who have bad allergies should follow my recommendations and purchase an iguana for the sake of their health.

Which of the following, if true, would demonstrate that following the professor's recommendation would not be helpful?

(A) There are a small number of people who would get never get sick if they kept an iguana in their home.
(B) Iguanas and cats do not get along well, so a person who purchases an iguana generally gets rid of his or her cats.
(C) Iguanas and dogs do get along well, so a person who purchases an iguana generally will not get rid of his or her dog.
(D) Purchasing and keeping an iguana does not inflame a person's allergies, nor does it mitigate the affects of other allergens in the environment.
(E) Health care professionals unanimously disapprove of certain people keeping iguanas as pets in their homes.

19. Psychiatrist: People who do not like any other people cannot be liked by other people. In the same vein, people who do like other people can, at times, be liked by other people.

Patient: But what relevance do these abstract contentions hold for me? I do not like other people, but I definitely want them to like me. Am I supposed to change my opinions in order to change their opinions?

Which of the following arguments is most analogous to the psychiatrist's argument?

(A) People who do not like rodents cannot be liked by rats. People who do like rodents can be liked by rodents.
(B) Aliens who do not visit earthlings cannot be visited by earthlings. Aliens who do visit earthlings cannot be visited by other earthlings.
(C) Aardvarks that do not appreciate animals cannot be appreciated by other animals. Aardvarks that do appreciate animals can be appreciated by other animals.
(D) People who do not like other people should begin to like other people, because that is the only way that they will be able to get other people to start liking them.
(E) Farmers who do tend their livestock cannot be tended by their livestock. Livestock that do not tend their farmers cannot be tended by their farmers.

GO ON TO THE NEXT PAGE

20. Macroevolution is one of the most well documented of all scientific phenomena; scientists have millions of years' worth of supporting evidence culminating in mineralized formations known as *fossils*. On the other hand, microevolution is less well documented. Since this kind of evolution occurs over shorter time periods, there is simply not a comparable trove of data available to verify its existence. Solely because of this lack of information, many people believe that evolution can occur over a long period of time, but few believe that it can occur over a short period.

Which of the following, if true, would cast the most doubt on the accuracy of the passage's reasoning?

(A) Microevolution and macroevolution involve substantively different biological processes.
(B) The theory of microevolution existed long before scientists arrived at a macroevolutionary theory.
(C) People who discredit microevolution equally discredit the evidence for macroevolution.
(D) The more educated people are, the more likely they are to believe in both types of evolution.
(E) Evolution cannot be proven by any of the data that are being used to support either theory.

21. Artist: It is absurd that graduate school art curricula mandate that painters and sculptors must pass up to three or four courses that have nothing at all to do with what we come to grad school for, namely the creation of art, but that focus instead on art history. In theory, this makes sense, since in order to create the new, it helps to understand the old, but in practice it amounts to teachers who know less about the reality of art and the making of art than do their students telling these students (not undidactically, I might add) what is and what is not veritable art. What will such an exercise contribute to the artist's improvement as an *artist*? Perhaps, then, art history students should be made to take studio art classes as well.

Which of the following best expresses the artist's main point?

(A) Art history students should be made to take studio art classes.
(B) Graduate programs in art are by and large a waste of time.
(C) Graduate art programs require coursework irrelevant to artistic training.
(D) Art history professors know less about art than do real artists.
(E) The standards by which art students versus art history students are graded and judged are unfair and should be revised.

GO ON TO THE NEXT PAGE

22. Proponents of spaceflight aimed at crossing galaxy borders argue that new types of engines are required to facilitate the interstellar quest. The current engine that uses rocket fuel is too heavy to achieve the necessary speeds for intergalactic travel. Presumably this travel will be possible with plasma engines that use fuel that has little or no mass. If we assume that this is the case, then in 10 years, when plasma engines are scheduled to be created, intergalactic travel will be possible.

Which of the following identifies a reasoning error in the passage?

(A) It relies on a fallacious assumption.
(B) Its evidence does not inadequately support its conclusion.
(C) It assumes what it sets out to prove.
(D) Its conclusion is based on an event that will happen in 10 years' time.
(E) Its conclusion is contradicted by one of its supporting premises.

23. More Americans than ever before are now attending colleges and universities, and consequently, these institutions are inundated more and more each year with applications. Whereas in the past, college applicants were admitted more uniformly on the basis of standardized scores and grade reports, now many intangible factors are far more important than ever before. What type of character qualities may be gleaned from an applicant's personal essays? What do her teacher recommendations say about the promise of her future? Today these questions are at the forefront of the mind of every admissions director.

Which of the following best summarizes the main point of the passage?

(A) College admission, especially at elite universities, is now more difficult than ever.
(B) Instead of focusing merely on classroom work, the aspiring college student should develop a wide array of interests and involvements.
(C) Now more than ever before, college admissions decisions are based on subjective factors.
(D) Teacher recommendations and personal essays have become the most important elements in a college application.
(E) The criteria upon which admissions decisions are made are always changing.

GO ON TO THE NEXT PAGE

24. People who hand out pamphlets professionally must be incredibly social in order to succeed at their job. I have never handed out pamphlets, but I have handed out newspapers, something that some people actually want, and it is still hard to approach people and give them the newspaper. For pamphlets, it must be many times harder because you know that people don't want to stop what they are doing to read the litter that you are handing out.

Which of the following, if true, would support the conclusion of the argument?

(A) People who are more sociable are more successful at handing out pamphlets than the people who hand out newspapers.

(B) Writers of newspaper articles are the best at handing out papers because they have a vested interest in getting the public to read their words.

(C) Handing out items that people do not want is more difficult than handing out items that they do want.

(D) It is many times more difficult to hire someone to hand out pamphlets than someone who will hand out newspapers.

(E) People who are professionals at something almost always tend to succeed.

25. Some say that the Spanish conquistadors did not conquer the Aztec people. Instead, they believe that sickness from foreign diseases coupled with the mistaken belief that the conquistadors were minions of a powerful god effectively conquered the Aztecs. This argument is moot, because if the Aztecs did not grow sick from foreign disease and if they did not believe that the conquistadors were agents of a god, the conquistadors still would have subjugated the Aztecs eventually through their army's brute force, brilliant military tactics, and superior technology.

Which of the following, if true, would most cast doubt on the passage's conclusion?

(A) Despite historical accounts, the Aztecs did not actually believe that the Spanish conquistadors were agents of a god.

(B) The plagues that killed many Aztecs originated from within the lands of the Aztec empire.

(C) The Spanish army of Cortés would have conquered the Aztecs regardless of their being sick and fearful of his supposed deity.

(D) The Spanish did not have the ability to transport an army overseas that could have overcome a healthy Aztec empire.

(E) The entire Spanish army was fighting in France at the time that the Aztecs fell to the Spanish conquistadors.

S T O P

IF YOU FINISH BEFORE TIME RUNS OUT, CHECK YOUR WORK ON THIS SECTION ONLY.

DO NOT GO ON TO ANY OTHER TEST SECTION.

SECTION 2
Time—35 minutes
25 questions

<u>Directions for Logical Reasoning Questions:</u> The questions in this section are based on brief statements or passages. Choose your answers based on the reasoning in each passage. Do not make assumptions that are not supported by the passage or by common sense. For some questions, more than one answer choice may be possible, so choose the *best* answer to each question, that is, the one that is most accurate and complete. After you have chosen your answer, mark the corresponding space on the Answer Sheet.

1. Student: Our professor's recent publication combines numerous works of many different authors. The compilation consists of partial works written by Kant, Marx, Weber, Rorty, and many others. Since no one portion of the book is original, it follows that our professor's publication cannot be considered original.

   Which of the following is a reasoning error committed by the student?

   (A) The student makes a claim based on the tenuous assumption that the works of Kant, Marx, Weber, Rorty, and the other authors were original to begin with.
   (B) The student makes a claim based on several parts of a whole without making a detailed examination of the compilations that first included the separate parts.
   (C) The student assumes that the characteristics of a representative group of texts apply to the entire body of the publication.
   (D) The student fails to recognize that even though something is true of each part of a whole, it is not necessarily true of the whole itself.
   (E) The student makes a conclusion based on a candid dislike for a professor instead of the substantive qualities of the professor's work.

2. Many people feel that the scariest thing in the ocean is the sea snake. Stories are told about sea snakes up to 12 feet long that are hundreds of times more poisonous than the king cobra. Additionally, for most sea snakes there is no antitoxin that could save a person from the effects of a bite. However, many scientists claim that even if you encountered an angry sea snake, the risk of being bitten is incredibly small because the snake's mouth is so tiny. The snake would have to bite you on your nose or between the folds of your fingers in order to puncture your flesh.

   Which of the following is assumed by the scientists?

   (A) People can avoid confronting sea snakes more easily than they can avoid confronting land snakes.
   (B) Sea snakes that are angry are more inclined to bite people than sea snakes that are not angry.
   (C) Having a tiny mouth causes the sea snake to be a voracious predator of small creatures in the ocean.
   (D) Sea snakes do not easily target areas that they could bite with their tiny mouths.
   (E) Sea snakes can unhinge their mouths and open them wider in order to bite.

GO ON TO THE NEXT PAGE

3. Psychologist: The administration of attention deficit hyperactivity disorder medication is a practice that has gotten way out of hand. Since parents and teachers certainly are not doing so, the AMA should look seriously at the rampant overprescription that occurs, especially in the case of young children whose natural youthful and hyperactive tendencies are, to make a pun, "bottled up" by parents and teachers for whom administering a sedative is far less trouble than doing a proper job of raising and teaching a child.

Which of the following, if true, would best corroborate the psychologist's argument?

(A) The behaviors for which psychiatrists, teachers, and parents are prescribing corrective medication not only are healthy but also are important to children's development.
(B) Last year alone, 75,000 children under the age of eight were given drugs to treat ADHD.
(C) A survey has shown that 84% of parents and teachers would rather administer a dose of prescription medication than punish an unruly child.
(D) The AMA has not, in the opinion of the psychologist, conducted enough tests to determine the long-term effects of such medications on children.
(E) A recent study conducted on adolescent mice proved that there may be serious side effects that are as yet undetected in humans.

4. John: The song "Ninety-Nine Bottles of Beer on the Wall" has been sung since the late 1600s, when English pirates were pilfering Spanish colonies in southern Central America for gold. After successfully raiding a ship, the pirates would begin singing the song in celebration.

Cindy: I am not sure if you have your facts straight. English pirates got the song from Swiss bartenders, who would sing the song to boast of their beer supplies and encourage patrons to drink.

Which one of the following, if true, would strengthen John's argument compared to Cindy's?

(A) Swiss bartenders were not the first people to sing the song.
(B) Many Swiss bartenders ended up becoming English pirates during the 1600s.
(C) The song has never been sung in a language other than English.
(D) No other pirate song has been preserved from the 1600s.
(E) Swiss bartenders titled the song "Nine Hundred and Ninety-Nine Bottles of Beer on the Wall" instead of "Ninety-Nine."

GO ON TO THE NEXT PAGE

5. A men's tennis tournament utilizes a ranking system and a single elimination bracket to determine a winner. Thirty-two players have entered the tournament, and the first seed will receive the easiest bracket, while the second seed is relegated to the opposite half of the bracket. If both first and second seeds win all of their matches, then they will face each other in the finals. Assuming that the second seed can never be beaten by a lower seed, the first seed is guaranteed to meet the second seed in the final match.

Which of the following, if true, would invalidate the passage's conclusion?

(A) The third seed of the tournament beats a seed that is ranked higher than he is.
(B) The first seed of the tournament loses a point to the fifth seed in the first round.
(C) The second seed wins all of his matches except for the finals.
(D) The first seed beats the second seed in the final match.
(E) The final match is delayed by rain until the next day.

6. Maximus was a great general who lived in Roman times. Historians base their ideas about his military prowess on parchments that describe his life and on books that tell of his deeds. Ethnologists have documented legends of his famous victories that have been passed down by people living in areas that were once part of the Roman Empire. Archeologists have excavated Maximus's tomb and former residence and have found great riches and inscriptions describing mighty battles that Maximus won for Rome.

In arguing that Maximus was a great general, the passage does which of the following?

(A) It reaches its conclusion after offering all of the evidence currently available that could possibly support of it.
(B) It ignores the possibility that Maximus was a poor fighter.
(C) It does not assume that the legends told by people in the former Roman areas are authentic.
(D) It appeals to the work done by experts on the subject.
(E) It is equivocal on the meaning of the word *great* in reference to Maximus.

GO ON TO THE NEXT PAGE

7. Studies on mice have demonstrated that the effects of starvation are similar to the effects of aging. Skin starts sagging, hair falls out, and the bodies of the mice grow thinner. The results of this study can be directly applied to humans. If you see a person whose body is thin, whose skin is sagging, and whose hair is falling out, you can assume that the person is suffering from starvation.

Which of the following is a reasoning error made by the passage?

(A) It claims that you cannot make valid assumptions about humans based entirely on studies of animals.

(B) It draws an analogy between humans and an animal species but then makes assumptions not based on that analogy.

(C) It mistakes a correlative relationship between two variables for a causal relationship between the variables.

(D) It unjustifiably implies that aging and starvation are both results of a third, more isolated variable.

(E) It uses data from a study of animals to make an invalid assumption about the cause of certain symptoms in humans.

8. Artist: If imitation is the highest form of flattery, then I am flattering people all the time. Wise men say that "every artist is a cannibal" because techniques that were developed during the Renaissance are still being used and copied by artists today. The same is true for the Modernist techniques that are being copied and elegantly modified by today's Postmodernists. This trend will be sure to continue as I myself modify Postmodernist techniques to form what will eventually be known as the characteristic style for this age. This cycle of modified regurgitation exhibits the reality that there is no real creativity in art, just adaptation.

Which of the following, if true, negates the artist's conclusion?

(A) The "regurgitation" that occurs in art is not limited to the techniques that artists use to create their works.

(B) Paintings in the Postmodernist style and those in the Renaissance style are so markedly different that it is impossible to see a connection.

(C) The modification of traditional artistic styles in order to form new artistic genres requires creativity.

(D) Imitation is flattery only when the focus is on specific people instead of goods or techniques; then imitation is more comparable to stealing.

(E) What wise men say is generally inapplicable to the study of art, since wise men philosophize and are largely disconnected from the lucid abstraction that is art.

GO ON TO THE NEXT PAGE

9. The phenomenon known as near-death experience, or NDE, has been the subject of much controversy in the medical world in the last two decades as a handful of scientists have attempted to use the scientific method to verify the reality of the lucid and often spiritual mental experiences that survivors report having had while in a technical state of death. This research crosses borders that many feel are best left uncrossed, linking medicine to religion in what critics says is potentially a very dangerous way. And yet, these researchers avow that their work is strictly secular, professional, and medicinal, in no way seeking to corroborate any dogmatic views whatsoever.

Which of the following is the main point of the passage?

(A) NDE is dangerous to study because it so closely links the objective with the subjective.
(B) Medicine must remain secularized in order to be professional.
(C) By studying near-death experiences, we will one day know more not only about ourselves but also about ethereal matters.
(D) NDE is a controversial, though staunchly defended, focus of study.
(E) Some people, while technically dead, experience lucid and often spiritual dreams.

10. Jill wants to go to the meeting without Frank. Frank wants to be at the meeting with Jill. If Bill is at the meeting, then Jill will want to go to the meeting with Frank. Frank does not want to go to the meeting with either Bill or Jill. If people follow their preferences, then Frank, Bill, and Jill will be in the meeting together.

Which of the following would also need to be assumed for the conclusion of the above argument to be true?

(A) If Jane is at the meeting, then Frank will want to go without Jill.
(B) If Bill goes without Emily, then he will tolerate Frank's presence at the meeting.
(C) If Jill and Frank go together, then Bill will not care about Jill or Frank's presence.
(D) If Cindy goes to the meeting, then Frank will not want to go with Jill but Bill will.
(E) If Andy is at the meeting, then Bill will go to the meeting with anyone.

GO ON TO THE NEXT PAGE

11. The Bantam soccer team has won numerous championships throughout the nation. The team is unsurpassed and exceptional. Juan is a player on this team, so he must be an exceptional player.

Which of the following possesses a similar logical flaw as the argument above?

(A) The Doris Company has a great management team. John is a manager at the Doris Company, so he must be nice to all of his employees.

(B) The local school system tries to educate every youngster that comes through its hallowed halls. Bill is a youngster in the halls of the school, so he must have been educated by the school system.

(C) The Asheville Homeowner's Association protects each of its members. Avery is a member of this association, so he must protect Asheville's scenic beauty.

(D) The government of a particular country is very kind to the country's poor citizens. Bill is a politician in this country, so he must be very kind to the poor.

(E) William is a member of the murderous Norse clan that raided and pillaged numerous villages. Since he is a member of this evil clan, William must not be a bad man.

12. Commissioner: That the players and the media are complaining about the condition of the golf course today is unreasonable, and I will not apologize for what we have done here. Indeed, the greens today were fast, the pin placements tricky, and the wind and the weather certainly were factors. But again, I emphasize the important distinction that we are here, not to humiliate the world's best golfers, but to prove who, exactly, they are. And in that regard, one glance at the names atop the leaderboard should leave no doubt in anyone's mind that we are accomplishing that purpose.

Which of the following can best be inferred by the commissioner's statement?

(A) The golfers whose names appear atop the leaderboard are, in the commissioner's opinion, the best golfers in the world.

(B) Some of the golfers feel humiliated by the course's tough conditions.

(C) The commissioner will not apologize because he does not agree with any of the players' complaints.

(D) The players' complaints focused especially on the speed of the greens, the difficult pin placements, and the challenging weather.

(E) The commissioner is not weary of and frustrated by the complaints of the players and the media.

GO ON TO THE NEXT PAGE

13. Teacher: Suzy, I know that you have been studying hard and that you have gotten perfect scores on the last four tests. I am sure that you will also get perfect scores on the remaining two tests.

    Suzy: I am going to study even harder than I have before. If I get a perfect score on these last two tests, then I will get a perfect score in the class.

Which of the following fashions an argument on the same grounds as the teacher's argument?

(A) The environmentalists have been right about every regulation up to this point, but they are sure to make an error at some point in the future.
(B) The lobbyists have lied in at least half their opportunities to testify before Congress. Thus, they will be sure to lie to Congress in one of their next two opportunities.
(C) The naturalist has shown that flamingos always stand on one leg. Some flamingoes will continue to stand on one leg in the future.
(D) The pitcher has struck out all 10 batters that he has faced so far in this game. He will inevitably strike out the next two batters.
(E) The dietitian has not broken her diet for the last four months. Undoubtedly, she will not stop exercising for the next two months.

14. For young professionals, cooking food is a process that simply takes more time and energy than they have to spare. These people toil in offices all day, and when they come home, they want to relax instead of spending another hour in the kitchen preparing food. This is why studies show that this age group tends to eat out at restaurants more than any other portion of the population. If we were to find some way to make cooking at home easier, then young professionals would be just as inclined to eat at home as the other portions of our population.

Which of the following is assumed by the argument?

(A) Cooking food at home is something that young professionals should be encouraged to do.
(B) There are not enough cookbooks aimed specifically at young professionals.
(C) Other portions of the population do not spend more time cooking food than young professionals do.
(D) For young professionals, the kitchen is the safest place to be in any house or restaurant.
(E) Social reasons for eating at restaurants are not important to young professionals.

GO ON TO THE NEXT PAGE

15. Several farmers in the southeastern portion of the state called 911 last night claiming that they had spotted UFOs. My own daughter called me to tell me that she had seen something strange in the night sky. However, even though everyone is jumping to the conclusion that aliens are coming in these UFOs, I have talked to the alien commander and he has told me that none of his or any other alien spaceships were in the vicinity of the southeastern portion of the state last night.

Which of the following would reconcile the ideas of the farmers with the claims of the author?

(A) The alien commander was not lying about the whereabouts of his spaceships last night.

(B) The alien commander does not know for certain the exact location of every single one of his spaceships.

(C) Last night in the area where the farmers live, the army was testing planes that most people would identify as UFOs.

(D) Farmers are especially quick to assume that aliens are responsible for strange lights in the sky.

(E) Last night farmers in the northeastern portion of the state saw UFOs that were alien spaceships.

16. Genetically modified crops will revolutionize the techniques that farmers use to grow their crops over the next 100 years. Genetically modified crops will not be as susceptible to disease, so farmers will not spray pesticides anymore to keep their crops disease-free. Farmers will not use fertilizers anymore either, because these crops will be able to glean a few nutrients from the natural soil and air. This will save the farming industry large amounts of money and create untold benefits for future generations.

Which of the following is a weakness in the argument?

(A) It treats measures that partially solve problems as measures that completely solve the problems.

(B) It focuses on the benefits to farmers as opposed to the benefits to humanity.

(C) It assumes that problem-solving methods used in the past will work just as well in the future.

(D) It ignores the fact that there are numerous minor costs associated with farming besides the major ones mentioned in the passage.

(E) It fails to differentiate between a case that is a probability versus a case that is a possibility.

GO ON TO THE NEXT PAGE

17. Baby mice raised in captivity display consistently competitive and confrontational behavioral patterns, tending, rather unusually, to coexist peaceably with same-gender mice close to their age, while quarreling, clawing, and wrestling with the opposite sex. Indeed, this behavior is at times so extreme that it seems a wonder that these same mice will ever learn to get along well enough to propagate their species.

Which one of the following can you conclude from the information above?

(A) Young mice display confrontational flirting techniques similar to those of young humans.
(B) Young mice raised in the wild tend to get along better with their same-sex peers than they do with the opposite sex.
(C) Male and female mice, with age, eventually become less antagonistic toward one another.
(D) Antagonism toward the opposite sex is a result of the mice being raised in captivity.
(E) While competition between opposite-gender mice occurs at early stages of development, once mice reach procreative age, their antagonism naturally turns toward mating competitors.

18. Churches that require people to donate money to them gain more spending power than neighboring churches that do not require donations. However, in general, churches that do not require donations from their congregations have more spending power than churches that do require donations.

Which of the following would explain the paradox presented in the passage above?

(A) Churches that do not require donations tend to receive money from donations.
(B) Churches that require a certain donation quota from each of their members have more faithful members than other types of churches.
(C) Donations are unrelated to the overall wealth of a church or religious body.
(D) Different religions have different requirements for their members.
(E) Most churches that require donations are located in poor parts of the world.

19. Doctors claim that getting children involved in sports when they are young will encourage them to engage in physical activities when they are older. Exercise is a good habit to encourage because it will confer many benefits on people as they grow older—it strengthens bones and muscles, it decreases the risk of heart disease and obesity, and it makes a person happier in general. But doctors' claims that encouraging children to exercise will encourage them to exercise as adults are patently false. I played sports when I was younger, and I never exercise now. And my brother engaged in no physical activity when he was younger, and now he runs 6 miles every day.

Which of the following is a logical error made by the author of the passage?

(A) He places more weight on his own experience than on the experiences of a much larger group of people.
(B) He makes an assumption about the health of an entire group of people without analyzing specific cases within the group.
(C) He bases his conclusion on evidence that is entirely irrelevant.
(D) He includes claims that are backed by nationwide data trends instead of data that can be gained only through case studies.
(E) He mistakenly identifies himself with a portion of the population that exercised when younger but does not exercise now.

GO ON TO THE NEXT PAGE

20. Cloning has received large amounts of publicity since Dolly the sheep was cloned, and some scientists, individuals, and corporations expect to be able to clone a human being in the relatively near future. Polymerase chain reaction ("PCR") is a technique that is used to copy DNA strands. Since cloning requires copying a person's entire genetic code, then PCR must be used at some point during the cloning process.

The author of the argument presupposes which of the following?

(A) A human being will eventually be cloned.
(B) PCR is the only way to copy DNA.
(C) The publicity given to cloning was warranted.
(D) DNA strands can be copied by splitting meiotic cells.
(E) Other sheep besides Dolly will be cloned.

21. Scarecrows placed in fields scare crows only when the scarecrow is portrayed as holding a gun. So many years have gone by, and the crow–farmer relationship has been so intense, that crows as a species have realized that a man will not harm them if he is not holding a long sticklike object in one of his hands. Therefore, any farmer serious about driving crows away should be careful to put not just one stick in a scarecrow's hand but three or four.

Which of the following is an assumption that is made by the argument?

(A) Crows cannot differentiate between a gun and long sticks that resemble guns.
(B) Having a scarecrow hold several gunlike objects is not more effective than having the scarecrow hold one gunlike object.
(C) Scarecrows placed outside of fields might have different effects than those placed within fields.
(D) Scarecrows are not the only effective way to combat the plague of crows that seek to destroy crops.
(E) Brave crows will try to dismantle the gunlike objects that the scarecrow is holding so that weaker crows can come and feed.

22. Ovens are the major fire hazard present in the home. If an oven is left on after cooking is done, often a fire will start. That is why it is so important to monitor your children when they use the oven, because children habitually forget to turn off the oven. Another group with this problem is adults who are very busy and too stressed out to remember seemingly insignificant details about mundane tasks such as cooking food. There are also many other groups who consistently forget to turn off the oven, but listing them is not necessary. Suffice it to say that buying a dog is the best oven-fire prevention measure because dogs are able to smell smoke.

In taking the position outlined, the author presupposes which of the following?

(A) Dogs cannot bark when they smell smoke and alert someone that a fire has started.
(B) Fire alarms are better than dogs at alerting people about potential oven fires.
(C) Putting a fire out immediately after it starts is better than preventing the fire.
(D) In an oven fire, smoke generally appears before the fire starts.
(E) Children will know to turn off the oven when the dog barks.

GO ON TO THE NEXT PAGE

23. The diaspora of poor people from the country to industrialized cities is a manifestation of the hope that our capitalist system inspires in our citizens. Poor people know that they can find jobs for themselves in the city, and they go there in order to provide a better life for their families. Most leave their families at home in the country and never correspond in any way with them again. However, urban centers offer a chance to individuals who want to succeed. All that is required of them is a little effort.

A flaw in this argument is that it

(A) appeals to an authority to support its conclusion
(B) deals entirely with abstract ideals and principles
(C) treats the key term *hope* as if it were indefinable
(D) allegorizes the story of poor country people
(E) has two premises that contradict each other

24. Admissions officer: Many students have an inordinate amount of trouble writing college admissions essays. There are a number of reasons this is so, the most important being the pressure that students are under as they write. Students know that the quality and substance of their writing could potentially procure them an acceptance or a rejection from the college of their choice. For this reason, students tend to overload their essay with idiosyncratic facts, hobbies, and other items that they hope will compel a bored admissions officer to offer them an acceptance. This practice of cramming essays with numerous personal facts is often counterproductive, since most admissions officers judge student essays by the quality of the writing rather than by the quantity of personal facts.

For the conclusion of the passage to be logically drawn, it is necessary to assume which of the following?

(A) Students often do not get into the college of their choice due to low test scores.
(B) Personal qualities can be described in other parts of the application besides the essay.
(C) Students feel the pressure of college admission more than they feel the pressure of high school deadlines.
(D) Overloading an essay with personal facts can cause the technical quality of the essay to decline.
(E) Athletes do not feel the same pressure to perform that prospective college students feel as they are drafting their essays.

GO ON TO THE NEXT PAGE

25. Sociologist: It is often claimed that people from the South tend to be more sociable on average than people from the North. I have not only found evidence to support these claims but also hypothesized that this marked divergence in behavioral norms is due entirely to the climate. Northerners have an incentive to remain indoors for the winter, which consumes approximately one-third of their lives. As they stay indoors in their homes, they grow accustomed to an independence and isolation that Southerners are never forced to deal with. Instead, Southerners are free to walk outside of their homes for the entire year where they continue to meet new and engaging people. It is no wonder that Southerners exhibit more developed social skills—they are conditioned to always be ready to meet new people.

Which of the following can be concluded on the basis of the passage?

(A) Northerners are not sociable people in general.
(B) The most sociable Southerner is more sociable than the most sociable Northerner.
(C) Southerners do not stay inside of their homes for periods of time during the winter.
(D) Scientists who study Northerners are aware of all of the pertinent information regarding Northerners' social skills.
(E) Weather can influence the sociability of people living in different geographic areas.

S T O P

IF YOU FINISH BEFORE TIME RUNS OUT, CHECK YOUR WORK ON THIS SECTION ONLY.
DO NOT GO ON TO ANY OTHER TEST SECTION.

SECTION 3
Time—35 minutes
25 questions

<u>Directions for Logic Games:</u> The questions in this section are divided into groups. Each group is based on a set of conditions. For each question, choose the answer that is most accurate and complete. For some questions, you may wish to draw a rough diagram to help you select your response. Mark the corresponding space on your Answer Sheet.

<u>Questions 1–5</u>

Seven children, A, B, C, D, E, F, and G, are to be chosen for two groups of three people in order to play tag. One child sits out each time. In order to make the teams fair, the teacher creates them according to the following constraints:

When A plays on a team, she plays with B.
When A sits out, B plays on a team with E.
D and E do not play in the same group.
E always plays.

1. Which of the following could NOT be the children on a team together?

   (A) E, C, F
   (B) B, F, G
   (C) D, B, A
   (D) B, E, G
   (E) A, B, E

2. If G sits out, then which of the following must be true?

   (A) F shares a group with E.
   (B) C shares a group with F.
   (C) A shares a group with D.
   (D) B shares a group with C.
   (E) E shares a group with B.

3. If A sits out, then which of the following must NOT be true?

   (A) C shares a group with D.
   (B) F shares a group with B.
   (C) G shares a group with E.
   (D) C shares a group with F.
   (E) D shares a group with B.

4. Who can never sit out?

   (A) A
   (B) B
   (C) C
   (D) D
   (E) G

5. If C, F, and E share a group, then all of the following could be true EXCEPT

   (A) B shares a group with A.
   (B) C shares a group with F.
   (C) D shares a group with G.
   (D) E does not share a group with B.
   (E) G shares a group with A.

GO ON TO THE NEXT PAGE

PART III / FIVE PRACTICE TESTS

Questions 6–12

At a logistics conference, programmers pair people with different specialties in booths in order to allow for a fuller knowledge base when people's questions are being answered. In a series of five booths, developers A, B, C, D, and E are paired with designers R, S, T, U, and V. Two people are in each booth, one from each specialty, and the order is governed by the following constraints:

A is in booth 1. T is in booth 2. B is in booth 3. V is in booth 5.
R is in a higher-numbered booth than C.
U is in a higher-numbered booth than T.
E is in a higher-numbered booth than U.

6. Which of the following is a possible order of developers in booths 1 to 5?

   (A) A, E, B, C, D
   (B) A, E, B, D, C
   (C) A, B, E, D, C
   (D) A, D, B, D, E
   (E) A, C, B, E, D

7. Which of the following is a possible order of the designers in booths 1 to 5?

   (A) U, T, R, S, V
   (B) R, T, S, T, V
   (C) S, T, U, R, V
   (D) R, T, S, U, V
   (E) S, T, R, V, U

8. If E is in booth 5, then which of the following must be true?

   (A) E is paired with U.
   (B) D is paired with V.
   (C) V is paired with E.
   (D) D is in a lower-numbered booth than C.
   (E) B and E are in consecutively numbered booths.

9. If D is paired with U, then which of the following must NOT be true?

   (A) E is paired with R.
   (B) A is paired with S.
   (C) V is paired with E.
   (D) C is paired with T.
   (E) C and B are in consecutively numbered booths.

10. If U is in a lower-numbered booth than R, then which of the following could be true?

    (A) E is in a higher-numbered booth than R.
    (B) U is in a lower-numbered booth than S.
    (C) T is in a higher-numbered booth than R.
    (D) C is in a higher-numbered booth than U.
    (E) U is in a lower-numbered booth than B.

11. Which of the following pairs of developers could both share booths with programmer D?

    (A) S, R
    (B) U, V
    (C) T, U
    (D) V, S
    (E) S, T

12. How many different configurations of variables are possible for this game?

    (A) one
    (B) two
    (C) three
    (D) four
    (E) five

GO ON TO THE NEXT PAGE

<u>Questions 13–19</u>

At a circular conference table in the Pentagon, important people A, B, C, D, E, F, G, and H are discussing important news. The seating arrangements are important, because important people like to sit next to other important people.

> G sits across from H.
> H sits next to B.
> G sits next to either E or F.
> Exactly one space is between A's and H's seats.
> If C sits next to G, then F sits next to H.

13. Which of the following people could NOT sit next to G?

    (A) A
    (B) F
    (C) C
    (D) D
    (E) E

14. If G sits next to E and F, then which of the following must NOT be true?

    (A) F sits next to B.
    (B) E sits next to C.
    (C) A sits next to D.
    (D) B sits next to C.
    (E) H sits next to D.

15. If F sits next to H, then which of the following must be true?

    (A) C sits next to G.
    (B) A sits across from C.
    (C) E sits next to G.
    (D) B sits across from F.
    (E) F sits next to A.

16. If C sits across from B, then who could B sit next to?

    (A) C
    (B) D
    (C) E
    (D) F
    (E) G

17. If A sits next to B and D, then which of the following could NOT be true?

    (A) C sits across from B.
    (B) E sits across from A.
    (C) F sits across from D.
    (D) H sits across from G.
    (E) B sits across from E.

18. If B does not sit next to A and A does not sit next to F or E, then which of the following must be true?

    (A) B sits next to F.
    (B) E sits next to G.
    (C) A sits next to B.
    (D) C sits next to H.
    (E) G sits next to F.

19. Who could never sit next to G?

    (A) A
    (B) C
    (C) D
    (D) E
    (E) F

GO ON TO THE NEXT PAGE

Questions 20–25

A little league soccer game ended in a tie, so it will go to a shootout. The shootout will consist of seven players from each team. The coach of the Bombers has developed an intricate strategy to win. The order in which his seven team members A, B, C, D, E, F, and G will shoot is governed by the following:

If C shoots before D, then E shoots sixth and F shoots seventh.

If E shoots before F, then C shoots first and D shoots second.

If A shoots before fifth, then G shoots fourth and B shoots third.

A, B, C, D, E, F, and G will all shoot only once.

20. Which one of the following could be an order that the coach uses?

   (A) E, F, A, G, B, C, D
   (B) D, C, F, A, G, B, E
   (C) C, D, B, G, A, E, F
   (D) F, E, A, D, C, G, B
   (E) C, D, E, F, A, D, G

21. If A shoots second, then which of the following must be true?

   (A) E shoots before F.
   (B) G shoots third.
   (C) E and D shoot consecutively.
   (D) D shoots before C.
   (E) E shoots sixth.

22. How many different places in the order can A shoot in?

   (A) three
   (B) four
   (C) five
   (D) six
   (E) seven

23. If C shoots before D, then we know the exact places in the order of how many people shooting?

   (A) three
   (B) four
   (C) five
   (D) six
   (E) seven

24. If A shoots first and F shoots second, then which of the following must NOT be true?

   (A) E shoots seventh.
   (B) Neither F nor D shoot first.
   (C) B shoots immediately before G.
   (D) G shoots immediately before E.
   (E) E shoots sixth.

25. If C, D, E, and F occupy the first four shooting slots, then which of the following must be true?

   (A) Neither B nor G shoots seventh.
   (B) Neither F nor D shoot first.
   (C) D and E occupy the second and third slots.
   (D) B shoots before G.
   (E) A does not shoot fifth.

STOP

IF YOU FINISH BEFORE TIME RUNS OUT, CHECK YOUR WORK ON THIS SECTION ONLY.
DO NOT GO ON TO ANY OTHER TEST SECTION.

SECTION 4
Time—35 minutes
25 questions

<u>Directions for Reading Comprehension Questions:</u> Each passage in this section is followed by a group of questions. Answer each question based on what is stated or implied in the passage. For some questions, more than one answer choice may be possible, so choose the *best* answer to each question. After you have chosen your answer, mark the corresponding space on the Answer Sheet.

In the early 20th century, with America steeped in the militarism surrounding the First and Second World Wars, peace education was vilified as being subversive. Peace educators who dreamed
(5) of a unified, peaceful world were considered un-American. In fact, these dark years for peace education continued through the following decades, fueled by the excesses of McCarthyism. This stigma greatly hampered the efforts of peace
(10) educators who overcame this setback by shifting their focus from negative peace, expressed as antimilitarism, to positive peace, with an emphasis on society-building through diminishing violence within and between nation-states. For example,
(15) peace education in the '80s took the form of "conflict resolution." In an effort to address issues surrounding youth, such as school violence and high drop out rates, young people were taught communication and negotiation strategies as part
(20) of student mediation initiatives. These programs included such elements as training in cross-cultural issues, interpersonal communication, and bias awareness with the belief that individuals must understand the nature of conflict and develop
(25) negotiating skills before the process of mediation can be effective.

Under the threat of nuclear war and planetary annihilation, peace education in the '80s saw a proliferation of curriculum guides and teaching
(30) materials targeted at children from preschool through high school in an effort to avoid earth's destruction. Curricular guides for younger children included nature study and care for the environment, teaching children that they can be responsible for
(35) the world they live in. Materials for older children included activity cards and videos presenting conflict scenarios aimed at teaching students to identify possible problems, to play roles, and to propose solutions. Educators began to see peace
(40) education not only as content but also as a process— a way of life that promotes personal and societal well-being.

In this decade, religious leaders across the denominational spectrum, making great efforts to
(45) unify common beliefs and decrease doctrinal differences, wrote and spoke extensively concerning the immorality of nuclear war, imploring congregations throughout America to consider alternatives to violence and war and to
(50) embrace peaceful coexistence. This leadership from the religious sector contributed hugely to a wider acceptance of peace education as a legitimate discipline for study in the schools.

Advances in technology and
(55) telecommunications made it possible to reach out internationally with gestures of goodwill and world friendship. Global awareness became an integral part of mainstream education. Educators believed that the study of cultures, customs, and beliefs of
(60) people around the world would enable students to appreciate differences, to discover similarities, and to develop empathy for others—all necessary skills for creating a harmonious society. Global awareness became peace education in action.
(65) Whatever the generational focus, peace education has consistently reflected the desire to improve the condition of human society.

GO ON TO THE NEXT PAGE

1. Which one of the following best describes the content of the passage as a whole?

   (A) As the generational focus of Americans shifted in the '80s, peace education was abandoned for "conflict resolution," which was actually just a masking term for a political movement toward national self-service.

   (B) The transformation of peace education to "conflict resolution" in the '80s marked the beginning of a new era of society building and global awareness studies in American schools.

   (C) As American bias awareness and global awareness increased through the '80s, more and more people turned to peace education as a means of recovering the losses suffered as a result of McCarthyism and the Cold War.

   (D) Despite his best intentions, McCarthy created an atmosphere in America of persecution of even the most innocent ideals.

   (E) The threat of nuclear war was the strongest factor in convincing schoolchildren that "conflict resolution" was important and cultural leaders that peace education was a legitimate discipline.

2. According to the author, peace education in the '80s differed from previous peace education in that

   (A) it approached peace from a capitalist perspective, instead of from what had been said to be a communist perspective

   (B) new technology in the classroom successfully pacified the former critics of peace education

   (C) the development of nuclear weapons required a focus on environmental conservation as much as on cultural conservation

   (D) it took on the more fundamental character of "conflict resolution" instead of promoting an idealized plan for world peace

   (E) a new generation of teachers, who had been educated during the Cold War, had never known peace in a traditional sense

3. The information in the passage provides the LEAST support for which one of the following claims?

   (A) Peace is a common goal for the religious leaders of many American denominations.

   (B) A key point in peace education is teaching students to be responsible for the world they live in.

   (C) Global awareness and international goodwill are both forms of peace education in action.

   (D) Peace education can be used to address both international and local issues.

   (E) Since peace education became accepted as a legitimate discipline of study, high school dropout rates have noticeably declined.

4. As used in line 52 of the passage, the meaning of *legitimate* is best paralleled by which one of the following words?

   (A) authentic
   (B) suitable
   (C) legal
   (D) logical
   (E) felicitous

5. It can be inferred that which of the following was a teaching goal in the '80s effort to discourage the acceptance of deliberate global destruction?

   (A) responsibility for local societal problems
   (B) appreciation of the well-being of the environment
   (C) dedication to antimilitarism
   (D) empathy for the poor in third-world countries
   (E) fear of nuclear weapons

6. The primary purpose of the first paragraph is to

   (A) explain an important transition
   (B) chronicle the history of the passage topic
   (C) introduce dual topics for debate
   (D) call the reader to attention and action
   (E) initiate a discussion

GO ON TO THE NEXT PAGE

Dominican society of the late 1980s reflected the country's Spanish-Caribbean heritage. It manifested significant divisions along the lines of race and class. A small fraction of the populace controlled (5) great wealth, while the vast majority struggled to get by. The middle stratum worked both to maintain and to extend its political and economic gains. Generally speaking, Dominican society offered relatively few avenues of advancement; most of (10) those available allowed families of middling means to enhance or to consolidate their standing.

The majority of the population was mulatto, the offspring of Africans and Europeans. The indigenous Amerindian population had been (15) virtually eliminated within half a century of initial contact. Immigrants—European, Middle Eastern, Asian, and Caribbean—arrived with each cycle of economic growth. In general, skin color followed the social hierarchy: Lighter skin was associated (20) with higher social and economic status. European immigrants and their offspring found more ready acceptance at the upper reaches of society than did darker-skinned Dominicans.

The decades following the end of the regime of (25) military strongman and dictator Rafael Leónidas Trujillo Molina (1930–1961) were a time of extensive changes as large-scale rural-urban and international migration blurred the gulf between city and countryside. Traditional attitudes persisted: (30) Peasants continued to regard urban dwellers with suspicion, and people in cities continued to think of rural Dominicans as unsophisticated and naive. Nonetheless, most families included several members who had migrated to the republic's larger (35) cities or to the United States. Migration served to relieve some of the pressures of population growth. Moreover, cash remittances from abroad permitted families of moderate means to acquire assets and to maintain a standard of living far beyond what they (40) might otherwise have enjoyed.

The alternatives available to poorer Dominicans were far more limited. Emigration required assets beyond the reach of most. Many rural dwellers migrated instead to one of the republic's cities. The (45) financial resources and training of these newcomers, however, were far inferior to those among typical families of moderate means. For the vast majority of the republic's population, the twin constraints of limited land and limited employment (50) opportunities defined the daily struggle for existence. In the midst of far-reaching changes, the republic continued to be a profoundly family-oriented society. Dominicans of every social

stratum relied on family and kin for social identity (55) and for interpersonal relationships of trust and confidence, particularly in the processes of migration and urbanization. Both this trend and the continuing of race-specific class divisions in Dominican society demonstrated what heavy social (60) influences were still left over from its Spanish heritage.

7. The author's primary purpose in this passage is to

(A) explicate the caste system of the Dominican Republic
(B) extol Dominican dictator Rafael Molina for his efforts in breaking down the class barriers
(C) describe Dominican society and explain why it was as it was in the late 1980s
(D) spell out that emigration is one of the only ways to cope with extreme poverty in the Dominican Republic
(E) account for the extensive changes that followed the reign of Rafael Molina

8. Which of the following claims about Dominican society is best supported by the passage?

(A) Emigration is the most viable option for the hopelessly poor families.
(B) Those who are able to leave the country are often of more value to their families than they were when living in the country.
(C) Dominican society is largely racist.
(D) The cruel class divisions could be mercifully remedied only by efforts of the governing wealthy class.
(E) Rafael Molina was a malevolent tyrant, more focused on his financial gains than on the well-being of his people.

GO ON TO THE NEXT PAGE

9. The author's use of the word *advancement* in line 9 most closely refers to which of the following aspects of life?

    (A) cultural
    (B) technological
    (C) financial
    (D) biological
    (E) familial

10. The main idea of the final paragraph is which of the following?

    (A) Even as the lower class has learned to undertake a daily struggle for existence, the social reliance on family has grown even more important.
    (B) Far-reaching changes have swept the Dominican Republic, but few of them have been good.
    (C) There are both good and bad reminders of Spanish heritage in the Dominican Republic.
    (D) Limited land and employment opportunities in the republic are the biggest constraints on the lower class.
    (E) Even citizens of the upper class traditionally hold their interpersonal relationships with their kin in high regard.

11. Which of the following words can be used to replace *middling* (line 10) without significantly changing the author's intended meaning?

    (A) intermediate
    (B) ample
    (C) illegitimate
    (D) down-turning
    (E) minimal

12. All of the following can be inferred about Dominican class distinction EXCEPT that

    (A) skin color is often indicative of one's class as it is clearly indicative of one's heritage and ancestry, whether rich European or poor slave, immigrant, or Amerindian
    (B) the middle class is relatively minimal in size
    (C) it is largely a result of colonial Spanish practices and customs
    (D) the vast majority of the population is on the poorer side of the spectrum
    (E) it has slowly but steadily lessened over the past several years

GO ON TO THE NEXT PAGE

The term *acid rain* is commonly used to mean the deposition of atmospheric acidic components by rain, snow, fog, dew, or dry particles. The more accurate term is "acid precipitation." Distilled
(5) water, which contains no carbon dioxide, has a neutral pH of 7. Liquids with a pH less than 7 are acid, and those with a pH greater than 7 are alkaline (or basic). "Clean" or unpolluted rain has a slightly acidic pH of 5.6, because carbon dioxide and water
(10) in the air naturally react together to form carbonic acid, a weak acid. Around larger cities, however, the average rain pH is often between 4.2 and 4.4. The extra acidity in rain comes from the reaction of air pollutants, primarily sulfur oxides and nitrogen
(15) oxides, with water in the air to form strong acids (like sulfuric and nitric acid). The main sources of these pollutants are vehicles and industrial and power-generating plants. In cities, the main sources are simply cars, trucks, and buses.
(20)   Acidity in rain is measured by collecting samples of rain and measuring its pH. To find the distribution of rain acidity, weather conditions are monitored and rain samples are collected at sites all over the country. The areas of greatest acidity are
(25) located in the Northeastern United States. This pattern of high acidity is caused by the large number of cities, the density of the population, and the concentration of power and industrial plants in the Northeast. In addition, the prevailing wind
(30) direction brings storms and pollution to the Northeast from the Midwest, and, chemically, dust from the soil and rocks in the Northeastern United States is less likely to naturally neutralize acidity in the rain.
(35)   When you hear or read in the media about the effects of acid rain, you are usually told about the lakes, fish, and trees in New England and Canada. However, we are becoming aware of an additional concern: Many of our historic buildings and
(40) monuments are located in the areas of highest acidity. In Europe, where buildings are much older and pollution levels have been 10 times greater than in the United States, there is a growing awareness that pollution and acid rain are
(45) accelerating the deterioration of buildings and monuments.
    When it is exposed to the environment, stone weathers as part of the normal geologic cycle through chemical, physical, and biological
(50) processes. This weathering process, over hundreds of millions of years, turned the Appalachian

Mountains from towering peaks as high as the Rockies to the rounded knobs we see today. Our concern is that air pollution, particularly in urban
(55) areas, may be accelerating the normal, natural rate of stone deterioration, so that we may prematurely lose buildings and sculptures of historic or cultural value.

13.   This passage is primarily concerned with

(A) explaining the causes and effects of acid precipitation
(B) reconciling several scientific theories pertaining to acid precipitation
(C) relaying a call for immediate action in preventing acid rain
(D) arguing that acid rain should more accurately be referred to as acid precipitation
(E) developing evidence that suggests relationships between geology, biology, and meteorology

14.   Which one of the following most accurately expresses the meaning of the word *deposition* as it is used in line 2 of the passage?

(A) documentation
(B) removal
(C) existence
(D) affirmation
(E) transfer

15.   The passage supports which one of the following claims about acid rain?

(A) Snow supports far more acidity as a precipitate than does rain.
(B) The effects of acid rain are substantial, but only ecological.
(C) The lowest levels of pH in precipitation can be found in the Northeastern section of the United States.
(D) There are no means for the environment to naturally neutralize acidic precipitation.
(E) The natural acidity of rain is required for stone to weather at all; however, the higher acidity in acid rain causes even faster weathering.

GO ON TO THE NEXT PAGE

16. Which of the following can be inferred from the information given in the third paragraph?

    (A) Much of America's trouble with acid rain is a result of Canadian pollutants.
    (B) Acid rain is an even more serious problem in Europe than it is in America.
    (C) Rain with a pH even as slightly acidic as 6.0 begins to deteriorate buildings faster than "clean" rain can.
    (D) The Appalachian Mountains were at one point as tall as many famous European mountain ranges, such as the Alps.
    (E) Prevailing winds from the Midwest that carry storms and pollution to the Northeast can travel even as far as Europe.

17. Which one of the following statements, if true, would most seriously undermine the author's suggestion that the high density of cars, trucks, and buses in cities is the main source of the air pollutants that cause acid rain?

    (A) Cars, trucks, and buses primarily produce sulfur oxides with only trace amounts of nitrogen oxides.
    (B) The physical structure of cities slows wind patterns in the area, increasing the amount of precipitation there.
    (C) Cars, trucks, and buses are popular in every United States city, but acid rain is worst in the Northeast.
    (D) Concrete and asphalt both have the chemical ability to absorb some of the sulfur and nitrogen oxides in the air.
    (E) Acid rain is often common far from densely populated areas and in areas without strong winds.

18. Which one of the following excerpts best relays the strongest means of provocation presented in the passage?

    (A) "Air pollution may be accelerating the natural rate of stone deterioration, so that we may prematurely lose buildings and sculptures of historic or cultural value."
    (B) "Chemically, dust from the soil and rocks in the Northeastern United States is less likely to naturally neutralize acidity in the rain."
    (C) "When it is exposed to the environment, stone weathers as part of the normal geologic cycle through chemical, physical, and biological processes."
    (D) "To find the distribution of rain acidity, weather conditions are monitored and rain samples are collected at sites all over the country."
    (E) "The extra acidity in rain comes from the reaction of air pollutants, primarily sulfur oxides and nitrogen oxides, with water in the air."

GO ON TO THE NEXT PAGE

A case selected for argument in the Supreme Court usually involves interpretations of the United States Constitution or federal law. At least four Justices must have selected the case as being of

(5) such importance that the Supreme Court must resolve the legal issues. An attorney for each side of a case will have an opportunity to make a presentation to the Court and answer questions posed by the Justices. Prior to the argument, each

(10) side will have submitted a legal brief—a written legal argument outlining each party's points of law. The Justices have read these briefs prior to argument and are thoroughly familiar with the case, its facts, and the legal positions that each

(15) party is advocating, so that the time spent in the courtroom is used as efficiently as possible.

Beginning the first Monday in October, the Court is scheduled to hear up to four one-hour arguments a day, three days a week, in two-week

(20) intervals, (with longer breaks in December and February), concluding the oral argument portion of the term in late April. Typically, two arguments are held in the mornings beginning at 10 A.M. and two in the afternoons beginning at 1 P.M. on

(25) Monday, Tuesday, and Wednesday. In the recesses between argument sessions, the Justices are busy writing opinions, deciding which cases to hear in the future, and reading the briefs for the next argument session. They grant review for approximately

(30) 100 of the more than 7000 petitions filed with the Court each term. No one knows exactly when a decision will be handed down by the Court in an argued case, nor is there a set time period in which the Justices must reach a decision. However, all

(35) cases argued during a term of Court are decided before the summer recess begins, usually by the end of June.

During an argument week, the Justices meet in a private conference, closed even to staff, to discuss

(40) the cases and to take a preliminary vote on each case. If the Chief Justice is in the majority on a case decision, he decides who will write the opinion. He may decide to write it himself, or he may assign that duty to any other Justice in the

(45) majority. If the Chief Justice is in the minority, the Justice in the majority who has the most seniority assumes the assignment duty.

Draft opinions are privately circulated among the Justices until a final draft is agreed upon. When

(50) a final decision has been reached, the Justice who wrote the opinion announces the decision in a Court session and may deliver a summary of the Court's

reasoning. Meanwhile, the Public Information Office releases the full text of the opinion to the

(55) public and news media. This form of legislative review is a vital part of the checks and balances system of American government, and it should be understood and appreciated by every American.

19. Which one of the following best describes the content of the passage as a whole?

(A) a detailed explanation of the judicial review process

(B) an advertising brochure encouraging tourists to visit the United States Supreme Court

(C) a short daily chronicle of the argument portion of the yearly Supreme Court term

(D) a description of the administrative and judicial practices of the United States Supreme Court

(E) a summarization of a government study on the legitimacy of United States Supreme Court's processes

20. The phrase "legislative review" (lines 55–56) can best be interpreted as referring to which of the following?

(A) the ability of a senior Justice to take some administrative control if the Chief Justice votes in the minority

(B) the capacity of the Supreme Court to reexamine the constitutionality of any federal law and reinterpret the Constitution itself

(C) the right of the people to have their cases decided by the time of summer recess in the same year

(D) the lack of a requirement for all decisions and written opinions of the Supreme Court to be published for public scrutiny and criticism

(E) the Supreme Court's review of case petitions so that only the most important ones are considered and no topics are repeated

GO ON TO THE NEXT PAGE

21. The author's claim in the final sentence of the passage reveals which of the following regarding his own attitude toward the American government?

    (A) He is bitter that Americans often take the success of our governmental system for granted.

    (B) He is grateful that the system has ways to double-check and revise itself.

    (C) He is indifferent toward the United States government, but he still appreciates the design of judicial review.

    (D) He is hopeful that the government will find a way to enforce education concerning its own intricacies.

    (E) He is astounded that the nation's founders were clever enough to come up with the "checks and balances" system.

22. The second paragraph primarily serves to

    (A) outline the essential scheduling and happenings of a single Supreme Court term

    (B) relate all of the basic administrative facts about the Supreme Court

    (C) explain why Supreme Court Justices need such long weekends to complete their work

    (D) astonish readers by telling them how extremely selective the Supreme Court is when choosing cases

    (E) justify a future argument the author makes regarding Supreme Court opinions

23. Based on the passage, the author would most likely claim that a good appreciation of the practices of the Supreme Court includes at the least which one of the following?

    (A) gaining a familiarity with several of the Chief Justice's officially documented opinions

    (B) understanding the process and importance of judicial review

    (C) expressing constant gratitude for the country's laws and legal system

    (D) memorizing the hours of the day when Court is in session

    (E) respecting the professions of the Justices and honoring their commitment to civic duty daily

24. The primary purpose of the third paragraph is to

    (A) explain how the Justices decide who writes the opinion regarding a particular case

    (B) emphasize that the Chief Justice is most often in the majority when a case is decided

    (C) provide a transition between the first paragraph and the final conclusory paragraph

    (D) underline the secrecy and importance of the judicial proceedings

    (E) illuminate what goes on inside the walls of the courthouse for those who are not privy to that information

25. When initial decisions are made as to whether or not to review individual cases, which of the following best approximates the fewest number of total votes that the Supreme Court Justices could give in a year to the cases that they do end up reviewing?

    (A) 100
    (B) 400
    (C) 800
    (D) 1200
    (E) 1400

STOP

IF YOU FINISH BEFORE TIME RUNS OUT, CHECK YOUR WORK ON THIS SECTION ONLY.

DO NOT GO ON TO ANY OTHER TEST SECTION.

ANSWER KEY

Section 1	Section 2	Section 3	Section 4
1. A	1. D	1. B	1. B
2. B	2. D	2. B	2. D
3. E	3. A	3. E	3. E
4. D	4. C	4. B	4. B
5. D	5. A	5. C	5. B
6. D	6. D	6. E	6. A
7. D	7. E	7. C	7. C
8. B	8. C	8. C	8. B
9. E	9. D	9. A	9. C
10. E	10. E	10. A	10. A
11. D	11. D	11. B	11. A
12. B	12. A	12. C	12. E
13. B	13. D	13. A	13. A
14. B	14. E	14. A	14. E
15. C	15. C	15. C	15. C
16. B	16. A	16. B	16. B
17. C	17. C	17. A	17. E
18. D	18. E	18. D	18. A
19. C	19. A	19. A	19. D
20. C	20. B	20. C	20. B
21. C	21. A	21. D	21. B
22. C	22. D	22. C	22. A
23. C	23. E	23. C	23. B
24. C	24. D	24. B	24. A
25. D	25. E	25. B	25. B

<u>Scoring Instructions:</u> To calculate your score on this Practice Test, follow the instructions on the next page.

CALCULATING YOUR SCORE

Now that you have completed this Practice Test 5, use the instructions on this page to calculate your score. Start by checking the Answer Key to count up the number of questions you answered correctly. Then fill in the table below.

Raw Score Calculator

Section Number	Question Type	Number of Questions	Number Correct
1	Logical Reasoning	25	_____
2	Logical Reasoning	25	_____
3	Logic Games	25	_____
4	Reading Comprehension	25	_____
		(Raw Score) Total:	_____

On the real LSAT, a statistical process will be used to convert your raw score to a scaled score ranging from 120 to 180. The table below will give you an approximate idea of the scaled score that matches your raw score. For statistical reasons, on real forms of the LSAT the scaled score that matches a given raw score can vary by several points above or below the scaled score shown in the table.

Write your scaled score on this test here:

Practice Test 5 scaled score: _____

Raw Score	Scaled Score	Raw Score	Scaled Score	Raw Score	Scaled Score
0	120	23	126	46	145
1	120	24	127	47	145
2	120	25	128	48	146
3	120	26	128	49	147
4	120	27	129	50	147
5	120	28	130	51	148
6	120	29	131	52	148
7	120	30	132	53	149
8	120	31	133	54	150
9	120	32	133	55	151
10	120	33	134	56	151
11	120	34	135	57	152
12	120	35	136	58	153
13	120	36	137	59	153
14	120	37	137	60	154
15	120	38	138	61	154
16	120	39	139	62	155
17	120	40	140	63	155
18	121	41	140	64	156
19	122	42	141	65	157
20	123	43	142	66	158
21	124	44	143	67	158
22	125	45	144	68	159

Raw Score	Scaled Score	Raw Score	Scaled Score	Raw Score	Scaled Score
69	159	80	166	91	174
70	160	81	166	92	175
71	160	82	167	93	175
72	161	83	167	94	176
73	161	84	168	95	177
74	162	85	169	96	178
75	162	86	170	97	179
76	163	87	170	98	180
77	163	88	171	99	180
78	164	89	172	100	180
79	165	90	173		

ANSWERS AND EXPLANATIONS

SECTION 1—LOGICAL REASONING

1. This question asks you to make an inference based on the information in the squib. You need to the letters that are certainly not beef. Those letters are: F, R, P, and letters A identify

   Correct answer: **A.** PAGE can be spelled using letters that cannot be beef.

   (B) You cannot be sure of O's characteristics.

   (C) You cannot be sure of T's characteristics.

   (D) You cannot be sure of T's characteristics.

   (E) You cannot be sure of Z's characteristics.

2. People who like animals *tend* to dislike zoos. However, large numbers of people who work in zoos like animals.

   Question type: "Resolve"

   Correct answer: **B.** If this statement were true, then the only people who would work in zoos would be those who like animals. This fact would explain why large numbers of people who like animals tend to work in zoos.

   (A) This answer would tend to refute information in the squib.

   (C–E) These points are irrelevant.

3. This squib says that the advertising campaigns of soft drinks cause people to engage in more communal behavior. However, it claims that the ads fail to achieve their main purpose because they do not motivate people to buy more soft drinks.

   Question Type: "Weaken"

   Correct answer: **E.** If increasing the incidence of communal behavior increases soft drink sales, then it would make sense for soft drink producers to run commercials that promote communal feeling.

   (A) This choice would support the conclusion.

   (B) This answer would undermine the part of the conclusion that claims that advertisers want to sell soft drinks.

   (C) This point does not relate to actually selling the drinks.

   (D) This answer would support the squib's claim that there is no link between soft drinks and an increase in communal behavior.

4. The squib claims that garage doors are necessary to prevent burglars from entering the house. The squib claims that without garage doors, entering someone's house would be just as easy as entering that person's garage.

   Question Type: "Strengthen"

   Correct answer: **D.** If these people did have other security measures in place, then the author's conclusion would be refuted.

   (A) There is no assumption that burglars can see inside someone's garage.

   (B) No assumption is made about the safety of a car in the garage, just about the house.

   (C) In many houses, friends come in through the garage more often than burglars.

   (E) This implication is not made.

5. This squib states two premises:

    1. Most politicians are moral.
    2. Most politicians are intelligent.

    Based on this information, John makes a leap of logic to draw the following conclusion: At least some immoral people are unintelligent.

    Question Type: Analogous reasoning

    Correct answer: **D.** This choice has exactly the same flawed argument structure as the squib. Most teachers care about students. Most teachers are well educated. Therefore, at least some teachers who do not care about students are not well educated.

    (A) This would be a rational argument.

    (B) This answer would have the same structure if the conclusion mentioned drivers who do not drive well.

    (C) This argument is similar, but it compares only one variable: pilots with bad eyes. In addition, it states a sufficient-necessary condition—Pilots → Good eyes.

    (E) The comparison of stylists to artists makes this choice completely different from the squib.

6. This squib states that with the help of computer programs, poor spellers can turn in papers that are spelled well. However, good spellers still turn in papers that are spelled better than those written by poor spellers. This means that the computer program is unable to overcome all the deficiencies of the poor spellers.

    Question Type: "Resolve"

    Correct answer: **D.** This answer would mean that the computer programs are not as skilled at spelling as good spellers are. It would thus be hard for them to create a paper spelled as well as a good speller would spell it.

    (A) This answer would confuse the information about good spellers.

    (B) This choice does not resolve the problem.

    (C) This point is irrelevant.

    (E) This answer does not mean that they are unable to create programs that spell well.

7. This squib is a sufficient-necessary problem.

    1. Green Martian → From Jupiter
    2. Blue Martian → From Jupiter
    3. Green Martian → Pointy Tails and Blue Eyes

    4. Blue Martian → Round Tails and Yellow Eyes
    5. Martian on the Landing Ship → No Tails

    This logic chain would mean that no blue or green Martians could be on the landing ship. You need to choose an assumption that supports the claim that all Martians on the landing ship are from Mars.

    Question Type: "Strengthen"

    Correct answer: **D.** This answer would mean that if the creature on the ship is a Martian, then it is from Mars, since it cannot be from Jupiter.

    (A) This answer tells us nothing about their planet of origin.

    (B) This assumption is a contradiction, because the squib says that the Martians on the ship have no tails and this statement says that they have pointy tails.

    (C) This point is irrelevant.

    (E) This does not mean that they are from Mars as opposed to Venus.

8. Philip assumes that since he and Billy have similar music tastes, Billy would not have bought a CD that he himself would not have bought. This assumption is not certain however, because it seems that Billy might know that Philip hates the singer, and Billy is therefore ashamed to tell Philip which CD he bought.

    Question Type: Reasoning strategy

    Correct answer: **B.** One important piece of evidence—Billy's refusal to tell Philip which CD he bought—suggests that Philip's conclusion is incorrect, yet Philip remains certain of its veracity.

    (A, C–E) These errors do not occur.

9. The teacher claims that there is no reason to apply external pressure to students who do not want to do something naturally. The principal claims that application of external pressure to students is sometimes useful.

    Question Type: Controversy

    Correct answer: **E.** What is debated is the value of applying external pressure to students.

    (A) This statement is not made in the arguments.

    (B) It appears that neither speaker would disagree with this statement.

(C) You cannot be sure about group tendencies.

(D) The speakers do not disagree over this idea.

10. The squib claims that most investment bankers work until their early 30s and then retire with all the money they made in order to pursue personal goals.

Question Type: "Strengthen"

Correct answer: **E.** More than likely, these rich bankers were not forced into early retirement, so if most retire when they are 30, the squib assumes it is because most *want* to retire when they are 30.

(A) You cannot be sure of the exact hours that bankers work. You know only that they work double the number of hours that other people work, which means that they work about 80 hours per week.

(B) No assumptions are made about 40-year-old bankers.

(C) The assumption is made that investment banking is a well-paid, not the best paid, profession.

(D) The squib makes assumptions only about the duration of the work, not the actual difficulty of the work.

11. This squib presents the idea that if people regularly disregard minor regulations, they will develop a disregard for the law as a whole. The squib claims that starting down this "slippery slope" will end in a revolt.

Question Type: Conclusion

Correct answer: **D.** This answer captures the majority of the points in the argument.

(A) This is a subsidiary point of the argument.

(B) The squib makes no surmise about which violation does more harm.

(C) Nothing is said about a cure. This statement is too general to present the main point of the argument.

(E) This point is not explicitly stated by the squib. The philosopher simply fears that a revolution might happen.

12. The squib claims that the only reason for giving safety booklets to employees is to place the burden of avoiding accidents on the employees' shoulders.

Question Type: "Strengthen"

Correct answer: **B.** This choice would provide the reason why safety booklets are given to employees.

(A) This statement does not mean that they are more likely to be able to waive liability.

(C) This answer does not mean that the sole purpose of the booklets is to waive liability.

(D) This point would undermine the conclusion.

(E) This point is irrelevant.

13. The squib says that even though daycare centers charge a lot, they do not make a lot of profit because of the high per-hour wages that they pay their employees. The squib claims that this situation is the result of the strength of the daycare worker's union.

Question Type: "Weaken"

Correct answer: **B.** This answer would mean that the high wage levels are most likely due to the shortage of workers, not to the strength of the union.

(A) This choice would support the claim that the union is responsible for the high wage levels.

(C and D) These points are irrelevant.

(E) This statement does not mean that excessively high employee salaries are absorbing the profits. Food and toys are fixed costs, but high salaries are not. Additionally, this answer choice does not relate to the conclusion regarding the strength of the daycare workers' union.

14. Brad claims that football players possess all kinds of amazing attributes. Evan claims that several of Brad's broad contentions do not apply to all football players.

Question Type: Reasoning strategy

Correct answer: **B.** Evan points out specific areas where Brad's claims do not apply.

(A, C–E) These tactics are not used.

15. Ben asks Sally to go to the beach, but she refuses, claiming that she needs to study. Ben suspects that she is lying, since she offers this excuse whenever he asks her out.

Question Type: Reasoning strategy

Correct answer: **C.** It could be possible that Sally is extremely studious, which is why she is refusing to forgo study time in order to go out with him.

(A) This preference is probably not true of most people and does not tell us anything about the relative importance of studying to Sally.

(B) Ben assumes that if Sally's reason for studying is *not* her only reason, then it cannot be a reason at all.

(D) This idea is probably the truth, so it is not a reasoning error.

(E) Ben does not assume that Sally dislikes the beach.

16. Lissy claims that dancing is her calling and that she will attend every dance this season.

Question Type: Conclusion

Correct answer: **B.** This inference is true, because May is in the same season as June and Lissy claims that she will attend all parades this season that have dancing.

(A) You cannot be sure of this occurence based on her statements.

(C) Nothing is said about Lissy's wish to become a professional dancer.

(D and E) You cannot make these inferences based solely on Lissy's claims.

17. This squib can be mapped out as follows:
    1. Fox Farm:
        a. Chardonnay
            i. Dry
            ii. Not heavy
        b. Riesling
            i. Nondry
        c. Zinfandel
            i. Dry
            ii. Not heavy
    2. Swan Song
        a. Chardonnay
            i. Nondry
        b. Merlot
            ii. Heavy
        c. Cabernet
            i. Nondry

Rita wants a heavy and dry wine.

Question Type: Conclusion

Correct answer: **C.** The only wine that could possibly meet these criteria is the Swan Song Merlot.

(A) This wine is not heavy.

(B) This wine is nondry.

(D) This wine is not heavy.

(E) This wine is nondry.

18. The professor claims that people who own iguanas have fewer allergy problems than those owning cats or dogs. He advises people with allergy problems to purchase an iguana so that their problems will dissipate. He does not advise people to avoid keeping cats or dogs or to get an iguana instead of a cat or a dog.

Question Type: "Weaken"

Correct answer: **D.** If this statement were true, then purchasing an iguana would have no effect on people's allergies.

(A) This answer does not mean that having an iguana caused these people to stay well. This choice could only support the conclusion.

(B) This answer would make it seem that the recommendation would be helpful.

(C) This point is irrelevant.

(E) This statement does not mean that iguanas would not normally aid a person's allergies.

19. This squib claims that those who do not like others *cannot* be liked by others. However, people who do like others can *sometimes* be liked by others.

Question Type: Analogous reasoning

Correct answer: **C.** This is almost the same statement as the psychiatrist's except that *people* is replaced by *aardvarks*.

(A) People are different from rats, so this choice is not analogous.

(B) This choice compares two very different things: aliens and earthlings. The squib compares people to people.

(D) This is a statement based on the argument. It does not display analogous reasoning.

(E) Livestock and farmers are different groups.

20. This squib is formed entirely from fallacious statements. Nevertheless, it claims that based on the "trove of data available," people believe in macroevolution more than they believe in microevolution.

Question Type: "Weaken"

Correct answer: **C.** This answer would mean that the evidence is not sufficiently convincing to

make disbelievers in microevolution believe in macroevolution.

(A) This point is irrelevant to people's beliefs about those processes.

(B and D) These points are irrelevant.

(E) This answer does not mean that people will not find the evidence to be compelling.

21. The artist claims that forcing graduate art students to take art history classes does not help the students at all.

Question Type: Conclusion

Correct answer: **C.** The claim is that the art history requirement is completely irrelevant to the creation of fine art.

(A) This argument is not made.

(B) This statement is not made.

(D) This is a subsidiary point of the argument.

(E) Nothing is said about the standard of judgment.

22. The passage assumes that plasma engines will allow for intergalactic space flight. Based on this assumption, it assumes that intergalactic space flight will occur as soon as plasma engines are available.

Question Type: Reasoning strategy

Correct answer: **C.** The squib first assumes that intergalactic space travel will be possible with plasma engines. It then sets out to prove that space travel will be possible with plasma engines based solely on this assumption.

(A) This assumption does not occur.

(B) This would not be a flaw.

(D) Accurate conclusions can often be drawn about future events.

(E) This contradiction does not occur.

23. The main point of the passage is that since more people are applying to college, standardized test scores are less relevant to their applications. More relevant are intangible factors such as teacher recommendations and personal essays.

Question Type: Conclusion

Correct answer: **C.** This answer is true based on the increased focus on intangible factors as opposed to standardized test scores.

(A) This is not the main point of the squib.

(B) No normative statement is made in the squib.

(D) The squib argues that recommendations and essays are becoming more important than standardized tests. It does not claim that they are the most important.

(E) This point is not stated; the squib merely says that they have changed.

24. The squib claims that people who hand out pamphlets must be very sociable people in order to succeed at their job. The squib further claims that handing out pamphlets must be harder than handing out newspapers, because people actually want newspapers at times.

Question Type: "Strengthen"

Correct answer: **C.** This answer would mean that handing out pamphlets is more difficult than handing out newspapers.

(A) This choice does not support the conclusion.

(B) This point is irrelevant.

(D) This answer does not mean that handing out pamphlets is actually harder than handing out newspapers.

(E) This point is irrelevant.

25. This squib claims that even if the Aztecs did not grow sick from foreign diseases or believe that Cortés was a minion of a god, the Spanish would still have conquered them eventually.

Question Type: "Weaken"

Correct answer: **D.** This answer would mean that if disease were not a factor, the Spanish could never have defeated the Aztecs.

(A) This choice would strengthen the squib's conclusion.

(B) This statement does not relate to whether the Spanish would have conquered the Aztecs eventually without the disease or the Aztecs' false beliefs about Cortés.

(C) This answer would strengthen the conclusion of the squib.

(E) This point is irrelevant to what eventually happened.

SECTION 2—LOGICAL REASONING

1. The student claims that the book is not original because no one part of the work is original. This is an invalid assumption, because the book can be original even if none of its parts is original.

   Question Type: Reasoning strategy

   Correct answer: **D.** This is the reasoning error; just because the parts are not original does not mean that the compilation is not original.

   (A–C, E) These errors do not occur.

2. The scientists claim that even though sea snakes are widely feared, they are not dangerous because of their tiny mouths.

   Question Type: "Strengthen"

   Correct answer: **D.** The scientists' claims would be weakened if sea snakes were able to target small areas to bite without any trouble.

   (A–C, E) These points are not assumed.

3. The psychologist claims that hyperactivity medication is overused. Instead of raising children the right way, parents try to bottle up emotions in order to make their job less taxing.

   Question Type: "Strengthen"

   Correct answer: **A.** If this statement were true, then children taking the medication would be deprived of healthy childhood phases.

   (B) This point is irrelevant.

   (C) This answer does not mean that the parents who administer the dose are doing the wrong thing.

   (D) This answer does not support the argument.

   (E) This statement does not apply to human beings.

4. John claims that the song "Ninety-Nine Bottles of Beer on the Wall" has been sung since the late 1600s by the English.

   Question Type: "Strengthen"

   Correct answer: **C.** If the song were always sung in English, then more than likely it was not sung first by Swiss bartenders.

   (A) This answer would not mean that the English were the first. It could have been a group that preceded both groups.

   (B) This statement would not strengthen John's argument.

   (D) This point is irrelevant.

   (E) This answer would not strengthen John's argument.

5. This squib relates the specifics of tennis tournaments and then makes an assumption that if the second seed can never lose to a lower seed, then he will meet the first seed in the finals. This does not mean that the first seed cannot lose before reaching the finals.

   Question Type: "Weaken"

   Correct answer: **A.** If this occurred, then the third seed or someone beating him (besides the first seed) would meet the second seed in the finals.

   (B) This answer does not mean he loses the match.

   (C–E) These points are irrelevant.

6. The squib bolsters its argument by appealing to the work of many experts: ethnologists, historians, and archaeologists.

   Question Type: Reasoning strategy

   Correct answer: **D.** All the passage did was appeal to the work of experts in the field.

   (A) This choice cannot be correct because you do not know if what it says is true. There may well be additional evidence that the author chose not to include.

   (B) This possibility is not really eliminated. It is merely claimed that he was a good general.

   (C) The passage does assume this.

   (E) This delay does not occur.

7. The reasoning error in this squib is that it uses data from a study of mice to conclude that what are likely signs of aging in humans must be caused by starvation.

   Question Type: Reasoning strategy

   Correct answer: **E.** The squib misapplies data from the study of mice to conclude that humans whose bodies are thin, whose skin is sagging, and whose hair is falling out must be suffering from starvation, even though these symptoms may simply be the signs of old age.

   (A) The exact opposite is claimed.

   (B) The squib makes an analogy between animals and humans and then makes an assumption that is based on that analogy.

(C) No claim is made that there is a causal relationship between aging and starvation.

(D) This implication does not occur.

8. The artist claims that there is no creation in art, just adaptation.

   Correct answer: **C.** If adaptability requires creativity, that would undermine the artist's claims.

   (A) This point is irrelevant.

   (B) This answer does not mean that there is not still a connection there.

   (D) This point is unrelated to the artist's conclusion.

   (E) This answer would be irrelevant.

9. The squib says that some medical researchers are trying to find a physical basis for the spiritual phenomenon known as near-death experience (NDE). The researchers defend their work in terms of its possible medical benefits, but others claim that mixing religion with secular scientific research can have harmful results.

   Question Type: Conclusion

   Correct answer: **D.** This is the main point of the squib.

   (A) The squib does not say that NDE is dangerous to study.

   (B) This point is not stated.

   (C) This is not really stated in the squib, nor is it the main point.

   (E) Nothing is said about people who are technically dead.

10. This is a sufficient-necessary question:
    1. Jill → ~~Frank~~
       a. Jill and Frank → Bill
    2. Frank → ~~Bill~~
    3. Frank → ~~Jill~~

    The conclusion is that if people follow their preferences, everyone will be in the meeting together. Something additional must be assumed for this conclusion to be true, and you need to select that assumption from among the answer choices.

    Question Type: Reasoning strategy

    Correct answer: **E.** This answer would allow them all to be in the meeting together.

(A) This is already a constraint.

(B) Bill is not currently constraining the situation.

(C) Bill is irrelevant.

(D) This answer would still cause Frank to prefer not to go to the meeting.

11. The squib assumes that because a team is exceptional, an individual player on that team must be exceptional. This assumption is not necessarily true.

    Question Type: Analogous reasoning

    Correct answer: **D.** This answer assumes that Bill must be kind to the poor solely because his government is kind.

    (A and B) These logical flaws are different from the one in the passage.

    (C) This answer would be close if it claimed that Avery must protect each of its members.

    (E) If it was assumed that William was a bad man, then this would be analogous logic.

12. The commissioner says that the purpose of the tournament is to prove who the world's best golfers are, not to humiliate them. He claims that the golfers' names on the leaderboard prove his point.

    Question Type: Conclusion

    Correct answer: **A.** This point can be assumed based on the Commissioner's last two sentences.

    (B) The golfers have complained about the course conditions, but you cannot tell if those golfers felt humiliated by those conditions.

    (C) You cannot determine what all of the players' comments are, so you cannot determine if the commissioner would disagree with all of them.

    (D) You cannot determine the exact nature of the players' comments.

    (E) Based on his words, it would seem based that he is frustrated with the players' comments.

13. The teacher assumes that since Suzy has performed well before, she will continue to perform well in the future.

    Question Type: Analogous reasoning

    Correct answer: **D.** This argument assumes that because the pitcher has performed well in the past, he will continue to perform well.

(A) This argument is opposite to the teacher's.

(B) If they lied to Congress in every single opportunity they had to testify, then this argument would be analogous to the squib's.

(C) This argument is completely different than the squib's.

(E) Exercising is different from dieting.

14. This squib assumes that the reason young professionals do not eat at home very often is because cooking at home takes too long and is such a lot of work.

Question Type: "Strengthen"

Correct answer: **E.** The passage claims that if home cooking could be made easier and less time consuming, young professionals would cook and eat at home instead of dining in restaurants. This claim assumes that young professionals dine in restaurants in order to save time and energy, and not for social reasons.

(A) The squib does not make this argument.

(B) Nothing in the squib indicates that what young professionals need to make home cooking easier is cookbooks.

(C and D) These points are irrelevant.

15. The author claims that there were no alien spaceships flying over the southeastern portion of the state last night despite sightings by his daughter and several farmers. He bases his claim on statements made to him by the alien commander.

Question Type: "Resolve"

Correct answer: **C.** This answer would mean that what the farmers and the author's daughter saw were not alien spaceships but rather army planes that appeared to be UFOs.

(A) This answer would not clear up anything.

(B) This answer does not mean that he does not know the general location of his spaceships. The southeastern portion of a state is a big area.

(D) This point is irrelevant as to whether it is actually aliens who are lighting up the sky.

(E) This point is irrelevant.

16. Since genetically modified crops "glean a few nutrients from the natural soil" and because they are not "as susceptible to disease," the author claims that farmers will not need to use any pesticides or fertilizers on these crops. But in all likelihood, the crops will still need fertilizers and pesticides, just not as much. The passage does not claim that the crops are entirely "disease-free" or that they are entirely "self-sustaining."

Question Type: "Weaken"

Correct answer: **A.** The genetically altered crops partially solve the problems of disease and lack of nutrients, but they do not solve them completely.

(B) This point does not matter.

(C) The squib makes no such assumption.

(D) This point is irrelevant.

(E) This failure does not occur.

17. The squib states that baby mice in captivity do not get along well with the opposite sex. It then asks how they ever procreate with so much aggression between the sexes.

Question Type: Conclusion

Correct answer: **C.** This would have to take place for reproduction to occur.

(A) This point could not be concluded.

(B) You cannot be sure how mice in the wild behave based on the information in the squib.

(D) There is no way of telling if mice in the wild behave any differently than those in captivity.

(E) There is no way of telling if male mice become more aggressive toward other males as they grow older.

18. This squib claims that churches that require donations have more money to spend than other churches in their area do. However, the squib also claims that in general, churches that require donations do not have as much spending power as churches that do not do this.

Question Type: "Resolve"

Correct answer: **E.** This answer would show why they have more money than other churches in the nearby area but not more than churches anywhere else.

(A) This answer does not explain the discrepancy in the squib.

(B) This answer does not explain the discrepancy.

(C) This explanation would confuse the situation.

(D) This point is true, of course, but it does not explain the financial situation described in the squib.

19. The squib describes the benefits conferred by exercise and relates doctors' claims that children who exercise when they are younger are more likely to continue the trend into adulthood. The author then claims, solely on the basis of personal experience, that the doctors' claims are false.

Question Type: Reasoning strategy

Correct answer: **A.** The author places too much weight on his personal experiences in evaluating the doctors' claims about children in general.

(B) The author does analyze some specific cases: his and his brother's.

(C) This is not the case.

(D) The author does not really include such claims.

(E) You cannot be sure that this identification occurs; more than likely, he identifies himself correctly.

20. This squib assumes that because the process of cloning involves copying an organism's DNA, a specific technique that is sometimes used to copy DNA will be used for cloning.

Question Type: "Strengthen"

Correct answer: **B.** The argument assumes that if DNA is copied, then it must be copied using the technique of PCR.

(A) This point is not assumed. It is merely stated as a possibility.

(C) Nothing in the squib allows you to comment on the author's opinions about this idea.

(D and E) These points are not assumed.

21. The squib assumes that crows are no longer deterred just by a scarecrow. Today a scarecrow needs accessories such as sticks that appear to be guns in order to scare off crows.

Question Type: "Strengthen"

Correct answer: **A.** If the crows could differentiate between the two, placing a stick in the hands of a scarecrow would not really have any effect on crows.

(B) The opposite is assumed.

(C) This point is not assumed.

(D) You cannot determine the author's opinion on this idea.

(E) This point is not assumed by the author.

22. The squib talks about the danger of leaving an oven on after it is no longer in use. It then talks about several categories of people who consistently do so. To prevent fires, the squib recommends buying a dog because the dog can smell smoke.

Question Type: "Strengthen"

Correct answer: **D.** If this answer were not true, then buying a dog would not be a very effective fire-preventive method because the dog would have no way of telling that a fire is starting.

(A and B) The exact opposite points are assumed.

(C) This assumption is not made.

(E) This point is not necessarily assumed. It is assumed that someone within the house will be able to do so.

23. This squib contradicts itself. It claims that poor people go to the city in order to provide for their families. Then it says that the poor people who go to the city never communicate with the family that they left behind. This is completely at odds with the idea that people go to the city to provide for their families.

Question Type: Reasoning strategy

Correct answer: **E.** The argument contains two contradictory premises: (1) that poor people go to cities to provide for their families, and (2) that they never talk to their families again once they leave them behind.

(A) There is no appeal to an authority in the passage.

(B) This is not a flaw.

(C) This does not occur.

(D) This does not really happen, nor would it be a flaw if it did.

24. In this passage, the admissions officer claims that students have trouble writing their essays because they tend to cram their essays with too many personal facts. When they do, the essay can become overloaded and technically deficient, since it is hard to include many details in a short essay while keeping it coherent.

Question Type: "Strengthen"

Correct answer: **D.** This assumption is necessary for the conclusion of the admissions officer to be logically drawn. If you assume the opposite—that

overloading essays with detail is irrelevant to technical quality—that would completely contradict the officer's conclusion. Thus, you know that this assumption is required for the conclusion to be logically drawn.

(A) Test scores are not mentioned in the squib.

(B) This assumptio is probably true, but it is not a necessary one for the argument.

(C) This assumption is made, but it is not necessary for the conclusion to be valid.

(E) This point is completely irrelevant.

25. This sociologist claims that Southerners are more sociable in general because they are not confined to their homes during the winter. This places them in situations where they continue to meet new people all winter long. This situation, for which the weather is responsible, makes Southerners more sociable on average than Northerners.

Question Type: Conclusion

Correct answer: **E.** If the statements in the passage are true, then it can be concluded that weather can influence sociability.

(A) This point cannot be concluded based on the passage. Maybe people living in the North are unsociable for a reason unrelated to the weather.

(B) You know about the general characteristics of each group, but you do not have information regarding specific outliers of each group. Therefore, you cannot make this conclusion.

(C) There are, of course, periods of time when Southerners enter their homes during the winter, spring, summer, and autumn.

(D) You do not know that they are aware of all information—just the information relating to the climate.

Section 3—Logic Games

Game 1: Grouping

Initial Setup:

1. Correct answer: **B.** This group could not play together, since if A is not with B, then A must be out. When A is out, B must be with E.

2. Correct answer: **B.** C must share a group with F. Notice that the two groups that are playing are interchangeable:

A	C	G
B	F	
D/E	E/D	

3. Correct answer: **E.** All of the answer choices could occur:

B		A
E	D	

4. Correct answer: **B.** If B is out, then A must play. When A plays, A must play with B. Therefore, B can never sit out.

5. Correct answer: **C.** D cannot share a group with G:

C	A	G/D
F	B	
E	D/G	

Game 2: Complex Linear

Initial Setup:

1	2	3	4	5
A		B		
	T			V

$C < R$

$T < U < E$

After looking at the sequential constraints of the game, it becomes clear that there are only two configurations for the variables:

A	C	B	D/E	E/D
S	T	U	R	V

A	C	B	D	E
S	T	R	U	V

6. Correct answer: **E.** A, C, B, E, D is the correct answer from scenario 1.

7. Correct answer: **C.** Scenario 1 gives this order.

8. Correct answer: **C.** This could occur in either scenario, but E must always be paired with V.

9. Correct answer: **A.** Scenario 2. E must not be paired with R.

10. Correct answer: **A.** This is scenario 1. E could be in booth 5, and R could be in booth 4.

11. Correct answer: **B.** D could share a both with U, R, and V. Therefore, any answer with S or T in it is incorrect.

12. Correct answer: **C.** There are two possible from scenario 1 and one from scenario 2. This is a total of 3.

Game 3: Mapping

Initial Setup:

Most of these lines are interchangeable, but you should still draw at least one possible outcome for each possible scenario so that you will get the idea of the game. For instance, in the following diagram, A could be on either side of the table, but for purposes of expediency, we can put her on one side:

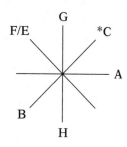

13. Correct answer: **A.** A could never sit next to G, because A must sit only two seats away from H, who sits across from G.

14. Correct answer: **A.** If this occurred, then F could not sit next to B, because B sits next to H, who is across from G:

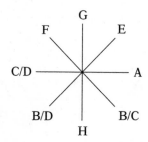

15. Correct answer: **C.** E would have to sit next to G, because G has to sit next to either F or E.

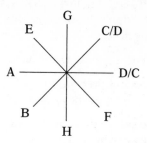

16. Correct answer: **B.** Remember here that the A and D lines are interchangeable, so B could sit next to D or A:

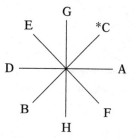

17. Correct answer: **A.** C would have to sit across from A or D:

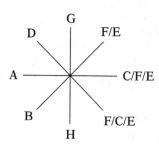

18. Correct answer: **D.** C must sit next to H:

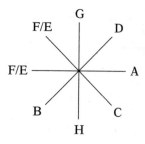

19. Correct answer: **A.** Since A must sit one seat away from H, who must sit exactly opposite from G, we know that A can never sit next to G.

Initial Setup:

Notice that the C < D constraint reciprocally operates with the E < F constraint. If one is true, then the other one has to be true:

$$\overline{\quad}_{1} \quad \overline{\quad}_{2} \quad \overline{\quad}_{3} \quad \overline{\quad}_{4} \quad \overline{\quad}_{5} \quad \overline{\quad}_{6} \quad \overline{\quad}_{7}$$

C < D → E$_6$, E$_7$
E < F → C$_1$, D$_2$
A < 5 → B$_3$, G$_4$

20. Correct answer: **C.** This could be an order.

    (A) If E is before F, then C must go first and D must go second and E must go sixth and F must go seventh.

21. Correct answer: **D.** This would not allow C to go first and D go second; therefore, F would have to go before E and D would have to go before C.

22. Correct answer: **C.** A can shoot everywhere except third and fourth because of the sufficient-necessary constraint that is in place if F goes before fifth.

23. Correct answer: **E.** We know that C and D must go first and second. Therefore, we know that E and F must go sixth and seventh. A must go fifth, since A cannot go in the third or fourth spots. Since A goes fifth, we know that G goes fourth and B goes third.

24. Correct answer: **B.** C cannot shoot fifth because that would force D to go after him. This would force the sufficient-necessary constraint to act when C < D. This would conflict with other spaces in the game:

    $$\underline{A} \quad \underline{F} \quad \underline{B} \quad \underline{G} \quad \underline{\quad} \quad \underline{\quad} \quad \underline{\quad}$$
    $$\cancel{C}$$

25. Correct answer: **B.** Due to constraints 1 and 2, D must shoot before C and F must shoot before E. Therefore, neither D nor F could shoot first.

1. Correct answer: **B.** The passage maps the transformation of "peace education" in American society from the '80s concept of "conflict resolution" that increased awareness in schools to religious leaders of present times.

   (A) Peace education was never abandoned; the term "conflict resolution" was added. There was no mention of national self-service in the passage.

   (C) McCarthyism and the Cold War were the backdrop of the peace education movement, but peace education was not seen as a way to recover from the losses suffered as a result of these circumstances.

   (D) This is a subsidiary point of the passage.

   (E) The threat of nuclear war is not the main thrust of the passage. Peace education was accepted more for reasons of moral sustainability than just the threat of nuclear war.

2. Correct answer: **D.** It took on the more pragmatic character of "conflict resolution" (line 16).

   (A) A capitalist approach to peace education is never mentioned.

   (B) New technology was applicable when reaching out globally, but the passage does not say anything about its use in the classroom.

   (C and E) These points are not stated.

3. Correct answer: **E.** This point is never stated.

   (A) The passage makes this claim (lines 43–43).

   (B) The passage makes this claim (lines 34–35).

   (C) The passage makes this claim (lines 54–57).

   (D) This is a common theme of the passage.

4. Correct answer: **B.** *Legitimate* is used to mean an "appropriate" discipline for children in schools.

   (A, C–E) These choices do not fit the meaning.

5. Correct answer: **B.** Appreciation for the environment was an important topic, as noted in lines 33–35.

   (A) This was a goal, but it was not the one mentioned in response to "planetary annihilation."

   (C) This is a type of "negative peace" that was not really the goal of this movement (lines 10–14).

(D) Empathy for third-world countries did not evolve until later, when telecommunications evolved.

(E) This fear was not something that the teachers were looking to engender in their students.

6. Correct answer: **A.** The purpose of this passage is to explain the transition from "negative peace" to "positive peace" to "conflict resolution" in the '80s.

(B) This chronicle occurs in the passage, but describing the transition is the most important purpose.

(C) Dual debate topics are not introduced.

(D) This call does not occur.

(E) This is a purpose of the passage, but not the main purpose.

7. Correct answer: **C.** The purpose of the passage is to describe Dominican society and the reasons for its current condition.

(A) This is only a minor theme in the passage.

(B) This is not the main point of the passage.

(D) This issue is addressed in the passage, but it is only a subsidiary issue.

(E) This is the purpose of the second half of the passage.

8. Correct answer: **B.** This claim is supported by the fact that many families used the remittances sent to them by their expatriate relatives to improve their standard of living (lines 37–40).

(A) This claim is not true. The most viable option was moving to a city from the country.

(C) The caste system was race-oriented, but describing the whole society as racist would be a great exaggeration.

(D) You have no reason to assume that this was the only way to remedy the situation.

(E) Not much is stated about Rafael Molina.

9. Correct answer: **C.** The context in which advancement occurs describes how a person could achieve financial advancement.

(A–B, D–E) These choices do not fit the context.

10. Correct answer: **A.** The final paragraph depicts the importance of the family for all classes, especially the poorer ones.

(B and C) These choices do not accurately characterize the paragraph.

(D and E) These are important parts of the paragraph, but they are subsidiary to the importance placed on families.

11. Correct answer: **A.** These families are described as middle class, so the word *intermediate* would be appropriate.

(B–E) These are not appropriate descriptions.

12. Correct answer: **E.** Nothing is said about any lessening of class distinctions.

(A) This point can be inferred from the passage (lines 18–20).

(B) This point can be inferred from the passage (lines 4–6).

(C) This point can be inferred from the passage (lines 1–2).

(D) This point can be inferred from the passage (lines 5–6).

13. Correct answer: **A.** This passage is concerned with explaining the effects of acid rain, especially as those effects relate to historic buildings.

(B) No theories are reconciled.

(C) The passage does not trumpet a call for action.

(D) This is a minor point of the first paragraph.

(E) This point does not apply.

14. Correct answer: **E.** Acid is transferred from the rain to the objects upon which the rain lands.

(A–D) These choices are not really appropriate.

15. Correct answer: **C.** This claim is true, because it means that this rain is more acidic.

(A) Nothing is said about acid in snow versus acid in water.

(B) There are also negatives for historic buildings.

(D) Some are mentioned regarding the minerals in the ground in the Northeast.

(E) The passage never says that stone requires acid in the rain to weather.

16. Correct answer: **B.** The passage states that Europeans have had up to 10 times more pollution than Americans have had.

(A) This point is never implied.

(C) This is not stated, since this rain cannot be considered to be acid rain; it is clean rain (line 8).

(D) The Appalachian Mountains are compared to the Rockies, not to the Alps. In addition, the comparison is not in this paragraph.

(E) This point is never implied.

17. Correct answer: **E.** This statement would indicate that there are other causes of acid rain besides these vehicles.

    (A) This point does not matter.

    (B) This choice would not undermine the author's contentions.

    (C) This answer does not mean that acid rain is not also bad in those other cities.

    (D) This statement does not mean that they absorb enough of it to make a difference.

18. Correct answer: **A.** This is the only emotionally charged sentence that is offered in this group. The rest are fairly dry and scientific.

    (B–E) These choices do not apply.

19. Correct answer: **D.** The passage is meant to describe the activity of the Supreme Court.

    (A) This answer is not specific enough. The judicial review process is very extensive, but this passage describes only the function of the United States Supreme Court.

    (B) This is not the point of the passage.

    (C) This statement is not accurate.

    (E) The passage does not summarize any study.

20. Correct answer: **B.** The sentence that includes the phrase "legislative review" functions as a short conclusion for the passage, so it tells the main point of the passage.

    (A and C) These are not the reference points.

    (D) Nothing is stated about any lack of a requirement for this type of accountability.

    (E) This is only a small part of legislative review.

21. Correct answer: **B.** The author praises the system for having a way to recheck itself through judicial review.

(A) You cannot infer that the author is expressing bitterness here.

(C) There is no reason to believe that a person who is writing a passage about the government is indifferent toward most of it.

(D) Nothing is said about enforcement.

(E) There is no mention in the passage of the nation's founders.

22. Correct answer: **A.** This passage outlines and discusses the system by which the Supreme Court deals with cases.

    (B) The paragraph is designed to present facts about what goes on during a term, not facts about the Supreme Court in general.

    (C) This is not the main purpose of the paragraph.

    (D) This paragraph makes no attempt to astonish readers.

    (E) This descriptive paragraph is not designed to justify a future argument.

23. Correct answer: **B.** The author says that people should be familiar with how the system's checks and balances operate, and judicial review is one of the most important of those checks and balances.

    (A) This is never represented as being especially worthwhile.

    (C and D) Nothing indicates that the author would require these.

    (E) This statement might be true, but the author does not state in the passage that this is necessary. The author merely stresses that knowledge of the system is important.

24. Correct answer: **A.** In this paragraph the author talks about the procedure that is followed to determine which Justice will write the opinion regarding a particular case.

    (B) This answer is not necessarily true, nor is it emphasized.

    (C) This provides a transition between the second and fourth paragraph, not the first and fourth paragraphs.

    (D) This is not the purpose of the paragraph.

(E) This statement is just too general to be the correct answer to this question. "What goes on inside the courthouse" could include all sorts of things unrelated to judicial opinions.

25. Correct answer: **B.** This question involves a bit of arithmetic. Justices have to decide whether or not to review a case in the first place. They submit votes on around 7000 cases, but they decide to review only around 100. The question asks what would be the fewest number of votes that the Justices would be required to submit in order to review these 100 cases. Four Justices must vote for a case in order for it to be accepted. Therefore, 400 votes is approximately the minimum number of total votes that the Justices could submit in a given year.

(A, C–E) These answers do not apply.

SOME FINAL ADVICE FOR TEST TAKERS

Now that you have finished reading the lessons and working your way through the sample tests, you might ask, "Where do I go from here?" It all depends on your goals, how satisfied you are with your performance, and how much time you have available to devote to studying for the LSAT.

Your LSAT score is the single most important ingredient in your law school application. Admissions officials call the LSAT "the great equalizer" for good reason: It is the single factor that allows them to compare applicants without regard to their different backgrounds, histories, interests, and the like. It also gives them a very good idea about your potential for success in the legal field.

It thus makes sense to spend whatever time you have left before test day to prepare yourself as well as you possibly can. Go back over the examples, exercises, and practice tests in this book. Refresh your memory regarding the characteristics of each type of LSAT question. Rework logic games that gave you trouble the first time through. Work on improving your pacing and on building up the stamina you'll need to get through all four hours of the test without tiring. If you have time, seek out supplementary materials and use the time you have left to keep practicing and improving your skills.

The Week before the LSAT

1. Get Up at 8:00 A.M. Every Day. For a week before the test, force yourself to get up each day at 8:00 A.M. and go to sleep before midnight. This will get your body accustomed to being awake during the hours of the LSAT. It will also ensure that you get enough sleep to be fully rested in time for the test. You don't want to be even a little sleepy during the LSAT!

2. Scout Out the Testing Center. It is a good idea to scout out your assigned testing center at some point during the week before test day. If you drive or walk past the testing center, you'll know exactly where you need to be, and that's one less thing you'll have to worry about. There's nothing worse that getting lost on the morning when you have to take the LSAT! It's no fun to be late either, so note the traffic patterns and figure out when you need to leave home in order to get to the testing center with time to spare.

3. Relax in the Two Days before the Test. During the two days just before the test, don't study at all. Any improvements that you could make in those two days would be marginal at best, and it's not worth tiring out your brain for test day. Give your brain time to rest and recharge so that it can perform at its peak on LSAT morning.

Do whatever works to minimize your stress level. For example, you might want to take a long break to relax and go out with friends. Make sure, though, to get to sleep before midnight on both nights before the exam.

During the Test

1. Sit Far Away from Others. The LSAT is not a group activity. It is something that you have to do by yourself, and having other people nearby can be distracting. Therefore, if at all possible, you should position yourself near the aisle or in a corner of the room so that people are not moving around you. Every movement is a potential distraction, and every distraction is a second or two that you could have spent improving your score.

2. Pace Yourself. Pay attention to the passage of time during the test so that you know whether or not you need to work faster. You might also want to set some time aside to work on a particularly difficult question. Consider bringing a personal stopwatch to the test to keep track of the time. If you decide to do so, train with the watch beforehand so that it doesn't cause you additional stress on test day.

3. Read Critically. Keep this tip in mind at all times. If you are able to train yourself to read critically and to pay attention to details, then you will have an advantage over other test takers. Small details are the points of entire passages, so if you pay close attention to each squib and every passage, then you will be better able to recall the information when a question asks for it.

Also, if you read critically, you will be less likely to make careless errors. Test makers love to use words like *not*, *except*, *only if*, and *and* that you might overlook if you aren't reading carefully but which can change the entire meaning of a question. If you miss one of these words because you aren't reading critically, chances are you'll pick the wrong answer.

4. Cross Out Obviously Wrong Answers. Now that you have practiced with many sample LSAT questions, you should be able to look at each actual test question and recognize the three out of every five answer choices that are typically obviously wrong. Take a moment to cross out those wrong choices. Then you'll be able to focus on the remaining two, of which one is the correct answer and the other is the seemingly plausible "second-best choice." In addition, if you are forced to guess, then narrowing down the choices will improve your chances of picking the correct answer.

5. Answer Every Question. On the LSAT there is no penalty for guessing, so mark an answer to every question even if you have no idea what the correct answer is. If you are able to eliminate a couple of choices before guessing, then all the better—you'll be

that much more likely to pick the right answer. Just know that it is never in your best interest to leave a question blank.

6. Diagram Whenever Possible. The diagramming tools that you learned in this book for logic games and certain sufficient-necessary logical reasoning questions set you apart from your competition. Don't forget these tools on the day of the test! Use them as often as you can so that you will derive the maximum benefit from them.

7. Don't Get Stressed. Speaking of stress, it is important to maintain a cool head during the test. Staying relaxed and in control will help you devote your full brainpower to answering questions instead of worrying about how you're doing. If you hit some questions that you can't answer, guess and move on. You have to. You can worry all you want when the test if over, but if you start to worry during the test, your concentration could suffer and your score could drop. This is a bad move.

Remember too that the section you're worried about could easily be the so-called experimental section, which doesn't even count toward your grade. Often the questions in that section, which are being field-tested to see if they work as well as they ought to, can seem more difficult than the questions on the rest of the test. So don't let a particularly tough section throw you. Keep a cool head and concentrate on doing well on the rest of the test.

APPENDIX

SURVIVING YOUR FIRST YEAR IN LAW SCHOOL

Advice from Curvebreakers

After you take the LSAT and submit all your applications, eventually you will receive a big packet emblazoned with the name of the law school you will call home for the next three years. The suspense is over, and you can finally relax, right? If only it were that easy. Your first year in law school is easily the most important part of the three years you will spend studying law, and arguably the most important year in determining the character of your entire legal career. It can also be one of the most enjoyable and illuminating experiences of your life. This 1L survival guide will serve as a roadmap to approaching this crucial year, and as a preview of what to expect from your teachers, fellow students, and the entire law school experience.

Why Your 1L Year Is so Important

You may wonder why there is such intense emphasis on the first year of law school. This question makes sense in the context of your education prior to law school. Many individuals who end up in law school are students who took some time to get their act together in college. Some of them may have changed their major multiple times, gotten some bad grades in freshman year, or even taken some time off to explore other options. In this context, it seems as though missteps early on did not matter all that much. Unfortunately, you have to completely let go of this type of thinking in law school. In fact, if there is any time when you cannot afford to lose sight of your goals or make bad decisions, it is the first year of law school as opposed to your 2L and 3L years.

The first explanation for why the 1L year is so important is an intuitive one. The first impressions you make on your fellow students, your teachers, and the

professionals you encounter your first year make a huge impact on your experience in law school and your subsequent career. Anyone who has ever started a new job or moved to a new school can attest to the validity of this insight.

Your Fellow Students: Like members of any other social group, law students begin to make judgments about each other very quickly. These first impressions are usually rather superficial evaluations of your goals, your intelligence, and your dedication to the study of law. You may be thinking this is strange behavior for a group of adults preparing for serious professional careers, but even at the most elite law schools there are tangible groupings of the students who are "serious" and "smart" and those who are determined to just be "along for the ride" or "slackers." There are a number of important reasons why you want to be in the first group.

The first reason is that your fellow students will haunt you for the rest of your life! Maybe that sounds more ominous than it ought to, but it is true in many ways. Law school is not like college, where graduating students spread to all four corners of the earth, never meeting again except when they see each other at reunions. Instead, your fellow classmates are all preparing for the same thing: to practice law. The majority of them will end up as practicing lawyers, often in very close proximity to one another. Most law schools send their graduates into concentrated markets, so the man or woman sitting to your left and right your first day of class will likely end up as your colleague, possibly at the same firm, or across the table from you in a future legal proceeding. For these reasons, you want to make a good impression. Your fellow students are a deep resource; they will form your network for your entire career and their initial impression of you could determine whether they introduce you to a prospective employer, recommend your services to potential clients, or even hire

you when you are looking for a career change. It can be difficult to think of your fellow students this way. When you look around the classroom you will see a bunch of other people who just like you are trying to figure out what law school is all about. Imagine instead a portion of your fellow students wearing the black robes of the judiciary, another fraction giving their victory speech after being elected to political office, and a large chunk of the remainder working for law firms and corporations that you will do business with, or may want to work for some day. When you see your classmates this way, you realize just how important it is to get off on the right foot with them.

Your Professors: Your fellow classmates are not the only people keeping a close eye on you your first year of law school. In a large first year law class it may be hard to imagine that a professor can keep track of all the students, and it is unlikely that he or she will remember every student's name by the end of the first year. At the same time, professors are always keeping their eyes open for students who show potential. They may be thinking of taking on students to do legal research, or even for potential co-authors for future articles. Law professors often fill these positions with students from their first-year classes, so standing out in class as a well-prepared and capable individual will pay dividends with them as well. If you are considering a legal career in academia or policy, your teachers are just as valuable a resource as your fellow students. They will be your future colleagues and their recommendations will often be a prerequisite for finding and retaining a great job as a legal academic.

Your Career: It should be clear to you now why starting off strong your first year is important in the context of students and professors, but there is another more tangible reason why the first year is so important, and it has to do with the structure of legal recruiting. Major law firms across the country are engaged in an intense struggle to attract well qualified law school graduates. This has resulted in a complex recruiting system (discussed in more detail in the "Finding a Summer Job" section). When employers begin interviewing you for your 1L summer job, they will only have your first semester grades to rely on. In some cases, they may not even have access to your grades and will have to rely on your resume and involvement outside of the classroom. Despite the fact that they have such a limited academic record to rely on, employers in general, and especially law firms place a great emphasis on grades. Those few grades could easily make the difference between a job at the organization of your choice, or having to stick out the summer at a workplace that does not fit your goals and desires.

For most students, the emphasis on first year grades only becomes more intense when they are looking for their 2L job. Most employers recruit and hire the majority of their summer employees during the fall of the 2L year. When they make these crucial decisions, they only have your full 1L grades to determine your quality as a candidate. There is much debate over whether 1L grades are a predictor for success as a lawyer, but among major law firms and other legal employers there seems to be a consensus that 1L grades are the best way to differentiate among the mass of law school applicants. The firm where you work during your 2L summer will likely give you a job offer upon graduation and you could easily spend many years working there. This entire trajectory is determined in many cases solely by the grades and experience you gain as a first-year law student! If you take this concept further, the quality of your initial employer will play a crucial role in your future job opportunities, earning potential, and in the quality of your working experience. Now it may be clearer to you why it is so very important for you to go into your first year of law school prepared to get it right the first time. There is no time to adjust or find your way in law school; the system is designed to heavily favor those who leap from the starting blocks and take an early lead.

Before You Set Foot in the Classroom

Living on Campus or Off: You should consider housing options early on. Where you live in relation to the law school can have a real impact on your study habits and ability to participate in law school functions and extracurricular activities. If you are planning on living in a dorm, you will likely need to complete a dorm application during the spring. Therefore you must make this decision very early. Living in the dorm can be a great experience for a 1L. For one thing, many dorms predominantly house 1L's who are less likely to have the resources or knowledge to confidently find off campus housing. You will likely meet a large number of 1L's this way, and that can make it much easier to find study partners, course outlines, or just someone to vent to. For these same reasons dorm life is not for every 1L. If you live in the dorms, it will be virtually impossible for you to escape the bubble of law school life. Everywhere you go, people will be studying law, discussing law, and generally creating an atmosphere of pressure and competitiveness. Especially during finals, dorms can turn into a pressure cooker of raging stressed-out personalities butting heads around every

corner. Many law students thrive in this sort of environment, but generally it can be somewhat counter-productive.

You may be thinking to yourself that you should clearly live off campus to avoid this situation. This may, however, not be the best advice for a 1L. Living off campus can isolate you from your classmates, and make it more difficult to stay involved with events on campus. What is most important, whether or not you live off campus, is finding a quiet place where you can study in peace. As this article will describe later, there is a huge workload of reading and review that goes along with a successful law school career and if you are attempting to keep up in a stressful environment, you may fail.

Making a Schedule: To enable you to devote all your time and energy to absorbing your first-year subjects, it is crucial to develop a daily and weekly schedule that will keep you on track in all of your classes. Before the first day of class you should create a basic schedule for yourself based on your class meeting times and when you plan on waking, and going to sleep. One of the keys to successful studying is to make sure that you have enough time to complete an entire assignment for a class in one sitting. This is important because law school textbooks often organize information in unconventional ways. For example, a reading assignment may contain a number of cases that only make sense once you read the explanation of basic legal concepts which follow them. Reading this type of assignment in chunks instead of all at once will reduce your ability to spot important concepts in the reading and will consequently hurt your in-class performance as well as your ability to retain what you have learned for the test. On your schedule, you should make sure to pencil in solid two to four hour blocks each day to concentrate on studying. By consistently studying in longer blocks every day, you will be better able to keep up with your classes and soak up the information you are learning. Beyond studying, you should make sure that you schedule time for physical fitness. Consistently working out will keep your energy levels up and improve performance.

Items You'll Need: One of the keys to succeeding your 1L year is to be fully prepared and to plan ahead. For this reason you need to make sure that you have everything you need for your classes well in advance.

- **Your Laptop:** For most law students the most important piece of the puzzle is getting a good laptop to take in-class notes. Unlike most undergraduate schools, law professors often encourage students to bring their laptops to class. Your laptop is an invaluable tool for organizing the huge amount of information that you will need to absorb for each class. When purchasing a laptop, try to buy a fully featured model that will last the entire three years of law school. Buying the cheapest laptop you can find at your local store may make financial sense on the spot, but when you have to replace your laptop at the beginning of your 2L year you may regret this decision. Also, resist the temptation to buy one of the desktop replacement models that is stuffed with enticing multimedia features. Even if the salesperson tries to sell you a big ten pound model that functions as a movie production facility and home theater system all in one, make sure that you buy a compact, lightweight laptop with a long battery life. You should try to buy a laptop which weighs less than 6 pounds and has at least a 4 hour battery life. This way you can make it through the longest classes without having to plug it in, to charge it up. You should also make sure that the computer you buy has a wireless connection, a CD/DVD burner, and that it is loaded with Microsoft Office. Your school will probably give you a list of compatibility requirements for its classroom software. Make sure you bring this list to the store with you to ensure that your laptop is compatible. In addition to a laptop, check that you have a printer that can handle a large volume of printing with good quality. You will have to print out hundreds of pages of cases, notes, and outlines in your 1L year alone and you do not want to have to deal with unreliable school printers or the same slow printer you bought four years ago. Make sure you stock up on printer cartridges and paper as well, because the worst thing is to be stuck scrambling late at night to find a 24 hour store that stocks ink when an important memo is due in your legal writing class.

- **Textbooks:** You should also make sure you buy all your books well in advance of the first day of class. Usually the school bookstore will be able to provide you with all of your assigned books if you bring in your class schedule. You can also usually buy your textbooks online on Amazon.com or a number of other online retailers. This will also save you a significant percentage over your school bookstore's prices and you get the added benefit of brand new copies. But be careful with this method. Law professors often assign older editions of textbooks or hard-to-find texts that are not available

online. The important thing is to make sure you have all your books in hand at least a week before class starts. You will often be assigned reading for the first day of class, and you do not want to be the student who is put on the spot the first day and has to admit that he or she does not have the textbook. It is also recommended that you purchase all the commercial outlines and hornbooks for your class as well.

- **Other Study Materials:** Once you have purchased your laptop, books, and study materials, make sure that you have all the other school supplies. In addition to the normal pencils and pens, many law students purchase a supply of yellow legal pads and multitude of highlighters in different colors. Yellow legal pads are ubiquitous in law firms and courtrooms. You may notice fellow students bringing these pads to presentations and lectures outside of class, and you should try to get used to doing so yourself. Multicolored highlighters will be used to brief cases.

Orientation

Make sure that you attend your law school's orientation sessions. Usually they are not mandatory, but by attending, you can gain valuable information about your law school and also get a head start on planning out your semester. Aside from administrative functions like getting a student ID and filling out required forms, you will also usually get the opportunity to meet the teachers who will teach your basic 1L classes, get a tour of the campus, and familiarize yourself with the extracurricular activities on campus. Make sure to remember the value of first impressions when you are interacting with your fellow students and with your professors.

Preparing for Class

The vast majority of law school classes are graded based on one cumulative final exam. There is virtually no opportunity in the form of tests or graded assignments during the year to check your progress and determine what the gaps in your knowledge and understanding are. For this reason, you may have to reevaluate the study methods used during your education career previous to law school.

The first step in successfully preparing for class is to make sure that you complete all your assigned reading in the casebook and supplemental materials in advance of class, preferably around two to three days in advance. This may seem like basic advice, but in the context of law school it takes on particular importance. One of the most often repeated complaints about the first year of law school is the sheer volume of reading. It is not unheard of for students to have hundreds of pages of reading every week, sometimes several hundred for a single class period. The frustrating part is that your professor will often only cover some of the cases that were assigned, or may gloss over important concepts that were extensively discussed in the textbook. Nonetheless, the professor will expect you to have a working knowledge of everything you have read when the final exam comes around, so you have to keep up. Often the professor will address the most complex or controversial legal issues dealt with in the text during class, but will expect you to absorb the more mundane and self evident rules that are contained in the casebook.

The Casebook: Hundreds of years ago, the law was taught much more like your average college class. Professors stood at a podium in front of the class and literally read the law out loud in a lecture format. Students took copious notes and were expected to be able to regurgitate the information in long cumbersome exams which were based on rote memorization. During the mid 1800's several administrators at Harvard Law School, including Christopher Columbus, Langdell, and John Barr Ames, began to experiment with different teaching styles. In the United States legal system, cases are argued through the use of existing legal decision and interpretation of statutes and laws. Lawyers use these persuasive tools to create convincing arguments in court documents and in front of judges. Langdell and Ames decided that the methods being used in law school at the time were ineffective and did not prepare students to be good advocates within this system. They began to use a new type of textbook called a casebook, which is basically a collection of the written opinions in influential cases along with snippets of actual law. These casebooks generally have very little contextual material to explain the relevance of their contents. Instead students are challenged to try to extract the legal precedents and implications of the cases themselves, instead of having the answers explicitly stated by the author. Casebooks contain no illustrations and often have confusing or dense formats.

Reading Cases: The first thing you should do when you read a case is to quickly and thoroughly skim the case from beginning to end, looking for certain characteristics that will assist you when you go back to read it word for word. First of all, note the overall structure of the case. Does the opinion have headings

to split up the major issues, or does the entire opinion consist of one passage? See if there are multiple opinions. When a panel of judges such as the U.S. Court of Appeals or the Supreme Court considers a case, often multiple opinions are filed. These opinions are as follow:

- The first opinion is always the majority decision. It states the final outcome of the case and is the only part of the published case that has the ability to form a binding precedent on future litigation.
- Another type of opinion is known as a concurring opinion. Often judges will agree with the majority on the proper ruling in the case, but will take specific issues with the legal reasoning used in the majority opinion. Sometimes judges just want to disassociate themselves from a few lines of the majority opinion, or want to add in their own two cents about additional theories that would support the outcome. Be careful to note that they do not have the same influence as the majority decision and should be treated as such.
- The third type of opinion that is often included at the end of a case in the casebook is called the dissent. Usually there are one or two judges who file dissenting opinions, because they disagree with the outcome of the case, or are so worried by the implications of the legal reasoning in the majority opinion that they cannot sign their names to it. They are not binding law even though they are often much longer than the majority opinion and can contain very persuasive legal arguments. Many casebooks include dissents from older cases to demonstrate how the reasoning used in the dissenting opinion has become the law in modern times. For all these reasons, it is very easy for law students to fall into the trap of confusing the text of the dissent with the majority opinion. You should always read every opinion included for each case, but make sure that you take them for what they are.

Next, try to identify the outcome of the case. Often this will be included right at the beginning of the case, especially if it is an appeal from a lower court. Look for language in the first few paragraphs or the last few paragraphs of the majority opinion that states something along the lines of "We affirm the ruling of the lower court" or "We reverse the holding of the lower court." If you know how the case is being decided, you can identify how the court has construed the facts and the lower court proceedings to support their decision.

The last step before you carefully read through the case is to come up with questions that you have about the case based on the limited information you have. Try to jot down a few basic pieces of information and rules of the law used in the case that you want to identify. While you are reading the case, try to answer these questions to your satisfaction, making sure to take notes in the margins when a particular part of the text brings a question to mind. You should also take notes when you have insights about the wording of a case, or its possible ramifications in the context of other legal situations.

Case Briefing: The second stage in proper class preparation is known as "briefing" cases. A "case brief" is a one-page summary of the important information in a given case. The case brief has been used by generations of law students to boil down the important aspects of each case into a format that can be easily referenced later on without needing to reread the case itself. Cases contain a huge amount of superfluous information, and it can be easy to lose track of the important issues. A case brief makes it easy to think about how the relevant decision in your cases interacts with different factual circumstances that will come up later in class. It also makes it easy to see overall concepts that the casebook is attempting to convey through the collection of cases. By going back over your case briefs, you should be able to see the similarities and differences much more easily and be better able to analyze the case in class. In addition, you should be able to use the case briefs to construct an excellent outline, a process which is discussed later in this article.

Most case briefs contain the following elements:

- **Heading:** This section generally contains the full name of the case, the court in which it was filed, the year of the opinion, and the page in the casebook on which the case can be found.
- **Procedural History:** In a modern casebook you will rarely read the original opinion of the trial court. Generally, you will be reading the ruling in an appeal from the original finding by the lower court. In the numerous Supreme Court cases that you will read in class, you will often find that the case has first made its way through multiple lower courts. This section should note the outcome of the case in each of the lower courts and include basic details on issues that were brought up on appeal.
- **Facts:** This section should contain the basic factual situation that led to the matter being brought to trial. You should attempt to keep

unnecessary factual information out of this section of the case and refrain from making value judgments. Often the court deciding the case will frame the facts in a light that makes its decision justifiable, so be careful to craft this section with as little bias as you can. This section should only contain the most important facts without any analysis.

- **Issue:** This section should describe the major legal issue that the court is attempting to decide. The issue should be framed in the form of a question and can often be lifted directly from the text of the case. There are often a number of other lesser issues brought up during the appeal of a case, but you should only contain the overarching purpose of the court action.

- **Reasoning:** This section is also sometimes referred to as the "rationale" of the case. In this section you should attempt to craft a brief synopsis of the court's explanation for its decision in the case. Try to determine if there were differing approaches that the court is considering in its decision making process. Identify important cases that provide precedents used in the ruling and note any cases that you have read that the court attempts to distinguish from the case at hand. Finally you can note the impact the decision will have on future cases that come before the court.

- **Holding:** This section should contain the ruling of the court. Many cases contain a number of smaller tangential rulings and findings of law, but a careful reading of the case should make it possible to determine what main "rule of law" the case is creating or altering. All the other legal determinations in the case are generally known as dictum and should be noted, but left out of the case brief.

This pattern is the classic design of a case brief and for many students it will fit their study methods perfectly. However, merely writing the case brief before class is only the first step in properly utilizing the case brief method.

Printing out the case brief and taking notes by hand is recommended. As the professor analyzes the case and your fellow students bring up valid points, take notes in the margins of your case brief. Make sure to note any information which seems as though it could improve your understanding of the case. Once the class is over, go back over the notes you took by hand. It will be much easier to determine which material is relevant and which seems unnecessary in retrospect. At this point, you should edit your case brief on your computer.

OTHER METHODS

- **"In-book Briefing":** Students who use this method try to identify the crucial parts of the case using notes in the margin identifying the various elements. When a professor asks for the holding of the case, the student will actually flip through the case trying to find the section labeled "holding" and then try to determine the correct answer. This method is probably not very effective, especially when it is used in class. Just because you were able to successfully identify the portion of the case that contains the holding does not mean that you will be able to coherently explain it in class a few days later just by glancing at it.

- **Color-Coded Briefing:** Another popular method for briefing cases is known as the "Technicolor" or color coding system. Students who practice this method use a set of multiple highlighters to highlight the various portions of the case in the book. An example would be using red highlighters for the holding, yellow for the facts, green for the issue, blue for the procedural history, and so on. Consistently color code your briefs so that, for example, your facts are always in yellow. That way, if the teacher has a difficult factual question, you can quickly refer back to that portion of the case without spending minutes aimlessly flipping through the case struggling to figure out where the answer is. Some students rely solely on color coded briefing to prepare for class. We do not recommend this practice, since you have so much material to wade through when your teacher asks you basic questions regarding the cases. Instead you should use the color coding as just one step in preparing a case for class. Once you have completely color coded a case in the book, it is much easier to go back and efficiently construct a fantastic case brief. Color coding can also help you stay alert and focused on the structure of the cases while you are reading through them.

Another Approach to Outlining: Formal case briefing can be very effective for your first few weeks of law school. But as the focus in class begins to shift from extensive examination of individual cases to a more thematic and policy based discussion, it may be counterproductive to produce full formalistic case briefs in the style described above. Your time could be put to better use reexamining the material learned in class and finding connections between the various cases.

The basic methods are similar to those described above. The main difference with this approach is the final step of creating the formal case brief. The first month or so of law school, most professors will take it kind of easy with the assigned reading. Two or three cases a night is the norm and most diligent students will find it relatively easy to create detailed case briefs for each class. The professor will also go over each case in great detail so the case brief is an invaluable tool. However, by the second month or so the honeymoon is over. Prepare to start reading eight to ten cases a night. Furthermore, the professor will spend less class time on each case and even skip large portions of the reading. This can be very frustrating for the typical 1L student who stays up half the night writing out detailed case briefs and never gets to use them. There is a solution and that is simplifying the process of briefing cases to derive the most useful information that can be used on exams. Use this three-step method:

- **Step 1.** Start by reducing the amount of information that you collect about each case. The first thing to eliminate should be overly detailed descriptions of the facts and procedural history. The only decision that can help you determine the outcome of a hypothetical on a test is the final rule created by the higher court. When you are reading and thinking about the case for class, you need to know exactly what the factual basis for the finding was, to understand how the court formulated the rules and holdings. However, focusing too much on the specific facts of a case can make you worse at applying the rules in an abstract way, to a completely different situation. As you begin to pare down your briefs, try to include the bare minimum of facts that are necessary for the reasoning in the case to make sense. This way it will be much easier to see how the decision in the case applies to other situations.
- **Step 2.** Next, streamline your brief by combining several sections of the case brief into one statement. The issue, reasoning, and holding of the case can be combined into one brief three or four sentence paragraph that is much easier to manage later on. The important thing is to try to boil down these three sections into a flexible and abstract legal rule that can be applied to other examples.
- **Step 3.** If your professor seems focused on the legal rule created by each case rather than on the actual fact patterns surrounding them, you can pare down your case brief even further. The ultimate compact case brief will include only two to four sentences that state the basic legal

rule that the case espouses and nothing else. You will have the bare minimum amount of context to properly utilize the material, but for many successful students this kind of abbreviated summary provides the perfect level of detachment from the irrelevant details of each case. Students use these summaries to identify how cases that seem completely irrelevant to a hypothetical could be used to analyze the proper outcome.

Hornbooks, Treatises, and Commercial Outlines:
There is another set of great resources that generations of first-year law students have relied on to help them grasp the enormous amount of material that they are responsible for. These secondary resources are similar to the Cliffs Notes you may have used in high school or your undergraduate institution. However, these resources do not focus on one book in particular, but rather address entire first-year courses. They are available in law school bookstores and online, and every law student swears by specific authors or series. It is important to note that many professors do not like students to bring these secondary sources into class with them. Some may specifically forbid it, or get annoyed when you quote directly from a secondary source in class.

- **Hornbooks:** The first type of resource is known as a hornbook. This genre of secondary resources is usually written by renowned professor(s) in a specific field of law, be it criminal procedure or property. A hornbook can be a refreshing change from a casebook that seems designed to confuse and misdirect first year law students. Hornbooks on the other hand read a lot more like regular textbooks. They are organized into cohesive sections and give a detailed overview of the history and modern application of legal principles and relevant case law. These guides are usually written in a plain text that can be easily understood and are formatted to improve retention. They generally include a multitude of perspectives on different aspect of legal principles, providing criticism, discussion of judicial interpretation, and the modern application of the legal rules. These books often have a focus on "black letter law." "Black letter law" is not found in any specific written form but is better understood as the simple distillation of basic legal principles and case law. These background elements are often crucial to understanding cases and solving final exam problems, but many professors gloss over them to talk about more complex policy issues in class. Professors nonetheless expect you to figure

out the "black letter law" on your own for the finals, but this is can be very difficult. Hornbooks can help you fill this gap.

- **Nutshells:** There are even more simplified versions of hornbooks often referred to as nutshells. These sources are extremely simplified and usually forgo a discussion of case law altogether. Instead, they contain simple overviews of current legal principles and are very dense. You should primarily use nutshells towards the end of the semester if you have extra time.

- **Commercial Outlines and Commercial Briefs:** These contain professionally prepared case briefs and detailed outlines for a number of first year topics. Usually the best examples are specifically matched up with the precise textbook assigned by your teacher. Often your law school bookstore or online source will offer the corresponding outline when you purchase your textbooks. This particular type of secondary source can be dangerous for first year law students; because it seems to eliminate the need to do the two most time consuming tasks: making case briefs and constructing a good outline.

- **The Commercial Brief:** Commercial briefs should be used only in specific circumstances. First of all, if circumstances beyond your control cause you to get behind in your reading or you skip a case, it is acceptable to use a commercial brief if you are called on. Just make sure you do not become dependent on these briefs for class. They often contain errors, and your professor's take on the case is much more useful to your final grade. It is advisable to use commercial briefs when you have finished your case brief and want to make sure you have not completely missed the legal significance of the case. Commercial briefs are often very good at stating the general legal rule established by a case, and you can use them to check if you got the right idea in your own analysis. Commercial briefs also contain great case summaries for your outline.

- **Commercial Outlines:** These secondary sources are professionally produced outlines that are also usually keyed to your specific textbook. Many law students think that they can just read through a commercial outline and use it on the finals and get a great grade. This is a fatal mistake! Commercial outlines are only useful as a guide to the relevant material that you need to glean from your reading. They are no substitute for reading the actual cases and supplemental reading. Use them when you launch into your reading so that the important information will jump out at you, when you are having a great deal of trouble determining what appropriate legal rule or doctrine is espoused by a given case, and when it is time for finals and you need good study aids.

- **Treatises:** These long, often multi-volume works are usually written by the reigning expert in a particular field of law. These treatises are identified by the scholar who produced them, and have names like *Williston on Contracts*. These works try to examine every aspect of the history and current state of a particular field of law with in depth analysis and doctrinal justification for the modern legal rules. They also often contain extensive explanations of the scholar's own take on various legal rules and complex arguments for their reform or repeal. They are geared towards legal academics and practicing lawyers, and are usually written at a level that is beyond the grasp of young law students. For your first year's success they are pretty much unnecessary.

Recommended Resources: The following recommendations for helpful secondary sources are by no means exhaustive. They are merely resources that the authors of this article found particularly illuminating and well organized.

Civil Procedure

- Joseph W. Glannon "Civil Procedure: Examples and Explanations" Aspen Law & Business Publishers; 4th edition (April 2001).
- Kane, Mary Kay "Civil Procedure in a Nutshell". West Group; 5th edition (July 2003).

Property

- Jesse Dukeminier "Gilbert Law Summaries: Property" Harcourt Legal & Professional Publications; 16th edition (January 2002).
- D. Barlow Burke "Property: Examples and Explanations" Aspen Publishers; 2nd edition (May 2004).
- Roger Bernhardt and Ann M. Burkhart "Real Property in a Nutshell" West Publishing Company; 4th edition (December 1999).

Contracts

- Joseph M. Perillo and John D. Calamari "Calamari and Perillo on Contracts" West Group; 5th edition (August 2003).
- Steven L. Emanuel "Contracts (Emanuel Law Outline)" Aspen Publishers; 7th edition (July 2003).

Criminal Law

- George E. Dix "Gilbert Law Summaries: Criminal Law" Harcourt Legal & Professional Publications; 17th edition (June 2001).
- Wayne R. Lafave "Criminal Law" West Group Publishing; 4th edition (July 2003).

Torts

- Kenneth S. Abraham "A Concise Restatement of Torts" West Group (October 2001).
- William Lloyd Prosser and W. Page Keeton "Prosser and Keeton on Torts" West Group; 5th Pkg edition (1984).

The First Day of Class

Finally it's time to attend your first day of class. The first thing you should do is relax! At this point your fellow students are in the exact same boat as you and are all feeling the same tension and anticipation about the year ahead. If you are well prepared for the classroom environment, you will be able to take advantage of early opportunities to define your law school career and set yourself apart from the crowd. Those other nervous students in your first year classes will end up being your most valuable resource, so it is important that you present yourself well in class and do not get an undeserved reputation. The most important things to consider when adjusting to the in-class learning experience are your professors' teaching style, your fellow students, and proper classroom behavior and etiquette.

Teaching Styles

One of the biggest differences between law school and any other educational experiences you have had, including undergrad, is the style of teaching employed by law school professors. You may have an inkling of what is in store for you from movies such as *The Paper Chase* or even *Legally Blonde*. In these fictional representations, domineering law professors rule a classroom, full of terrified students, by alternating difficult questions that may or may not have an answer with confusing hypotheticals designed to stump those who try to answer them.

Fortunately, the real law school experience is not quite this harrowing. It is, however, a good idea to be prepared for a new style of learning that is the hallmark of legal education. This method is known as the Socratic Method and has been used in legal education since the nineteenth century.

Socratic Method: This method was originally developed by Socrates himself and is a dialectic method of teaching and learning that was originally employed to help explore complex moral and ethical concepts for which no cut and dried answers exist. The classic application of the Socratic Method was a dialogue between two individuals in which questions were posed and then the answers received were either accepted or criticized and challenged, by the other participants. Through this process, philosophers and teachers hoped to achieve greater understanding of the important moral and ethical dilemmas of life by finding the strengths and weaknesses in various arguments for and against different positions. During the late nineteenth and early twentieth centuries, the Socratic Method became the preeminent method used for teaching in U.S. law schools.

A typically Socratic professor will rarely lecture to the class on law. Instead these professors will usually give a brief introduction or outline of the topics that will be covered in that day's class and then launch immediately into questions. Some professors may forgo any introductory remarks and immediately begin calling on students. First year classes generally have assigned seating and the professors are given seating charts so that they can "cold call" unsuspecting students. "Cold Calling" is one way of using the Socratic Method to begin posing questions to a student who has not volunteered to participate. Usually a professor will make it clear early on in the semester whether or not it is acceptable to pass when you are "cold called."

The professor often begins by asking simple questions about the cases that were assigned for that day. She or he may ask for an explanation of the facts in the case or of the ruling. These deceptively simple questions are often followed by a series of more difficult questions. The professor may ask you to explain something, and then question the assumptions that provided the basis of your answer. These methods are designed to make you unsure of the validity of your conclusions and reveal the weaknesses in your arguments. During the course of these questions the professor will often turn to other students and challenge them to take the opposite position, or to criticize the statements of their fellow law students.

"Hiding the Ball": "Hiding the ball" is one of the classic Socratic professor's favorite methods. This technique is used when a professor wants to identify a core legal concept without explicitly stating it or explaining it to the class. Therefore the professor is "hiding" the proverbial "ball." which in this case is the actual point that he or she is trying to make. Instead

the professor will ask a number of carefully crafted statements in order to lead the students to identify the principle on their own. These questions are often structured to create greater confusion and are incredibly frustrating for many students. Often professors ask a series of such questions without their being a clear "right answer" or possibly without there being any answer at all!

Alternatives to the Socratic Method: In many law school classrooms, modified forms of the Socratic Method have become more popular. These are often designed to make the in-class discussion more topical and to improve the quality of the classroom discourse.

- **The Panel Method:** Professors who use this strategy will split up the class into groups of two or three students who form a panel. The professor will then create a schedule for the time when these panels will be responsible for answering the questions that are posed that day in class. This method is preferred by many students who enjoy knowing in advance when they will be called on. The flip side is that those students who are on the panel are expected to be very well versed in the material being covered. Professors who use this method can be quite unforgiving toward students who are "on panel" on any given day. They will ask tougher questions than would normally be asked during random "cold calling" and the intensity level remains high for the entire class period.
- **Passing:** Other variations on the Socratic Method include professors who allow passing in limited circumstances, and in some cases at all times. In these classrooms, if a professor asks a question for which you are unprepared, you may pass, and they will move on to other students. Some professors may ask you to give them a note or write them an email prior to class explaining that you are unprepared. If these rules apply, you must follow these instructions; professors who allow you to opt out, often become upset if you are unprepared and do not let them know.
- **Other Methods:** Some professors pose the same questions as would be used in a Socratic classroom, but address the questions to the entire class. This type of voluntary participation is more relaxing for students who would rather just listen and take notes, but if you are brave enough to volunteer well prepared answers, it is an opportunity to stand out. Some teachers will lecture to the class or use PowerPoint presentations to teach the material, usually with some time for discussion at the end. These classes are often preferred by students, but in some ways you're missing out on a valuable learning experience if the class lacks interaction.

Your Classmates

Law school students are generally very diverse in terms of age, experience, and background. The ratio of men to women is usually around fifty: fifty, and there is a mix of students who have come straight through from college in their early twenties and older students who have returned to pursue a new career or gain new skills. For this reason it is important to be prepared for some of the challenges that can be posed by your fellow classmates. It is also important to know how to deal with difficult members of your class, because you will be spending the next three years in close proximity to them. Here are two common law schools "types" that you are likely to meet:

- **The "Laid-back" Student:** Some of your fellow students will be very laid back and will not take themselves too seriously. These students will rarely volunteer in class and will often seem distracted. You may even catch them playing solitaire or shopping online in class. But these behaviors can be deceptive! These students are often some of the most prepared, but perhaps they do not feel it necessary to constantly remind everyone else of how brilliant they are.
- **The Gunner:** The polar opposite of the laid-back student is a type of individual that is generally known in law school as the "gunner." Every 1L section will have a few and they are usually easily identified early on in the semester. The first sign that someone is a gunner is that whenever the professor solicits answers or opinions from the class, this student always raises a hand. Gunners always have a long winded and superficially intellectual comment prepared, usually containing conspicuous references to obscure concepts, or theories that were buried in the casebook, or mentioned by the professor. Another key characteristic of gunners is that they like creating situations in which they can appear to have outdone a fellow student in correctly answering a question. If another student is cold called and fails to answer a very difficult question, a gunner will always be ready to follow it up with a smartly worded answer that also manages to make the other student look bad.

Don't be a gunner! Even if you know the correct answer most of the time, it is important that you keep your contributions to class balanced with those of

your fellow students. Whether or not your behavior reaches the level described above, your fellow students usually have just as many insightful and valuable comments to make, and they will appreciate you allowing them room to share their opinions.

In-Class Etiquette

Beyond class participation, there are some other in-class etiquette rules that should be followed. As we have emphasized earlier, your fellow classmates are one of your most important resources, and you want them to hold you in high esteem. Here are some ways you can make this happen. First of all, when a fellow student is struggling to make a point but the professor is not following, it is acceptable to say something along the lines of "What I think he/she is saying is this..." This might seem counterintuitive when considered in conjunction with the comments on "gunner" behavior above. However, when a student is being grilled with questions that she or he cannot answer, that student will usually be thrilled to be taken off the hook. The key to this is your approach. Make sure to credit the student for his or her contribution and then build on the foundation to make your point. This will garner you goodwill with your fellow students while still conveying the quality of your grasp of the material. This is definitely a judgment call on a case by case basis, but if used judiciously it is a great tool for creating lasting camaraderie with fellow students.

Another good rule is to not attempt to make up answers to questions for which you are unprepared. If a professor asks you a question and you draw a blank, it is acceptable to explain that you do not know the answer. Though this may seem embarrassing, if you are truly lost it is advisable to allow the professor to move onto someone new rather than drag on the charade of attempting to answer for a long time. Your professors and fellow students will have very little patience for this obfuscation and it will reflect poorly on you. If you do pass, it is often prudent to try to make a contribution later in the discussion when you are more comfortable participating.

Taking Notes in Class

One of the more challenging aspects of your first year of law school can be figuring out exactly what you should be writing down in your in-class notes. First of all, as noted above, you should be writing relevant notes directly on the material you have produced while reading, be it a case brief or notes. That way you

can easily organize the additional insight you receive from class with the information you gained on your own. Beyond these notes, you should type important information that comes up in class. One common mistake that you will often see repeated by first-year students is an attempt to create a transcript of the class. This is antithetical to the whole Socratic learning process. In an undergraduate lecture, the professor has usually carefully prepared the teaching materials, so everything that is being said has value. However, in a Socratic learning environment there is going to be a lot of dialogue between student and teacher which does not have any value beyond the classroom. The teacher will often ask students to explain complex legal concepts that they do not understand. If you write down their error-filled answers, then later on you could easily assume that those statements are true.

You should also not fall prey to the strategy of merely listening in class and not taking notes. Some students feel that it helps them engage in the discussion and not miss the thrust of the professor's questions, but even if you are more alert to what is going on in class, you will forget it soon after. If you do not take some notes to remind yourself of what was elucidated in class, those ideas will get buried in the literal tidal wave of information that will be rushing at you every week. The optimal method is to take limited notes in class. Try to limit much of your note-taking to written notes or annotations to the case briefs and notes you create while studying. When you are typing out notes in class, make sure to only write down valid conclusions or theories that are given some credence by the professor.

Once Class Is Over

Once you have read all your material for class, carefully prepared case briefs, answered difficult questions in class, and taken great in-class notes, you may think that your job is done. Sorry, but succeeding in law school is not going to be that easy! You still need to take the proper steps to follow up on and consolidate everything that you have learned from your reading and class discussion. This step will help you retain what you have learned more effectively and is one of the tools that very successful law students use, to stay ahead of their peers.

Try to schedule your review of the day's material for the same day you covered it, preferably before you continue your reading for the same class. The first step is to read back though your case briefs and reading notes, making sure to read all the additional comments

and information you added during class. Then read through the notes that you took during class. Try to see where you made mistakes in your own analysis and try to add anything you missed into your class notes. This is also a great time to look back over the concepts and analysis in your hornbook and other supplemental materials.

You should not only reread all your notes and scan your supplemental materials, but also you should make a conscious effort to pare down the notes you have taken for class on your laptop. Even if you avoid the problem of transcribing everything that is said in class, you will start to realize that your professors and fellow students are constantly repeating themselves and restating points that have already been made in slightly different ways. You will also find that professors will reiterate what you have learned over the previous few class sessions at the beginning of class. This is great for stimulating discussion, but probably better left out of the notes that you will use to construct your outline. You may find it useful to keep a copy of your original notes from class, but you should make a duplicate set of notes where you delete and revise what you have taken down.

Extracurricular Activities

There are numerous chances outside of class to further your success in law school and to lay the groundwork for an outstanding career. These myriad opportunities include chances to sharpen your legal writing skills, pursue the legal aspects of your personal interests, and even to defend real clients in court! This section will introduce the types of opportunities that usually exists for 1L's, the job responsibilities that go along with various commitments, and the skills that each will nurture. There are three common types of extracurricular activities that this section will cover in depth:

- Student affinity groups, which are usually focused around the legal interests of a certain section of the student body, be it by gender, ethnic group, sexual orientation, or area of common interest.
- Student practice organizations, which focus on providing pro bono legal services in a number of different areas of law.
- Student-run law journals, which publish the latest legal scholarship, short written analyses of groundbreaking legal decisions, and surveys of the changes in various areas of substantive law.

This section will briefly cover a number of other extracurricular opportunities that are available at some law schools that might be of interest to 1L's.

Student Affinity Groups: Until the middle of the last century, the students who attended law school were pretty homogenous. The vast majority of student bodies were made up of white males, often from upper-middle-class or wealthy backgrounds. In the 1950s and 1960s all that began to change as more and more law schools began to admit women and eventually significant numbers of racial minorities. This sweeping change inevitably led to growing pains as faculty members and legal professionals had to adjust to the integration of women and racial minorities into the legal world at large. These changes coincided with the vast social movements of the era, which likewise brought many changes in law and judicial practice. The campuses of law schools were hotbeds of debate and advocacy during this time period.

One response to all of these factors was the creation of many student affinity groups. Student affinity groups are organizations loosely affiliated with the law school that the members attend. There are now literally dozens of active groups on most modern law school campuses. Here are some that you are most likely to encounter:

- **Ethnic-based Organizations:** These are organizations that define themselves by ethnic group. Some of the most common include the Black Law Students Association (BLSA), the Asian-Pacific American Law Students Association (APALSA), and La Alianza, which is a Latino student organization. When these student organizations were first formed, they often focused on issues related to the treatment of their members on campus and issues of civil rights law on a national basis. Now, organizations like BLSA and APALSA have expanded their focus to all issues that are relevant to their constituent group, both in the context of their own law school campus and the legal world. They also often reach out to the local community to extend a helping hand when there are pressing issues that can be ameliorated through legal means.
- **Religious Organizations:** These organizations are dedicated to specific religious beliefs and the pressing issues of law that are important to their members.
- **Women's Organizations:** These organizations are dedicated to issues that are unique to female students. They seek to further improve the experience of women in law school and to enhance their career attainment after graduation. They also focus on issues such as violence against women, reproductive law issues, and employment discrimination.

- **Political Organizations:** Some of the strongest organizations on campus are dedicated to political causes. The major conservative group on campus is the Federalist Society, which has its counterpoint in the more progressive American Constitution Society. Both of these groups hold numerous events on most law school campus and inspire some of the fieriest debates. These groups are great for any law student who has an interest in pursuing a career in politics or government. Students who are involved will be exposed to many influential political figures and will also gain the opportunity to network with the future politicians and power brokers of American politics.
- **Other Groups:** There are also student groups dedicated to environmental law, national security law, and a plethora of other interest areas.

These student groups host social events in order to foster unity among their members and to provide opportunities for useful discussion of the topics that are important to them. They also often present a variety of lecture events. These usually feature a knowledgeable member of legal academia who has done particularly interesting work in the organization's area of interest.

As a 1L, you can volunteer to help publicize or organize these events. The best way to get involved is to attend the regular meetings of the student organization and to begin networking with the leadership. Once you have established some connections, ask for projects or tasks that will help publicize the events being put on. You can offer to publicize the event to your fellow students or assist in staffing the event. Student organizations often need someone to meet visiting speakers at the airport and assist in their transportation to and from the event. If you are particularly ambitious, you can take it upon yourself to set up one of the events by coordinating with the venue and handling all the logistics. Even better, if you have the time to dedicate to the task, you can offer to do the research and contact potential speakers to create an event on your own.

Generally it is difficult for 1L's to take on true leadership roles in student affinity groups, but there are some exceptions. It is important to get started early. If your research on the Internet introduces you to a particular organization in which you are sure you want to play an active role, you should contact them and determine what types of opportunities exist for first year law students. Some student organizations have section representatives who play the permanent role of publicizing events and keeping members of their section aware of the group's activities. Still other organizations have leadership positions that serve as liaison to the entire 1L class and are usually filled by whichever student demonstrates the earliest interest in the role.

Later on in the year, usually at the mid-point of the second semester, student affinity groups hold elections to determine who will make up the leadership for the following year. This is much like election in high school and the positions usually include a president, secretary, treasurer, and various officers to deal with internal and external communications, events, and other organization specific roles. Usually the voting is done by the active members of the organization, so the best way to succeed is to get as involved as your schedule will allow, but even more importantly, to network and communicate with your fellow members so that they are aware of your dedication to the group and your achievements. Some student organizations have positions appointed by the previous leadership. In these types of groups your best bet is to make sure you are well acquainted with the existing leaders of the group so that when the time comes to pick their successors, you will be on the list.

Student Practice Organizations: Despite what you see on television or how you envision legal practice, very few lawyers ever actually spend a significant amount of time in court. But if you have an interest in going in front of a judge and arguing your case the old fashioned way, law school offers several good opportunities to do so. The best way to pursue this interest is to participate in student practice organizations. Student practice organizations function much like small public interest-oriented law firms within the law school. They are able to function because most states allow law students to represent clients in certain types of matters on a pro-bono basis, even in their first year of law school! They provide a fantastic chance to learn valuable legal skills, hone your writing, and become comfortable in the role of an advocate for your clients. They are also very rewarding on an individual level, because student practice organizations usually serve populations that would not otherwise be able to afford legal counsel. Here are some common practice organizations that you may be able to join:

- **Legal Aid Bureaus:** In most law schools there is usually a large legal aid bureau, which may or may not allow 1L's to participate. In many schools you have to apply at the end of your first year to become a part of the legal aid bureau, and the time commitments during your second and third year can be substantial.

- **Tenant Law Programs:** Law schools in urban areas often have strong programs dedicated to issues of tenancy law. Students in these groups represent tenants who are embroiled in various legal battles with their landlords. These cases can range from fighting an eviction attempt to suing for various violations of the local building codes. In these types of cases, there is often no requirement for the government to provide a lawyer, so student attorneys play a valuable role for clients who would otherwise have to deal with unfamiliar courts and sophisticated legal tactics from their opponents on their own.

- **Family Law Programs:** Student practice organizations have also been created to deal with issues of family law, often to help individuals trapped in the foster care system or suffering from abuse at home. These organizations let students represent some of the most vulnerable members of our society, and their work makes a tangible difference in the quality of life for many young individuals. Another common focus area is defending indigent clients who have been accused of petty crimes or claim to have been the victims of unfair police tactics. Some schools have organizations that provide students with the ability to represent incarcerated individuals during disciplinary hearings within the prison system.

To get involved in a student practice organization, make sure to attend the early meetings of the group, which are often held during orientation or soon after. This is particularly important because these groups usually have mandatory training requirements. Some states have mandatory training and testing before you can represent individuals in certain contexts such as arbitration for public housing cases. Stay on top of the schedule to make sure you don't miss your chance to become certified to represent these clients.

When you join one of these groups, here are some of the responsibilities and benefits that you can expect:

- **Intake:** Once you have received the proper training, the first major role that 1L's participate in is known as intake. Almost every student practice organization has many more clients seeking assistance than they can provide with student attorneys. Therefore, the process of determining which client's needs are the greatest is a difficult and crucial process. Some student organizations rely on local groups to process their intake. In many cities, these legal aid organizations hold weekly open houses where clients can come and describe their legal issues to the intake staff. Once the staff has created reports detailing their needs, they select the clients who can most benefit from their services and pass them on to the student practice organization. Other student practice organizations rely on law students to man phones and receive the calls directly from potential clients. As a 1L, you can often sign up for weekly office hours where you answer phone calls, determine the needs of various individuals, and answer some basic legal questions.

- **Arbitration/Negotiation Opportunities:** Many student practice organizations let 1L's represent real clients or assist second and third years during cases. It is rare that 1L's will represent clients in an actual trial; the majority of the chances will occur in administrative hearings or negotiation settings. Many types of housing and family laws have the requirement that the parties engage in arbitration or negotiation to resolve the dispute before it goes before a judge. For many of your clients it will be the first time they have encountered such a legal setting and they will be going up against parties who have participated in these types of processes many times. Though the context of your eventual practice will probably be very different, representing these clients gives you a chance to hone your negotiation skills—an opportunity that is often missing from the core law school curriculum.

- **Leadership and Career Development Benefits:** Much like student affinity groups, student practice organizations often have opportunities to run for leadership positions in the spring of the 1L year. The same advice applies here as does for the affinity groups: participate early and often, network with the existing leadership, and try to take on extra responsibility in order to demonstrate your dedication and potential. When you are interviewing with potential employers, they will be very interested to see that you have already gained real substantive legal skills outside of the classroom, so it is a great opportunity to build your resume.

Student-run Journals: Every major profession has a number of journals that are dedicated to presenting the latest research and theory at the cutting edge of the subject area. The law is no exception, but there is one significant permutation that makes a big difference for law students. While most journals dedicated to other topics consist of peer-reviewed articles, selected and edited by established professionals in the

field, most law journals are completely staffed by law students. Current law students who have not yet proven their worth in the legal arena are responsible for everything from selecting appropriate articles to determining the accuracy and originality of the pieces selected for submission.

The most prestigious journal at any law school is generally the Law Review, but 1L's are almost always precluded from participating. The process for getting onto the Law Review staff will be discussed in more detail later in this article, but there are many other journals that are happy to provide work to 1L students. Most schools have journals that are related to a wide range of topics from business or securities law to environmental and technology law. Every single journal determines its own structure, and they vary widely in their approach. This section will introduce you to the most common ways of running a journal and give you general advice on how to get involved and secure leadership roles for later in law school. Keep in mind that most employees would like to see some kind of journal experience on your resume, so it is probably a good idea to find some way to participate on a journal.

One of the most time-consuming jobs on a journal is known as subcitation or "subciting". This task is often assigned to 1L's, because it requires relatively little training and is easily broken up into manageable assignments for a large number of willing volunteers. Part of the journal's responsibility for the accuracy of the articles it prints is to verify that every single source is cited correctly and that it supports the proposition that the author is making in the article. Journals tackle this enormous task by taking on any students who are interested in participating on the journal as subciters.

The subciting process follows these steps:

- **Step 1.** Once the articles have been selected, the journal staff will distribute the articles to a number of more senior members of the journal often referred to as article editors. Article editors in turn are assigned a number of line editors, who each take on a section of the article as their responsibility. Each of these line editors is assigned a number of subciters to supervise. The line editors are responsible for breaking up the sections into manageable chunks and assigning them to individual subciters.
- **Step 2.** A subciter's first responsibility is to locate the original version of the cited source. Many journals do not allow you to merely locate the electronic versions of the source;

instead you have to track down the hard copy version and photocopy it. Many of the citations are to other law review articles, and these are usually relatively easy to locate in your school's library.

- **Step 3.** The next step is to read the original source and compare it to the reference in the article. Subciters usually have to complete small reports on each citation and determine whether they believe the citation is appropriate and if it references the correct pages.
- **Step 4.** If there is an issue with a citation, subciters will often make the case to their line editors that the reference should be removed or that a new source should be located to support the proposition being made by the author. Subciters are also responsible for editing their section for style and grammar errors. Though there are multiple levels of review, subciters often catch the majority of mistakes at this crucial first step.
- **Step 5.** After you have determined if the cite is appropriate, you must make sure it is written in the proper form. The correct format for legal citations is determined by referring to a lengthy rulebook known as The Bluebook. This source of authority is created by the staff of the Harvard Law Review and is regularly edited and updated. As a first year law student, you will increasingly rely on the complex rules promulgated by this influential text. The bluebook has hundreds of pages of obscure rules about every type of legal source available, and those rules are often far from intuitive. For each citation you have, you will need to determine which combination of bluebook rules applies and make sure that the proper format is followed. This step is emphasized, because when filing briefs and motions in a real court of law, there are often serious repercussions if formatting and style rules are not adhered to flawlessly. The process of subciting can be up to an hour per citation and subciters are often assigned upward of twenty citations.
- **Step 6.** Once you have completed the entire process, you will turn in a completed subciter report to your line editor who will carefully review your work. Line editors will communicate with subciters if they have a difference of opinion and will eventually produce an edited version of the section. Once all the line editors have completed their edits, they will usually combine the sections into a full article and hold another line-by-line review of the article with the article editor. Subciters are often invited to

join this step, which is sometimes known as a technical edit. A technical edit can be a tedious experience because each line of what could be a very lengthy article is read out loud and discussed to make sure that it is in top shape. These marathon sessions can take many hours, but it is crucial to make sure that the article is flawless when it is published. Once the tech edit is finished, the articles editor will present the final product to the editor(s) in chief who will give the final sign off for publication.

The main reason that the process has so many steps is that the participants are not practicing lawyers with the experience or judgment to figure it all out on their own. Instead, the model moves forward on the concept that if many talented but relatively inexperienced individuals collectively apply their abilities to editing the article, they can produce a professional result. The more practical benefit of this process is that it is very similar to how work is produced in a modern law firm.

Here are some other journal opportunities that may be open to 1L's:

- **Line editing:** If you do a good job subciting for a journal on multiple occasions you may be able to get a position as a line editor in your spring semester. Take time early on to find out exactly what the requirements are, so you know what your goals should be.
- **Reading submissions:** Law journals receive a huge number of submissions throughout the year, far too many for a small staff to handle. For this reason, many journals have a large volunteer group who read submissions to the journal to determine if they are high quality and if the piece is appropriate for a journal. Many journals have an editor who farms out all the submissions to rotating teams of students to review articles. If a team decides that the article is good enough to warrant further review, it is passed onto the entire committee that will read and review the submission as a group. If it is determined to be appropriate, once again, it will go to the editor(s) in chief for final approval.
- **Running for leadership positions:** Most law journals have a large number of subciters, a smaller but still substantial group of line editors and article editors, and the executive editors of the journal who are known as "the masthead." Most journals have elections during the spring semester for various editorial positions. As a 1L, your chances of winning the election for editor in chief are pretty slim. But if

your journal has a submissions editor and you have been very involved with the submissions process then that would be a great position to run for. You should also make sure to apply to be an article editor and continue line editing. Subcite at every possible opportunity, do your best to be selected as a line editor, and try to participate in the submissions process. If your journal has any events, such as a symposium on its specific area of law, make sure that you volunteer to help with the planning and execution of the event. As in any other form of politics, make sure that you get to know the leadership of the journal and try to demonstrate your dedication and interest through hard work.

Law Review: Most 1L students are aware of the most prestigious journal at any law school, which is known as the Law Review. Generally staffed by only a small percentage of any given class, these journals present articles that represent the most prestigious and groundbreaking legal research in the field. For a legal writer, being accepted for publication in the Law Review is the ultimate achievement, and many students consider getting onto Law Review to be the most impressive achievement that you can put on your resume.

Making Law Review can open up career possibilities that are not available to some of your peers. Many top-tier law firms will hire students from less-prestigious schools if they have managed to make it onto the Law Review. For this reason, every student should seriously consider going through the application process. The requirements for making Law Review vary from school to school, but generally there are two components. The first component is your 1L grades and the second is a legal writing and editing competition that is generally held after your second semester final exams.

Most Law Reviews create a competition packet that is distributed a few days after spring finals end. The content is determined by the current staff and is designed to require that you work for the entire designated period. The classic competition is made up of two portions. The first is a grueling and exceptionally difficult section of subciting and editing that will test your concentration. The second is a writing assignment that is often to write a commentary on a recent case that is reproduced within the competition packet.

The process for determining who wins the competition is created by the Law Review staff. They also review the applications and select the winners. The weight given to grades in the decision is substantial,

but a great performance in the competition is needed to be selected.

Students who make it onto Law Review often find that the work consumes a vast amount of their free time. Law Reviews often come out with more issues than other journals and generally accept scholarship that is more complex and thus a greater challenge to edit. Many Law Review staff members may find themselves dedicating upward of thirty hours a week to their duties.

Other Extracurricular Activities: Law school has a wealth of opportunities besides journals and student practice organizations. Many students who were involved in community service activities during their high school and undergraduate years still find some time every week to volunteer at a local homeless center, soup kitchen, or engage in some kind of public service to the community. In this same spirit, some law students become Big Brothers or Big Sisters to a local child who is in need of guidance.

Some students find it very exciting and educational to work on a political campaign if their 1L year falls during an election cycle. Political campaigns often seek out law students for their writing and advocacy skills, and there are a number of roles that law students can play without traveling or interrupting their focus on preparing for exams. Law students may even get the opportunity to write position papers or advocacy pieces in support of their political beliefs.

Most law schools have a student newspaper that hires law students as writers, editors, and administrative staff. This presents a great opportunity for creative writing outside of the legal arena and may also give you the opportunity to meet many members of the faculty and student body that you would have missed otherwise. Some students become involved in theater productions. Many law schools have an annual parody that gives students the opportunity to laugh at exaggerated representations of the trials and tribulations of law school life.

Applying for a Summer Job

There is one other very important task that you must focus on during your 1L year, and that is getting a great job for the summer. The summer job you take after your 1L year is a golden opportunity for you to get experience in a legal job without locking yourself into a certain career or field of law. The summer job you take as a 2L generally leads to full time employment, but you should remember that most employers do not look for a certain type of 1L job when considering you for a position.

There are a number of different options available in your 1L summer, and it is important that you start researching early. The first place you should stop by is the career services office at your law school. This office employs advisors who are often graduates of the school or former lawyers. Their job is to help students like you find fantastic careers so that one day they will give generous donations back to the law school! They are a deep resource for you and have a wealth of knowledge about not only what jobs are available, but which ones will be right for your career goals. Often the services of these offices are unavailable the first few months of the school year because they are tied up assisting 2L's and 3L's with the busy fall interviewing season. In addition, there is a generally accepted rule at most law schools that does not permit 1L's to apply for jobs prior to December 1. Law firms also almost always decline to accept applications from 1L's prior to this date, so there is a lot of focus among hardcore students to be completely prepared when the moment arrives.

As a 1L, you have a wealth of options. There are a number of obvious choices: work for a private law firm, the government, or a public interest organization. All of these are great choices, but you should also be aware of the wealth of opportunities in other areas that you might not be able to pursue as a 2L or beyond law school.

Law Firms: Generally, law firms that hire 1L's are trying not to waste their recruiting budgets and effort on students who are just looking for a cushy summer job and then moving on to their 2L year. In general, firms are seeking students who they believe have a genuine interest in working for the firm after graduation. For this reason, it is very important that you have some kind of experience or ties to the city or region in which they are located. Therefore, the first logical place you have a chance of finding a job is your hometown or its closest major city. You should also focus on regions with which you have close ties, such as the city where you attended college. You should also look at regions where your immediate family lives or where you have had significant work experience. If you attend a regional law school that places many students in the same city in which it is located, another great bet is to focus on firms in that city. Chances are that many of the firm's lawyers will have attended your law school and the firms will often be competing for the best students during the 1L summer.

Go to your career services office or the career services website maintained by your law school. Many schools

keep binders at these offices with lists of law firms that hire on campus and that have hired law students in the past. If you are lucky, they may even contain reviews of the students' experiences while working for the firms. If you can locate these binders, or find the same type of information on the website, start making lists of firms that are located in the cities of your choice and practice the type of law that you are interested in. You should begin to seek this information prior to December 1.

Another great way to discover law firms is to use the National Association of Legal Professionals (NALP) Directory. The NALP Directory is a compendium of most mid-size to large law firms in the entire United States. Each year, NALP produces a printed guide, several copies of which should be available in your career service office. However, many students find it even easier to use the electronic version at www.nalpdirectory.com. On this site, the information is available as a fully searchable database that makes it easy to narrow down appropriate firms in any city. Beyond the demographic information, the NALP Directory has details about the summer associate pay. Most importantly, the firms report whether or not they hire 1L's. The NALP Directory also contains a number of public interest organizations that choose to list themselves.

Government Jobs: Other than law firms, the most common employers for 1L students, and indeed law students in general, are state and local governments. One great thing about government jobs is that they are a little easier for a 1L to get than law firm jobs. In addition, the deadlines for seeking these jobs are a bit more relaxed and vary depending on the position and the location. Working for the government as a 1L is a great idea, even if you are sure you will work for a firm your second summer and after law school. Firms love to see experience in government work because a huge amount of time at a private law firm is spent negotiating with government entities in various matters. It is also a great opportunity to make sure that government work is not right for you without getting stuck in the public service career track.

On the state and regional level, there are often summer internships available in the offices of district attorneys and in the office of the state attorney general. There are also positions available at state governmental organizations that hire lawyers such as the state legislature and even state governmental offices like the Department of Labor or Health. At the federal level, there are United States District Attorney Offices in almost every major city throughout the lower forty eight states. These offices are also located in places

like Alaska, Guam, and Hawaii. These locations would be really fun places to work as a 1L! Another major source of employment is the Federal Department of Justice. The Justice Department has many subdivisions with offices throughout the United States, though many of the jobs are concentrated in the Washington D.C. area. No matter what your area of interest, be it labor relations, environment, or antitrust, there is probably a division of the DOJ that is focused in the area. The best way to find these jobs is to start at www.doj.gov. This website contains information on all available jobs and specific information on how to apply.

Another opportunity is to clerk for a judge. Many law students seek judicial clerkships after they finish law school, but it is a fact that many judges hire current law students to fill out their staff. These positions have some drawbacks. First of all they are generally unpaid. In addition, many law schools that provide funding for summer public interest work do not provide funding for these types of clerkships. Lastly, many judges give inexperienced law students very basic work, which can often amount to file keeping and document management. On the other hand, a good experience as a judicial clerk can give you unparalleled skills in analyzing written legal work and drafting opinions. The best way to avoid pitfalls when applying for a clerkship is to get detailed information about the judges from former clerks and the advisors at your school.

Besides the Department of Justice, many other government entities seek legal interns. Almost every government organization constantly seeks expert legal advice and employs large numbers of in-house counsel. Some examples of government organizations that hire 1L's are the National Labor Relations Board, the Equal Employment Opportunity Commission, and the Securities and Exchange Commission. These types of organizations give you significant experience in interpreting complex statutes as well as in arbitration and mediation solutions.

Public Interest Jobs: A public interest organization is generally understood to mean a group that either provides free legal services to a needy portion of the community or a group that advocates on behalf of the public in a beneficial way. There are legal organizations in urban areas that are focused on assisting the urban poor and homeless with issues related to welfare services, public housing, and family law. There are groups that specialize in environmental issues, suing private and public organizations on behalf of endangered wildlife or threatened natural habitats. There are also a number of firms and organizations

that focus on problems in the U.S. criminal justice system, including lack of representation, prison issues, and fighting death penalty cases. In addition to causes that can be identified as "liberal," there are also many public interest organizations dedicated to advocating for traditionally "conservative" causes such as encouraging the free market and reforming the tax code.

Finding these organizations can be the hard part. Many law schools have offices or websites specifically dedicated to public interest advising, or they may be included in the general career services offerings. If you are lucky, they will contain records of the public interest organizations that seek students on campus and even reviews by students who were previous employed. The advisors in these offices can also help you narrow down the many potential employers and suggest options that you may have overlooked.

Your Resume: The resume you send out must serve many purposes. Most employers are going to decide whether or not to give you an interview based on the information you include in this document. You want to convey all of your accomplishments in a clear and concise manner while making sure that you do not overwhelm the employer with too much information. This can be tricky for law students who have a laundry list of accomplishments, because you need to restrict your resume to one page. Law firms are looking for a one-page summary that contains no "fat," only the most relevant information to help distinguish you from the big stack of applications they have in front of them. There are a number of different formats for resumes and there will probably be several examples available through your career services office or websites.

First include your name, email address, and phone number prominently centered at the top of the page. The next section should be your education information. After the education section, you should list your most significant work and extracurricular experiences in reverse chronological order including the location. Below the description of your experience, you can include headings for other important skills you would like to share with potential employers.

You may need to make several different versions of your resume for different potential employers. For example, for a private law firm you will want to emphasize any employment, internships, or extracurricular involvement that demonstrates leadership ability or creates the impression of a skill set that will be valuable to the firm. If you spent some time working in banking, then emphasizing the finance skills you gained will look great for a corporate law firm. How-

ever, if you are applying to an environmental defense group, they would probably be much more interested in your volunteer efforts as an undergraduate. It is important to tailor your resume to your audience.

Your Cover Letter: Though the resume is a very important part of a successful law school job application, the cover letter can be even more crucial. When employers are reviewing big stacks of applications, the first thing they will read is the cover letter. If the letter does not draw them in, they may not read through the resume and give you an interview. Just like the resume, it is important to be brief and concise in your cover letter. No one is going to read a five-page essay on why you would be the best summer associate of all time. They want to know why you are applying, what makes you stand apart from your peers, and why you are interested in working for them specifically. They also want to see that you have the ability to produce a decently written letter with no spelling or grammar errors. One of the biggest mistakes is to leave a small error in your cover letter. It is impossible to determine how many thousands of great applicants have been tossed in the reject pile because they misspelled a word in the first paragraph of their cover letter!

The first paragraph is designed to introduce you to the employer and emphasize the connections you have to the area where the employer is located. This first sentence should mention that you are a 1L and the law school that you attend.

The second paragraph is where you should summarize the most important parts of your resume. Talk about your undergraduate and graduate work and discuss the most relevant work experiences. The key in this paragraph is to fill in all the connections that you are trying to convey in your resume. Think back on why you included what you did in the experience section of your resume and articulate these reasons in this paragraph. The third paragraph is where you ask for an interview. Emphasize how interested you are in the position and ask politely for the opportunity to be considered for a summer job. Make sure to demonstrate that you have researched the employer by mentioning some particular strengths of the organization.

Career Advisors: Be sure to visit any advisors who are available to you through the law school. Make an appointment for the earliest date, and make sure that you bring a copy of your resume and cover letter with you. Also bring a list of the firms that you are interested in working for. The advisor should go through your resume and cover letter with a fine-tooth comb and make sure that there are no errors. The advisor

will also help you to format your documents perfectly and shape the content so that they convey the unique skills and characteristics that make you a great choice for employers. Advisors also have a wealth of knowledge about various summer jobs. First of all, they will help you eliminate employers who are unlikely to hire you as a 1L. They will also help you identify jobs that you may have initially missed during your job search.

The advisors in the office of career services can also help you in other ways. One of the best ways to find a 1L job is to get to know an attorney who works for your employer of choice. The office of career services can help you find graduates of your law school who are employed across the country. Generally these attorneys are happy to help students from their alma mater.

Job Fairs: Job fairs are a great way to meet potential employers. After the rush of 2L hiring early in the year, many employers decide that they need to hire still more law students. At this point, many employers participate in 1L job fairs on law school campuses. These are usually hosted by student affinity groups or by the law schools themselves. Be sure to attend. Wear formal clothes to the job fair, and bring many copies of your resume printed on high-quality paper. The various employers will be manning tables containing tons of free recruiting materials, and they will usually accept resumes. An impressive number of jobs result from resumes dropped off at job fairs, so you should be sure to be on your best behavior. Even if you just talk to the representatives of various law firms, make sure to get their cards. If you email them a few days later and follow up by meeting them, you could create a precious contact that could lead to a potential job.

Spring On-Campus Interviewing: At most law schools, law firms do all their on-campus interviewing (OCI) with 2L's during September and October. However, at some law schools, the firms return in the spring for another round of hiring. 1L's are often encouraged to participate in this process, and many organizations are indeed looking to fill open spots with first year law students. The employers usually hold a number of brief interviews on campus. They ask potential candidates to bring their transcript with their first semester grades, resumes, and sometimes a writing sample. You will want to wear a suit to these interviews and be prepared to field some pretty tough questions about your experience and your transcripts. Employers use these brief on-campus interviews to weed out applicants who do not meet their basic requirements. You should be prepared to explain why you are interested in the firm. Find out some specific information about the firm's practice to

ensure that you can demonstrate that you have a genuine interest. Employers will also ask you about your law school experience so far. Make sure that you have some interesting experiences to share with them.

Be prepared to explain any poor grades on your transcript or glaring omissions from your resume. Many on-campus interviewers try to throw students off track by asking them why they received a particular grade, or why their resume is lacking a particular type of experience. You should be well prepared to fend off these questions and find a way to emphasize your positive attributes. Many interviewers just want to see how you handle tough situations, and a poor grade will rarely preclude you from getting an interview if it is handled gracefully. If you manage to do well in the on-campus interview, you will move on to the final stage of summer hiring.

The Final Interview: Depending on the type of employer, most final job interviews will either be completed over the telephone or in a call back interview. Law firms often fly their candidates to their offices for interviews, but due to budget constraints public interest organizations and the government often interview by phone. Each type of interview presents a unique challenge so you must vary your approach to achieve the desired result: a summer job!

Telephone Interviews: The greatest benefit of a telephone interview is that you do not have to go through airport security, put on a suit, or shave for an in-person interview! The downside is that the interviewer will have a hard time getting to know your personality or demeanor so she or he will be much more likely to ask tough questions to try and determine your quality as a candidate. The first thing that you usually have control of is where and when you will be interviewed. Make sure to schedule your telephone interview in a large open time slot so you will not feel rushed. Next, make sure that you are using a reliable phone that you can use comfortably for an extended period of time. If you still happen to have a home phone connected to a land line, now would be the time to use it. Make sure you have plenty of water so that you can speak clearly during the entire interview.

It can be difficult to project your personality through a telephone interview, but by following these simple rules you should be able to make a good impression.

- Be very patient with your interviewer.
- When your interviewer is asking questions or telling a story, wait for him or her to finish completely before beginning to speak. In fact, you should wait a second or two after you think the

interviewer is finished to make sure that she or he is completely done.

- Once it is your turn to speak, answer clearly and try to convey your experiences without embellishing them too much or trying to be funny.
- Be relaxed, but maintain a professional attitude, even if your interviewer is very informal. If you get too comfortable, it can be very easy to cross that invisible line between what is appropriate and what isn't. This line can be a lot harder to identify over a phone line.

Thank the interviewer when the interview is over and never ask how you performed. It is generally acceptable to ask an interviewer when you can expect a response. If you are told a date and it passes, feel free to call for a follow-up. Just make sure to limit your follow-up calls to the absolute minimum.

The Call-back Interview: If you make it past the initial interview, or if a law firm selects your resume and cover letter as promising, you will usually be invited for what is known as a call-back interview. If the firm is located in a different city from your school, you will be flown into town and put up at a local hotel for the night. Then you will visit the firm for a round of interviews. The process varies from firm to firm, but usually you will interview with a number of different partners and associates from around the firm, usually one after another. These attorneys are usually members of the firm's recruiting committee and are seasoned interview veterans. Once law firms have selected a student for a call-back they are usually trying to determine if the student is a good fit for the personality of the firm. This can come as a surprise to some who are expecting tough treatment and instead receive softball questions about their favorite sports teams and law school experiences. The important thing in a call-back is to remain positive and to explain why you are a good candidate. Two of the toughest and most common questions asked at call-back are "Why are you interested in working for this firm?" and "Do you have any questions for me about the firm?" One of the best ways to answer these questions is to research the firm's strengths and to discuss how they attracted you to the firm.

Once you have finished interviewing with all the lawyers, you will likely be treated to a great lunch with a couple of young associates. These lunches can seem pretty informal, but it is crucial to remember that you are still being evaluated. Once you have finished lunch you may receive an acceptance or rejection on the spot. Generally, you will receive an offer or be rejected within a few days of the interview.

Preparing for Final Exams

Throughout this survival guide, there has been an emphasis on the importance of your 1L grades. This final section will discuss how to prepare for final exams, what you should bring into the exam with you, and how to write great answers for different final exam formats. You'll learn how to

- create a great outline for each one of your classes
- use your outline and textbook materials effectively while taking exams
- practice writing exam answers under time pressure

Outlines: Well before exam day, prepare an outline for each of your classes. The outline should be a carefully constructed guide to the definitions, rules, case summaries, and policy theories that make up the course. You should be comfortable with the structure of your outline so that you can quickly find the relevant information once you're taking final exams. Here are three pitfalls to avoid:

- Don't try to write a detailed transcript of every concept you encountered both in and out of class.
- Don't focus too heavily on recounting every exhaustive detail of each case. The typical law professor is much more interested in the legal rule or concept demonstrated by the case, rather than the actual facts that led to the outcome.
- Don't worry about how the outline looks because you are the only one using it.

Plan to have your outline complete at least a week before the final exam. This will give you plenty of time to work through the outline so that you can navigate it easily when it is test time. You will also have the time to take practice exams with your outline, to identify any ways in which it might be lacking.

Your outline should contain the following elements and structure:

Headings

- Create a separate heading for each main section of the course. Under each heading, list the specific rules of law that you covered in class and in your reading.
- Before you dive into the cases and the rules themselves, define all the relevant terms under the headings.

Rules

- Write a short summary of the rule and the elements that make up the doctrine.
- For each of the elements, explain briefly how they are applied.
- Once you have summarized the rule, follow up with brief case summaries that illustrate the application of the rule.
- If your professor gave any relevant hypotheticals in class, this is where you should include them in your outline.
- Highlight the exceptions to the rule as well as any cases you read that interpreted the doctrine differently.
- In some cases there is a split on a certain rule of law between different states. If your professor highlighted such a split in class, you should probably mention it in your outline.

Policies

- Once you have gotten through all the rules and case law, the last consideration should be the policy arguments and doctrines that were discussed in the reading and class.
- You can often score extra points on a law school exam by discussing policy once you have applied the rules.

Making Connections

- The last things to include in your outline are the connections between different legal concepts.
- Most law school exams contain complex hypotheticals that can be solved using multiple approaches.
- If you acknowledge the connections between various legal doctrines, it will help you to write a more complete exam answer.

As you prepare your outline, think carefully about how you approach the different elements listed above. Follow these guidelines:

- **Themes:** To get an idea of the overall theme of your course, a great place to start is with your class syllabus or the table of contents of your casebook. Another way is to look at old outlines if they are available from your professor. Some schools maintain online outline banks, or you may be able to obtain good outlines from students who have already taken the course. Don't use this resource as an excuse to neglect making your own outline. Much of the value of the outline is a result of the process of putting it together. Instead, just use these sources to determine the overall theme and also to help

check if you missed anything important in your own work.

- **Rules:** When you begin to write about a specific rule identify the characteristics of that rule by synthesizing the material available to you. The best way to do this is to start by reviewing the holdings in all the cases related to the rule. Look at each of the rules separately and try to harmonize the outcomes so that you can create a rule. The rule should be an abstract but flexible statement of the boundaries of that particular legal framework. You need to identify a generality, not just the specific holding in a case. This can be difficult, because your professor will probably be confusing you further in class. You should work through the cases in order and try to extract the general holding. As each subsequent case is considered, try to modify your original rule to reflect that court's holding. If a court case adds an exception to the rule, you should modify your initial rule in the outline to contain a "but" or "if then" that addresses it. Even if your rule seems to become a little cumbersome, remember that if you do not reflect the detail of the case law you will end up with a less than complete exam answer.
- **Cases:** Now add in the cases and hypotheticals. Refer back to your case briefs and include the information that supplements the rule that you have created. Only include the bare minimum facts to remind you of the situation in the case. There is an exception to this rule. If you have a professor who places heavy emphasis on discussing the specifics of the casebook, you may want to consider including more factual analysis in your outline.
- **Hypotheticals:** Including hypotheticals in your outline will help you tackle the gray zone that exists for many of the rules of law. Professors like to explore the edge of legal rules where it is unclear how to apply the general rule of law. They often discuss these gray areas in class through the use of hypotheticals. When adding these hypotheticals to your outline, try to think about how your professor used these hypotheticals to figure out how your professor approaches applying the legal rules to new factual situations. If you can reflect this thought process on your exam, it will generally help you earn a better grade.
- **Policy:** Policy issues can take on a number of different forms. In general, they can be defined as arguments for or against an existing legal rule. If your professor places an emphasis in class on the philosophical and theoretical justifications for a rule, you can be pretty sure that

policy will show up on your exam. You should include these elements on your outline if they show up in class: 1) discussion of whether or not a particular legal rule is fair as applied, 2) any explanations of who the law was created to protect, 3) the history of the law and how it shaped the rulings of the court, and 4) the impact the law has had on American society. These types of arguments may not be in your casebook or secondary commercial sources, but they will probably show up in class on a regular basis.

Practice Exams: Next, assess your mastery of each course by tackling practice exams. These are usually kept on file by your school, and if they are not in a central location, many professors are happy to share their old exams with students as a study aid. It is very important to take practice exams under actual test conditions. If your professor gives an eight-hour take-home exam, you should take only the allotted time period to work on the test. Only use the materials that the professor will allow on the real exam and do not collaborate with anyone.

One of the best ways to tackle practice exams is to work with your friends. Everyone in a practice exam study group should email each other one's final answers. Take a day or so to read over your fellow students' final products. Identify the issues that you missed but the others in your group successfully identified, and go back to the original exam to see how the question was worded. Also note when your analysis was lacking in depth or if you forgot to mention an exception to the rule or policy argument. Once you have reviewed each other's test answers, meet to discuss the results. Once you have exhaustively gone over the answers, you should go back to your outline and fill in all the information that you were missing. If you found the style of your outline cumbersome or difficult to use, now is the time to try a new format or to reorganize the information in a new way.

Test-taking Strategies: Even though professors use a multitude of different exam formats, there are still some great strategies that can be applied to the majority of law school exams. By applying these concepts, you will find it easier to answer tough exam questions and perform better.

- **Watch for "Issue Spotters":** The most common type of law school exam question is what is known as the issue spotter. A professor will concoct a long and convoluted set of circumstances referred to as the fact pattern. Woven into this narrative are numerous legal issues

discussed in class that you need to identify and discuss in the answer. The fact patterns can be intimidating due to their length or because of the complexity of the situation. With practice, however, issue spotters can become much easier to handle. The first step is to focus on what the professor is looking for in the answer. Try to determine what role you are assuming when you are writing your answer (e.g, judge, lawyer, etc.).

- **Focus on the Facts:** Remember to focus on the facts presented in the question. It can be easy to determine the substantive rules of law that the question is related to and just regurgitate everything from your outline onto the page. This is a great way to get a mediocre grade on an exam. Your professors are already aware that you have most of the relevant rules and cases summarized in your outline. They are much more interested in your original application of that information to the facts they have created. They put a lot of time and effort into creating the questions and they want to see numerous references to specific facts in your analysis.

- **Identify All the Issues:** One way to make sure that you incorporate all the relevant facts into your exam answer is to be sure that you have identified all the relevant issues as well as the individuals involved in the fact pattern. Consider making a list or chart as you read through the question for the first time to create a summary of individuals and questions of law. Once you have created this list, try to identify the facts in the case as well as the rules of law that apply to each individual. This will also prevent a common problem in exam answers where students accidentally apply the same legal issues to multiple individuals separately. Instead, discuss the relevant rule and legal issues in an introductory paragraph, and then apply that rule to every individual for whom it is relevant.

- **Explain Your Reasoning:** It is important that you justify any claims that you make on a test. Just because you are applying a concept of black letter law or one of the most tried and true legal rules discussed in class, it does not mean that your professor is not looking for an explanation of why you made that particular choice. Any conclusion on a rule of law you make on an exam should be followed by a detailed explanation of the relevant rule and how it applies to the facts. This will also show your ability to analyze an unusual fact pattern with well-known legal rules.

- **Manage Your Time Wisely:** Though many professors have begun using take home formats, the classic law school exam consists of a three or four hour in-class open book exam. In these types of exams, professors will typically construct an exam that contains too many issues to adequately tackle within the allotted time. Therefore, it is pretty much impossible to identify every last issue and exception. If you attempt to do this, you will end up not finishing the exam which will severely hurt your grade. Instead, divide up the allotted time by the number of questions that are on the test. Try not to spend more than that amount of time when you are answering each question. While you are writing your answer, note all the issues that you identified and try to mention them in your answer. Even if you have to merely include brief notes mentioning their relevance you may be able to salvage some points. However, it will be much worse if you do not get to one of the questions. Once you have finished all the questions, if there is time remaining, you can go back and tackle any remaining issues that you did not fully address in the first round.

- **Make an Outline:** Don't start writing without having some idea of how you are going to organize your arguments. A good rule of thumb is to spend the first quarter of the time allotted to each question outlining your issues into a basic framework. This may seem like an unnecessary waste of time, but it will result in a much better answer. When your answer is separated into distinct issues, it is much easier for the professor to see how you analyzed the issue and reward you with big points.

- **Use the IRAC Method:** One effective way of answering law school exam questions is known as the IRAC method. IRAC stands for Issue, Rule, Application, and Conclusion and should be the basic starting point for tackling any issue spotter exam.

- **Issue:** The first step is to identify the legal issue. This may sound easy, but most issue spotters contain multiple issues that you must tackle. Therefore, the first step is to identify every issue and list it in your chart of individuals and issues. Once you have identified the issues, you need to determine a logical order to place them in your answer in order to effectively make your argument. Begin by writing an introductory paragraph that discusses the main context of the case and which area of law the conflict relates to. Once you have gotten that out of the way, structure the remainder of the answer as a series of lengthy paragraphs beginning with a couple of sentences identifying the issue and the individuals who are related to it.

- **Rule:** Next, discuss the rule that applies to the issue. You should identify the legal rule, but you must also explain its legal basis and origins. This may be easy for certain rules that have a clear set of elements such as adverse possession in property law. In other situations, it may be necessary to go further. In your outline you likely synthesized a number of different legal holdings and information from the classroom discussion to determine the relevant rule. You should try to convey this process when you describe the rule. Explain the relevant cases that use the rule, and what the judges in the cases had to say about its application. Also note the major exceptions to the rule and why the courts chose not to apply it. It can also be useful to point out the policy arguments that have been made on the subject of the rule. Cite the cases that you are discussing in the rule section to demonstrate your grasp of the material.

- **Application:** Now apply the rule to the facts in the question. Law professors are much less interested in your conclusions than in the deductive path that lead you there. Applying the rule will generally be tough. Law professors like to create fact patterns that present a very close legal issue. Valid arguments can usually be made on both sides, so the quality of your analysis is the key factor. If the rule you have written contains specific elements, apply each one to the facts in the question in order. Discuss similarities and differences between the fact patterns in key cases with the question on the test. Also discuss why you rejected other possible conclusions. To make sure that you do not miss any important facts, consider creating a chart with headings for each of the major issues. Then place each important fact in the issue column to which it is relevant. When you have completed your answer, check back to make sure that you included all the relevant information. This will also help you identify "red herrings." "Red herrings" are facts included in an exam question that are designed to throw you off and lead you to apply the wrong rules to the fact pattern. When you have all the facts together to compare, it is much easier to identify these grade-killers.

Conclusion: The last step is to state a conclusion. It is very important for you to state a definitive answer to the issues that you have identified. If you are writing from the perspective of the judge, state who will win the case. If you are writing as a lawyer giving advice, make predictions about how a judge will decide various issues facing your client. In most cases it is advisable to use language that indicates the probability of a given legal argument succeeding. However, if you are completely sure that the law is on your side, it is acceptable to take a firm position. Professors like to see their students state their arguments confidently even if they ultimately disagree with the analysis.

The 1L Experience

There is no avoiding the fact that the grades and experience you receive during the first year will play a crucial role in the eventual trajectory of your career. Despite this fact, it should not be an unhappy time for you as a student. The best way to get through the 1L year is to focus on the rewards of your hard work. You will learn to "think like a lawyer" and the skills you gain will serve you for the rest of your life, even if you end up pursuing a career outside of law. You will learn to zealously advocate for any position and to express yourself eloquently in speech and in writing. You will improve your work ethic and learn to push yourself beyond what you thought you were capable of. Most important, you will be preparing to enter a profession full of some of the best people you will ever meet, and you will likely forge new friendships that will last for a lifetime.

The 1L year is a trial by fire, designed to push you to find skills that you may not have realized you possess. The importance of the 1L year cannot be overstated. Your 1L record will influence your job prospects in the legal profession, and it will determine whether you can participate in selective student organizations like Law Review. So you need to choose: will you coast through doing just enough work to get by, or will you apply yourself to achieve your maximum potential? This article has given you advice and specific strategies for success if you have decided to take the second path. Use this information to make your efforts efficient and to avoid the pitfalls that derail so many law students' success. Best of luck in your first year of law school!